MICROSOFT° VISUAL BASIC .NET 2003 UNLEASHED

Heinrich Gantenbein, Greg Dunn, Amit Kalani,
Chris Payne, Thiru Thangarathinam

SAMS

Sams Publishing, 800 East 96th St., Indianapolis, Indiana, 46240 USA

Microsoft Visual Basic .NET 2003 Unleashed

Copyright © 2005 by Sams Publishing

International Standard Book Number: 0-672-32677-9

Library of Congress Catalog Card Number: 2004095064

Printed in the United States of America

First Printing: December 2004

07   06   05   04   4   3   2   1

Trademarks

All terms mentioned in this book that are known to be trademarks or service marks have been appropriately capitalized. Sams Publishing cannot attest to the accuracy of this information. Use of a term in this book should not be regarded as affecting the validity of any trademark or service mark.

Warning and Disclaimer

Every effort has been made to make this book as complete and as accurate as possible, but no warranty or fitness is implied. The information provided is on an "as is" basis. The authors and the publisher shall have neither liability nor responsibility to any person or entity with respect to any loss or damages arising from the information contained in this book or from the use of the CD or programs accompanying it.

Bulk Sales

Sams Publishing offers excellent discounts on this book when ordered in quantity for bulk purchases or special sales. For more information, please contact

> **U.S. Corporate and Government Sales**
> 1-800-382-3419
> corpsales@pearsontechgroup.com

For sales outside of the U.S., please contact

> **International Sales**
> international@pearsoned.com

Associate Publisher
Michael Stephens

Acquisitions Editor
Neil Rowe

Development Editor
Mark Renfrow

Managing Editor
Charlotte Clapp

Senior Project Editor
Matthew Purcell

Copy Editor
Krista Hansing

Indexer
Tom Dinse

Proofreader
Paula Lowell

Technical Editor
Ramesh Mani

Publishing Coordinator
Cindy Teeters

Multimedia Developer
Dan Scherf

Designer
Gary Adair

Page Layout
Cheryl Lynch

Contents at a Glance

Table of Contents

Part V: Advanced Programming

About the Authors

Heinrich Gantenbein is a solutions architect at Avanade specializing in .NET security, scalability, and multitier architectures. He is an expert in C#, VB .NET, Enterprise Services, and Java to .NET interoperability. Heinrich influences the future of .NET technologies through his participation in Microsoft's Preview Labs and has presented at many events, including Microsoft's Security Summit 2004, Comdex's Web Services Innovation Center, and user groups and webinars. With more than 20 years of experience in software engineering and engineering management, Heinrich combines architectural excellence and commitment to a productive development process. Before Avanade, he was a principal software architect at the .NET consulting company IDesign. Heinrich was named a BEA technical director in recognition of his work on interoperability.

Greg Dunn is the president of Instinctive Webware and Database, a software consulting and training business based in Pleasanton, California. He teaches object-oriented programming, SQL, Visual Basic, and mathematics for the University of Phoenix and has been writing database apps since the 1980s in dBase, Clipper, FoxPro, Access, and VB. He holds a Master's degree in operations research from the University of Texas at Austin.

Amit Kalani has authored or coauthored 10 programming books, including Que Certification's *MCAD/MCSD Training Guides for the Microsoft Exams 70-315, 70-316, and 70-320*. He is president of TechContent Corporation, where he provides contract programming, consulting, and training services. Amit lives in Michigan and can be reached at amit@techcontent.com.

Chris Payne has had a passion for computers and writing from a young age. He holds a Bachelor of Science in biomedical engineering from Boston University, and he supported himself through college as an independent consultant and writer of technical articles focused on web development. He currently makes his home with his wife, Eva, in Orlando, Florida, where he works as a web developer and is continuing his career as an author of both technical and fictional material.

Thiru Thangarathinam works at Intel Corporation in Chandler, Arizona. He specializes in architecting, designing, and developing distributed enterprise-class applications using .NET-related technologies. He has coauthored a number of books in .NET-related technologies as well and has been a frequent contributor to leading technology-related online publications. He can be reached at thiru.thangarathinam@intel.com.

Dedications

To my wife, Denyse
—Heinrich Gantenbein

To my beloved girls, Gay, Leela, and Aminta, who are my heart; and to Ron Greenstein, for being a matchless friend when it mattered most.
—Greg Dunn

To my wife, Priti
—Amit Kalani

I would like to dedicate this book to my wife, Thamiyadevi, for providing me with all the help and motivation while I was working on this book.
—Thiru Thangarathinam

Acknowledgments

I would like to thank my wife, Denyse, for her invaluable help in the writing of this book. Thanks also to my friend Juval Lowy, of IDesign.NET, who introduced me to .NET and continues to be a great force in that field.

Heinrich Gantenbein

Thanks to Evan Lim for recommending me, and to Heinrich Gantenbein for inviting me to seek involvement in this project; to the talented and dedicated volunteers of the Bay.NET user group, through whose efforts San Francisco–area .NET developers are provided with a steady flow of world-class educational opportunities; and to the skilled and cheerful Sams editors for their guidance, suggestions, expert corrections, and, above all, patience.

Greg Dunn

I would like to thank the excellent team of publishing professionals at Sams Publishing and my co-authors for making this work possible. I would also like to thank my wife, Priti, for her careful reviews and suggestions.

Amit Kalani

Thanks again to Neil Rowe for getting me involved in this project.

Chris Payne

We Want to Hear from You!

As the reader of this book, *you* are our most important critic and commentator. We value your opinion and want to know what we're doing right, what we could do better, what areas you'd like to see us publish in, and any other words of wisdom you're willing to pass our way.

As an associate publisher for Sams Publishing, I welcome your comments. You can email or write me directly to let me know what you did or didn't like about this book—as well as what we can do to make our books better.

Please note that I cannot help you with technical problems related to the topic of this book. We do have a User Services group, however, where I will forward specific technical questions related to the book.

When you write, please be sure to include this book's title and author, as well as your name, email address, and phone number. I will carefully review your comments and share them with the author and editors who worked on the book.

Email: feedback@samspublishing.com

Mail: Michael Stephens
            Associate Publisher
            Sams Publishing
            800 East 96th Street
            Indianapolis, IN 46240 USA

For more information about this book or another Sams Publishing title, visit our website at www.samspublishing.com. Type the ISBN (0672326779) or the title of a book in the Search field to find the page you're looking for.

INTRODUCTION

Overview of Visual Basic (VB)

Before the arrival of VB, programming (especially user interface programming) involved tedious work to understand the minute internals of processor and operating systems. This refers not to the early days of computing in the 1960s, but to the late 1980s and 1990s. The tasks were achieved with primitive (by today's standards) languages such as C and Pascal or with overly complex languages such as C++. The libraries exposed details of the underlying operating system, such as message queues and WinProcs in Windows 3.1.

VB together with ActiveX controls changed this by introducing a simple environment to create user interfaces with little effort. The programming model was indeed so simple that it enabled many untrained programmers to enter the field and produced an explosion of useful (and some not-so-useful) programs for Windows. Many geeks argued that this development decreased the overall quality and maintainability. Although this is likely true, the huge increase in productivity outweighed the downside. However, this model of programming worked best for standalone programs and simple client/server systems.

Meanwhile, the geeks also wanted productivity increases to keep up with the demand for more complex programs, so Microsoft introduced Visual C++ and MFC, which was a great improvement. Unfortunately, this new environment was based on C++, a language so complex that even seasoned engineers produced bad mistakes. Sun invented a new, simpler language called Java, which eliminated many C++ pitfalls. Microsoft initially supported this language as a solution to the problem of complexity with COM and C++. However, the old rivalries between Sun and Microsoft soon surfaced again, and Microsoft's support of Java descended this temporary alliance into a legal mud fight. Whose fault that was has been argued endlessly, and the arguments undoubtedly will continue for a long time.

VB had moved on and made the initial concept even more powerful. However, the language provided a glass ceiling for the kind of programs that could be reasonably written.

Visual Basic .NET (and C#)

Microsoft had three systems: the simple but limited VB; the overly complex and powerful C++; and the reasonably complex Java, which was stopped by legal issues. The desire was to combine the power of C++ without its pitfalls, the language simplicity of Java, and the unbeatable simplicity of working in VB. At the same time, the concept of web-connected applications emerged (this was later known as web services). Thus was born the idea for Microsoft .NET.

In .NET, all languages are created equal. For example, VB .NET can do everything C# can. Both are fully object-oriented, support component-oriented development, and enable developing everything from simple Windows and web applications to complex multitier distributed systems. The power of .NET is achieved through the shared .NET Framework and its common language runtime, which allows for binary components that can be shared by all .NET-compliant languages.

Visual Basic .NET 2003 Unleashed

Despite the parity of language capabilities between C# and VB.NET, many geeks consider VB.NET programmers to be second-rate programmers. This is unfair to many because bad programming is not the exclusive domain of programmers who use a specific programming language.

The vision was to write a book that enables VB .NET (and VB6) programmers to take full advantage of the new capabilities for writing high-quality advanced software, while continuing the unprecedented productivity inherent in VB.

If you master the material in this book, your understanding of .NET and your command of its capabilities will exceed that of the vast majority of .NET programmers—including those whose language of choice is C#.

How This Book Is Organized

This book covers the entire breadth of .NET, from fundamentals to Enterprise Services. At the end of each chapter, a suggested reading list is included, to deepen your already considerable knowledge. This book has nine parts.

Part I: Fundamentals

You will learn the fundamentals of .NET Framework and its evolution. Additionally, you will learn about concepts of .NET Framework such as the common language runtime, the class library, object-oriented programming in .NET, and .NET Framework data types.

Part II: Windows Forms Applications

Windows Forms technology is the cornerstone for creating Windows applications in .NET. In this section, you will learn about Windows-based applications such as Windows Forms controls, drawing techniques, deployment techniques, printing and graphics, and advanced Windows Forms techniques.

Part III: Database Programming

After an introduction to the most important ADO.NET classes, you will be guided through a thorough dissection of code produced by the Data Form Wizard, illustrating important points not only about the design of data-aware applications, but also, more generally, of Windows Forms. You will then be introduced to working with SQL Server databases from within Visual Studio. Next, you will dive deep into data binding—radically redesigned in Visual Studio .NET—to discover its reborn power and flexibility. Finally, you will learn how to produce and consume XML representations of data and data schemas using the ADO.NET classes.

Part IV: Web Applications (ASP.NET)

ASP.NET provides a greatly enhanced paradigm for building web applications. You will learn the fundamentals of applications distributed over the Internet and also learn how to leverage the powerful .NET common language runtime and VB .NET to create everything from simple data-driven websites to complex applications that go deeper into server technologies than ever.

Part V: Advanced Programming

The .NET Framework enables you to develop robust and scalable applications. In this part of the book, you'll learn about advanced programming features such as versioning and the Global Assembly Cache, IO and persistence, events and delegates, multithreading, and reflection.

The .NET Framework also supports interoperability with the existing COM code. In this part, you will learn how to take advantage of the interoperability feature to migrate your existing applications to Visual Basic .NET.

Part VI: Securing Applications

You will learn how to use .NET Code Access Security (CAS) to prevent bad code from attacking good code, and to sandbox code from untrusted or partially trusted sources. Additionally, you will learn how to use role-based security to defend your application from unauthorized users.

Part VII: Remoting

You will learn how to write distributed components that behave almost the same as local components. This is only the first of three methods of writing distributed systems, and it is the weakest of the set.

Part VIII: Web Services

Web Services enables you to develop distributed applications that work across hetero-geneous environments and over the Internet. In this part, you will learn how to create your own web services and how to make use of web services available from other vendors. You will also learn how to take advantage of the web service enhance-ments to customize and secure your web services.

Part IX: Enterprise Services

Enterprise Services are the most robust way to program distributed systems. You will learn how to program serviced components, correctly request services, deploy components, and administer deployed components. You will learn each service used for scalability, transactions, loosely coupled systems, concurrency protection, and security.

How to Use This Book

At the beginning of each chapter you will find a "What You Need" section that will outline the minimum requirements, in terms of hardware, software, and skills to obtain maximum benefit the chapter. Immediately following this section will be an "At a Glance" table that will show the main topics in the chapter. Throughout the book, there are many code listings, tables, figures, tips, and sidebars. Many code listings will also contain sections of code that are shaded, numbered, and referenced in the surrounding discussion. Should you need more information on a particular topic, the "Further Reading" section is provided at the end of each chapter.

Part I

Fundamentals

1

INTRODUCTION TO .NET

IN BRIEF

This chapter discusses what .NET is, how it works, how developers can benefit from it, and its many new features. It covers all aspects of the objectives of the .NET Framework, its architecture, and its various components in details.

Simply put, .NET can be referred to as Microsoft's next-generation platform for Windows and Internet software development. However, .NET is much more than just a new software-development platform. To understand what .NET really is and what it can do for you, it's best to discuss the primary goals of .NET and the way the ideas for .NET came about. .NET is Microsoft's newly redesigned, revolutionary software-programming architecture aimed at achieving Microsoft's vision of "software as a service." Microsoft was dedicated to turning this idea into reality; .NET is the first step toward this reality. One of the important features of this architecture is Software as a Service, which is exactly what you will see in the next section.

INTRODUCTION TO .NET AT A GLANCE

1

Software as a Service

The idea of Software as a Service is not as baffling and complex as you might imagine. Many companies are already using this technology without your even noticing it. They have started to transform their Win32 applications into software services, or these applications have at least been modified to integrate with the services that the company might provide down the track.

Using .NET and technologies it supports (such as web services), developers can easily create software services. These services can then be published online and made available to other developers instantly. .NET is made up of three key parts:

- ▸ .NET products
- ▸ .NET services
- ▸ .NET Framework

The next section takes a look at each of these.

.NET Products

.NET products include any current and future products released by Microsoft that can take part in .NET. The major product in this area is Visual Studio .NET. Visual Studio .NET is designed to enable developers to create tightly knit applications with ease and also to give them a wider range of features to use when developing these applications. The Visual Studio IDE includes easy access to all of the tools currently available to developers.

.NET Services

.NET services refer to the services provided by Microsoft that enable developers to utilize several sets of premade functionality in their own applications. Microsoft is currently providing only one service, which is its Passport service. The Microsoft Passport service is an authentication service and is used on sites such as HotMail and NineMSN. The Passport service is currently provided to developers for providing integrated authentication.

.NET Framework

Because of the fact that the .NET Framework is completely seamlessly integrated with the Windows operating system—and, therefore, completely transparent to the developer and the user—it enables developers to create applications that are fast, flexible, scalable, and efficient. In addition, developers now can create applications that can interact with other .NET applications and components that were created in a totally different programming language.

Software as a Service

This is a new and exciting concept that is possible only because of the way that the .NET Framework has been developed. Microsoft planned to implement this sort of functionality right from the start. This means that you can create a component in a .NET–compatible language, such as C#, and consume that same component with an application that was written in VB .NET. The concepts and technologies that have been added to the .NET Framework include the .NET Framework Class Library, the common language runtime, Windows Forms (WinForms), and ASP.NET. The next section takes a high-level look at each of these elements.

.NET Framework Base Class Library

The .NET Framework base classes are a collection of built?in functions, objects, properties, and methods that can be utilized by any .NET–compatible language. ADO.NET resides in this part of the .NET architecture and provides developers with functions, objects, properties, and methods to access, view, and manipulate databases. The tools that developers require to work with XML are also included in these base classes.

NOTE

XML capabilities are one of the strengths of the .NET Framework. The XML handling capabilities are native to the platform, and the syntax is intuitive.

The Common Language Runtime

The common language runtime is the heart of the .NET Framework and is responsible for the execution and management of .NET applications, as well as the compilation of .NET applications into native code. It is the environment under which .NET applications are run. The common language runtime offers developers many useful and important features and benefits: simpler Rapid Application Development (RAD), memory management, scalability, and common approach programming/cross-language integration.

CROSS LANGUAGE INTEGRATION CAPABILITY

The cross-language integration benefits are lessons learned from the COM/DCOM world. In COM, most of the low-level component code was written in C++ (occasionally, even in C) and the classes used from VB. There are large gaps in the use of these technologies because C++ programming and VB programming generally do not go together. In .NET, however, creating such class libraries in C# and accessing them from VB. NET (sometimes even vice versa) is a cakewalk.

Simpler Rapid Application Development

The concept of rapid application development is not a new one. Because the .NET Framework base classes provide developers with prewritten, built?in functionality and the capability to reuse source code that already exists, the amount of code that a developer needs to write to create an application is reduced by a significant amount.

Memory Management

Memory management is one of the most important features that the common language runtime provides. It works behind the scenes and gives developers more of an opportunity to concentrate on building their application than having to worry about the nitty?gritty aspects of memory management.

Scalability

Increased scalability is a direct result from the issues already discussed, including rapid application development and memory management. Rapid application development enables you to spend more time tweaking and improving your application's performance, while the built?in memory management features of the common language runtime improve the in?memory performance and number of resources available to your application at any given time.

TIP
Remember that you can also convert the MSIL into native code so that you will have native executables, just as in C/C++.

Cross-Language Integration

This feature is probably the most talked about when developers are discussing .NET. It is a radical and very significant change from the traditional concepts because it brings all of the .NET languages up to par with each other. For example, although C++ is generally considered and accepted as being more powerful than Visual Basic, .NET has discarded this idea. All .NET applications are compiled into Intermediate Language (IL). The Intermediate Language equalizes the power, complexity, and optimization across all of the .NET languages before they are compiled into native machine code. For a programming language to be considered .NET compatible, its source code must be capable of being compiled into Intermediate Language.

The section "Advantages of the Common Language Runtime," later in this chapter, takes an in-depth look at all these features.

Windows Forms–Based Applications (WinForms)

WinForms are an essential part of the Win32 application-development system in .NET. They are the .NET equivalent of the graphics and drawing APIs and controls, and they are available to all of the .NET–compatible languages. WinForms are equivalent to MFC for C++ developers and the Win32 API for VB developers. Because of the unification and the way they are built, structured, and integrated into the common language runtime, WinForms provide developers with features such as a drag-and-drop designer, which can be used to visually create forms for .NET applications.

Software as a Service

ASP.NET

ASP.NET is the next generation of Microsoft's Active Server Page (ASP), a feature of Internet Information Server (IIS). The biggest and most popular change within the .NET Framework occurred during the transformation of ASP to ASP.NET. ASP.NET is a completely different platform compared to the older, classic version of ASP. A lot of people seem to get confused by ASP.NET and some of its newer features. To clear up a couple of things, ASP.NET is not written in VBScript anymore. It now supports all the compiled .NET languages, such as VB .NET, C#, and JScript .NET. ASP.NET is based on an event?driven, object?oriented paradigm, not a sequential paradigm, as with classic ASP. ASP and ASP.NET share very few similarities besides their name.

ASP.NET is a server-side event-driven language that is created using any of the .NET languages. Because ASP.NET utilizes an event?driven, object?oriented programming paradigm, stronger, more formal syntax is enforced. This helps increase performance significantly and makes the use of components, events, properties, and methods easier. ASP.NET's most significant benefits over traditional ASP relate directly to its integration with the common language runtime. ASP.NET takes a lot of features from the common language runtime, including support for common-approach programming. In addition, ASP.NET pages are compiled and cached in the server's memory after they are first executed. This provides a huge speed increase in comparison to traditional ASP pages, which are compiled every time they are executed.

Scalability is another big issue with traditional ASP. Traditional ASP code and HTML can be written, mixed, and matched on any one page, making it nearly impossible to keep track of which code is where. Sure, COM objects helped to separate code into tiers, but a lot of developers still just plunked their business logic directly into their ASP pages. That wasn't good.

ASP.NET is a vital part of .NET for many reasons. The most important of these reasons is that ASP.NET pages act as the superglue to bind the Internet and Win32 applications closer together. Web services are considered to be part of ASP.NET. Web services utilize the Simple Object Access Protocol (SOAP) as their core communication protocol. SOAP is based heavily on XML, which makes it ideal for Internet-era computing.

The purpose of a web service is to enable other developers to access ASP.NET components, functions, or even prebuilt web applications (that are configurable online) over the Internet. Web services allow developers to keep the code and logic for their applications private, exposing only a minimal amount of methods and member variables to implement the web services functionality. This all ties back into Microsoft's vision of Software as a Service. Web services are an extremely powerful and popular addition to .NET and really do need to be experienced to be fully appreciated.

WEB SERVICES AND THEIR POTENTIAL

With web services, clients can expect a whole new range of advanced Internet-equipped components and services to help meet their demands more easily. Just imagine a couple of years down the road: You might be the developer creating a web service to help your clients train their new employees online, without any human intervention. The possibilities are endless with .NET, and things can only get better from here.

Now that you understand the important components of the .NET Framework, the next section discusses its objectives.

Objectives of the .NET Framework

.NET is Microsoft's greatest invention since the development of MS?DOS back in 1982. .NET has advantages for developers and clients alike. Developers now have all the necessary tools at their fingertips to create, manage, and distribute applications with ease. They can utilize the Internet like never before. .NET's common language runtime also means that applications are less likely to crash and more likely to provide the results developers are looking for: a clean, quick, and sturdy implementation with maximum uptime and minimum downtime.

The .NET Framework is designed to fulfill the following objectives:

- ▸ A consistent object-oriented programming environment, where object code can be stored and executed locally, executed locally but Internet distributed, or executed remotely

- ▸ A code-execution environment that minimizes software deployment and versioning conflicts

- ▸ A code-execution environment that guarantees safe execution of code, including code created by an unknown or semitrusted third party

- ▸ A code-execution environment that eliminates the performance problems of scripted or interpreted environments

- ▸ Consistency for developers across widely varying types of applications, such as Windows-based applications and web-based applications

- ▸ All communication built on industry standards to ensure that code based on the .NET Framework can integrate with any other code. For example, Borland has created a framework for .NET components to talk to Java components; this is already in evidence in the C# Builder development tool.

The next section delves into the architecture of .NET Framework and how it provides for all of these features.

Understanding the .NET Framework Architecture

The .NET Framework has two components:

- ▸ .NET Framework class library
- ▸ Common language runtime

Understanding the .NET Framework Architecture

The .NET Framework class library facilitates types (CTS) that are common to all .NET languages. The common language runtime consists of a class loader that loads the IL code of a program into the runtime. Then it compiles the IL code into native code, executes, and manages the code to enforce security and type safety while providing thread support. Figure 1.1 shows the .NET Framework architecture and its various components.

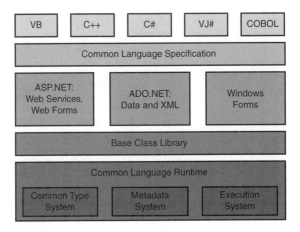

FIGURE 1.1　.NET Framework architecture.

The .NET Framework architecture has languages such as VB .NET, C#, VJ#, and VC++ .NET at the top; developers can develop (using any of these languages) applications such as Windows Forms, Web Forms, Windows services, and XML web services. The bottom two layers consist of the .NET Framework class library and the common language runtime.

Understanding the Role of the .NET Framework

As you have already seen, the .NET Framework has two main components: the common language runtime and the .NET Framework class library. The common language runtime is the foundation of the .NET Framework. It acts as an agent that manages code at execution time, providing core services such as memory management, thread management, and remoting. It also enforces strict type safety and facilitates code accuracy that ensures security and robustness. The concept of code management is a fundamental principle of the common language runtime. Code that targets the common language runtime is known as managed code, while code that does not target it is known as unmanaged code.

The class library, which is an integral component of the .NET Framework, consists of an object-oriented collection of reusable classes or types that you can use to develop applications ranging from traditional command-line applications or any graphical user interface (GUI) applications, such as Windows Forms, ASP. NET Web Forms and Windows services, and the newly invented XML web services.

The code written in a CLS-compliant language should be compliant with the code written in another CLS-compliant language, because the code supported by a CLS-compliant language is compiled into an intermediate language (IL) code and then the common language runtime engine executes the IL code. This ensures interoperability between CLS-compliant languages. The Microsoft .NET Framework supports languages such as Microsoft Visual Basic .NET, Microsoft Visual C#, Microsoft Visual C++ .NET, and Microsoft Visual J# .NET.

The language compilers generate an Intermediate Language code, called Microsoft Intermediate Language (MSIL), which makes programs written in the .NET languages interoperable across languages.

The Common Language System (CLS), defines the specifications for the infrastructure that the IL code needs for execution. The CLI provides a Common Type System (CTS) and services such as type safety, managed code execution, and side-by-side execution.

What Is MSIL?

MSIL can be defined as a CPU-independent instructions set into which .NET applications are complied. It contains instructions for loading, storing, and initializing objects. When you compile your C# application or any application written in a CLS-compliant language, the application is compiled into MSIL. When the common language runtime executes the application, a Just-In-Time (JIT) compiler converts the MSIL into native CPU instructions that the machine can understand. Figure 1.2 illustrates this process.

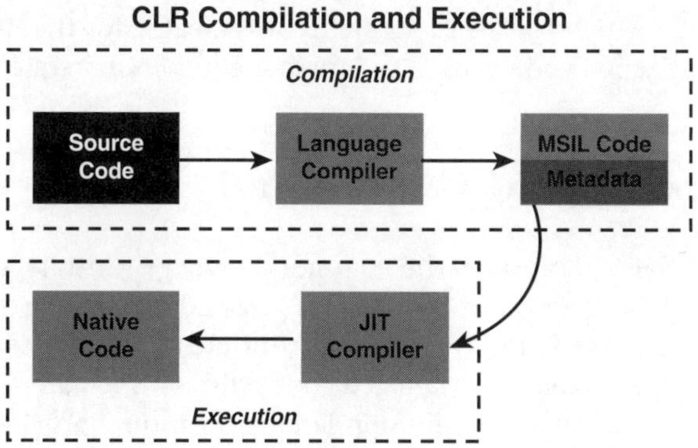

CLR Compilation and Execution

FIGURE 1.2   Converting the MSIL into native code.

1

MSIL makes cross-language integration possible in conjunction with metadata and the Common Type System. As you have already seen, the Common Type System is the core of the .NET Framework that provides cross-language integration by supporting the types and operations found in most of the programming languages.

What Is a Portable Executable (PE) File?

When you compile your application, along with MSIL, the compiler generates metadata that is simply a collection of information about your application. This metadata persists in binary form in the portable executable file. Microsoft has designed PE file format for use in all of its Win32-based systems. This is the role of a portable executable file in the execution of a .NET program.

- You write source code in any .NET language.

- You then compile the source code using a .NET language–specific compiler.

- The compiler outputs the MSIL code and a manifest into a read-only part of the EXE that has a standard PE (Win32 portable executable) header.

- When you execute the application, the operating system loads the PE and all the other dependent dynamic libraries.

- Then the operating system starts the execution of the MSIL code that was placed in the PE. Because MSIL code is not in machine-executable format, it cannot be executed directly. The common language runtime then compiles the MSIL into native code using the Just-In-Time compiler as it continues to execute the MSIL code.

Understanding the JIT Compiler

As you have already seen, the JIT compiler is an integral part of the common language runtime. It compiles the MSIL code to native code and executes the batch of code just-in-time which will be cached after it is created for the first time. Subsequently, the cached code is used to satisfy the incoming requests.

Common Language Runtime

At the core of the .NET platform is the common language runtime, which is responsible for managing the execution of code that is targeted toward the .NET platform. The code that requires the common language runtime at runtime to execute is referred to as managed code. The managed code relies on the core set of services (discussed in a moment) that the common language runtime provides. The services provided by the common language runtime are listed in the next section.

1

Components of the Common Language Runtime

Figure 1.3 shows the architecture of the common language runtime and its various components.

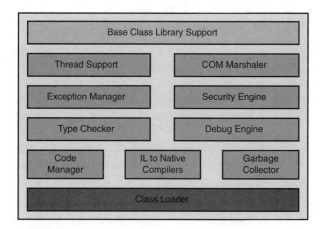

FIGURE 1.3   .NET common language runtime architecture.

This list takes a look at each of the elements in detail:

▶ **Class loader**—This is responsible for loading classes into the common language runtime.

▶ **MSIL-to-native-code compilers**—These compilers convert MSIL code into native code, which is machine dependent.

▶ **Code Manager**—The code manager manages the code during execution.

▶ **Memory allocation and garbage collector**—This performs automatic memory management.

▶ **Security engine**—This enforces security restrictions posed by the code access security. You can configure machine-level security using tools provided by Microsoft .NET under the Control Panel.

▶ **Type checker**—This enforces strict type checking.

▶ **Thread support**—This component provides multithreading support to applications.

▶ **Exception manager**—This provides a mechanism to handle the runtime exceptions handling using `try..catch..finally` blocks.

▶ **Debug engine**—This enables developers to debug different types of applications.

1

▶ **COM marshaler**—This allows .NET applications to exchange data with COM applications.

▶ **Base class library support**—This provides the classes (types) that the applications need at runtime.

.NET Framework Class Library

As you can see from its name, the class library is merely a collection of classes and related structures that can be leveraged as base building blocks for application development. As such, it is safe to think of this collection of classes as an API: They are a boundary interface between your applications and the operating system. This concept, of course, is really nothing new to Visual Basic developers: the ADO library, the Win32 API, and the COM+ services library all have enabled you to reference and use existing code in applications. The class library is a massive library of existing code that you can use as a foundation for your application features.

The .NET Framework includes classes, interfaces, and value types that not only provide access to system functionality, but also optimize the development process. To facilitate interoperability between languages, the .NET Framework types are CLS compliant and, therefore, can be used from any programming language whose compiler conforms to the Common Language System.

Classes in the .NET Framework are the foundation on which .NET applications, components, and controls are built. The .NET Framework includes types that perform the following functions:

▶ Represent base data types and exceptions

▶ Encapsulate data structures

▶ Perform I/O

▶ Access information about loaded types

▶ Invoke .NET Framework security checks

▶ Provide data access; rich client-side GUI; and server-controlled, client-side GUI

Referencing preexisting libraries of code has traditionally been pretty easy with Visual Basic. One of the main issues, however, was that many times these code libraries weren't initially consumable by Visual Basic developers. If you were a C++ programmer, the world was open to you in terms of functionality. VB programmers had to wait for Microsoft or some other entity to make a wrapper or interface available that they could use from VB. Documentation also tended to be a problem. The .NET Framework helps solve this problem by providing a unified interface that all languages in the .NET Framework can take advantage of. The way classes are organized in the .NET Framework class library also makes programmers' lives much easier than in the past.

How Classes Are Organized in the .NET Framework Class Library

The primary units of organization for the class library are namespaces. A namespace is just a bucket for functionality: It describes a grouping of like-focused classes and constructs. You can liken the concept of a namespace to that of a file system folder: Both attempt to implement organization across objects with parent and child relationships. Just as a folder can contain other folders and actual documents, a namespace can contain other namespaces or actual classes, delegates, and so on.

All namespaces stem from a common root: the System namespace. The System namespace is the one and only common root for all other namespaces. For instance, the System namespace contains the actual structures that define the common data types used in .NET, such as Boolean, DateTime, and Int32. It also contains the most important data type: Object, which is the base object inherited by all other .NET objects.

Benefits of the .NET Framework Class Library

So far, you have learned about the structure of the .NET Framework class and its various components. Some of the core benefits of the .NET Framework Class Library are listed in the following sections.

Enhancing Developer Productivity

An important design goal of the framework class library is to enhance developer productivity. It might surprise you to learn that the class library primarily targets the goal of enhanced productivity not by introducing new functionality, but by repackaging functionality in an object-oriented way. That is, although the framework class library does introduce some new features, much of the functionality exposed by the namespaces was previously available through the Win32 API, ActiveX controls, COM-based DLLs, and so on. Now, however, it is wrapped in a way that enables you to program them at an abstracted level at which you don't have to deal with the complexities and granular pieces of data required by the Win32 API. As a direct result, you have to deal with only one over-arching design pattern in your applications: one that uses and promotes components in an object-oriented environment. Moreover, the functionality is available across all of the common language runtime–targeted languages.

In case you were wondering, the framework class library does not replace the Win32 API. The class library still relies on the actual Win32 API classes to talk directly to the Win32 API to execute code through something called a P/Invoke (platform invoke).

Finding the Code That You Need

If you start to examine the ways that the class library helps to make for a more productive development experience, you can see a few things immediately. First, the class library enables you to easily find the functionality that you are seeking. The size of the class library might seem daunting at first, but its logical presentation inside of the namespaces allows functionality to be discovered in a straightforward fashion. For instance, the System.Drawing namespace contains classes that will provide you with drawing functions. The System.IO namespace exposes classes for basic input/output operations, and so on. And inside the System.Drawing namespace, you find objects that will be familiar to any Windows graphics programmer: the Pen object, the Brush object, and so on.

Common Language Runtime

1

With any sufficiently sized API, the task of actually locating the code or function that you need for a given task is not an inconsiderable issue. Contrast the organization of the namespaces discussed thus far with the organization of the flat, monolithic namespace offered up by the Win32 API. The problem is that, as the Win32 API has grown at its core, its developers have had to be more creative with their function names. The capability to look at a function name and know without some research what its purpose is has started to deteriorate. To be fair, it is possible to be productive using the Win32 API from Visual Basic. It just takes some determination and a lot of reference information. The framework class library is a more approachable API: Things are where you expect them to be. It appeals to the OO programmer in everyone who, after all, is just interested in simplifying software by using objects.

Any code that runs under the control of the .NET runtime is known as managed code. Unmanaged code is any code that runs outside of the .NET runtime, such as the Win32 API, COM components, and ActiveX controls. Currently, the only development tool available from Microsoft for writing unmanaged code is Visual C++.

Using the Class Library

Finding the class that you need is the first step; after you have found it, the framework class library also makes utilizing it easy. By exposing functionality through properties and methods, you have straightforward access to features that are extremely complicated under the hood. In the true spirit of data hiding and encapsulation, you are dealing with black boxes; you neither know nor care about what takes place in the box. What you do care about is that you talk to the black box in a standard and predictable way.

This element of productivity is not insignificant. Again, consider the effort required to work directly with the Win32 API. Because Visual Basic was talking to an API that had a different type system, there was not a clear one-to-one mapping between API calls and actual Visual Basic syntax. Now, because of the integral role that the Common Type System plays, all languages talk to runtime components through the same data types. This ensures that the classes in the Framework Class Library can be consumed evenly by any of the .NET languages. For the first time, Visual Basic developers have the full range of framework functionality open to them, with no corresponding drop in productivity.

There is little to no disjoint when a programmer hops between language-intrinsic functions and the class library. In other words, Visual Basic developers are finally free to accomplish their application programming without jumping in and out of different coding paradigms (such as moving from procedural Win32API patterns to VB component patterns). Design patterns can remain consistent throughout your code, regardless of the actual type of component being consumed. This is because the entire library was built to support object- and component-based programming. What's more, the class library usage follows familiar design patterns for VB developers. No esoteric syntax is required; instead, you reference the component, instantiate it, and then use its methods and properties.

Because the Framework Class Library is written in managed code that runs on top of the .NET common language runtime, it reaps all the benefits of any other piece of managed code, such as these:

- ▶ Freedom from GUIDs, window handles, hResults, and so on

- ▶ Automatic garbage collection of unused resources and memory

- ▶ Support for structured exception handling

Advantages of the Common Language Runtime

The common language runtime provides a host of benefits to the managed code, including cross-language integration, enhanced security, versioning and deployment support, debugging and profiler services, and memory management through garbage collection. This section looks at each of these benefits in detail.

Cross-Language Integration

The common language runtime allows managed code written in one language to seamlessly integrate with code written in another language. This is made possible through CLS, which defines a set of rules that every language in the .NET Framework has to abide by. The list of possible cross-language integration capabilities includes inheritance, exception handling, and marshalling. For example, you can define an interface in COBOL and implement it in languages such as VB .NET and C#.

Enhanced Security

Today you can get code into your machine not only through a setup application that you execute, but also from the Internet via a web page or an email message. Recent experiences have shown that this can be harmful to your system. So how does .NET answer this threat?

.NET provides code access security, which enables you to control access to protected resources and operations. Code is trusted to varying degrees, depending on its identity and where it comes from. These are some of the features of code access security:

- ▶ Administrators can define security policies that assign specific permissions to defined groups of code.

- ▶ Code can demand that the caller have specific permissions to execute it.

- ▶ Code can request the permissions that it requires to run and the permissions that would be useful, as well as explicitly state which permission it must never have.

Versioning and Deployment Support

The common language runtime supports side-by-side execution of multiple versions of the same component, even within the same process. Applications produced in the .NET Framework can be installed into the system using a simple XCOPY with zero-impact install to the system. XCOPY means just copying the files to the bin directory of the application; the application starts picking up the changes immediately.

Common Language Runtime

1

This is possible because compilers in the .NET Framework embed identifiers or meta-data into compiled modules, and the common language runtime uses this information to load the appropriate version of the assemblies. The identifiers contain all the information required to load and run modules, and also to locate all the other modules referenced by the assembly.

Debugging and Profiler Services

The common language runtime provides necessary features to enable the developer to debug and profile managed code. After you attach an executing .NET program to the debugger, you can perform operations such as walking through the stack of a managed code, examining its dependencies, interrogating the objects, and much more. These features are available to all the applications, regardless of the language in which they were written.

Garbage Collection

In unmanaged code, memory leaks can occur very often. A memory leak is caused when memory allocated by an application is not freed after it is no longer referenced by the application. Applications written using programming languages such as C++, which enable the developers to allocate memory on the heap, are vulnerable to memory leaks. But in managed code, the garbage collector (GC) is responsible for cleaning up all the objects that the application no longer references. Whenever a memory is allocated for a managed-code application, the memory is always associated with the object. GC takes care of collecting these objects when they are no longer referenced by the application, so it is not possible for managed code to experience memory leaks. The GC uses a process called elimination to identify the objects that need to be cleaned up.

At runtime, GC accomplishes this elimination process by making use of the information that the common language runtime maintains about a running application. The GC first gets a list of root objects that the application directly references. The GC then finds a list of the objects that the root objects reference. When the GC identifies all the objects that the application directly or indirectly references, the GC is free to clean up all remaining objects on the managed heap. The garbage collector can be automatically invoked by the common language runtime, or sometimes the application can explicitly invoke the GC by calling the `GC.Collect` method to clean up the memory that is allocated in the heap.

Rich Object Models and Class Libraries

The common language runtime furnishes a rich set of object models and class libraries that expose a wealth of functionality for performing operations such as accessing a relational database, performing input and output operations, dealing with XML-related data, inspecting metadata, and so on. Because all the object models are at the runtime level, you can easily design tools to work across all the languages that target the common language runtime. The core namespace in the .NET Framework that encapsulates most of the functionality is the `System` namespace. Namespace is a new concept introduced with .NET that enables you to logically group related classes into a single entity. All the classes within a namespace must be unique.

So far, you have learned about the architecture of the common language runtime and its different components. In the next section, you learn what an assembly is and different types of assembly.

What Is an Assembly?

For .NET to live up to the bill that it will revolutionize the future of computing, it must have all the possible innovative features implemented in its framework. One of those innovations is the way the applications are executed and versioned; it goes a long way in eliminating the infamous DLL hell problem. Microsoft has tried to address this problem by introducing what is known as an assembly, which is the unit of deployment of a .NET application.

Assemblies are extensively used in .NET applications. An assembly is a primary building block of a .NET Framework application. It represents a logical collection of one or more executables or dynamic link libraries (DLLs) that contain an application's code and resources. The assembly provides the formal structure for visibility and versioning in the runtime. Assemblies also contain a manifest, which is a metadata description of the code and resources inside the assembly. Because the manifest contains all the information about the assembly, it is responsible for the self-describing nature of the assembly. Before moving on to the different types of assemblies and the advantages, it is important to look at the structure of an assembly.

Structure of an Assembly

An assembly has the general structure shown in Figure 1.4.

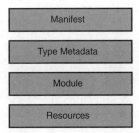

FIGURE 1.4   Structure of an assembly.

As you can see, an assembly consists of four elements:

- ▶ Assembly metadata or manifest
- ▶ Type data or metadata that describes the types
- ▶ Module
- ▶ Set of resources

What Is an Assembly?

Out of these elements, the manifest must be present in every assembly. All the other elements, such as types and resources, are optional and are required to give the assembly meaningful functionality. The next section takes an in-depth look at the different components of the assembly.

Manifest

The manifest makes an assembly self-describing. It contains the following information:

▸ **Identity**—This is made up of a name, a version number, an optional locale, and a digital signature (if the assembly is to be shared across multiple applications).

▸ **File list**—A manifest includes a list of all the files that make up the assembly. A manifest also contains additional information for every file that is part of the assembly, including its name and a cryptographic hash of its contents at the time of manifest creation. This hash is verified at runtime to ensure that the deployment unit is consistent and has not been tampered with. Dependencies between assemblies are stored in the calling assembly's manifest. The dependency information includes a version number that is used at runtime to load the correct version of the dependency.

▸ **Types and resources**—This consists of a list of types exposed by the assembly and the resources. It also consists of information about whether these types are visible to other assemblies (exposed) or are private to this application.

▸ **Security permissions**—Assemblies are the unit at which code access security permissions are applied.

Module

A module is either a DLL or an executable in the Windows PE executable format. The compiled code in the module is in Microsoft Intermediate Language (MSIL).

> **NOTE**
>
> The module is actually an extended form of the PE format. This is needed because the native PE format does not provide for accommodating such things as version information and metadata.

Type Metadata

A type is a combination of data and methods that work on that data. It consists of properties, fields, and methods. Fields are more like public variables and can be accessed directly. Properties are similar to fields, except that you can associate a set of statements to be executed when the properties are accessed. Methods are actions or behaviors of the type.

1

How Assembly Enables XCOPY Deployment and Zero-Impact Install

One of the primary goals of the .NET Framework is to simplify the deployment by making possible what is known as XCOPY deployment. Before covering how .NET enables XCOPY deployment, it is important to tell what XCOPY deployment is. Before .NET, installing a component required copying the component to appropriate directories, making appropriate Registry entries, and so on. But now in .NET, to install the component, all you have to do is copy the assembly into the bin directory of the client application; the application starts using it right away because of the self-describing nature of the assembly. This is also called a zero-impact install because you are not impacting the machine by configuring the Registry entries and the component.

TIP

The installation of Microsoft .NET itself is an implementation of the side-by-side install technique. For instance, if you install both versions of .NET Framework (1.0 and 1.1), you will find that there are two directories for .NET 1.0 and 1.1 as follows: C:\WINNT\Microsoft.NET\Framework\v1.0.3705 and C:\WINNT\Microsoft.NET\Framework\v1.1.4322.

Design Considerations of an Assembly

An assembly can be a single file that contains all the elements of the assembly, including the manifest, type metadata, IL code, and resources. When you use tools such as Visual Studio .NET to build your application, each project most likely corresponds to a single assembly. As an alternative, you can spread the contents of an assembly into multiple files; in this case, the assembly resides in more than one file in the same directory. The manifest of the assembly also then resides in one of the executables or DLLs of the assembly. It is important to remember that in a multifile assembly, the file system does not tie files together. The only thing that makes these files part of the assembly is the fact that they are mentioned in the manifest. Using a command-line utility such as al.exe (the Assembly Linker utility), you can add or remove files from a multifile assembly.

In Figure 1.5, the contents of the Main assembly have been split into three different files. Utility code is in a separate DLL, and the large resource file is kept in its original location. One of the advantages of this approach is that it optimizes code download to a greater extent. The .NET Framework downloads a file only when it is referenced, so if the assembly contains code or resources that are not accessed frequently, breaking them out into individual files increases download efficiency.

What Is an Assembly?

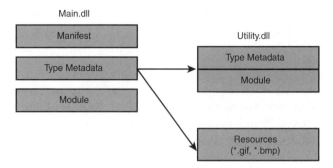

FIGURE 1.5   A multifile assembly.

Types of Assemblies

Before categorizing assemblies, the following two factors should be considered:

▸ **How assemblies are used**—Whether they are private to one application or shared among many applications

▸ **How assemblies are constructed**—Whether the assembly is constructed at design time or runtime

Based on the pattern of their usage, you can classify assemblies as private assemblies and shared assemblies. Based on the way assemblies are constructed (at design time or at runtime), you can classify them as static assemblies and dynamic assemblies. This section looks at each of these assemblies in detail.

Private Assemblies

A private assembly is an assembly that is visible to only one application. Most of the .NET applications are deployed as private assemblies because one of the selling points of the .NET Framework is its capability to isolate an application from changes that other applications make to the system. When you create private assemblies, you deploy them within the bin directory of the application in which it is used. Because the scope of the private assembly is only within the current application, the naming requirements for private assemblies are simple: The names must be unique only within the application. Each deployed private assembly is specific to only that particular application that uses it, so you need not maintain version information for private assemblies. When the common language runtime receives a request for loading an assembly, it maps the assembly name to the name of the file that contains the manifest. This process is called probing.

Shared Assemblies

Another kind of assembly is a shared assembly, which is shared by multiple applications on the machine. Shared assemblies are stored in the Global Assembly Cache, which is a centralized repository for storing all the shared assemblies in the machine. It is important to note that in .NET, the developer makes the decision to share code between applications.

This approach is completely different from the COM scenario, in which developers were forced to share their components and, hence, ran the risk of some other installation overwriting their components. If you use Visual Studio .NET to add a reference to an external assembly (shared assembly) that is already deployed in the Global Assembly Cache, Visual Studio .NET does not make a local copy of the assembly. Instead, it directly refers to the one that is deployed in the global cache. This behavior is determined by the `CopyLocal` property, which is automatically set to `false` when you add a reference to a shared assembly. You can access this property by right-clicking on the referenced assembly and selecting Properties from the context menu.

Shared assemblies are designed to avoid the sharing problems faced today. However, shared assemblies should meet the following requirements:

▶ Must have cryptographically strong names that are globally unique.

▶ Must have the built-in infrastructure to prevent someone else from releasing a subsequent version of your assembly and falsely claim that it came from you. This is made possible through public key cryptography.

▶ Must provide identity on reference. When resolving a reference to an assembly, shared assemblies are used to guarantee the assembly that is loaded came from the expected publisher.

Static Assemblies and Dynamic Assemblies

As already mentioned, an assembly consists of a collection of physical files. An assembly that is built at compile time and whose dependencies are resolved at link time itself is called a static assembly. Most of the assemblies that you will be creating in this book fall into this category. In addition, the .NET Framework exposes a set of classes through Reflection API that you can use to create code on the fly and execute it directly. These assemblies are called dynamic assemblies; they can be stored on disk, if required.

Metadata

Metadata is information that enables components to be self-describing. Metadata is used to describe many aspects of components, including classes, methods, fields, and the assembly. The common language runtime uses metadata to facilitate all sorts of things, such as validating an assembly before it is executed and performing garbage collection while the code is being executed.

Is Metadata an Evolution of IDL?

If you have done COM programming, you are probably somewhat familiar with the Interface Definition Language (IDL) and type libraries. They are used to store all the necessary information for COM automation. You can think of metadata as being similar to IDL in the COM world. However, unlike IDL, metadata is much more accurate and complete, and it is not optional.

What Is an Assembly?

1

Metadata can be defined simply as the information that the common language runtime uses to identify everything about the classes, functions, properties, resources, and other items in an executable file. The important point to be noted is that metadata is always associated with the file that contains the code—that is, the metadata is always embedded in the same executable or DLL, making it impossible for the code and metadata to go out of synch.

All .NET–compliant compilers are required to give full metadata information about every type class that is present in the compiled source code module. In the world of COM, metadata is stored separately from the executable. The COM developer has an option to store the component's type library as a separate file. In addition, important COM metadata used at runtime, such as the component's GUID and supported threading model, is stored in the Registry. Because metadata is stored separately from the COM or COM+ component, installing and upgrading components can be a nightmare. The component must be registered before it can be used, and if the type library is stored in a separate file, it must also be installed in the proper directory.

After the component is installed, upgrading to a new version can be problematic. You might end up installing a new binary for the component without updating its corresponding metadata (that is spread everywhere in the machine), only to find out that the application has suddenly stopped working. The process of installing and upgrading a .NET component is greatly simplified. Because all metadata associated with a .NET component resides within the file that contains the component itself, no registration is required. After a new component is copied onto the system, it can be immediately used without having to do any of the configurations that you are used to doing in COM world. This is called XCOPY deployment.

Upgrading a component is also less problematic because the component and its associated metadata are always packaged together; they cannot go out of synch.

Common Language System (CLS)

The Common Language System defines a specific set of constructs and constraints that serves as a guide for people who write libraries and compilers. Languages that fit into the .NET Framework must satisfy the guidelines set by the CLS. This enables any language that supports CLS to fully access the libraries written using those languages. You can consider CLS to be a subset of the Common Type System. From the developer's perspective, when developers design publicly accessible classes following the specifics of CLS, other programming languages easily can use their classes. To create an application that is CLS compliant, you need to make sure that you use only CLS-specific features in the following places of the application:

- ▶ Definitions of the public classes

- ▶ Definitions of the public members and protected members

- ▶ Parameters to public methods of public classes and protected methods

1

From these constraints, you can understand that CLS enforces constraints only in certain parts of the application. This means that the other parts of the application are free to implement any language-specific features and still create a CLS-compliant component.

Integration of Languages into the .NET Platform

A .NET language can subscribe to three levels of CLS compliance:

- **Compliant producer**—The components developed in the language can be used by any other language.

- **Consumer**—The language can consume the classes produced in any other language.

- **Extender**—Languages in this category can extend the classes produced in any other language using the inheritance features of .NET.

All the predefined languages in Visual Studio .NET (VB.NET, VC++, and C#) satisfy all three levels of CLS compliance. If you are writing a language that targets the common language runtime, you can select a level of compliance that fits your requirements. Fully supporting a third-party language in the .NET Framework requires a lot of work from the language vendors. The vendor needs to create a compiler for the language that has the capability to create intermediate language code instead of native code. The features of the language must be in compliance with the specifications laid out in the CLS. If you go through the process of rearchitecting your language to contain only those features, your language can enjoy the following benefits in return:

- Complete access to the full set of optimized, scalable .NET Framework class libraries.

- Advanced IDE for development.

- Sophisticated debugging tools.

- Complete cross-language integration. An example for this is creating an interface in COBOL and implementing it in C#.

These are some of the third-party languages that are integrated into the .NET platform:

- APL
- Python
- COBOL
- Eiffel
- Mercury

- Perl
- SmallTalk
- Scheme
- Oberon

What Is an Assembly?

The previous sections gave you an overview of the .NET Framework class library. In the next section, you take an in-depth look at the .NET Framework class library and its benefits.

Summary

Microsoft's .NET Framework provides a much-needed new set of tools to rapidly develop enterprise-grade applications. The tight integration of APIs geared for the Internet, such as web services, XML, and ASP.NET, make the platform especially compelling for next-generation applications. Furthermore, integration with other languages gives the .NET Framework an advantage over other platforms that are architecture and language dependent. The independence of the platform makes the .NET Framework an emerging leader in distributed application development.

This chapter covered quite a bit of ground. It started with the objectives of .NET and detailed the important components of the .NET platform. Then it offered an introduction to the common language runtime and discussed the set of services that the common language runtime provides to applications that are targeted toward the .NET platform. This chapter also discussed the three important entities of a .NET application: assemblies, modules, and types. It then reviewed CTS and the rules that third-party language vendors need to follow while creating a language so that it can take advantage of the services provided by the .NET platform.

Further Reading

Microsoft .NET site: http://msdn.microsoft.com/netframework.

MacKenzie, Duncan, and Kent Sharkey. *Sam's Teach Yourself VB. NET in 21 Days*. Pearson Education, 2001.

2 LANGUAGE FUNDAMENTALS

IN BRIEF

Although Visual Basic .NET makes it easy to write a simple program without using much code, any program simpler than a demo needs to keep track of information and do simple calculations and similar tasks. To write code that performs these tasks, you need a good understanding of variables. By understanding the use and types of variables, you lay the foundation for your understanding of Visual Basic .NET. Similarly, just as when you began learning simple arithmetic, you need to learn concepts such as modules and namespaces, and how to work with them in your programs.

This chapter focuses on the concepts of variables and also demonstrates the constructs that Visual Basic .NET provides for controlling execution flow.

WHAT YOU NEED

SOFTWARE REQUIREMENTS	Windows 2000, XP, or 2003 .NET Framework 1.1 SDK Visual Studio .NET 2003 with Visual Basic .NET installed Visual Studio
HARDWARE REQUIREMENTS	PC desktop or laptop

LANGUAGE FUNDAMENTALS AT A GLANCE

LANGUAGE FUNDAMENTALS AT A GLANCE

Variable Declaration

You declare a variable to specify its name and characteristics. To declare a variable in VB .NET, you use the `Dim` statement. Its location and contents determine the variable's characteristics. Variables have different scope levels that determine the life of the variable. The following sections delve into the accessibility and scope of the variables. This is the basic syntax for declaring and initializing a variable:

```
{Dim|Private|Public|Static} <VariableName> [As Type] [=expression]
```

After the keyword for a variable declaration, you code the name of the variable. This is followed by the keyword `As` and the data type for the variable. When you type this keyword followed by a space in the Code Editor window in Visual Studio .NET, a list of the available data types is displayed so that you can select the one you are interested in. If you want to assign an initial value to the variable you are declaring, you can follow the data type with an equals sign and the initial value coded as an expression. If you don't assign an initial value, the variable is assigned a default value depending on its data type.

Variable Declaration

NOTE
Note that when you declare two or more variables in the same statement, you can't specify initial values for the variables.

TIP
One of the nice features of Visual Studio .NET is that the VB .NET Code Editor automatically adjusts the capitalization of variable names to the way you entered them when you declared them. Do your best to type each variable name properly when you declare it. After that, you can enter the name in all lowercase and the editor will adjust it for you.

Keyword Meaning

Visual Basic.NET provides a number of keywords related to variable declaration that you need to be aware of:

- ▶ `Dim`—Declares a variable that can be used within a single procedure or within just a part of that procedure. This is determined by the location of the `Dim` statement within the procedure.

- ▶ `Private`—Declares a variable that more than one procedure within a class or module can use.

- ▶ `Public`—Declares a variable that all the classes and modules in a project can use.

- ▶ `Static`—Declares a variable that retains its value from one execution of a procedure to another.

The following lines of code provide an example of various declarations:

```
Dim sErrorMessage As String 'declares string variable
Dim iIndex As Integer = 1 'declares integer variable with initial value of 1
Dim tMonth As Short, dRate As Decimal 'declares 2 variables
Dim iStatus, iRunningValue As Integer 'declares 2 integer variables
Private bAddMode As Boolean = True 'declares Boolean variable with initial value of
➥True
Public iUserStatus As Integer 'declares Public integer variable
Static iRunningValue As Integer 'declares Static integer variable
```

You will learn more about the .NET data types in Chapter 4, ".NET Framework Data Types."

Declaration Levels

A local variable is one that is declared within a procedure. A module variable is declared at the module level, inside the module but not within any procedure internal to that module. In a class or structure, the category of a nonlocal variable depends on whether it is shared. If it is declared with the Shared keyword, it is a shared variable and it exists in a single copy shared among all instances of the class or structure. Otherwise, it is an instance variable, and a separate copy of it is created for each instance of the class or structure. A given copy of an instance variable is available only to the instance for which it was created.

Declaring Data Type

The As clause in the declaration statement enables you to define the data type or object type of the variable you are declaring. You can specify any of the following types for a variable:

▶ An elementary data type, such as Boolean, Long, or Decimal

▶ A composite data type, such as an array or structure

▶ An object type, or class, from Visual Basic or another application, such as a Label or TextBox

It is also possible for you to declare several variables in one statement without having to repeat the data type. In the following statements, the variables I, J, and K are declared as type Integer; L and M are declared as Long; and X is declared as Single:

```
Dim I, J, K As Integer  ' All three are Integer variables.
Dim L, M As Long, X As Single 'L and M are Long, X is Single.
```

TIP
Try to use the best variable type for the situation. Although there is no harm in using a variable designed to hold larger values than needed, it wastes memory. In addition, it could cause your program to run slower because it must keep track of larger sections of memory, even when that memory is never used.

Declaring Lifetime

The lifetime of a variable is the period of time during which it is available for use. A local variable declared with a Dim statement exists only as long as its procedure is executing. When the procedure terminates, all its local variables disappear, and their values are lost. However, if you declare a local variable using the Static keyword, it continues to exist and preserve its value even when the procedure ends. Module, shared, and instance variables retain their values as long as your application continues to run.

Declaring Scope

The scope of a variable is the set of all code that can refer to it without qualifying its name. A variable's scope is determined by where the variable is declared. When considering scope, keep in mind that local variables are a good choice for any kind of temporary calculation. They consume memory only when their procedure is running, and their names are not susceptible to conflict. For example, you can create several different procedures containing a variable named `temp`. As long as each `temp` is declared as a local variable, each procedure recognizes only its own version of `temp`. Any one procedure can alter the value in its local `temp` without affecting `temp` variables in other procedures.

TIP

Module, shared, instance, and static variables consume memory resources until your application stops running, so use them only when necessary. In general, when declaring any variable or constant, it is good programming practice to make the scope as narrow as possible. This helps conserve memory and minimizes the chance of code erroneously referring to the wrong variable. Similarly, you should declare a variable to be `Static` only when it is necessary to preserve its value between procedure calls.

Code located in a given region can use the variables defined in that region without having to qualify their names. When declaring scope, the following rules apply:

- ▶ The scope of a module variable is the entire namespace in which the module is defined.

- ▶ The scope of a shared or instance variable is the structure or class in which it is declared.

- ▶ The scope of a local variable is the procedure in which it is declared.

However, if you declare a local variable within a block, its scope is that block only. A block is a set of statements terminated by an `End`, `Else`, `Loop`, or `Next` statement—for example, a `For...Next` or `If...Then...Else...End If` construction.

Declaring Accessibility

A variable's accessibility is determined by the keyword you use in the declaration statement. You can choose from the following keywords: `Dim`, `Public`, `Protected`, `Friend`, `Protected Friend`, and `Private`. You can declare a module, structure, class, or instance variable with any of these keywords. Within a procedure, only the `Dim` keyword is allowed, and the accessibility is always private.

Variables and Assignment

Variables and assignment are at the core of every programming language. Variables enable you to store information for later use. Assignment is the way you get information into variables. You often need to store values temporarily when performing calculations with Visual Basic. For example, you might want to calculate several values, compare them, and perform different operations on them, depending on the result of the comparison. You need to retain the values if you want to compare them, but you don't need to store them in a property.

Like most programming languages, Visual Basic uses variables for storing values. A variable has a name (the word you use to refer to the value the variable contains) and a data type (which determines the kind of data the variable can store). A variable can represent an array if it needs to store an indexed set of closely related data items.

TIP
You can declare a variable with any of the data types that VB .NET supports. If you omit the `As` clause, the `Object` data type is used as the default. However, this usually isn't what you want, so it's a good idea to always specify a data type.

You use assignment statements to perform calculations and assign the result to a variable, as shown in the following code:

```
Dim applesSold as Integer = 10  ' value 10 is assigned
applesSold = applesSold + 1  ' The variable is incremented.
```

Note that the equals sign (=) in this example is an assignment operator, not an equality operator. The value is being assigned to the variable `applesSold`.

Use of Namespaces

A namespace can be seen as a container for some classes in much the same way that a folder on your file system contains files. Namespaces are needed because there are a lot of .NET classes. Microsoft has written many thousands of base classes, and any reasonably large application defines many more. By putting the classes into namespaces, you can group related classes and also avoid the risk of name collisions: If your company happens to define a class that has the same name as the class written by another organization and there were no namespaces, there would be no way for a compiler to figure out which class a program is actually referring to. With namespaces, there isn't a problem because the two classes are placed in different namespaces; this compares with, for example, the Windows files system, where files with the same name can be contained in different folders.

Use of Namespaces

It is also possible for namespaces to contain other namespaces, just as folders on your file system can contain other folders as well as files. When Visual Studio generates your projects, it automatically puts your classes in a namespace. For example, imagine that you use Visual Studio .NET to create a VB Windows application project called MyProject. If you do this and look at the code generated for you, you'll see something like this:

```
Public Class Form1
  Inherits System.Windows.Forms.Form
  'Implementation goes here
End Class
```

This code does not provide any information about the namespace that this class is part of. You can view this information by selecting Properties from the Project menu and selecting General node under the Common Properties root node in the project properties dialog box. This is shown in Figure 2.1.

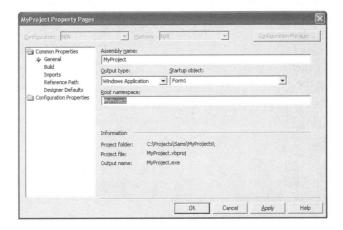

FIGURE 2.1   General panel that enables you to specify the namespace for the project.

You can change the namespace by typing the new namespace into the Root Namespace text box. Apart from setting the namespace through the Project Properties dialog box, you can specify namespaces directly in code using the Namespace keyword. For example, consider the following lines of code:

```
Namespace MyProject
  Public Class Form1
    Inherits System.Windows.Forms.Form
    'Implementation goes here
  End Class
End Namespace
```

The initial `Namespace` command indicates that everything following that is part of a namespace called `MyProject`. Later in the file, a class called `Form1` is declared. Because this class has been declared inside the namespace, its "real" name is not `Form1`, but `MyProject.Form1`, and any other code outside this namespace must refer to it as such. This name is correctly known as its fully qualified name. However, you can use the `Imports` statement to import the namespace and then directly use the `Form1` class without having to specify the fully qualified name. This is covered in the next section.

Notice that in the earlier line, `Form1` is derived from a class called `Form`. This class is defined inside the namespace `Windows`, which, in turn, is defined inside the namespace `System` (recall that it is possible for namespaces to contain other namespaces). This code sample refers to the `Form` class using its fully qualified name.

`Imports` **Keyword**

When you create a new VB .NET Windows application project, you don't see the list of namespaces that are imported by default in the code generated by the form designer. However you can see these namespaces by selecting Properties from the Project menu. In the project Property Pages dialog box, select the Imports node under the Common Properties root node. In this tab, you will see the list of namespaces that are imported by default in the Project Imports list box. Apart from viewing the imported namespaces, you can import other namespaces by typing in the namespace in the `Namespace` text box and clicking the Add Import button. Figure 2.2 shows the Imports panel.

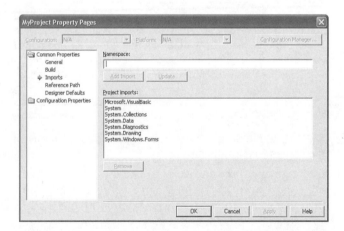

FIGURE 2.2   Imports panel in the Project Properties dialog box.

Apart from adding the namespaces through the Add Import option, you can add them in the code directly using the `Imports` statement. The `Imports` command is basically a way to avoid having to write fully qualified names everywhere because the fully qualified names can get quite long and make your code hard to read.

Use of Namespaces

For example, consider this line:

```
Imports System.Windows.Forms
```

It specifies that, later in the code, you can use classes from the System.Windows.Forms namespace without indicating the fully qualified name. The same applies for every other namespace mentioned in an Imports command. For example, consider this line of code also generated by the developer environment:

```
Public Class Form1
   Inherits System.Windows.Forms.Form
```

Because of the earlier Imports command, you could equally well write this as follows:

```
Public Class Form1
   Inherits Form
```

In this latter case, the compiler locates the class by searching all the namespaces that have been mentioned in an Imports command. If it finds a class named Form in more than one of these namespaces, it generates a compilation error. In that case, you need to use the fully qualified name in your source code.

TIP

Note that the only purpose of the Imports command in this context is to save you typing and make your code simpler. It does not, for example, cause any other code or libraries to be added to your project. If your code uses base classes or any other classes that are defined in libraries (they are stored in assemblies), you need to separately ensure that the compiler knows which assemblies to look in for the classes.

Using Aliases

If you have a very long namespace and you want to use it several times in your code, you can substitute a short word for the long namespace name and can refer to it in the code as often as you want. The advantages of doing this are that the code becomes easier to read and maintain, and it saves you typing very long strings. For example, consider the following lines of code:

```
Imports ConsoleAlias = System.Console 'Create an alias
Public Class MyConsole
   Public Shared Sub Main()
     ConsoleAlias.WriteLine("Hello World")
   End Sub
End Class
```

Here, an alias named `ConsoleAlias` is created to represent the `System.Console` class. After the alias is created, you can invoke the methods of the `System.Console` class without having to type in the fully qualified name every time. In the `Main` method, the `WriteLine` method of the `System.Console` class is invoked using the `ConsoleAlias` that you created earlier.

How to Create Modules in Visual Basic .NET

Modules are a reference type similar to classes, but with some important distinctions. The members of a module are implicitly shared and scoped to the declaration space of the standard module's containing namespace instead of just to the module itself. A module can only be declared in a namespace and cannot be nested in another type.

NOTE

Classes and modules have many similarities, but there are important differences as well. Previous versions of Visual Basic recognized two types of modules: class modules and standard modules. The current version calls these classes and modules, respectively. In a class, you can control whether a member of a class is a shared or instance member; for the module, all the members are implicitly shared.

Classes are object oriented, meaning that you can create one or more instances of a class, with each instance becoming an object with a lifetime that starts when it is created and ends when it is released. A class can inherit from another class, can be nested within another class or a module, and can implement one or more interfaces. Modules are not object oriented. Unlike classes, modules can never be instantiated, do not support inheritance, and cannot implement interfaces. For each module type, there is exactly one copy of it in an application, with the same lifetime as that of the application itself.

Listing 2.1 shows an example of how to declare a module and then invoke its methods from a Windows form.

LISTING 2.1
Declaring a Module and Invoking Its Methods

```
Imports System.Windows.Forms
Imports System.Drawing
Namespace WindowsFormsExample
  Public Module MathModule
    Public Function Add(ByVal firstVal As Integer, ByVal secondVal As Integer) As
    ➥Integer
      Return firstVal + secondVal
    End Function
  End Module
```

How to Create Modules in Visual Basicπ .NET

LISTING 2.1
Continued

```
Public Class Form1
    Inherits Form
    Private Sub Form1_Load(ByVal sender As System.Object, _
        ByVal e As System.EventArgs) Handles MyBase.Load
        'Invoke the Module's method
        MessageBox.Show(Add(10, 20))
    End Sub
    Public Shared Sub Main()
        Application.Run(New Form1)
    End Sub
End Class
End Namespace
```

The code shown in Listing 2.1 first imports all the required namespaces. After that, it declares a namespace named WindowsFormsExample. Inside the namespace, a module named MathModule is declared. As the name suggests, MathModule contains mathematic functions. In this example, it contains only one method, Add, which basically sums up the two input arguments and returns the result to the caller. Next, the listing contains a form named Form1; inside the form, the form Load **1** method is used to invoke the Add method that is contained in MathModule. You will see more on form events in Chapter 5, "Windows Forms." For this example, understand that the form load event is fired before the form is displayed to the user. Then the Main method is used to create an instance of the Form1 class, and the created form object is supplied to the Application.Run **2** method. When you execute this code, the Add method is invoked and the results of the operation are displayed to the user. As you can see, you could invoke the Add method directly without having to qualify the name of the method with the name of the module.

Creating Multiple Modules

It is possible to have multiple modules in a project. However, when you declare multiple modules, you need to be careful defining the members for those modules. Members with the same name that are defined in two or more modules must be qualified with their module name when accessed outside their module. For example, create another module named MathModuleNew, as shown here, and add it to Listing 2.1.

```
Public Module MathModuleNew
    Public Function Add(ByVal firstVal As Integer, ByVal secondVal As Integer) As
    ➡Integer
        Return firstVal + secondVal
    End Function
    Public Function Subtract(ByVal firstVal As Integer, _
        ByVal secondVal As Integer) As Integer
```

```
      Return firstVal - secondVal
   End Function
End Module
```

After you add MathModuleNew, you have two `Add` methods, one in MathModule and another one in MathModuleNew. Because the members in a module are shared by default, you now need a way to differentiate the two `Add` methods in MathModule and MathNewModule. This means that the form `Load` event needs to be rewritten as follows:

```
Private Sub Form1_Load(ByVal sender As System.Object, ByVal e As
➥System.EventArgs) _
   Handles MyBase.Load
   'Invoke the Module's method
   MessageBox.Show(MathModule.Add(10, 20)) 'Add method is qualified with module
   ➥name
End Sub
```

As you can see from this code, the module name (MathModule) is prefixed with the method name (Add) while invoking that method.

Control Structures

This section dives into VB .NET's control structures to show you how to control the order of events in your programs. Visual Basic's sequence, selection, and repetition structures are used to select and repeat various statements and, thereby, execute complex algorithms. In the process, this section introduces commonly used short-hand operators that enable the programmer to quickly calculate and assign new values to variables.

Normally, statements in a program are executed one after another in the order in which they are written. This process is called sequential execution. However, various Visual Basic statements enable the programmer to specify that the next statement to be executed might not be the next one in sequence. A transfer of control occurs when a statement other than the next one in the program executes.

Visual Basic provides seven types of repetition structures:

- ▶ `While`
- ▶ `DoWhile/Loop`
- ▶ `Do/LoopWhile`
- ▶ `DoUntil/Loop`
- ▶ `Do/LoopUntil`
- ▶ `For/Next`
- ▶ `ForEach/Next`

Control Structures

Apart from providing repetition structures, Visual Basic .NET provides conditional statements such as If/Then and Select/Case. The following sections demonstrate these conditional statements.

If/Then **Selection Structure**

In a program, a selection structure chooses among alternative courses of action. For example, suppose that the passing grade on an examination is 75 (out of 100).

```
If studentGrade >= 75 Then
  Console.WriteLine("Passed")
End If
```

This Visual Basic .NET code determines whether the condition studentGrade>=75 is true or false. If the condition is true, Passed is printed, and the next statement in order is "performed." If the condition is false, the Console.WriteLine statement is ignored, and the next statement in order is performed. A decision can be made on any expression that evaluates to a value of Visual Basic's Boolean type (that is, any expression that evaluates to True or False).

If/Then/Else **Selection Structure**

The If/Then selection structure performs an indicated action only when the condition evaluates to true; otherwise, the action is skipped. The If/ThenElse/Selection structure enables the programmer to specify that a different action should be performed when the condition is True than what is performed when the condition is False.

```
If studentGrade >= 75 Then
  Console.WriteLine("Passed")
Else
  Console.WriteLine("Failed")
End If
```

For example, the previous statement prints Passed if the student's grade is greater than or equal to 75; it prints Failed if the student's grade is less than 75. In either case, after printing occurs, the next statement in sequence is executed.

Select/Case **Statement**

Occasionally, an algorithm contains a series of decisions in which the algorithm tests a variable or expression separately for each value that the variable or expression might assume. The algorithm then takes different actions based on those values. Visual Basic provides the SelectCase structure to handle such decision making. The syntax of the SelectCase statement is as follows:

```
Select [Case] testexpression
  [Case expressionlist
    [statements]]
  [Case Else
      [elsestatements]]
End Select
```

The statement `Select Case` begins the `Select Case` structure. The expression following the keywords `Select Case` is called the controlling expression. The controlling expression is compared sequentially with each `Case`. If a matching `Case` is found, the code in the `Case` executes and program control proceeds to the first statement after the `SelectCase` structure.

```
Dim marks As Integer = 75
Select marks    'Evaluate marks
  Case 90 To 100    'Marks between 90 and 100, inclusive.
    Debug.WriteLine("Grade A")
  Case 80 to 89    'Marks between 80 and 89, inclusive.
    Debug.WriteLine("Grade B")
  Case 70 to 79    'Marks between 70 and 79, inclusive.
    'The following is the only Case clause that evaluates to True
    Debug.WriteLine("Grade C")
  Case 60 to 69    'Marks between 60 and 69, inclusive.
    Debug.WriteLine("Grade D")
  Case 0 to 59    'Marks between 0 and 59, inclusive.
    Debug.WriteLine("Grade F")
  Case Else    'Other values.
    Debug.WriteLine("No Grade")
End Select
```

This code uses a `SelectCase` structure to calculate the grade for the students in an exam. Assume that the exam is graded as follows: 90 and above is an A, 80–89 is a B, 70–79 is a C, 60–69 is a D, and 0–59 is an F. Students not present for the exam receive a 0. Line 7 in Figure 3.8 declares a variable grade as type `Integer`. The `marks` variable stores each mark that is input. In the previous example, the `marks` variable contains a hard-coded value. Because of the hard-coded value, it always executes the `Debug.WriteLine("Grade C")` line.

`While` **Repetition Structure**

A repetition structure enables the programmer to specify that an action should be repeated a number of times, depending on the value of a condition. As you have already seen, Visual Basic .NET provides seven repetition structures, one of which is the `While` repetition structure.

Control Structures

As an example of a `While` structure, consider a program segment designed to find the first power of 2 that is larger than 1,000. Suppose that the `Integer` variable product contains the value 2. When the following `While` structure finishes executing, `product` contains the result:

```
Dim product As Integer = 2
While product <= 1000
    product = product * 2
End While
```

When the `While` structure begins executing, `product` is 2. The variable product is multiplied by 2 repeatedly, taking on the values 4, 8, 16, 32, 64, 128, 256, 512, and 1024, successively. When `product` becomes 1024, the condition `product<=1000` in the `While` structure becomes `false`. This condition causes the repetition to terminate, with 1024 as the final value of `product`. Execution continues with the next statement after the `While` structure.

TIP

Note that if a `While` structure's condition is initially `false`, the body statement(s) never are executed.

DoWhile/Loop **Repetition Structure**

The `DoWhile/Loop` repetition structure behaves like the `While` repetition structure. As an example of a `DoWhile/Loop` structure, consider another version of the segment designed to find the first power of 2 larger than 1,000:

```
Dim product As Integer = 2
Do While product <= 1000
  product = product * 2
Loop
```

When the `DoWhile/Loop` structure is entered, the value of `product` is 2. The variable product is multiplied by 2 repeatedly, taking on the values 4, 8, 16, 32, 64, 128, 256, 512, and 1024 successively. When product becomes 1024, the condition in the `DoWhile/Loop` structure, `product<=1000`, becomes `false`. This condition causes the repetition to terminate, with 1024 as the final value of `product`. Program execution continues with the next statement after the `DoWhile/Loop` structure.

`Do/LoopWhile` **Repetition Structure**

The `Do/LoopWhile` structure tests the loop-continuation condition after the body of the loop is performed. Therefore, in a `Do/LoopWhile` structure, the body of the loop is always executed at least once. When a `Do/LoopWhile` structure terminates, execution continues with the statement after the `LoopWhile` clause. As an example of a `Do/LoopWhile` repetition structure, again consider the segment designed to find the first power of 2 larger than 1,000:

```
Dim product As Integer = 1
Do
  product = product * 2
Loop While product <= 1000
```

The `Do/LoopWhile` repetition structure is similar to the `While` and `DoWhile/Loop` structures. In the `While` and `DoWhile/Loop` structures, the loop-continuation condition is tested at the beginning of the loop, before the body of the loop is performed.

`DoUntil/Loop` **Repetition Structure**

Unlike the `While` and `DoWhile/Loop` repetition structures, the `DoUntil/Loop` repetition structure tests a condition for falsity for repetition to continue. Statements in the body of a `DoUntil/Loop` are executed repeatedly, as long as the loop-continuation test evaluates to `false`. As an example of a `DoUntil/Loop` repetition structure, again consider the segment designed to find the first power of 2 larger than 1,000:

```
Dim product As Integer = 2
Do Until product >= 1000
      product = product * 2
Loop
```

In this code, the condition is evaluated first. If the condition is true, the code inside the loop then is executed.

`Do/LoopUntil` **Repetition Structure**

The `Do/LoopUntil` structure is similar to the `DoUntil/Loop` structure, except that the loop-continuation condition is tested after the body of the loop is performed; therefore, the body of the loop executes at least once. When a `Do/LoopUntil` terminates, execution continues with the statement after the `LoopUntil` clause.

Control Structures

As an example of a Do/LoopUntil repetition structure, again consider the segment designed to find the first power of 2 larger than 1,000:

```
Dim product As Integer = 1
Do
  product = product * 2
Loop Until product >= 1000
```

Because the condition is evaluated at the end, the code inside the loop is executed at least once.

For/Next **Repetition Structure**

The variations of the Do loops that you saw in the previous sections work well when you do not know in advance how many times you need to execute the statements in the loop. However, when you expect to execute the loop a specific number of times, a For/Next loop is a better choice. Unlike a Do loop, a For loop uses a variable called a counter that increases or decreases in value during each repetition of the loop. The syntax is as follows:

```
For counter [ As datatype ] = start To end [ Step step ]
    'Statement block to be executed for each value of counter.
Next [counter]
```

The variable counter is usually an Integer. The iteration values start, end, and step are expressions that must evaluate to the same data type used by counter. The optional step can be positive or negative. If it is omitted, it is taken to be 1.

TIP

If counter is not declared outside the loop, you can use the As clause to declare it as part of the For statement.

When execution of the For/Next loop begins, Visual Basic evaluates start, end, and step. It then assigns start to counter. Before it executes the statement block, it compares counter to end. If counter is already past the end value, the For loop terminates and control passes to the statement following the Next statement. Otherwise, the statement block is executed. Each time Visual Basic encounters the Next statement, it increments counter by step and returns to the For statement. Again it compares counter to end, and again it either executes the block or terminates the loop, depending on the result. This process continues until counter passes end or an Exit For statement is executed.

> **TIP**
>
> You can optionally specify `counter` in the `Next` statement. This improves the readability of your program. When you do specify this information, you must use the same variable as the one that appears in the `For` statement.

2

In the following procedure, named `Calculate`, the `For` statement specifies the `counter` variable `i` and specifies its start and end values as `1` and `10`, respectively. The `Next` statement increments the counter by `1` because `step` is not supplied.

```
Sub Calculate()
  Dim i, total As Integer
  For i = 1 To 10
    total = total + i
  Next i
  MsgBox("The total is " & total)
End Sub
```

If required, you can also decrease the `counter` variable by specifying a negative step value. When you do this, you should specify an end value that is less than the start value.

`ForEach/Next` **Repetition Structure**

The `ForEach/Next` loop is similar to the `For/Next` loop, but it executes the statement block for each element in a collection instead of a specified number of times. The syntax of the `ForEach/Next` statement is as follows:

```
For Each elementvariable [As datatype] In collection
   'Statement block to be executed for each value of elementvariable.
Next [elementvariable]
```

The elements of `collection` can be of any data type. The data type of `elementvariable` must be such that each element of the collection can be converted to it.

For each iteration of the loop, Visual Basic sets the variable `elementvariable` to one of the elements in the collection and executes the statement block. When all the elements in the collection have been assigned to `elementvariable`, the `For Each` loop terminates and control passes to the statement following the `Next` statement. As with the `For/Next` loop, you can optionally specify the element variable in the `Next` statement. This improves the readability of your program.

Control Structures

The following procedure accepts a form and sets the background color of every control in that form to light blue:

```
Sub ConvertBackground(ByVal currentForm As System.Windows.Forms.Form)
  Dim ctl As System.Windows.Forms.Control
  For Each ctl In currentForm.Controls
    ctl.BackColor = System.Drawing.Color.LightBlue
  Next ctl
End Sub
```

NOTE

The collection must be an object that implements the `IEnumerable` interface of the `System.Collections` namespace. `IEnumerable` defines the `GetEnumerator` method, which returns an enumerator object for the collection. The enumerator object exposes the `Current` property and the `MoveNext` method. Visual Basic uses the `Current` property and the `MoveNext` methods of the enumerator object to traverse the collection.

`Exit` Statement

Sometimes you want to leave a loop while executing a repetition structure such as a `Do/Loop`, `For/Loop`, `Select/Case`, or `Do/While`. The `Exit` statement is used to exit a procedure or block and transfer control immediately to the statement following the procedure call or the block definition. The syntax of the exit statement is as follows:

```
Exit { Do | For | Function | Property | Select | Sub | Try | While }
```

As you can see, you can use the `Exit` statement to exit directly from any decision structure, loop, or procedure. The following versions of the `Exit` statement are possible when dealing with looping structures:

- `Exit Select`
- `Exit Try`
- `Exit Do`
- `Exit While`
- `Exit For`

This is an example of how to use the `Exit` statement:

```
Sub ExitStatement()
  Dim number as Integer
  number = Int(Rnd * 1000) 'Generate random numbers.
  Select Case number 'Evaluate random number.
    Case 1:
      Debug.WriteLine("Generated random number is 1")
    Case 2:
      Debug.WriteLine("Generated random number is 2")
```

```
   Case 3 to 10:
      Exit Select
   End Select
   'Add the remaining code here
End Sub
```

In this code, when the randomly generated number is between 3 and 10, the code immediately exits the SelectCase structure.

Assignment Operators

Visual Basic .NET provides several assignment operators for abbreviating assignment statements. For example, the statement

```
value = value + 3
```

can be abbreviated with the addition assignment operator (+=) as follows:

```
value += 3
```

The += operator adds the value of the right operand to the value of the left operand and stores the result in the left operand's variable. Any statement of the form

```
<variable> = <variable> <operator> <expression>
```

where operator is one of the binary operators +, -, *, ^, &, /, or \, can be written in this form:

```
<variable> <operator>= <expression>
```

Although the symbols =, +=, -=, *=, /=, \=, ^=, and &= are operators, you do not include them in operator-precedence tables. When an assignment statement is evaluated, the expression to the right of the operator always is evaluated first and subsequently is assigned to the variable on the left. Unlike Visual Basic's other operators, the assignment operators can occur only once in a statement.

Logical Operators

So far, you have studied only simple conditions, such as count<=10, total>1000, and total <> 100. Each selection and repetition structure evaluated only one condition with one of the operators >, <, >=, <=, =, or <>. To make a decision that relied on evaluating multiple conditions, you performed these tests in separate statements or in nested If/Then or If/ThenElse structures.

Assignment Operators

To handle multiple conditions more efficiently, Visual Basic provides logical operators that can be used to form complex conditions by combining simple ones. The logical operators are AndAlso, And, OrElse, Or, Xor, and Not. The next sections consider examples of how to use each of these operators.

Suppose that you want to ensure that two conditions are both true in a program before a certain path of execution is chosen. In such a case, you can use the logical AndAlso operator, as follows:

```
If gender = "M" AndAlso age >= 65 Then
  seniorCitizen += 1
End If
```

This If/Then statement contains two simple conditions. The condition gender="M" determines whether a person is male, and the condition age>=65 determines whether a person is a senior citizen. The two simple conditions are evaluated first because the precedences of = and >= are both higher than the precedence of AndAlso. The If/Then statement then considers the combined condition

```
gender = "F" AndAlso age >= 65
```

This condition evaluates to true only if both the simple conditions are true. When this combined condition is true, the count of seniorCitizen is incremented by one. However, if either or both of the simple conditions are false, the program skips the incrementation step and proceeds to the statement following the If/Then structure.

TIP

Note that you can increase the readability of the preceding combined conditions by adding parentheses:

```
(gender = "F") AndAlso (age >= 65)
```

Now consider the OrElse operator. Suppose that you want to ensure that either or both of two conditions are true before you choose a certain path of execution. You use the OrElse operator in the following program segment:

```
If (semesterAverage >= 90 OrElse finalExam >= 90) Then
  Console.WriteLine("Student grade is A")
End If
```

This statement also contains two simple conditions. The condition semesterAverage >=90 is evaluated to determine whether the student deserves an A in the course because of an outstanding performance throughout the semester. The condition finalExam >= 90 is evaluated to determine whether the student deserves an A in the course because of an outstanding performance on the final exam.

The `If/Then` statement then considers the combined condition and awards the student an A if either or both of the conditions are true:

```
(semesterAverage >= 90 OrElse finalExam >= 90)
```

Note that the text `Student grade is A` is always printed unless both of the conditions are false.

The `AndAlso` operator has a higher precedence than the `OrElse` operator. An expression containing `AndAlso` or `OrElse` operators is evaluated only until truth or falsity is known. For example, evaluation of this expression stops immediately if gender is not equal to `F` (that is, the entire expression is false):

```
(gender = "F" AndAlso age >= 65)
```

The evaluation of the second expression is irrelevant because the first condition is false. Evaluation of the second condition occurs only if gender is equal to `F` (that is, the entire expression could still be true if the condition `age>=65` is true). This performance feature for evaluating `AndAlso` and `OrElse` expressions is called short-circuit evaluation.

TIP

In expressions that use the operator `AndAlso`, if the separate conditions are independent of one another, place the condition most likely to be false as the leftmost condition. In expressions that use the operator `OrElse`, make the condition most likely to be true the leftmost condition. Each of these techniques can reduce a program's execution time.

The logical AND operator without short-circuit evaluation `And()` and the logical inclusive OR operator without short-circuit evaluation `Or()` are similar to the `AndAlso` and `OrElse` operators, respectively, with one exception: The And and Or logical operators always evaluate both of their operands. No short-circuit evaluation occurs when And and Or are employed. For example, the expression `(gender = "F" And age >= 65)` evaluates `age>=65` even if gender is not equal to F.

Normally, there is no compelling reason to use the And and Or operators instead of `AndAlso` and `OrElse`. However, some programmers make use of them when the right operand of a condition produces a side effect (such as a modification of a variable's value) or when the right operand includes a required method call, as in the following program segment:

```
Console.WriteLine("What is your age?")
If (gender = "M" And Console.ReadLine() >= 65) Then
   Console.WriteLine("You are a male senior citizen.")
End If
```

Assignment Operators

Here, the And operator guarantees that the condition Console.ReadLine()>=65 is evaluated, so ReadLine is called regardless of whether the overall expression is true. It would be better to write this code as two separate statements; the first would store the result of Console.ReadLine in a variable, and the second would use that variable with the AndAlso operator in the condition.

A condition containing the logical exclusive OR (Xor) operator is true only if one of its operands results in a true value and the other results in a false value. If both operands are true or both are false, the entire condition is false.

Visual Basic's Not (logical negation) operator enables a programmer to "reverse" the meaning of a condition. Unlike the logical operators AndAlso, And, OrElse, Or, and Xor, which each combine two conditions (that is, they are all binary operators), the logical negation operator is a unary operator and requires only one operand. The logical negation operator is placed before a condition to choose a path of execution if the original condition (without the logical negation operator) is false. The following program segment demonstrates the logical negation operator:

```
If Not (grade = sentinelValue) Then
    Console.WriteLine("The next grade is " & grade)
End If
```

The parentheses around the condition grade = sentinelValue are necessary because the logical negation operator (Not) has a higher precedence than the equality operator. In most cases, the programmer can avoid logical negation by expressing the condition differently with relational or equality operators. For example, the preceding statement can be written as follows:

```
If grade <> sentinelValue Then
    Console.WriteLine("The next grade is " & grade)
End If
```

This flexibility aids programmers in expressing conditions more naturally.

Conditional Statements

As you write Visual Basic code, you often need to determine when certain operations should be done. For instance, you'll want to execute one or more statements if a certain condition is true and other statements if the condition is false. To get you started, this section first shows you how to code condition expressions. Then it shows you how to code two kinds of conditional statements that use those expressions.

How to Code Conditional Expressions and Use Them in Conditional Statements

A conditional expression is an expression that evaluates to either a `True` or a `False` value when it's used in certain statements. You can use conditional expressions in assignment statements to assign a value to Boolean variables or properties.

You also use these expressions in conditional statements such as `If` and `Select Case` statements.

To evaluate a conditional expression, Visual Basic performs the operations from left to right, based on the order of precedence. If you review this order, you can see that arithmetic operations are done first, followed by relational operations and logical operations. Although you can use six logical operators with Visual Basic, the ones you'll use the most are `Not`, `And`, and `Or`. Here are some examples of conditional expressions:

```
switch <> "Yes"
newCustomer = True
thisDay > lastDay
value = 1
value Not > 99
monthlyInvestment > 0 And interestRate > 0 And months > 0
```

These lines of code show how to create conditional expressions.

Using Assignment Operators

Assignment has been simplified in Visual Basic .NET. Earlier Visual Basic versions (Visual Basic 4.0 to 6.0) had two different ways of assigning a value to a variable: one for simple variables (including structures and arrays) and one for object variables. Fortunately, the developers of Visual Basic .NET removed the assignment method used for object variables and relied only on the method used for simple variables. You assign values to variables (either simple or object) by putting the variable to the left of an equals sign, as shown in the following code:

```
count = 1
custObj = New Customer()
```

In the first line, the `count` variable is assigned the value of `1` and the second line is used to create an instance of the `Customer` object.

Using Assignment Operators

> **TIP**
>
> In Visual Basic 4.0 to 6.0, the assignment lines shown previously would have appeared like this:
>
> ```
> iSomeVar = 1234
> Set oObjectVar = New Something
> ```
>
> However, the rules of when to use Set were confusing, so Microsoft removed the need for the Set keyword.

Constants

Constants are another class of values that you can use in your Visual Basic .NET programs. Constants are values that do not change, either for the lifetime of your program or ever. For example, the months in a year, the value of pi, and the database server from which your program retrieves data are all constant values. You can define a value as being constant when you declare it. Any attempts to change the value of a constant are marked as an error while you are still in the Integrated Development Environment (IDE) and before you attempt to run the application. Constants are declared using one of the two forms shown in the following code:

```
Const PI As Double = 3.1415
Const MONTHS_IN_YEAR As String = "12"
```

If the type of the constant is not described in a declaration, the compiler must use the value type that best fits. However, it does not always select the best possible type.

> **TIP**
>
> Declare the type you want to use when declaring constants, just as you do when declaring variables.

Generally, when declaring constants, if you do not include the type of the value, Visual Basic .NET creates the following variable types:

- ▶ Long—For any undeclared whole numbers.
- ▶ Double—For any undeclared decimal numbers. (Note that if the value is actually too large for a Double, it will be truncated.)
- ▶ String—For any character values.

Using Operators

In Visual Basic .NET, operators perform simple calculations and similar "functions." Most of the operators in Visual Basic .NET should be familiar to you as common algebraic symbols. However, some of them are unique to programming. Table 2.1 lists the most commonly used operators.

TABLE 2.1

Common Operators in Visual Basic .NET

Operator	Use	Example
=	Assigns one value to another	`X = 6`
+	Adds two values	`Y = X + 7` (Y holds 13)
–	Subtracts one value from another	`Y = X – 4` (Y holds 2)
*	Multiplies two values	`Y = X * 2` (Y holds 12)
/	Divides one value by another	`Y = X / 2` (Y holds 3)
\	Divides one value by another, but returns only a whole number	`Y = X \ 3` (Y holds 1)
Mod	Short for modulus, returns the remainder for a division	`Y = X Mod 3` (Y holds 2)
&	Combines two strings	`S = "Hello " & "World"` (S holds "Hello World")
+=	Shorthand for adds a value and assigns the result	`X += 2` (X holds 8)
-=	Shorthand for subtracts a value and assigns the result	`X -= 3` (X holds 5)
*=	Shorthand for multiplies a value and assigns the result	`X *= 6` (X holds 30)
/=	Shorthand for divides by a value and assigns the result	`X /= 5` (X holds 6)
&=	Shorthand for combines with a string and assigns the result	`S &= ", John"` (S holds "Hello World, John")
^	Raises one value to the power of an exponent	`3^4` (3 to the power of 4, returns 81)

Table 2.1 also provides examples of how to use those operators in your code.

Built-In Functions

In addition to the functions that the .NET Framework provides, Visual Basic .NET has many built-in functions. These functions provide many useful capabilities, including the capacity to convert from one data type to another, mathematical calculations, string manipulation, and so on. You should know about some of these functions to be able to get around in Visual Basic .NET.

Built-In Functions

Conversion Functions

Some of the most important functions available to you in Visual Basic are the conversion functions. They enable you to convert one type of data into another. With Visual Basic .NET, conversion functions have become even more important because this version of Visual Basic is much stricter about data types and does not automatically convert one type into another, as previous versions did.

TIP

If you want Visual Basic .NET to automatically convert data types for you, you can turn off the strict type checking by adding Option Strict Off to the top of your files. You should know, however, that this could lead to unexpected results in your code if Visual Basic .NET converts a variable when you don't expect it to.

The conversion functions in Visual Basic .NET all begin with the letter *C* (as in *conversion*) and end with an abbreviated form of the new type. In addition, there is a generic conversion function, CType, which can convert to any type. Table 2.2 describes the main conversion functions.

TABLE 2.2

Conversion Functions in Visual Basic .NET

Function	Description
CBool	Converts to a Boolean. Anything that evaluates to False or 0 will be set to False; otherwise, it will be True.
CByte	Converts to a Byte. Any value greater than 255 or any fractional information will be lost.
CChar	Converts to a single character. If the value is greater than 65535, it will be lost. If you convert a String, only the first character is converted.
CDate	Converts to a Date. One of the more powerful conversion functions, CDate can recognize some of the more common formats for entering a date.
CDbl	Converts to a Double.
CInt	Converts to an Integer. Fractions are rounded to the nearest value.
CLng	Converts to a Long. Fractions are rounded to the nearest value.
CSht	Converts to a Short. Fractions are rounded to the nearest value.
CStr	Converts to a String. If the value is a Date, this will contain the Short Date format.
CType	Converts to any type. This is a powerful function that enables you to convert any data type into any other type. Therefore, the syntax for this function is slightly different than the others.

The syntax for CType is shown here:

```
newVariable = CType(oldVariable, <Type_Name>)
```

Here, `newVariable` and `oldVariable` are placeholders for the variables that you're converting to and from, respectively. `Type_Name` is the type you are converting to. This can be any variable that you could put after the `As` in a declaration, so you can use this function to convert to enumerations, structures, and object types as well as simple types.

String-Manipulation Functions

Most of Visual Basic's earlier string-related functions have been replaced in Visual Basic .NET with the functionality internal to the `String` class. However, you might see some of the functions listed in Table 2.3 in older code, so you should be familiar with these functions.

TABLE 2.3

String-Related Functions in Visual Basic .NET

Function	Description	Example
Len	Returns the length of a string.	value = Len("Hello") ('value holds 5)
Chr	Returns the character based on the entered ASCII or Unicode value.	value = Chr(56) ('value holds the letter A)
Asc	Returns the ASCII or Unicode value.	value = Asc("A") ('value holds 56)
Left	Returns characters from a string, beginning with the leftmost character. Also requires the number of characters to return.	value = Left("Hello World", 2) ('value holds He)
Right	Returns characters from a string, beginning with the rightmost character (the opposite of Left). Also requires the number of characters to return.	value = Right("Hello World",4) ('value holds orld.)
Mid	Returns characters that are not at either end of a string. Mid returns any number of characters. The syntax for Mid is retValue = Mid(String, Start, Length), in which Start is the character to begin returning from and Length is the number of characters (including Start) to return. One nice feature is that if you omit Length, you return all the characters from Start on.	value = Mid("Hello World", 4, 5)) ('value holds lo Wo)
Instr	Finds one string within another. This is useful when searching a file for some string.	value = Instr(1,"Hello World","l")) ('value holds 3)
LCase	Converts a string to all lowercase.	value = LCase("Hello World") ('value holds hello world)

Built-In Functions

TABLE 2.3

Continued

Function	Description	Example
UCase	Converts a string to all uppercase.	value = UCase("Hello World") ('value holds HELLO WORLD)
LTrim	Removes all leading spaces from a string.	value = LTrim(" Hello World ") ('value holds Hello World)
RTrim	Removes all trailing spaces from a string.	value = RTrim(" Hello World ") ('value holds Hello World)
Trim	Removes all leading and trailing spaces from a string.	value = Trim(" Hello World ") ('value holds Hello World)

As explained before, all the functions listed in Table 2.3 are used with the System.String class.

Other Useful Functions

Some useful functions don't fit into the other categories. These include functions that enable you to determine the type of a variable, as well as date-manipulation functions. Table 2.4 lists some of these miscellaneous built-in functions.

TABLE 2.4

Miscellaneous Built-in Functions

Function	Description
IsArray	Returns True if the parameter is an array
IsDate	Returns True if the parameter is recognizable as a date
IsNumeric	Returns True if the parameter is recognizable as a number
IsObject	Returns True if the parameter is some object type
TypeName	Returns the name of the data type of the parameter
Now	Returns the current date and time
Today	Returns the current date, with the time set to 0:00:00 a.m.

TIP

You can also find a quick description of other built-in functions using the Object Browser. You can open Object Browser by selecting View, Other Windows, Object Browser. The built-in functions are contained in the Microsoft.VisualBasic.dll section.

Writing Your Own Routines

Although the built-in functions are quite useful, there will always be times when you need to create your own routines. Perhaps you need to select a set of built-in functions that are all called in the same way, or perhaps you need to create some unique functionality. Either way, Visual Basic .NET makes creating your own routines easy.

Visual Basic .NET uses two types of routines. One type is a routine that does something but doesn't return any value. This is called a subroutine (or sub, for short). The other type of procedure does something but returns a value. These are called functions. The following sections look at both of these routines.

Subroutines

A subroutine is a block of Visual Basic .NET code that performs some task—for example, the `Console.WriteLine` method that you see in many of the examples prints information to the screen but does not return any value. You use subroutines to perform tasks in your programs.

Generally, anytime you have some code that you perform more than once, you should think about putting it into a subroutine. Similarly, if you have some code that you might use in multiple applications, you should put it into a subroutine. Subroutines let you isolate a small chunk of your program so that, rather than repeating the whole block of code, you simply refer to it by name. This does not mean that the subroutine will always do exactly the same steps; it will do just some task.

To create your own subroutines, you use the `Sub` keyword:

```
Sub <MethodName>(Parameter1 As Type, Parameter2 As Type, ............ParameterN As Type)
  'Add code here
End Sub
```

In this syntax, each of the parameters defines a value that is to be passed into the routine. The following code shows how to declare a subroutine:

```
Sub ShowMessage(ByVal Message As String)
  Console.WriteLine(Message)
End Sub
```

The subroutine begins with the `Sub` keyword. The subroutine is called `ShowMessage`, and it takes one parameter when you call it. The subroutine ends with the `End Sub` keyword. In between is the actual code that the subroutine executes. In this case, it simply displays the contents of the parameter to the Console window.

Writing Your Own Routines

When you have the previous subroutine declared, you can invoke the subroutine using the following line of code:

```
ShowMessage("Hello World")
```

This line shows one possible way of calling the subroutine, passing in the string Hello World.

Functions

Creating your own functions enables you to create new capabilities within your application. Creating a new function is similar to defining new subroutines, except that you define the return value type. Within the procedure, you identify the value to be returned, as shown here:

```
Function <FunctionName>(Parameter1 As <Type>, ... ParameterN As <Type>) As
➥<ReturnType>
  'Add code here
  Return returnVal
End Function
```

In this syntax, each of the parameters defines a value that is to be passed into the routine, <ReturnType> is the data type the function returns, and returnVal is the value that will be returned from the function. The following code shows the declaration of a simple function:

```
Function Volume(ByVal Length As Integer, ByVal Width As Integer, _
  ByVal Height As Integer) As Integer
  Return Length * Width * Height
End Function
```

The Volume function can now be invoked using the following line of code:

```
Console.WriteLine(Volume(3,4,5))
```

To the Volume function, you also supply the parameters.

Scope of Variables

Scope can be defined as the attribute that defines the visibility of variables within a program—that is, which routines could use a given variable. You might not want all routines to access all variables. Allowing all routines to see all variables could lead to one routine "accidentally" changing the value of a variable, introducing a bug in your program.

Until now, you have usually declared variables using the `Dim` keyword inside procedures. However, you can also declare variables outside procedures to make the variable available to multiple procedures. If you do this, you can use two other keywords, `Public` and `Private`:

- ▶ Public variables are available throughout an application. These are global variables, which exist throughout the application—that is, globally. Public variables should be used sparingly but are useful when you need some value that will be used at many points in your program, such as the connection to a database, or a file.

- ▶ Private variables are available within the module or class where they are declared. Private variables are used frequently in applications when you need a single variable that can be used in multiple procedures. By creating it with the keyword, you allow all the procedures within one module or class to access the variable. Private variables are useful for sharing common information required for a task, such as an intermediate value that different functions can access to perform a calculation.

TIP

When you create a variable, you should declare it a newly created variable as close as possible to where it is needed. If you use a variable in only one procedure, you should declare that variable within that procedure. Also note that you should use module-level private and public variables sparingly.

Why Is Scope Important?

Scope enables you to isolate the data that your applications' procedures use. Much older versions of BASIC did not have the capability for scope, and all variables were accessible and changeable from all parts of the program. Imagine writing a program back then: You might often reuse a variable elsewhere in a program. This could possibly lead to a bug if you changed the value in one spot in the program, only to mistakenly read the changed value later when you expected to get the original value.

Scope and Procedures

Just as variables can have scope, procedures (subroutines and functions) have scope. Scope for procedures means the same as scope for variables: It describes where else in your program you can use the procedure. Procedure scope is defined using the same keywords used for variable scope. Generally, scope has the same meaning here as well. These are the two commonly used scope levels:

- ▶ **Public**—The procedure can be called from any other part of the application. This is the default if you don't add any other keyword.

Writing Your Own Routines

▸ **Private**—The procedure can be called only from another procedure within the same module or class where it is defined. This is useful when you are writing a number of support routines used throughout a calculation, but other routines would not need to use them.

You will see more on this topic in Chapter 3, "Object-Oriented Programming Fundamentals," which covers objects and classes.

Summary

In this chapter, you learned the basics of variables and how to use them in your VB .NET applications. After that, this chapter covered such various concepts as modules and namespaces. It also focused on the constructs that VB .NET provides for controlling execution flow.

Further Reading

MSDN documentation on VB .NET.

.NET Framework Fundamentals, http://msdn.microsoft.com/netframework/ programming/fundamentals/default.aspx.

Visual Basic Developer Center, http://msdn.microsoft.com/vbasic/.

3 OBJECT-ORIENTED PROGRAMMING FUNDAMENTALS

IN BRIEF

With the introduction of a new set of object-oriented features, Visual Basic .NET has become a full-fledged object-oriented language. Visual Basic .NET provides built-in support for all the object-oriented concepts, including abstraction, encapsulation, polymorphism, and inheritance. In this chapter, you will learn the concepts of object-oriented programming and get a complete understanding of how to implement these concepts in Visual Basic .NET.

WHAT YOU NEED

SOFTWARE REQUIREMENTS	Windows 2000, XP, or 2003 .NET Framework 1.1 SDK Visual Studio .NET 2003 with Visual Basic .NET installed
HARDWARE REQUIREMENTS	PC desktop or laptop
SKILL REQUIREMENTS	Basic knowledge of .NET Framework

OBJECT-ORIENTED PROGRAMMING FUNDAMENTALS AT A GLANCE

Object-Oriented Concepts

VB .NET provides a simplified object-oriented syntax and provides the core foundation for implementing object-oriented applications by supporting the four major defining concepts required for a language to be fully object oriented. Those four concepts are listed here:

▶ **Abstraction**—This is merely the capability of a language to create "black box" code—to create an abstract representation of a concept within a program. A Customer object, for instance, is an abstract representation of a real-world customer.

▶ **Encapsulation**—This is the concept of separation between interface and implementation. The idea is that you can create an interface (Public methods in a class) and, as long as that interface remains consistent, the application can interact with your objects. This remains true even if you entirely rewrite the code within a given method—thus, the interface is independent of the implementation. Encapsulation enables you to hide the internal implementation details of a class. For example, the algorithm used to compute pi might be proprietary. You can expose a simple API to the end user, but you hide all of the logic used by the algorithm by encapsulating it within the class.

▶ **Polymorphism**—This is reflected in the capability to write one routine that can operate on objects from more than one class, treating different objects from different classes in exactly the same way. For instance, if both Customer and Vendor objects have a Name property, and you can write a routine that calls the Name property regardless of whether you're using a Customer or Vendor object, then you have polymorphism.

▶ **Inheritance**—VB .NET is the first version of VB that supports inheritance. Inheritance is the idea that a class can gain the pre-existing interface and behaviors of an existing class. This is done by inheriting these behaviors from the existing class through a process known as subclassing. With the introduction of full inheritance, VB is now a fully object-orientated language by any reasonable definition.

To start, the next section takes a look at how to create classes and how to create objects by creating instances of the classes.

Creating Classes

Using objects is fairly straightforward and intuitive; even the most novice programmers can pick this up and accept rapidly. Creating classes and objects is a bit more complex and interesting, however; that is covered in the next section.

Creating Basic Classes

As discussed earlier, objects are merely instances of a specific template (or a class). The class contains the code that defines the behavior of its objects and also defines the instance variables that will contain the object's individual data.

Classes are created using the `Class` keyword. A class includes definitions (declaration) and implementations (code) for the variables, methods, properties, and events that make up the class. Each object created based on this class has the same methods, properties, and events, and has its own set of data defined by the variables in the class.

The `Class` Keyword

If you want to create a class that represents a `Customer`, you can use the `Class` keyword:

```
Public Class Customer
   'Implementation code goes here
End Class
```

When you create a new Windows application in Visual Basic using Visual Studio .NET, by default, the project is composed of a set of files with the `.vb` extension. Each file can contain multiple classes. This means that, within a single file, you could have something like this:

```
Public Class Person
   'Implementation code goes here
End Class


Public Class Employee
   'Implementation code goes here
End Class


Public Class Dept
   'Implementation code goes here
End Class
```

Even though you can have multiple classes in a single file, the most common approach is to have a single class per file. This is because the VS .NET Solution Explorer and the code-editing environment are tailored to make it easy to navigate from file to file to find your code. For instance, if you create a single class file with all these classes, Solution Explorer simply shows a single entry, as shown in Figure 3.1.

However, the VS .NET IDE provides the Class View window. If you decide to put multiple classes in each physical `.vb` file, you can use the Class View window to quickly and efficiently navigate through your code, jumping from class to class without having to manually locate those classes in specific code files. To bring up the Class View window, select Class View from the View menu from within Visual Studio .NET. This is shown in Figure 3.2.

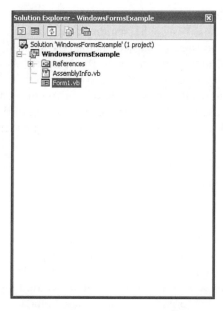

FIGURE 3.1   Classes displayed in
Solution Explorer.

FIGURE 3.2   Showing classes in the Class
View window.

The Class View window shown in Figure 3.2 is incredibly useful, even if you keep one
class per file, because it provides you with a class-based view of your entire
application.

Creating Classes

Creating a Class Using Visual Studio .NET

To start, create a new Visual Basic .NET Windows application by selecting File, New Project from the menu. In the New Project dialog box, select Visual Basic Projects as the project type and Windows Application as the template. After entering the name and location in the dialog box, click OK. When the project is created, you can add a new class by selecting Add Class from the Project menu. You are presented with the standard Add New Item dialog box. Change the name of the class to **Customer.vb**, and click Open. The result is the following code that defines the Customer class:

```
Public Class Customer


End Class
```

It is worth noting that all VB .NET source files end with a .vb extension, regardless of which type of VB source file you choose (form, class, module, and so on) when you are adding the file to the project. In fact, any forms, classes, components, or controls that you add to your project are actually class modules—they are just specific types of classes that provide the appropriate behaviors. The exception is the Module, which is a special construct that enables you to include code within your application that is not directly contained within any class. As with previous versions of Visual Basic, methods placed in a Module can be called directly from any code within a project.

Objects, Classes, and Instances

An object is a code-based abstraction of a real-world entity or relationship. For instance, you might have a Customer object that represents a real-world customer, or you might have a File object that represents a file on your computer's hard drive.

A closely related term is *class*. A class is the code that defines an object, and all objects are created based on a class. A class is an abstraction of a real-world concept, and it provides the basis from which you create instances of specific objects. For example, to have a Customer object, you must first have a Customer class that contains all the code (methods, properties, events, variables, and so on) necessary to create Customer objects. Based on that class, you can create any number of Customer objects. All the Customer objects are identical in terms of what they can do and the code they contain, but each one contains its own unique data. This means that each object represents a different physical customer.

Creating Constructors

In VB .NET, classes can implement a special method that is always invoked as an object is created. This method is called the constructor, and it is always named New.

The constructor method is an ideal location for such initialization code, since it is always run before any other methods are ever invoked—and it is always run only once for an object. Of course, you can create many objects based on a class, and the constructor method will be run for each object that is created.

The constructor method of a VB .NET class is similar to the `Class_Initialize` event in previous versions of Visual Basic, but it is far more powerful in VB .NET because you can also supply parameter values to the constructor.

You can easily implement a constructor in your class simply by implementing a public method named `New`. For example, add the following lines of initialization code to the constructor of the `Customer` class:

```
Public Class Customer
  Private _country as String
  Public Sub New()
    _country = "US"
  End Sub
  'Implementation code goes here
End Class
```

In this example, you are simply using the constructor method to initialize the country for any new `Customer` object that is created.

Parameterized Constructors

You can also use constructors to allow parameters to be passed to your object as it is being created. This is done by simply adding parameters to the `New` method. For example, you can modify the constructor method that was created in the previous section and make it look like as follows:

```
Public Sub New(ByVal countryName As String)
    _country = countryName
End Sub
```

With this change, any time a `Customer` object is created, you are provided with values for the country name parameter. This changes how you can create a new `Customer` object, however. Originally, you used code such as this:

```
Dim custObj As New Customer()
```

Now you have code such as this:

```
Dim custObj As New Customer("US")
```

In fact, because your constructor expects these values, they are mandatory: Any code that wants to create an instance of your `Customer` class must provide these values.

Objects, Classes, and Instances

Fortunately, there are alternatives in the form of optional parameters and method overloading (enabling you to create multiple versions of the same method, each accepting a different parameter list).

Constructors with Optional Parameters

In many cases, you want a constructor to accept parameter values for initializing new objects, but you also want to have the capability to create objects without providing those values. This is possible by using optional parameters.

Optional parameters on a constructor method follow the same rules as optional parameters for any other `Sub` routine: They must be the last parameters in the parameter list, and you must provide default values for the optional parameters.

For instance, you can change your `Customer` class as shown:

```
Public Sub New(Optional ByVal country As String = "US")
  _country = country
End Sub
```

Here you changed the country parameter to be optional and provided a default value for the country. With this constructor in place, you have the option of creating a new `Customer` object with or without the parameter values:

```
Dim custObj As New Customer("US")
```

or

```
Dim custObj As New Customer()
```

If you don't provide a value for the country parameter, the default value of `US` will be used and your code will work just fine.

Composition of an Object

You use an interface to get access to an object's data and behavior. The object's data and behaviors are contained within the object, so a client application can treat the object like a black box accessible only through its interface. This is a key object-oriented concept called encapsulation. The idea is that any programs that make use of this object won't have direct access to the behaviors or data; instead, those programs must make use of the object's interface.

This list walks through each of the elements related to object in detail:

▶ **Interface**—The interface is defined as a set of methods (`Sub` and `Function` routines), properties (`Property` routines), events, and fields (variables or attributes) that are declared `Public` in scope.

▶ **Attribute**—*Attribute* means one thing in the general object-oriented world and something else in .NET. The OO world often refers to an object's variables as attributes, whereas, in .NET, an attribute is a coding construct that you can use to control compilation, the IDE, and so on.

▶ **Method**—This is the place where you actually write code that operates on the data. You can also have `Private` methods and properties in your code. Although these methods can be called by code within your object, they are not part of the interface and cannot be called by programs written to use your object. Another option is to use the `Friend` keyword, which defines the scope to be the current project; this means that any code within your project can call the method, but no code outside your project (that is, from a different .NET assembly) can call the method. To complicate things a bit, you can also declare methods and properties as `Protected`, which are available to classes that inherit from your class.

For example, you might have the following code in a class:

```
Public Function ReturnResult() As Integer
End Function
```

Because this method is declared with the `Public` keyword, it is part of your interface and can be called by client applications that are using your object. You might also have a method such as this:

```
Private Sub DoSomething()
End Sub
```

This method is declared as being `Private` and so is not part of your interface. This method can be called only by code within your class, not by any code outside your class, such as the code in a program that is using one of your objects.

On the other hand, you can do something like this:

```
Public Function ReturnResult() As Integer
  DoSomething()
End Function
```

In this case, you are calling the `Private` method from within a `Public` method. Although code using your objects can't directly call a `Private` method, you will frequently use `Private` methods to help structure the code in your class to make it more maintainable and easier to read.

Finally, you can use the `Friend` keyword:

```
Friend Sub DoSomething()
End Sub
```

Objects, Classes, and Instances

In this case, the DoSomething method can be called by code within your class or from other classes or modules within your current VB .NET project. Code from outside the project will not have access to the method.

The Friend scope is very similar to the Public scope, in that it makes methods available for use by code outside your object itself. However, unlike Public, the Friend keyword restricts access to code within your current VB .NET project, preventing code in other .NET assemblies from calling the method.

Implementation or Behavior

The code inside of a method is called the implementation. Sometimes it is also called behavior because this code actually makes the object do useful work. For instance, you might have a Name property as part of your object's interface. Within that property, you can write code to combine the first name and last name and return the name:

```
Public Class Customer
  Private _firstName as String
  Private _lastName as String
  Public ReadOnly Property Name() As Integer
    Get
      Return _firstName + "" + _lastName
    End Get
  End Property
End Class
```

In this example, the code returns the full name by combining the first name and the last name. The key concept here is to understand that client applications can use your object even if you change the implementation—as long as you don't change the interface. As long as your method name and its parameter list and return data type remain unchanged, you can change the implementation of the Name property all you want.

The code necessary to call the Name property looks something like this:

```
Dim name as String = cust.Name
```

The result of running this code is the Name value returned for your use. Although your client application will work fine, you might suddenly discover that you want to return the name in a different format, meaning that you need to improve upon the code. Fortunately, you can change your implementation without changing the client code:

```
Public Class Customer
  Private _firstName as String
  Private _lastName as String
  Public ReadOnly Property Name() As Integer
```

```
    Get
      Return _lastName + ", " + _firstName
    End Get
  End Property
End Class
```

In this code, the implementation of the Name property is changed behind the interface without changing the interface itself. Now if run your client application, you will find that Name property returns the new format without breaking the client.

> **NOTE**
>
> It is important to keep in mind that encapsulation is a syntactic tool: It allows your code to continue to run without change. However, it is not semantic. Just because your code continues to run doesn't mean that it continues to do what you actually wanted it to do.

Member or Instance Variables

The third key part of an object is its data, or state. In fact, it might be argued that the only important part of an object is its data. After all, every instance of a class is identical in terms of its interface and its implementation—the only thing that can vary is the data contained within that particular object.

Member variables are declared so that they are available to all code within your class. Typically, member variables are Private in scope, meaning that they are available only to the code in your class itself. They are also sometimes referred to as instance variables or attributes. The .NET Framework refers to them as fields.

> **TIP**
>
> Don't confuse instance variables with properties. In VB, a property is a type of method that is geared toward retrieving and setting values, whereas an instance variable is a variable within the class that can hold the value exposed by a property.

For instance, you might have a class that has instance variables such as first name and last name, as shown in the following code:

```
Public Class Customer
  Private _firstName As String
  Private _lastName As String
End Class
```

Objects, Classes, and Instances

Each instance of the class (each object) will have its own set of these variables in which to store data. Because these variables are declared with the `Private` keyword, they are available only to code within each specific object. Although member variables can be declared as `Public` in scope, this makes them available to any code using your objects in a manner that you can't control. Such a choice directly breaks the concept of encapsulation because code outside your object can directly change data values without following any rules that might otherwise be set in your object's code.

If you want to make the value of an instance variable available to code outside your object, you should use a property and let the client application invoke the property to set or get the value of the instance variable. Listing 3.1 shows the implementation of the `Customer` class and demonstrates how properties can be used to access the private variables.

LISTING 3.1
`Customer` **Class with Properties**

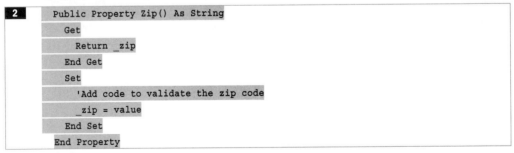

```
Public Class Customer
    Private _city As String
    Private _zip As Date
1       Public Property City() As String
        Get
            Return _city
        End Get
        Set
            'Add code to validate the value of the city
            _city = value
        End Set
    End Property

2       Public Property Zip() As String
        Get
            Return _zip
        End Get
        Set
            'Add code to validate the zip code
            _zip = value
        End Set
    End Property
End Class
```

Because the private City █1 and ZIP █2 attributes are accessed through the properties, you are not directly exposing your internal variables to the client application, thereby preserving encapsulation of data. At the same time, through this mechanism, you can safely provide access to your data as needed.

> **TIP**
>
> Member variables can also be declared with `Friend` scope, meaning that they are available to all code in your project. As with declaring them as `Public`, this breaks encapsulation and is strongly discouraged.

Now that you have a grasp of some of the basic object-oriented terminology, you are ready to explore the creation of classes and objects. First, you will see how VB enables you to interact with objects. Then you will move on to the actual process of authoring those objects.

Working with Objects

In the .NET environment—and within VB, in particular—you use objects all the time without even thinking about it. Every control on a form—and, in fact, every form—is an object. When you open a file or interact with a database, you are using objects to do that work.

Object Declaration and Instantiation

Objects are created using the `New` keyword, indicating that you want a new instance of a particular class. A number of variations exist for how or where you can use the `New` keyword in your code. Each one provides different advantages in terms of code readability or flexibility. The most obvious way to create an object is to declare an object variable and then create an instance of the object:

```
Dim cust As Customer
cust = New Customer()
```

The result of this code is a new instance of the `Customer` class ready for your use. To interact with this new object, you use the `cust` variable that you declared. The `cust` variable contains a reference to the object.

You can shorten this by combining the declaration of the variable with the creation of the instance:

```
Dim cust As New Customer()
```

In previous versions of VB, this was a very poor thing to do because it had both negative performance and maintainability effects. However, in VB .NET, there is no difference between the first example and this one, other than that this line of code is shorter.

The following code both declares the variable `cust` as the data type `Customer` and immediately creates an instance of the class that you can use from your code:

```
Dim cust As Customer = New Customer()
```

Working with Objects

The previous syntax provides a great deal of flexibility while remaining compact. Even though it is a single line of code, it separates the declaration of the variable's data type from the creation of the object. Such flexibility is very useful when working with inheritance or multiple interfaces. You might declare the variable to be of one type—say, an interface—and instantiate the object based on a class that implements that interface. To demonstrate this, create an interface as shown here:

```
Public Interface ICustomer
  Sub GetCustomer()
End Interface
```

After you have created the Customer interface, you can implement that interface, meaning that your class now has its own native interface and also a secondary interface called ICustomer. This is how the declaration of the class looks:

```
Public Class Customer
  Implements ICustomer
  Public Sub GetCustomer() Implements ICustomer.GetCustomer
    'Implementation goes here
  End Sub
End Class
```

You can now create an instance of the Customer class but reference it via the secondary interface by declaring the variable to be of type ICustomer.

```
Dim cust As ICustomer = New Customer()
```

You can also do this using two separate lines of code:

```
Dim cust As ICustomer

cust = New Customer()
```

Either technique works fine and achieves the same result: You have a new object of type Customer that is accessed via its secondary interface.

Object References

Typically, when you work with an object, you are using a reference to that object. On the other hand, when you are working with simple data types such as Integer, you are working with the actual value rather than a reference. In this section, you explore these concepts and see how they work and interact.

When you create a new object using the New keyword, you store a reference to that object in a variable. For instance, this line of code creates a new instance of the Customer class:

```
Dim cust As New Customer()
```

To gain access to this new object, use the cust variable. This variable holds a reference to the object. When you have the reference, you can also do something like this:

```
Dim custObjRef As Customer
custObjRef = cust
```

Now you have a second variable, custObjRef, which also has a reference to that same object. You can use any one of these variables interchangeably because they both reference the exact same object. Remember, however, that the variable you have is not the object itself, but just a reference or pointer to the object itself.

Dereferencing Objects

When you are done working with an object, you can indicate that by dereferencing the object. To dereference an object, simply set your object reference to Nothing:

```
Dim cust As Customer
Cust = New Customer()
cust = Nothing
```

This code has no impact on your object itself. In fact, the object can remain blissfully unaware that it has been dereferenced for some time. After all the variables that reference an object are set to Nothing, the .NET runtime can tell that you no longer need that object. At some point, the runtime destroys the object and reclaims the memory and resources that the object consumes.

Between the time that you dereference the object and the time that .NET gets around to actually destroying it, the object simply sits in memory, unaware that it has been dereferenced. Right before .NET destroys the object, the framework calls the Finalize method on the object (if it has one).

Handling Events

Using methods and properties, you can write code that interacts with your objects by invoking specific functionality as needed. It is often useful for objects to provide notification as certain activities occur during processing. You can see examples of this with controls, with a button indicating that it was clicked via a Click event, or a text box indicating that its contents have changed via the TextChanged event.

Handling Events

Objects can raise events of their own, thereby providing a powerful and easily implemented mechanism by which objects can notify the client code of important activities or events.

TIP

Delegates are used to provide a mapping between the event and the event handlers that will respond to the event. They are the .NET equivalent of function pointers in C++.

Handling Single Events

Before you learn how to handle events, you first will add a button control to the form that you created in the previous sections. Double-click the button to bring up the following code in the code editor:

```
Private Sub button1_Click (ByVal sender As System.Object, _
  ByVal e As System.EventArgs) Handles button1.Click
End Sub
```

Typically, you just write your code in this routine without paying a lot of attention to the code that the VS .NET IDE creates. However, take a second look at that code here, to take note of a couple important things.

First, notice the use of the `Handles` keyword. This keyword specifically indicates that this method will be handling the `Click` event from the `button1` control. Of course, a control is just an object, so you are indicating here that this method will be handling the `Click` event from the `button1` object. Also notice that the method accepts two parameters. The `Button` control class defines these parameters. It turns out that any method that accepts two parameters with these data types can be used to handle the `Click` event. For instance, you could create a new method to handle the event:

```
Private Sub ButtonClickEvent(ByVal s As System.Object, _
  ByVal args As System.EventArgs) Handles button1.Click
End Sub
```

Even though you have changed the method name and the names of the parameters, you are still accepting parameters of the same data types, and you still have the `Handles` clause to indicate that this method will handle the event.

Handling Multiple Events

The `Handles` keyword offers even more flexibility. Not only can the method name be anything you choose, but a single method can handle multiple events, if you desire.

Again, the only requirement is that the method and all the events being raised must have the same parameter list. This explains why all the standard events that the .NET system class library raises have exactly two parameters: the sender and an `EventArgs` object. By being so generic, it is possible to write very generic and powerful event handlers that can accept virtually any event that the class library raises.

One common scenario in which this is useful is having multiple instances of an object that raises events, such as two buttons on a form:

```
Private Sub ButtonClickEvent(ByVal sender As System.Object, _
  ByVal e As System.EventArgs) Handles button1.Click, button2.Click
End Sub
```

Notice that you have modified the `Handles` clause to have a comma-separated list of events to handle. Either event causes the method to run, giving you a central location to handle these events.

The `WithEvents` Keyword

The `WithEvents` keyword tells VB that you want to handle any events raised by the object within your code:

```
Private WithEvents button1 As System.Windows.Forms.Button
```

The `WithEvents` keyword makes any events from an object available for your use, and the `Handles` keyword is used to link specific events to your methods so you can receive and handle them. This is true not only for controls on forms, but also for any objects that you create.

The `WithEvents` keyword cannot be used to declare a variable of a type that doesn't raise events. In other words, if the `Button` class didn't contain code to raise events, you would get a syntax error when you attempted to declare the variable using the `WithEvents` keyword. The compiler can tell which classes will and won't raise events by examining their interface. Any class that will be raising an event will have that event declared as part of its interface. In VB .NET, this means that you will have used the `Event` keyword to declare at least one event as part of the interface for your class.

Raising Events

Objects can raise events just like a control, and the client code that uses your object can receive these events by using the `WithEvents` and `Handles` keywords. Before you can raise an event from your object, however, you need to declare the event within your class by using the `Event` keyword.

Handling Events

In your `Customer` class, for instance, you might want to raise an event any time the `LoadCustomer` method is called. For instance, if you call this method `Loaded`, you can add the following declaration to your `Customer` class:

```
Public Class Customer
  Private _firstName As String
  Private _secondName As String

  Public Event Loaded()

  Public Sub LoadCustomer()
    'Implementation goes here
  End Sub
End Class
```

Events can also have parameters so that you can supply values to the code receiving the event. A typical button's `Click` event receives two parameters, for instance. In the `Loaded` method, perhaps you want to also indicate the number of customers that were loaded. You can do this by changing the event declaration:

```
Public Event Loaded(ByVal count As Integer)
```

Now that the event is declared, you can raise that event within your code, where appropriate. In this case, you raise that within the `LoadCustomer` method so that any time a `Customer` object is used to load customers, it fires an event indicating the number of customers loaded. Modify the `LoadCustomer` method to look like the following:

```
Public Sub LoadCustomer()
  'Add code to load the customer objects into a result set
  Dim count as Integer = 10   'Assign the number of loaded  customers to the count
  ➥variable
  RaiseEvent Loaded(count)
End Sub
```

The `RaiseEvent` keyword is used to raise the actual event. Because the event requires a parameter, that value is passed within parentheses and is delivered to any recipient that handles the event. In fact, the `RaiseEvent` statement causes the event to be delivered to all code that has the `Customer` object declared using the `WithEvents` keyword with a `Handles` clause for this event, or any code that has used the `AddHandler` method.

If more than one method will be receiving the event, the event will be delivered to each recipient one at a time. The order of delivery is not defined, so you can't predict the order in which the recipients will receive the event, but the event will be delivered to all handlers. Note that this is a serial, synchronous process.

The event is delivered to one handler at a time, and it is not delivered to the next handler until the current handler is complete. After you call the RaiseEvent method, the event is delivered to all listeners, one after another, until it is complete; there is no way for you to intervene and stop the process in the middle.

Receiving Events

So far, you have seen how to raise events using the RaiseEvent keyword. After you raise the event, the next step is to handle the raised event and do some processing based on that event. You can handle raised events in two ways, as discussed in the next two sections.

Receiving Events with WithEvents

Now that you have implemented an event within your Customer class, you can write client code to declare an object using the WithEvents keyword. For instance, in the project's Form1 code module, you can write the following:

```
Public Class Form1
    Inherits System.Windows.Forms.Form
    Private WithEvents cust As Customer
```

By declaring the variable WithEvents, you are indicating that you want to receive any events that this object raises. You can also choose to declare the variable without the WithEvents keyword, although, in that case, you would not receive events from the object as described here. Instead, you would use the AddHandler method, discussed shortly.

You can then create an instance of the object as the form is created by adding the following code:

```
Private Sub Form1_Load(ByVal sender As System.Object, ByVal e As System.EventArgs) _
   Handles MyBase.Load
   cust = New Customer()
End Sub
```

At this point, you have declared the object variable using WithEvents and have created an instance of the Customer class so that you actually have an object with which to work. You can now proceed to write a method to handle the Walked event from the object by adding the following code to the form. You can name this method anything you like. The Handles clause is important because it links the event from the object directly to this method, so it is invoked when the event is raised:

```
Private Sub OnCustomerLoad(ByVal count as Integer) Handles cust.Loaded
   MessageBox.Show("No of Customers Loaded" & count)
End Sub
```

Handling Events

In his code, you are using the `Handles` keyword to indicate which event this method should handle. You are also receiving an `Integer` parameter. If the parameter list of the method doesn't match the list for the event, you will get a compiler error indicating the mismatch.

Finally, you need to call the `LoadCustomer` method on your `Customer` object. Add a button to the form and write the following code for its `Click` event:

```
Private Sub Button1_Click(ByVal sender As System.Object, ByVal e As
➥System.EventArgs) _
  Handles button1.Click
  cust.LoadCustomer()
End Sub
```

When the button is clicked, you simply call the `LoadCustomer` method. This causes the code in your class—including the `RaiseEvent` statement—to be run. The result is an event firing back into your form because you declared the `cust` variable using the `WithEvents` keyword. The `OnCustomerLoad` method is run to handle the event because it has the `Handles` clause linking it to the event. The `RaiseEvent` causes the `OnCustomerLoad` method in the form to be invoked; control returns to the `Walk` method in the object afterward. Because you have no code in the `Walk` method after you call `RaiseEvent`, the control returns to the `Click` event back in the form, and then you are finished.

Receiving Events with `AddHandler`

Now that you understand how to receive and handle events using the `WithEvents` and `Handles` keywords, this section takes a look at an alternative approach. You can use the `AddHandler` method to dynamically add event handlers through code.

`WithEvents` and the `Handles` clause require you to declare both the object variable and event handler as you build your code, effectively creating a linkage that is compiled right into your code. `AddHandler`, on the other hand, creates this linkage at runtime, which can provide you with more flexibility. Before going deep into that, you should see how `AddHandler` works.

In Form1, you can change the way your code interacts with the `Customer` object, first eliminating the `WithEvents` keyword:

```
Private Customer As Person
```

Then you eliminate the `Handles` clause:

```
Private Sub OnCustomerLoad(ByVal count As Integer)
  MessageBox.Show("No of Customers Loaded" & count)
End Sub
```

With these changes, you have eliminated all event handling for your object, so your form no longer receives the event, even though the `Customer` object raises it. Now you can change the code to dynamically add an event handler at runtime by using the `AddHandler` method. This method simply links an object's event to a method that should be called to handle that event. Any time after you've created your object, you can call `AddHandler` to set up the linkage:

```
Private Sub Form1_Load(ByVal sender As System.Object, ByVal e As
➥System.EventArgs)  _
  Handles MyBase.Load
  cust = New Customer()
  AddHandler cust.Loaded, AddressOf OnCustomerLoad
End Sub
```

This single line of code does the same thing as the earlier use of `WithEvents` and the `Handles` clause, causing the `OnCustomerLoad` method to be invoked when the `Loaded` event is raised from the `Customer` object.

TIP
With this approach of using `AddHandler` to receive events, it is important to note that it does the linkage at runtime. More control over the process also is provided than you have with the `WithEvents`-based approach.

Inheritance in Visual Basic .NET

Inheritance is often considered one of the most exciting features of Visual Basic .NET and is considered fundamental to the creation of object-based systems. Objects are a way to represent concepts or entities in code. Each of the object features of Visual Basic is designed to help you make the most useful representation possible. In many situations, one entity or concept is really what you would call a subobject of a more basic entity or concept. Consider the class of objects designed to represent animals, such as a cat, a tiger, or a lion. The class would have various properties, such as `Color`, `Weight`, and `Height`.

In this example, the general `Animal` class really contains several subclasses of objects, such as `Cats` and `Tigers`. Those classes, of course, would have all the properties of their parent class, `Animal`, such as `Color`, `Weight`, and `Height`, but they could also have unique properties of their own. For example, a `Tiger` class could have properties that describe the size and behavior of a tiger. This relationship between `Animal` and its subclasses of `Tiger` and `Cat` would be considered a parent-child relationship; the method for representing this relationship in your systems is called inheritance. The class `Tiger` is said to inherit from its base class, `Animal`. This relationship means that, in addition to any properties and methods created in the child class, the child also possesses all the properties and methods of the parent.

Inheritance in Visual Basic .NET

This section demonstrates the concepts of inheritance by looking at an example. To start, you could have a base class of `Animal`, which could represent any type of animal (tiger, cat, lion) and has the properties of `Color`, `Weight`, and `Height`. You could easily represent this class in Visual Basic code, as shown in Listing 3.2.

LISTING 3.2
`Animal` Class

```
Public Class Animal
  Public Property Color() As String
    Get
    End Get
    Set
    End Set
  End Property
  Public Property Weight() As Long
    Get
    End Get
    Set
    End Set
  End Property
  Public Function Description() As String
  End Function
End Class
```

The code that goes within the various procedures in the `Animal` class is not really relevant to this example, so it is left blank for now. If you were to jump to some code to try using your object (for instance, in the `Sub Main()` section), you would see that you can create objects of type `Animal` and work with their properties:

```
Shared Sub Main()
  Dim animalObj As Animal
  animalObj = New Animal
  animalObj.Color = "Red"
  animalObj.Weight = 100
End Sub
```

Now add another class, named `Tiger`, to your project by selecting Add Class from the Project menu. This class will inherit from `Animal`, just as the real class of object `Tiger` is a subclass or child of the `Animal` class of objects. Because you are creating a class designed to deal with just tigers, you can add properties (such as `Speed`) specific to this subclass of `Tiger`:

```
Public Class Tiger
  Inherits Animal
  Public Property Speed() As Long
    Get
    End Get
    Set
    End Set
  End Property
End Class
```

3

The key to this code is the line `Inherits Animal`, which tells Visual Basic that this class is a child of the `Animal` class and, therefore, should inherit all that class's properties and methods. Again, no code is actually placed into any of these property definitions because they are not really relevant at this time. When that code is in place, without having to do anything else, you can see the effect of the `Inherits` statement.

Returning to your `Main()` procedure, add code to create an object of type `Tiger`, and you will quickly see that it exposes both its own properties and those of the parent class.

Overriding Methods

When an inherited class adds new methods or properties, it is said to be extending the base class. In addition to extending, it is possible for a child class to override some or all of the functionality of the base class. This is done when the child implements a method or property that is also defined in the parent or base class. In such a case, the code in the child is executed instead of the code in the parent, enabling you to create specialized versions of the base method or property.

NOTE

For a child class to override some part of the base class, that portion must be marked `Overridable` in the base class definition. For instance, in the version of `Animal` listed earlier, none of its properties had the keyword `Overridable`, so child classes would be incapable of providing their own implementations.

As an example of how overriding is set up in the base and child classes, the code in Listing 3.3 marks the `Description()` function as being overridable and then overrides it in the `Tiger` child class. Note that nonrelevant portions of the two classes have been removed for clarity.

Inheritance in Visual Basic .NET

LISTING 3.3
Using the `Overridable` **and** `Overrides` **Keywords**

```
Public Class Animal
    Overridable Public Function Description() As String
        Return "This is the description for a generic animal"
    End Function
End Class

Public Class Tiger
    Inherits Animal
    Overrides Public Function Description() As String
        Return "This is the description for tiger"
    End Function
End Class
```

When overriding a method or property, as you did in Listing 3.3, you can refer to the original member of the base class by using the built-in object `MyBase`. For example, to refer to the existing `Description()` method **1** of the `Animal` class, you could call `MyBase.Description()` from within the `Description` method of `Tiger`. This functionality enables you to provide additional functionality through overriding, without having to redo all the original code as well.

> **TIP**
>
> In addition to marking code as `Overridable`, it is possible to mark a method or property as `MustOverride` and a class as `MustInherit`. The `MustOverride` keyword indicates that any child of this class must provide its own version of this property or method. The `MustInherit` keyword means that this class cannot be used on its own (you must base other classes off it). It is important to note that if a class contains a method marked `MustOverride`, the class itself must be marked as `MustInherit`.

Summary

VB .NET offers you a fully object-oriented language with all the capabilities you would expect. This chapter covered the basic concepts surrounding classes and objects, as well as the separation of interface from implementation and data. It also demonstrated how to use the `Class` keyword to create classes and how those classes can be instantiated into specific objects.

These objects have methods and properties that client code can invoke, and they can act on data that is stored in member or instance variables of the object. The chapter also explored advanced concepts, such as shared properties, shared methods, events, and the use of delegates.

Further Reading

MSDN documentation on Visual Basic .NET.

Visual Basic Developer Center: http://msdn.microsoft.com/vbasic/.

Mackenzie, Duncan, and Kent Sharkey. *Sam's Teach Yourself Visual Basic .NET in 21 Days*. Pearson Education, 2001.

3

4 .NET FRAMEWORK DATA TYPES

IN BRIEF

As you learned in the previous chapter, an important fundamental element in the .NET Framework is the managed execution environment provided by the common language runtime. One of the important components of the common language runtime is the Common Type System (CTS), which provides all the types and classes found in all the .NET languages. It is important to understand the various types contained in the CTS because the rich type support that it provides enables you to create object-oriented, flexible .NET applications. By enforcing typing, you can clearly determine what type of data will be in each variable, which will go a long way toward reducing bugs. This also enables you to optimize memory by using the smallest-size data type for the job. This chapter discusses the CTS and its components.

Finally, this chapter delves into the concepts of boxing and unboxing, to give you an in-depth understanding of data type conversion.

WHAT YOU NEED

SOFTWARE REQUIREMENTS	Windows 2000, Windows XP, or 2003
	.NET Framework 1.1 SDK
	Visual Studio .NET 2003 with Visual Basic .NET installed
	Internet Information Server (version 5 or later)
	SQL Server or Microsoft Desktop Database Engine (MSDE)
HARDWARE REQUIREMENTS	PC desktop or laptop system
SKILL REQUIREMENTS	Advanced knowledge in HTML
	Intermediate knowledge in the .NET Framework

.NET FRAMEWORK DATA TYPES AT A GLANCE

What Is the Common Type System?

When working with VB .NET, one concept that you need to be sure to understand is that of data types. A data type is a blueprint for the layout of a section of memory. This blueprint determines the range of values that the memory can store and the operations you can perform on the memory. Of course, every variable, array, constant, property, procedure argument, and procedure return value has a data type. You'll see shortly that understanding data types goes far beyond simple numeric types—it extends to every object.

The Common Type System (CTS) is a rich type system built into the common language runtime that provides the types and operations found in most programming languages. Although a language in which everything is an object enables developers to consume the language in a truly object-oriented manner, it has its own disadvantages. The biggest disadvantage is poor performance, resulting from the allocation of the objects in the heap even for trivial operations, such as for adding two numbers. Needless to say, the allocation of an object is extremely inefficient when all that was necessary was to sum two numbers. The .NET Framework design team was faced with the task of creating a rich type system in which everything is an object but that still works in an efficient way, when required. Its solution to this problem was to separate the CTS into two families: value types and reference types. This classification is based on the following considerations for the types:

▶ Memory allocation

▶ Initialization

▶ Behavior when being tested for equality

▶ Treatment in assignment statements

▶ Dependence on the garbage collection (GC) mechanism of the common language runtime

> **NOTE**
>
> Not that although the value types used in .NET are stored efficiently as primitive types, you can call methods on the value types themselves. This is because, for each value type, the .NET Framework provides a corresponding boxed type. However, the value types are sealed, and you cannot derive classes and types from them.

Figure 1.1 shows the CTS and the various types present within it. Now that you have taken a look at CTS, the chapter moves on to talk about the System.Object class, which is the root type from which all the types are derived.

What Is the Common Type System?

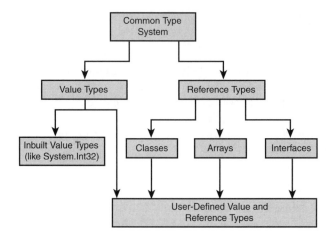

FIGURE 4.1   Common Type System.

System.Object: **The Root of Everything**

All the types in the Common Type System are ultimately derived from the
System.Object type, ensuring that every type in the system has a minimum set of
expected behaviors. By supporting all the classes in the .NET Framework, the
System.Object class provides low-level services to derived classes.

TABLE 4.1

Public Methods of the System.Object Class

Method	Description
Equals	This method returns True or False and is used to check whether two objects are equal. For reference types, if the two variables refer to the same object, the return value is True. In the case of value types, this method returns True if the two types are identical and have the same value.
GetHashCode	Generates a number that is mathematically derived from the value of an object. The handling of collections in the .NET Framework is based on the return value of this method.
GetType	Used to get the Type object that contains useful information about the object. it is mainly used with Reflection methods to retrieve the type information of an object.
ToString	For primitive types such as int, bool, and string, returns the string representation of the type's value. For other types, the default implementation of this method returns the fully qualified name of the class of the object. However, it is usually overridden to return a more user-friendly string representation of the object.
ReferenceEquals	Determines whether the specified object instances are the same.

Types and Aliases

Although the CTS is responsible for defining the types that are required to have cross-language interoperability across languages, most language compilers have chosen to implement aliases to those types. For example, a 2-byte integer is represented by the CTS type `System.Int16`. VB .NET defines an alias for this called `Short`. Even though there is no advantage to using one technique over the other, using an alias provides the developers with more options to choose from. Table 4.2 provides a listing of the various CTS types and their aliases.

TABLE 4.2

CTS Types and Aliases

Type	VB .NET Alias	Description
System.Object	Object	Base class for all CTS types
System.String	String	Represents the string
System.SByte	SByte	Represents the signed 8-bit value
System.Byte	Byte	Represents the unsigned 8-bit value
System.Int16	Short	Represents the signed 16-bit value
System.Int32	Integer	Represents the signed 32-bit value
System.Int64	Long	Represents the signed 64-bit value
System.Char	Char	Represents the Unicode character value
System.Single	Single	Represents the single-precision floating-point number (32 bits)
System.Double	Double	Represents the double-precision floating-point number (64 bits)
System.Boolean	Boolean	Represents the Boolean value of either True or False
System.Decimal	Decimal	Represents the 128-bit data type

Getting to Know Data Types

A variable is really the name of a memory location that is used to store data. When you dimension a variable, you give it a name and a data type. The variable's data type determines how the data is stored in the computer's memory.

Many classic Visual Basic programmers have had limited exposure to data types. These programmers occasionally use variables that are not dimensioned; other times, they use `Variant` variables to hold string, integer, or Boolean values. Earlier versions of Visual Basic allowed you to play fast and loose with data types in this manner. If you didn't dimension a variable, Visual Basic gave the variable the default data type: a 16-byte `Variant`.

Types and Aliases

Although the Variant type has valid uses, such as holding a reference to an Excel spreadsheet object, it is usually the last refuge of a sloppy programmer. This lack of precision not only wastes memory, but it also is dangerous. For example, you can assign a Double value to a Variant and then inadvertently assign a string to the same variable. Previous Visual Basic compilers didn't even blink at this blatant mismatch of data types. Visual Basic .NET is far stricter about how you use variables. The value that you assign to a variable must be assignment compatible with the variable's type. If you declare a variable to be an integer, you can't automatically assign a Short value to it. Visual Basic .NET also disallows type coercion. Those of you who like to write code similar to myStringVariable = "The number is " + 10 will really need to pay attention.

Garbage Collection

In Visual Basic 6, when you finished with an object, you had two means to free up memory it occupied. The lazy way was simply to wait for the object to go out of scope. The second and more professional way was to use SET myObject = Nothing. Because Visual Basic 6 relied on COM, whenever a new instance of an object was created or a new reference to an existing object was set, an internal reference counter was incremented. When a reference to the object was released, the internal reference counter was decremented. When all references were released, the object was terminated and its memory and resources were released. At this point, the Class_Terminate event fired predictably. We knew for sure when this event happened and could place any cleanup code, such as code-releasing connections to databases, in that event. This method of clearly terminating an object is known as deterministic finalization. Visual Basic 6 programmers always knew exactly when an object would be released.

The Stack and the Managed Heap

When you write a Visual Basic .NET program, the operating system allocates a chunk of memory exclusively for the program's use. The application has many different areas inside its own memory map that are used to store different objects. The program's memory has a code segment (the instructions that tell the computer what to do) and a data segment (in-memory objects, variables, and other temporary storage). The data segment is further broken up into the stack (value variables) and the heap (reference variables). Now you see why it's important to understand the difference between value and reference variables. The ways they are stored in memory and are released when finished are different. A solid understanding of how reference variables are stored can materially help you increase the performance of your code.

Value objects, such as integers, are stored on the stack. The stack is also used to hold data passed to functions and methods. As more items are placed on the stack, such as when you pass parameters to a procedure, the stack grows toward the heap. The compiler can determine the size of the stack because it knows the exact size of the value types used in procedures, function calls, and so on. As value variables go out of scope, they are immediately released and memory is freed up, shrinking the stack.

This is not the case with reference variables, which are placed on the managed heap. Whereas you could use `Set myObject = Nothing` in Visual Basic 6 to release memory, Visual Basic .NET operates in a completely different way. In Visual Basic .NET, when an object goes out of scope, it is internally flagged for deletion. At some later time, a low-level background thread examines heap memory to see what objects can safely be released. Now it's the system, not the programmer, that must manage memory. This memory management is called nondeterministic finalization.

> **NOTE**
>
> Because of the nondeterministic nature of the garbage-collection mechanism, you will have no idea when the type references will be removed from memory. The algorithm used to determine when the references are no longer required is complicated and uses some sophisticated techniques to determine reference type lifetimes.

4

Although setting an object to `Nothing` in Visual Basic 6 immediately releases memory, in Visual Basic .NET, this process might take a while. In some cases, several minutes might elapse before the garbage collector (GC) gets around to releasing objects on the managed heap. The good news is that this delay typically provides a performance benefit. Rather than using CPU cycles to release objects that are no longer needed, the system usually waits until the application is idle, which decreases the impact on the user. You can signal the garbage collection to start its work programmatically by calling the `System.GC.Collect` method. But note that this method is used only in rare circumstances when it is imperative to release many large objects immediately. Most programs never make use of this.

The stack grows toward the heap (and vice versa). If they meet, that application has run out of memory—and when this happens, it is just a matter of time before the application crashes. Although crashes like these used to be a problem with complex programs, the .NET runtime uses advanced memory-allocation algorithms to ensure it won't happen.

Value Types

The first thing to be noted is that value type variables are allocated memory on the stack and are initialized to an appropriate value at the time of declaration itself. When you have a variable that is of value `type`, it means that you have a variable that contains actual data, which ensures that they cannot be null. Consider the following statement, which creates a variable of the CTS type `System.Int16` in VB:

```
Dim s As Integer = 10
```

In this declaration, 32-bit space is allocated on the stack for the variable s. In addition, the assignment of a value to s results in that 32-bit value being moved into this allocated space.

Types and Aliases

The list of value types in the .NET Framework includes enumerators, structures, and primitives. Any time that you declare a variable of one of these types, you allocate the number of bytes for that type on the stack. You also then work directly with the allocated array of bits instead of with the reference to that allocated memory. In addition, when you assign a variable that is a value type, the copy of the value of the variable is assigned and is not a reference to its underlying object. Finally, value types do not expect the GC to reclaim the memory that they use.

Numeric Data Types

This section covers various numeric data types that are used for handling numbers in various representations. Numeric data types can be classified into the following two categories:

▸ **Integral types**—Consist of Short, Integer, Long, and Byte data types

▸ **Nonintegral types**—Consist of Decimal, Single, and Double data types

The next sections take an in-depth look at each of the numeric data types.

Integral Types

Integral data types are data types that represent only whole numbers. The signed integral data types are Short (16-bit), Integer (32-bit), and Long (64-bit). If you want a variable to store whole numbers rather than numbers with a fractional amount, you should declare it as one of these types.

The Byte data type is an unsigned integral type that is made up of 8 bits. If you want to store a value that contains binary data or data of an unknown nature, you can use this data type. If you need more than 8 bits of data, you can use an array of Byte elements. Because Byte is an unsigned type with a range of 0 to 255, it cannot represent a negative number. If you use the unary minus (–) operator on an expression that evaluates to type Byte, Visual Basic converts the expression to Integer first.

In terms of performance, arithmetic operations are faster with integral types than with other data types. They are fastest with the integer type in Visual Basic .NET. You can also use integral types as counter variables in For ... Next loops. If you try to set a variable of an integral type to a number outside the range for that type, an error occurs. If you try to set it to a fraction, the number is rounded, as in the following example:

```
Dim K As Integer  ' Valid range is -2147483648 to +2147483647.
K = 2147483648    ' Causes an error.
K = CInt(5.9)     ' Sets K to 6.
```

Binary data stored in Byte variables and arrays is preserved during format conversions. String variables should not be used for storing binary data because its contents can be corrupted during conversion between ANSI and Unicode formats. Such conversion can happen automatically when Visual Basic reads or writes files, or when it calls DLLs, methods, and properties. For integral types, the literal type characters are S for Short, I for Integer, and L for Long. No literal type character exists for Byte.

Nonintegral Types

Nonintegral data types are those that represent numbers with both integer and fractional parts. The nonintegral numeric data types are `Decimal` (128-bit fixed point), `Single` (32-bit floating point), and `Double` (64-bit floating point). They are all signed types. If you need to store a value that contains a fraction, you should declare the type of the variable as one of these types.

Using a `Decimal` data type variable, you can store up to 29 significant digits and store values up to 7.9228×1028. This type is particularly suitable for mission-critical calculations, such as financial calculations, that require a large number of digits but cannot tolerate rounding errors.

To assign a large value to a `Decimal` variable or constant, you must append the literal type character to a numeric literal if it is too large for the `Long` data type, as the following example shows:

```
Dim decVar As Decimal
decVar = 9223372036854775808   'Overflow; too big
decVar = 9223372036854775808D  'No overflow; Decimal data type.
```

Floating-point (`Single` and `Double`) numbers have larger ranges than decimal numbers but can be subject to rounding errors. Floating-point types support fewer significant digits than `Decimal` types but can represent values of greater magnitude. Floating-point values can be expressed as `mmmEeee`, in which `mmm` is the mantissa (the significant digits) and `eee` is the exponent (a power of 10). The highest positive value of a `Single` data type is `3.4028235E+38`, and the highest positive value of a `Double` data type is `1.79769313486231570E+308`.

Declaring a Built-in Value-Type Variable

You can declare a built-in value-type variable in two ways: with the full struct name or with the alias. For instance, the following are identical:

```
'Using the full struct name
Dim length As System.Int32
```

```
'Using the VB.NET alias
Dim length As Integer
```

Both of these statements declare 32-bit integer variables. Using the alias produces more compact, readable code and is the preferred method, although the compiled IL code is identical.

```
Dim length As Integer = 4
```

As you can see from this code, you can initialize a value type when it is declared by including a value in the variable-declaration statement.

Types and Aliases

> **NOTE**
>
> .NET data types are either structures or classes, part of the `System` namespace. For example, these are some of the data types that are implemented as struct in .NET:
>
> ▶ Int16   ▶ Double
>
> ▶ Int32
>
> You can use structs as if they are simple data types.

4

User-Defined Value Types

The VB .NET language allows the creation of user-defined value types. A user-defined value type is defined as a struct that derives from the `System.ValueType` class. A user-defined value type can contain fields, properties, methods, and events. If the user-defined type is boxed, it has access to the virtual methods defined in the `System.ValueType` and `System.Object` classes. Boxing is described later in this chapter. Value types are, by their nature, sealed; no other type can derive from them.

Structures

In Visual Basic .NET, structures are similar to classes, in that they associate one or more members with each other. A structure is also similar to a class, in that it can contain member data, properties, methods, and events. Structures do, however, have distinct differences from classes:

- ▶ Structures aren't inheritable.

- ▶ Structures are implicitly derived from `System.ValueType`.

- ▶ A variable of a structure type directly contains its own copy of data.

- ▶ Structures are never terminated. The common language runtime doesn't call the `Finalize` method on a structure.

- ▶ Structures require parameters when they have unshared constructors. However, all structures implicitly have a public `New()` constructor without parameters that initializes the members to their default value.

- ▶ Declarations of a structure's data members can't include initializers.

- ▶ The default access for members declared with the `Dim` statement is public.

- ▶ Members can't be declared protected in a structure.

- ▶ Equality testing must be performed with a member-by-member comparison.

- ▶ Structures can't have abstract methods.

To declare structures, you use the `Structure` statement. In previous versions of Visual Basic, you used the `Type` statement to declare a structure. When a structure is declared, it is implicitly derived from `System.ValueType`, which gives the structure the same properties as other value types. The following shows a simple structure declaration:

```
Structure MyStruct
   Public Name As String
   Public Address As String
   Public City As Boolean
End Structure
```

Note that, with structures, each structure element can have its own scope modifier (for example, it can be public, private, and so on). Structures in .NET behave a lot like classes. They support most of the constructs of a class, including properties, methods, and events.

Why Use a Structure?

Structures are useful in defining new value types that encapsulate a group of variables. For example, an employee can be represented as a structure that includes all the employee's information. The advantages of using a structure instead of a class as a value type are that a structure isn't allocated on the heap and each instance of the structure has its own copy of the data. For example, if structure A is assigned to structure B, each has its own copy of the data; modifications to one don't affect the other. The same example with a class would assign only a reference to B, and any modifications to either one would be reflected in the other because they share the same memory. If you are designing a new data type that represents a new data element and doesn't need to be extended through inheritance, a structure is a better choice. Table 4.3 summarizes some of the key similarities and differences between classes and structures.

TABLE 4.3

Structures Versus Classes

Characteristic	Class	Structure
Parameterless constructors used	Yes	No
Support for properties, methods, and events	Yes	Yes
Capability to inherit from	Yes	No
Capability to implement interfaces	Yes	Yes
Support for destructors	Yes	No

In the class library, structures are used to represent value types such as integers (`Int16`, `Int32`, `Int64`). As you have already seen, the actual structure object inherits directly from the class `ValueType` in the root `System` namespace.

Enumerations

An enumeration is essentially a named constant: It is an aid to developer productivity because it enables you to reference values using a recognizable name. Using enumerations greatly improves code readability and speeds up coding because enumerations provide a way to name or reference a value that maps to one of the underlying data types defined by the CTS. Visual Basic developers should be familiar with the concept of enums—the syntax has not changed moving into Visual Basic .NET.

Types and Aliases

The .NET runtime allows enumerations to evaluate to any of the signed or unsigned integer data types that are defined (such as Int32, Int64, and so on). Essentially, an enumeration has a name, a set of fields, and an underlying type.

In addition, the following restrictions apply to enumerations:

- ▸ They cannot define their own methods.
- ▸ They cannot implement interfaces.
- ▸ They cannot define properties or events.

As far as the .NET Framework class library is concerned, enumerations are in many of the namespaces. One example of an enumeration in the class library is `CommandType`, contained in the `System.Data` namespace.

To use an enumeration from your code, simply reference the enumeration's name and the name of the value that you want to use:

```
myCommand.CommandType = CommandType.StoredProcedure
```

In the preceding code, you use the `CommandType` enumeration to specify that the code you are trying to execute is a stored procedure.

Enumerations are derived from the `System.Enum` class, which means that you can reference enumerations in some very cool ways. For instance, you can call the `GetValues()` method to get an array of all values defined by an enumeration. You can also call the `GetNames()` method to get an array of all names for the values defined by an enumeration. The underlying type of an enumeration is an integral value and can be specified as either a `Byte`, a `Short`, an `Integer`, or a `Long`. By default, enumerations are defined as `Integer`. You declare an enumeration by using the `Enum` keyword, followed by the enumeration name and type. If no type is specified, `Integer` is the default. The following shows the declaration of the enumeration `Color`:

```
Enum Color
  Red
  Green
  Blue
End Enum
```

Each value defined in the `Color` enumeration receives an integer value starting with 0—for example, Red (0), Green (1), Blue (2). If you need to define an enumeration in which the values have specific associated integer values, assign the values as follows:

```
Enum Color
  Red = 1
  Green = 2
  Blue = 3
End Enum
```

Now each enumeration value has a specific value. Assigning values is useful in enumerations in which each value is fixed, as it is with colors. Values are fixed and can't be changed at runtime. Using enumerations is similar to using other variables. All enumeration values must be prefaced by the containing enumeration. For example, the following statement gives `MyColor` the value of `Red`:

```
Color = Color.Red
```

You can avoid prefacing enumerations by importing them with the `Imports` statement. In this case, the following code imports the `Color` enumeration and then makes the same assignment as before:

```
Imports MyApplication.Color
Dim colorObject As Color = Red
```

You can define enumerations as part of a module, class, or structure. If an enumeration is part of a class or structure, you must preface it with the class or structure, as follows:

```
Structure TestStruct
   Public IsValidColor As Boolean
   Enum Color
      Red = 1
      Green = 2
      Blue = 3
   End Enum
End Structure
```

You can display the value of an enumeration by either its name or its integral value. The following sample code segment shows how to display both the name and the value of `Color.Red` in a message box:

```
MessageBox.Show(TestStruct.Color.Red.ToString() + " = " _
   + CType(TestStruct.Color.Red, Integer).ToString())
```

Reference Types

The second major branch of the type hierarchy tree corresponds to reference typ Reference types contain a pointer to a location on the heap where the object it stored. Because they contain only a reference, not the actual values, reference variables passed into method calls are affected by any changes made to the within the body of the method. Therefore, they are similar in some ways parameters.

Types and Aliases

Reference-type variables are allocated memory on the heap and are always initialized to null. They do not contain a reference to a valid object until they are assigned such a reference, either by creating a new instance of the class or by assigning a reference from an existing valid object. In the following example, a reference type of `string` is allocated to the variable `s`:

```
Dim s as String = "This is a reference type"
```

When this statement is executed, the value is allocated on the heap, and a reference to that value is assigned to the variable. As with value types, several types—such as classes, arrays, delegates, and interfaces—are defined as reference types in the .NET Framework. Any time you declare a variable of one of these types, you allocate the number of bytes associated with that type on the heap; you are working with the reference to that object instead of directly with the bits, which is the case with value types. Even after the reference-type variables go out of scope, they sit around the memory waiting for the garbage collector to run through its elimination process.

Reference types include pointer, interface, and self-describing types. Pointer types are used to store the address of another object and are permitted only in unsafe code in C#. An interface defines the contract that implementing classes or structs must adhere to (the methods, properties, fields, and so on that they must expose), but it doesn't provide any implementation for those members.

Self-describing reference types include class types and arrays. An array represents a set of elements, which can be value or reference types. An array is a reference type, even if its elements are value types. Classes are user-defined reference types (very similar in ⌐ctionality to structs). They can contain data members (fields and constants) and ⌐ members (methods, properties, events, operators, constructors, and destruc- ⌐ng to object-oriented programming principles, a class defines all of the ⌐d to manipulate its data members.

⌐ne that refers to a method, similar to a function pointer in ⌐ delegates include the object on which the method is ⌐fe and secure way to reference a method defined ⌐ virtual, or instance method. Delegates are ⌐at you have a basic understanding of the ⌐ each one of its type in detail.

⌐f the most commonly used classes in .NET ⌐an immutable sequence of Unicode characters.

This immutability means that after a string has been allocated on the heap, its value never changes. If the value is altered, .NET creates an entirely new `String` object and assigns that to the variable. This means that, in many ways, strings behave like value rather than reference types: If you pass a string into a method and alter the parameter's value within the method body, that doesn't affect the original string (unless, of course, the parameter is passed by reference). VB .NET provides the alias `String` to represent the `System.String` class.

Strings can be created using the usual constructor syntax or by using what is called a string literal. The following two expressions are valid ways to create a `String` object:

```
Dim strA As New String("A"c, 5)
```

```
Dim strB As String = "Test"
```

The first version uses one of the `String` class constructors (other overloads can take a char array or a pointer to a char array). The second statement simply assigns a string literal to the variable. The `String` class defines methods that can be used to concatenate two strings. You can also use the + operator for this purpose:

```
Dim str As String = "Hello"
```

```
Dim str2 As String = str + " There"
```

You can extract a character at a given position in the `String` by using an indexer syntax as shown below:

```
String str = "Bye Bye";
char firstChar = str[0];
```

The `String` class provides a number of methods, shown in Table 4.4.

TABLE 4.4

Members of the `String` Class

Member	Description
`Clone`	Instance method that returns a new `String` with the same value
`Compare`	Shared method that compares two strings and returns an `Integer` specifying the result
`CompareOrdinal`	Shared method that compares two strings and returns an `Integer` specifying the result, without taking into account the language or culture

Types and Aliases

TABLE 4.4

Continued

Member	Description
CompareTo	Instance method that compares this instance with a given object
Concat	Shared method that creates a new String from one or more strings or objects
Copy	Shared method that creates a new instance of a String with the same value as the specified string
CopyTo	Instance method that copies a portion of the string to a character array
Empty	Shared constant representing an empty string
EndsWith	Instance method that determines whether a given string matches the end of this string
Equals	Both a shared and an instance method that determines whether two strings have the same value
Format	Shared method used to format the string with the given format specification
IndexOf	Instance method that returns the index of the first occurrence of a string within this string
Insert	Instance method that inserts the given string at a given position within this string
Join	Shared method that concatenates a given separator between each element in a given array
LastIndexOf	Instance method that returns the last occurrence of a given string within this string
PadLeft, PadRight	Instance methods that align the current string with spaces or a specified character for a specified length
Remove	Instance method that deletes the specified number of characters from this instance of the string at the specified location
Replace	Instance method that replaces all occurrences of a specified string with the given string
Split	Instance method that splits the string into an array of strings based on a separator
StartsWith	Instance method that determines whether this string is prefixed with a given string
SubString	Instance method that retrieves a substring from the string
ToCharArray	Instance method that copies the characters of the string to a character array
ToLower, ToUpper	Instance methods that return a copy of the string in lower- or uppercase
Trim, TrimEnd, TrimStart	Instance methods that remove spaces or a set of characters from the string

Mutable Strings

Because strings are immutable, three separate strings are needed every time you perform a concatenation. For example, consider the following VB .NET code:

```
Dim strA As String = "Hello"
Dim strB As String = strA + " There"
Dim strC As String s3 = strB + " John"
```

Because of the immutability of the strings, this code requires five separate strings to be loaded. Besides the three hard-coded strings, two strings are created by the calls to String::Concat(); each change to the string results in a new String object being allocated on the heap.

Before .NET, VB programmers were used to the String data type. It was easy to use, flexible, and often inevitable. Besides, there was no choice. When they upgraded to VB .NET, they found the same String data type wrapping the .NET Framework System.String class. It is still as easy to use, as flexible, and as important as the old String data type. However, there is now an alternative if you need to manipulate strings and avoid resource-hungry and time-consuming object creation. The alternative is somewhat hidden in the System.Text namespace: the StringBuilder class.

The StringBuilder Object

The System.Text.StringBuilder class is faster because it allocates an initial space when an instance of it is created. By default, a StringBuilder object created using the StringBuilder class reserves a space for 16 characters in memory. Therefore, if you later append more characters to it, as long as there is room for the new characters, no new StringBuilder needs to be created. The initial space depends on the implementation. This could be different in a non-Windows implementation of the .NET Framework.

You can obtain the size of a StringBuilder object's storage the class's Capacity property. For example, the following code instantiates a StringBuilder object using the no-argument constructor and writes the capacity to the console:

```
Dim sb As New System.Text.StringBuilder()
System.Console.WriteLine(sb.Capacity)
```

The code prints 16. You can change the capacity by assigning a different value to the Capacity property. The same capacity is also set aside if you construct an instance by passing a String object, such as in the following code:

```
Dim sb As New System.Text.StringBuilder("Test")
System.Console.WriteLine(sb.Capacity)
```

Mutable Strings

This code also results in the output of 16. However, if the string passed to the constructor exceeds 16 characters, the StringBuilder object allocates enough space to accommodate all of the characters in the string. In this case, the initial capacity is double the lower capacity. For example, the following code constructs a StringBuilder object by passing a string consisting of 20 characters. To accommodate the whole string, an initial capacity of 32 is allocated.

```
Dim sb As New System.Text.StringBuilder("12345678901234567890")
System.Console.WriteLine(sb.Capacity)
```

This code results in the output of 32. The next initial capacity, supposing that you pass a string of 33 characters, will be 64 (2 × 32), not 48 (3 × 16). The length of the string in a StringBuilder object can be obtained from its Length property. As an example, the following code prints both the capacity and the string length:

```
Dim sb As New System.Text.StringBuilder(
    "12345678901234567890")
System.Console.WriteLine(sb.Capacity)    ' prints 32
System.Console.WriteLine(sb.Length)      ' prints 20
```

The capacity must be equal to or greater than the length. If you change the Capacity property value to a number less than the length of the internal string, it throws an exception named System.ArgumentOutOfRangeException. However, if you append a string to a StringBuilder object and the operation results in a string whose length exceeds the StringBuilder object's capacity, the capacity is increased automatically. Keep in mind that the key to getting the most benefit from the StringBuilder class is to make sure that the length of the string it contains is always less than the capacity. In other words, the performance will degrade if a StringBuilder object has to allocate more memory to increase its capacity. To ensure that you can assign a big enough initial capacity, the StringBuilder class provides another constructor that accepts an integer. This integer is the initial capacity for the StringBuilder object.

TIP

Incidentally, such constructors are called overloaded constructors. Generally, methods with the same name but different parameters (of different data types or a different number of data types) are overloaded methods.

```
Public Sub New (ByVal capacity As Integer)
```

If you want to instantiate a `StringBuilder` object by passing a `String`, but you want to define your own initial capacity, use the constructor that accepts a `String` and an integer:

```
Public Sub New (ByVal value As String, _
    ByVal capacity As Integer)
```

The `StringBuilder` class also enables you to specify the maximum capacity that an instance can grow to, using the following constructor:

```
Public Sub New (ByVal capacity As Integer, _
ByVal maxCapacity As Integer)
```

The maximum capacity can be obtained from the `MaxCapacity` property. If you construct a `StringBuilder` object without specifying a maximum capacity, the default is the same as `Int32.MaxValue`. As with the `Capacity` property, the default value of `MaxCapacity` is implementation dependent. Now you can take a look at other features that come with the `StringBuilder` class.

Accessing Individual Characters

As with the `System.String` class, the `StringBuilder` class enables you to access each individual character of its internal string by using the `Chars` property. For example, the following code constructs a `StringBuilder` object by passing the string `test` and then prints the first character of the string:

```
Dim sb As New System.Text.StringBuilder("test")
System.Console.WriteLine(sb.Chars(0))    ' prints t
```

The `Chars` property of the `StringBuilder` class is more flexible than the same property in the `String` class because, in `StringBuilder`, the `Chars` property is read-write, whereas the `String` class's `Chars` property is read-only. This makes `StringBuilder` objects very flexible because you can also write to individual characters. Consider the following example:

```
Dim sb As New System.Text.StringBuilder("test")
sb.Chars(0) = "m"c
sb.Chars(3) = "s"c
System.Console.WriteLine(sb)    ' prints mess
```

Appending a Value

You can use the `Append` method to append a value to the existing string. This method has 19 overloads to make sure you can append values in any format.

Mutable Strings

Therefore, you can append a string, a byte, an integer, a long, an `Object`, a `Single`, a `Double`, an array of characters, and so on. For example, the following snippet appends a string and an integer to a `StringBuilder` object:

```
Dim sb As New System.Text.StringBuilder()
Dim text As String = "Total product(s): "
Dim count As Integer = 19
sb.Append(text).Append(count)
System.Console.WriteLine(sb) ' prints Total product(s): 19
```

Inserting a Value

To insert a new value into an existing `StringBuilder` object, you can use the `Insert` method. This method has 18 overloads that accept a value of any format. Each overload accepts two or more arguments, the first being the index indicating the insertion point. For example, here is the signature of the `Insert` method overload that you can use to append an integer:

```
Overloads Public Function Insert( _
  ByVal index As Integer, ByVal value As Integer) _
  As StringBuilder
```

Note that the `Insert` method returns a `StringBuilder` object that is the reference to the same instance. For example, the following code constructs a `StringBuilder` object with an initial string value and then inserts a new string at index 0:

```
Dim sb As New System.Text.StringBuilder("product(s): 20")
sb.Insert(0, "Total ")
System.Console.WriteLine(sb) 'prints Total product(s): 20
```

Removing a Substring

You can remove a range of characters from a `StringBuilder` object using the `Remove` method. The signature of this method is as follows:

```
Public Function Remove( _
  ByVal startIndex As Integer, _
  ByVal length As Integer) As StringBuilder
```

Here, `startIndex` is the start index at which the removal begins, and `length` is the number of characters to be removed. For example, the following code removes the `or` from `War and or Peace`:

```
Dim sb As New System.Text.StringBuilder("Come and Go")
sb.Remove(4,4)
System.Console.WriteLine(sb) ' prints Come Go
```

Replacing Characters and Substrings

You can also replace an individual character in a `StringBuilder` object with another character or a substring with another substring using the `Replace` method. In particular, you use one of the following overloads:

```
Overloads Public Function Replace( _
  ByVal oldChar As Char, _
  ByVal newChar As Char ) _
  As StringBuilder

Overloads Public Function Replace( _
  ByVal oldValue As String, _
  ByVal newValue As String ) _
  As StringBuilder
```

For example, in the following code, you replace all occurrences of x with y:

```
Dim sb As New System.Text.StringBuilder("xxxyyy")
sb.Replace("x"c, "y"c)
System.Console.WriteLine(sb)    ' prints yyyyyy
```

As another example, the following replaces the word and with or:

```
Dim sb As New System.Text.StringBuilder("xyz and xyz")
sb.Replace("and", "or")
System.Console.WriteLine(sb)    ' prints xyz or xyz
```

Using the methods of the `StringBuilder` class, you can also replace a range of positions of characters.

Converting a `StringBuilder` Object into a `String`

Many methods in various .NET classes expect a `String` object as an argument. Therefore, it is important to convert a `StringBuilder` object into a `String` object before you pass it to one of those methods. The `StringBuilder` class provides you with the `ToString` method. Using this method is very simple. For instance, here is the code that converts a `StringBuilder` object into a `String`:

```
Dim sb As New System.Text.StringBuilder("Test")
System.Console.WriteLine(sb.ToString()) ' prints Test
```

What Is a GUID?

A GUID represents a unique identifier, meaning that you cannot generate the same GUID more than once. A GUID has a very low (almost practically impossible) probability of being duplicated.

A GUID is a 128-bit integer that has a variety of applications.

TIP

You can use a GUID as a primary key in your database table or in a several other scenarios. As an example, if you have a distributed application in which data is generated and stored in various locations, and you want to merge all that data at some intervals of time, you could use a GUID as the primary key.

GUIDs can be generated in a number of ways, most often, as a hash of several things that might be unique at any given point in time. For example, the combination of the machine's IP address plus the clock date/time can be used to generate unique identifiers. Each system might have a slightly different algorithm to generate the unique ID.

In .NET, you can use the `System.Guid` class to generate a GUID. For example, in the following code, `System.Guid.NewGuid()` returns a `Guid` object:

```
Dim guid As System.Guid = System.Guid.NewGuid()
Dim id As String = guid.ToString()
```

You can use the `ToString()` method to convert it to a string. When you execute this code, you get a string that is somewhat similar to the following GUID:

```
c91c9121-0a17-4b26-a09d-d5980eb532df
```

Boxing and Unboxing

Boxing a value means implicitly converting a value type to the type object. When a value type is boxed, an object instance is allocated and the value present in the value type is copied into the new object. Consider the following VB code:

```
Dim i As Integer = 10
Dim o as Object = i
O = 20
Console.WriteLine ("{0}{1}", i, o)
```

The assignment in the second line implicitly involves a boxing operation, and the value of variable i is copied to the object o. After the value is copied, the two variables are independent of each other, and there is no link between them. Because of that, when you change the value of the oNumber variable, it does not affect the value of the i variable. If you execute the code, you should get the following output:

```
10 20
```

Unboxing refers to converting object type to any value type. In contrast to boxing, unboxing is an explicit operation and you must explicitly tell the compiler what value type you want to extract from the object type. To understand unboxing, consider the following VB.NET code:

```
Dim i As Integer = 10
Dim o As Object = i
Dim j As Integer = CType(o, Integer)
```

Here, you unbox the o object and assign the extracted integer variable to a variable of type Integer.

4

Summary

In this chapter, you looked at CTS and the various types that it provides. The two major types contained in CTS are reference types and value types. Reference data types contain a pointer that references another location in memory. This referenced location might contain a large object, a string, or some other data. You can have several reference data types pointing to the same memory location. Changes to anything in that location are reflected in all variables referencing that memory location.

Value types, on the other hand, are primitive types, which contain a data type whose size is known ahead of time, such as an integer. Because an integer always is 4 bytes, the common language runtime can map the 4-byte memory location that will hold a value. In other words, there is no need to reference another memory location to hold an unknown size variable.

Further Reading

Microsoft .NET website, http://msdn.microsoft.com/netframework.

MacKenzie, Duncan, and Kent Sharkey. *Sam's Teach Yourself VB. NET in 21 Days.* Pearson Education, 2001.

Part II

Windows Forms Applications

5 WINDOWS FORMS

IN BRIEF

This chapter takes a look at some of the basics of creating Visual Basic .NET Windows Forms projects: adding forms to a project, manipulating their properties, and showing and hiding them using Visual Basic code. When you have learned these nuts and bolts, you'll be ready for more advanced form techniques.

With few exceptions, forms are the cornerstones of every Windows application's interface. Forms are essentially windows, and the two terms are often used interchangeably. More accurately, *window* refers to what's seen by the user and what the user interacts with, whereas *form* refers to what you see when you design. Forms let users view and enter information in a program. Such information might be text, pictures, graphs, or almost anything that can be viewed on the screen. Understanding how to design forms correctly enables you to begin creating solid interface foundations for your programs.

The next section starts by helping you create a new project in Visual Studio .NET 2003.

WHAT YOU NEED

SOFTWARE REQUIREMENTS	Windows 2000, XP, or 2003 .NET Framework 1.1 SDK Visual Studio .NET 2003 with Visual Basic .NET installed
HARDWARE REQUIREMENTS	PC desktop or laptop
SKILL REQUIREMENTS	Knowledge of Visual Basic .NET Knowledge of the .NET Framework

WINDOWS FORMS AT A GLANCE

WINDOWS FORMS AT A GLANCE

Creating a New Project

5

When you create a new Visual Basic project, you use the New Project dialog box to set the basic options for the project, such as the project's name and the location where the project is saved. This dialog box lets you select the type of project you want to create by choosing one of several templates.

To create a Windows Forms application, for example, you select the Windows Application template. Among other things, this template includes references to all of the assemblies that contain the namespaces you're most likely to use as you develop a Windows application.

The New Project dialog box also lets you specify the name for the project and identify the folder in which it will be stored. By default, projects are stored in the Visual Studio Projects folder under the My Documents folder. However, you can change this default, as you'll learn shortly. You can also click the Browse button to select a different location, you can display the drop-down list to select a location you've used recently, or you can type a path directly. If you specify a path that doesn't exist, Visual Studio creates the necessary folders for you. When you click on the OK button, Visual Studio automatically creates a new folder for the project, using the project name you specify. Figure 5.1 shows the New Project dialog box, with the project name specified as WindowsFormsExample and the location as C:\Projects\SAMS.

As a result, Visual Studio creates a folder named WindowsFormsExample in the SAMS folder. You can see the complete path for the new project near the bottom of the New Project dialog box. When you create a new project, Visual Studio also creates a new solution to hold the project. By default, the solution is given the same name as the project and is stored in the same folder. If that's not what you want, you can click the More button in the New Project dialog box for additional options that let you create a solution folder above the project folder and provide a separate name for the solution.

Creating a New Project

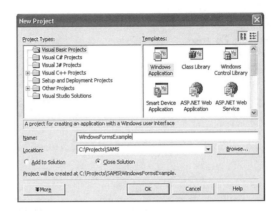

FIGURE 5.1   New Project dialog box.

How to Run a Project

After you correct any syntax errors that are detected as you enter the code for a project, you'll want to run the project. When the project runs, you'll want to test it to make sure it works the way you want it to and debug it to remove any programming errors you find.

Before you can run a project, you need to build it into an assembly containing the Intermediate Language that the common language runtime then can run. You can build the project by selecting the Build Solution option from the Build menu.

To run a project, click the Start button in the Standard toolbar, select the Start command from the Debug menu, or press the F5 key. This builds the project, if it hasn't been built already and causes the project's form to be displayed. When you close the form for a project, the application ends. Then you're returned to Visual Studio .NET, where you can continue working on your program.

TIP

If your project contains two or more forms, you can designate which one of them is displayed when you start your project. You can do this by right-clicking the project from Solution Explorer and selecting Properties from the context menu. In the Properties menu, selecting Common Properties node from tree view displays a `DropDownList` named Startup Object; using this, you can specify the form you want to use as a startup object.

Introduction to Forms

Visual Basic .NET uses a new forms engine called Windows Forms, which is different than the engine used in previous versions of Visual Basic. You can think of a form as a canvas on which you build your program's interface.

On this canvas, you can print text, draw shapes, and place controls with which users can interact. The wonderful thing about Visual Basic forms is that they behave like a dynamic canvas: Not only can you adjust the appearance of a form by manipulating what's on it, but you can also manipulate specific properties of the form itself.

The `Form` Class

All windows in a Windows Forms application are represented by objects of some type that derive from the `Form` class. Of course, the `Form` class derives from `Control`, as do all classes that represent visual elements. You will rarely use the `Form` class directly—any forms you define in your application will be represented by a class that inherits from `Form`. Adding a new form in Visual Studio .NET simply adds an appropriate class definition to your project. The Forms Designer enables this key functionality.

The Forms Designer

Most forms are designed using the Forms Designer in Visual Studio .NET. This is not an essential requirement—the designer just generates code that you could write manually instead. It is simply much easier to arrange the contents of a form visually than it is to write code to do this. When you add a new form to a project, a new class definition is created. The designer always uses the same structure for the source code of these classes. To start, this structure contains `Friend` fields to hold the contents of the form. The Designer inserts new fields in this location as you add controls to the form. Next is the constructor, followed by the `Dispose` and `InitializeComponent` methods. Finally, any event handlers for controls on your form are added at the end of the class.

> **NOTE**
>
> The Forms Designer does not make it obvious where you are expected to add code of your own, such as fields or methods other than event handlers. This is because it doesn't matter: Visual Studio .NET is pretty robust about working around you. You even can move most of the code that it generates if you don't like the way it arranges things. The only the exception is the code inside the `InitializeComponent` method, which you should avoid modifying by hand. The editor hides the code, by default, to discourage you from changing it.

Any newly created form contains a constructor and an `InitializeComponent` method. The purpose of these methods is to make sure that a form is correctly initialized before it is displayed. The generated constructor is very simple: It just calls the `InitializeComponent` method. The intent here is for the Forms Designer to place all its initialization code in `InitializeComponent`, and you will write any initialization that you require in the constructor. The designer effectively owns `InitializeComponent`, and it is recommended that you avoid modifying its contents because this is liable to confuse the designer. When you look at the source code for a form class, Visual Studio .NET conceals the `InitializeComponent` method by default.

Introduction to Forms

You can see this code by clicking the + symbol at the left of this line in the editor. You must not make any modifications to the overall structure of the InitializeComponent method; any changes to the form must be made by using the Forms Designer or by modifying values in its Properties window, causing Visual Studio to update the InitializeComponent method automatically.

Although the theory is that you will never need to modify anything inside this generated code, you occasionally might have to make edits. If you do make such changes by hand, you must be very careful not to change the overall structure of the method. To this end, it is useful to understand how this method is arranged. It begins by creating the objects that make up the UI: Each control on the form has a corresponding line that calls the New operator and stores the result in the relevant field. For example if you have a Button, a Label, and a TextBox control in your form, you will see that the InitializeComponent method contains the following lines of code as part of its declaration.

```
Me.Button1 = New System.Windows.Forms.Button()
Me.Label1 = New System.Windows.Forms.Label()
Me.TextBox1 = New System.Windows.Forms.TextBox()
```

Next comes a call to the SuspendLayout method, which is inherited from the Control class. The purpose of this call is to prevent the form from attempting to rearrange itself every time a control is set up. Then each control is configured in turn, to set the necessary properties such as position, name, tab order, and so on.

```
Me.TextBox1.Location = New System.Drawing.Point(112, 136)
Me.TextBox1.Name = "TextBox1"
Me.TextBox1.TabIndex = 2
Me.TextBox1.Text = "TextBox1"
```

After this, the form's size is set and all the controls are added to its Controls collection. Note that simply creating controls and storing them in private fields is not enough to make them appear onscreen—they must be explicitly added to the form on which they are to appear. Finally, the ResumeLayout method, which is inherited from the Control class, is called. This is the counterpart of the earlier call to SuspendLayout, and it indicates to the form that the various additions and modifications are complete and that it won't be wasting CPU cycles when it manages its layout. This call also causes an initial layout to be performed, causing any docked controls to be positioned appropriately.

The other method created on all new forms is the Dispose method. This runs when the form is destroyed and frees any resources that were allocated for the form. In fact, all controls have two Dispose methods: one public, supplied by the framework, and one protected, which you usually implement yourself.

Adding Controls to a Form

You can add a control to a form in four ways:

▶ The easiest way is to click on the control in the toolbox and then click the form where you want to add the control. You can then resize the control by dragging one of its adjustment handles, and you can move the control by dragging it to a new location on the form.

▶ Place and size the control in a single operation by clicking the control in the toolbox and then clicking and dragging in the form.

▶ Simply double-click the control you want to add in the toolbox. This places the control in the upper-left corner of the form. You can then move and resize the control.

▶ Drag the control from the toolbox to the form. The control is placed wherever you drop it. You can then resize the control.

Figure 5.2 shows how you can use the toolbox to add controls to a form.

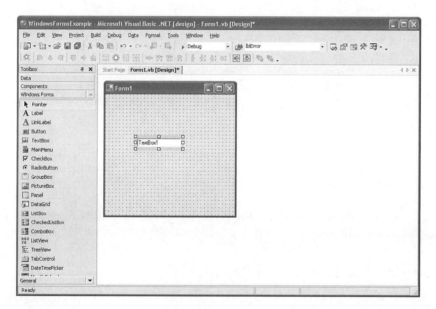

FIGURE 5.2   Using the toolbox to add controls to a form.

Note that if the AutoHide feature is activated for the toolbox and you move the mouse pointer over the toolbox tab to display it, the display frequently obscures some or all of the form. This makes it difficult to add controls. As a result, it's a good idea to turn off the AutoHide feature by clicking the push-pin button in the upper-right corner of the toolbox.

TIP

After you have added controls to the form, you can work with several controls at once. For example, let's say that you have four text box controls on your form and you want to make them all the same size with the same alignment. To do that, you would first select all four controls by holding down the Shift key as you clicked on them or by using the mouse pointer to drag around the controls. Then you would use the commands in the Format menu or the buttons in the Layout toolbar to move, size, and align the first three controls relative to the fourth control (the primary control).

Modifying a Form's Properties

You will want to manipulate these basic properties of a form's appearance:

- Text
- Name
- Height
- Left
- Top
- Width

The capability to tailor your forms, however, goes far beyond these simple manipulations. More complex actions can include these:

- Adding controls to a form
- Positioning, aligning, sizing, spacing, and anchoring controls
- Creating intelligent tab orders
- Creating transparent forms
- Creating forms that always float over other forms
- Creating multiple document interfaces

The following sections walk you through the process of manipulating a form's properties, methods, and events.

Changing the Name of a Form

The first thing you should do when you create a new object is give it a descriptive name. Start Visual Basic now (if it's not already running), and open the Windows application WindowsFormsExample that you created earlier. Using the Properties window, change the name of the form to `SampleForm`. When you need to create a new instance of this form, you'll use this name rather than the default generic name of `Form1`. This is shown in Figure 5.3.

Figure 5.3 shows how you can set various properties of the form using the Properties window.

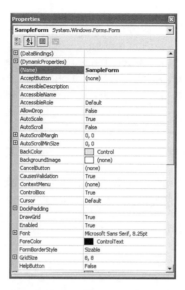

FIGURE 5.3   Changing the name of the form using the Properties window.

TIP

To get help on any property at any time, select the property in the Properties window and press F1.

Take a moment to browse the rest of the form's properties in the Properties window. The following sections show you how to use some basic properties of the form to tailor its appearance.

Displaying Text on a Form's Title Bar

You should always set the text in a form's title bar to something meaningful. The text displayed in the title bar is the value placed in the form's Text property. Generally, the text should be one of the following:

▶ The name of the program

▶ The purpose of the form

▶ The name of the form

Change the Text property of your form to First Windows Form. As with most other form properties, you can also change the text at runtime using Visual Basic code.

Changing a Form's Background Color

Although most forms appear with a gray background (this is part of the standard 3D color scheme in Windows), you can change a form's background to any color you like. To change a form's background color, you change its `BackColor` property. The `BackColor` property is a unique property, in that you can specify a named color or an RGB value in the format Red, Green, Blue.

By default, `BackColor` is set to the color named Control. This color is a system color and might not be gray. When Windows is first installed, it's configured to a default color scheme. In the default scheme, the color for forms and other objects is the familiar "battleship" gray. However, as a Windows user, you're free to change any system color you desire. For instance, some people with color blindness prefer to change their system colors to colors that have more contrast than the defaults so that objects are more clearly distinguishable. When you assign a system color to a form or control, the appearance of the object adjusts itself to the current user's system color scheme. This doesn't just occur when a form is first displayed; changes to the system color scheme are immediately propagated to all objects that use the affected colors.

Change the background color of your form to blue now by selecting the appropriate color from the color palettes. To view color palettes from which you can select a color for the `BackColor` property, click the drop-down arrow in the `BackColor` property in the Properties window. Figure 5.4 shows the color palette from which you can choose a color.

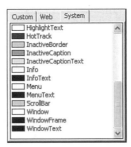

FIGURE 5.4 System tab in the color palette that displays the list of colors.

Select the System tab to see a list of the available system colors, and choose Control from the list to change the `BackColor` of your form back to the default Windows color.

Adding an Image to a Form's Background

In addition to changing the color of a form's background, you can place a picture on it. Simply set the form's `BackgroundImage` property. When you add an image to a form, the image is "painted" on the form's background. All the controls that you place on the form appear on top of the picture.

Add an image to your form now by following these steps:

1. Select the form.

2. Click the `BackgroundImage` property in the Properties window.

3. Click the Build button that appears next to the property (the small button with three dots).

4. Use the Open dialog box that appears to locate and select a GIF file from your hard drive. Visual Basic always tiles an image specified in a `BackgroundImage` property. This means that if the selected picture isn't big enough to fill the form, Visual Basic will display additional copies of the picture, creating a tiled effect. If you want to display a single copy of an image on a form, anywhere on the form, you should use a picture box.

Notice that to the left of the `BackgroundImage` property is a small box that contains a plus sign. This indicates that there are related properties, or subproperties, of the `BackgroundImage` property. Click the plus sign now to expand the list of subproperties. In the case of the `BackgroundImage` property, Visual Basic shows you a number of properties related to the image assigned to the property, such as its dimensions and image format.

5

TIP

Removing an image from a form is just as easy as adding the image in the first place. To remove the picture that you just added to your form, right-click the `BackgroundImage` property name and choose Reset from the shortcut menu that appears. Note that this is true for all of the form's properties that were demonstrated in the previous examples.

Displaying an Icon in the Form

The icon assigned to a form appears on the left side of the form's title bar, in the taskbar when the form is minimized, and in the iconic list of tasks when you press Alt+Tab to switch to another application. The icon often represents the application; therefore, you should assign an icon to any form a user can minimize. If you don't assign an icon to a form, Visual Basic supplies a default icon to represent it when the form is minimized. This default icon is generic and unattractive, and you should avoid it.

You assign an icon to a form in much the same way you assign an image to the `BackgroundImage` property. Add an icon to your form now by clicking the form's `Icon` property in the Properties window, clicking the Build button that appears, and selecting an icon file from your hard drive. After you've selected the icon, it appears in the form's title bar to the left.

Modifying a Form's Properties

Run your project by pressing F5, and then click the form's Minimize button to minimize it to the taskbar. Look at the form in the taskbar; you'll see both the form's caption and the form's icon displayed. As you can see, assigning meaningful icons to your forms makes your application easier to use. Stop the project now by choosing Stop Debugging from the Debug menu.

Specifying the Initial Display Position of a Form

The location on the display (monitor) where a form first appears isn't random, but is controlled by the form's StartPosition property. The StartPosition property can be set to one of the values shown in Table 5.1.

TABLE 5.1

Values for the StartPosition Property

Value	Description
Manual	The location property of the form determines where the form first appears.
CenterScreen	The form appears centered in the display.
WindowsDefaultLocation	The form appears in the Windows default location, which is toward the upper left of the display.
WindowsDefaultBounds	The form appears in the Windows default location with its bounds (size) set to the Windows default bounds.
CenterParent	The form is centered within the bounds of its parent form.

Generally, it's best to set the StartPosition property of all your forms to CenterParent, unless you have a specific reason to do otherwise. However, if your application has only one form, it makes sense to set the StartPosition property to CenterScreen.

Controlling Size and Location of the Form

You already know that there are two ways to control the size of your form: with the Width and Height properties. These properties simply take numeric values to set the size of the form in pixels. For example:

```
SampleForm.Width = 100
SampleForm.Height = 200
```

Here, the Width and Height properties of the SampleForm are set to 100 and 200 pixels, respectively.

You can set the size relative to the user's screen as well by using the Screen object. Listing 5.1 shows an example of this in action ▪1▪.

TIP

You can also set the size using the `Size` property and a `Size` object:
 	
`    SampleForm.Size = New Size(100, Form1.Size.Height)`
`    SampleForm.Size = New Size(100, Form1.Size.Width)`
 	
Both methods do the same thing, but you'll typically use the first method because it's simpler.

LISTING 5.1
Setting Form Height Based on Screen Size in VB .NET

```
Imports System
Imports System.Windows.Forms

Public Class MultiForm : Inherits Form
   Public Sub New()
      Me.Text = "Main form"
      Me.Height = Screen.GetWorkingArea(Me).Height / 2      1
   End Sub
End Class


Public Class StartForm
   Public Shared Sub Main()
      Application.Run(New MultiForm)
   End Sub
End Class
```

In Listing 5.1, the `GetWorkingArea` method of the `Screen` object returns a `Rectangle` object that represents the user's screen. You pass in the current form object (using the `Me` keyword) to tell the common language runtime which screen to use (this is just in case the user has more than one monitor). `Rectangle` objects, in turn, have `Height` and `Width` properties that return integers that describe the height and width of the screen. You then divide the height value by 2. Compile this application and run it; note that the window now takes up half the vertical height of your screen.

To control where the form pops up on the screen, you can use the `Location`, `DesktopLocation`, `Top`, or `Left` properties. The last two set the position of the upper-left corner of your form to a location on the user's desktop. They work just like the `Height` and `Width` properties. Note that you can set these properties to some location way off the user's screen, such as `Top = 9999` and `Left = 9999`, but that's generally not a good idea.

The `Location` and `DesktopLocation` properties are similar. For a `Form` object, they do the same thing: set the starting location for the top-left corner of your form.

Modifying a Form's Properties

For example, both of the following lines do the same thing:

```
Form1.DesktopLocation = New Point(100,300)
Form1.Location = New Point(100,300)
```

`Location` is a property that is inherited from the `Control` class. Because the `Form` class inherits from the `System.Windows.Forms.Control` class, all the properties and methods of the `Control` class are available within the `Form` class as well. This property is used to set the location of a control within another control. In this case, the containing control for the form is simply the user's desktop. You could use the `Location` property for any other object that inherits from the `Control` object, such as the `TextBox` or `Label` controls, to set its location within another object, such as your form. The `DesktopLocation` property, however, applies only to the `Form` object. For consistency, you'll use the `Location` property from now on, so you need to use only one property for all Windows Forms objects. As you can see, the earlier code invokes the `Application.Run` method in the `Shared Main` method to invoke the form. Next you take a brief look at the important properties and methods of the `Application` object.

Application Object

In the previous example, to exit the application, you called the `Application.Exit` method. The `Application` object is similar to the `App` object in Visual Basic 6; it contains information about the current running application. It's important to note that the `Closing` event won't fire when you call the `Application.Exit()` method. In the later section "Controlling Execution," you will be introduced to the `Closing` event. Make sure that you gracefully close your windows, and then call `Application.Exit()`. Table 5.2 lists some common properties of the `Application` object.

TABLE 5.2

Important Properties of the `Application` Object

Property	Description
AllowQuit	Gets a value indicating whether the caller can quit this application
CommonAppDataPath	Gets the path for the application data that's shared among all users
CommonAppDataRegistry	Gets the Registry key for the application data that's shared among all users
CompanyName	Gets the company name associated with the application
ExecutablePath	Gets the path for the executable file that started the application
LocalUserAppDataPath	Gets the path for the application data of a local, nonroaming user

TABLE 5.2

Continued

Property	Description
ProductName	Gets the product name associated with this application
ProductVersion	Gets the product version associated with this application
StartupPath	Gets the path for the executable file that started the application
UserAppDataPath	Gets the path for the application data of a roaming user
UserAppDataRegistry	Gets the Registry key of the application data specific to the roaming user

Table 5.3 lists some common methods of the Application object that you'll find useful.

TABLE 5.3

Important Methods of the Application Object

Method	Description
AddMessageFilter	Adds a message filter to monitor Windows messages as they're routed to their destinations
DoEvents	Processes all Windows messages currently in the message queue
Exit	Informs all message pumps that they must terminate, and then closes all application windows after the messages have been processed
ExitThread	Exits the message loop on the current thread and closes all windows on the thread
OnThreadException	Raises the ThreadException event
RemoveMessageFilter	Removes a message filter from the message pump of the application
Run	Begins running a standard application message loop on the current thread

Controlling the Appearance of the Form

As you have already seen, the Text property is used to determine the text displayed in the form's title bar. Next you explore a few things you can do with font (the typeface in which the text appears). The Font property sets the font that will be used on the form, unless otherwise overridden by a control's Font property. The ForeColor property then sets the color of that text. Take a look at the following code snippet:

```
Form1.Font = New Font(new FontFamily("Wingdings"), 23)
Form1.ForeColor = Color.Blue
```

Modifying a Form's Properties

The first line creates a new `Font` object. In that line, it also sets the font face by using the `FontFamily` object, which contains predefined font names. The second parameter is the size of the font. The second line sets the text color to blue, using the `Blue` property of the `Color` object.

The `BackColor` and `BackgroundImage` properties enable you to change the default appearance of the form. `BackColor` is used just like `ForeColor`:

```
Form1.BackColor = Color.LightSalmon
```

The `BackgroundImage` property takes an `Image` object as a parameter. Typically, you use the `Image`'s `FromFile` method to load an image. For example:

```
Form1.BackgroundImage = Image.FromFile("c:\Projects\Arch.bmp")
```

Because `FromFile` is a static method, there is no need to create an instance of the class to be able to use that method.

The `FormBorderStyle` property represents the type of border around a Windows Form. The main reason you modify this property is to allow or disallow resizing of the form, although changing border styles sometimes also changes the form's appearance. For example:

```
Form1.FormBorderStyle = FormBorderStyle.Sizable
```

TIP

Mostly it is useful to disable sizing of the form because this distorts the position of the controls on the screen. Alternatively, you can build logic into the application to reposition the controls and resize them if the container form is resized.

The `FormBorderStyle` enumeration has several predefined styles to choose from, as shown in Table 5.4.

TABLE 5.4

`FormBorderStyle` Enumeration Values

Style	Description
Fixed3D	Nonresizable 3D border around a form.
FixedDialog	A thick, nonresizable border.
FixedToolWindow	A nonresizable form with a smaller title bar, useful for displaying ToolTips and Help windows. It does not provide Minimize or Maximize buttons.
None	A nonresizable form with no border.
Sizable	A resizable form. This is the default value.

TABLE 5.4

Continued

Style	Description
SizableToolWindow	A resizable form with a smaller title bar, useful for displaying ToolTips and Help windows. It does not include Minimize or Maximize windows.

Showing and Unloading Forms

Knowing how to create forms does nothing for you if you don't have a way to show and hide them: Visual Basic can display a single form automatically only when a program starts. To control this process on your own, you need to write code.

Showing Forms

In Visual Basic .NET, everything is an object, and objects are based on classes. Because the definition of a form is a class, you have to create a new `Form` object using the form class as a template. The process of creating an object from a class (or template) is called instantiation. You need this syntax to instantiate a form:

```
Dim <NameOfVariable> As New <NameOfFormClass>
```

> **TIP**
>
> Unlike in classic VB, you need not necessarily rely on a sophisticated development environment such as Visual Studio .NET to create forms; all code can be written using a simple editor such as Notepad.

This declaration has four parts:

- `Dim` **statement**—A reserved word that tells the compiler that you're creating a variable.

- **Name of the variable**—The name of the form that you will use in code.

- **Keyword** `New`—Indicates that you want to instantiate a new object for the variable.

- **Name of form class**—Specifies the name of the class to use to derive the object your form class.

If you have a form class named `SampleForm`, for example, you could create a new `Form` object using the following code:

```
Dim sample As New SampleForm()
```

Showing and Unloading Forms

Three properties control how—and if—your form is displayed onscreen. First, the Visible property determines whether your form is visible to the user. If a form is not visible, the user cannot interact with it. This is a good way to hide things from the user—if you want your application to stay open but you don't want it to interfere with the user's desktop, for example.

Displaying the Forms

As long as the variable that represents the form remains in scope, you can manipulate the Form object using the variable. For instance, to display the form, you call the Show method of the form or set the Visible property of the form to True using code such as this:

```
SampleForm.Show
SampleForm.Visible = True
```

You can see this with a simple example. To begin, choose Add Windows Form from the Project menu to display the Add New Item dialog box. Change the name of the form to SecondForm.vb, as shown in Figure 5.5. Click Open to create the new form.

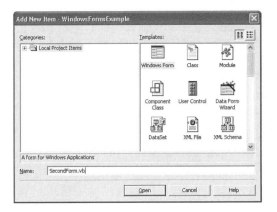

FIGURE 5.5 Adding a new form to the Windows Forms project.

Your project now has two forms, as you can see by viewing the Solution Explorer window. The new form is displayed in Forms Designer, but right now you need to work with the main form. At the top of the main design area is a set of tabs. Currently, the tab SecondForm.vb [Design] is selected.

1. Click the tab titled SampleForm.vb [Design] to show the designer for the first form.

2. Add a new button to your form by double-clicking the Button item on the toolbox.

3. Set the button's properties as shown in Table 5.5.

TABLE 5.5

Property Values for the Button

Property	Value
Name	btnShowForm
Location	150, 112
Text	Show Form

Double-click the button to access its `Click` event, and enter the following code:

```
Dim secondFormObj As New SecondForm()
secondFormObj.Show()
```

The first statement creates a new object variable and instantiates an instance of the `SecondForm` form. The second statement uses the object variable, now holding a reference to a `Form` object, to display the form. Press F5 to run the project and click the button. (If the button doesn't appear on the form, you might have accidentally added it to the wrong form.) When you click the button, a new instance of the second form is created and displayed. Move this form and click the button again. Each time you click the button, a new form is created. Stop the project now and click Save All on the toolbar.

Differences Between Modal and Nonmodal Dialog Boxes

All forms that Visual Studio .NET creates will conform to the predefined structure just described. But as with dialog boxes in classic Windows applications, these boxes can be shown in two ways: Forms can exhibit either modal or nonmodal behavior. A modal form is one that demands the user's immediate attention and blocks input to any other windows the application may have open. The application enters a mode in which it will allow only the user to access that form, hence the name. Forms should be displayed modally only if the application cannot proceed until the form is satisfied. Typical examples are error messages that must not go unnoticed or dialog boxes that collect data from the user that must be supplied before an operation can be completed (such as the File Open dialog box—an application needs to know which file it is supposed to load before it can open it). You select between modal and nonmodal behavior when you display the form. The `Form` class provides two methods for displaying a form:

- ▶ `ShowDialog`—This method displays the form modally.

- ▶ `Show`—As you have already seen in the previous section, this method displays the form nonmodally.

A nonmodal form has a life of its own after it has been displayed; it might even outlive the form that created it.

Showing and Unloading Forms

By contrast, the ShowDialog method does not return until the user has dismissed the dialog box. Of course, this means that the thread will not return to the Application class's main event-handling loop until the dialog box goes away, but this is not a problem because the framework will process events inside the ShowDialog method. However, events are handled differently when a modal dialog is open: Any attempts to click on a form other than the one being displayed modally are rejected. Other forms will still be redrawn correctly, but they will simply beep if the user tries to provide them with any input. This forces the user to deal with the modal dialog box before progressing.

> **NOTE**
>
> One more minor difference exists between modal and nonmodal use of forms: Resizable forms have a subtly different appearance. When displayed modally, a form always has a resize grip in the bottom-right corner. Nonmodal forms have a resize grip only if they have a status bar. Be careful with your use of modal dialog boxes because they can prove somewhat annoying for the user. Dialog boxes that render the rest of the application inaccessible for no good reason are just frustrating. To avoid making this kind of design error in your own applications, follow this guideline: Do not make your dialog boxes modal unless they really have to be.

Unloading Forms

After a form has served its purpose, you'll want it to go away. However, "go away" can mean one of two things. First, you can make a form disappear without closing it or freeing its resources (this is called hiding). To do so, set its Visible property to False. This hides the visual part of the form, but the form still resides in memory and can be manipulated by code. In addition, all the variables and controls of the form retain their values when a form is hidden so that if the form is displayed again, it looks the same as it did when its Visible property was set to False.

Second, you can completely close a form and release the resources it consumes. You should close a form when it's no longer needed so that Windows can reclaim all resources used by the form. To do so, you invoke the Close method of the form:

```
Me.Close()
```

Because Me represents the current Form object, you can manipulate properties and call methods of the current form using the identifier Me. The Close method tells Visual Basic to not simply hide the form, but to destroy it completely. If variables in other forms are holding a reference to the form you close, their references will be set to Nothing and will no longer point to a valid Form object.

Select the SecondForm.vb [Design] tab to display the Forms Designer for the second form, add a new button to the form, and set the button's properties as indicated in Table 5.6.

TABLE 5.6

Property Values for the Button

Property	Value
Name	btnCloseMe
Location	150, 112
Text	Close

Double-click the button to access its `Click` event and then enter the following statement:

```
Me.Close()
```

Next, run the project by pressing F5. Click the Show Form button to display the second form, and then click the second form's button. The form disappears. Again, the form isn't just hidden; the form instance is unloaded from memory and no longer exists. You can create a new one by clicking the Show Form button on the first form. When you're finished, stop the running project and save your work.

Configuring Control Boxes

Most of the Windows application will have standard features, such as Minimize, Maximize, Close, and sometimes Help buttons in the upper-right corner of the window, and a "gripper" on the bottom right to resize the form. Each of these control boxes can be hidden or shown on your forms with the following properties:

- ► `MaximizeBox`
- ► `MinimizeBox`
- ► `HelpButton`
- ► `ControlBox`
- ► `SizeGripStyle`

The first four properties simply take a `True` or `False` value. `ControlBox` determines whether the previous buttons should be shown at all. This means that if you set `ControlBox` to `False`, you might not be able to close your application.

TIP

The Help button appears only if the Maximize and Minimize buttons are not visible. This is a standard feature of .NET.

The `SizeGripStyle` property takes a `SizeGripStyle` enumeration, which can have any one of the following values: `Auto`, `Hide`, or `Show`. Auto displays the sizing grip when necessary (in other words, depending on the `FormBorderStyle`), while `Hide` and `Show` determine whether the sizing grips are shown.

Showing and Unloading Forms

Two special keys often are associated with applications: the Enter key and the Esc (Escape) key. For example, many applications exit if you press the Esc key. You can control these functions with the `AcceptButton` and `CancelButton` properties. Listing 5.2 shows an example of this in action **1**.

LISTING 5.2
Handling Enter and Esc Key Events in a Form

```
Imports System
Imports System.Windows.Forms
Imports System.Drawing

Namespace WindowsFormsExample
    Public class FormButtonEvents
        Inherits Form
      Private btnAccept as Button = New Button()
      Private btnCancel as Button = New Button()
      Private lblMessage as Label = New Label()
      Public Sub New()
        lblMessage.Location = New Point(75,150)
        lblMessage.Width = 200
        btnAccept.Location = new Point(100,25)
        btnAccept.Text = "Accept"
        AddHandler btnAccept.Click, AddressOf Me.AcceptEvent
        btnCancel.Location = new Point(100,100)
        btnCancel.Text = "Cancel"
        AddHandler btnCancel.Click, AddressOf Me.CancelEvent
        Me.AcceptButton = btnAccept
        Me.CancelButton = btnCancel
        Me.Text = "Accept and Cancel Button Example"
        Me.Height = 200
        Me.Controls.Add(lblMessage)
        Me.Controls.Add(btnAccept)
        Me.Controls.Add(btnCancel)
      End Sub
      Public Sub AcceptEvent(Sender as Object, e as EventArgs)
        lblMessage.Text = "Accept button pressed"
      End Sub
      Public Sub CancelEvent(Sender as Object, e as EventArgs)
        lblMessage.Text = "Cancel button pressed"
      End Sub
    End Class
    Public Class StartForm
      Public Shared Sub Main()
```

LISTING 5.2
Continued

```
        Application.Run(new FormButtonEvents())
    End Sub
  End Class
End Namespace
```

Much of this code shown in Listing 5.2 is already familiar to you, so you can just breeze through most of it. To start, you import all the required namespaces. Next, you declare the controls you'll be using in your form. Note that these are declared outside of any method, but inside the class so that they can be used from every method in the class. Then the code simply sets a few properties for your controls and associates event-handler methods to the `Click` event of the command buttons. These event handler methods (named `AcceptEvent` and `CancelEvent`) simply print a message in the `Label` control.

Then the code sets some properties and adds the controls to the form. After that, the code sets the `AcceptButton` and `CancelButton` properties of the `Form` object to the Accept and Cancel buttons, respectively. Essentially, this means that clicking the Accept and Cancel buttons with your mouse does the same thing as pressing the Enter and Esc keys. Finally, the code contains another class that is used simply to hold the `Main` method and call the `Application.Run` method. Figure 5.6 shows the output of the application after pressing the Enter key.

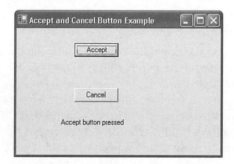

FIGURE 5.6   Output produced by the form.

Figure 5.6 shows the output produced by the form when then Accept button is pressed.

5

> **TIP**
>
> If the Cancel button on the form gets the focus, pressing Enter causes that button to be pressed and, consequently, the `CancelEvent` method to execute. In other words, the button receives the input before the form does. Unfortunately, there's no easy way to get around this. Some controls, such as the `Button` and `RichTextBox` controls, automatically handle the Enter key press when they have the focus, before anything else can execute. As a result, when you give the Cancel button focus (by clicking it or tabbing to it), pressing the Enter key always causes the `CancelEvent` method to execute. Note that although the `AcceptButton` and `CancelButton` properties need to point to `Button` controls, those `Buttons` do not have to necessarily be visible to the user. By setting their `Visible` properties to `False`, the buttons will be invisible, but you can still retain their functionality.

Finally, the `AllowDrop` property specifies whether the form can handle drag-and-drop functionality—that is, when a user drags some item into the form and releases it there. This property accepts a `True` or `False` value.

Form Methods

The `Form` object has quite a few methods, and most are inherited from the `Object` and `Control` classes, so they are common to almost all the objects you work with in Windows Forms. You have already been introduced to some of these methods in this chapter. The following sections cover a few of them here, grouped by category.

Dealing with Display Issues

The first two methods you will learn in terms of displaying a form are `Show` and `Hide`. As the name suggests, these two methods make your form visible and invisible, respectively, by modifying the `Visible` property. These functions don't do anything to the form, such as remove it from memory or activate other functions. They only control what the user sees. The `Close` method, on the other hand, completely gets rid of a form (and its controls), removing it from memory. Use this method when you want to close your application or simply when you don't need a form anymore.

Because Windows is a multitasking environment, you can have many windows open at once. Each window must compete for the user's attention. The `Form` object has a few methods that help you deal with this issue. The `Activate` method "activates" your form. This can mean two different things:

> ▸ If your application is the active one (the one the user happens to be using at the moment), `Activate` brings the form to the front of the screen, ensuring that it is on top of all other forms.

▶ If it is not the active application, the title bar and the taskbar icon flash, grabbing the user's attention. More than likely, you've seen this type of attention grabber before; the most common usage is for instant-messaging applications. If someone sends you an instant message while you're working on another application, the IM window pops up in the background and flashes its title bar.

The `BringToFront` and `SendToBack` methods are more direct than `Activate` at getting a user's attention. The first method brings your form to the front of all other windows onscreen, forcing the user to look at it. This is useful, for example, when something happens with your application that demands the user's attention (such as getting an instant message pop-up). `SendToBack`, conversely, places your form behind all others on screen. `SendToBack` isn't used as often, but it's there just in case.

TIP

You can set the `TopMost` property to `True` to have your form always stay on top of other windows. This is especially useful for forms that deliver error or warning messages.

5

Finally, the `Refresh` method works much like the Refresh button on your web browser; it simply redraws everything on the form, updating, if necessary.

Resetting Properties

The `Form` object has a series of reset methods that enable you to change modified properties back to their default values. All of these methods follow the naming scheme `Reset<NameOfProperty>`. These are a few of the more common ones:

▶ `ResetBackColor`   ▶ `ResetForeColor`

▶ `ResetCursor`   ▶ `ResetText`

▶ `ResetFont`

These methods are very convenient when you've modified something and need to go back, but you don't know or don't care what the original value was. For example, if in a word processor the user changes the font several times but then wants to go back to default values, you could use `ResetFont`.

Event Handling

An event is something that happens as a result of an action. Going back to the car object analogy, imagine that when you press the brake (an action), the car stops (an event). When you press the gas pedal (an action), the car moves (an event). An event is always the effect of some action taking place.

Event Handling

Windows Forms have events, too, although many of them might not seem very obvious. For example, open and close are two events that occur when you start and stop your application. When you move your mouse cursor into the form, an event takes place; when your mouse cursor leaves the form, another event occurs. Without events, Windows Forms would be very bland because they would never do anything, no matter what the user tried. The next section takes a brief look at how events are handled with Windows Forms and .NET.

The Message Loop

Events are wonderful ways of dealing with user input. Let's look at two different application models—one with events and one without events—before examining how applications use events.

First, imagine an event-driven application. *Event-driven* means that the application responds to events caused by user actions. In fact, without these events, the application would do nothing. The events drive the application. In this model, an application sits around and waits for things to happen. It uses events as its cues to perform actions. For example, a user presses a letter on the keyboard. The application sees that an event has occurred (the key being pressed), performs an action to display that letter onscreen, and then waits for another event.

A non–event-driven application doesn't allow users free reign of the application: They can only respond to prompts from the application. With an event-driven application, users can interact with any part of the application they want, in any order or time they want. Imagine a non–event-driven calculator application. When you start the application, it retrieves two values from text boxes, performs the mathematical calculations, and spits out the result. If there are no values in the text boxes, the calculator does nothing. The calculator cannot detect when a number has changed because it isn't aware of events. Anytime you want to change the numbers to calculate a different value, you have to change the numbers first and then run the application again.

Both models have their advantages and disadvantages. After they are started, non–event-driven applications can execute without user intervention. Event-driven applications typically require user input but are often more interactive. Because interactivity is a must with any Windows-based application, all your programs will use the event-driven model.

You might be wondering how an application detects events. When a typical Windows application starts, it enters a message loop. This is simply a period of time when the application is waiting for input or messages from the user. This period continues until the application quits, so it is known as a loop. During this loop, the application does nothing except wait for user input (the period of inactivity is known as *idling*). When some input is received, the application does some work and then goes back into the message loop. This cycle continues until the application is closed.

TIP

When you provide some input, the Windows OS is the first stop for processing. Windows determines to what application the event applies and sends it along to the application. These communications are known as Windows messages (hence, the name message loop).

For example, when you first open a Microsoft Word document, nothing happens; Word just idles, waiting for you to type. When you press a key, an event occurs, a method is executed (to display the character onscreen), and Word goes back into the message loop waiting for more input. Every time you press a key, the message loop stops for a moment to do some processing and then continues the wait. Windows Forms are typically the main user interface for your applications. Thus, they'll be dealing with quite a few different events.

Form Events

Now that you understand the basics of events, you can take a look at the important events of the Form object.

Controlling Execution

To give you, the developer, the most control over your applications, some events fire both before and after an action occurs. For example, when you close your form, the Closing event occurs immediately before the form begins to close, and the Closed event occurs immediately afterward.

NOTE

These types of event names always follow the "ing" and "ed" suffixes, such as Closing and Closed. Not all events come in pairs like this. If you see an "ing" event name, though, you can be sure there's also an "ed" event as well, but not the other way around.

You might wonder why this approach of two events per action is needed. Imagine that a user makes a large number of changes to a word-processing document and then closes the application using the Close control box, but forgets to save the document. What would happen? If the user waited for the Closed event to fire before doing anything, it would be too late; the document would have closed and all changes would be lost. With .NET, however, the Closing event fires before closing actually takes place. Here, you can prompt the user to save the document before changes are lost and can conditionally save the changes. After the window closes, the Closed event fires, and then you can do whatever other processing you need to (such as display a message to the user).

Form Events

Take a look at an example using this two-step process. Listing 5.3 uses the Closing and Closed events of the Form object to illustrate the previous example ▇1▇.

LISTING 5.3
Handling the Form Closing Events

```
Imports System
Imports System.Windows.Forms
Imports System.Drawing
Imports System.ComponentModel

Namespace WindowsFormsExample
    Public Class FormEvents : Inherits Form
        Public Sub New()
            Me.Text = "Form Event Example"
            AddHandler Me.Closing, AddressOf Me.ClosingEvent
            AddHandler Me.Closed, AddressOf Me.ClosedEvent
        End Sub
        Public sub ClosingEvent(Sender as Object, e as
            CancelEventArgs)
            MessageBox.Show("Form closing")
        End Sub
        Public Sub ClosedEvent(Sender as Object, e as EventArgs)
            MessageBox.Show ("Form closed")
        End Sub
    End Class
    Public Class StartForm
        Public Shared Sub Main()
            Application.Run(new FormEvents)
        End Sub
    End Class
End Namespace
```

Listing 5.3 starts by importing the required namespaces. One namespace that you might not be familiar with is System.ComponentModel. This namespace has objects that apply to events that you'll need later in the code. In the constructor of the FormEvents class, the AddHandler method is invoked to tell the common language runtime to execute the ClosingEvent and ClosedEvent methods. The ClosingEvent method takes two parameters: an Object and System.ComponentModel.CancelEventArgs object. CancelEventArgs is a specialized object that applies only to events—and only to Closing events, in particular. It has a special property named Cancel, which you can use to stop the form from closing. If at any point in time you want to stop the form from closing inside the Closing event, set the Cancel property to True:

```
e.Cancel = true
```

The code inside `ClosingEvent` and `ClosedEvents` are very similar: They simply call the `MessageBox.Show` method to display a message box to the user.

You should know about a few important events when dealing with Windows Forms. You've already learned about `Closed`, which fires when a form closes. A `Load` event fires immediately before a form is displayed for the first time. The event handler for this event is often a good place to initialize components on your form that you haven't already initialized in the constructor. The `Activated` event occurs when your form gains focus and becomes the active application. Deactivate, on the other hand, is fired when your form is deactivated—that is, when it loses focus or another application becomes the active one.

Keyboard and Mouse Events

Mouse and keyboard actions are one of the most important types of events—after all, those are typically the only forms of user input. As such, quite a few events pertain to these two input devices. You can begin with the keyboard events.

Keyboard Events

First is the `KeyPress` event. This occurs anytime a key is pressed, no matter what key it is. If this event doesn't provide enough control, there are also the `KeyDown` and `KeyUp` events, which fire when a key is pressed and then released, respectively. Because of their nature, these events provide additional information (such as the specific key that is pressed) that you can use in your application. As such, their event handlers (the methods that execute when the event is fired) are specialized. Declaring these handlers in VB .NET is the same process that you're used to:

```
AddHandler Form1.KeyPress, AddressOf <MethodName>
AddHandler Form1.KeyDown, AddressOf <MethodName>
AddHandler Form1.KeyUp, AddressOf <MethodName>
```

As with the `CancelEventArgs` object, the `KeyPressEventHandler` and `KeyEventHandler` objects have special properties that aid your application in determining the action that caused the event: `Handled` and `KeyChar`. The `Handled` property is simply a `True` or `False` value indicating whether your method has handled the key press. It is recommended that you set this property to `True`, unless you specifically want the OS to process that specific key. The `KeyChar` property simply returns the key that was pressed. Listing 5.4 shows an example of this in action.

LISTING 5.4
Handling Key Presses

```
Imports System
Imports System.Windows.Forms
Imports System.Drawing
Imports System.ComponentModel
```

Form Events

LISTING 5.4
Continued

```
Namespace WindowsFormsExample
  Public Class FormKeyPressEvents : Inherits Form
    Public Sub New()
      Me.Text = "Keypress Example"
      AddHandler Me.KeyPress, AddressOf Me.KeyPressed
    End Sub
    Public Sub KeyPressed(Sender as Object, e as
      KeyPressEventArgs)
      MessageBox.Show(e.KeyChar)
      e.Handled = True
    End Sub
    Public Shared Sub Main()
      Application.Run(new FormKeyPressEvents)
    End Sub
  End Class
End Namespace
```

In the constructor of the form, the `KeyPressed` event handler **1** is associated with the `KeyPress` event. The `KeyPressed` event declaration takes a `KeyPressEventArgs` object as one of its parameters. Inside the `KeyPressed` event, you simply display the character pressed in a message box and then set the `Handled` property to `True`.

Note that only the character and numeric keys and the Enter keys fire the `KeyPress` event. To handle other keys (such as Ctrl, Alt, and the F1–F12 function keys), you need to use the `KeyUp` and `KeyDown` events. Also note that these events use handlers of the type `KeyEventHandler`, so the second parameter of your event-handler methods must be `KeyEventArgs`:

```
Public Sub KeyReleased(Sender as Object, e as KeyEventArgs)
  'Some code
End Sub
```

As long as your form has the focus, any key press executes the `KeyPressed` method. The `KeyEventArgs` object has several properties that are useful in determining which key was pressed:

- `Alt`—Boolean value that indicates whether the Alt key was pressed
- `Control`—Indicates whether the Ctrl key was pressed
- `Handled`—`True` or `False`, to indicate whether the method handled the key press.

- ▶ KeyCode—Provides the keyboard code for the key that was pressed

- ▶ KeyData—Provides the key data for the key that was pressed

- ▶ KeyValue—Provides the keyboard code for the key that was pressed

- ▶ Modifiers—Returns flags indicating which keys and modifiers (such as Shift, Ctrl, or Alt) were pressed

- ▶ Shift—Indicates whether the Shift key was pressed

Every key on the keyboard has unique KeyCode, KeyData, and KeyValue values. The KeyCode and KeyValue properties are typically the same. KeyData is the same as the other two for most keys, but it is different on modifier keys.

Mouse Events

So far, you have been introduced to the key press events that the form supports. This section discusses the mouse events that the form supports. These are some of the important mouse events that the form control supports:

- ▶ MouseEnter—When the mouse cursor enters the region of the form

- ▶ MouseMove—When the mouse cursor moves over the region of the form

- ▶ MouseHover—When the cursor simply hovers over the form (without moving or clicking)

- ▶ MouseDown—When you press a mouse button on the form

- ▶ MouseUp—When you release the mouse button

- ▶ MouseLeave—When the mouse cursor leaves the form (moves out from over the form)

> **TIP**
>
> The MouseEnter, MouseLeave, and MouseHover events typically used provide visual cues to the user. For example, you can use these events to change the button face color in a button control or to display hyperlinks and clickable hotspots.

The MouseEnter, MouseLeave, and MouseHover events don't provide any special information and, therefore, use the standard EventHandler event handler and EventArgs event parameter objects. The MouseMove, MouseDown, and MouseUp events, however, provide special information by using the MouseEventHandler as their EventArgs objects:

```
Public Sub MouseClick(Sender as Object, e as MouseEventHandler)
```

Form Events

The `MouseEventHandler` object provides information such as the cursor's exact position onscreen, which button was clicked, and so on. These are some of the important properties of the `MouseEventHandler` object:

- ▸ `Button`—Gets which mouse button was pressed. This property returns an object of type `MouseButtons` enumeration. Values provided by the `MouseButtons` enumeration are `MouseButtons.Left`, `MouseButtons.Middle`, `MouseButtons.None`, `MouseButtons.Right`, `MouseButtons.XButton1`, and `MouseButtons.XButton2`.

- ▸ `Clicks`—The number of times the mouse was clicked (an integer value).

- ▸ `Delta`—The number of detents (or rotational notches) the mouse wheel has moved.

- ▸ `X`—The x screen coordinate of the mouse cursor.

- ▸ `Y`—The y screen coordinate of the mouse cursor.

Summary

The `System.Windows.Forms.Form` object, derived indirectly from `Object`, is the core component of your Windows Forms applications. It provides the frame and background for other user interface pieces, and it provides a lot of functionality by itself.

In this chapter, you learned about the properties of the `Form` object that enable you to control nearly every single visual aspect of the UI. You can make your form transparent with the `Opacity` property, make it nonresizable with the `FormBorderStyle` property, and control how the user can interact with the form by modifying the `MaximizeBox`, `MinimizeBox`, `HelpButton`, `ControlBox`, and `SizeGripStyle` properties. Additionally, this chapter talked about the many methods of the `Form` class, such as `BringToFront` and `Focus`, that you can execute to control the display.

Finally, you learned about events and the message loop, which enables an application to sit idly by until a user provides some input. The `Form` object has events that fire for many user actions, including mouse clicks, key presses, and dragging and dropping. This is only the bare minimum involved in creating forms. You've learned how to add them to your project, how to set basic appearance properties, and how to show and hide them using Visual Basic code.

Further Reading

Microsoft .NET site, http://msdn.microsoft.com/netframework.

Mackenzie, Duncan, and Kent Sharkey. *Sam's Teach Yourself VB .NET in 21 Days*. Sams, 2001.

5

6 CONTROLS

IN BRIEF

Microsoft Visual Studio .NET controls are the graphical tools you use to build the user interface of a Visual Basic program. Controls are located in the toolbox in the development environment, and you use them to create objects on a form with a simple series of mouse clicks and dragging motions. Windows Forms controls are specifically designed for building Windows applications; you will find them organized on the Windows Forms tab of the toolbox.

WHAT YOU NEED

SOFTWARE REQUIREMENTS	Windows 2000, XP, or 2003 .NET Framework 1.1 SDK Visual Studio .NET 2003 with Visual Basic .NET installed
HARDWARE REQUIREMENTS	PC desktop or laptop
SKILL REQUIREMENTS	Knowledge of Visual Basic .NET Knowledge of the .NET Framework

CONTROLS AT A GLANCE

Controls   147

Working with the Visual Studio .NET Form Designer

CONTROLS AT A GLANCE

The ComboBox Control	**165**		

Menu	**169**		
Building the Menu Groups	170	User Interface Control Events for	
Adding Menu Levels	171	MenuItems	177
Creating Menus Programmatically	172	Defining a MenuItem as a Separator	178
Adding a Menu Shortcut	174	Arranging Menu Items	178
Adding Hotkeys	175	Right-to-Left Menus	180
Responding to the Click Event	176	Context Menu	180

Working with the Visual Studio .NET Form Designer

The Visual Studio .NET Form Designer enables you to design your application's user interface visually by dragging controls onto a design-time representation of your application. When the controls are on the form, you can visually position the controls, set their properties through the Properties window, and create event handlers for the events the controls fire. When you create a VB .NET Windows application project, Visual Studio .NET opens the project in Designer view. You can also select the Designer option from the View menu to put the project in Designer view. The Form Designer is usually the window in the middle of the Visual Studio .NET environment that contains the design-time representation of the application's form object.

Figure 6.1 shows the Form Designer of a VB .NET Windows application in Designer view.

Notice the MainMenu1 component at the bottom of the Designer window. This region of the designer is reserved for controls that do not have visual representations, such as the MainMenu control, the ContextMenu control, and the Timer control.

The Toolbox Window

The Toolbox window contains all of the .NET Windows Forms controls that can be added to an application. Adding a control to an application at design time is as easy as dragging the control from the toolbox and dropping it onto the application's form in the Form Designer window. Figure 6.2 shows the toolbox for a VB .NET Windows Forms application.

Working with the Visual Studio .NET Form Designer

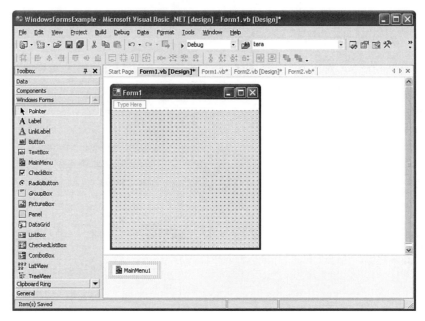

FIGURE 6.1   Form Designer in a VB .NET Windows application.

FIGURE 6.2   Toolbox window.

As you can see, the toolbox contains multiple tabs, such as Data, Components, Windows Forms, and General, that contain the right set of controls based on the classification.

The Properties Window

The Properties window contains all the public properties of the control currently selected in the Form Designer window. You can change these properties by typing values into the textbox controls next to the property names. If the property has a limited number of predefined values, a drop-down box is displayed next to the property name that contains the possible values for the property. If the property's value is a collection of objects or a complex object, there might be an ellipsis located next to the property name. Clicking this ellipsis displays a dialog box that enables you to edit the value of the property further. Figure 6.3 displays the Properties window when a text box is selected.

FIGURE 6.3 The Properties window for a `TextBox` control.

Note that most of the properties that you can set through the Properties window can also be set programmatically using code.

Working with the Visual Studio .NET Form Designer

Adding Event Handlers

As you have seen in the Windows Forms chapter, when a control is manipulated at runtime, it fires an event to notify the application that the control's state has changed. This event notification follows the same event-handling convention used throughout the .NET Framework. To handle an event published by a control, you must first create a method containing the code to execute when the event is fired. Then attach the method to the control's published event. In Visual Basic .NET, events are found in drop-down boxes above the code editor. You can assign a method as the event handler by clicking the event and selecting a method from the drop-down control next to the event name. In Visual Basic .NET, selecting the event name from the drop-down box automatically generates a method to handle the event.

You can also add an event handler by double-clicking the control in design view. Doing so switches the project to code view and leaves the editor inside the event-handler method. Code to wire the event handler to the control is also automatically generated. The following code wires a `Click` event handler to the `Click` event of a `Button` control.

```
Private Sub Button1_Click(ByVal sender As System.Object, ByVal e As
➡System.EventArgs)  _
    Handles Button1.Click


End Sub
```

Working with the `Form` Control

The `Form` control is the container for an application's entire user interface. The `Form` control is the actual window that contains the application's controls. All the controls used for creating the user interface of a Windows application are placed in the `Form` control.

Now that you have had an overview of the Windows Form Designer and the windows associated with it, this section introduces you to the Windows Forms controls. The discussion starts by focusing on the `TextBox` control.

`TextBox` Control

The `TextBox` control is used to accept input from the user. The `TextBox` control is generally used for editable text, although it can also be made read-only. Text boxes can display multiple lines, wrap text to the size of the control, and add basic formatting. The `TextBox` control supports the `BackColor` and `ForeColor` properties. The `TextBox` control does not support the `Click` event, but it provides support for other events, such as `KeyPress`, `KeyUp`, and `KeyDown` events. It also supports a `PasswordChar` property that enables you to specify the character to show in the display.

> **TIP**
>
> The `TextBox` control provides a single format style for text displayed or entered into the control. To display multiple types of formatted text, use the `RichTextBox` control.

The text that the control displays is contained in the `Text` property. By default, you can enter up to 2,048 characters in a text box. If you set the `MultiLine` property to `true`, you can enter up to 32KB of text. The `Text` property can be set in any of the following ways:

- ▸ At design time with the Properties window

- ▸ At runtime in code

- ▸ Through user input at runtime

The current contents of a text box can be retrieved at runtime by reading the `Text` property. This code sets the text of the control at runtime:

```
Private Sub InitializeControls()
  'Put some text into the control first.
  TextBox1.Text = "This text is set at runtime"
End Sub
```

6

Creating a Password Text Box

To create a password text box, set the `PasswordChar` property of the `TextBox` control to a specific character. The `PasswordChar` property specifies the character displayed in the text box. For example, if you want asterisks displayed in the password box, specify * for the `PasswordChar` property in the Properties window. Then, regardless of what character a user types in the text box, an asterisk is displayed. The following code shows an example of this in action.

```
Private Sub New()
  'Set to no text.
  TextBox1.Text = ""
  'Password character is an asterisk.
  TextBox1.PasswordChar = "*"
  'Control will allow no more than 14 characters.
  TextBox1.MaxLength = 14
End Sub
```

Another important property of the `TextBox` control that is closely related to the `PasswordChar` property is the `MaxLength` property. This property determines how many characters can be typed in the text box. If the maximum length is exceeded, the system emits a beep and the text box does not accept any more characters.

Note that you might not want to do this because hackers trying to guess the password might have an easier time if they know the maximum length of a password.

Creating a Read-Only Text Box

You can transform an editable Windows Forms text box into a read-only control. For example, the text box can display a value that is usually edited but that might not be currently because of the state of the application. To create a read-only text box, set the ReadOnly property to true. Even with the ReadOnly property set to true, you can scroll and highlight text in a text box without allowing changes. Note that the ReadOnly property affects user interaction only at runtime. You can still change text box contents programmatically at runtime by changing the Text property of the text box.

By default, the Windows Forms TextBox control displays a single line of text and does not display scrollbars. If the text is longer than the available space, only part of the text is visible. You can change this default behavior by setting the MultiLine, WordWrap, and ScrollBars properties to appropriate values.

To view multiple lines in the TextBox control, set the MultiLine property to true. If WordWrap is true (the default), the text in the control will appear as one or more paragraphs; otherwise, it will appear as a list, in which some lines might be clipped at the edge of the control.

Events Raised by the TextBox Control

When you are using the TextBox control, the focus events occur in the following order:

- ▸ Enter—Fired when the control is entered
- ▸ GotFocus—Fired when the control receives the focus
- ▸ Leave—Occurs when the focus leaves the control
- ▸ Validating—Occurs when the control is validating
- ▸ Validated—Occurs when the control is finished validating
- ▸ LostFocus—Occurs when the control loses the focus

If the CausesValidation property of the text box is set to false, the Validating and Validated events are suppressed. If the Cancel property of the CancelEventArgs object is set to true in the Validating event delegate, all events that would normally occur after the Validating event are suppressed.

The `Button` **Control**

The Windows Forms `Button` control enables the user to click it to perform an action. When the button is clicked, it looks as if it is being pushed in and released. Whenever the user clicks a button, the `Click` event handler is invoked. You place code in the `Click` event handler to perform any action you choose. The text displayed on the button is contained in the `Text` property. If your text exceeds the width of the button, it wraps to the next line. However, it will be clipped if the control cannot accommodate its overall height. You can also set the `Text` property of the control at runtime.

TIP

The `Text` property of the button control can contain an access key that enables a user to click the control by pressing the Alt key with the access key. For example, if you set the `Text` property of a button control to `&File`, you can access the `Click` event of the button by pressing Alt+F. You will notice this behavior in almost all Microsoft applications, including Microsoft Word.

The appearance of text is controlled by the `Font` property and the `TextAlign` property. Set the `AcceptButton` or `CancelButton` properties of a form to enable users to click a button by pressing the Enter or Esc keys even if the button does not have focus. This gives the form the behavior of a dialog box.

You can change the appearance of the button control by setting the `FlatStyle` property to any of the values listed in Table 6.1.

TABLE 6.1

Values for the `FlatStyle` Property

Value	Description
`Flat`	The control appears flat.
`Popup`	When set to this value, the button appears flat. When you move the mouse pointer over it, however, it appears three-dimensional.
`Standard`	The control appears three-dimensional.
`System`	The appearance of the control is determined by the operating system of the user's computer.

The button control can also display images using the `BackgroundImage` property. To set the image for the button control, follow these steps:

1. Select the button control and select the Properties window from the View menu. In the Properties window, select the `BackgroundImage` property of the control; then click the ellipsis button (...) to display the Open dialog box.

2. In the File Open dialog box, select the file you want to display in the background.

Selecting a Button Control

You can use a Windows Forms button (raise the `Click` event) in a number of ways:

▸ You can use the mouse to click the button control in the form.

▸ You can explicitly invoke the button's `Click` event in code.

▸ You can move the focus to the button by pressing the Tab key, and then choose the button by pressing the spacebar or Enter.

▸ You can also press the access key (Alt + the underlined letter) for the button.

▸ If the button is the "accept" button of the form, pressing Enter chooses the button.

▸ If the button is the "cancel" button of the form, pressing Esc chooses the button.

▸ In the code, you can call the `PerformClick` method of the button class to select the button programmatically. The `PerformClick` method basically raises the `Click` event of the button.

The most basic use of a button control is to run some code when the button is clicked. Clicking a button control also generates a number of other events, such as the `MouseEnter`, `MouseDown`, and `MouseUp` events. If you attach event handlers for these related events, you need to ensure that their actions do not conflict. If the user attempts to double-click the button control, each click will be processed separately; this means that the button control does not support the double-click event.

Responding to a Button Click

When the user clicks the button, a `Click` event is raised. You can handle this event by implementing a `System.EventHandler` delegate. Listing 6.1 shows the code required for handling the `Click` event of the command button.

LISTING 6.1
Handling the `Click` Event of the Button

```
Imports System.Windows.Forms
Imports System.Drawing

Public Class ButtonExample
  Inherits Form
  Private btnDisplayDate As Button = New Button
  Private lblDisplayDate As Label = New Label
```

LISTING 6.1
Continued

```
Public Sub New()
    btnDisplayDate.Location = New Point(50, 75)                                    1
    btnDisplayDate.Width = 150
    btnDisplayDate.Text = "Display Current Time"
    lblDisplayDate.Location = New Point(50, 120)
    lblDisplayDate.Width = 150
    AddHandler btnDisplayDate.Click, AddressOf Me.btnDisplayDate_Click             2
    Me.Controls.Add(btnDisplayDate)
    Me.Controls.Add(lblDisplayDate)
End Sub

Public Sub btnDisplayDate_Click(ByVal Sender As Object, ByVal e As EventArgs)
    lblDisplayDate.Text = DateTime.Now.ToLongDateString()
End Sub
Public Shared Sub Main()
    Application.Run(New ButtonExample)
End Sub
End Class
```

6

Listing 6.1 starts by declaring objects of type button and a label control. In the constructor, the code sets the various properties of the button, such as `Width`, `Text`, and `Location`. **1** After that, it associates the `btnDisplayDate_Click` method with the `Click` event of the button by using the `AddHandler` method. **2** Finally, the constructor adds the button to the `Controls` collection of the `Form` class by invoking the `Controls.Add` method. Inside the `btnDisplayDate_Click` event, it simply displays the current date and time in a label control.

Figure 6.4 shows the resultant output after the user clicks the command button.

FIGURE 6.4 Capturing the `Click` event of the button.

The `Label` Control

The `Label` control enables you to display text to the user. This is a simple control that does not warrant much explanation. The `Text` property of the control determines what text will be visible to the user. The display text can have a different alignment based on the `TextAlign` property. The possible align values are `TopLeft`, `TopCenter`, and `TopRight`. The `TextChanged` event is fired when the text in a `Label` control changes.

Labels have a `Location` property, keeping track of where the label is placed on the screen. The `Location` property accepts a `Point` structure, which is a member of the `System.Drawing` namespace. The `Point` struct is used frequently in Windows Forms applications to specify x and y screen coordinates. In the following line of code, the `Location` of the `lblDisplay` is 12 pixels from the left and 116 pixels from the top of the main form.

```
lblDisplay.Location = new Point (12, 116)
```

The static text of a label is set through the `Text` property. The following statement sets the text of the label to the string:

```
lblDisplay.Text = "Hello World!"
```

A label also has a `Size` property that takes a `Size` structure. To set the size of a label, set the `Size` property.

```
lblDisplay.Size   = new Size (267, 40)
```

In the previous code, the size of `lblDisplay` is set to 267 pixels wide by 40 pixels high. The `AutoSize` property accepts a Boolean value that tells whether a label can automatically resize itself to accommodate its contents. Here's how the `AutoSize` property of the `lblDisplay` label is set:

```
lblDisplay.AutoSize = True
```

A label can change its typeface through the `Font` property. It accepts a `Font` object. The constructor for the `Font` object in the following statement accepts three parameters: the font name, the font size, and a font style. The font style is from the `FontStyle` enum in the `System.Drawing` namespace.

```
lblDisplay.Font = new Font("Microsoft Sans Serif", 26,
➥System.Drawing.FontStyle.Bold)
```

When there are multiple controls on a form, each control that can accept input can have its `TabIndex` property set. This permits the user to press the Tab key to move to the next control on the form, based on `TabIndex`. Here's how you can set the `TabIndex` property of the `lblDisplay` label:

```
lblDisplay.TabIndex = 0
```

The `RadioButton` **Control**

`RadioButton` controls are mainly used when you need to present a set of two or more mutually exclusive choices to the user. For example, a group of `RadioButton` controls might display a choice of package carriers for an order, but only one of the carriers will be used. Therefore, only one `RadioButton` at a time can be selected, even if it is a part of a functional group.

Although radio buttons and check boxes might appear to function similarly, there is an important difference: When a user selects a radio button, the other radio buttons in the same group cannot be selected as well. In contrast, any number of check boxes can be selected. Defining a radio button group tells the user, "Here is a set of choices from which you can choose only one."

When a `RadioButton` control is clicked, its `Checked` property is set to `true` and the `Click` event handler is called. The `CheckedChanged` event is raised when the value of the `Checked` property changes. If the `AutoCheck` property is set to `true` (the default), when the radio button is selected, all others in the group are automatically cleared. The text displayed within the control is set with the `Text` property, which can contain access key shortcuts. The `RadioButton` control can appear like a command button when you set the `Appearance` property to `Appearance.Button`. Radio buttons can also display images using the `Image` and `ImageList` properties.

You group radio buttons by drawing them inside a container such as a `Panel` control, a `GroupBox` control, or a form. All radio buttons that are added directly to a form become one group. To add separate groups, you need to place them inside panels or group boxes. An application can have multiple radio button groups by putting radio buttons in different `Panel` controls or `GroupBox` controls. You will see more about `Panel` control in the later sections of this chapter.

To group `RadioButton` controls as a set to function independently of other sets, follow these steps:

1. Drag a `GroupBox` or `Panel` control from the Windows Forms tab on the toolbox onto the form.

2. Draw `RadioButton` controls on the `GroupBox` or `Panel` control.

6

The `RadioButton` **Control**

The `RadioButton` class publishes two events that are fired when the checked state of a RadioButton changes: `Click` and `CheckedChanged`. The `Click` event is raised when a user clicks the radio button. You can handle this `Click` event just as you handled the `Click` event for the `Button` class. The `CheckedChanged` event is raised when the `RadioButton`'s checked state changes, either programmatically or visually.

```
Private Sub RadioButton2_CheckedChanged(ByVal sender As System.Object, _
  ByVal e As System.EventArgs) Handles RadioButton2.CheckedChanged
  If RadioButton2.Checked Then
    MessageBox.Show ("Radio button checked")
  End If
End Sub
```

Note that the `Click` event is not raised if the `RadioButton`'s Checked property is changed programmatically.

The `CheckBox` **Control**

The `CheckBox` control indicates whether a particular condition is on or off. It is commonly used to present a Yes/No or True/False selection to the user. You can use CheckBox controls in groups to display multiple choices from which the user can select one or more.

The `CheckBox` control provides the `CheckState` property, which determines whether the `CheckBox` is checked. The `CheckState` property is actually an enumeration, the `CheckState` enumeration. Its members are `Unchecked`, `Checked`, and `Indeterminate`. Unchecked and `Check` are self-explanatory, but the `Indeterminate` member warrants explanation. The `Indeterminate` state can be used only when the `CheckBox` control's `ThreeState` property is set to `true`. When the `CheckState` is `Indeterminate` and the `ThreeState` property is `true`, the control is grayed out but still checked. This signifies that the check state cannot be determined.

TIP

The `CheckBox` control is similar to the `RadioButton` control, in that both the controls are used to indicate a selection that the user makes. They differ in that only one radio button in a group can be selected at a time. With the group of `Checkbox` controls, however, any number of check boxes can be selected.

Multiple check boxes can be grouped using the GroupBox control. This is useful for visual appearance and also for user interface design because grouped controls can be moved together on the form designer. The CheckBox control has two important properties:

- ▶ Checked—The Checked property returns either true or false, depending on whether the check box is checked.

- ▶ CheckState—The CheckState property returns either CheckState.Checked or CheckState.Unchecked. However, if the ThreeState property is set to true, CheckState can also return CheckState.Indeterminate. In the Indeterminate state, the box is displayed with a dimmed appearance to indicate that the option is unavailable.

Responding to Check Box Clicks

Whenever a user clicks a CheckBox control, the Click event occurs. You can program your application to perform some action depending upon the state of the check box. You can use the Checked property to determine the control's state and perform any necessary action.

```
Private Sub CheckBox1_Click(ByVal sender As Object, ByVal e As System.EventArgs) _
  Handles CheckBox1.Click
  'The CheckBox control's Text property is changed each time the control is clicked
  If CheckBox1.Checked = True Then
    CheckBox1.Text = "Checked"
  Else
    CheckBox1.Text = "Unchecked"
  End If
End Sub
```

This code uses the Click event handler to determine the state of the control.

The ListBox Control

The ListBox control enables you to display a list of items to the user. It is best suited for situations in which users need to see a large number of items at once or be able to select more than one item from a list. If the total number of items in a list box exceeds the number that can be displayed, a scrollbar is automatically added to the control. When the MultiColumn property is set to true, the list box displays items in multiple columns and a horizontal scrollbar appears. When the MultiColumn property is set to false, the list box displays items in a single column and a vertical scrollbar appears. When ScrollAlwaysVisible is set to true, the scrollbar appears regardless of the number of items.

Selecting Items in the `ListBox` Control

The `SelectedIndex` property returns an integer value that corresponds to the first selected item in the list box. You can programmatically change the selected item by changing the `SelectedIndex` value in code. The selected item in the list appears highlighted on the Windows Form. If no item is selected, the `SelectedIndex` value is `-1`. If the first item in the list is selected, the `SelectedIndex` value is `0`. When multiple items are selected, the `SelectedIndex` value reflects the selected item that appears first in the list. The `SelectedItem` property is similar to `SelectedIndex` but returns the item itself, usually a string value. The `Items.Count` property reflects the number of items in the list; the value of the `Items.Count` property is always one more than the largest possible `SelectedIndex` value because `SelectedIndex` is zero based.

Finding Items in a `ListBox` Control

`ListBox` provides two new features that enable you to search a list box for a specific item: `FindString` and `FindStringExact` methods. If you want to perform a search for a particular item instead of manually looping through all the items, you can simply use the `FindString` and `FindStringExact` methods. The `FindString` method finds the first item that starts with a particular string, whereas `FindStringExact` searches for an exact match.

The `SelectionMode` property of the `ListBox` control is used to control how many items the user can select and how those items can be selected:

```
lstItems.SelectionMode = SelectionMode.MultiSimple
```

A user can select items from a `ListBox` control in three ways. The `SelectionMode` property determines how many list items can be selected at a time. The `SelectionMode` enumeration can be set to any one of the values shown in Table 6.2.

TABLE 6.2

Property Values for the `SelectionMode` Enumeration

Value	Description
`MultiExtended`	Multiple items can be selected; the user can use the Shift, Ctrl, and arrow keys to make selections.
`MultiSimple`	Multiple items can be selected using the mouse or the spacebar.
`None`	No items can be selected.
`One`	Only one item can be selected.

Manipulating Items in a `ListBox` Control

To add or delete items in a `ListBox` control, use the `Items.Add`, `Items.Insert`, `Items.Clear`, or `Items.Remove` methods. Alternatively, you can add items to the list by using the other methods of the `Items` property, such as `Insert` and `AddRange`. These are the different ways of adding items to a `ListBox` control:

▶ Add the string or object to the list by using the `Add` method of the `ObjectCollection` class. The collection is referenced using the `Items` property:

```
ListBox1.Items.Add("Tokyo")
```

▶ Insert the string or object at the desired point in the list with the `Insert` method:

```
ListBox1.Items.Insert(0, "Copenhagen")
```

▶ Assign an entire array to the `Items` collection:

```
Dim itemArray(9) As System.Object
Dim i As Integer
For i = 0 To 9
  itemArray(i) = "Item" & i
Next i
ListBox1.Items.AddRange(itemArray)
```

Previously, you saw how to use the `Items` collection to add items to a `ListBox` control. Apart from using the `Items` property, you can populate the list box using data binding via the `DataSource`, `DisplayMember`, and `ValueMember` properties. Data sources include any objects instantiated from classes that implement the `IList` interface, such as the `Array` class, the `Collection` class, and the `DataView` class. You will learn more about data binding concepts in Chapter 14, "Data Binding in Windows Applications."

TIP

A great new feature of .NET Framework is the capability to speed up the rendering of a control by preventing it from redrawing itself every time an item is added to it. This is done via the `BeginUpdate` and `EndUpdate` methods. The following example demonstrates the use of these methods:

```
With lstSelectedItems
    .Items.Clear()
    .BeginUpdate()
    Dim fi As FileInfo
    For Each fi In lstMultiSelect.SelectedItems
        .Items.Add(fi.Name)
    Next
    .EndUpdate()
End With
```

The `ListBox` **Control**

Listing 6.2 shows an example of how to use the `ListBox` control to add multiple items to a list box in an efficient way. It also shows how to programmatically select items in a list box.

LISTING 6.2

Adding and Selecting Items in a `ListBox` **Control**

```
Imports System
Imports System.Drawing
Imports System.Windows.Forms

Public Class ListBoxExample
  Inherits System.Windows.Forms.Form
  Private btnAdd As New Button

  Public Sub New()
    MyBase.New()
    Me.InitializeComponent()
  End Sub

  Private Sub InitializeComponent()
    Me.btnAdd.Location = New Point(10, 10)
    Me.btnAdd.Size = New Size(40, 20)
    Me.btnAdd.TabIndex = 1
    Me.btnAdd.Text = "Add"
    AddHandler Me.btnAdd.Click, AddressOf Me.btnAdd_Click
    Me.AutoScaleBaseSize = New Size(5, 13)
    Me.ClientSize = New Size(292, 273)
    Me.Controls.AddRange(New Control() {Me.btnAdd})
    Me.Text = "ListBox Example"
  End Sub

  Private Sub btnAdd_Click(ByVal sender As Object, ByVal e As System.EventArgs)
    'Create an instance of the ListBox.
    Dim lstItems As New ListBox
```

LISTING 6.2
Continued

```
'Set the size and location of the ListBox
lstItems.Size = New Size(200, 100)
lstItems.Location = New Point(30, 60)
'Add the ListBox to the form
Me.Controls.Add(lstItems)
lstItems.MultiColumn = True                                        1
lstItems.SelectionMode = SelectionMode.MultiExtended
'Stop the painting of the ListBox as items are added.
lstItems.BeginUpdate()                                            2
'Loop through and add 50 items to the ListBox
Dim x As Integer
For x = 1 To 50
    lstItems.Items.Add("Item " & x.ToString())
Next x
'Allow the ListBox to repaint and display the new items
lstItems.EndUpdate()                                             3
'Select three items from the ListBox
lstItems.SetSelected(1, True)
lstItems.SetSelected(3, True)
lstItems.SetSelected(5, True)
'Display the first selected item in the ListBox
 MessageBox.Show(lstItems.SelectedItems(0).ToString())
End Sub

Shared Sub Main()
  Application.Run(New ListBoxExample)
End Sub
End Class
```

Listing 6.2 not only shows how to add items to a ListBox control, but it also demonstrates how to select a set of items in a ListBox control using the SetSelected method. To display multiple columns in a list box, you set the MultiColumn property to true. **1** When you are adding a large number of items to a list box, use the BeginUpdate method to prevent the control from repainting the ListBox each time an item is added to the list. **2** When you have completed the task of adding items to the list, call the EndUpdate method to enable the ListBox to repaint. **3** This method of adding items can prevent flickered drawing of the list box when a large number of items are being added to the list. This approach is demonstrated in Listing 6.2. To select a specific item in the list box, you invoke the SetSelected method and pass in the index of the list item you want to select. To this method, you also send in a Boolean value as the second argument, to indicate whether you want the list item to be selected. Figure 6.5 shows the output produced by Listing 6.2.

6

The `ListBox` **Control**

FIGURE 6.5 Adding and selecting items in a `ListBox` control.

Because the list box is dynamically created within the `Click` event of the button, each time you click the button, the list box is re-created and its contents are refreshed.

Common Methods Supported by the List Controls

The `ListBox`, `CheckedListBox`, and `ComboBox` controls have a lot in common in terms of the methods they expose. Table 6.3 looks at some of the important methods that these controls provide.

TABLE 6.3

Methods Supported by `ListBox`, `ComboBox`, **and** `CheckedListBox` **Controls**

Method	Description
`BeginUpdate`	Provides better performance while items are added to the control by preventing the control from drawing until the `EndUpdate` method is called
`EndUpdate`	Resumes painting the control after painting is suspended by the `BeginUpdate` method
`FindString`	Finds the first item in the control that starts with the specified string
`FindStringExact`	Finds the first item in the control that exactly matches the specified string
`GetTextItem`	Returns the text representation of the specified item in the control

These methods are discussed in detail when the ComboBox control is explained in the next section.

The ComboBox Control

The ComboBox control is the ideal control to present a list of choices in a confined amount of screen space. The combo box appears as a TextBox control with an arrow on the right side. A list of options drops down below the control when the user clicks the arrow. When the user selects an option or clicks the arrow again, the list of options rolls up. To make a selection, the user can either choose an existing item from the list or enter text into the text box. Items can be added to the ComboBox control both at design time and at runtime.

By default, the ComboBox control appears in two parts: The top part is a text box in which the user can type a list item. The second part is a list box that displays a list of items from which the user can select one. The DropDownStyle property is an important property that enables you to determine the following two options:

▸ Whether the user can enter a new value in the text portion

▸ Whether the list portion of the ComboBox is always displayed

Table 6.4 illustrates the different values that can be set for the DropDownStyle property.

TABLE 6.4

Property Values for the ComboBoxStyle Enumeration

Value	Description
DropDown	When you set the DropDownStyle property to this value, the text portion becomes editable and the user must click the arrow button to display the list portion.
DropDownList	The text portion becomes read-only, and the user must click the arrow button to display the list portion.
Simple	The text portion is always editable, and the list portion is always visible.

The SelectedIndex property returns an integer value that corresponds to the selected list item. You can programmatically change the selected item by changing the SelectedIndex value in code; the corresponding item in the list appears in the text box portion of the combo box. ComboBox provides a number of properties that enable you to control its behavior at both design time and runtime. Table 6.5 lists some of the important properties of the ComboBox control.

The `ComboBox` **Control**

TABLE 6.5

Important Properties of the `ComboBox` **Control**

Property	Description
`DropDownStyle`	Gets or sets an enumeration that specifies the style of the combo box
`DropDownWidth`	Gets or sets the list portion of the `ComboBox` control
`Items`	Gets an object that represents the collection of items contained in the combo box
`MaxLength`	Gets or sets the maximum number of characters allowed in the editable portion of the combo box
`SelectedIndex`	Gets or sets the index of the currently selected item
`SelectedItem`	Gets or sets the currently selected item
`SelectedText`	Gets or sets the text that is selected in the text portion of the combo box
`Sorted`	Gets or sets a value that indicates whether the items in the combo box are sorted

To add or delete items in a `ComboBox` control, use the `Items.Add`, `Items.Insert`, `Items.Clear`, or `Items.Remove` methods. Alternatively, you can add items to the list by using the `Items` property in the designer.

6

CHOOSING BETWEEN A `ComboBox` **AND A** `ListBox`

The `ComboBox` and `ListBox` controls have similar behaviors and, in some cases, can be interchangeable. Sometimes, however, one is more appropriate to a task. A combo box is appropriate when there is a list of suggested choices. A list box is appropriate when you want to limit user input to what is on the list. A combo box contains a text box field, so choices not on the list can be typed in. The exception is when the `DropDownStyle` property is set to `ComboBoxStyle.DropDownList`. In that case, the control selects an item if you type its first letter.

In addition, combo boxes save space on a form. Because the full list is not displayed until the user clicks the down arrow, a combo box can easily fit in a small space where a list box would not fit. An exception is when the `DropDownStyle` property is set to `ComboBoxStyle.Simple`: The full list is displayed, and the combo box takes up more room than a list box would.

As with the `ListBox` control, to add a new item to the `Items` collection of the `ComboBox` control, simply call the `Items.Add` method. To remove a particular item from the `Items` collection, call the `Items.Remove` method. To remove all the items in the combo box, call the `Items.Clear` method. You can even determine whether an item exists by using the `Contains` method. As with any other collection, you can use a `For/Each` loop to iterate on the members, and you can use the `Count` property to determine the total number of items in the control.

Listing 6.3 shows how to add, find, and select items in a `ComboBox` control.

LISTING 6.3

Adding, Finding, and Selecting Items in a ComboBox

```
Imports System
Imports System.Drawing
Imports System.Windows.Forms

Public Class ComboBoxExample
  Inherits System.Windows.Forms.Form

  Private btnAdd As New Button
  Private txtMessage As New TextBox
  Private cboItems As New ComboBox
  Private btnShowSelected As New Button
  Private btnFind As New Button
  Private lblDisplay As New Label

  Public Sub New()
    MyBase.New()
    Me.InitializeComponent()
  End Sub

  Private Sub InitializeComponent()
    Me.btnAdd.Location = New Point(248, 32)
    Me.btnAdd.Size = New Size(40, 24)
    Me.btnAdd.TabIndex = 1
    Me.btnAdd.Text = "Add"
    AddHandler Me.btnAdd.Click, AddressOf Me.btnAdd_Click
    Me.cboItems.Anchor = ((AnchorStyles.Bottom Or AnchorStyles.Left) Or _
      AnchorStyles.Right)
    Me.cboItems.DropDownWidth = 280
    Me.cboItems.Items.AddRange(New Object() {"Item 1", "Item 2", _
      "Item 3", "Item 4", "Item 5"})
    Me.cboItems.Location = New Point(8, 248)
    Me.cboItems.Size = New Size(280, 21)
    Me.cboItems.TabIndex = 7
    Me.btnShowSelected.Location = New Point(8, 128)
    Me.btnShowSelected.Size = New Size(280, 24)
    Me.btnShowSelected.TabIndex = 4
    Me.btnShowSelected.Text = "What Item is Selected?"
    AddHandler Me.btnShowSelected.Click, AddressOf Me.btnShowSelected_Click
    Me.txtMessage.Location = New Point(8, 32)
    Me.txtMessage.Size = New Size(232, 20)
    Me.txtMessage.TabIndex = 5
    Me.txtMessage.Text = ""
    Me.btnFind.Location = New Point(248, 64)
```

6

The ComboBox **Control**

LISTING 6.3
Continued

```
    Me.btnFind.Size = New Size(40, 24)
    Me.btnFind.TabIndex = 3
    Me.btnFind.Text = "Find"
    AddHandler Me.btnFind.Click, AddressOf Me.btnFind_Click
    Me.lblDisplay.Location = New Point(8, 224)
    Me.lblDisplay.Size = New Size(144, 23)
    Me.lblDisplay.TabIndex = 0
    Me.lblDisplay.Text = "Test ComboBox"
    Me.AutoScaleBaseSize = New Size(5, 13)
    Me.ClientSize = New Size(292, 273)
    Me.Controls.AddRange(New Control() {Me.cboItems, Me.txtMessage, _
       Me.btnShowSelected,Me.btnFind, Me.btnAdd, Me.lblDisplay})
    Me.Text = "ComboBox Example"
End Sub


Private Sub btnAdd_Click(ByVal sender As Object, ByVal e As System.EventArgs)
```
1   `cboItems.Items.Add(txtMessage.Text)`
```
End Sub


Private Sub btnFind_Click(ByVal sender As Object, ByVal e As System.EventArgs)
    Dim index As Integer
```
2   `index = cboItems.FindString(txtMessage.Text)`
```
    cboItems.SelectedIndex = index
End Sub


Private Sub btnShowSelected_Click(ByVal sender As Object, ByVal e As
➥System.EventArgs)
    Dim selectedIndex As Integer
    selectedIndex = cboItems.SelectedIndex
    Dim selectedItem As Object
    selectedItem = cboItems.SelectedItem
    MessageBox.Show("Selected Item Text: " & selectedItem.ToString() & _
       Microsoft.VisualBasic.Constants.vbCrLf & "Index: " & selectedIndex.ToString())
End Sub

Shared Sub Main()
    Application.Run(New ComboBoxExample)
End Sub
End Class
```

As you can see, Listing 6.3 uses the Items.Add method to add an item to the combo box. **1** To find an item in the combo box, it uses the FindString method. **2**

When an item is found, this method sets the SelectedIndex property to the value returned by the FindString method. This enables the item that the FindString method finds to be displayed in the ComboBox control. Listing 6.3 also contains a button named btnShowSelected that is used to display the selected item in a message box. To get a reference to the selected item and the selected index, use the SelectedItem and SelectIndex properties, respectively. Figure 6.6 shows the output produced by executing Listing 6.3.

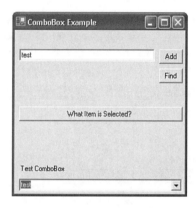

FIGURE 6.6   Adding, finding, and displaying items in a ComboBox control.

You can also add items to a combo box at runtime by binding the control to a collection object. This is done by setting the DataSource property to the collection object. When the ComboBox control attempts to add items to the drop-down list, it calls the ToString method on each item in the DataSource and adds that string to the drop-down list. The string can be customized by setting the ComboBox control's DisplayName property. The ComboBox calls the property specified in the DisplayName property and adds the returned string to the drop-down list.

Menu

One of the most important things in any application is to allow users to easily access all its functions. Users are accustomed to accessing most functions with a single mouse click. Most users also want all functions located conveniently in one place. One way to accomplish this is to use menus. A Windows application without a menu is a rare thing. A Windows Forms application is no exception. Like the button and label you saw earlier, the menu component can be added to the Menu member of the main application, and events from the menu items can be hooked to handlers. Visual Basic enables you to quickly and easily create menus with the new MainMenu control, which you create using the actual menu bars located at the top of a form. Pop-up menus that users typically access by right-clicking are created by using the new ContextMenu control.

Building the Menu Groups

When creating a menu, you must display the form that you want to add the menu to. Double-click the `MainMenu` control in the toolbox to add it to the form. You can see in Figure 6.7 that you can enter the menu items on the form directly.

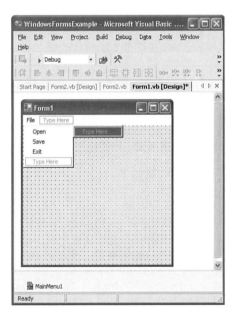

FIGURE 6.7   Adding menu items to the `MainMenu` control using the Menu Editor.

When the `MainMenu` control is on the form, you can start adding the items that you want in the menu. For each item that you want on a menu, you enter the `Text` property directly on the menu control at the top of the form. However, the `Name` property must be changed separately. The `Text` property is what users see on the menu when using your application; the `Name` property is what you use in your application code to access the menu item. After you enter a menu item, use the arrow keys to move the cursor to the next menu item. Remember to change the `Name` property for each menu item; otherwise, all menu items will look almost the same in the code, except for the number added to the control name.

When you finish entering the menu items for the application, click away from the menu. Your menu will appear on the form exactly as you've entered it.

Adding Menu Levels

It is important to group similar menu items according to the application you're creating. In fact, to be consistent with other Windows applications, you should use groups that your users are already familiar with. This way, they have an idea of where to find a particular menu item, even if they've never used this application. You might find the following standard menu groups in a Windows application:

▸ **File**—This menu contains any functions related to the opening and closing of files that your application uses. Some standard items included in this menu are New, Open, Close, Save, Save As, Print, and Page Setup. The File menu also is the location of the most recently used file list that many applications have. Finally, a File menu generally appears where the Exit command is located.

▸ **Edit**—The functions on this menu pertain to editing text and documents. Some typical Edit items are Undo, Cut, Copy, Paste, and Clear.

▸ **View**—This menu can be included if your program supports different views for the same document. For example, a word processor might include a normal view for editing text and a page layout view for positioning document elements.

▸ **Tools**—This menu is a catchall for any optional programs that might be available from within the application. For example, a spelling checker might be included for a word processor.

▸ **Window**—If your application supports working with multiple documents at the same time, you should have this menu included in your application. The Window menu is set up to let users arrange multiple documents or switch rapidly among them.

▸ **Help**—The Help menu enables users to access your application's help system. It usually includes menu items for a table of contents, an index, a search feature, and an About box.

Use these six menu types as a starting point when creating the menu system for your application. You can include any of them as you need them, but don't think that you need to add all six. Also, if you need other menu groups for your application, you can add whatever groups you might need.

Under each one of these menus, you can set up a menu that uses multiple levels to display multiple menu items. When you click the menu item on the menu bar, the first level of the menu drops down. This level is called a submenu. Adding subitems to the menu is very easy to do: First select the menu item you want to add the subitem to. This displays a new item entry to the right of the select item.

6

Menu

Now click the new subitem displayed and enter the required text. If you want to insert a new item in the menu list, right-click the item below the point where you want to insert the new item, and select Insert Item from the pop-up menu.

TIP

One other option to use for separating menu items in a menu is a separator bar. This is a line that enables you to group different menu items together with a single menu item's sublevel list. These bars break up a long list of menu items without creating submenus.

Creating Menus Programmatically

When you visually create menus using the menu editor, the editor automatically creates all the underlying code required for the menus to work. Apart from creating the menus visually using the menu editor, you can programmatically create menu-related classes in the code. As you have already seen, menus under .NET come in two forms. MainMenu is applied to a form to provide the main user interface menu, and ContextMenu is used to respond to right mouse clicks. In both cases, the individual items within the menus are objects of type MenuItem. Table 6.6 lists some of the important properties of the MenuItem class.

TABLE 6.6

Important Properties of the MenuItem Class

Value	Description
Checked	Determines whether a check mark is displayed next to a menu item when it is selected. This is used to indicate that a particular option has been selected.
RadioCheck	Determines whether a dot is displayed instead of a check mark.
Enabled	Sets or gets a value that indicates whether the menu item is enabled.
Visible	Enables you to hide menu items that aren't needed for a particular function or form.
MergeType	Determines whether the top-level items are displayed while another form is active and contains its own menu.
MDIList	Available only within MDI applications. It displays a list of the current child windows displayed.

A menu is constructed as a hierarchy of parent and child objects. The main menu owns the individual drop-downs, which, in turn, own their menu items. Listing 6.4 shows an example of constructing a menu using code.

LISTING 6.4
Constructing a Menu

```
Dim menu as MainMenu = New MainMenu()                                    1
Dim filemenu as MenuItem = New MenuItem()
filemenu.Text = "File"
menu.MenuItems.Add(filemenu)
Dim openMenu as MenuItem = New MenuItem()
openMenu.Text = "Open"
filemenu.MenuItems.Add(openMenu)
Dim saveMenu as MenuItem = New MenuItem()
saveMenu.Text = "Save"
filemenu.MenuItems.Add(saveMenu)
Dim exitmenu as MenuItem = New MenuItem()
exitMenu.Text = "Exit"
filemenu.MenuItems.Add(exitMenu)
Dim editmenu  as MenuItem = New MenuItem()
editmenu.Text = "Edit"
menu.MenuItems.Add(editmenu)
Dim cutMenu as MenuItem = New MenuItem()
cutMenu.Text = "Cut"
editmenu.MenuItems.Add(cutMenu)
Dim copyMenu as MenuItem = New MenuItem()
copyMenu.Text = "Copy"
editmenu.MenuItems.Add(copyMenu)
Dim pasteMenu as MenuItem = New MenuItem()
pasteMenu.Text = "Paste"
editmenu.MenuItems.Add(pasteMenu)
Me.Menu = menu                                                          2
```

6

Listing 6.4 starts by creating an instance of the MainMenu object. **1** Then it creates menus such as File, Edit directly under the MainMenu object. Under each of these menus, it also creates submenus and adds them under their appropriate parent menus. For example, the Cut, Copy, and Paste menus are added under the Edit menu. When all the menus and submenus are added, it sets the Menu property of the current form to the MainMenu object created earlier. **2** Figure 6.8 shows the output produced by Listing 6.4.

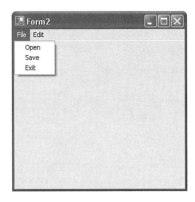

FIGURE 6.8
A simple application with a menu.

Adding a Menu Shortcut

Apart from selecting the menu by clicking the mouse, you can select the menu using shortcuts. Shortcut keys provide direct access to any function in a menu, no matter what level it's actually on. You can perform shortcuts with a key combination (such as Ctrl+C for a copy function) or with a single key (such as Delete for the delete function). Assigning shortcut keys is simply a process of selecting the key or keys that you want to use from the Shortcut drop-down list. Shortcut keys are displayed to the right of the menu item both in the selection list in the Menu Editor and in the actual menu in your application. Because of the way shortcut keys work, only one shortcut key can use a given key combination. A new property for each menu item also enables you to choose whether a shortcut key is displayed to the user at any point in the application.

TIP

As with hotkeys, the shortcut key should correspond to the first letter of the menu item, whenever possible. However, if a key combination already exists for the command in Microsoft Windows or Microsoft Office, you should use the same key combination. Placing an ampersand before a character in the menu text automatically gives the menu item an underscore when the Alt key is pressed. The key combination of Alt+F followed by O can be used to invoke the menu handler as if the menu were selected with the mouse.

A direct key combination can also be added to the menu item by using one of the predefined `Shortcut` enumerations. The File, Open menu item handler can be made to fire in response to a Ctrl+O key press by adding the shortcut, as shown in Listing 6.5.

LISTING 6.5
Adding a Shortcut to the Menu

```
Dim menu as MainMenu = New MainMenu()
Dim fileMenu as MenuItem = New MenuItem()
filemenu.Text = "&File"
menu.MenuItems.Add(filemenu)
Dim openMenu as MenuItem = new MenuItem()
openMenu.Text = "&Open"
filemenu.MenuItems.Add(openMenu)
openMenu.Shortcut = Shortcut.CtrlO
openMenu.ShowShortcut = true
Me.Menu = menu
```

Note how the Open menu is appended with the shortcut key press combination Ctrl+O by the `MenuItem.ShowShortcut` property setting.

When you press the Alt key, the F in the File menu is underlined. You can press F to pop up the menu and press O to invoke the menu's function, as shown in Figure 6.9.

FIGURE 6.9
Menu shortcuts in action.

Adding Hotkeys

Hotkeys are something that you already know about and use, probably without thinking about it. A hotkey is identified by an underscore beneath the letter in the item's text (for example, the *E* in Edit). To create a hotkey, place an ampersand (&) in the `Text` property immediately before the letter you want to use as the hotkey. For the File menu item, the value of the `Text` property would be `&File`. Hotkeys can be used for any item in your menu, including the top-level menu items.

6

Menu

> **NOTE**
>
> At any given level of a menu, only one unique value can be used as a hotkey. For example, the Visual Basic menu has File and Format at the same top level. If you look closely at them, you'll see that the File menu item has the *F* as the hotkey, but the Format menu has the *o* as the hotkey. If you used the *F* for both menu items, Windows wouldn't know which one you really wanted. However, the same letter can be used in items that appear in different groups, such as the File menu's Print option and the View menu's Page Layout option. For each group or level, you can have at most 36 hotkeys—one for each letter and one for each number.

After you include hotkeys in your menu, you can open a top-level menu simply by holding down the Alt key and pressing the hotkey of choice. When the menu appears, you can press the hotkey for the menu item you want to execute. For example, if you want to start a new project in Visual Basic, you would press Alt+F and then N for the File menu's New Project option.

> **TIP**
>
> If there's no conflict with letter selection, you should use the first letter of a menu item as the hotkey. This is what users expect; it also makes it easy to guess what the hotkey is for a particular function.

Responding to the `Click` Event

Adding code for the menu is the same as adding code for any other control in your application. A `Click` event exists for each menu item added to the form. For this reason, giving each menu item a unique name is important. The `Click` event is triggered whenever you select the menu item by clicking it, by using the hotkey or the shortcut key. To display the `Click` event routine for a menu item, simply double-click the menu item you want to work with; its related `Click` event appears in the Code Editor window.

In Listing 6.6, a handler that pops up a message box is defined and added to the methods of the `MenuExample` class.

LISTING 6.6
A Simple Event Handler

```
Imports System
Imports System.Windows.Forms
Imports System.Drawing

Public Class MenuExample
   Inherits System.Windows.Forms.Form
   Public Sub New()
      Dim menu As MainMenu = New MainMenu
```

LISTING 6.6
Continued

```
    Dim fileMenu As MenuItem = New MenuItem
    fileMenu.Text = "&File"
    menu.MenuItems.Add(fileMenu)
    Dim openMenu As MenuItem = New MenuItem
    openMenu.Shortcut = Shortcut.CtrlO
    openMenu.Text = "&Open"
    fileMenu.MenuItems.Add(openMenu)
    Me.Menu = menu
    AddHandler openMenu.Click, AddressOf Me.OnFileOpen                1
  End Sub
  Public Sub OnFileOpen(ByVal sender As Object, ByVal e As EventArgs)
    MessageBox.Show("You selected File-Open!")
  End Sub
  Shared Sub Main()
    Application.Run(New MenuExample)
  End Sub
End Class
```

6

The event handler has the standard method signature for events `Sub(Object, EventArgs)` and is added to the File, Open `MenuItem`'s `Click` event in Listing 6.6. **1**

This line is added to the menu-setup code after the shortcut initialization. Whenever the menu item is selected with the mouse, the Alt+F+O key sequence, or the Ctrl+O shortcut, the menu handler fires and the message box pops up.

User Interface Control Events for `MenuItems`

Other events are fired by `MenuItems` to enable you to give better feedback to the user or to customize the user experience. Just before a `MenuItem` is shown, the `Popup` event is fired to give you time to decide whether to show, check, or change the appearance of a menu item. You can trap this event by adding an event handler to the `Popup` event source:

```
AddHandler filemenu.Popup, AddressOf Me.OnPopupFilemenu
```

The handler for this event is defined in Listing 6.7.

LISTING 6.7
Handling the PopUp Event

```
Private popupChecked as boolean
Public Sub OnPopupFilemenu(sender as Object, e as EventArgs)
  'handler illustrates the Popup event and the MenuItem UI properties.
  popupChecked = Not popupChecked
  Dim item  as MenuItem = CType(sender, MenuItem)
  item.MenuItems(0).Checked = popupChecked
  item.MenuItems(1).Enabled = popupChecked
  item.MenuItems(2).Visible = popupChecked
End Sub
```

Listing 6.7 shows some of the standard things you can do with MenuItems: checking, enabling, hiding, and so on. The class has a Boolean variable called popupChecked. Every time the File menu is expanded, the program toggles this variable to true or false, depending on its previous state. The Sender object is known to be a MenuItem, so it's possible to cast to that type safely. The three menu entries in the File menu are then checked, disabled, or hidden entirely, depending on the state of the variable.

Defining a MenuItem as a Separator

Often a group of menu entries is strongly associated with one another, or one menu item is separated from another by strategic placement of a menu separator. Under Windows Forms, the menu separator is a menu item that does nothing but draw a line across the menu. This is simple: Just set the text of a menu item to a single dash.

This code shows an example of setting the menu separator for a group of menus:

```
Dim dummymenu as MenuItem = New MenuItem()
dummymenu.Text = "Separator"
menu.MenuItems.Add(dummymenu)
dummymenu.MenuItems.Add(new MenuItem("Above"))
dummymenu.MenuItems.Add(new MenuItem("-"))
dummymenu.MenuItems.Add(new MenuItem("Below"))
```

Arranging Menu Items

Menus are built up from MenuItem components. These can be arranged across the screen on the menu bar and are most often arranged vertically in drop-down menus. You can change the default layout of MenuItems to give a different UI style. The Break and BarBreak methods are used to create menus that are arranged horizontally rather than vertically. Setting the BarBreak property in a MenuItem causes the item to be drawn in a new column. BarBreak adds a vertical separator bar to the menu between the columns. Break makes a new column but doesn't add the vertical bar. Listing 6.8 shows an example of this in action.

LISTING 6.8
Setting the `BarBreak` and `Break` Properties

```
Dim menu as MainMenu = New MainMenu()
Dim filemenu as MenuItem = New MenuItem()
filemenu.Text = "&File"
menu.MenuItems.Add(filemenu)
Dim openMenu as MenuItem = New MenuItem()
openMenu.Text = "&Open"
AddHandler openMenu.Select, AddressOf Me.ShowInfo
filemenu.MenuItems.Add(openMenu)
Dim saveMenu as MenuItem = New MenuItem()
saveMenu.Text = "&Save"
AddHandler saveMenu.Select, AddressOf Me.ShowInfo
filemenu.MenuItems.Add(saveMenu)
saveMenu.BarBreak= True
Dim exitMenu as MenuItem = new MenuItem()
exitMenu.Text = "E&xit"
AddHandler exitMenu.Select, AddressOf Me.ShowInfo
filemenu.MenuItems.Add(exitMenu)
exitMenu.Break = True
Me.Menu = menu
```

Executing Listing 6.8 results in the output shown in Figure 6.10.

FIGURE 6.10 `BarBreak` and `Break` properties in use.

As you can see in Figure 6.10, each time you set the `BarBreak` and `Break` properties, the `MenuItem` is placed in a new column.

Right-to-Left Menus

To cater to cultures that read right to left, or to add an unconventional style to your menus, you can modify the menu's `RightToLeft` property:

```
Dim menu as MainMenu = New MainMenu()
menu.RightToLeft = RightToLeft.Yes
Dim filemenu  as MenuItem = New MenuItem()
filemenu.Text = "&File"
menu.MenuItems.Add(filemenu)
Me.Menu = menu
```

In this code, the second line sets the `RightToLeft` property to `Yes`, which results in output shown in Figure 6.11.

FIGURE 6.11   Right-to-left menus.

As you can see from the output, the File menu appears starting from the right.

Context Menu

A context menu is a floating menu that can pop up wherever it's needed for selections in a particular editing or user interface context. The convention is for the context menu to appear in response to a right mouse button click. The context menus appear only when needed and directly next to the area you're working with. After you select an option from the menu, it disappears from the screen. These types of menus often are used to handle functions related to a specific area of the form. For an example of this type of menu, right-click anywhere in Visual Basic's Code Editor window for a code-related menu.

Setting Up a Context Menu

To create a context menu, add the `ContextMenu` control to the form; then add all the required menu items using the same techniques as for the `MainMenu` control.

> **NOTE**
>
> If you want a menu item to appear on the main menu and on the context menu, you must add the same item twice: once on the main menu and once on the context menu.

To see how the context menu works, add one to your form and insert at least one menu item. When you are done adding the menu items, you need to change the `ContextMenu` property for the control with which you want to associate the context menu. The techniques of adding, showing, and modifying the appearance of a context menu and specifying its handler are largely the same as those used for the main menu. The following adds a context menu with three items to the main window of the form:

```
Dim cmenu as ContextMenu = New ContextMenu()
cmenu.MenuItems.Add(New MenuItem("&First"))
cmenu.MenuItems.Add(New MenuItem("&Second"))
cmenu.MenuItems.Add(New MenuItem("-"))
cmenu.MenuItems.Add(New MenuItem("&Third"))
Me.ContextMenu = cmenu
```

A simple right mouse click brings up the context menu. Output produced by the previous code is shown in Figure 6.12.

FIGURE 6.12 Context menu displayed in a form.

Summary

In this chapter, you learned about the different controls that the Visual Basic .NET Framework provides and how to use them in your applications. This chapter started with an introduction to the Toolbox window and the Properties window and showed how to use those windows. It went on to discuss the advanced features of Windows Forms controls for creating Windows Forms–based applications. To this end, this chapter covered how to use the input controls such as the `TextBox`, `Button`, `Label`, `RadioButton`, `CheckBox`, `ListBox`, and `ComboBox` controls to process user input. It also demonstrated how to use the `Menu`, `MenuItem`, and `ContextMenu` components to create menus and context menus.

Further Reading

MSDN documentation on Visual Basic .NET Windows Forms applications.

Payne, Chris. *Sams Teach Yourself .NET Windows Forms in 21 Days*. Pearson Education, 2002.

6

7 DRAWING

IN BRIEF

Whatever you do in your application does not get to the user's screen without the aid of a drawing function. This includes images, colors, and even text. The OS must render all things visually by drawing pixels to an output device (monitor, printer, and so on). Even though Windows does a good job of hiding drawing functions from you, you still need to understand the high-level .NET drawing API so that you can create customized output. The .NET drawing library provides you with a host of classes that make adding drawing capabilities to your application easy and fun.

This chapter illustrates common programming tasks using the namespaces related to drawing in the .NET Framework Class Library. The chapter starts by illustrating the key classes used to execute drawing functions. Then it provides a detailed discussion of these key classes and related code examples.

WHAT YOU NEED

SOFTWARE REQUIREMENTS	Windows 2000, XP, or 2003 .NET Framework 1.1 SDK Visual Studio .NET 2003 with Visual Basic .NET installed
HARDWARE REQUIREMENTS	PC desktop or laptop
SKILL REQUIREMENTS	Knowledge of Visual Basic .NET Knowledge of the .NET Framework

DRAWING AT A GLANCE

The Graphics Device Interface (GDI)

To write a GUI application, you need to write some kind of visual interface in the form of windows and controls. The visual interface can be seen in only one way: through hardware, such as a printer and monitor. The Graphic Device Interface (GDI) provides a way to work with painting graphic objects, such as painting on Windows, forms, or other media.

> **NOTE**
>
> GDI is a set of classes that provides functionality to render data to a program to hardware devices with the help of device drivers. It sits between the program and the hardware and transfers data from one to other.

GDI+: A Higher-Level API

Working with GDI objects in earlier versions of Microsoft products was a pain. Now, with the advanced version of GDI named GDI+, Microsoft has taken care of most of the GDI problems and made the GDI easy to use.

> **TIP**
>
> GDI+ is the next evolution of GDI; it's a much improved and easier-to-use version. The best part is that you don't need to know any details of drivers to render data on printers and monitors; GDI+ takes care of it for you.

7

In other words, GDI was a low- to middle-level programming API, in which you needed to know about devices as well. By contrast, GDI+ is a higher-level programming model that provides functions to do work for you. For example, if you want to set the background or foreground color of a control, you just set `ForeGroundColor` property of the control, and GDI+ takes care of the rest for you.

Features of GDI+

Besides the fact that the GDI+ API is easier and flexible than that of GDI, many new features have been added:

- Improved colors. GDI+ comes with more colors, which are compatible with other colors, such as those colors in Windows.

- Antialiasing support.
- Gradient brushes.
- Splines.

- Transformation and matrices.
- Scalable reasons.
- Alpha blending.

GDI+ Namespaces in .NET

GDI+ is defined in the Drawing namespace and its five subnamespaces. All drawing code resides in the System.Drawing.DLL assembly. These namespaces are as follows:

- System.Drawing
- System.Drawing.Design
- System.Drawing.Printing
- System.Drawing.Imaging
- System.Drawing.Drawing2D
- System.Drawing.Text

The following sections provide a detailed look at these namespaces. When you have a high-level understanding of these namespaces, you then can learn how to make use of the classes contained in those namespaces.

System.Drawing Namespace

The System.Drawing namespace provides basic GDI+ functionality. It contains the definition of basic classes such as Brush, Pen, Graphics, Bitmap, and Font. The Graphics class plays a major role in GDI+ and contains methods for drawing to the display device. Table 7.1 shows some of the classes in the System.Drawing namespace.

TABLE 7.1

Classes in the System.Drawing Namespace

Class	Description
Bitmap, Image	Bitmap and image classes.
Brush, Brushes	Brush classes used to define objects to fill GDI objects such as rectangles, ellipses, pies, polygons, and paths.
Font, FontFamily	Classes that define a particular format for text, including font face, size, and style attributes. Not inheritable.
Graphics	Class that encapsulates a GDI+ drawing surface. Not inheritable.
Pen	Class that defines an object used to draw lines and curves. Not inheritable.
SolidBrush, TextureBrush	Class that defines a brush of a single color. Brushes are used to fill graphics shapes such as rectangles, ellipses, pies, polygons, and paths. Not inheritable.

Now that you understand the classes, Table 7.2 shows some of the structures contained in the System.Drawing namespace.

TABLE 7.2

Structures in the `System.Drawing` Namespace

Structure	Description
`Color`	Represents an ARGB color.
`Point, PointF`	Represents 2D x- and y-coordinates. `Point` takes x, y values as a number. You can use `PointF` if you want to use floating number values.
`Rectangle, RectangleF`	Represent a rectangle with integer values. A rectangle represents two point pairs: top, left and bottom, right. You can use floating values in `RectangleF`.
`Size`	Encapsulates a GDI+ drawing surface. Not inheritable.

Later sections of this chapter provide a complete discussion on some of the important classes in the `System.Drawing` namespace.

`System.Drawing.Design` **Namespace**

The `System.Drawing.Design` namespace is somewhat similar to the `System.Drawing` namespace. It extends design-time user interface (UI) logic and drawing functionality, and provides classes for customizing toolbox and editor classes. For beginners, there is nothing in this namespace.

▶ **Editor classes**—`BitmapEditor`, `FontEditor`, and `ImageEditor` are the editor classes. You can use these classes to extend functionality and provide an option in the properties window to edit images and fonts.

▶ **Toolbox classes**—`ToolBoxItem` and `ToolBoxItemCollection` are the two major toolbox classes. Using these classes, you can extend the functionality of the toolbox and provide the implementation of toolbox items.

`System.Drawing.Printing` **Namespace**

The `System.Drawing.Printing` namespace defines classes for printing functionality in your applications. Some of its major classes are discussed in Table 7.3. You will learn more about the concepts of printing in Chapter 9, "Printing."

TABLE 7.3

Classes in the `System.Drawing.Printing` Namespace

Class	Description
`PageSettings`	Enables you to define page settings
`PrintController`	Controls document printing
`PrintDocument`	Sends output to a printer
`PrinterResolution`	Sets resolution of a printer
`PrinterSettings`	Enables you to configure printer settings

7

System.Drawing.Imaging **Namespace**

This namespace provides advanced GDI+ imaging functionality. It defines classes for metafile images. This namespace also defines the class PropertyItem, which enables you to store and retrieve information about the image files.

System.Drawing.Drawing2D **Namespace**

This namespace consists of classes and enumerations for advanced two-dimensional and vector graphics functionality. It contains classes for gradient brushes, matrix and transformation, and graphics paths. Important classes in this namespace are shown in Table 7.4.

TABLE 7.4

Classes in the System.Drawing.Drawing2D **Namespace**

Class	Description
Blend, ColorBlend	Define the blend for gradient brushes. ColorBlend defines the array of colors and position for a multicolor gradient.
GraphicsPath	Represents a set of connected lines and curves.
HatchBrush	Acts as a brush with hatch style, a foreground color, and a background color.
LinearGradientBrush	Provides brush functionality with linear gradient.
Matrix	Works as a 3×3 matrix that represents geometric transformation.

Apart from providing a number of classes, the System.Drawing.Drawing2D namespace provides the enumerations shown in Table 7.5.

TABLE 7.5

Enumerations in the System.Drawing.Drawing2D **Namespace**

Enumeration	Description
CombineMode	Different clipping types
CompositingQuality	The quality of compositing
DashStyle	The style of dashed lines drawn with a Pen
HatchStyle	Different patterns available for HatchBrush
QualityMode	Specification of the quality of GDI+ objects
SmoothingMode	Specification of the quality of GDI+ objects

System.Drawing.Text **Namespace**

Even though most of the font's functionality is defined in the System.Drawing namespace, the System.Drawing.Text namespace provides advanced typography functionality, such as creating a collection of fonts. Right now, this class has only three classes: FontCollection, InstalledFontCollection, and PrivateFontCollection. All of these classes are self-explanatory and are not discussed in detail here.

The Graphics **Class**

The Graphics class is the center of all GDI+ classes. After discussing this class, this section shows some of the common GDI+ objects and their representation. After that, it offers some examples of applying this theory in your applications and shows how it works.

> **TIP**
>
> The Graphics class plays a vital role in GDI+: It encapsulates GDI+ drawing surfaces. Before you draw any object, such as a circle or rectangle, you must create a surface using the Graphics class.

7

You can get a Graphics object in your application by using your form's Paint event or by overriding the OnPaint() method of a form. These methods have an argument of type System.Windows.Forms.PaintEventArgs. You call its Graphics member to get the Graphics object in your application. For example:

```
protected overrides sub OnPaint(ByVal e As System.Windows.Forms.PaintEventArgs)
  Dim g As Graphics = e.Graphics
End Sub
```

When you have the reference to the Graphics object, you can do anything you want. The Graphics class has lots of methods for drawing Graphics objects, such as fonts, pens, lines, path and polygons, images and ellipses, and so on. Table 7.6 describes some of the Graphics class members.

TABLE 7.6

Methods of the Graphics Class

Method	Description
DrawArc	Draws an arc representing a portion of an ellipse specified by a pair of coordinates, a width, and a height.
DrawBezier, DrawBeziers, DrawCurve	These methods draw simple and Bezier curves. These curves can be closed, cubic, and so on.

The Graphics Class

TABLE 7.6

Continued

Method	Description
DrawEllipse	Draws an ellipse defined by a bounding rectangle based on the height and width coordinates.
DrawImage	Enables you to draw the specified Image object at the specified location with the original size.
DrawLine	Enables you to draw a line connecting the two points specified by coordinate pairs.
DrawPath	Draws the path using the GraphicsPath object.
DrawPie	Draws a pie shape defined by an ellipse specified by a coordinate pair, a width and a height, and two radial lines.
DrawPolygon	Draws a polygon defined by an array of Point structures.
DrawRectangle	Enables you to draw a rectangle specified by a coordinate pair, a width, and a height.
DrawString	Enables you to draw the specified text string at the specified location with the specified Brush and Font objects.
FillEllipse	Enables you to fill the interior of an ellipse defined by a bounding rectangle specified by a pair of coordinates, a width, and a height.
FillPath	Fills the interior of a path.
FillPie	Fills the interior of a pie section.
FillPolygon	Fills the interior of a polygon defined by an array of points.
FillRectangle	Fills the interior of a rectangle with a Brush.
FillRectangles	Fills the interiors of a series of rectangles with a Brush.
FillRegion	Fills the interior of a Region.

Now, say, if you want to draw an ellipse using the same method shown before, you override the OnPaint method and write the following code:

```
protected overrides sub OnPaint(ByVal e As System.Windows.Forms.PaintEventArgs)
  Dim g As Graphics = e.Graphics
  'Code to write the ellipse
End Sub
```

The following sections show you the code required for creating various shapes.

Common Graphics Objects

Graphics objects are the objects you use to draw your GDI+ items, such as images, lines, rectangles, and path. For example, to fill a rectangle with a color, you need a color object and type of style that you want to fill, such as a solid, texture. You'll use four common GDI+ objects using throughout your GDI+ life to fill GDI+ items:

- ▶ Brush—Used to fill enclosed surfaces with patterns, colors, or bitmaps
- ▶ Pen—Used to draw lines and polygons, including rectangles, arcs, and pies
- ▶ Font—Used to describe the font to be used to render text
- ▶ Color—Used to describe the color used to render a particular object

> **TIP**
>
> In GDI+ color can be alpha-blended. Each of these objects is represented by a class (also called type).

The Pen Class

A pen draws a line of specified width and style. You always use Pen constructor to create a pen. The constructor initializes a new instance of the Pen class. The constructor is overloaded and provides the following variations.

Initializes a new instance of the Pen class with the specified color:

```
Public Sub New(Color)
```

Initializes a new instance of the Pen class with the specified Brush:

```
Public Sub New(Brush)
```

Initializes a new instance of the Pen class with the specified Brush and width:

```
Public Sub New(Brush, Single)
```

Initializes a new instance of the Pen class with the specified Color and Width:

```
Public Sub New(Color, Single)
```

Table 7.7 discusses the important properties of the Pen class.

TABLE 7.7

Important Properties of the Pen Class

Property	Description
Alignment	Gets or sets the alignment for objects drawn with this Pen
Brush	Gets or sets the Brush that determines attributes of this Pen
Color	Gets or sets the color of this Pen
Width	Gets or sets the width of this Pen

Drawing Lines

So far, you have learned about pens and drawing methods but have not yet rendered anything to the screen. Now you will use a Pen object to draw a line on a form.

A line is a set of pixels linked by a start point and an endpoint. Line attributes are defined by the Pen object with which they are drawn. To draw a line, use the DrawLine method of the Graphics class. This method is overloaded and defines a number of ways you can pass it parameters. For instance, you can pass it a Pen object and two Point structures between which GDI+ will draw the line. A Point structure stores the x and y coordinates of a point on a 2D plane.

Listing 7.1 uses the DrawLine method and a Pen instance to draw a blue line on a form. You can test this code, create a new form-based application, add a button to it, and add the code in the listing to the button's click event.

LISTING 7.1
Drawing a Line Using the Pen Class

```
Imports System
Imports System.Drawing
Imports System.Drawing.Printing

Public Class LineExample
   Inherits System.Windows.Forms.Form
   Private WithEvents btnDraw As New System.Windows.Forms.Button

   Public Sub New()
     InitializeComponent()
   End Sub

   Private Sub InitializeComponent()
     Me.btnDraw.Location = New System.Drawing.Point(86, 180)
     Me.btnDraw.Name = "btnDraw"
     Me.btnDraw.Size = New System.Drawing.Size(96, 32)
     Me.btnDraw.Text = "Draw"
     Me.Controls.Add(Me.btnDraw)
     Me.Name = "LineExample"
     Me.Text = "LineExample"
   End Sub

   Private Sub btnDraw_Click(ByVal sender As System.Object, _
     ByVal e As System.EventArgs) Handles btnDraw.Click
     Dim graphicsObj As Graphics
     Dim penObj As Pen
```

LISTING 7.1
Continued

```
'Return the current form as a drawing surface
graphicsObj = Graphics.FromHwnd(hwnd:=ActiveForm().Handle)               1
'Instantiate a new pen object using the color structure
penObj = New Pen(Color:=Color.Blue, Width:=4)
'Draw the line on the form using the pen object
graphicsObj.DrawLine(Pen:=penObj, x1:=1, y1:=1, x2:=25, y2:=50)          2
End Sub

Public Shared Sub Main()
    Application.Run(New LineExample)
End Sub
End Class
```

Note that in Listing 7.1, before you can draw anything to the screen, you need to return a valid drawing surface that provides you with an object to draw on. This is accomplished by invoking the FromHwnd method **1** of the Graphics class. To this method, you pass in the handle of the currently active form.

Next, a Pen instance is created. You pass its constructor a valid color and width. Finally, the DrawLine method of the Graphics object is called to render the line on the form. **2** The version of the DrawLine method that is used in the earlier example requires a Pen instance and a set of start and end coordinates. These coordinates are simply passed in order as two points defined as (x1, y1) and (x2, y2). The method connects the two coordinate points with a blue line based on the Pen object.

7

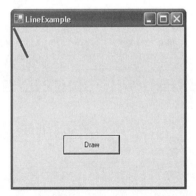

FIGURE 7.1   Drawing a line using the Pen class.

Figure 7.1 shows the output produced by Listing 7.1.

The `Graphics` **Class**

Dashes and Caps

Sometimes you want to add an arrow at the end of your line, or you want the line to be a dotted one. In addition to defining color and width, you can use the `Pen` class to create dashed lines and to attach start and end line caps. Line caps can be as simple as an arrowhead or as complex as a custom-defined cap. Table 7.8 lists the properties of the `Pen` class that are specific to dashes and caps.

TABLE 7.8

Dash- and Cap-Related Properties of the `Pen` Class

Property	Description
CustomStartCap	Used to set or get a custom-defined line cap. It defines the cap at a line's start. It is of type `CustomLineCap`.
CustomEndCap	Used to set or get a custom-defined line cap. It defines the cap at a line's end. It is of type `CustomLineCap`.
DashCap	Used to set or get the style used for the start or end caps of dashed lines.
DashOffset	Used to set or get the distance between the start of a line and the start of the dash pattern.
DashPattern	Sets or gets an array of integers that indicates the distances between dashes in dash-patterned lines.
DashStyle	Sets or gets the style used for dashing a line. The property is of the type `DashStyle` enumeration. `DashStyle` enumeration members include the following: `Dash`, `DashDot`, `DashDotDot`, `Dot`, and `Solid`.
EndCap	Sets or gets the `LineCap` object used to define the end of the line. `EndCap` is of the type `LineCap`. The `LineCap` enumeration includes the following members: `AnchorMask`, `ArrowAnchor`, `Custom`, `DiamondAnchor`, `Flat`, `NoAnchor`, `Round`, `RoundAnchor`, `Square`, `SquareAnchor`, and `Triangle`.
StartCap	Sets or gets the `LineCap` object used to define the start of the line. It is of the type `LineCap`. The `LineCap` enumeration includes the following members: `AnchorMask`, `ArrowAnchor`, `Custom`, `DiamondAnchor`, `Flat`, `NoAnchor`, `Round`, `RoundAnchor`, `Square`, `SquareAnchor`, and `Triangle`.

Add a new form; then add a button to your form and modify the `click` event of the button to look like Listing 7.2.

LISTING 7.2

Drawing a Dashed Line Using `DashStyle`

```
Private Sub btnDraw_Click(ByVal sender As System.Object, _
  ByVal e As System.EventArgs) Handles btnDraw.Click
  'Dimension a local variable of type Pen
  Dim penObj As Pen
```

LISTING 7.2
Continued

```
'Instantiate a Pen using the color structure and width constructor
penObj = New Pen(color:=Color.Blue, Width:=5)
'Set the Pen's end cap to be of type arrow
penObj.EndCap = Drawing.Drawing2D.LineCap.ArrowAnchor
'Set the Pen's dash style to be a dash followed by a dot
penObj.DashStyle = Drawing.Drawing2D.DashStyle.DashDot
End Sub
```

Listing 7.2 demonstrates how to set the styles and cap properties of a Pen object. The code first creates a Pen object of the color blue. It then sets the EndCap property to an arrow using the LineCap enumeration. Finally, it indicates the line's DashStyle to be a dash followed by a dot (DashDot).

Joins

If you have multiple lines that are joined to indicate a shape or routing direction through a diagram and you need to render those joins in a specific style, you can use the enumerations supplied in the LineJoin enumeration. The Pen class defines how lines are joined. To do so, it provides the LineJoin property. This property is of the type LineJoin enumeration that includes the following members:

- ▶ Bevel—The Bevel member indicates a beveled join between the lines.

- ▶ Miter—The Miter member specifies an angled join.

- ▶ Round—The Round member creates a smooth and rounded join.

To join lines, you must add each line to a Path object, which is drawn to the surface using one Pen instance. Intersecting lines are then joined based on the LineJoin property ■1■ of the given Pen instance. Listing 7.3 illustrates this with code.

LISTING 7.3
Using the LineJoin Property to Join Lines

```
Private Sub btnDraw_Click(ByVal sender As System.Object, _
  ByVal e As System.EventArgs) Handles btnDraw.Click
  Dim myPath As New System.Drawing.Drawing2D.GraphicsPath
  Dim graphicsObj As Graphics
  Dim penObj As New Pen(Color:=Color.Blue, Width:=8)
  'Return the current form as a drawing surface
  graphicsObj = Graphics.FromHwnd(hwnd:=ActiveForm().Handle)
  'Add 2 intersecting lines to a path
  myPath.AddLine(10, 10, 50, 10)
  myPath.AddLine(50, 10, 50, 50)
```

7

The Graphics Class

LISTING 7.3
Continued

```
'Set the line join property
penObj.LineJoin = Drawing.Drawing2D.LineJoin.Miter
'Draw the line to the form
graphicsObj.DrawPath(Pen:=penObj, path:=myPath)
End Sub
```

You can see the output shown in Figure 7.2.

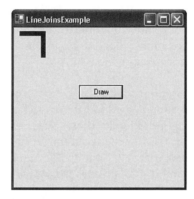

FIGURE 7.2   Setting the `LineJoin`
property of the `Pen` class.

Drawing Basic Shapes

This section continues the exploration of the namespace by looking at some of the
drawing functionalities. Because of the large number of features contained in this
namespace, this section focuses only on the shapes that you will most likely employ
in building your application.

Rectangles

The `Rectangle` structure is the backbone of the shapes presented in this section;
classes such as `Ellipse` and `Pie` use it to bind their shape. The structure stores the
size and location of a rectangular region. Table 7.9 shows the members of the
`Rectangle` structure.

TABLE 7.9

Members of the `Rectangle` **Structure**

Member	Description
Bottom	Gets the y-coordinate of the lower-right corner of the rectangular region defined by this `Rectangle`
Height	Gets or sets the width of the rectangular region defined by this `Rectangle`
IsEmpty	Tests whether this `Rectangle` has a `Width` or a `Height` of 0
Left	Gets the x-coordinate of the upper-left corner of rectangular region defined by this `Rectangle`
Location	Gets or sets the coordinates of the upper-left corner of the rectangular region represented by this `Rectangle`
Right	Gets the x-coordinate of the lower-right corner of the rectangular region defined by this `Rectangle`
Size	Gets or sets the size of this `Rectangle`
Top	Gets the y-coordinate of the upper-left corner of the rectangular region defined by this `Rectangle`
Width	Gets or sets the width of the rectangular region defined by this `Rectangle`
X	Gets or sets the x-coordinate of the upper-left corner of the rectangular region defined by this `Rectangle`
Y	Gets or sets the y-coordinate of the upper-left corner of the rectangular region defined by this `Rectangle`

7

Two constructors are available to create an instance of the `Rectangle` structure. One creates the rectangle based on the upper-left x and y coordinates, the width of the rectangle, and its height. To the other constructor, you pass both location as an instance of the `Point` structure and size as an instance of the `Size` structure.

Listing 7.4 illustrates both rectangle constructors. The code is simply fired by a button's `Click` event **1**. The rectangles are displayed in the active form.

LISTING 7.4

Creating Rectangles Using the `Rectangle` **Class**

```
Private Sub btnDraw_Click(ByVal sender As System.Object, _
    ByVal e As System.EventArgs) Handles btnDraw.Click
  Dim graphicsObj As Graphics
  Dim rectangleObj As Rectangle
  Dim penObj As New Pen(Color.Red)
  'Return the current form as a drawing surface
  graphicsObj = Graphics.FromHwnd(ActiveForm().Handle)
  'Create a rectangle based on x,y coordinates, width, & height
  rectangleObj = New Rectangle(x:=5, y:=5, Width:=10, Height:=40)
  'Draw rectangle from pen and rectangle objects
  graphicsObj.DrawRectangle(Pen:=penObj, rect:=rectangleObj)
```

The `Graphics` **Class**

LISTING 7.4
Continued

```
'Create a rectangle based on Point and Size objects
rectangleObj = New Rectangle(Location:=New Point(10, 10), _
Size:=New Size(Width:=20, Height:=60))
'Draw another rectangle from Pen and new Rectangle object
graphicsObj.DrawRectangle(Pen:=penObj, rect:=rectangleObj)
'Draw a rectangle from a Pen object, a rectangle's x & y, width, & height
graphicsObj.DrawRectangle(Pen:=penObj, x:=20, y:=20, _
   Width:=30, Height:=80)
End Sub
```

When executed, Listing 7.4 produces the output shown in Figure 7.3.

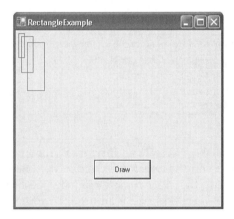

FIGURE 7.3   Drawing rectangles.

TIP

The `DrawRectangle` method of the `Graphics` object enables you to draw the outline of a rectangle to the drawing surface. The method is overloaded with three different sets of parameters. The first set enables you to create a rectangle based on `Pen` and `Rectangle` instances. The other two sets create a rectangle directly from a `Pen` instance and the rectangle's x and y coordinates (width and height). The difference between these two is the data types used to define the coordinates and size. One uses the `Int32` data type, and the other uses a `Single`.

Ellipses
An ellipse is simply a circle or oval bound inside a rectangle structure. You can use the `DrawEllipse` method of the `Graphics` class to draw an ellipse. This method requires a `Pen` object and some semblance of a rectangle definition (structure instance, coordinates, and so on). Listing 7.5 illustrates drawing an ellipse inside a defined rectangle instance using the `DrawEllipse` method **1**.

LISTING 7.5
Drawing an Ellipses Using the DrawEllipse Method

```
Private Sub btnDraw_Click(ByVal sender As System.Object, _
  ByVal e As System.EventArgs) Handles btnDraw.Click
  Dim graphicsObj As Graphics
  'Return the current form as a drawing surface
  graphicsObj = Graphics.FromHwnd(ActiveForm().Handle)
  'Draw an ellipse inside a bounding rectangle with a Pen instance
  graphicsObj.DrawEllipse(Pen:=New Pen(Color.Blue), _
    rect:=New Rectangle(x:=5, y:=5, Width:=70, Height:=25))
End Sub
```
1

Running Listing 7.5 produces the output shown in Figure 7.4.

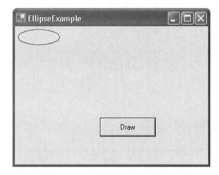

FIGURE 7.4 Drawing an ellipses using the DrawEllipse method.

Filling Shapes

So far, you have dealt with the outline of a shape. Now you will learn about the interior, or fill area, of a shape. GDI+ gives you the concept of a brush to indicate how a shape is filled. Brushes are useful when blending colors for a desired effect, such as a fade, or indicating a shape's texture, such as sand, stone, or brick. Brushes can be a single solid color, a blend of colors, a texture, a bitmap, or a hatched pattern.

To create brush objects, you use a derivative of the Brush class. Brush is an abstract base class. Classes that derive from Brush are SolidBrush, TextureBrush, RectangleGradientBrush, LinearGradientBrush, and HatchBrush. This section discusses the various Brush-related classes.

SolidBrush
The SolidBrush class works just as it sounds: It provides a single-colored brush with which to fill shapes. It has one constructor and one property, Color.

The Graphics **Class**

Of course, this property is of the type Color structure. The following is an example of how to create a SolidBrush object:

```
Dim myBrush as New SolidBrush(color:=Color.Red)
```

TextureBrush

You can use the TextureBrush class to create custom fill effects. Custom fills are useful when you need to apply your own design to the interior of a shape. For example, suppose you've created a bar graph and you want to fill each bar with the logo of a different company. The TextureBrush class would enable you to use a bitmap of each company's logo to fill each rectangle or bar in the graph. You can use the combination of TextureBrush class and bitmap images to create endless fill patterns.

The following code creates a TextureBrush instance based on a simple bitmap made up of three 45° lines. The bitmap is defined inside an ImageList control named imageList1. When you create the object instance, you set the WrapMode parameter to the TileFlipXY enumeration member. This reverses the image both vertically and horizontally before it is applied to the graphic surface.

```
Dim textureBrushObj As TextureBrush
'Create a new instance of TextureBrush
textureBrushObj = New TextureBrush(imageList1.Images.Item(0), _
   Drawing.Drawing2D.WrapMode.TileFlipXY)
```

TIP
You can use the WrapMode enumeration to tile an image inside the TextureBrush object to create a desired effect.

LinearGradientBrush

In Windows 9x and above, you might have already seen how you can blend two colors across the title bar of a window from within the Display Settings control panel. The LinearGradientBrush class enables you to do just that: You can blend two colors across a given shape.

To do so, you first create an instance of the class based on two colors and a blend style. Blend styles are defined by the LinearGradientMode enumeration. You then use a fill method of the Graphics object to paint your shape with the blended style. Listing 7.6 illustrates this by creating a Rectangle object and then using the blended LinearGradientBrush to fill its interior by calling FillRectangle.

LISTING 7.6
Using the LinearGradientBrush Class

```
Private Sub btnDraw_Click(ByVal sender As System.Object, _
  ByVal e As System.EventArgs) Handles btnDraw.Click
  Dim graphicsObj As Graphics
  Dim brushObj As System.Drawing.Drawing2D.LinearGradientBrush
  Dim rectangleObj As Rectangle
  'Return the current form as a drawing surface
  graphicsObj = Graphics.FromHwnd(hwnd:=ActiveForm().Handle)
  'Create a rectangle object
  rectangleObj = New Rectangle(x:=5, y:=5, Width:=40, Height:=50)
  'Draw the rectangle to the surface
  graphicsObj.DrawRectangle(Pen:=New Pen(Color.Black), rect:=rectangleObj)
  'Create the gradient brush
  brushObj = New System.Drawing.Drawing2D.LinearGradientBrush( _       1
  rect:=rectangleObj, color1:=Color.White, color2:=Color.DarkSlateBlue, _
  LinearGradientMode:=System.Drawing.Drawing2D.LinearGradientMode.Vertical)
  'Fill the rectangle using the gradient brush
  graphicsObj.FillRectangle(Brush:=brushObj, rect:=rectangleObj)
End Sub
```

Notice that when you created the brush, you set the LinearGradientMode parameter ■1 to indicate a blend from the top of the shape to its bottom (Vertical).

Listing 7.6 produces the output displayed in Figure 7.5.

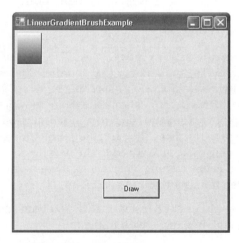

FIGURE 7.5 Using the LinearGradientBrush class.

7

Collections of Shapes

It is often useful to collect various "building block" shapes into a single unit. Rather than managing each rectangle in a bar graph, for instance, it is often easier to group these objects into a single, manageable unit. If the objects need to be moved or redrawn, you can simply make one method call. Similarly, if you are transforming the objects, maybe rotating them all 45°, it is much easier to transform a group than to transform each item independently. The System.Drawing.Drawing2D namespace provides the Path class that can be used for grouping shapes.

TIP

Additionally, after you have defined your various object groups, it is often necessary to indicate how those groups interact with one another. If you've ever used a drawing application, you are undoubtedly familiar with the concepts of "bring to front" and "send to back." These features enable you to indicate how shapes (or groups of shapes) relate to one another in layers. The System.Drawing namespace gives you the Region class for indicating object interaction and layers.

Paths

Paths enable you to leverage advanced drawing techniques in .NET. A path is made up of one or more geometric shapes (rectangle, line, curve, and so on). By grouping shapes in a path, you can manage and manipulate the group as one object. You add shapes to a path for storage in what is called the world coordinate space. This coordinate system is essentially virtual; it is the place where the shapes logically exist in memory relative to one another. The graphic can then be manipulated as a whole. It can be drawn to the screen over and over. In addition, it can be transformed (rotated, sheared, reflected, or scaled) when moving from this logical world space to the physical device space (form).

To create a path, you use the GraphicsPath class. This class provides methods such as AddLine, AddRectangle, and AddArc that add their shape to the path. Paths can contain multiple figures or groups of shapes that represent one object. When adding a shape to a path, it is best to indicate the figure to which the shape belongs. You do this by calling the StartFigure method. Each subsequent call to an add function adds the shape to the figure. If you call StartFigure again, a new figure is started and all following shapes are added to the new figure. You call the CloseFigure method before starting a new figure if you want the figure to be closed off, or connected from start point to endpoint.

Listing 7.7 creates a GraphicsPath instance **1**. You then add a few shapes to the GraphicsPath class and display the path to the form.

LISTING 7.7
Using the GraphicsPath Class

```
Private Sub btnDraw_Click(ByVal sender As System.Object, _
  ByVal e As System.EventArgs) Handles btnDraw.Click
  Dim graphicsObj As Graphics
  Dim penObj As New Pen(Color:=Color.Blue, Width:=2)
  Dim pathObj As System.Drawing.Drawing2D.GraphicsPath            1
  Dim pointsArray(2) As Point
  'Create a new GraphicsPath instance with default values
  pathObj = New System.Drawing.Drawing2D.GraphicsPath
  'Start the figure
  pathObj.StartFigure()
  'Add an ellipse for the head
  pathObj.AddEllipse(x:=0, y:=0, Width:=50, Height:=70)
  'Add 2 ellipses to the eyes
  pathObj.AddEllipse(x:=10, y:=10, Width:=10, Height:=8)
  pathObj.AddEllipse(x:=30, y:=10, Width:=10, Height:=8)
  'Add bezier for the nose
  pathObj.AddBezier(pt1:=New Point(x:=25, y:=30), _
    pt2:=New Point(x:=15, y:=30), pt3:=New Point(x:=20, y:=40), _
    pt4:=New Point(x:=25, y:=40))
  'Add a points to make a curve for the mouth
  pathObj.StartFigure()
  pointsArray(0) = New Point(x:=10, y:=50)
  pointsArray(1) = New Point(x:=25, y:=60)
  pointsArray(2) = New Point(x:=40, y:=50)
  pathObj.AddCurve(points:=pointsArray)
  'Return the current form as a drawing surface
  graphicsObj = Graphics.FromHwnd(hwnd:=ActiveForm().Handle)
  'Output the Path to the drawing surface of the form
  graphicsObj.DrawPath(Pen:=penObj, path:=pathObj)
End Sub
```

Executing Listing 7.7 produces the output shown in Figure 7.6.

TIP

If you use paths a lot, you will want to check out the Flatten method of the GraphicsPath class. This method enables you to change how items are stored within the object instance. By default, state is maintained for each item added to the path. This means that if a curve and an ellipse, for instance, are stored in a GraphicsPath, data for the curve's points and control points, as well as data that defines the ellipse, is stored in the object. By flattening the path, you allow the object to manage the shape as a series of line segments, thus reducing overhead. In a completely flattened path, all points are stored as points to be connected by line segments.

7

The `Graphics` **Class**

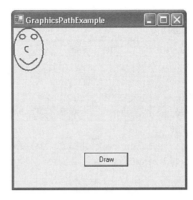

FIGURE 7.6   Using the
`GraphicsPath` class.

Regions and Clipping

A region is a section of the screen defined by a given path or rectangle. Using regions, you can define clip areas and do hit testing based on a graphics area. Clipping involves one shape defining the border, or area, of another shape. Additional items drawn within a defined region are constrained by the region; that is, a line with a width of 50 drawn within a rectangular region whose width is 20 will be cropped to 20 for display.

> **NOTE**
>
> Hit testing simply allows your application to know when the user has placed the mouse over a given region or whether another shape is contained within the area defined by the region. For example, if you define a region based on a rectangle, you can trap when a user clicks on the rectangle or when his or her mouse travels over the rectangle.

You use the `Region` class to create regions with the namespace. An instance of the `Region` class can be created with either a valid `Rectangle` instance or a `Path` object. To hit-test, you use the `IsVisible` method of the `Region` class. After a region has been defined, you can pass a point or a rectangle and a valid graphics surface as parameters to the `IsVisible` method. This method simply returns `True` if the given point or rectangle is contained within the `Region`; otherwise, it returns `False`. The following is an example of this method call; it displays the return of the `IsVisible` method to a message box.

```
MsgBox(prompt:=regionObj.IsVisible(x:=75, y:=75, g:=graphicsObj))
```

You still draw with the `Graphics` class, but the `Region` class enables you to set parameters for drawing. For example, you set the `region` parameter of the `SetClip` method of the `Graphics` object to your instance of `Region`. This tells the `Graphics` object that your `Region` further defines the graphics area on the given drawing surface.

Listing 7.8 presents a clipping example. You first draw a rectangle and add it to a Path object. You then define a Region instance **1** based on the Path object. After that, you call the SetClip method **2** of the Graphics container and pass in the Region object. Finally, you draw a number of strings to the graphic surface; notice how the defined region clips them.

LISTING 7.8
Clipping with the Region Class

```
Private Sub btnDraw_Click(ByVal sender As System.Object, _
  ByVal e As System.EventArgs) Handles btnDraw.Click
  Dim graphicsObj As Graphics
  Dim penObj As New Pen(Color:=Color.Blue, Width:=2)
  Dim pathObj As New System.Drawing.Drawing2D.GraphicsPath
  Dim pointsArray(2) As Point
  Dim regionObj As Region
  Dim i As Short
  'Define a triangle
  pathObj.StartFigure()
  pointsArray(0) = New Point(x:=100, y:=20)
  pointsArray(1) = New Point(x:=50, y:=100)
  pointsArray(2) = New Point(x:=150, y:=100)
  'Add triangle to the path
  pathObj.AddPolygon(points:=pointsArray)
  'Create a region based on the path
  regionObj = New Region(path:=pathObj)                              1
  'Return the current form as a drawing surface
  graphicsObj = Graphics.FromHwnd(hwnd:=ActiveForm().Handle)
  'Draw the region's outline to the screen
  graphicsObj.DrawPath(Pen:=penObj, path:=pathObj)
  'Set the clipping region
  graphicsObj.SetClip(Region:=regionObj, _                           2
      combineMode:=Drawing.Drawing2D.CombineMode.Replace)
'Draw the string multiple times
  For i = 20 To 100 Step 20
    'Draw clipped text
    graphicsObj.DrawString(s:="Clipping Region", _
      Font:=New Font(familyName:="Arial", emSize:=18, style:=FontStyle.Regular, _
      unit:=GraphicsUnit.Pixel), Brush:=New SolidBrush(Color:=Color.Red), x:=50, _
      ➥y:=i)
  Next
End Sub
```

7

The Graphics Class

As you can see from the listing, when you called SetClip, you also set the combineMode enumeration to Replace. This indicates how the two regions or shapes should be combined. In this example, you have a triangular Region object and a few strings that you draw. By setting the combineMode enumeration to Replace, you indicate that the string information should replace the region inside the triangle. Output produced by this listing is shown in Figure 7.7.

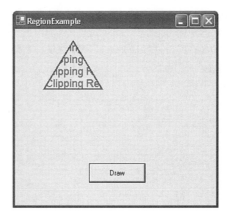

FIGURE 7.7   Clipping with the Region class.

Working with Images

In this section, you will see how to use two of the most common graphic types a programmer interacts with: bitmaps and icons. As stated earlier in the chapter, all user-interface objects in Windows are some form of a bitmap; a bitmap is simply a collection of pixels set to various colors.

Images

The namespace library gives you three classes for working with images: Image, Bitmap, and Icon. Image is simply the base class from which the others inherit. Bitmap enables you to convert a graphics file into the native GDI+ format (bitmap). This class can be used to define images as fill patterns, transform images for display, define the look of a button, and more. Although the bitmap format is used to manipulate images at the pixel level, GDI+ can actually work with the following image types:

- ▶ Bitmaps (BMP)

- ▶ Graphics Interchange Format (GIF)

- ▶ Joint Photographic Experts Group (JPEG)

- ▶ Exchangeable Image File (EXIF)

- ▶ Portable Network Graphics (PNG)

- ▶ Tagged Image File Format (TIFF)

Creating an instance of `Bitmap` requires a filename, a stream, or another valid `Image` instance. For example, the following line of code instantiates a `Bitmap` object based on a JPEG file:

```
Dim bitMapObj As New System.Drawing.Bitmap(fileName:="MyBitmap.jpg")
```

After the image is instantiated, you can do a number of things with the image. For instance, you can change its resolution with the `SetResolution` method, or you can make part of the image transparent with `MakeTransparent`. Of course, you will also want to draw your image to the form. You use the `DrawImage` method of the `Graphics` class to output the image to the screen. The `DrawImage` method has more than 30 overloaded parameter sets. In its simplest form, you pass the method an instance of `Bitmap` and the upper-left coordinate of where you want the method to begin drawing:

```
graphicsObj.DrawImage(image:=bitmapObj, point:=New Point(x:=5, y:=5))
```

Unit of Measurement

One of the excellent features of the `Graphics` class is the capability to reset the graphics unit used by the `Graphics` class by setting the `PageUnit` property. This property takes a valid member of the `GraphicsUnit` enumeration. Members include `Inch`, `Millimeter`, `Pixel`, `Point`, and so on. After setting the `PageUnit` property, subsequent calls to the `Graphics` object interpret your values as the new unit of measurement. For instance, the following code sets the unit to inches and creates a rectangle an inch wide and a half-inch high:

```
graphicsObj.PageUnit = GraphicsUnit.Inch
graphicsObj.DrawRectangle(pen:=New Pen(Color.Red, Width:=0.1F), _
  x:=0, y:=0, Width:=1, Height:=0.5F)
```

Working with Fonts

The `Font` class in the `System.Drawing` namespace defines a particular format for text, such as font type, size, and style attributes. You use a font constructor to create a font. As with the `Color` class, this class provides overloaded constructors that can be used while creating an instance of the `Font` class:

Initializes a new instance of the `Font` class with the specified attributes:

```
Public Sub New(String, Single)
```

7

Working with Fonts

Initializes a new instance of the Font class from the specified existing Font and FontStyle:

```
Public Sub New(Font, FontStyle)
```

where FontStyle is an enumeration; its members are shown in Table 7.10.

TABLE 7.10

Members of FontStyle Enumeration

Member	Description
Bold	Sets the text to bold
Italic	Sets the text to italic
Regular	Sets the text to regular text
Strikeout	Sets the text with a line through the middle
Underline	Enables you to underline the text

Apart from providing a number of overloaded constructors, the Font class provides a number of properties that you can use, as shown in Table 7.11.

TABLE 7.11

Common Properties of the Font Class

Property	Description
Bold	Gets a value indicating whether this Font is bold
FontFamily	Gets the FontFamily of this Font
Height	Gets the height of this Font
Italic	Gets a value indicating whether this Font is italic
Name	Gets the face name of this Font
Size	Gets the size of this Font
SizeInPoints	Gets the size, in points, of this Font
Strikeout	Gets a value indicating whether this Font is strikeout (has a line through it)
Style	Gets style information for this Font
Underline	Gets a value indicating whether this Font is underlined
Unit	Gets the unit of measure for this Font

7

Summary

This chapter provided a complete walkthrough of the key classes related to drawing using managed code. All of the key points explained in this chapter are summarized as follows:

GDI+ is the underlying technology that the managed code uses to execute drawing tasks. The Graphics class provides the core foundation required for executing nearly all drawing tasks. The Brush class is an abstract class from which all the brush-related classes are derived. Brush classes include SolidBrush, TextureBrush, and HatchBrush. The GraphicsPath class enables you to group shapes. Using this class, you can manipulate various shapes as a whole. The Bitmap class encapsulates an image. You can use the DrawImage method of the Graphics class to render it to the surface. The Font class can be used to define a particular format for the text.

Further Reading

MSDN documentation on System.Drawing namespace.

Mackenzie, Duncan, Andy Baron, Erik Porter, Joel Semeniuk. *Microsoft Visual Basic .NET 2003 Kick Start.* Pearson Education, 2003.

7

8 DEPLOYING YOUR APPLICATION

IN BRIEF

In the early days of personal computing, constructing an application that could be installed successfully on another computer was often as simple as compiling an .exe file and copying it to a floppy disk. As applications have become increasingly complex and sophisticated, the number of files needed for a typical installation has grown from a handful of files to several hundred. This is especially true with Windows applications that have historically required sophisticated setup programs to copy the correct dynamic link libraries and support files to the end user's computer and to register the applications appropriately with the operating system.

This chapter discusses the features that the .NET Framework provides for deploying Windows applications onto the end user's machine, and it discusses the different types of deployment options that the .NET Framework provides. Then it takes a look at the architecture of the Windows Installer and discusses the differences between XCOPY and Windows Installer. Along the way, this chapter also demonstrates the process of packaging Windows Forms applications using the setup and deployment project types that Visual Studio .NET supports.

WHAT YOU NEED

SOFTWARE REQUIREMENTS	Windows 2000, Windows XP, or Windows Server 2003 .NET Framework 1.1 SDK Visual Studio .NET 2003 with Visual Basic .NET installed Internet Information Server (version 5 or later) SQL Server or Microsoft Desktop Database Engine (MSDE)
HARDWARE REQUIREMENTS	PC desktop or laptop system
SKILL REQUIREMENTS	Advanced knowledge in HTML Intermediate knowledge in the .NET Framework

DEPLOYING YOUR APPLICATION AT A GLANCE

DEPLOYING YOUR APPLICATION AT A GLANCE

Introduction to Deployment

Before diving into the processes involved in setting up and deploying applications, it is important to understand the difference between setup and deployment. A setup is an application or process that enables you to package your application into an easy-to-deploy format that can then be used to install the application on another machine. Deployment is the process of installing the application on another machine, usually by using a setup application.

Planning for Deployment

At some time, most computer users have experienced the dark side of installing Windows programs. For example, before the .NET era, when you installed a new version of your Windows application, the installation program copied the new version of DLLs into the system directory and made all the necessary Registry changes. This installation potentially had an impact on other applications running on the machine, especially if an existing application was using the shared version of the installed component. If the installed component was backward compatible with the previous versions, all was fine, but in many cases, it was not possible to maintain backward compatibility. If you cannot maintain backward compatibility, you often end up breaking the existing applications as a result of new installations.

One of the areas Visual Studio .NET was designed to address was the installation shortcomings of Windows applications that relied heavily on COM components. In Visual Studio .NET, it is possible to simplify the installation process because Visual Studio .NET applications rely on .NET assemblies (that are built on a completely different programming model) for much of their functionality. In addition, Visual Studio .NET applications are compiled as assemblies, a deployment unit consisting of one or more files. To understand how Visual Studio .NET simplifies the deployment process, the next section takes a brief look at the structure of the assembly that provides for this simplification.

8

Structure of an Assembly

An assembly consists of the following four elements:

- ▶ **Microsoft Intermediate Language (MSIL) code**—Language code (C#, VB .NET, and others) is compiled into this intermediate common language that can be understood by the common language runtime.

- ▶ **Metadata**—Contains information about the types, methods, and other elements defined in the code.

- ▶ **Manifest**—Contains name and version information, a list of included files in the assembly, security information, and so on.

- ▶ **Nonexecutable content**—These include supporting files and resources.

As you can see, assemblies are so comprehensive and self-describing that Visual Studio .NET applications don't need to be registered with Registry. This means that Visual Studio .NET applications can be installed by simply copying the required files to the target machine that has the .NET Framework installed. This is called XCOPY installation. However, it is also possible to automate the setup process by making use of the deployment projects that Visual Studio .NET provides. The next section considers the various deployment options that Visual Studio .NET supports.

Deployment Options Supported by .NET

It is possible to deploy Windows Forms applications using the following two deployment options:

- ▶ XCOPY deployment

- ▶ Deployment using the Visual Studio .NET Installer

The following sections discuss both of the deployment options and demonstrate the right method to choose for different scenarios.

Using XCOPY to Deploy Applications

One of the primary goals of the .NET Framework is to simplify the deployment by making possible what is known as XCOPY deployment. Before talking about how .NET enables XCOPY deployment, you need to see what XCOPY deployment is. Before .NET, installing a component required copying the component to the appropriate directories and making appropriate Registry entries. But now in .NET, to install the component, all you need to do is copy the assembly into the bin directory of the client application, and the application can start using it right away because of the self-describing nature of the assembly. An XCOPY deployment is also called a zero-impact install because you are not impacting the machine by configuring the Registry entries and configuring the component.

> **NOTE**
>
> The compilers in the .NET Framework embed identifiers or metadata into compiled modules, and the common language runtime uses this information to load the appropriate version of the assemblies. The identifiers contain all the information required to load and run modules, as well as to locate all the other modules that the assembly references.

This zero-impact installation also makes it possible to uninstall a component without affecting the system in any manner. All that is required to complete the uninstall is to remove specific files from the specific directory.

Using Visual Studio .NET Installer to Deploy Applications

Even though XCOPY deployment is very simple and easy to use, it does not lend itself well to all of the deployment requirements. For example, if your application requires more robust application setup and deployment requirements, Visual Studio .NET Installer can be used to perform that. Because the Visual Studio .NET Installer is built on top of Windows Installer technology, it takes advantage of all the features of Windows Installer. This discussion of Visual Studio .NET Installer starts by taking a look at the architecture of Windows Installer.

Windows Installer Architecture

Windows Installer is a software installation and configuration service that ships with the Windows 2000 and Windows XP operating systems and is freely available to all Win9*x* and NT4 platforms. Windows Installer Service maintains a record of information about every application that it installs. The Windows Installer runtime (MSI) inspects these records during the execution of deployment packages. When you try to uninstall the application, Windows Installer checks the records to make sure that no other applications rely on its components before removing it.

Windows Installer divides applications into the following three levels:

- ▶ **Product**—This is something that a user can install and use to take advantage of its features. For example, MS Word is a product that a user can install and use to perform word processing.

- ▶ **Feature**—A product is composed of multiple features. A feature is also the smallest unit of functionality of a product. For example, the AutoCorrect functionality is a feature of MS Word.

- ▶ **Component**—A component can be considered as the smallest unit that can be shared across multiple features. It is very important to understand that the term *component* in Windows Installer terms is not the same as in the .NET Framework. A Windows Installer component can be a single file or multiple files that logically belong together. It can be an executable, a DLL, or a simple text file. A collection of components can come together to provide a feature, and a component also can be shared across multiple features.

8

Deployment Options Supported by .NET

Although features are specific to a product and are identified by a name unique only within the product, components are global across all products installed on a machine. For example, the spell-checker component of MS Word can be shared across all the applications that want to implement the spell-checking feature.

Information related to a product such as a feature's components are described in a centralized repository known as the Installation Database. The Installation Database is nothing but a file with the extension .msi that contains information not only about the features and components of the product, but also about the sequence of user interfaces displayed during the installation of the product. Because the Windows Installer is registered as the default application for files with the .msi extension, the shell automatically invokes it when a user opens an .msi file. When invoked in this way, the Installer reads product information from the Installation Database file and determines whether the product is already installed. If the product is not yet installed, it launches the product's installation sequence, which is described in the database. If the product is installed, different logic can be invoked, such as to add and remove features or to uninstall the product.

The installation database is a relational database and can be queried and modified using a query tool that understands the MSI database format. Most often, the tools used to directly modify the installation database are Installation tools like InstallShield. These tools can open a MSI database and display the tables in much the same manner that any other RDBMS client displays data from its server. However, it is pertinent to note that directly modifying Installer tables is very rare and not warranted in normal circumstances. Each package (.msi) file is a relational database that stores all of the instructions and data required to install and remove the program across various installation scenarios. For example, a package file can contain instructions for installing an application when a prior version of the application is already installed. The package file also contains instructions for installing the software on a computer where that application has never been present.

Additional Features Provided by Visual Studio .NET

In addition to the features of Windows Installer, the deployment projects in Visual Studio .NET provide the following features:

- ▶ Reading or writing of Registry keys

- ▶ The capability to create directories in the Windows file system

- ▶ A mechanism to register both COM components and .NET components (in the GAC)

- ▶ The capability to gather information from users during installation

- ▶ The capability to set launch conditions, such as checking the username, computer name, current operating system, software application installed, presence of .NET common language runtime, and so on

> ▶ The capability to run a custom setup program or script after the installation is complete

Later parts of this chapter (which look at creating deployment projects using Visual Studio .NET) give an in-depth overview of all these features.

Trade-Offs Between XCOPY and Windows Installer

As you have seen, XCOPY is ideal for deployment scenarios that are simple and manually executed. Although XCOPY works well for simple scenarios, in many cases, a more robust deployment solution is required. In those scenarios, it is recommended that you use the Windows Installer technology to install applications. The following advantages of Windows Installer make it an ideal candidate for creating setup and deployments for applications created using the .NET Framework:

TIP
If an application installed using the Windows Installer is corrupted, the applications can do self-repair by using the repair feature of Windows Installer packages. In XCOPY-based deployments, you need to manually replace the corrupted component with the newer version.

By using the Windows Installer, you can also take advantage of the automatic rollback feature, which ensures not only that the installed components are uninstalled, but also that, if the installation fails, the machine is brought back to the same stage as before the installer started.

Because Windows Installer uses an MSI Installation Database for storing all of the information, it is possible to get information about what files are copied, what Registry keys are created, and so on.

If you're developing an application that you want to distribute to multiple users (or sell as a package), you need a more convenient, automated approach to deploying them. A manual-deployment process such as XCOPY is not desirable and might not work because of the complexity work involved. However by using a sophisticated installer technology such as Windows Installer, you can automate the entire installation process, thereby simplifying the deployment.

Different Types of Deployment Project Templates Provided by Visual Studio .NET

By default, Visual Studio .NET comes bundled with five types of project templates that can be used to set up and deploy applications created using the .NET Framework.

8

Different Types of Deployment Project Templates Provided by Visual Studio .NET

These project templates can be accessed in the same way as any other projects in Visual Studio .NET, by choosing File, New Project and using the resulting dialog box, shown in Figure 8.1.

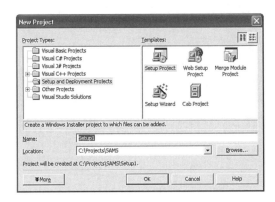

FIGURE 8.1   New Project dialog box.

Figure 8.1 shows the different setup and deployment project types available in Visual Studio .NET. The following list takes a brief look at each of the available project types:

- **Setup Project template**—The Setup Project template is used to create a standard Windows Installer setup for a Visual Studio .NET application.

- **Web Setup Project template**—The Web Setup Project template is used to create a Windows Installer setup program that can be used to install a web application onto a virtual directory of a web server.

- **Merge Module Project template**—Microsoft introduced merge modules as part of the Windows Installer technology to enable a set of files to be packaged into an easy-to-use file that could be reused and shared between setup programs that are based on Windows Installer technology. The idea is to package all the files and any other resources that are dependent on each other into the merge module. As you can imagine, this type of project can be very useful for packaging a component and all its dependencies into a single unit, which can then be merged into the setup program of each application that uses the component. During the installation, the merge module component is installed only if the component is not present in the machine. The merge module Windows Installer package files are identified by the file extension .msm. For example, the latest versions of MSXML (Microsoft XML) Parser are also available in the form of merge modules. If your application uses MSXML Parser, you can easily package the merge module into the setup program of your application.

- **Setup Wizard template**—The Setup Wizard guides you through the process of creating one of the setup and deployment project templates mentioned earlier.

▶ **Cab Project template**—As the name suggests, the Cab Project template is used to create a cabinet file (`.cab`). A cabinet file can contain any number of files but has no installation logic. It is generally used to package components into a single file that can then be deployed on a web server to enable the browser-based clients to download them onto their local machine and then install them. For example, controls hosted in a web page are often packaged into a cabinet file and placed on the web server. When the browser encounters the control, it checks that the control isn't already installed in the local computer; then it downloads the cabinet file, extracts the control from it, and installs it into the user's computer.

> **TIP**
>
> For those who come from other technologies, CAB files are a bit like JAR files introduced in Java. CAB files are also the default format for packaging ActiveX controls.

Creating an Installer Package

Now that you have had a look at the different setup project types, you need to understand the steps involved in creating a setup and deploy project for a Windows application. For the purposes of this example, you will create a simple Windows application named FormattingApplication and then explore the deployment features. As the name suggests, this application simply enables you to format the contents entered in a rich-text box to the desired format. The main focus of this chapter is on creating Windows Installer packages, so not much time is spent on what this application does. However, you can download the source code for this project, along with the support material for this chapter, from the Sams website.

Start by adding a Windows Installer project to the solution that contains the VB .NET formatting application project.

Now add a setup project to the existing solution (FormattingApplication) by selecting File, Add Project, New Project from the New Project dialog box. Name the project FormattingApplicationSetup.

Configuring Deployment Properties

Now that the project is created, you can configure the deployment-related properties in the deployment project. To do this, right-click the FormattingApplicationSetup project from the Solution Explorer and select Properties. Then open the Configuration Properties tree view and select Build. Click the Configuration Manager command button to bring up the Configuration Manager dialog box. Now change the Active Solution Configuration setting from Debug to Release for both projects to create a release build.

8

Configuring Deployment Properties

Also check the Build option for the setup project. By setting the configuration settings to Release, you create a release build that can be installed onto the end user's computer. By default, when you are working with a VS .NET project, you are creating a debug build, which creates the debugging information as part of the project output; the project output is also not optimized for performance. Before you deploy the application, you need to change this to release build, which not only optimizes the project output for performance, but also ignores the unnecessary debugging information.

After modification, the dialog box should look as shown in Figure 8.2.

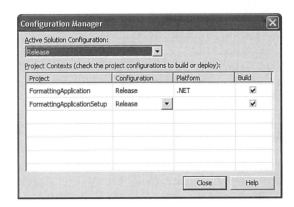

FIGURE 8.2 Configuration Manager dialog box.

The files that are part of the deployment project can be packaged into any of the following three formats:

▶ **As loose, uncompressed files**—No compression takes place, and the entire program and data files are stored as they are.

▶ **In the setup file**—When selected, this option merges all the files and compresses them into an MSI file.

▶ **In cabinet file(s)**—All files are packaged into one or more cabinet files. The MSI file contains entries about all the project CAB files and uses that information at runtime to load and install the CAB files. These files are placed in the same directory as the MSI file.

In this example, you want to compress all the files into a single MSI file, so select the option In Setup File. The next property that needs to be configured is the `BootStrapper` property; set this property to Bootstrapper.

TIP

A bootstrapper is a program that must be executed before the actual application can be run.

When you install an application created using Visual Studio .NET Installer, Windows Installer version 1.5 must be present in the target computer. The Windows XP operating system is the first operating system that comes bundled with Windows Installer 1.5. If you want to deploy your application on earlier systems, you need to include the bootstrapper as part of the installation program. If you include this option, it increases the file size by about 3MB. Because the bootstrapper is required to support earlier systems, it is recommended that you select that option. However, if you are deploying your application only on Windows XP–based systems, you can safely ignore this option, thereby decreasing the size of the final installation program. If you use the Web Bootstrapper option, you need to make the bootstrapper available for download over the web because it isn't included in the MSI download. When selecting this option, you are asked to provide the URL of the download. The user installing the application to install the bootstrapper will then use this URL. The main benefit to this approach is that no additional space is required in the installation package, thereby reducing the size of the install.

Finally, set the Compression property to Optimized for Speed, meaning that you want the files to be compressed to install faster.

Configuring Project Properties

Apart from setting the configuration properties for the entire solution, you need to set the following deployment-specific properties for the deployment project FormattingApplicationSetup. These properties are accessed through the properties window. Table 8.1 discusses some of the important properties that can be set for a deployment project.

TABLE 8.1

Deployment Project Properties

Method	Description
AddRemoveProgramsIcon	Specifies the icon to be displayed in the Add/Remove Programs dialog box on the target computer
Author	Enables you to specify the name of the author of the application
Description	Enables you to specify the description that is displayed during the installation
Keywords	Specifies the keywords that can be used to search for an installer on the target machine
DetectNewerInstalledVersion	Enables you to specify whether you want to check for the newer versions of the application during the installation
RemovePreviousVersions	Enables you to indicate whether you want to remove the previous versions of the application during the installation
Manufacturer	Specifies the name of the manufacturer of the application
ManufacturerUrl	Specifies the URL of the manufacturer's web site
ProductCode	Specifies a unique identifier (GUID) for the application
ProductName	Specifies the name of the product
SupportUrl	Specifies the URL for the website that contains support information about the application

8

Configuring Project Properties

TABLE 8.1

Continued

Method	Description
Title	Specifies the title for the installer
Version	Specifies the version number of the installer

After you make these changes, the FormattingApplicationSetup properties window looks as shown in Figure 8.3.

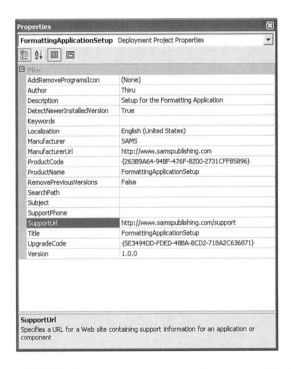

FIGURE 8.3   Deployment project Properties dialog box.

Now that you understand the different properties that need to be configured, the next section discusses the setup and deployment projects that provide the foundation required for performing advanced deployment-related configurations.

Different Types of Setup Editors

Because of the great deal of flexibility the deployment projects in Visual Studio .NET offer, it is very easy to specify how and where a solution will be deployed. The bulk of an installer's work is copying files to the right places, so there is obviously a file system configuration editor within the setup editors. However, a setup can also include Registry configuration options, a check for special conditions, and so on. It is also useful to be able to customize the installer's user interface. For these reasons, VS includes a number of editors within the setup projects. All these editors can be accessed through View, Editors:

▶ **File System Editor**—Used to add files and shortcuts, such as Start menu items, to the installation package.

▶ **Registry Editor**—Enables you to manipulate Registry entries on the target computer.

▶ **File Types Editor**—Enables you to associate file extensions with applications. This is useful if your application uses custom file extensions and you want to associate a specific application with that file extension.

▶ **User Interface Editor**—Enables you to configure the dialog boxes that are shown during the installation.

▶ **Custom Actions Editor**—Enables you to start external programs during installs and uninstalls.

▶ **Launch Conditions Editor**—Enables you to specify the requirements for your application to be installed on the target computer.

The following section takes an in-depth look at each of these editors. The discussion starts with the File System Editor.

Configuring File System Editor

As the name suggests, this editor enables you to add project output files, assemblies, and other files to the deployment project. Using this editor, you can also specify the directory location where these files will be installed on the end user's computer.

> **TIP**
>
> Using the File System Editor, you can also create shortcuts to your application on a target computer's desktop.

You can open the File System Editor by selecting View, Editor, File System. When opened, the File System Editor looks as shown in Figure 8.4.

Different Types of Setup Editors

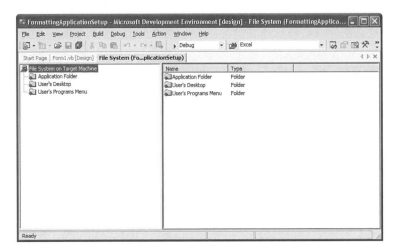

FIGURE 8.4   File System Editor.

By using any of the predefined folders in the File System Editor, you can choose a destination folder on a target computer without even having to know the actual path to that folder; the installer works it out from the virtual path at installation. The following list takes a brief look at each of these folders and their purposes:

▶ **Application folder**—The Application folder is normally represented by the path [*ProgramFilesFolder*] [*Manufacturer*] \ [*ProductName*]. On English systems, by default, the [ProgramFilesFolder] folder resolves to [*Drive Name*]\Program Files. The names for the Manufacturer and ProductName directories are taken from the settings that you defined while setting the project properties. It is also possible for the end users to override these settings while installing the application.

▶ **Global Assembly Cache folder**—Enables you to specify the assemblies that need to be installed as shared assemblies on the target computer.

▶ **User's Desktop**—This folder acts as a placeholder for files and folders that should appear on the user's desktop. The default location of this folder is [*DriveName*]\Documents and Settings\[*UserName*]\Desktop, with the username representing the name of the user who performs the installation.

▶ **User's Programs Menu**—This folder acts as a placeholder for entries that should appear in the programs group of the user. The default location of this folder is [*DriveName*]\Documents and Settings\[*UserName*]\Start Menu\Programs, with the Username representing the name of the user who performs the installation.

> **TIP**
>
> Apart from the four predefined folders, you can add custom folders from a predefined list of folders to the File System Editor. To display the list of special folders that can be added to the File System Editor, right-click on the File System on Target Machine folder from the File System Editor, and then select Add Special Folder from the context menu.

Adding Items to Special Folders

Using the File System Editor, you can add any of the following four items to the special folders:

- **Folder**—Enables you to create a folder on the target machine in the specified directory.

- **Project Output**—Enables you to specify where the output of one or more projects (.dll or .exe files) in the solution will be deployed on a target computer. It also adds all the dependencies to the folder.

- **File**—Using this option, you can also deploy loose (zero-compression) files to a target computer. This can be very useful for deploying help files, such as Readme.txt.

- **Assembly**—Enables you to specify the assemblies that need to be added. When this option is selected, it adds all the referenced assemblies as well.

Now that you have had a look at the different editors, you can configure your deployment project using the File System Editor. The first step in creating a setup is specifying what files you want to be copied to the target computer using the File System Editor.

8

1. Add the primary output of FormattingApplication to the installer by choosing Project, Add, Project Output. Select Primary Output in the Add Project Output Group dialog box when the Application Folder directory is selected. When you click OK in the dialog box, the primary output of the FormattingApplication project is added to the Application folder of the File System Editor. At the same time, this adds the dependencies to the installer project.

2. Because FormattingApplication requires the .NET runtime, it automatically is added to the installer project. As a result, the merge module for the .NET runtime, dotnetfxredist_x86_enu.msm, becomes visible in the Solution Explorer. This merge module includes all files for the .NET runtime. If the .NET runtime is not already installed on the target system, it is installed along with the application. In this case, assume that you require the .NET runtime to be already present in the target machine. Exclude this file from the package by selecting the file dotnetfxredist_x86_enu.msm and then setting the Exclude property to True through its properties window.

Different Types of Setup Editors

3. Now add the additional folders and files. Right-click on Application Folder in the File System Editor and select Add, Folder. Name the created folder Support. This folder will be used as a placeholder where all the supporting files for the application are stored.

4. Right-click on the Support folder and select Add, File. Add the `readme.rtf`, `license.rtf`, `Readme.txt`, and `sams.bmp` files to the Support folder.

5. Because you want the Readme.txt file to be available as an individual file, to allow the end user to read that information before the installation, keep this file as a loose (uncompressed) file in the installer package. To do this, select the Readme.txt file from the Support folder and select View, Properties Window. Change the `PackageAs` property to `vsdpaLoose`.

TIP

Note that a merge module cannot contain loose files (files whose `PackageAs` property is set to `vsdpaLoose`). Also note that the Loose Files option should not be used for applications that will be distributed over the Web. Files packaged in this manner can be downloaded without any security prompt, creating a security risk for users.

---

6. In this step, add the provision for the users to create a shortcut to FormattingApplication in their desktop. As mentioned before, this requires the shortcut to be added to the User's Desktop folder. To add the shortcut, right-click on the Primary output from the FormattingApplication (Active) item in the Application folder and select Create Shortcut to Primary Output from FormattingApplication (Active) from the context menu. Rename the shortcut as Formatting Application. Drag and drop this shortcut to the User's Desktop folder. However, you should install this only if the user wants to install it. Therefore, set the `Condition` property of the User's Desktop folder to `SHORTCUTDEMO`. This ensures that the shortcut will be installed only if this condition is set to True. When you learn about the User Interface Editor later in this chapter, you will create a dialog box where this property can be set.

7. You also want to make the program available from the Start, Programs menu, so you should add a shortcut to the User's Program Menu folder. To add the shortcut, create another shortcut as before, and rename it again as Formatting Application. Drag and drop this shortcut to the User's Program's Menu folder. This time, because you always want this shortcut to install, don't alter the `Condition` property.

Configuring Registry Editor

This editor enables you to manage the Registry settings in the target computer where the application will be installed. By default, the Registry Editor displays the standard Windows Registry keys, such as HKEY_CLASSES_ROOT, HKEY_CURRENT_USER, HKEY_LOCAL_MACHINE, and HKEY_USERS. Using the Registry Editor, it is also possible to add custom Registry keys under any of these keys. Selecting View, Editor, Registry from the menu displays the Registry Editor, which is shown in Figure 8.5.

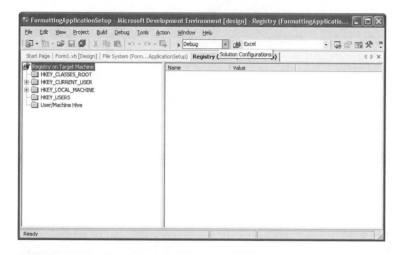

FIGURE 8.5 Registry Editor.

To add information to the Registry that your application requires at runtime, you can use either HKEY_LOCAL_MACHINE\Software\[*Manufacturer*] or HKEY_CURRENT_USER\Software\[*Manufacturer*]. You can add entries to this editor by right-clicking on a specific node and selecting various options from the context menu. Using this editor, you can perform all the activities that you would normally perform using the Registry Editor that is accessed using the regedit command in the command prompt. It is a good practice to add the application-specific information under the value specified in the Manufacturer property that is available in the Project properties window.

Configuring File Types Editor

The File Types Editor enables you to set up file associations on the target computer. This is accomplished by assigning an application to a file extension so that double-clicking the file launches the correct application. When the initial association is done, the extension and the file type description appear in the file types list in Windows Explorer.

Different Types of Setup Editors

This is very useful if your application uses custom file types that require a separate external application to be launched. The following list describes the important properties associated with the File Types Editor:

- ▸ Name—Enables you to specify the name used in the File Types Editor to identify a particular file type
- ▸ Command—Can be used to set the executable file that should be launched when the user opens a file with this type
- ▸ Description—Provides the description for the file type
- ▸ Extensions—Enables you to specify the file extensions with which the executable should be registered
- ▸ Icon—Specifies an icon to be displayed for the file type
- ▸ MIME—Specifies one or more MIME types to be associated with the selected file type
- ▸ Verb—Enables you to specify the verbs (such as open, edit, and play) that are used to invoke the selected action for the file type

Configuring Custom Actions Editor

This editor enables you to link to another program that can be launched at the end of the application installation. To create a custom action, you need to create a .dll or .exe file that performs the custom action and then add it to the deployment project. It is also important to note that the custom actions can be launched only at the end of the installation. These custom actions can be associated with any one of the following four installation outcomes:

- ▸ Install
- ▸ Commit
- ▸ Rollback
- ▸ Uninstall

For example, if you want to launch a specific external program after installing the application, you can accomplish this by associating that external program with the Install node.

Configuring Launch Conditions Editor

Using this editor, you can specify conditions that must be met for the setup to run. If the user tries to install the application on a system that does not meet the launch condition, the setup will not run.

NOTE

While setting the launch condition, it is also possible to specify that searches be performed on the target computer to determine the existence of a particular file, Registry key, component, and so on.

As you can see from the following list, this editor has two sections to specify the requirements:

- **Search Target Machine**—Enables you to specify the kind of search that needs to be performed on the target computer. This can include a search for a specific file, Registry key, and so on.

- **Launch Conditions**—Enables you to define the conditions that need to be met before the application setup can be launched.

For example, using the Launch Conditions Editor, you can configure any of the following conditions:

- **File Launch**—Searches for installed files on the target system

- **Registry Launch**—Searches for Registry keys before the start of the installation

- **Windows Installer Launch**—Searches for Windows Installer files

- **.NET Framework Launch**—Checks for the existence of the .NET Framework on the target computer

- **Internet Information Services Launch**—Checks for the installed version of IIS

While adding the primary output of the FormattingApplication project to the installer, you excluded the .NET runtime file (`dotnetfxredist_x86_enu.msm`) from the installer package. Because you did not include the .NET runtime with the installer package, add code to check for the existence of the .NET runtime on the target computer by using the .NET Framework launch condition.

For the purposes of this example, add a search condition that enables you to check whether the .NET Framework is installed on the target machine. To do this, you need to perform the following steps:

1. Open the Launch Conditions Editor by selecting View, Editor, Launch Conditions.

2. Add a launch condition by choosing Action, Add .NET Framework Launch Condition. Set the `Name` property to `CHECKDOTNETCONDITION`.

Now that you have set the .NET Framework launch condition, if the user tries to run the installation without having the .NET Framework installed, the installation will not run.

Configuring User Interface Editor

As indicated by the name, this editor permits you to specify the sequence of user interface dialog boxes that are displayed during the installation of the application on the target computer. You will see an example of this in action when you look at configuring these dialog boxes later in this chapter.

Different Types of Setup Editors

The User Interface Editor consists of two different high-level installation modes:

▸ **Install**—Lists all the dialog boxes that will be displayed when the end user runs the installer. An example of how to configure this type of install is presented in the later sections.

▸ **Administrative Install**—Lists all the dialog boxes that will be displayed when a system administrator uploads the installer to a network location.

The predefined dialog boxes present in the Install and Administrative sections can be further subdivided into the following three categories:

▸ **Start dialog boxes**—Are displayed before the installation begins.

▸ **Progress dialog box**—Enable you to provide users with feedback on the progress of the installation.

▸ **End dialog boxes**—Displays that the installation has successfully completed. It can also be used to allow users to look at the Readme file or launch the application.

It is easy to rearrange the dialog boxes by dragging and dropping them onto proper locations. The default set of dialog boxes mentioned earlier always shows up in the installation sequence of the application, even if you have not configured these dialog boxes.

Now that you have taken a look at these dialog boxes, you must understand how you can configure these dialog boxes for the setup of FormattingApplication. Here are the steps:

1. Select the Welcome dialog box, and then select View, Properties to display its properties window. Set the `BannerBitmap` property to `sams.gif` by clicking Browse in the combo box and navigating to `Application Folder\Support` (where you already placed all the support files). Also set the `CopyrightWarning` and `WelcomeText` properties to appropriate values that suit your requirements.

2. You want the logo bitmap to be displayed on all of the default dialog boxes, so set the `BannerBitMap` property to `sams.gif` in the Installation Folder, Confirm Installation, Progress, and Finished dialog boxes as well.

How to Add Custom Dialog Boxes

In the last section, you configured the properties of the default dialog boxes. The default dialog boxes are very flexible and can form the core foundation for many of the simple installations. However, sometimes you want to customize the installation sequence to support your application's requirements. You can accomplish this by adding a new set of dialog boxes by using the Add Dialog menu. Select Start from the User Interface Editor and then choose Action, Add Dialog. You will see the dialog box shown in Figure 8.6.

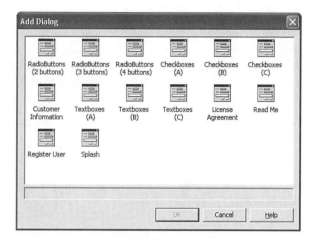

FIGURE 8.6   Add a custom dialog box.

From the previous set of dialog boxes, you can choose the dialog box that you want to add to your installation sequence. The following list briefly discusses the use of these dialog boxes and the dialog boxes already present by default.

- ▶ **Welcome**—Enables you to display an introductory window that can display text information from `CopyrightWarning` and `WelcomeText` properties.

- ▶ **Customer Information**—Enables you to display a window that requires customer information such as name and organization name. You can also force the user to enter a serial number and perform simple validations using this dialog box.

- ▶ **License Agreement**—Enables you to display licensing information to the users that requires them to agree to the licensing conditions. This licensing information is obtained from an external file, which is linked to this dialog box through the `LicenseFile` property that can be assigned a Rich Text Format (`.rtf`) file.

- ▶ **Read Me**—Displays information from the `.rtf` file specified by the `ReadMeFile` property.

- ▶ **Register User**—Enables users to complete the installation by asking them to register the installation. It displays a Register Now button that can either be used to launch an external executable or take them to a website. You specify the information about the external application and the arguments to be passed to them through the `Executable` and `Arguments` properties, respectively.

- ▶ **Splash**—Displayed at the beginning of the install to display the company logo that can be set through the `SplashBitmap` property.

Different Types of Setup Editors

As you can see, the Windows Installer is very restricted: You can't design custom windows and add them to the deployment project. However, by adopting a standard approach defined by Windows Installer, you can create installers that are not only consistent, but also simple to use. In this section, you add some additional dialog boxes to the installation sequence by using the Add Dialog menu. Here are the required steps:

1. Select Start from the User Interface Editor and then choose Action, Add Dialog.

2. In the Add Dialog box, select the Check Boxes (A), License Agreement, Read Me, and Splash dialog boxes, and add them to the Start sequence.

3. Drag and drop the dialog boxes to arrange them in proper sequence, as displayed in Figure 8.7.

FIGURE 8.7   User Interface Editor after adding custom dialog boxes.

4. Because you want the Sams logo bitmap to be displayed on all of these additional default dialogs also, set the `BannerBitMap` property to `sams.gif`.

5. Select the License Agreement dialog box and view its properties window. Change the `LicenseFile` property to `license.rtf`.

6. Select the Read Me dialog box and select View, Properties Window to bring up its properties window. Change the `ReadMeFile` property to `readme.rtf`.

7. You use the Checkboxes (A) dialog box to ask the user whether the demo shortcut placed in the User's Desktop folder should be installed. Modify the properties of this dialog box according to Figure 8.8.

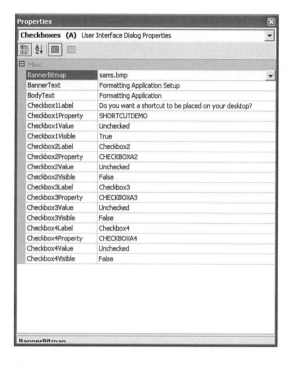

FIGURE 8.8   The Checkboxes (A) custom dialog box properties window.

8. Keep in mind that `CheckBox1Property` is already set to `SHORTCUTDEMO`. This value is the same as the `Condition` property that you set for the User's Desktop folder in the File System Editor. During installation, if the user selects this check box, the value of the `SHORTCUTDEMO` condition is set to `True`; as a result, the shortcut will be installed to the user's desktop. If the user does not select this check box, the `SHORTCUTDEMO` condition is set to `False` and the shortcut is not installed. In the previous window, note that you also set the `Visible` property for the rest of the check boxes to `False`, to prevent them from being displayed.

Building the Installer Package

Now that you have configured all the editors and set all the options, you can now build the installer project. To build the installer project, select Build, Build Solution to create the MSI installer package. After the installer has been successfully built, you will see `FormattingApplicationSetup.msi` and `Setup.exe` files in the Release directory.

Installing FormattingApplication

To install FormattingApplication, you can use any one of these options:

▶ Double-click on either the `FormattingApplicationSetup.msi` file or the `Setup.exe` file from Windows Explorer to start the installation.

▶ Right-click on the `FormattingApplication.msi` file and then choose Install from the context menu.

Now go through the actual steps involved in installing FormattingApplication on the end user's computer. Start the installation by double-clicking the `FormattingApplicationSetup.msi` file from Windows Explorer. You will see the following steps as you go through the installation.

1. **Splash screen**—This first dialog box appears after a pop-up window that states Preparing to Install. In this dialog box, you will see the bitmap that you specified using the `SplashBitmap` property.

2. **Welcome**—The next dialog box that is displayed is the Welcome dialog box. Because you set the `BannerBitMap` property to the Sams logo, you will see that displayed in the dialog box.

3. **Readme**—This dialog box displays the contents of the `readme.rtf` file that you specified using the `ReadMeFile` property.

4. **License Agreement**—This dialog box displays the contents of the `license.rtf` file that you specified using the `LicenseFile` property. The Next button in the dialog box is enabled only when the user selects the I Agree option, thereby making sure that the user agrees to the licensing terms and conditions.

5. **Shortcut Check Box**—This dialog box asks the users whether they want a shortcut to the application to be installed on the desktop. When the user checks the check box, the condition `SHORTCUTDEMO` is set to `True`, and a shortcut to the application is installed on the user's desktop.

6. **Installation Folder**—This dialog box displays the path to the installation folder where the application will be installed. It also provides the users with an option to change the installation folder, if required. Using this dialog box, you can also specify whether you want to install the application only for yourself or whether you want to make this application available to everyone who will be using this computer. In addition, you can find out how much disk space is required for installing the application by clicking the Disk Cost button.

7. **Disk Cost**—This dialog box helps you to identify the suitable drive (one that has enough space) in which the application can be installed. Apart from displaying the amount of disk space required for installing the application, it displays the free space available in each drive.

8

8. **Confirm Installation**—This dialog box enables you to provide the final confirmation before the application installation can proceed. Clicking the Next button on this dialog box installs the application on the user's computer.

9. **Finished Installation**—When you click the Next button in the Confirm Installation dialog box, the installation starts and the progress of the installation is displayed in the Progress dialog box through a progress bar. When the installation is complete, you get the Installation Complete dialog box, which shows that the installation has been successfully completed.

Uninstalling the Application

Now that you have successfully installed the application, you can see what it takes to uninstall the application from the end user's computer. The process of uninstalling the application is very simple: It just requires you to open the Add/Remove Programs window by going to Start, Control Panel and then double-clicking the Add/Remove Programs icon. Now all you have to do is to click the Remove button. A confirmation dialog box (asking you to confirm the uninstall process) appears. If you click Yes, the uninstall process begins and the application is completely removed.

TIP

When you right-click on the `FormattingApplicationSetup.msi` file from Windows explorer, you will also see the Repair option in the context menu. This is very useful when you have accidentally deleted any of the application-related files from the machine and you want to repair the application so that it is returned to its original state.

8

It is also possible for you to uninstall the application by right-clicking `FormattingApplicationSetup.msi` from Windows Explorer and selecting Uninstall from the context menu.

Summary

In this chapter, you gained an understanding of the different aspects of deploying a Windows Forms application. This chapter started with an introduction to deployment by considering the fundamentals of deployment, and then went on to discuss the different types of deployments supported by .NET. Specifically, this chapter covered the following two deployment types:

▸ XCOPY deployment

▸ Windows Installer–based deployment

Summary

After considering both types of deployments, this chapter highlighted the features of Windows Installer that make it the preferred choice for deploying Windows Forms applications. After the initial discussion on the deployment methods, it then considered a walk-through and demonstrated the procedures to be followed for deploying a Windows Forms application using the Visual Studio .NET installer. Along the way, it demonstrated how to customize the installation sequence by making use of the various editors. It then discussed the steps involved in actually installing the application on the end user's computer. Finally, it covered how to uninstall the application by using the Add/Remove Programs dialog box.

Further Reading

Microsoft Windows Installer SDK site, http://msdn.microsoft.com/library/default.asp?url=/library/en-us/msi/setup/windows_installer_start_page.asp.

8

9 PRINTING

IN BRIEF

Developers familiar with Visual Basic 6 will recall that whenever printing functionality was required in their application, they would use the `Printer` object to implement the required functionality. With the release of Visual Basic .NET, the `Printer` object has been rendered obsolete by the new GDI+ library. Now, whenever developers wants to add printing functionality to their application, they import the `System.Drawing.Printing` namespace.

This chapter looks at the classes that are used to provide printing support in your applications. It also demonstrates its properties and methods and gives an example of how to use them in your applications.

WHAT YOU NEED

SOFTWARE REQUIREMENTS	Windows 2000, XP, or 2003 .NET Framework 1.1 SDK Visual Studio .NET 2003 with Visual Basic .NET installed Administrative rights on the machine
HARDWARE REQUIREMENTS	PC desktop or laptop
SKILL REQUIREMENTS	Knowledge of Visual Basic .NET Knowledge of the .NET Framework

PRINTING AT A GLANCE

Printing in .NET

Printing is an integral part of every complete Windows-based application. Providing robust printing capabilities is essential to the success of an application. .NET provides a rich set of classes through which you easily can create sophisticated printing capabilities in your application.

The .NET Framework provides a document-centric approach to creating print functionalities. Whereas the `System.Windows.Forms` namespace provides seamless integration with all the standard print dialog boxes (such as Print Preview, Page Setup, and Print), the `System.Drawing.Printing` namespace offers numerous classes for extensibility and customization. Before discussing those classes, this section looks at a simple example to demonstrate how to enumerate all the printers available to a computer. Listing 9.1 provides an example of how to accomplish this.

LISTING 9.1
Enumerating All the Installed Printers

```
Imports System
Imports System.Drawing
Imports System.Drawing.Printing

Public Class InstalledPrintersExample
  Inherits System.Windows.Forms.Form
  Private WithEvents ComboBox1 As New System.Windows.Forms.ComboBox

  Public Sub New()
    InitializeComponent()
  End Sub

  Private Sub InitializeComponent()
    Me.ComboBox1.DropDownStyle = System.Windows.Forms.ComboBoxStyle.DropDownList
    Me.ComboBox1.Location = New System.Drawing.Point(48, 88)
    Me.ComboBox1.Name = "ComboBox1"
    Me.ComboBox1.Size = New System.Drawing.Size(226, 30)
    Me.Controls.Add(Me.ComboBox1)
    Me.Name = "InstalledPrintersExample"
    Me.Text = "Installed Printers"
  End Sub

Private Sub Form1_Load(ByVal sender As System.Object, ByVal e As System.EventArgs)
➥ _
```

9

Printing in .NET

LISTING 9.1
Continued

```
    Handles MyBase.Load
    Dim printerName As String
    For Each printerName In PrinterSettings.InstalledPrinters
        ComboBox1.Items.Add(printerName)
    Next printerName
  End Sub

  Public Shared Sub Main()
    Application.Run(New InstalledPrintersExample)
  End Sub
End Class
```

Note that Listing 9.1 imports the `System.Drawing.Printing` namespace so that all of its print-related classes can be used from within the application. After that, it declares a combo box control and then set its properties in the `InitializeComponent` method. The `Load` event of the form is used to enumerate all the installed printers in the computer. `InstalledPrinters` is a property exposed by the `PrinterSettings` object that returns all the installed printers in the form of a `StringCollection` object. **1** You will see more on the `PrinterSettings` class in the "`PrinterSettings` Class" section of this chapter. For now, understand that it provides information about how a document is printed, including the printer that prints it. When you execute the code in Listing 9.1, you will see output that is somewhat similar to Figure 9.1.

FIGURE 9.1 Enumerating all the installed printers.

The output shown in Figure 9.1 will vary in your machine: It will display the printers connected to your machine.

Defining a Document

As mentioned, the `System.Drawing.Printing` namespace contains all the classes required for providing printing support. The main class in this namespace is the `PrintDocument` class, which represents an object that sends output to the printer. The role of this class is so central that you can achieve simple and complex printing tasks by using this class alone.

A print job consists of one or more pages printed on a particular printer, and it is represented by the `PrintDocument` class. Generally, a program begins the process of printing by creating an object of type `PrintDocument`:

```
Dim printDoc As New PrintDocument()
```

You could create this object for each print job. However, if you're using the standard print dialog boxes, you might want to retain those settings in the `PrintDocument` object and use the same instance for the duration of the program. In that case, you would define `printDoc` as a field and create it only once. `PrintDocument` has only four properties, which are shown in Table 9.1.

TABLE 9.1

Properties of the `PrintDocument` Class

Property	Description
`PrinterSettings`	Gets or sets the settings of the printer that prints the document, in the form of a `PrinterSettings` object.
`DefaultPageSettings`	Gets or sets page settings that are used as defaults for all pages to be printed.
`DocumentName`	Gets or sets the document name that is displayed while printing the document. By default, this property is initialized to the string value `"document"`.
`PrintController`	Gets or sets the print controller that guides the printing process.

When you create a new `PrintDocument` object, the `PrinterSettings` property indicates the default printer. If you want, you can change the `PrinterSettings` property or individual properties of the `PrinterSettings` property. For example, this code retrieves the `PrinterSettings` object by invoking the `PrinterSettings` property of the `PrintDocument` object and then sets the `Copies` property of the `PrinterSettings` object to 2:

```
printDoc.PrinterSettings.Copies = 2
```

9

Defining a Document

The `DefaultPageSettings` property is initially set from the `DefaultPageSettings` property of the `PrinterSettings` object. You can also change that property by using the following line of code:

```
printDoc.DefaultPageSettings.Landscape = True
```

Here the `Landscape` property of the `PageSettings` object is set to `true`, to indicate that the page will be printed in landscape format.

Events Supported by the `PrintDocument` Class

So far, you have seen the properties of the `PrintDocument` class. This section walks you through the different events triggered by the `PrintDocument` class. Table 9.2 provides a listing of these events.

TABLE 9.2

Events Supported by the `PrintDocument` Class

Event	Description
BeginPrint	Invoked when the `Print` method is called but before the first page of the document prints
EndPrint	Fired when the last page of the document has printed
PrintPage	Occurs when output to print the current page is needed and also to indicate whether there are more pages to be printed
QueryPageSettings	Fired immediately before each `PrintPage` event

Out of the four events supported by the `PrintDocument` class, the `BeginPrint` and `EndPrint` events are triggered once for every print job. The `QueryPageSettings` and `PrintPage` events are triggered for every page in the print job. You can use the `PrintPage` event to configure different page settings for each page. The `PrintPage` event handler receives an argument of type `PrintPageEventArgs`. The `PrintPageEventArgs` object provides important properties that you might need in your application. Table 9.3 provides the listing of the properties of the `PrintPageEventArgs` object that are specific to the `PrintPage` event.

TABLE 9.3

Properties Supported by the `PrintPageEventArgs` Class

Property	Description
Cancel	Used to indicate whether the current job should be canceled
Graphics	Gets the `Graphics` object that is used to paint the page

TABLE 9.3

Continued

Property	Description
HasMorePages	Gets or sets a value that indicates whether additional pages need to be printed
MarginBounds	Fired immediately before each PrintPage event
PageBounds	Gets the rectangular area that represents the total area of the page
PageSettings	Gets the page settings for the current page

TIP

The Cancel property of the PrintPageEventArgs object is very useful, in that you can set that property to True to abort the current printing job. Setting Cancel to True causes the operating system to attempt to cease the printing of pages already in the queue.

Methods of the PrintDocument Class

To initiate printing, you need to call the Print method, which is the only method in PrintDocument that isn't associated with an event. The Print method does not return until the program is finished printing the document. The application cannot respond to any user input during this time. In the interim, the PrintDocument event handlers installed by the program are called—first is the BeginPrint handler, then come the QueryPageSettings and PrintPage handlers for each page, and, finally, the EndPrint handler is called.

The PrintPage method is an important event that can be used to wire an event handler to the PrintPage event and write the code to send output to the printer. The event handler receives an argument of type System.Drawing.Printing. PrintPageEventArgs, containing data related to the PrintPage event. As you have already seen, the Graphics property of the PrintPageEventArgs object can be used to obtain a System.Drawing.Graphics object. This Graphics object represents a print page. To send a string to the printer, for example, you use the DrawString method of the Graphics class. Of course, you can also call other methods of the Graphics class, such as FillRectangle and DrawEllipse.

The Graphics class encapsulates a GDI+ drawing surface and is involved in essentially all graphics operations that a program performs. It provides methods for drawing text and a wide variety of shapes. Now that you understand the basics of the PrintDocument object, the next section walks through the procedures involved in printing a document.

9

Printing a Document

Now that you have understood the methods exposed by the PrintDocument class, you are ready to look at the steps involved in printing a document. This section starts by detailing the steps involved in printing a document:

1. Write a procedure that uses the Graphics class to create the desired output.

2. Create an instance of the PrintDocument class.

3. Connect the procedure created in step 1 to the PrintPage event of the PrintDocument object. You do this with Visual Basic's AddressOf operator.

4. Call the PrintDocument object's Print method.

Listing 9.2 provides an example that illustrates these steps.

LISTING 9.2

Using the PrintDocument Object to Print a Document

```
Imports System
Imports System.Drawing
Imports System.Drawing.Printing

Public Class PrintingExample
  Inherits System.Windows.Forms.Form
  Private WithEvents btnPrint As New System.Windows.Forms.Button
  Public Sub New()
    InitializeComponent()
  End Sub

  Private Sub InitializeComponent()
    Me.btnPrint.Location = New System.Drawing.Point(86, 180)
    Me.btnPrint.Name = "btnPrint"
    Me.btnPrint.Size = New System.Drawing.Size(96, 32)
    Me.btnPrint.Text = "Print"
    Me.Controls.Add(Me.btnPrint)
    Me.Name = "PrintingExample"
    Me.Text = "PrintingExample"
  End Sub

  Private Sub btnPrint_Click(ByVal sender As System.Object, _
    ByVal e As System.EventArgs) Handles btnPrint.Click
    'Create a PrintDocument object
    Dim printDoc As New PrintDocument
    'Link the printing procedure with the PrintPage event.
    AddHandler printDoc.PrintPage, AddressOf Me.OnPrintPage
```

9

LISTING 9.2
Continued

```
    'Start printing.
    printDoc.Print()
  End Sub
  Private Sub DrawPage(ByVal g As Graphics)                                    1
    'Define a rectangle.
    Dim r As New Rectangle(25, 25, 200, 150)
    'Draw it with a black pen.
    g.DrawRectangle(Pens.Black, r)
    'Add some text.
    Dim f As New Font("Times", 24)
    g.DrawString("Printing", f, Brushes.Red, 70, 80)
  End Sub

  Private Sub OnPrintPage(ByVal sender As Object, ByVal e As PrintPageEventArgs)
    DrawPage(e.Graphics)
  End Sub

  Private Sub Form1_Paint(ByVal sender As Object, _
    ByVal e As System.Windows.Forms.PaintEventArgs) Handles MyBase.Paint
    DrawPage(e.Graphics)
  End Sub

  Public Shared Sub Main()
    Application.Run(New PrintingExample)
  End Sub
End Class
```

As mentioned before, the first step is to write the procedure that uses Graphics class methods to create the output. This procedure can have any name you like, but it must have the correct signature. Listing 9.2 uses a procedure named DrawPage that performs this. **1**

You should pay attention to two things in the DrawPage procedure. First, it is passed a Graphics object as part of the PrintPageEventArgs object. This is the Graphics object that is connected to the printer and, therefore, is the Graphics object that you'll use to create output. Second, the same code is used in the Paint event of the Form object to draw the screen contents.

The remaining three steps are accomplished together in the Click event of the command button. The result is the box and text printed on the system's default printer. In this example, the code used for screen display and for producing printer output are located in a single procedure and shared by both of them. From both of these places, the DrawPage method is invoked and passed in a reference to the Graphics method. This enables the same drawing code to perform double duty, for screen display and printing.

9

Using the Print Dialogs

The beauty of printing in .NET is the way that the print document so elegantly fits together with the print dialogs.

The `System.Drawing.Printing` namespace has three different print dialogs:

- `PrintPreviewDialog`
- `PrintDialog`
- `PageSetupDialog`

In addition, there is a `PrintPreviewControl` class that doesn't include the surrounding dialog, providing you with greater UI design flexibility. The next few sections demonstrate the usage of these dialogs.

Using `PrintPreviewDialog` Control

The Windows Forms `PrintPreviewDialog` control is a preconfigured dialog box that is used to display how a `PrintDocument` will appear after it is printed. This control can be used to create a simple and quick solution for displaying the print preview. The control contains buttons for printing, zooming in, displaying one or multiple pages, and closing the dialog box.

TIP

To use the `PrintPreviewDialog` control at runtime, you must have a printer installed on your computer, either locally or through a network, because this is partly how the `PrintPreviewDialog` component determines how a document will look when printed.

A key property of the `PrintPreviewDialog` control is `Document`, which enables you to set the document to be previewed. The document that is set through the `PrintDocument` object must be of type `PrintDocument`. When you have set the document property to an appropriate value, you can invoke the `ShowDialog` method of the control to display the preview dialog box. Another property of the `PrintPreviewDialog` control that you will use frequently is `UseAntiAlias`. Using this Boolean property, you can make the text appear smoother. Note, however, that it can also make the display slower.

The `PrintPreviewDialog` control uses the `PrinterSettings` class to configure printer settings. Additionally, the `PrintPreviewDialog` control uses the `PageSettings` class for configuring page-related settings. The print document specified in the `PrintPreviewDialog` control's `Document` property refers to instances of both the `PrinterSettings` and `PageSettings` classes, and these are used to render the document in the preview window.

> **NOTE**
>
> Note that because `PrintPreviewControl` is contained within a `PrintPreviewDialog` control, you can access the properties of `PrintPreviewControl` through the `PrintPreviewDialog` control. For example, you can access the `Columns` property of `PrintPreviewControl` using the following line.
>
> ```
> MessageBox.Show(PrintPreviewDialog1.PrintPreviewControl.Columns)
> ```
>
> The `Columns` property determines the number of pages displayed vertically on the control.

How to View Pages Using the `PrintPreviewDialog` Control

You can use the `ShowDialog` method to display the dialog box specifying the `PrintDocument` to use. In the example shown in Listing 9.3, the `Button` control's `Click` event handler opens an instance of the `PrintPreviewDialog` control. The print document is specified in the `Document` property.

LISTING 9.3

Using the `PrintPreviewDialog` control

```
Imports System
Imports System.Drawing
Imports System.Drawing.Printing

Public Class PrintPreviewDialogExample
  Inherits System.Windows.Forms.Form

  Private WithEvents PrintPreviewDialog1 As New PrintPreviewDialog
  Private WithEvents printDoc As New PrintDocument
  Private WithEvents btnPrint As New System.Windows.Forms.Button

  Public Sub New()
    InitializeComponent()
  End Sub

  Private Sub InitializeComponent()
    'Set the size, location, and name.
    Me.PrintPreviewDialog1.ClientSize = New System.Drawing.Size(400, 300)
    Me.PrintPreviewDialog1.Location = New System.Drawing.Point(29, 29)
    Me.PrintPreviewDialog1.Name = "PrintPreviewDialog1"
    'Set the minimum size the dialog can be resized to.
    Me.PrintPreviewDialog1.MinimumSize = New System.Drawing.Size(375, 250)
    'Set the UseAntiAlias property to true, which will allow the
```

9

Using the Print Dialogs

LISTING 9.3
Continued

```
    'operating system to smooth fonts.
    Me.PrintPreviewDialog1.UseAntiAlias = True
    Me.btnPrint.Location = New System.Drawing.Point(86, 180)
    Me.btnPrint.Name = "btnPrint"
    Me.btnPrint.Size = New System.Drawing.Size(96, 32)
    Me.btnPrint.Text = "Print"
    Me.Controls.Add(Me.btnPrint)
    Me.Name = "PrintingExample"
    Me.Text = "PrintingExample"
    AddHandler printDoc.PrintPage, AddressOf Me.OnPrintPage
  End Sub

  Private Sub OnPrintPage(ByVal sender As Object, ByVal e As _
    System.Drawing.Printing.PrintPageEventArgs)
    'The following code will render a simple message on the document in the control
    Dim text As String = "PrintPreviewDialog Example"
    Dim printFont As New Font("Arial", 35, System.Drawing.FontStyle.Regular)
    e.Graphics.DrawString(text, printFont, System.Drawing.Brushes.Black, 10, 10)
  End Sub

  Private Sub btnPrint_Click(ByVal sender As System.Object, _
    ByVal e As System.EventArgs) Handles btnPrint.Click
    'Link the printing procedure with the PrintPage event
    PrintPreviewDialog1.Document = printDoc
    'Call the ShowDialog method
    PrintPreviewDialog1.ShowDialog()
  End Sub

  Public Shared Sub Main()
    Application.Run(New PrintPreviewDialogExample)
  End Sub
End Class
```

1 `PrintPreviewDialog1.Document = printDoc`

In Listing 9.3, the InitalizeComponent method sets the various properties of the PrintPreviewDialog control. In the Click event of the button, the Document property of the PrintPreviewDialog control is assigned the instance of the PrintDocument object. **1** Output produced by the listing is shown in Figure 9.2.

As you can see from the output, the Print Preview dialog box provides functionalities such as zooming in, zooming out, printing, and displaying multiple pages.

FIGURE 9.2   Displaying print preview using `PrintPreviewDialog`.

Using `PrintDialog` Control

The `PrintDialog` control is a predefined dialog box that can be used to perform a number of activities, such as selecting a printer, choosing the pages to print, and determining other print-related settings in Windows applications. The `PrintDialog` class inherits from the `CommonDialog` class.

To display the print dialog box, use the `ShowDialog` method to display the dialog box at runtime. When you add a `PrintDialog` control to the form, it appears in the tray at the bottom of the Windows Forms designer. To use the `PrintDialog` class, you need to perform the following steps:

1. Create an instance of the `PrintDialog` class.

2. Set the `PrintDialog` object's `Document` property to the `PrintDocument` object that is being used for the print job.

3. Display the Printer Settings dialog box by calling the `ShowDialog` method.

4. Verify that the user closed the Printer Settings dialog box by clicking OK. Then start the print job by calling the `PrintDocument.Print` method. Because the `PrintDialog` object was already associated with the print job in step 2, the settings that the user chooses in this dialog box are automatically applied to the print job.

Listing 9.4 shows how to use the `PrintDialog` class to display the Printer Settings dialog box.

LISTING 9.4
Using `PrintDialog` to Configure Print Settings

```
Imports System
Imports System.Drawing
```

Using the Print Dialogs

LISTING 9.4
Continued

```vb
Imports System.Drawing.Printing
Public Class PrintDialogExample
  Inherits System.Windows.Forms.Form
  Private WithEvents btnPrint As New System.Windows.Forms.Button
  Public Sub New()
    InitializeComponent()
  End Sub

  Private Sub InitializeComponent()
    Me.btnPrint.Location = New System.Drawing.Point(86, 180)
    Me.btnPrint.Name = "btnPrint"
    Me.btnPrint.Size = New System.Drawing.Size(96, 32)
    Me.btnPrint.Text = "Print"
    Me.Controls.Add(Me.btnPrint)
    Me.Name = "PrintDialogExample"
    Me.Text = "PrintDialogExample"
  End Sub

  Private Sub btnPrint_Click(ByVal sender As System.Object, _
    ByVal e As System.EventArgs) Handles btnPrint.Click
    'Create a PrintDocument object
    Dim printDoc As New PrintDocument
    'Link the printing procedure with the PrintPage event.
    AddHandler printDoc.PrintPage, AddressOf Me.OnPrintPage
    Dim prDlg As New PrintDialog
    prDlg.Document = printDoc
    'If the user closes dialog box with OK, start printing
```

1   `If prDlg.ShowDialog = DialogResult.OK Then`

2
```vb
        'Start printing
        printDoc.Print()
```
```vb
    End If   End Sub

  Private Sub DrawPage(ByVal g As Graphics)
    'Define a rectangle.
    Dim r As New Rectangle(25, 25, 200, 150)
    'Draw it with a black pen.
    g.DrawRectangle(Pens.Black, r)
    'Add some text.
    Dim f As New Font("Times", 24)
    g.DrawString("Printing", f, Brushes.Red, 70, 80)
  End Sub
```

9

LISTING 9.4
Continued

```
Private Sub OnPrintPage(ByVal sender As Object, ByVal e As PrintPageEventArgs)
  DrawPage(e.Graphics)
End Sub

Private Sub Form1_Paint(ByVal sender As Object, _
  ByVal e As System.Windows.Forms.PaintEventArgs) Handles MyBase.Paint
  DrawPage(e.Graphics)
End Sub

Public Shared Sub Main()
  Application.Run(New PrintDialogExample)
End Sub
End Class
```

In the `Click` event of the button, an instance of the `PrintDialog` class is created. After that, the `Document` property of the `PrintDialog` object is set to the `PrintDocument` object that is being used for the print job. Then the code displays the Printer Settings dialog box by calling the `ShowDialog` method. ■1 In the dialog box, if the user clicks OK, the print job is started by invoking the `Print` method of the `PrintDocument` object. ■2

Executing the code in Listing 9.4 results in the output that is shown in Figure 9.3.

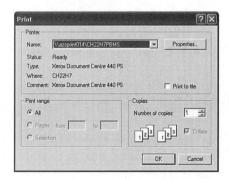

FIGURE 9.3   Configuring printer settings using the `PrintDialog` control.

Using the `PageSetupDialog` Control

As the name suggests, the `PageSetupDialog` control is used to set page details for printing in Windows applications. You can use this dialog box to let users set page preferences before printing. Some of the page preferences you can set through this control are border and margin adjustments, headers and footers, and portrait versus landscape orientation.

Using the Print Dialogs

You use the `PageSetupDialog` class in a manner that parallels the technique for `PrintDialog` class, covered in the previous sections. Even with this control, you need to associate it with the `PrintDocument` object and then display it to the user.

TIP

When possible, you should use the default dialogs, such as `PrintPreviewDialog`, `PrintDialog`, and `PageSetupDialog`, because they enable you to create applications whose basic functionality is immediately familiar to users.

To display this dialog, use the `ShowDialog` method. The `PageSetupDialog` class has properties that relate to either a single page or any document. Additionally, the `PageSetupDialog` class can be used to determine specific printer settings, which are stored in the `PrinterSettings` class. Table 9.4 lists some of the important properties of the `PageSetupDialog` control.

TABLE 9.4

Important Properties of the `PageSetupDialog` Control

Property	Description
PageSettings	Enables you to get or set a value that specifies the page settings
PrinterSettings	Enables you to get or set the printer settings that are modified when the user clicks the Printer button in the dialog
ShowHelp	Gets or sets a value indicating whether the Help button is visible
ShowNetwork	Gets or sets a value indicating whether the Network button is visible

You can see an example of how to use the printer settings in Listing 9.5.

LISTING 9.5

Using `PageSetupDialog` to Configure Page Settings

```
Imports System
Imports System.Drawing
Imports System.Drawing.Printing

Public Class PageSetupDialogExample
  Inherits System.Windows.Forms.Form

  Public Sub New()
    InitializeComponent()
  End Sub


  Private WithEvents btnShowDialog As New System.Windows.Forms.Button
  Private WithEvents lstSettings As New System.Windows.Forms.ListBox
  Private WithEvents PageSetupDialog1 As New System.Windows.Forms.PageSetupDialog
```

LISTING 9.5
Continued

```
Private Sub InitializeComponent()
  Me.btnShowDialog = New System.Windows.Forms.Button
  Me.lstSettings = New System.Windows.Forms.ListBox
  Me.btnShowDialog.Location = New System.Drawing.Point(90, 206)
  Me.btnShowDialog.Size = New System.Drawing.Size(80, 30)
  Me.btnShowDialog.Name = "btnShowDialog"
  Me.btnShowDialog.Text = "Show Dialog"
  Me.lstSettings.Location = New System.Drawing.Point(60, 18)
  Me.lstSettings.Name = "lstSettings"
  Me.lstSettings.Size = New System.Drawing.Size(195, 180)
  Me.Controls.Add(Me.lstSettings)
  Me.Controls.Add(Me.btnShowDialog)
  Me.Name = "PageSetupDialogExample"
  Me.Text = "PageSetupDialog Example"
End Sub


Private Sub btnShowDialog_Click(ByVal sender As System.Object, _
  ByVal e As System.EventArgs) Handles btnShowDialog.Click
  'Initialize the dialog's PrinterSettings property to hold user-defined printer
  ➥settings
  PageSetupDialog1.PageSettings = New PageSettings                        1
  'Initialize dialog's PrinterSettings property to hold user-defined printer
  ➥settings
  PageSetupDialog1.PrinterSettings = New PrinterSettings
  PageSetupDialog1.ShowNetwork = False
  Dim result As DialogResult = PageSetupDialog1.ShowDialog()              2
  'If the result is OK, display selected settings in lstSettings
  If (result = DialogResult.OK) Then
    With PageSetupDialog1
      lstSettings.Items.Add(.PageSettings.PrinterResolution)
      lstSettings.Items.Add(.PageSettings.PaperSize)
      lstSettings.Items.Add(.PageSettings.Landscape)
      lstSettings.Items.Add(.PrinterSettings.PrinterName)
      lstSettings.Items.Add(.PrinterSettings.PrintRange)
    End With
  End If
End Sub
End Class
```

In the Click event of the button, the PageSetupDialog class is initialized with
the user-defined page settings and print settings by setting its PageSettings and
PrinterSettings properties. **1** Then the dialog box is displayed using the
ShowDialog method. **2** The dialog box is shown in Figure 9.4.

Using the Print Dialogs

FIGURE 9.4   Configuring page settings using the PageSetupDialog control.

If the user clicks OK in the dialog box in Figure 9.4, the code retrieves the selected settings and adds them to the list box. This is shown in Figure 9.5.

FIGURE 9.5   Displaying selected settings in a list box.

Using PrintPreviewControl

PrintPreviewControl is used to display a PrintDocument as it will appear when printed. As with the PrintPreviewDialog control, a key property of this control is Document, which sets the document to be previewed. The document must be a PrintDocument object. The Columns and Rows properties determine the number of pages displayed horizontally and vertically on the control. You can also use the UseAntiAlias property to make text appear smoother.

TIP
`PrintPreviewControl` **has no buttons or other user-interface elements, so typically you use it only if you want to write your own print-preview user interface. If you want the standard user interface, use a** `PrintPreviewDialog` **control.**

Listing 9.6 demonstrates how to use `PrintPreviewControl` to display the print preview.

LISTING 9.6
Using `PrintPreviewControl`

```
Imports System
Imports System.Drawing
Imports System.Drawing.Printing

Public Class PrintPreviewControlExample
  Inherits System.Windows.Forms.Form
  Private WithEvents PrintPreviewControl1 As New PrintPreviewControl
  Private WithEvents printDoc As New PrintDocument
  Private WithEvents btnPrint As New System.Windows.Forms.Button

  Public Sub New()
    InitializeComponent()
  End Sub

  Private Sub InitializeComponent()
    'Set location, name, and dock style for PrintPreviewControl1.
    Me.PrintPreviewControl1.Location = New Point(88, 80)
    Me.PrintPreviewControl1.Name = "PrintPreviewControl1"
    Me.PrintPreviewControl1.Dock = DockStyle.Fill
    'Set the Document property to the PrintDocument                    1
    Me.PrintPreviewControl1.Document = printDoc
    'Set the zoom to 50 percent.
    Me.PrintPreviewControl1.Zoom = 0.5
    'Set the document name. This will be displayed when the document loads into the
    ➥control
    Me.PrintPreviewControl1.Document.DocumentName = "c:\Temp\DocumentName.txt"
    'Set the UseAntiAlias property to true so fonts are smoothed
    Me.PrintPreviewControl1.UseAntiAlias = True
    'Add the control to the form.
    Me.Controls.Add(Me.PrintPreviewControl1)
    AddHandler printDoc.PrintPage, AddressOf Me.OnPrintPage
  End Sub
```

Using the Print Dialogs

LISTING 9.6
Continued

```
Private Sub OnPrintPage(ByVal sender As Object, ByVal e As System.Drawing.Printing
.PrintPageEventArgs)
    'The following code will render a simple message on the document in the control
    Dim text As String = "PrintPreviewControl Example"
    Dim printFont As New Font("Arial", 35, System.Drawing.FontStyle.Regular)
    e.Graphics.DrawString(text, printFont, System.Drawing.Brushes.Black, 10, 10)
End Sub

Public Shared Sub Main()
    Application.Run(New PrintPreviewControlExample)
End Sub
End Class
```

In this example, the `InitalizeComponent` method is used to initialize the various properties of `PrintPreviewControl` such as `Document` and `Zoom`. **1** As with the previous examples, the key property is the `Document` property, which is used to associate the `PrintDocument` object with the `PrintPreviewControl`. When you execute the code, you will see output as in Figure 9.6.

FIGURE 9.6   Displaying the print preview using `PrintPreviewControl`.

As shown in Figure 9.6, `PrintPreviewControl` simply displays the Print Preview dialog box without displaying any of the related functionalities, such as zoom in and zoom out.

Dealing with Settings

So far, you have looked at .NET printing at its simplest. There's a lot more to it, as you might well suspect. It's unavoidable that printing involves certain complications that are not present for screen display:

- ▶ Printer settings associated with a print job—These settings are related to the printer hardware, controlling things such as the printer to use, the paper source, and the number of copies.

- ▶ Page settings—These control page-related characteristics, such as paper size and margin.

.NET makes it relatively painless to deal with these settings. The `PrinterSettings` class handles printer settings. The following sections discuss the `PrinterSettings` and `PageSettings` classes in detail.

PrinterSettings **Class**

This class specifies information about how a document is printed, including the printer that prints it. Typically, you access `PrinterSettings` through `PrintDocument.PrinterSettings` or `PageSettings.PrinterSettings` properties to modify printer settings. One of the most common printer settings that you are likely to use is `PrinterName`, which specifies the printer to print to. Table 9.5 lists the important properties of the `PrinterSettings` class.

TABLE 9.5

Important Properties of the `PrinterSettings` **Class**

Property	Description
CanDuplex	(Read-only) Gets a value indicating whether the printer supports double-sided printing
Collate	Enables you to get or set a value indicating whether the printed document is collated
Copies	Enables you to get or set the number of copies of the document to print
DefaultPageSettings	Gets the default page settings for this printer in the form of a `PageSettings` object
FromPage	Gets or sets the page number of the first page to print
InstalledPrinters	Gets the names of all printers installed on the computer in the form of a `StringCollection` object
IsDefaultPrinter	Returns `true` or `false`, depending on whether the current printer is the default printer

9

Dealing with Settings

TABLE 9.5

Continued

Property	Description
IsValid	Gets a value indicating whether the PrinterName property references a valid printer
MaximumCopies	Gets the maximum number of copies that can be printed at a time
PaperSizes	Gets the paper sizes that the printer supports
PaperSources	Gets the paper source trays that are available on the printer
PrinterName	Gets or sets the name of the printer to use
PrintToFile	Gets or sets a value that specifies whether the printing output is sent to a file instead of a port
SupportsColor	Enables you to determine whether the printer supports color printing

The following lines of code demonstrate how to use the PrinterSettings property of the PrintDocument class to retrieve the PrinterSettings object. When you have a reference to the PageSettings object, you can set various properties, such as PrinterName.

```
'Create a PrintDocument object
  Dim printDoc As New PrintDocument
  Dim printerName As String = "TestPrinter"
  'Link the printing procedure with the PrintPage event.
  AddHandler printDoc.PrintPage, AddressOf Me.OnPrintPage
  Dim prtSettings As PrinterSettings = printDoc.PrinterSettings
  prtSettings.PrinterName = printerName
  If prtSettings.IsValid Then
    printDoc.Print()
  Else
    MessageBox.Show("Supply a Valid Printer Name")
  End If
```

Before invoking the Print method of the PrintDocument object, the code checks to see whether there is a valid printer with the assigner printer name by checking the IsValid property of the PrinterSettings object.

Role of PageSettings Class in Printing

As you have already seen, the PageSettings class is used to specify settings that modify the way a page will be printed, such as paper orientation, the size of the page, and the margins. Each of these settings is represented as a property of the PageSettings class. Important properties of the PageSettings class are shown in Table 9.6.

TABLE 9.6

Important Properties of the `PageSettings` Class

Property	Description
Bounds	Enables you to get the size of the page, taking into account the page orientation specified by the Landscape property
Color	Enables you to get or set a value that indicates whether the page should be printed in color
Landscape	(Boolean) Enables you to get or set a value indicating whether the page is printed in landscape or portrait orientation
Margins	Enables you to get or set the margins for this page
PaperSize	Enables you to get or set the paper size for the page
PaperSource	Enables you to get or set the paper source for the page

In the following lines of code, the `DefaultPageSettings` property of the `PrintDocument` object is used to get a reference to the `PageSettings` object. When it has the reference to the `PageSettings` object, you can set the various properties of the `PageSettings` class.

```
'Create a PrintDocument object
Dim printDoc As New PrintDocument
Dim pgSettings As PageSettings = printDoc.DefaultPageSettings
pgSettings.Color = True
pgSettings.Landscape = True
'Link the printing procedure with the PrintPage event.
AddHandler printDoc.PrintPage, AddressOf Me.OnPrintPage
'Start printing.
printDoc.Print()
```

Finally, the `Print` method of the `PrintDocument` object is invoked to print the document. Because the `Color` property is set to `True`, you will find that the document is printed in color.

Summary

The rich class library that the .NET Framework supplies offers truly significant improvements in the way printing from an application is handled. As you have seen in this chapter, .NET treats printing as just like any other graphical operation. Printing in .NET is accomplished using a set of classes contained in the `System.Drawing.Printing` namespace, whose classes combine the fine-grain control of the Win32 API with the relative ease of Visual Basic's classic `Printer` object. The `PrintDocument` class is the most important of these classes; it enables you define an object that can then be sent to a destination such as a printer or a Print Preview display dialog box.

Further Reading

MSDN documentation on Visual Basic .NET

Payne, Chris. *Sam's Teach Yourself .NET Windows Forms in 21 Days*. Pearson Education, 2002.

Mackenzie, Duncan, and Kent Sharkey. *Sam's Teach Yourself VB .NET in 21 Days*. Pearson Education, 2001.

9

10 ADVANCED WINDOWS FORMS TECHNIQUES

IN BRIEF

So far you've looked at different types of simple user interface controls and learned how to use them to create Windows applications. In this chapter, you will expand your knowledge beyond these simple controls by taking a look at some of the advanced Windows Forms techniques that enable you to create effective Windows applications that are not only easy to use, but also intuitive.

To start, this chapter discusses how to add controls dynamically in code and also demonstrates how to hook up events with those dynamic controls. It moves on to advanced Windows Forms technique and then controls and their usage. After the initial discussion, this chapter demonstrates how to incorporate those concepts into your Windows applications.

WHAT YOU NEED

SOFTWARE REQUIREMENTS	Windows 2000, XP, or 2003 .NET Framework 1.1 SDK Visual Studio .NET 2003 with Visual Basic .NET installed
HARDWARE REQUIREMENTS	PC desktop or laptop
SKILL REQUIREMENTS	Knowledge of Visual Basic .NET Knowledge of the .NET Framework

ADVANCED WINDOWS FORMS TECHNIQUES AT A GLANCE

ADVANCED WINDOWS FORMS TECHNIQUES AT A GLANCE

Adding Controls Dynamically in Code

Sometimes you've want to add controls to a form dynamically using code. For example, you might want to create a diagramming program that enables users to drag and drop various symbols onto a form. Instead of manually painting the individual graphics, a better way to handle this problem is to use button or picture controls. With this technique, you can easily move pictures using their properties and let the Windows operating system worry about painting the form in such a way that the existing controls aren't overwritten. This approach also enables you to easily capture mouse clicks and enables the user to drag and move your icons after they have been placed.

> **TIP**
>
> In Visual Basic .NET, the distinction between controls added at runtime and those added at design time has been blurred. All the controls that you add using the Windows Forms Designer are really created by the code in the `InitializeComponent` routine when your form is first loaded. This code looks almost exactly the same as the code you use to add a control later in a program's execution. The only difference is its location in your program.

One easy way to dynamically add a control is to add it at design time and configure its properties. Then find the corresponding automatically generated code, and cut and paste it into another method. Be aware that this code might exist in several different places in the Windows Designer code region.

Examine the following code created by the Windows Forms Designer, which is used to create a new label:

```
Friend WithEvents Label1 As System.Windows.Forms.Label

Private Sub InitializeComponent
    Me.Label1 = New System.Windows.Forms.Label
    Me.Label1.Location = New System.Drawing.Point(96, 100)
```

10

Adding Controls Dynamically in Code

```
    Me.Label1.Name = "Label1"
    Me.Label1.Size = New System.Drawing.Size(112, 48)
    Me.Label1.Text = "Test"
    Me.Controls.Add(Me.Label1)
End Sub
```

With some minor modifications, this code could be inserted into a button's `Click` event to create the label dynamically, as shown in the following example:

```
Private Sub Button1_Click(ByVal sender As System.Object,
➥ByVal e As System.EventArgs)    _
    Handles Button1.Click
    Dim label1 As New System.Windows.Forms.Label
    label1.Location = New System.Drawing.Point(96, 200)
    label1.Name = " label1"
    label1.Size = New System.Drawing.Size(112, 48)
    label1.Text = "Dynamically created label"
    Me.Controls.Add(label1)
End Sub
```

One significant change is present in this code. The declaration for the label has been changed to a `Dim` statement because the `Friend` and `WithEvents` keywords are not valid inside a subroutine. The previous code also has a couple drawbacks. First, the control variable is created inside the button's `Click` event, so it is destroyed as soon as the `Click` event is finished. You might be wondering whether the control disappears after the `Click` subroutine ends. The fact is, the control remains, but it is a little bit more difficult to access. The only way you can reach it is through the `Controls` property of your form. For example, you can use something like `myForm.Controls("label1")` to get a reference to the label control. The `Controls` collection contains a collection of all the controls on the form.

10

TIP
A better solution to create controls dynamically is to use your own collection for groups of dynamically added controls. To use your own collection, add this line to your form class:

```
Private dynamicControls As Collection = New Collection()
```

Use the following line to add a reference to your label, and then store it:

```
dynamicControls.Add(label)
```

Of course, if you are creating a control that you won't need to access again, you don't need to worry about any of these methods.

Dynamic Event Hookup

Alternatively, you might be adding a control whose primary purpose is to receive events (such as a button control). In this case, you might not need to explicitly keep track of the control, but you do need a way to receive its events. Unfortunately, controls that are created at runtime can't be defined with the `WithEvents` keyword. Even if they could, it wouldn't help you; all `WithEvents` really does is make it easy for you to write event handlers by choosing the appropriate control and event in the code display window.

You can solve this problem by dynamically wiring up a new control at runtime with the `AddHandler` statement. Consider the example shown in Listing 10.1, which adds a new button at a random location and sets it to use the same event handler as the first button.

LISTING 10.1
Handling the `Click` Event of the Button

```
Private Sub Button1_Click(ByVal sender As System.Object,
➥ ByVal e As System.EventArgs)  _
  Handles Button1.Click
  'Create a random number generator for choosing the new    button's position.
  Dim Rand As New Random()
  'Generate and configure the new button.
  Dim newButton As System.Windows.Forms.Button
  newButton = New System.Windows.Forms.Button()
  newButton.Left = Rand.Next(Me.Width)
  newButton.Top = Rand.Next(Me.Height)
  newButton.Size = New System.Drawing.Size(88, 28)
  newButton.Text = "New Button"
  'Add the button to the form.
  Me.Controls.Add(newButton)
  'Wire up the new button's Click event.
  AddHandler newButton.Click, AddressOf Button1_Click
End Sub
```

In Listing 10.1, every time you click on this button, you add a new button that, when clicked, adds yet another new button. This is shown in Figure 10.1.

The capability to create controls dynamically gives you flexibility in the user interface and enables you to create complete forms based on user settings that might be stored in a database or configuration file.

10

Adding Controls Dynamically in Code

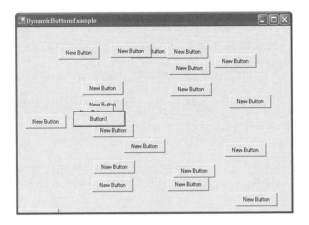

FIGURE 10.1 Dynamically adding controls to a Windows form.

Creating Owned Forms

Visual Basic .NET introduces the concept of owned forms. An owned form belongs to another form. When the owner window is minimized, all of its owned forms are also minimized automatically. When an owned form overlaps its owner, it is always displayed on top.

> **TIP**
>
> Owned forms are usually used for floating toolbox and command windows. One example of an owned form is the Find and Replace window in Microsoft Word.

10

Any form can own another form, and you don't need to set up the relationship at design time. Instead, you just set the Owner property, as shown here:

```
'Show the main window.
Dim main As New MainForm()
main.Show()
'Create and display an owned form.
Dim search As New SearchForm()
search.Owner = main
search.Show()
```

Place the preceding code within the Click event of a button control. In this code, SearchForm sets its owner property to MainForm.

MDI Interfaces

A Multiple Document Interface (MDI) program is generally based on a single parent window that can contain numerous child windows. Usually, this model is used to allow a user to work with more than one document at a time. A document might be a report, a data grid, a log, a text listing, or something entirely different.

Any window can become an MDI parent (container) if you set the `IsMdiContainer` property to `True`. Many of the restrictions that were placed on MDI parents in previous versions of Visual Basic have now been lifted. For example, parent windows can now contain regular controls, such as buttons, along with the standard menus and command bars. This makes it possible to create a wide variety of bizarre forms that look nothing like a conventional window should. For respectable interfaces, an MDI parent should contain only dockable controls, such as status bars and menu bars, which latch onto an edge of the window and provide a clear working area for any child windows.

Turning a window into an MDI child is very simple and straightforward:

```
Private Sub button1_Click(ByVal sender As System.Object,
➥ ByVal e As System.EventArgs) _
  Handles button1.Click
  Dim child As New ChildForm()
  child.MdiParent = Me
  child.Show()
End Sub
```

As you would expect, at the end of this subroutine, the child variable is lost, and you cannot use it to access the MDI child. However, MDI forms include some extra conveniences that make them easy to work with and that free you from manually keeping track of forms. Every MDI parent has a special `MdiChildren` collection, which contains all of the currently opened MDI forms. Every MDI parent also has an `ActiveMdiChild` property, which tells you which child window currently has focus. This allows the following kind of information exchange and the following code in the MDI child class:

```
Public Sub RefreshData()
  'Some code here to update the window display.
End Sub

Private Sub InfoChanged(ByVal sender As System.Object, _
  ByVal e As System.EventArgs) Handles button1.Click
  'Calls a function in the parent.
  CType(Me.MdiParent, ParentForm).RefreshAllChildren()
End Sub
```

10

MDI Interfaces

Note that to call the `RefreshAllChildren` subroutine, the code needs to convert the reference to the MDI parent form into the appropriate form class. Otherwise, you can access only the standard form properties and methods through the reference, not the custom ones you might have added to the class. The `RefreshAllChildren` subroutine is found in the parent:

```
'This code is in the MDI parent class.
Public Sub RefreshAllChildren()
  Dim child As ChildForm
  For Each child in Me.MdiChildren
    If Not Me.MdiChildren Is Me.ActiveMdiChild
      child.RefreshData()
    End If
  Next
End Sub
```

This form has an extra feature that determines whether an MDI child is the one that called it and, if it is, does not bother to call the refresh procedure. The reasoning here is that the active MDI child already is up-to-date because it is the one that originated the refresh request. Of course, the real reason this code is included is to demonstrate the `ActiveMdiChild` property. Notice that the code uses the `Is` statement instead of an equals sign to compare the forms. This is because both forms are objects (reference types), which cannot be compared with an equals sign.

Implementing Inheritance with Visual Studio .NET

An important property that controls inheritance in VB .NET is the `Modifiers` property. Every control in the toolbox has a `Modifiers` property, which specifies the accessibility of the control in the derived forms. For example, when you set the modifier to `Public`, you are indicating that properties of this control can be modified in an inherited form. This means that you have complete control over each object on a form, and you can specify what inheritance capabilities can be used. The following list defines each modifier:

- ▸ `Private`—The control can be modified only in the base form.

- ▸ `Protected`—The control can be modified only by the deriving form.

- ▸ `Public`—The control can be modified only by any form or code module.

- ▸ `Friend`—The control can be modified only within the base form's project.

To see how this works, create a new VB .NET Windows application project named InheritanceProject. After the project is created, add a new form to the project and then inherit that form. To start, right-click InheritanceProject in the Solution Explorer and select Add Windows Form from the Project menu. Change the Name to BaseForm, and click the OK button to add it to your solution. On the BaseForm in the Windows Forms Designer, drag a few TextBox controls and Button controls from the toolbox to the form. In the Properties window, change the modifier for one of the controls on your form to Public. Leave the remaining controls properties the same. From the Build menu, select Build Solution to make sure that the forms are saved and the controls are up-to-date. Now you need to add a new form to your application. But instead of adding a Windows form, right-click the project name in the Solution Explorer and select Add Inherited Form from the Project menu. This brings up the Add New Item dialog box, as if you were adding a regular form. In the Add New Item dialog box, change the name to InheritedForm, and click the OK button. Now the Inheritance Picker dialog pops up, as shown in Figure 10.2.

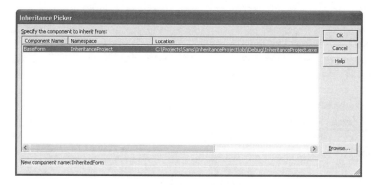

FIGURE 10.2   The Inheritance Picker dialog box.

From the Inheritance Picker, select the BaseForm form and click the OK button. You will notice that every form in your solution is also listed. Because a form is a class, and every class can be inherited, you can inherit any form. After InheritedForm is added to the solution, notice that you can't double-click the controls that aren't set to Public. Notice also that all the properties for the controls are disabled in the Properties window. By setting modifiers on controls and making their properties overridable, you can implement a very robust inheritance mechanism for your Windows Forms solutions.

The NotifyIcon Control

With the release of .NET, Visual Basic provides an easy way to add and use a system tray icon. All you need to do is place the NotifyIcon control on your component tray and associate an appropriate icon. The icon appears immediately when the form is displayed and disappears when the form is unloaded.

10

The `NotifyIcon` Control

A more useful way to use the `NotifyIcon` control is to create it in code. This enables you to use an application-wide system tray icon even when no corresponding forms are visible. For example, you might have a utility application that loads an icon onto the system tray when it starts but displays no other user interface. Instead, it might linger in the background, performing periodic tasks automatically, or enable you to display forms or choose functions from a context menu when you need them.

Listing 10.2 is exactly that kind of program. The startup object for the project is the `Main` subroutine of the App module, not a form, so no windows are displayed. **1** Instead, a system tray icon and the required context menu elements are created manually in code. Then all the program needs to do is wait for a context-menu click. If the user clicks Exit, the program ends; if the user clicks Show Clock, the current time is displayed.

LISTING 10.2
Using the `NotifyIcon` Control to Add an Item to the System Tray

```
Public Module App
    Public appIcon As New NotifyIcon()
    Public sysTrayMenu As New ContextMenu()
    'Our menu items are defined using WithEvents to receive the Click event.
    Public WithEvents displayClockMenu As New MenuItem("Show Clock")
    Public WithEvents exitAppMenu As New MenuItem("Exit")
    Public Sub Main()
        'Assign an icon from a file
        Dim ico As New Icon("c:\icon.ico")
        appIcon.Icon = ico
        'Place the menu items in the menu
        sysTrayMenu.MenuItems.Add(displayClockMenu)
        sysTrayMenu.MenuItems.Add(exitAppMenu)
        appIcon.ContextMenu = sysTrayMenu
        'Set the tooltip text
        appIcon.Text = "My .NET Application"
        'Show the system tray icon
        appIcon.Visible = True
        'Because no forms are being displayed, you need this
        'statement to stop the application from automatically ending.
        Application.Run()
    End Sub

    Public Sub exitAppMenu_Click(ByVal sender As Object, _
        ByVal e As System.EventArgs) Handles exitAppMenu.Click
        Application.Exit()
    End Sub
```

LISTING 10.2
Continued

```
Public Sub displayClockMenu_Click(ByVal sender As Object, _
    ByVal e As System.EventArgs) Handles displayClockMenu.Click
      MessageBox.Show(Date.Now.ToString, "Date", MessageBoxButtons.OK)
  End Sub
End Module
```

The possible uses for an application like this are countless. For example, you could create a task-logging program that records the amount of time spent on each project. All you would need to do is "punch in" and "punch out" on the system tray icon menu. The program would then take care of writing the appropriate information to a file or database.

The Use of Providers in Windows Forms Applications

Providers extend the properties of other controls on the current form. For example, you can add a ToolTip to a button just by dragging a `ToolTipProvider` onto the component tray and modifying the corresponding ToolTip property for the button control. You can also tweak various properties of the provider to configure global settings, such as how many milliseconds your program waits before showing the ToolTip, or how long the ToolTip remains displayed if the user does not move the mouse. Usually, however, the default settings are best. The next few sections discuss the various providers the .NET Framework supplies, such as HelpProvider and the ToolTip Provider. To start, the next section focuses on the HelpProvider component and demonstrates how to use that to provide rich help systems for your applications.

HelpProvider

One of the important providers is HelpProvider, which enables you to add context-sensitive help to every control through the `SetHelpNamespace` property (which specifies the help file) and the `SetHelpKeyword` property (which specifies the topic or uses a built-in value to show the Contents tab or Index tab). Most applications use form-specific help and set only these properties for the form.

Visual Basic .NET help features now support the HTML Help standard (.chm files) and enable you to specify a help string right in your program for use in a simple pop-up message. To use this text string instead of a help file, use the `SetHelpString` method and leave the `HelpNamespace` property empty.

10

Providing Help in a Windows Forms Application

The .NET Framework provides several means for hooking up external help systems into Windows applications, thereby providing rich context-sensitive and timely help for Windows applications. It is mainly accomplished through the classes contained in the System.Windows.Forms namespace. These classes are as follows:

- Help
- HelpProvider

The following sections provide a detailed look at these classes by explaining their properties and methods and then giving an example.

Help Class

The Help class encapsulates the HTML Help 1.0 engine. You cannot create an instance of the Help class because it exposes all its functionalities only by means of static methods. Because the Help class encapsulates the HTML Help engine, it can be used to display not only compiled help files, but also files that are in HTML format. The Help class supplies these static methods:

- ShowHelp—As the name suggests, enables you to display the contents of a help file. This method is overloaded to provide for variations in displaying the help content to the user.

- ShowHelpIndex—Enables you to display the index of the specified help file.

- ShowPopup—Enables you to display pop-up messages.

HelpProvider Class

Using the HelpProvider class, you associate an HTML help file (.chm file) or an HTML file (.html file) with a Windows application. After the initial association is established, you can use it as a repository of help for the individual controls contained in the Windows form. This initial association is required for you to display appropriate help information for different controls.

10

> **TIP**
>
> You can create compiled HTML files (.chm files) by combining several individual pieces, such as text, graphics, and HTML files, into a help project (.hhp file) and then compiling it using tools such as HTML Help Workshop. The help project manages all the files in the help system. After this help project is compiled, you get a single compiled help file with the extension .chm that represents the entire help system.

Using the HelpProvider class, you can display the help in a variety of ways:

- Provide context-sensitive help for controls on Windows forms
- Provide context-sensitive help on a dialog box or specific controls on a dialog box

▶ Open the specific parts of the help file, such as a table of contents, an index, or search functions, while launching the help file

▶ Display help information in a pop-up window for specific controls

To link help systems to individual controls using the HelpProvider class, you need to do the following steps:

1. Create an instance of the HelpProvider class.

2. Associate an external help file with the HelpProvider object by setting the HelpNamespace property.

3. Finally, hook up the individual controls to the specific topics of the help file by invoking the SetHelpNavigator method of the HelpProvider object. To this method, you pass the name of the control and a value from the HelpNavigator enumeration.

The HelpNavigator enumeration is used to provide access to the specific elements of the help file. Keep in mind that it is always used in conjunction with the Help and HelpProvider classes. Table 10.1 shows the constants defined by the HelpNavigator enumeration.

TABLE 10.1

HelpNavigator Enumeration Values

Member Name	Description
AssociateIndex	Enables you to specify constants indicating which elements of the help file to display
Index	Enables you to display the index function of the specified help file with the selected keyword highlighted when the help system is launched
KeywordIndex	Displays the Index function of the help system, which enables you to specify the keyword to search for in the index function of the help file
TableOfContents	Enables you to display the TableOfContents function of the specified help file when the help system is launched
Topic	Enables you to display the specified topic referenced in the specified help file when the help system is launched

10

Using the HelpProvider class, you can also optionally display context-sensitive help information that appears when the user presses F1. To accomplish this, you need to use the SetHelpString method (which enables you to specify the help string information to be displayed) of the HelpProvider class. To this method, you need to pass as arguments the name of the control and the help string to be associated with that control. At runtime, when the user presses F1 for help, the help string associated with the HelpProvider class is displayed in a pop-up window. Table 10.2 lists the important methods of the HelpProvider class.

HelpProvider

TABLE 10.2

Methods of the `HelpProvider` Class

Method	Description
GetHelpKeyword	Enables you to get the help keyword for the specified control. This method takes the name of the control for which to retrieve the help keyword.
GetHelpNavigator	Enables you to get the current `HelpNavigator` setting for the specified control. This method takes the name of the control for which to retrieve the help topic.
GetHelpString	Enables you to get the contents of the pop-up window for the specified control.
GetShowHelp	Enables you to get the value indicating whether the specified control's help should be displayed. This is useful when you want to dynamically determine the help topic to display for the controls.
SetHelpKeyword	Enables you to set the help keyword used to retrieve help when the user invokes help for the specified control.
SetHelpNavigator	Enables you to set the help command to use when retrieving help from the help file for the specified control.
SetHelpString	Enables you to set the `hstring` associated with the specified control.
SetShowHelp	Specifies whether help should be displayed for the specified control.

Using the `SetHelpXXX()` methods (shown in Table 10.3) repeatedly, you can use the single instance of the `HelpProvider` object to maintain a collection of references to individual controls and their related help content. Listing 10.3 shows an example of this in action.

LISTING 10.3

Using `Help` and `HelpProvider` Classes to Display Dynamic Help

```
Public Class HelpExample
  Inherits System.Windows.Forms.Form

  Private btnBold As New System.Windows.Forms.Button
  Private btnItalic As New System.Windows.Forms.Button
  Private btnCenter As New System.Windows.Forms.Button
  Private btnHelp As New System.Windows.Forms.Button

  Public Sub New()
    InitializeComponent()
  End Sub

  Private Sub InitializeComponent()
    Me.btnBold.Location = New System.Drawing.Point(32, 216)
    Me.btnBold.Name = "btnBold"
    Me.btnBold.TabIndex = 0
```

10

LISTING 10.3
Continued

```vb
    Me.btnBold.Text = "Bold"
    Me.btnItalic.Location = New System.Drawing.Point(136, 216)
    Me.btnItalic.Name = "btnItalic"
    Me.btnItalic.TabIndex = 1
    Me.btnItalic.Text = "Italic"
    Me.btnCenter.Location = New System.Drawing.Point(240, 216)
    Me.btnCenter.Name = "btnCenter"
    Me.btnCenter.TabIndex = 2
    Me.btnCenter.Text = "Center"
    Me.btnHelp.Location = New System.Drawing.Point(352, 216)
    Me.btnHelp.Name = "btnHelp"
    Me.btnHelp.TabIndex = 3
    Me.btnHelp.Text = "Help"
    AddHandler btnHelp.Click, AddressOf Me.btnHelp_Click
    Me.Controls.Add(Me.btnHelp)
    Me.Controls.Add(Me.btnCenter)
    Me.Controls.Add(Me.btnItalic)
    Me.Controls.Add(Me.btnBold)
    Me.Name = "HelpExample"
    Me.Text = "HelpExample"
End Sub


Private Sub btnHelp_Click(ByVal sender As System.Object, _
    ➥ ByVal e As System.EventArgs)
    Help.ShowHelp(Me, "C:\temp\HTMLHelpProject\FormattingAppHelp.chm", _    1
        HelpNavigator.TableOfContents)
End Sub


Private Sub HelpExample_Load(ByVal sender As System.Object, _
    ➥ByVal e As System.EventArgs) Handles MyBase.Load
    Dim helpProv As HelpProvider = New HelpProvider
    helpProv.HelpNamespace = "C:\temp\HTMLHelpProject\FormattingAppHelp.chm"
    'For the Form level context sensitive help, show the TableOfContents tab    2
    helpProv.SetHelpNavigator(Me, HelpNavigator.TableOfContents)
    'For the individual controls, show the index tab with the appropriate text
selected
    helpProv.SetHelpKeyword(btnBold, "Bold")
    helpProv.SetHelpKeyword(btnItalic, "Italic")
    helpProv.SetHelpKeyword(btnCenter, "Center")
End Sub
End Class
```

10

HelpProvider

In Listing 10.3, four button controls are added to the form. When the user clicks on the Help button, the `ShowHelp` method of the `Help` class is used to display the help information in a compiled HTML file format. **1** Also, by setting the second argument to `HelpNavigator.TableOfContents`, you indicate that when the help file opens, you want the table of contents to open by default. Inside the form load event, a `HelpProvider` class is created and its `HelpNamespace` property is set to the name of the help file that contains the help contents. After that, the `SetHelpNavigator` method is invoked to open the help file with the table of contents by default. **2** Then the `SetHelpKeyword` method of the `HelpProvider` class is used to assign the help keywords for the Bold, Italic, and Center buttons. After you do this association, any time one of these three controls has the focus and you press F1, the help file opens with the corresponding topic highlighted by default. This is shown in Figure 10.3.

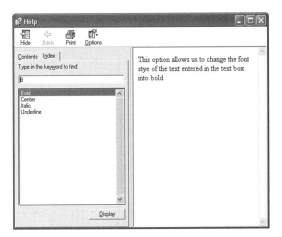

FIGURE 10.3   Displaying HTML help file contents.

Figure 10.3 shows the output produced when the user presses F1 with focus on the Bold button.

Providing Help Using ToolTips

Another popular and widely used way of providing help information in an application is to use ToolTips. By using ToolTips, you can provide a brief description of a control's purpose when the user moves the mouse over the control. This is a familiar behavior that can be seen in all of the Microsoft products. In addition to providing static help information about a control, you can configure the ToolTip to display help information that is created dynamically. For example, in a data entry form, the ToolTip for a text box control can be configured to display dynamic help information based on the values the user enters in the other controls in the form. The ToolTip class is contained in the `System.Windows.Forms` namespace.

TIP
Remember that ToolTips should be reserved for graphical controls such as toolbar buttons, not label controls or ordinary buttons.

It is possible to use a single ToolTip component to provide help information for multiple controls. For example, by having a single instance of the `ToolTip` component, you can provide help for a button control, a label control, and so on. The ToolTip component exposes a method named `SetToolTip()`, which enables you to specify the ToolTip text displayed for each control on the form. The ToolTip component is very flexible, in that it can be configured in such a way that there is a delay before the ToolTip is shown. Table 10.3 discusses the important properties of the ToolTip class.

TABLE 10.3

Important Properties of the ToolTip Control

Property	Description
Active	Enables you to get or set a value that specifies whether the ToolTip is currently active
AutoPopDelay	Enables you to get or set the amount of time the ToolTip remains active when the mouse pointer is stationary
InitialDelay	Enables you to get or set the initial delay that elapses before the ToolTip appears
ShowAlways	Enables you to get or set a value indicating whether the ToolTip is shown even when the parent control is not active

Now that you understand the important properties of the ToolTip class, Table 10.4 discusses the important methods exposed by this class.

TABLE 10.4

Important Methods of the ToolTip Control

Method	Description
SetToolTip	Enables you to associate ToolTip text with the specified control
GetToolTip	Enables you to retrieve the ToolTip associated with the specified control
RemoveAll	Removes all the ToolTip text associated with the ToolTip component

Listing 10.4 shows an example of how to use the properties and methods.

10

Providing Help Using ToolTips

LISTING 10.4
Using the ToolTip Control to Display a ToolTip for a Windows Forms Application

```vb
Public Class ToolTipExample
  Inherits System.Windows.Forms.Form

  Private btnBold As New System.Windows.Forms.Button
  Private btnItalic As New System.Windows.Forms.Button
  Private ToolTip1 As New System.Windows.Forms.ToolTip

  Public Sub New()
    InitializeComponent()
  End Sub

  Private Sub InitializeComponent()
    Me.btnBold.Location = New System.Drawing.Point(32, 216)
    Me.btnBold.Name = "btnBold"
    Me.btnBold.TabIndex = 0
    Me.btnBold.Text = "Bold"
    Me.btnItalic.Location = New System.Drawing.Point(136, 216)
    Me.btnItalic.Name = "btnItalic"
    Me.btnItalic.TabIndex = 1
    Me.btnItalic.Text = "Italic"
    Me.Controls.Add(Me.btnItalic)
    Me.Controls.Add(Me.btnBold)
    Me.Name = "ToolTipExample"
    Me.Text = "ToolTip Example"
  End Sub
  Private Sub ToolTipExample_Load(ByVal sender As System.Object, _
➡ ByVal e As System.EventArgs) Handles MyBase.Load
    ToolTip1.SetToolTip(btnBold, "Change the font style to bold")
    ToolTip1.SetToolTip(btnItalic, "Change the font style to Italic")
  End Sub
End Class
```

In Listing 10.4, apart from declaring the button controls, a new component named
`ToolTip` is also declared. The `InitializeComponent` event is used to initialize all
the controls and then add them to the form. In the form load event, the
`SetToolTip` method of the `ToolTip` component is invoked. To this method, you
supply the name of the control and the ToolTip to display as arguments. The output
produced by the Listing 10.4 is shown in Figure 10.4.

In the screenshot, if you hover the mouse over the buttons, you will see the ToolTip
that is associated in the form load event.

FIGURE 10.4   Displaying a ToolTip
button control.

Dialog Box Controls

The common dialog box controls in Windows Forms enable you to perform dialog-related tasks. After you add a control, you can use its properties and methods to display the dialog box. Using dialog box controls, you can display standard Windows dialog boxes, such as those for font or color selection. The common dialog box controls are nonvisual controls that are added to a form. Table 10.5 lists all the common dialog box controls.

TABLE 10.5

Common Dialog Box Controls

Control	Description
ColorDialog	Displays the color picker dialog box that enables users to set the color of an interface element
FontDialog	Displays a dialog box that enables users to set a font and its attributes
OpenFileDialog	Displays a dialog box that enables users to navigate to and select a file
PrintDialog	Displays a dialog box that enables users to select a printer and set its attributes
PrintPreviewDialog	Displays a dialog box that shows how a PrintDocument object appears when printed
SaveFileDialog	Displays a dialog box that enables users to save a file

10

Dialog Box Controls

These controls really don't need to be added to the component tray. It is more intuitive to define them in your code just before you display them, as shown here:

```
Dim dlgFile As New OpenFileDialog()
dlgFile.InitialDirectory = "c:\"
dlgFile.Filter = "txt files (*.txt)|*.txt|All files (*.*)|*.*"
dlgFile.FilterIndex = 2
If dlgFile.ShowDialog() = DialogResult.OK Then
  'You can now open the selected file, which is dlgFile.FileName.
End If
```

Here the code shows the dialog box in the same line that it checks the result. This means that you don't need to declare a separate results variable.

> **NOTE**
>
> Notice that you no longer have to perform error trapping to determine whether a user has clicked the OK button or the Cancel button. Instead, you use the familiar DialogResult object discussed earlier in this chapter.

In Listing 10.5, the OpenFileDialog box control is used to select the cursor files.

LISTING 10.5

Using the `Filter` Property of `OpenFileDialog` to Prompt the User for Cursor Files

```
'Display an OpenFileDialog so the user can select a Cursor.
Dim openFileDialog1 As New OpenFileDialog()
openFileDialog1.Filter = "Cursor Files|*.cur"
openFileDialog1.Title = "Select a Cursor File"
'Show the Dialog.
'If the user clicked OK in the dialog and
'A .CUR file was selected, open it.
If openFileDialog1.ShowDialog() = DialogResult.OK Then
  If openFileDialog1.FileName <> "" Then
    'Assign the cursor in the Stream to the Form's Cursor property.
    Me.Cursor = New Cursor(openFileDialog1.OpenFile())
  End If
End If
```

In Listing 10.5, the ShowDialog method is used to display the File Open dialog box. When you display the File Open dialog box, the FileName property is used to check whether the user has selected a valid file in the File Open dialog box.

10

Using Cursors in Windows Forms Applications

The cursor is the (usually flashing) line or block that indicates where input or output text will be inserted or where deletion will take place. A cursor appears on a particular row, at a particular column; the arrow keys usually move the cursor up, down, left, and right. When the user moves the pointing device, the operating system moves the cursor accordingly.

Different shapes provided by the `Cursor` class are very useful, in that they can be used to inform the user of the kind of operation performed by the application. For example, when you perform a time-consuming operation, you want to provide users with a visual clue about the executing process. This is normally accomplished by setting the mouse cursor to indicate a wait state (an hourglass), which provides an indication to the user. You might want to change the cursor shape when the user retrieves a large amount of data, opens a file, saves a file, and so on.

The `Cursor` property exposed by the `Control` class enables you to perform operations related to the cursor. Because all the controls in the `System.Windows.Form` namespace derive from `Control` class, the `Cursor` property is available to all the controls. The `Cursor` object can be created from any one of the following sources:

- The handle of an existing cursor object. To perform this, you need to use the `CopyHandle` method that returns the handle of the cursor.

- An external cursor file (a file that is saved with extension `.cur`).

- An external resource.

- A data source.

TIP

The `DrawStretched` method of the cursor class enables you to stretch the size of the cursor. This is very useful when you are using an external resource as a cursor image and the image is too small for the cursor. In this case, you can use the `DrawStretched` method to stretch the image of the cursor to its desired size.

10

The `Cursor` class also exposes other useful methods, such as `Show` and `Hide`. As the name suggests, these methods are used to control the cursor display behavior. Table 10.6 summarizes the important properties of the `Cursor` class.

Using Cursors in Windows Forms Applications

TABLE 10.6

Important Properties of the `Cursor` Class

Property	Description
Current	Enables you to get or set the mouse cursor that determines the mouse cursor shown on the screen
Handle	Read-only property. Enables you to retrieve the handle of the cursor. This is useful when you are creating a new cursor object from an existing cursor object.
Size	Read-only property. Used to get the size of the cursor object in the form of a `Size` object.
Clip	Enables you to clip the cursor within the specified clipping rectangle

In Table 10.7, the most frequently used property that you will be requiring in your application is the `Current` property. Using this property, you can set the mouse cursor from the collection of cursor shapes that the `Cursors` class contains. Some of the important values the `Cursors` collection class contains include `AppStarting`, `Arrow`, `Cross`, `Default`, `Hand`, `Help`, `IBeam`, and `WaitCursor`. Listing 10.6 shows an example of how to use the `Cursor` class to change the mouse pointer.

LISTING 10.6

Changing a Mouse Pointer Using the `Cursor` Object

```
Imports System.Windows.Forms
Imports System.Drawing
Public Class CursorExample
  Inherits Form
  Private btnStartProcess As Button = New Button

  Public Sub New()
    btnStartProcess.Location = New Point(50, 75)
    btnStartProcess.Width = 150
    btnStartProcess.Text = "Start Process"
    AddHandler btnStartProcess.Click, AddressOf Me.btnStartProcess_Click
    Me.Text = "Cursor Example"
    Me.Controls.Add(btnStartProcess)
  End Sub

  Public Sub btnStartProcess_Click(ByVal Sender As Object, ByVal e As EventArgs)
    Cursor.Current = Cursors.WaitCursor
    'Dummy variable used to simulate the real processing behavior
    Dim counter As Long = 100000000
    'Replace these set of statements with your time consuming process invocation
    For counter = 0 To 100000000
      'Do Nothing inside the loop
    Next counter
```

10

LISTING 10.6
Continued

```
    'Set the cursor back to the default shape                          2
    Cursor.Current = Cursors.Default
  End Sub
  Public Shared Sub Main()
    Application.Run(New CursorExample)
  End Sub
End Class
```

If you run the previous code and then click the Start Process command button, you will see the mouse pointer change to WaitCursor shape to indicate that it is executing a long process. **1** When the process is completed, the mouse pointer changes back to the default shape. In the previous code, a long running process is simulated through the use of a for loop statement. Before executing the for loop, the cursor is set to Cursors.WaitCursor to indicate that the user needs to wait for the processing to complete. When the processing is complete, the cursor is set back to the default cursor. **2**

Advanced User Interface Controls

In the previous chapters, you learned about the basic controls that can be used in a Windows Forms application. The following sections talk about some of the important advanced user interface controls, such as TreeView, DateTimePicker, MonthCalendar, and Cursor. While looking at these controls, you will look at not only the basics of these controls, but also the important properties and methods of the controls. Along the way, you see an example of how to use these controls and their properties and methods. To start, the next section demonstrates the TreeView control.

The TreeView Control

As you might have seen in many places, a TreeView control enables you to display a set of related information using a hierarchical structure. Using TreeView, you can organize related information into easy-to-manage blocks. For example, you can use the TreeView control to display a common list of disk drives and directories, like the one shown in the left side of Windows Explorer.

The important classes that encapsulate the core functionality of the TreeView are TreeView, TreeNode, and TreeNodeCollection. Each individual item displayed in the TreeView is represented by a TreeNode object. To get references to the list of child nodes under a specified node, you use the Nodes collection property of the TreeNode object that returns an object of type TreeNodeCollection.

10

Advanced User Interface Controls

The important methods of the `TreeNodeCollection` object that enable you to add or delete a node from the `TreeView` are `Add` and `Remove`.

At runtime, the `TreeView` can be expanded to display the next level of child nodes. The user can expand the `TreeView` by clicking the + sign that is displayed next to the node, if the node has child nodes. It is also possible to programmatically expand a `TreeView` by invoking the `Expand()` method of the `TreeNode` object. When you are displaying nodes in the `TreeView`, it is also possible to display images right next to the nodes. To display images, you need to perform these steps:

1. Add a set of images that you want to display in the `TreeView` to an `ImageList` control.

2. Associate the `ImageList` with the `TreeView` by setting the `ImageList` property of the `TreeView` to refer to the `ImageList` object.

3. When the initial association is done, you can easily reference the images contained in the `ImageList` object from the `TreeView` by using the `ImageIndex` property.

Table 10.7 discusses important properties of the `TreeView` control and Listing 10.7 shows its use.

TABLE 10.7

Important Properties of the `TreeView` Control

Property	Description
CheckBoxes	Enables you to specify whether you want to display check boxes next to the nodes in the `TreeView`
HotTracking	Enables you to specify whether the tree node label looks like a hyperlink when the mouse pointer is moved on top of it
ImageList	Enables you to associate an `ImageList` object that is used as the repository for all the images used by the `TreeView`
ImageIndex	Enables you to refer to the images stored in the `ImageList` by using the index number
Indent	Enables you to specify the indent that is used for each of the child tree node levels
Nodes	Enables you to get the collection of tree nodes that are part of the `TreeView` control
PathSeparator	Enables you to get or set the delimiter string used by the tree nodes
SelectedImageIndex	Enables you to get or set the index of the image (that is stored in the `ImageList`)
SelectedNode	Enables you to get or set the tree node that is currently selected in the `TreeView` control
ShowLines	Enables you to get or set the value that determines whether lines are drawn between the nodes in the `TreeView` control
ShowPlusMinus	Determines whether you want to set or get a value indicating that you want to display a plus sign (+) and minus sign (–) next to the nodes in the `TreeView`
ShowRootLines	Determines whether you want to draw lines between the root nodes in the `TreeView`

10

LISTING 10.7
`TreeView` Control to Create Windows Explorer–Style Application

```
Imports System
Imports System.Drawing
Imports System.IO

Public Class TreeViewExample
  Inherits System.Windows.Forms.Form

  Public Sub New()
    InitializeComponent()
  End Sub

  Private folder As DirectoryInfo
  Private WithEvents splExplorer As New System.Windows.Forms.Splitter
  Private WithEvents tvwExplorer As New System.Windows.Forms.TreeView
  Private WithEvents lvwExplorer As New System.Windows.Forms.ListView
  Private WithEvents colName As New System.Windows.Forms.ColumnHeader
  Private WithEvents colModified As New System.Windows.Forms.ColumnHeader

  Private Sub InitializeComponent()
    Me.tvwExplorer.Location = New System.Drawing.Point(0, 0)
    Me.tvwExplorer.Name = "tvwExplorer"
    Me.tvwExplorer.SelectedImageIndex = -1
    Me.tvwExplorer.Size = New System.Drawing.Size(256, 438)
    Me.lvwExplorer.Columns.AddRange(New System.Windows.Forms.ColumnHeader() _
    ➥{Me.colName, Me.colModified})
    Me.lvwExplorer.Location = New System.Drawing.Point(256, 0)
    Me.lvwExplorer.MultiSelect = False
    Me.lvwExplorer.Name = "lvwExplorer"
    Me.lvwExplorer.Size = New System.Drawing.Size(280, 438)
    Me.lvwExplorer.View = System.Windows.Forms.View.Details
    Me.colName.Text = "Name"
    Me.colName.Width = 109
    Me.colModified.Text = "Modified"
    Me.colModified.Width = 105
    Me.AutoScaleBaseSize = New System.Drawing.Size(5, 13)
    Me.ClientSize = New System.Drawing.Size(536, 438)
    Me.Controls.Add(Me.splExplorer)
    Me.Controls.Add(Me.lvwExplorer)
    Me.Controls.Add(Me.tvwExplorer)
    Me.Name = "TreeViewExample"
    Me.Text = "TreeViewExample"
  End Sub
```

10

Advanced User Interface Controls

LISTING 10.7
Continued

```
Private Sub TreeViewExample_Load(ByVal sender As System.Object, _
➡ ByVal e As System.EventArgs) Handles
    MyBase.Load
```

1   `LoadTree()`

```
End Sub


Private Sub LoadTree()
    Dim directory As DirectoryInfo
    'Clear the treeview
    tvwExplorer.Nodes.Clear()
    'Loop through the drive letters and find the available drives.
    Dim drive As String
    For Each drive In Environment.GetLogicalDrives()
        Try
            'Get the directory information for this path
            directory = New DirectoryInfo(drive)
            'If the retrieved directory is valid, add it to the treeview
            If (directory.Exists = True) Then
                Dim newNode As TreeNode = New TreeNode(directory.FullName)
                tvwExplorer.Nodes.Add(newNode)
```

2   `'Add the new node to the root level.`
        `GetSubDirectories(newNode)`

```
                'scan for any sub folders on this drive
            End If
        Catch ex As Exception
            'Ignore Exceptions
            Return
        End Try
    Next
End Sub


Private Sub GetSubDirectories(ByVal parent As TreeNode)
    Dim directory As DirectoryInfo
    Try
        'Check if we have already scanned this folder
        If (parent.Nodes.Count = 0) Then
            directory = New DirectoryInfo(parent.FullPath)
            Dim dir As DirectoryInfo
            For Each dir In directory.GetDirectories()
                Dim newNode As TreeNode = New TreeNode(dir.Name)
                parent.Nodes.Add(newNode)
            Next
```

10

LISTING 10.7
Continued

```
      End If
      Dim node As TreeNode
      'Scan the first level of sub folders to create + or - sign
      For Each node In parent.Nodes
        'If we have not scanned this node before
        If (node.Nodes.Count = 0) Then
          'Get the folder information for the specified path
          directory = New DirectoryInfo(node.FullPath)
          'Check this folder for any possible subdirectories
          Dim dir As DirectoryInfo
          For Each dir In directory.GetDirectories()
            'Create a new TreeNode and add it to the TreeView
            Dim newNode As TreeNode = New TreeNode(dir.Name)
            node.Nodes.Add(newNode)
          Next
        End If
      Next
    Catch ex As Exception
      'Ignore Exceptions
      Return
    End Try
  End Sub


  Private Sub tvwExplorer_BeforeSelect(ByVal sender As Object, ByVal e As
    System.Windows.Forms.TreeViewCancelEventArgs) Handles tvwExplorer.BeforeSelect
    'Get all the subdirectories for the selected node
    GetSubDirectories(e.Node)
    'Get the DirectoryInfo object and assign it to the module level variable
    folder = New DirectoryInfo(e.Node.FullPath)
  End Sub


  Private Sub tvwExplorer_BeforeExpand(ByVal sender As Object, ByVal e As
    System.Windows.Forms.TreeViewCancelEventArgs) Handles tvwExplorer.BeforeExpand
    'Get all the subdirectories for the selected node
    GetSubDirectories(e.Node)
    'Get the DirectoryInfo object and assign it to the module level variable
    folder = New DirectoryInfo(e.Node.FullPath)
  End Sub

  Private Sub tvwExplorer_AfterSelect(ByVal sender As Object, ByVal e As        3
    System.Windows.Forms.TreeViewEventArgs) Handles tvwExplorer.AfterSelect
    'Get reference to the selected node
    Dim dirInfo As DirectoryInfo = New DirectoryInfo(e.Node.FullPath)
```

10

Advanced User Interface Controls

LISTING 10.7
Continued

```
     'Clear all the items in the listview
     lvwExplorer.Items.Clear()
     'Check if the Directory exists or not
     If (dirInfo.Exists) Then
       'Get reference to all the files
       Dim fileInfos As FileInfo() = dirInfo.GetFiles()
       'Add all the files to the ListView
       Dim info As FileInfo
       For Each info In fileInfos
         Dim item As ListViewItem = New ListViewItem
         item = lvwExplorer.Items.Add(info.Name)
         item.SubItems.Add(info.LastAccessTime.ToString())
       Next
     End If
   End Sub
End Class
```

In the form load event shown in Listing 10.7, the LoadTree method is invoked, populating not only the root elements in the TreeView, but also their child nodes. **1** This is done to display + or − signs next to the individual elements. To populate the child nodes, the LoadTree method internally calls the GetSubDirectories method. **2** As the name suggests, the GetSubDirectories method is used to retrieve all the directories under the specified parent directory. The core class that enables you to perform this operation is the DirectoryInfo class that is contained in the System.IO namespace. Whenever the user selects a folder from the TreeView, it displays the files contained in that folder in the ListView. This is accomplished by providing code in the AfterSelect event of the TreeView control. **3**

An alternative approach to loading the tree is to use recursive programming. Recursion is a programming technique by which you can write a function that has the capability to call itself. The most important thing to keep in mind while doing recursive programming is to make sure that you have an end condition in place. Programs that use recursion can be made to do all sorts of things, from calculating the factorial of a number to loading a complex TreeView such as the one used in the earlier example.

The DateTimePicker Control

The DateTimePicker control enables you to display a placeholder that allows easy date selection. It is also possible to format the date field so that it displays the format according to your requirements. In addition, the DateTimePicker can be customized to select the date from a drop-down calendar interface. Table 10.8 summarizes the important properties of the DateTimePicker control and Listing 10.8 shows its use.

TABLE 10.8

Properties of the `DateTimePicker` Control

Property	Description
CustomFormat	Enables you to specify the custom date-time format string to control the way in which the date and time are displayed in the `DateTimePicker`
MaxDate	Enables you to set or get the maximum date that can be selected in the control
MinDate	Enables you to set or get the minimum date that can be selected in the control
ShowCheckBox	Enables you to determine whether you want to show a check box to the left of the selected date
ShowUpDown	Enables you to determine whether an up-down control is displayed to adjust the date-time value

As you might have already guessed, by using the combination of MinDate and MaxDate properties, you can perform validations without even writing a single line of code. Apart from the properties mentioned already, you can change attributes such as font, foreground color, and background color using the following properties: CalendarFont, CalendarForeColor, CalendarMonthBackground, CalendarTitleBackColor, CalendarTitleForeColor, and CalendarTrailingForeColor.

LISTING 10.8

`DateTimePicker` to Select a Date

```
Private Sub DateTimePickerSample_Load(ByVal sender As System.Object, _
➥ ByVal e As System.EventArgs) Handles
   MyBase.Load
  'Set the Default date style for both the controls to Long style    1
   dtpStartDate.Format = DateTimePickerFormat.Long
   dtpEndDate.Format = DateTimePickerFormat.Long
  'Get the current Date and Time
   Dim now As DateTime = DateTime.Now
  'Set the MaxDate and MinDate to values which only allow the user to
  'select the start date that falls within the last month
   dtpStartDate.MaxDate = now                                         2
   dtpStartDate.MinDate = now.AddDays(-30)
  'Allow the user to select the maximum date that falls in the next month
   dtpEndDate.MaxDate = now.AddDays(30)
End Sub


Private Sub Button1_Click(ByVal sender As System.Object, _
➥ ByVal e As System.EventArgs) Handles Button1.Click
   Dim noOfDays As Integer = dtpEndDate.Value.Subtract(dtpStartDate.Value).Days
   MessageBox.Show(noOfDays.ToString())
End Sub
```

10

Advanced User Interface Controls

In Listing 10.8, you start by setting the Format properties of the dtpStartDate and dtpEndDate controls to DateTimePickerFormat.Long, which sets the format of the selected date. **1** The MaxDate and MinDate properties of the dtpStartDate control ensure that the user selects a date that falls within the last month. **2** The MaxDate of the dtpEndDate control is set to a value that should fall within the next month. The Click event of the button is used to calculate the difference between the start date and end date and then display that information in a message box. Figure 10.5 shows the output produced by the DateTimePicker control.

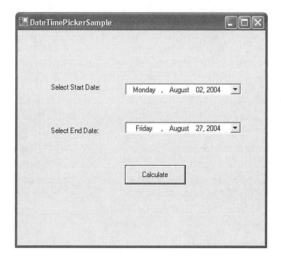

FIGURE 10.5   DateTimePicker control to set start and end dates.

The MonthCalendar **Control**

This control is similar to the DateTimePicker control, except that it provides a user interface in which you can select a range of dates. Similar to the DateTimePicker, this control also enables users to set the minimum and maximum dates by means of MaxDate and MinDate properties.

TIP

Note that the MonthCalendar control does not allow the user to provide a custom-formatting string for the selected date(s). If your application needs custom formatting, it is recommended that you use the DateTimePicker control and take advantage of the built-in custom-formatting capabilities.

Table 10.9 summarizes the important properties of the MonthCalendar control, and Listing 10.9 shows its use.

10

TABLE 10.9

Properties of the `MonthCalendar` Control

Property	Description
MaxSelectionCount	Using this property, you can set or get the maximum number of days that can be selected in the `MonthCalendar` control.
SelectionStart	If you want to select a group of dates, this property can be used to provide the starting date for that range of dates.
SelectionEnd	This property is similar to `SelectionStart`, except that it enables you to provide the end date for the range of dates.
SelectionRange	This property can be used to set or get the range of dates in the `MonthCalendar` control. It is normally used as an alternative to the combination of the `SelectionStart` and `SelectionEnd` properties to select a date range.
ShowToday	This property enables you to specify whether you want to display today's date at the bottom of the control.
ShowTodayCircle	This enables you to specify whether you want to circle today's date at the bottom of the control.
TodayDate	This enables you to get or set today's date in the `MonthCalendar` control.

LISTING 10.9

`MonthCalendar` Control to Select a Range of Dates

```
Private Sub MonthCalendarExample_Load(ByVal sender As System.Object, _
➥ ByVal e As System.EventArgs) Handles
 MyBase.Load
  'Get the current Date and Time
  Dim now As DateTime = DateTime.Now
  'Set the default properties
  monCalendarSelection.ShowToday = True
  monCalendarSelection.ShowTodayCircle = True
  monCalendarSelection.TodayDate = now
  'Set the MinDate and MaxDate properties
  monCalendarSelection.MinDate = now.AddDays(-30)
  monCalendarSelection.MaxDate = now.AddDays(30)
  'Select the last 7 days as the default range
  monCalendarSelection.SelectionStart = now.AddDays(-7)
  monCalendarSelection.SelectionEnd = now
End Sub


Private Sub btnCalculate_Click(ByVal sender As System.Object, _
➥ ByVal e As System.EventArgs) Handles
  btnCalculate.Click
```

10

Advanced User Interface Controls

LISTING 10.9
Continued

```
'Get the Start and End Dates
Dim startDate As DateTime = monCalendarSelection.SelectionRange.Start
Dim endDate As DateTime = monCalendarSelection.SelectionRange.End
'Get the difference in number of days
Dim noOfDays As Integer = endDate.Subtract(startDate).Days
MessageBox.Show(noOfDays.ToString())
End Sub
```

In Listing 10.9, the form load event is used to set the various properties of the
MonthCalendar control. These properties include ShowToday and
ShowTodayCircle, which are set to True. The TodayDate property is set to the
current date. The MinDate and MaxDate properties are set to specific values to
ensure that the selected date is within a specific range. Finally, the
SelectionStart, and SelectionEnd properties are used to select the last seven
days. This means that when the form is loaded, the last seven days are selected in the
MonthCalendar control. In the Click event of the btnCalculate button, the
SelectionRange.Start and SelectionRange.End properties are used to get
the start and end date, respectively, onto local variables. When they are available in
local variables, the difference between them is then calculated and displayed in a
message box. Figure 10.6 shows the output produced by Listing 10.9.

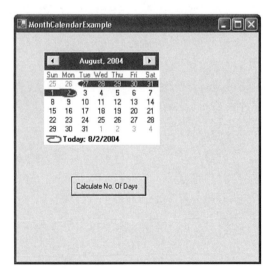

FIGURE 10.6 MonthCalendar Control
to set start and end dates.

10

Summary

In this chapter, you learned about the support that the .NET Framework provides for hooking up external help systems into Windows Forms applications for providing help. This chapter also discussed the advanced user interface controls and their properties and methods. In addition, this chapter discussed how to use these controls to create sophisticated Windows applications.

Further Reading

Payne, Chris. *Sams Teach Yourself .NET Windows Forms in 21 Days*. Pearson Education, 2002

10

Part III

Database Programming

11 ADO.NET CLASSES

IN BRIEF

Some ADO.NET classes are provider-specific classes (which, therefore, must be supplied in different versions for different database products), and some are provider-independent classes. The provider-specific classes are grouped into collections referred to as data providers; these classes are used for connecting to a database, executing commands, and retrieving results. This chapter covers the four core classes of a .NET data provider: `Connection`, `Command`, `DataReader`, and `DataAdapter`.

Provider-independent ADO.NET classes also play a crucial role in database-connected applications. The `DataSet` class, a kind of in-memory database, is pivotal in facilitating one of ADO.NET's key design goals: disconnected data access. This chapter covers the `DataSet` class, along with the classes for the subordinate objects that populate a `DataSet`: `DataTables`, `DataColumns`, `DataRows`, `Constraints`, and `DataRelations`. Finally, the chapter takes a look at the `DataView` class, another provider-independent class that provides sorting, filtering, and data-binding capabilities for the data in a `DataSet`.

WHAT YOU NEED

SOFTWARE REQUIREMENTS	Windows 2000, Windows XP, or Windows Server 2003 .NET Framework 1.1 Visual Studio .NET 2003 with Visual Basic .NET installed SQL Server 2000 or Microsoft Desktop Database Engine (MSDE)
HARDWARE REQUIREMENTS	PC desktop or laptop
SKILL REQUIREMENTS	Intermediate knowledge of the .NET Framework Intermediate knowledge of Windows Forms Understanding of relational database concepts and applications

ADO.NET CLASSES AT A GLANCE

ADO.NET CLASSES AT A GLANCE

Data Providers

The .NET Framework provides different varieties of the four data provider objects, optimized for different back-end databases. The Framework includes a data provider for Microsoft SQL Server (version 7.0 or later), OLE DB, ODBC, and Oracle. The last two, for ODBC and Oracle, were not included in version 1.0 of the .NET Framework but are present in 1.1 and can be downloaded separately by those running version 1.0 of the .NET Framework.

You should be aware that the formal specification for a .NET data provider requires only that it support the execution of commands and the retrieval of read-only, forward-only result sets. These facilities comprise the common denominator for .NET data providers; support for any feature over and above these is up to the discretion of the provider's vendor (whether this is Microsoft or another company). The discussion in this chapter encompasses the facilities supplied by full-featured providers such as `SqlClient` and `OleDb`.

The `SqlClient` and `OleDb` Data Providers

Let's look in a bit more detail at the providers for SQL Server and OLE DB, to see an example of the similarities and differences between data providers. .NET makes these providers available through the namespaces `SqlClient` and `OleDb`. Each of these namespaces includes classes for the four core objects and their subordinate objects (such as the `Parameter` object used by `Command` objects). Both versions of the `Connection` class implement the IDBConnection interface; and if you look in your IDE's object browser under `System.Data`, you will see several additional interfaces

11

that serve as common strains between the `OleDb` and `SqlClient` data providers: `IDbCommand`, `IDataReader`, and `IDataAdapter`.

The data providers for the two namespaces are summarized in Table 11.1.

TABLE 11.1

`OleDb` and `SqlClient` Data Provider Classes

Data Provider Class (Generic Name)	OleDb	SqlClient
Connection	OleDbConnection	SqlConnection
Command	OleDbCommand	SqlCommand
DataReader	OleDbDataReader	SqlDataReader
DataAdapter	OleDbDataAdapter	SqlDataAdapter

These two data providers provide very similar functionality. The `OleDb` version is more general than the `SqlClient` version because it can facilitate connection and operations with a number of data sources, including SQL Server, Oracle, and Microsoft Access, as well as XML files, Microsoft project files, Microsoft Directory Services, Microsoft Outlook, ISAM files, OLAP Services, and anything with an ODBC driver. The `SqlClient` provider, on the other hand, is exclusive to and optimized for work with SQL Server databases.

Not surprisingly, the `SqlClient` data provider yields the best performance when working with SQL Server.

In this chapter, the data providers mainly are discussed generically, although the code examples presented generally use the `SqlClient` classes. In most cases, the code samples can be adapted for the `OleDb` providers simply by declaring and coding to those instead. Occasionally, differences in facilities are noted. Otherwise, programming statements and techniques are virtually the same.

The `Connection` Object

A `Connection` object establishes a connection to a database. It requires a `ConnectionString`—that syntactically abstruse monstrosity database developers love to hate—and features `Open()` and `Close()` methods as its main attractions. With that one property and those two methods, you can do most of the basic things you need to do in connection with a database. For enterprise applications, the `BeginTransaction()` method is also quite important (it is addressed later).

You can get Visual Studio to generate `SqlClient` and `OleDb` connection strings for a SQL Server database by using the DataAdapter Wizard.

11

ConnectionString **Property**

The Connection object's ConnectionString property supplies parameters for connecting to a database, in a series of keyword/value pairs separated by semicolons.

Keywords may contain spaces. Key values typically are not enclosed in quotation marks, although there are some exceptions, as with the key value for the data source key in a SqlClient connection string, or the Provider key value in an OleDb connection string.

The particular keywords and values that can be supplied are database specific but include items such as server and database name, security-related settings, and performance parameters. The connection string can contain a user ID and password, but it is generally not advisable to include these because anyone with even momentary access to your source code can quickly locate and steal them.

If you're familiar with connection strings, you can simply type them in a statement that assigns them to the Connection object's ConnectionString property. If you aren't so familiar with connection strings, you can get the Visual Studio DataAdapter Wizard to generate one for you pretty quickly. You'll see how to do that in the section "The DataAdapter Object," later in this chapter.

The following is a SqlClient connection string generated using the DataAdapter Configuration Wizard against a SQL Server database. (That wizard runs automatically when you drag a SqlDataAdapter from the toolbox onto a Windows form.)

```
Me.conNw.ConnectionString = "workstation id=DIM4300;packet size=4096;" & _
    integrated security=SSPI;datasource=""(local)""; & _
persist security info=False;initial catalog=Northwind"
```

Note that the string contains key values that are specific to the machine on which it was generated and the server and database it targets.

Many of the key names shown in the previous string are set to default values and can be eliminated. For simple work, you could shorten the connection string previously shown to this:

```
data source=localhost;initial catalog=pubs;integrated security=SSPI
```

That defines a connection to the instance of SQL Server running on your local machine, declares pubs as the default database, and tells the connection to use Windows authentication for its security mode. As long as the username with which you logged into Windows has rights to the specified database, you can access that database without having to supply a further username or password.

11

The Connection **Object**

The following is an OleDb connection string as generated using the DataAdapter Configuration Wizard. (Again, this wizard is launched automatically when an OleDbDataAdapter object is dragged from the toolbox onto a Windows form.)

```
Me.conNw.ConnectionString = "Integrated Security=SSPI;User ID=sa;" & _
"Data Source=DIM4300;Tag with column collation when possible=False;" & _
"Initial Catalog=pubs;Use Procedure for Prepare=1;Auto Translate=True;" & _
"Persist Security Info=False;Provider="SQLOLEDB.1";" & _
"Workstation ID=DIM4300;Use Encryption for Data=False;Packet Size=4096"
```

As with the SqlClient connection string, this one can be simplified for basic use. You can use something like the following:

```
Data Source=localhost;Initial Catalog=pubs;Provider="SQLOLEDB.1";Integrated
➥Security=SSPI;
```

Note that the only additional piece of required information here is the OleDb provider name ("SQLOLEDB.1" for a connection to a SQL Server database).

For more specifics on key names that can be included in a SqlClient connection string, see the entry "SqlConnection.ConnectionString Property" in the MSDN Help file that installs with Visual Studio. For more information on connection string key names for the OleDb, ODBC, and Oracle data providers, see the help file entries for "OleDbConnection.ConnectionString Property," "OdbcConnection.ConnectionString Property," or "OracleConnection.ConnectionString Property," respectively.

Open() **Method**

The Open() method of the Connection object opens a database connection with the property settings specified in your connection string. Open connections that go out of scope do not close automatically: You must close an open connection explicitly using the Close() method. For example, the following code would leave open a connection, even though the Connection object, conPubs, goes out of scope as soon as the procedure OpenConnection() completes:

```
Private Sub OpenConnection
        Dim conPubs As New System.Data.SqlClient.SqlConnection
        conPubs.ConnectionString = "data source=localhost;initial catalog=pubs;" & _
                "integrated security=SSPI"
        conPubs.Open()
End Sub
```

If your code attempts to open a connection that is already open, an exception is thrown. To prevent this, you can test the state of the connection as follows:

```
If conPubs.State = ConnectionState.Closed Then
    conPubs.Open()
End If
```

Close() Method

The Close() method of the Connection object closes the connection to a database. It must be called explicitly; as noted earlier, open connections that go out of scope do not close automatically. The following code completes the code shown in the discussion of the Open() method by using the connection and then closing it:

```
Private Sub OpenConnection
      Dim conPubs As New System.Data.SqlClient.SqlConnection
      conPubs.ConnectionString = "data source=localhost;initial catalog=pubs;
➥integrated security=SSPI"
      conPubs.Open()
      Do something with the connection: e.g., read some data using a DataReader
      conPubs.Close()
End Sub
```

BeginTransaction() Method

The BeginTransaction() method of the Connection object begins a database transaction. If your database is SQL Server, this command maps to the TRANSACT-SQL's BEGIN TRANSACTION command. The description of the latter command from the Transact-SQL Reference (in SQL Server books online) reads as follows:

> BEGIN TRANSACTION represents a point at which the data referenced by a connection is logically and physically consistent. If errors are encountered, all data modifications made after the BEGIN TRANSACTION can be rolled back to return the data to this known state of consistency. Each transaction lasts until either it completes without errors and COMMIT TRANSACTION is issued to make the modifications a permanent part of the database, or errors are encountered and all modifications are erased with a ROLLBACK TRANSACTION statement.

You can see from that statement why, in ADO.NET, BeginTransaction() is a method of the Connection class. The connection is the domain within which a transaction can ensure integrity in the data through changes made by perhaps many SQL commands. Of course, it wouldn't help much if other processes, operating through other connections, were busily clobbering the same collection of data whose integrity you were attempting to ensure by operating on it inside a transaction. The Transact-SQL reference continues:

11

The Connection Object

> BEGIN TRANSACTION starts a local transaction for the connection issuing the statement. Depending on the current transaction isolation-level settings, many resources acquired to support the Transact-SQL statements issued by the connection are locked by the transaction until it is completed with either a COMMIT TRANSACTION or ROLLBACK TRANSACTION statement. Transactions left outstanding for long periods of time can prevent other users from accessing these locked resources.

As you see, your transaction also protects the data you're working on from changes by other users or processes. Just how fiercely your transaction protects the data depends upon a property known as the IsolationLevel of the transaction. You can set this property, if you want, at the time you initiate the transaction. The code on the website includes an application called TransactionIsolationLevels that permits you to see the effect of various IsolationLevel settings. This application is discussed later in this section.

To establish a transaction, you open a connection, invoke that connection's BeginTransaction() method, and assign the transaction thus begun to the Transaction property of a command:

```
Me.conNw.Open()
Dim transX As System.Data.SqlClient.SqlTransaction = Me.conNw.BeginTransaction
Me.cmdProductsInsert.Transaction = transX
```

When the command is subsequently executed (either directly or indirectly by means of a call to a DataAdapter's Update() method), all changes that it makes to the back-end database remain within the jurisdiction of the transaction.

You can assign the same transaction to many different commands, and you can execute any or all of those commands multiple times. As long as the transaction remains in force, all changes made by all those invocations of all those commands are reversible. There is no limit to the number of tables that can be affected by changes and yet still returned to their original state if necessary.

When your code has completed a set of operations under the control of a transaction, if everything went well, you can make the changes permanent by calling the transaction's Commit() method:

```
transX.Commit()
```

On the other hand, if things did not go well, the entire set of changes can be reversed using the RollBack() method:

```
transX.Rollback()
```

When might you want to do that? Well, let's say that you were attempting to place an order for a specified number of units of a given product. You first check the inventory level for the product, determine that there is sufficient inventory to fill the order, and decrement the inventory count by the number of units ordered to reserve those units for the order in progress. But then, in the process of attempting to create an order record, you learn that some problem exists with the account of the customer placing the order, so new orders by that customer are temporarily disallowed. You could then roll back the change to the Products table, freeing up the inventory temporarily reserved.

That covers the basics of using transactions. However, depending upon which database you're using, some additional facilities enable you to fine-tune your use of a given transaction:

▶ Specifying a nondefault `Isolation` level

▶ Nesting transactions

▶ Using named transactions

Specifying a Nondefault `IsolationLevel`

Every transaction has a property known as its `IsolationLevel`, which determines the locking behavior for the connection on which a transaction is started. ADO.NET supports five distinct isolation levels, shown in Table 11.2.

TABLE 11.2

Members of the `IsolationLevel` Enumeration

Member Name	Description	Comments
Chaos	The pending changes from more highly isolated transactions cannot be overwritten.	Not supported by SQL Server.
ReadUncommitted	Shared locks are held while the data is being read, to avoid dirty reads, but the data can be changed before the end of the transaction, resulting in nonrepeatable reads or phantom data.	
ReadCommitted	A dirty read is possible, meaning that no shared locks are issued and no exclusive locks are honored.	The default value.
RepeatableRead	Locks are placed on all data that is used in a query, preventing other users from updating the data. This prevents nonrepeatable reads, but phantom rows are still possible.	
Serializable	A range lock is placed on the `DataSet`, preventing other users from updating or inserting rows into the `DataSet` until the transaction is complete.	

Source: MSDN Help File entry for "`IsolationLevel` Enumeration."

11

The Connection Object

When a transaction is active on a given connection, any command issued against the data source at the other end of that connection must be placed under the control of that transaction. Recall that this is accomplished by setting the command's Transaction property to the active transaction:

```
Me.cmdProductsInsert.Transaction = transX
```

If you attempt to execute a command that has not been placed under the control of the active transaction, you get an error message similar to the following:

```
Execute requires the command to have a transaction object when the connection
assigned to the command is in a pending local transaction. The Transaction
property of the command has not been initialized.
```

Within the connection associated with a pending transaction, changes made by a given command are visible to any other command issued against that connection (and, therefore, under the control of the same transaction). This is true regardless of the isolation level you have set on the transaction.

You should also be aware that the isolation level that you specify guarantees only that the back-end database will conduct the transaction with no *lower* isolation level than that specified: It goes not guarantee that it won't conduct it using a higher isolation level if it decides that this is necessary or prudent. If the database has elected to use a different IsolationLevel than the one specified, but the level used cannot be determined, the transaction's IsolationLevel property is set to IsolationLevel.Unspecified.

Nesting Transactions

The OleDbTransaction class exposes a Begin() method that permits you to start a nested transaction within an existing one:

```
Me.conFoo.Open()
Dim transX As OleDb.OleDbTransaction = Me.conFoo.BeginTransaction
'Make some data changes…
Dim transY As OleDb.OleDbTransaction = transX.Begin()
'Make some data changes...
transY.Rollback()    'Rolls back the nested transaction
transX.Commit()      'Commits the outer transaction
Me.conFoo.Close()
```

Not all database products support nested transactions: Oracle and Microsoft Access support them, for example, but SQL Server does not.

11

Using Named Transactions

The good news is, SQL Server supports an alternate facility that permits you to accomplish much the same thing as the nested transactions of Oracle and Access. This facility is called *named transactions*. This code illustrates the use of a named transaction:

```
Me.conNw.Open()
Dim transX As SqlClient.SqlTransaction = _
Me.conNw.BeginTransaction(IsolationLevel.ReadCommitted, "TranMain")
'Make first set of data changes, then...
transX.Save("GoodSoFar")  'Save them
'Make second set of data changes, then...
transX.Rollback("GoodSoFar") 'Roll them back
'Make third set of data changes, then...
transX.Commit() 'Commit them
Me.conNw.Close()
```

These statements result in the first and third set of data changes being committed to the database, but not the second set.

Transaction-Related Applications on the Code Website

Two applications that illustrate the use of transactions are included in the code for this chapter. TransactionsAndDataSets illustrates a number of basic behaviors of transactions, some related functionality of the DataSet, and interactions between the two. TransactionIsolationLevels illustrates the effect of IsolationLevel settings on the various read and write operations.

Both applications employ most of the ADO.NET objects discussed in this chapter, including connections, commands, DataSets, DataTables, and DataAdapters, so it is suggested that you defer your examination of these apps until after you have read the material on each of those objects. Accordingly, the discussion of the apps is deferred to the section "Illustrative Applications on the Code Website," near the end of this chapter.

Connection Pooling

An overhead is associated with opening connections, caused by the check of security credentials and other low-level operations that must be performed each time a connection is opened. For applications that never see more than a few concurrent users, this does not ordinarily become an issue, but in a large enterprise applications with hundreds or even thousands of concurrent users, the cumulative overhead can be significant.

For this reason, most ADO.NET providers implement some form of *connection pooling*, a technique wherein similar connections are grouped into pools and kept available for reuse even when they are no longer immediately needed. With most of the .NET

11

The `Connection` **Object**

data providers, connection pooling is done automatically. When you execute the `Open()` method of a `Connection` object, any existing connection pools are automatically examined to see whether a suitable one is available. If so, and if that pool has a connection that is not already being used, that connection is loaned to you. If the suitable pool has no available connection but is not already filled with its maximum number of connections, a new connection is created, added to the pool, and allocated to satisfy your request. If the suitable pool is already filled, your request is queued. If no suitable pool is found, a new pool is opened, `Connection` objects are added to it as required to satisfy a minimum pool size, and one of those connections is allocated to satisfy your request.

A pooled connection is released back into its pool when you call its `Close()` or `Dispose()` method. If you never do that, your connection is returned to the connection pool only if the maximum pool size is reached while the connection is still valid. If your connection times out before the maximum pool size is reached (*if* it is reached), it isn't reused.

The bottom line is, you always should use `Close()` or `Dispose()` for your connections explicitly!

> **NOTE**
>
> You should not call `Close()` or `Dispose()` on a `Connection` object, a `DataReader`, or any other managed object in the `Finalize` method of your class. In a finalizer, you should release only unmanaged resources that your class owns directly. For more information, see the Visual Studio Help file entry "Programming for Garbage Collection," listed in the "Further Reading" section at the end of this chapter.

The determination about which connections to pool is based on their `ConnectionStrings`. To be placed in an existing pool, the connection string of the requesting `Connection` object must be the same as the one associated with the `Connection` object that originally opened the available connection. The specifics of what constitutes an *exact* match are up to the provider, but many require a string that includes the same values for the same parameters and also specifies them in the same order, possibly with the same capitalization. In other words, this is a letter-for-letter, identical string. This means that your provider might not consider any two of the following three connection strings as matches:

```
integrated security=SSPI;data source=localhost;initial catalog=pubs
data source=localhost;initial catalog=pubs;integrated security=SSPI
Data Source=localhost;Initial Catalog=pubs;Integrated Security=SSPI
```

The best way to ensure that connection strings that you *want* to be considered the same *are* considered the same by your provider is to store them centrally in your application—for example, in a configuration file or in a public property to which

11

you can refer as needed. Then whenever you need to specify that connection string anywhere in your code, you obtain it from that single location. This ensures that the same set of connection parameters always equates to the same connection string.

Most providers supply connection string parameters that enable you to control various aspects of connection-pooling behavior, if you need to. For example, with both the SQL Server and Oracle data providers, you can set a limit on how long reusable connections are kept alive, set minimums and maximums on the number of connections kept alive in the pool, or even turn off connection pooling altogether. These settings are controlled with key/value pairs that can be added to the connection's ConnectionString. Keys include such items as Pooling (a Boolean, to turn pooling on or off), Connection Lifetime, Max Pool Size, and Min Pool Size.

Exception Handling with Connection **Objects**

Attempts to open or use a connection can fail for a variety of reasons, including external conditions that you can't control and that might vary among instances of application use. The maximum number of concurrent connections allowed by your company's database license might be reached under heavy usage, a network connection might act up, or an invalid parameter in your connection string might derail the attempt. Also, as noted earlier, it is critical that you explicitly close any connection that you open.

For all of these reasons, connections should always be opened and closed within a Try-Catch-Finally block, such as the following:

```
Try
    conPubs.Open()
    drX = cmdAuthorSelect.ExecuteReader()
    Me.txtOutput.Text = "
    While drX.Read()
        Me.txtOutput.Text = Me.txtOutput.Text & _
            drX("au_id") & ControlChars.Tab & _
            drX("au_lname") & ", " & _
            drX("au_fname") & ControlChars.NewLine
    End While

Catch ex As Exception
    Console.WriteLine(ex.Message)

Finally
    conPubs.Close()
End Try
```

Besides writing an entry to the console, you could throw the exception up to a higher-level handler, write an entry to a log file or to the Windows event log, or call a method that automatically sends some appropriate person an email.

11

The `Connection` **Object**

Placing the call to the `Close()` method in the `Finally` block ensures that the connection always gets closed, even if an error occurred after it was opened.

You can also determine the state of a connection at any point through its `State` property. The `State` property takes values—`Broken`, `Closed`, `Connecting`, `Executing`, `Fetching`, and `Open`—from the `ConnectionState` enumeration.

The `Command` Object

The `Command` object (`SqlCommand` or `OleDbCommand`, for example) houses an SQL statement (or stored procedure name or database table name) and associated parameters. It can be executed in a variety of ways to retrieve data from or change data in its target database.

The `Command` object can be used in a variety of ways. Its own `ExecuteReader()`, `ExecuteScalar()`, and `ExecuteXmlReader()` methods can be invoked to return a `DataReader` object, a single value, or an `XmlReader` object, respectively. Its `ExecuteNonQuery()` method can be invoked to execute a `Transact-SQL` statement against the connection. Alternatively, the command object can be assigned to one of the `Command` properties of a `DataAdapter` object (`SelectCommand`, `InsertCommand`, `DeleteCommand`, or `UpdateCommand`), where it then is used in a `SELECT`, `INSERT`, `DELETE`, or `UPDATE` action against the `DataAdapter`'s data source.

Important properties of the `Command` object include its `Name`, `CommandType`, `CommandText`, `Connection`, and `Parameters`. A `Command` object's `CommandType` can be `Text`, `Stored Procedure`, or `TableDirect`. (Note that `TableDirect` is supported by only the OLE DB data provider, specifically *not* by the `SqlClient` provider). Its `CommandText` can be a complete SQL statement or simply the name of a stored procedure or table. Its `Connection` property must be assigned a `Connection` object that establishes a connection to the required database. Finally, its `Parameters` collection must include `Parameter` objects for all parameters referenced in its `CommandText` property.

Preparing a `Command` Object to Execute an SQL Statement

Here, for example, are statements that initialize a `Command` object to perform an SQL `SELECT` operation against the authors table in the pubs database:

> **NOTE**
>
> Several examples in this chapter (and other chapters in the "Database Programming" section) use the Pubs and Northwind sample databases. These ship with SQL Server and can be installed when that product is installed. Alternatively, they can be installed by running the `instpubs.sql` and `instnwnd.sql` SQL scripts, which are typically found in `C:\Program Files\Microsoft SQL Server\MSSQL\Install`.

11

```
Dim conPubs As New System.Data.SqlClient.SqlConnection
Dim cmdAuthorSelect As New System.Data.SqlClient.SqlCommand

conPubs.ConnectionString = "data source=localhost;initial catalog=pubs;"
    & "integrated security=SSPI"
cmdAuthorSelect.CommandType = CommandType.Text
cmdAuthorSelect.CommandText = "SELECT a.au_id, a.au_lname, a.au_fname "
    & "from authors a ORDER BY au_lname, au_fname"
cmdAuthorSelect.Connection = conPubs
```

This Command object requires no parameters, so none is declared or added to it. But now consider an INSERT statement to add a record to the same table:

```
dim strSql as string
strSql = "INSERT INTO authors(au_id, au_lname, au_fname) "
strSql += "VALUES (@au_id, @au_lname, @au_fname); "
strSql += "SELECT au_id, au_lname, au_fname FROM authors WHERE (au_id = @au_id)"
Me.cmdAuthorsInsert.CommandText = strSql
Me.cmdAuthorsInsert.CommandText = "INSERT INTO authors(au_id, au_lname, au_fname) "
Me.cmdAuthorsInsert.CommandText += "VALUES (@au_id, @au_lname, @au_fname); "
Me.cmdAuthorsInsert.CommandText += "SELECT au_id, au_lname, au_fname "
Me.cmdAuthorsInsert.CommandText += "FROM authors WHERE (au_id = @au_id)"
Me.cmdAuthorsInsert.Connection = Me.conPubs

Dim prmAu_Id As New System.Data.SqlClient.SqlParameter( _
     "@au_id", System.Data.SqlDbType.VarChar, 11, "au_id")
Dim prmAu_LName As New System.Data.SqlClient.SqlParameter( _
     "@au_lname", System.Data.SqlDbType.VarChar, 40, "au_lname")
Dim prmAu_FName As New System.Data.SqlClient.SqlParameter( _
     "@au_fname", System.Data.SqlDbType.VarChar, 20, "au_fname")
Me.cmdAuthorsInsert.Parameters.Add(prmAu_Id)
Me.cmdAuthorsInsert.Parameters.Add(prmAu_LName)
Me.cmdAuthorsInsert.Parameters.Add(prmAu_FName)
```

The latter statements, which declare and instantiate Parameter objects and then add them to the command's Parameters collection, can be written more concisely as follows:

```
Me.cmdAuthorsInsert.Parameters.Add(New System.Data.SqlClient.SqlParameter( _
     "@au_id", System.Data.SqlDbType.VarChar, 11, "au_id"))
Me.cmdAuthorsInsert.Parameters.Add(New System.Data.SqlClient.SqlParameter( _
     "@au_lname", System.Data.SqlDbType.VarChar, 40, "au_lname"))
Me.cmdAuthorsInsert.Parameters.Add(New System.Data.SqlClient.SqlParameter( _
     "@au_fname", System.Data.SqlDbType.VarChar, 20, "au_fname"))
```

11

The `Command` Object

Note that the `Parameter` objects in the previous statements are instantiated with four parameters: *parameterName*, its *dbType*, its *size*, and its *sourceColumn*. The `Parameter` object has additional properties, including *direction* (Input or Output) and *isNullable*. Different overloads of the `Parameter`'s constructor can accommodate explicit settings for those properties as well.

The `OleDbCommand` Object and Named Parameters

Named parameters such as those used earlier are not supported by the OleDB provider, either for SQL statements or for stored procedures. When using this provider, you must use a question mark (?) in your SQL statement or statements to indicate parameters, and the order of `Parameters` in the `Parameters` collection of the command object must correspond exactly to the order in which you want their values substituted for the question mark placeholders.

Here is the `OleDb` version of the previous INSERT command:

```
Dim conPubsOleDb As New System.Data.SqlClient.SqlConnection
Dim cmdAuthorsInsertOleDbAs New System.Data.SqlClient.SqlCommand

conPubsOleDb.ConnectionString = "Data Source=localhost;Initial Catalog
    =pubs;" + Provider="SQLOLEDB.1";Integrated Security=SSPI;"
cmdAuthorsInsertOleDb.CommandType = CommandType.Text
Me.cmdAuthorsInsertOleDb.Connection = Me.conPubsOleDb

Me.cmdAuthorsInsertOleDb.CommandText = _
    "INSERT INTO authors(au_id, au_lname, au_fname) " + _
    WHERE (au_id = ?)"VALUES (?, ?, ?); SELECT au_id, au_lname,
    au_fname FROM authors
Me.cmdAuthorsInsertOleDb.Parameters.Add(New System.Data.OleDb.OleDbParameter
    ("au_id", System.Data.OleDb.OleDbType.VarChar, 11, "au_id"))
Me.cmdAuthorsInsertOleDb.Parameters.Add(New System.Data.OleDb.OleDbParameter
    ("au_lname", System.Data.OleDb.OleDbType.VarChar, 40, "au_lname"))
Me.cmdAuthorsInsertOleDb.Parameters.Add(New System.Data.OleDb.OleDbParameter
    ("au_fname", System.Data.OleDb.OleDbType.VarChar, 20, "au_fname"))
Me.cmdAuthorsInsertOleDb.Parameters.Add(New System.Data.OleDb.OleDbParameter
    ("Select_au_id", System.Data.OleDb.OleDbType.VarChar, 11, "au_id"))
```

11

With the `SqlClient` version of the `Command` object, you could have changed the order in which you added `Parameters` to the collection without causing problems. Here you cannot.

Preparing a `Command` **Object to Call a Stored Procedure**

The statements to set up a `Command` object to call a stored procedure are similar to those used earlier for executing an SQL statement. However, instead of setting the `CommandType` to `CommandType.Text`, you must set it to `CommandType.StoredProcedure`:

```
cmdAuthorSelect.CommandType = CommandType.StoredProcedure
```

You must then set the `CommandText` property to the name of the stored procedure that you want to execute:

```
cmdAuthorSelect.CommandText = SelectAuthors
```

If your stored procedure requires parameters, you declare, instantiate, and initialize them just as you do for the *Text* `CommandType`.

```
Me.cmdAuthorsInsertSP.CommandType = System.Data.CommandType.StoredProcedure
Me.cmdAuthorsInsertSP.CommandText = "[InsertAuthors]"
Me.cmdAuthorsInsertSP.Connection = Me.conPubs
Me.cmdAuthorsInsertSP.Parameters.Add(New System.Data.SqlClient.
SqlParameter("@RETURN_VALUE", System.Data.SqlDbType.Int, 4, System.Data.
ParameterDirection.ReturnValue, False, CType(0, Byte), CType(0, Byte), ",
 System.Data.DataRowVersion.Current, Nothing))
Me.cmdAuthorsInsertSP.Parameters.Add(New System.Data.SqlClient.
SqlParameter("@au_id", System.Data.SqlDbType.VarChar, 11, "au_id"))
Me.cmdAuthorsInsertSP.Parameters.Add(New System.Data.SqlClient.
SqlParameter("@au_lname", System.Data.SqlDbType.VarChar, 40, "au_lname"))
Me.cmdAuthorsInsertSP.Parameters.Add(New System.Data.SqlClient.
SqlParameter("@au_fname", System.Data.SqlDbType.VarChar, 20, "au_fname"))
```

In the previous code, the parameters were declared, instantiated, and initialized in the same statement in which they were added to the `Command` object's `Parameters` collection. Note that, for the first parameters, an overload of the `SqlParameter` constructor was used with the maximum number of arguments.

If you split the declaration, instantiation, and initialization of the new `Parameter` from the statement that adds it to the `Parameters` collection, it would look like the following:

11

The `Command` Object

```
Dim prmRetVal As New System.Data.SqlClient.SqlParameter( _
    "@RETURN_VALUE", System.Data.SqlDbType.Int, _
    4, System.Data.ParameterDirection.ReturnValue, _
    False, CType(0, Byte), CType(0, Byte), _
    ", System.Data.DataRowVersion.Current, Nothing)
Me.cmdAuthorsInsertSP.Parameters.Add(prmRetVal)
```

Here's the signature for this 10-argument constructor:

```
Public Sub New( _
    ByVal parameterName As String, _
    ByVal dbType As SqlDbType, _
    ByVal size As Integer, _
    ByVal direction As ParameterDirection, _
    ByVal isNullable As Boolean, _
    ByVal precision As Byte, _
    ByVal scale As Byte, _
    ByVal sourceColumn As String, _
    ByVal sourceVersion As DataRowVersion, _
    ByVal value As Object _
)
```

I used this overload because I needed to specify that the `@RETURN_VALUE` parameter was *ReturnValue* (`ParameterDirection.ReturnValue`) rather than *Input*, *Output*, or *InputOutput*. The 10-argument overload is the only one that permits that property to be specified.

Alternatively, you could have used a less complex overload and then specified the `Parameter`'s direction in a separate statement:

```
Dim foo As SqlClient.SqlParameter("@RETURN_VALUE", SqlDbType.Int, 4)
foo.Direction = ParameterDirection.ReturnValue
```

Procedure overloads in .NET frequently provide you with many different ways to accomplish the same thing. Having so many choices can at first be bewildering, but as you become more comfortable with .NET, it begins to feel more like having a conversation with someone in your native language. You can say something in many different ways, and you can finely tailor your choice to the specific situation.

Preparing a `Command` Object to Call a `TableDirect`

Only the OleDB data provider supports a third `CommandType` for `Command` objects: `TableDirect`. With this `CommandType`, you set the `CommandText` property to the name of the table to be accessed. If the table name contains special characters, you might need to use escape character syntax or include qualifying characters.

```
cmdTitlesPublishersSelect.CommandType = CommandType.TableDirect
cmdTitlesPublishersSelect.CommandText = "titles"
```

In the upcoming section "The DataReader Object," you can see an example of an OleDbCommand object that uses TableDirect.

Execute Methods of the Command Object

ExecuteReader()
The ExecuteReader() method of the Command object returns an ADO.NET DataReader object. An example of the use of this method is provided later in the section "The DataReader Object."

ExecuteScalar()
The ExecuteScalar() method of the Command object returns a single value, the contents of the first column of the first row of the result set. In the following code, the result set consists of a single row of one column, a calculated one representing an author's name.

```
Dim conPubs As New System.Data.SqlClient.SqlConnection
Dim cmdGetOneAuthor As New System.Data.SqlClient.SqlCommand
conPubs.ConnectionString = "data source=localhost;" + _
    "initial catalog=pubs;integrated security=SSPI"
cmdGetOneAuthor.CommandType = CommandType.Text
cmdGetOneAuthor.CommandText = "SELECT a.au_fname +' '+ a.au_lname as AuthorName "+ _
    "from authors a WHERE a.au_id = '341-22-1782'"
cmdGetOneAuthor.Connection = conPubs

Try
    conPubs.Open()
    Me.txtAuthorName.Text = cmdGetOneAuthor.ExecuteScalar()

Catch ex As Exception
    MessageBox.Show(ex.Message)

Finally
    conPubs.Close()
End Try
```

11

The Command Object

The WHERE clause in the CommandText string ensures that only a single row is returned. However, that is not an ExecuteScalar() requirement: ExecuteScalar() is perfectly willing to ignore extra rows. If you want the name of the author with the highest year-to-date sales, you could do so by retrieving a multi-row result set ordered descendingly on the sales:

```
cmdGetYtdSales.CommandText = "SELECT '('+ CAST(titles.ytd_sales As
➡Char(6)) + ') ' "+ _
        "authors.au_lname + ' '+ authors.au_fname as YtdSales FROM authors "+ _
        "INNER JOIN titleauthor ON authors.au_id = titleauthor.au_id " + _
        "INNER JOIN titles ON titleauthor.title_id = titles.title_id ORDER BY
➡titles.ytd_sales DESC"
```

ExecuteScalar() would return the value from the first row.

ExecuteNonQuery()

The ExecuteNonQuery() method of the Command object executes an SQL statement against the specified connection and returns the number of rows affected. The following code inserts a record into the authors table of the pubs database and writes the number of rows affected to a textbox control:

```
Dim conPubs As New System.Data.SqlClient.SqlConnection
Dim cmdInsertAuthorsRecord As New System.Data.SqlClient.SqlCommand

conPubs.ConnectionString = "data source=localhost;initial catalog=pubs;
➡integrated security=SSPI"
cmdInsertAuthorsRecord.CommandType = CommandType.Text
cmdInsertAuthorsRecord.CommandText = "INSERT INTO authors(au_id, au_lname,
➡au_fname, phone, contract) VALUES ('987-65-4321', 'Diesel', 'Danny', '555 289-
➡9382', 1)"
cmdInsertAuthorsRecord.Connection = conPubs

Try
    conPubs.Open()
    Me.txtRowsAffected.Text = cmdInsertAuthorsRecord.ExecuteNonQuery()

Catch ex As Exception
    MessageBox.Show(ex.Message)

Finally
    conPubs.Close()
End Try
```

ExecuteXmlReader()

The ExecuteXmlReader() method of the Command object sends the CommandText to the connection and builds an XmlReader object. This method and the XmlReader object are discussed in Chapter 15, "ADO.NET and XML."

The DataReader **Object**

A DataReader object retrieves a read-only, forward-only stream of data from a database. Compared to the combination of a DataAdapter and DataSet, it is very fast, so it's perfect for situations in which you simply need to retrieve some data from the database for display or use in computations.

The code that follows shows the basics of using a DataReader. You can find the form that incorporates this code on the website, or you can duplicate it on your system with the following steps:

1. Create a new Windows form.

2. Place a TextBox on the form, set its Multiline property to True, size it about 250×350 pixels, and name it "txtOutput."

3. Place a button control on the form, name it "btnReadData," and set its Text property to "Read Data." Your form should appear approximately as shown in Figure 11.1.

4. Double-click the button to create the code stub for its Click event, and enter this code:

```
Private Sub btnReadData_Click(ByVal sender As System.Object, _
        ByVal e As System.EventArgs) Handles btnReadData.Click

    Dim conPubs As New System.Data.SqlClient.SqlConnection
    Dim cmdAuthorSelect As New System.Data.SqlClient.SqlCommand
    Dim drX As System.Data.SqlClient.SqlDataReader

    conPubs.ConnectionString = "data source=localhost;" + _
        "initial catalog=pubs;integrated security=SSPI"
    cmdAuthorSelect.CommandType = CommandType.Text
    cmdAuthorSelect.CommandText = "SELECT a.au_id, a.au_lname, " + _
        "a.au_fname from authors a ORDER BY au_lname, au_fname"
    cmdAuthorSelect.Connection = conPubs

    Try
        conPubs.Open()
        drX = cmdAuthorSelect.ExecuteReader()
        Me.txtOutput.Text = "
```

11

The DataReader Object

```
        While drX.Read()
            Me.txtOutput.Text = Me.txtOutput.Text & _
                drX("au_id") & ControlChars.Tab & _
                drX("au_lname") & ", " & _
                drX("au_fname") & ControlChars.NewLine
        End While

    Catch ex As Exception
        MessageBox.Show(ex.Message)

    Finally
        conPubs.Close()
    End Try

End Sub
```

When you click the Read Data button, you should see something like what is shown in Figure 11.2.

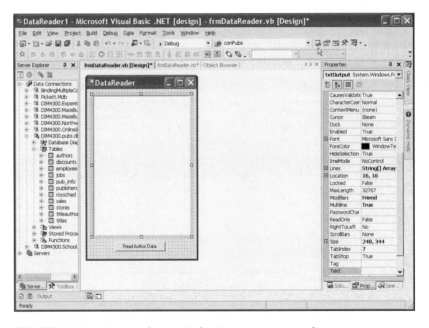

FIGURE 11.1   Layout of controls for the DataReader form.

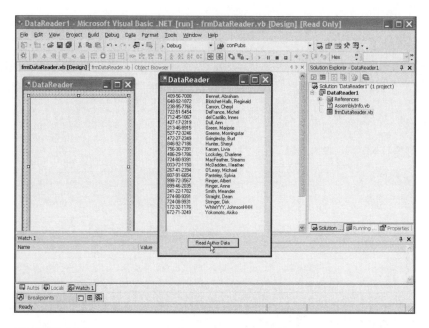

FIGURE 11.2   `DataReader` form after clicking the Read Data button.

For comparison, here's the `Click` event handler for a button that fills the
`txtOutput` TextBox using a `DataReader` that gets its data from an `OleDbCommand`
object whose `CommandType` is `TableDirect`:

```
Private Sub btnFillWithTableDirect_Click( _
        ByVal sender As System.Object, _
        ByVal e As System.EventArgs) _
        Handles btnFillWithTableDirect.Click

    Dim conPubsOleDb As New System.Data.OleDb.OleDbConnection
    Dim cmdTitlesPublishersSelect As New System.Data.OleDb.OleDbCommand
    Dim drX As System.Data.OleDb.OleDbDataReader

    conPubsOleDb.ConnectionString = "Data Source=localhost;Initial
➥Catalog=pubs;" + _
        "Provider="SQLOLEDB.1";Integrated Security=SSPI;"
    cmdTitlesPublishersSelect.CommandType = CommandType.TableDirect
    cmdTitlesPublishersSelect.CommandText = "titles"
    cmdTitlesPublishersSelect.Connection = conPubsOleDb

    Try
        conPubsOleDb.Open()
```

11

The `DataReader` Object

```
drX = cmdTitlesPublishersSelect.ExecuteReader()
Me.txtOutput.Text = "
While drX.Read()
    Me.txtOutput.Text = Me.txtOutput.Text & _
        drX("title") & " (" & _
        drX("price") & ")" & ControlChars.NewLine
End While

Catch ex As Exception
    MessageBox.Show(ex.ToString)

Finally
    conPubsOleDb.Close()
End Try

End Sub
```

The `DataSet` **Object**

As mentioned earlier, the `DataSet` object is not one of the provider-specific set of objects, but it plays a critical role in the functioning of the `DataAdapter`, which *is* one of that set. This section considers it now before moving on to the `DataAdapter`.

A `DataSet` is like an in-memory version of a database. It can contain multiple `DataTables`, which are the in-memory equivalent of their persistent sisters, database tables. Similar to a database, the `DataSet` permits relationships (`DataRelations`) to be defined among those tables, and constraints to be defined on records and values that can be entered into them.

Not provider-specific, the `DataSet` object has only one flavor, living a level of abstraction away from any "real-world" persistent databases. You can't do some things with a `DataSet` that you can do with a database: For example, a `DataSet` won't accommodate stored procedures. However, particularly when used in combination with a `DataAdapter` (discussed shortly), a `DataSet` can be the key to beautifully managed and sophisticated facilities for performing data manipulation without requiring a constant connection to a database.

The following code declares and instantiates a `DataSet` named "pubs":

```
Dim dsData As New DataSet
dsData.DataSetName = "pubs"
```

11

Here's another way to do the same thing, using an overload of the DataSet constructor:

```
Dim dsData As New DataSet("pubs")
```

Strongly Typed versus Weakly Typed DataSets

Two flavors of the DataSet object are provided for in ADO.NET. DataSets instantiated directly from the System.Data.DataSet are of a variety known as *untyped* because they contain little specialized schema information. You will see examples of this type later in this chapter (for example, in the section "The DataRow Object").

The other DataSet flavor is the *strongly typed* DataSet. A strongly typed DataSet is instantiated from a collection of classes that inherit from System.Data.DataSet and related classes but that contain detailed schema information. Visual Studio builds a strongly typed DataSet class from information stored in an XML schema. The latter is a text file, stored with an extension of .xsd, that describes a database structure in XML. The most common way to obtain such a file is to let the Visual Studio DataAdapter Wizard create it for you. The DataAdapter Wizard reads schema information from a back-end database and translates what it learns into XML that it places in an .xsd file. It adds the .xsd file to your project and then generates a custom class from it. The generated class is stored in a file with the same name as the schema, but with a .vb extension. It becomes visible in your project if you toggle the "Show All Files" button in the Solution Explorer. You will find it located hierarchically under the corresponding .xsd file.

An XSD file can also be created using the WriteXmlSchema() method of a DataSet object; by running the XML Schema Definition Tool (XSD.EXE), available in the bin directory of the .NET SDK (Software Developer's Kit) downloadable from MSDN.Microsoft.com; with various third-party tools; or manually (although most will find that method to be way too much trouble). A new DataSet class can be generated from the .xsd file any time by opening the latter in the Visual Studio Designer (which you can do simply by double-clicking the file in the Solution Explorer), right-clicking, and selecting Generate DataSet from the shortcut menu. When the schema file is open in the designer, you will also find a Generate DataSet option on the Schema submenu of the main Visual Studio menu. Figure 11.3 shows a schema file open in the designer, the schema menu with the Generate DataSet option, and the schema (.xsd) file and associated class in the project hierarchy in the Solution Explorer.

11

The DataSet Object

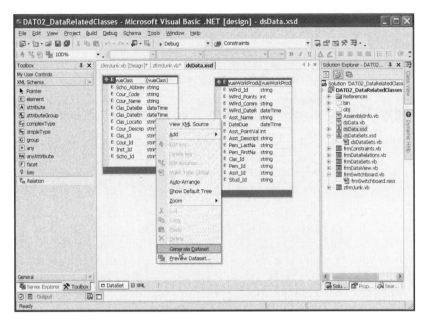

FIGURE 11.3 XSD schema file and custom DataSet class.

When the custom DataSet class is available in your project, you can use it as the blueprint for DataSet objects that you declare and instantiate in your application. Unlike untyped DataSet objects, these strongly typed objects permit you to refer to contained table and column names through properties rather than indexer arguments. Thus, instead of getting the value for a particular column of a particular table row through this syntax:

```
strLastName = dsUntyped.Tables("Authors").Rows(0)("au_lname")
```

you can get it through this much simpler and more intuitive syntax:

```
strLastName = dsTyped.authors(0).au_lname
```

Here are those same statements, with a little more code around them for context. Note that "dsDataSets" is a custom class generated from an .xsd file of the same name.

```
Dim dsUntyped As New DataSet
Dim tblAuthors As New DataTable
Dim strLastName As String
```

```
'Create an untyped DataSet object with one three-column table
tblAuthors = New DataTable("Authors")
dsUntyped.Tables.Add(tblAuthors)

tblAuthors.Columns.Add("au_id", GetType(Integer))
tblAuthors.Columns.Add("au_lname", GetType(String))
tblAuthors.Columns.Add("au_fname", GetType(Integer))

strLastName = dsUntyped.Tables("Authors").Rows(0)("au_lname")

'Create a strongly typed DataSet object from an existing custom
    DataSet class
Dim dsTyped As New dsDataSets
strLastName = dsTyped.authors(0).au_lname
```

Besides offering the advantage of more intuitive syntax (and design-time IntelliSense assistance), strongly typed `DataSets` can prevent type mismatch errors and also errors resulting from misspelled string-valued indexer arguments—for example, `Tables("Auhtors")`—or out-of-bounds integer-valued indexer arguments—for example, `Tables(1)`. These errors can be identified at compilation rather than runtime.

Nevertheless, there are some disadvantages to using strongly typed `DataSets`. The biggest is that they must be regenerated whenever the data structure changes, and all applications that use them must then be rebuilt using a reference to the new version. Strongly typed `DataSets` also add a small amount of overhead to code execution and can thus affect performance slightly.

Subordinate Objects of the `DataSet`

`DataSets` contain two public collections: `Tables` and `Relations`. The first contains `DataTable` objects, and the second contains `DataRelation` objects.

The `DataTable` Object

A `DataTable` is an in-memory version of the database equivalent. It contains several public collections, including `ChildRelations`, `Columns`, `Constraints`, `ExtendedProperties`, `ParentRelations`, and `Rows`. The most basic of these are the `DataTables` `Columns` and `Rows` collections.

The following code declares and instantiates a `DataTable` named "authors" and adds the table to the `pubs` `DataSet`:

```
Dim dsData As New DataSet
dsData.DataSetName = "pubs"
Dim tblAuthors As New DataTable
```

11

The `DataSet` Object

```
tblAuthors.TableName = "authors"
dsData.Tables.Add(tblAuthors)
```

The following statements accomplish the same result using more concise constructor overloads:

```
Dim dsData As New DataSet("pubs")
dsData.Tables.Add(New DataTable("authors"))
```

The `DataColumn` Object

The `DataColumn` object represents the schema of a column in a `DataTable`. It has *ColumnName* and *Caption* properties, which house its internal and display names, respectively; a *DataType* property; and numerous other properties similar to what you see for a column in a database table. Table 11.3 shows a complete list of the public properties of a `DataTable`.

TABLE 11.3

Selected `DataColumn` Public Properties (from the MSDN Help File for Visual Studio 2003)

Property	Purpose
`AllowDBNull`	Gets or sets a value indicating whether null values are allowed in this column for rows belonging to the table
`AutoIncrement`	Gets or sets a value indicating whether the column automatically increments the value of the column for new rows added to the table
`AutoIncrementSeed`	Gets or sets the starting value for a column that has its `AutoIncrement` property set to `True`
`AutoIncrementStep`	Gets or sets the increment used by a column with its `AutoIncrement` property set to `True`
`Caption`	Gets or sets the caption for the column
`ColumnMapping`	Gets or sets the `MappingType` of the column
`ColumnName`	Gets or sets the name of the column in the `DataColumnCollection`
`DataType`	Gets or sets the type of data stored in the column
`DefaultValue`	Gets or sets the default value for the column when creating new rows
`Expression`	Gets or sets the expression used to filter rows, calculate the values in a column, or create an agGTDate column
`ExtendedProperties`	Gets the collection of custom user information associated with a `DataColumn`
`MaxLength`	Gets or sets the maximum length of a text column
`Ordinal`	Gets the position of the column in the `DataColumnCollection` collection
`Prefix`	Gets or sets an XML prefix that aliases the namespace of the `DataTable`

11

TABLE 11.3

Continued

Property	Purpose
ReadOnly	Gets or sets a value indicating whether the column allows changes after a row has been added to the table
Table	Gets the DataTable to which the column belongs
Unique	Gets or sets a value indicating whether the values in each row of the column must be unique

The following code declares and instantiates a DataColumn named "au_id" and adds it to an existing DataTable object named tblAuthors:

```
Dim colAu_Id As New DataColumn
colAu_Id.ColumnName = "au_id"
colAu_Id.DataType = GetType(String)
tblAuthors.Columns.Add(colAu_Id)
```

Here's a more concise way to do the same thing:

```
Dim colAu_Id As New DataColumn("au_id", GetType(String))
tblAuthors.Columns.Add(colAu_Id)
```

And here's an even more concise way:

```
tblAuthors.Columns.Add(New DataColumn("au_id", GetType(String)))
```

Here's how to add an identity column:

```
'Add an autoincrement column
Dim colAu_Id As New DataColumn("au_id", GetType(Integer))
tblAuthors.Columns.Add(colAu_Id)
With colAu_Id
    .AutoIncrement = True
    .AutoIncrementSeed = 1
    .AllowDBNull = False
    .Unique = True
End With
```

SQL Server's uniqueidentifer data type maps to a string type in a DataTable. You can define a uniqueidentifer column in a DataTable as follows:

```
Dim colAu_Id As New DataColumn("au_id", GetType(String))
tblAuthors.Columns.Add(colAu_Id)
With colAu_Id
```

11

The `DataSet` Object

```
    .AllowDBNull = False
    .DefaultValue = System.Guid.NewGuid.ToString
End With
```

There's a more concise way to do that, as well:

```
With tblAuthors.Columns.Add("au_id", GetType(String))
    .AllowDBNull = False
    .DefaultValue = System.Guid.NewGuid.ToString
End With
```

Note that this code uses the `NewGuid` method from the `System.Guid` namespace to get a globally unique identifier value. The `NewGuid` method is similar to SQL Server's `NewId()` function.

The `DataRow` Object

A `DataRow` object represents a single row of data within a `DataTable` and supports methods to view, insert, update, and delete its own data. Distinguishing it from its ADO counterpart, the ADO.NET `DataRow` can contain multiple versions of its data, designated Current, Default, Original, and Proposed. A `DataRow` also has a `RowState` property to indicate its relationship to the `DataTable` of which it is (or is not) a member. `RowStates` and versions are discussed shortly, but first, here are the basics.

The following code creates a `DataSet`, adds to it a single `DataTable`, defines three `DataColumns` for the `DataTable`, and populates the `DataTable` with two `DataRows`:

```
Dim dsData As New DataSet
dsData.DataSetName = "pubs"
Dim tblAuthors As New DataTable
tblAuthors.TableName = "authors"
dsData.Tables.Add(tblAuthors)

Dim colAu_Id As New DataColumn
colAu_Id.ColumnName = "au_id"
colAu_Id.DataType = GetType(String)
tblAuthors.Columns.Add(colAu_Id)

Dim colAu_Lname As New DataColumn
colAu_Lname.ColumnName = "au_lname"
colAu_Lname.DataType = GetType(String)
tblAuthors.Columns.Add(colAu_Lname)
```

11

```
Dim colAu_Fname As New DataColumn
colAu_Fname.ColumnName = "au_fname"
colAu_Fname.DataType = GetType(String)
tblAuthors.Columns.Add(colAu_Fname)

Dim objValues(2) As Object
objValues(0) = "987-65-4321"
objValues(1) = "Smithfield"
objValues(2) = "Stephanie"
tblAuthors.Rows.Add(objValues)
objValues(0) = "876-54-3210"
objValues(1) = "Johnson"
objValues(2) = "Wilfred"
tblAuthors.Rows.Add(objValues)

Me.DataGrid1.DataSource = dsData
Me.DataGrid1.DataMember = "authors"
```

Here is the same set of operations done with a more concise syntax, courtesy of the
.NET overloads for the `DataSet`, `DataTable`, and `DataColumn` constructors:

```
Dim dsData As New DataSet("pubs")
dsData.Tables.Add(New DataTable("authors"))

'The following statements illustrate some of the many ways you can
   create and add columns

'Method 1
Dim colAu_Id As New DataColumn
colAu_Id.ColumnName = "au_id"
colAu_Id.DataType = GetType(String)
tblAuthors.Columns.Add(colAu_Id)

'Method 2
Dim colAu_Lname As New DataColumn("au_lname", GetType(String))
tblAuthors.Columns.Add(colAu_Lname)

'Method 3
tblAuthors.Columns.Add(New DataColumn("au_fname", GetType(String)))

Dim objValues(2) As Object
objValues(0) = "765-43-2109"
objValues(1) = "Rigby"
objValues(2) = "Eleanor"
```

11

The `DataSet` Object

```
tblAuthors.Rows.Add(objValues)
objValues(0) = "654-32-1098"
objValues(1) = "Hickok"
objValues(2) = "Wild Bill"
tblAuthors.Rows.Add(objValues)


Me.DataGrid1.DataSource = dsData
Me.DataGrid1.DataMember = "authors"
```

With an identity column present, you need to use a different overload of the `Add()` method for the `Rows` collection. The following code adds a row to a `DataTable` in which the `au_id` column has been defined as an identity (as discussed earlier in the section "The `DataColumn` Object"):

```
Dim row As DataRow = tblAuthors.NewRow
row("au_lname") = "Brown"
row("au_fname") = "James"
tblAuthors.Rows.Add(row)
```

`RowStates` and Versions of a `DataRow`

The following code creates and manipulates a `DataRow` object in various ways, while tracking the `RowState` and versions. The code calls a `RowStateDescription()` method that accepts as parameters the `DataRow` object and a string version of the last code line executed. This returns a string that describes various aspects of the row's condition and values. So as not to distract from the main point at hand, that method isn't listed, but you can find that in the code files for the chapter, in the application `RowStateAndVersions`. Most important, you can see its output following the code listing.

```
Private Sub DemonstrateRowState()
    Dim tblX As DataTable = CreateTable()
    Dim rowX As DataRow

    Console.WriteLine()
    Console.WriteLine()
    Console.WriteLine("Row State & Versions")
    Console.WriteLine("----------------------")
    Console.WriteLine()

    ' Create a new DataRow.
    rowX = tblX.NewRow()
    Console.WriteLine(RowStateDescription(rowX, "rowX = tblX.NewRow()"))

    'Change a column value in the row
    rowX("ProductName") = "Ginzu Knife"
```

```
        Console.WriteLine(RowStateDescription(rowX, "rowX("ProductName") = "Ginzu
➥Knife""))

        'Add the row to a table
        tblX.Rows.Add(rowX)
        ' New row.
        Console.WriteLine(RowStateDescription(rowX, "tblX.Rows.Add(rowX)"))

        'Accept changes on the table
        tblX.AcceptChanges()
        Console.WriteLine(RowStateDescription(rowX, "tblX.AcceptChanges()"))

        'Change a column value in the row
        rowX("ProductName") = "Waffle Iron"
        Console.WriteLine(RowStateDescription(rowX, "rowX("ProductName") = "Waffle
➥Iron""))

        'Reject changes on the table
        tblX.RejectChanges()
        Console.WriteLine(RowStateDescription(rowX, "tblX.RejectChanges()"))

        'Delete the row
        rowX.Delete()
        Console.WriteLine(RowStateDescription(rowX, "rowX.Delete()"))

        MessageBox.Show("Actions completed - check Output Window.")
        Me.Dispose()
    End Sub

    Private Function CreateTable() As DataTable
        Dim tblX As DataTable = New DataTable("tblX")
        Dim colProductName As DataColumn = New DataColumn("ProductName",
➥Type.GetType("System.String"))
        tblX.Columns.Add(colProductName)
        CreateTable = tblX
    End Function
```

11

If run inside Visual Studio, the previous code writes the following output to the
Output window:

```
Row State & Versions
---------------------

Statement executed: rowX = tblX.NewRow()
Resulting RowState: Detached
```

The DataSet Object

```
Versions of Row being maintained: Proposed
    Proposed ProductName Value:

Statement executed: rowX("ProductName") = "Ginzu Knife"
Resulting RowState: Detached
Versions of Row being maintained: Proposed
    Proposed ProductName Value: Ginzu Knife


Statement executed: tblX.Rows.Add(rowX)
Resulting RowState: Added
Versions of Row being maintained: Current
    Current ProductName Value: Ginzu Knife


Statement executed: tblX.AcceptChanges()
Resulting RowState: Unchanged
Versions of Row being maintained: Current, Original
    Current ProductName Value: Ginzu Knife
    Original ProductName Value: Ginzu Knife


Statement executed: rowX("ProductName") = "Waffle Iron"
Resulting RowState: Modified
Versions of Row being maintained: Current, Original
    Current ProductName Value: Waffle Iron
    Original ProductName Value: Ginzu Knife


Statement executed: tblX.RejectChanges()
Resulting RowState: Unchanged
Versions of Row being maintained: Current, Original
    Current ProductName Value: Ginzu Knife
    Original ProductName Value: Ginzu Knife


Statement executed: rowX.Delete()
Resulting RowState: Deleted
Versions of Row being maintained: Original
    Original ProductName Value: Ginzu Knife
```

11

Table 11.4 breaks down the output, showing the effect of the various operations performed on the DataRow's RowState and versions.

TABLE 11.4

Effect of Various Operations on the `RowState` and Version

Statement Executed	Effect
Statement executed: `rowX = tblX.NewRow()` Resulting RowState: `Detached` Versions of row being maintained: `Proposed` Proposed ProductName value:	After the new row is created, its `RowState` is listed as "Detached" (that is, as `DataRowState.Detached`), indicating that it is not associated with a `DataTable`. At that point, the only version of the row that is available is the `Proposed` version, and it contains a null value for the `ProductName`.
Statement executed: `rowX("ProductName") = "Ginzu Knife"` Resulting `RowState`: `Detached` Versions of row being maintained: `Proposed` Proposed ProductName value: `Ginzu Knife`	When the `ProductName` is changed, the `RowState` and available versions of the `DataRow` remain as before, but the `ProductName` value in the `Proposed` version of the row holds the new value.
Statement executed: `tblX.Rows.Add(rowX)` Resulting `RowState`: `Added` Versions of row being maintained: `Current` Current ProductName value: `Ginzu Knife`	After it is added to a table, the `RowState` changes to `Added` and the version changes to `Current`. The `ProductName` value in the `Current` version is the one set before the record was added.
Statement executed: `tblX.AcceptChanges()` Resulting `RowState`: `Unchanged` Versions of row being maintained: `Current, Original` Current ProductName value: `Ginzu Knife` Original ProductName value: `Ginzu Knife`	When `AcceptChanges()` is subsequently called on the containing `DataTable`, the `RowState` changes to `Unchanged`, meaning that no changes have been made to it since it was loaded from another source or since its `AcceptChanges()` method was called. `AcceptChanges()` is typically called after changes in a `DataTable` are communicated to a back-end database so that the changes will not continue to be committed and recommitted to the database. Note however, that even though it's `RowState` is marked as `Unchanged`, an `Original` version of the `DataRow` is maintained and made available so that it remains possible to revert to the values in that version.

11

The DataSet Object

TABLE 11.4

Continued

Statement Executed	Effect
Statement executed: rowX("ProductName") = "Waffle Iron" Resulting RowState: Modified Versions of row being maintained: Current, Original Current ProductName value: Waffle Iron Original ProductName value: Ginzu Knife	The program's next action on the DataRow is to change the value of its ProductName column again. That results in an automatic change in its RowState to Modified. Again, Current and Original versions of the row remain available: the Current version contains the ProductName as just modified, whereas the Original version contains the premodification version of the ProductName. Obviously, because the old value is still around and accessible, you can revert to it before committing changes to the back-end database.
Statement executed: tblX.RejectChanges() Resulting RowState: Unchanged Versions of row being maintained: Current, Original Current ProductName value: Ginzu Knife Original ProductName value: Ginzu Knife	Calling the containing DataTable's RejectChanges() method restores the column values in the DataRow to their premodification state and leaves the RowState designation as Unchanged because it's back where it started (or, at least, to the state it had when AcceptChanges() was last invoked on its containing DataTable).
Statement executed: rowX.Delete() Resulting RowState: Deleted Versions of row being maintained: Original Original ProductName value: Ginzu Knife	Deleting the row results in a RowState of DataRowState.Deleted. But the Original version of the row remains available, leaving open the possibility of reversing the deletion before committing any changes to the back-end database.

The Constraint Object

As in a database, constraints in a DataSet can help prevent incorrect data from finding its way into a DataTable. Two types of constraint are provided for: the UniqueConstraint and the ForeignKeyConstraint. These are discussed later. Before entering that discussion, it is important to note that the DataSet class includes an EnforceConstraints property that can be used in an instantiated DataSet to suspend the enforcement of any constraints defined on DataTables contained in that DataSet. This avoids constraint violations that might otherwise result from harmless temporary conditions created during the loading of data sequentially into multiple tables. It also makes it possible to programmatically repair conditions that produce such violations.

The `UniqueConstraint`

The `UniqueConstraint` prevents nonunique values from being entered into a specified column or group of columns in a `DataTable`. For example, the following statements create and add a constraint on the `ID` field of a table of publishers:

```
Dim tblTitleAuthor As New DataTable("TitleAuthor")
Dim cstPub As New UniqueConstraint("Id", tblPublishers.Columns("pub_id"))
tblPublishers.Constraints.Add(cstPub)
```

`UniqueConstraints` can also be placed on multicolumn keys (also known as "compound" keys). To do that, you must first create an array of `DataColumns` that contains all the columns to be considered part of the key. Then you pass that array to an overload of the `UniqueConstraint` constructor that accepts a `DataColumns` array as a parameter. As before, you then add the constraint to the `DataTable`'s `Constraints` collection:

```
Dim tblTitleAuthor As New DataTable("TitleAuthor")
Dim acolKey(1) As DataColumn
acolKey(0) = tblTitleAuthor.Columns.Add("au_id")
acolKey(1) = tblTitleAuthor.Columns.Add("title_id")
Dim ucnTitleAuthor As New UniqueConstraint("TitleAuthor", acolKey)
tblTitleAuthor.Constraints.Add(ucnTitleAuthor)
```

There's a simpler way to add a `UniqueConstraint` to a `DataColumn`, however. The `DataColumn` object has a `Unique` property that, when set to `True`, automatically generates a `UniqueConstraint` and adds it to the host table's `Constraints` collection. Setting the property to `False` automatically removes any `UniqueConstraint` that is present for that column.

The `ForeignKeyConstraint`

The `ForeignKeyConstraint` is a tool for enforcing referential integrity. Options also permit you specify what to do with related rows in a child table when you update or delete parent rows.

To create a `ForeignKeyConstraint`, you specify a `DataColumn` in the parent table, a `DataColumn` in the child table, and, optionally, a name for the constraint:

```
Dim fkcPubTitle As New ForeignKeyConstraint( _
    tblPublishers.Columns("pub_id"), tblTitles.Columns("pub_id"))
```

or

```
Dim fkcPubTitle As New ForeignKeyConstraint( _
    tblPublishers.Columns("FkPubTitle", _
    tblPublishers.Columns("pub_id"), _
    tblTitles.Columns("pub_id"))
```

11

The `DataSet` Object

Before adding the `ForeignKeyConstraint` (to the child `DataTable`), you should add a `UniqueConstraint` to the key column in the parent table. This ensures that every child record can be linked uniquely to a single parent record.

```
Dim cstPub As New UniqueConstraint("Id", tblPublishers.Columns
    ("pub_id"))
tblPublishers.Constraints.Add(cstPub)
tblTitles.Constraints.Add(fkcPubTitle)
```

Besides preventing unwanted data changes, a `ForeignKeyConstraint` can be used to introduce certain kinds of desired changes. This is done using three of its properties: `DeleteRule`, `UpdateRule`, and `AcceptRejectRule`.

`DeleteRule` determines what ADO.NET does to related child rows when a parent row is deleted. The default setting for this rule is Cascade, which means that the delete operation is cascaded to the children: They also are deleted. Other settings are listed here:

- **None**—The orphaned child rows are left alone.
- **SetDefault**—The foreign key column in the linked child rows is set to the default value for that column.
- **SetNull**—The foreign key field in the linked child rows is set to null.

`UpdateRule` determines what ADO.NET does to related child rows when a parent row is updated. The default setting for this rule also is Cascade, which means that if the key value for a parent row is changed, the corresponding foreign key in the linked child rows is updated correspondingly. In practice, this facility is seldom used because, in most databases, after primary keys have been established, they seldom, if ever, get changed. Other settings for `UpdateRule` are the same as those listed for `DeleteRule`.

`AcceptRejectRule` determines what ADO.NET does to related child rows when a parent row's `AcceptChanges()` method is invoked. The default setting for this rule is None, which means that the child rows are left alone. The only other setting available is Cascade, which causes the `AcceptChanges()` method to be called on the child rows. You should be careful about doing that, however: If the updates in the child rows haven't been committed to the data source when a cascading `AcceptChanges()` method is called on their parent row, those child row updates might never get committed (because their `RowState` will have been reset to Unchanged, and only an additional change will set it back).

The `DataRelation` Object

The `DataRelation` object establishes a relationship between two tables in a `DataSet`. It has some similarities to a `Constraint`, but unlike a `Constraint`, it

11

can be used to keep child records automatically synchronized with parent records during table navigation.

A DataRelation also bears functional similarities to a DataTable. It can be used, for example, to supply rows of data to a data-aware control such as the DataGrid control. But unlike a DataTable, it automatically guarantees that rows supplied are only those linked to the currently selected record in its parent table. The Master-Detail forms produced by the Visual Studio Data Form Wizard (whose code is thoroughly dissected in Chapter 13, "Using the Data Form and DataAdapter Wizards in Windows Applications") provide an excellent example of DataRelations performing this function. In those forms, the detail (or "child") records are always displayed in a DataGrid control, and the records displayed there are always those that are linked to the currently displayed or selected master record by a user-designated foreign key. This is accomplished by binding the DataGrid not to a DataTable, but instead to a DataRelation between the master (parent) table and the detail (child) table.

The code that follows does several things: creates a DataSet and adds two DataTables to it, after first defining them; adds three rows to the first table and six rows to the second; creates a DataRelation between the two; binds two text box controls on a Windows form to columns of the parent table; and, finally, binds a DataGrid control on that form to the DataRelation. It represents a stripped-down, fully inclusive version (no external database involved) of a master-detail relationship such as used by Data Form Wizard forms.

```
dsDataRelational = New DataSet
Dim tblPublishers As New DataTable("Publishers")
dsDataRelational.Tables.Add(tblPublishers)
Dim tblTitles As New DataTable("Titles")
dsDataRelational.Tables.Add(tblTitles)
tblPublishers.Columns.Add("pub_id", GetType(Integer))
tblPublishers.Columns.Add("pub_name", GetType(String))
tblTitles.Columns.Add("title_id", GetType(Integer))
tblTitles.Columns.Add("title", GetType(String))
tblTitles.Columns.Add("pub_id", GetType(Integer))
Dim objValues(1) As Object
objValues(0) = 1
objValues(1) = "Cockeyed Views Books"
tblPublishers.Rows.Add(objValues)
objValues(0) = 2
objValues(1) = "PU Press"
tblPublishers.Rows.Add(objValues)
objValues(0) = 3
```

11

The DataSet Object

```
objValues(1) = "Portentous Publications"
tblPublishers.Rows.Add(objValues)

ReDim objValues(2)
 objValues(0) = 1
objValues(1) = "How to Raise Healthy Brundleflies"
objValues(2) = 1
tblTitles.Rows.Add(objValues)

objValues(0) = 2
objValues(1) = "Dimebox, Texas"
objValues(2) = 2
tblTitles.Rows.Add(objValues)

objValues(0) = 3
objValues(1) = "My Big Mouth Can Make You a Millionaire"
objValues(2) = 2
tblTitles.Rows.Add(objValues)

objValues(0) = 4
objValues(1) = "Don't Let the Sun Set on Your Plaid Sofa"
objValues(2) = 2
tblTitles.Rows.Add(objValues)

objValues(0) = 5
objValues(1) = "Rise and Fall of the Spaghetti Empire"
objValues(2) = 3
tblTitles.Rows.Add(objValues)

objValues(0) = 6
objValues(1) = "Bonding with Bozo"
objValues(2) = 3
tblTitles.Rows.Add(objValues)

Dim colParent As DataColumn = tblPublishers.Columns("pub_id")
Dim colChild As DataColumn = tblTitles.Columns("pub_id")
Dim relPubsTitles As New DataRelation("PublishersTitles", colParent, colChild)

dsDataRelational.Relations.Add(relPubsTitles)

'Set bindings
Me.txtPubId.DataBindings.Add(New System.Windows.Forms.Binding("Text",
➥dsDataRelational, "Publishers.pub_id"))
```

11

```
Me.txtPubName.DataBindings.Add(New System.Windows.Forms.Binding("Text",
➥dsDataRelational, "Publishers.pub_name"))

Me.grdTitles.DataSource = dsDataRelational
Me.grdTitles.DataMember = "Publishers.PublishersTitles"
```

In the sample code on the book's website, this code is the body of a form's `Load` event handler. I suggest that, after reviewing it here, you look at it there, in context and experiment with the navigational facilities provided on that form.

By default, a `DataRelation` automatically creates a `UniqueConstraint` for the parent column specified in the relationship and adds that constraint to the parent table, if one does not already exist. It adds a `ForeignKeyConstraint` for the child column to the child table. Those constraints then work according to the rules already discussed for `Constraints`.

However, you can create a `DataRelation` without generating constraints. To do that, you use a different overload of the `DataRelation` constructor that accepts a Boolean fourth argument, `createConstraints`. You can suppress the automatic generation of constraints by setting that argument to `False`:

```
        Dim relPubsTitles As New DataRelation("PublishersTitles", colParent,
➥colChild, False)
```

The `DataView` Object

Another important date-related object that is not provider-specific is the `DataView`. This object provides a means of sorting and filtering the rows in a single `DataTable`. It can filter based not only on column values (with the kind of criteria you're accustomed to seeing in an SQL "WHERE" clause), but also on the `RowState` (unchanged, deleted, inserted) of the targeted rows.

The `DataView` is somewhat analogous to a view in a database, but it has important differences:

> ▶ It references only a single `DataTable`, so any joins must be done before the `DataSet` is filled rather than being done by the `DataView`.

> ▶ It is expressly designed to be a mechanism for sorting rows, whereas, in a database view, sorting might be frowned upon for performance reasons.

Here are examples of statements that create `DataViews`:

```
        Dim vueTitles As New DataView(tblTitles)
        Dim vueTitles As New DataView(tblTitles, "pub_id = 1 or pub_id = 3",
➥"title", DataViewRowState.CurrentRows)
```

11

The DataView **Object**

The DataView object plays an important role in ADO.NET data binding. You'll find more discussion of it in the earlier section "The DataView Object."

The DataAdapter **Object**

The DataAdapter, a particularly powerful and interesting ADO.NET object, is designed to function as a mediator between a back-end data source and an ADO.NET DataSet. The cycle of its use is as follows:

1. Use the DataAdapter to retrieve some subset of that database from the back-end database for temporary storage in a DataSet.

2. Perform (or allow your user to perform) maintenance of the data in that retrieved subset.

3. At a time or processing stage of your choosing, call upon the DataAdapter to communicate the changes back to the back-end database.

The DataAdapter is a key element in .NET's strategy for facilitating disconnected database access and the associated scalability in distributed applications.

The object's two most important methods are Fill() and Update(). Fill() retrieves data from the database and stores it to an in-memory DataSet. Update() works in the opposite direction: it uses changes from a DataSet to update the back-end database. The DataAdapter, used in this way in conjunction with a DataSet, can thus handle extensive and complex changes to data without requiring complex code to manage such changes in the form or other component that receives them from the user. The front end can therefore act like a desktop database app, with bound controls that automatically track changes in the current record. But it's even better than a desktop database app because its "database" (the DataSet) resides in memory and can therefore respond to the changes at RAM speed rather than disk controller speed. (Forget about turtle-esque LAN or glacial Internet connection speed!) Commitment of local changes to the database can be handled in batch mode at such times or in such situations as the developer deems appropriate. In an extreme case, a user with only a very slow dial-up connection to the back-end database could work all morning making vast and sweeping changes to the data, and then click an Update button when ready for a short break to answer the phone or refresh the teacup.

In practice, you might want to implement some temporary persistent storage of the data to protect against power outages or other catastrophic events on the local computer. .NET gives you some excellent ways to do that as well, but we'll leave that discussion for another time. You get the idea.

11

Using the DataAdapter Wizard to Generate a Connection String

When you drag a `SqlDataAdapter` or `OleDbDataAdapter` object from the Visual Studio toolbox onto a Windows form, a wizard called the DataAdapter Configuration Wizard is automatically launched. The output of this wizard is not only a configured `DataAdapter`, but also (if no appropriate `Connection` object is already present) a `Connection` object with a fully fleshed-out connection string. To use the wizard, follow these steps:

1. Create a new form.

2. Drag a `SqlDataAdapter` onto the form.

3. Click Next in the Welcome panel.

4. If you have an existing data connection for the pubs database (pubs is a sample database from Microsoft that gets installed with SQL Server), select it and click Next. Otherwise, do the following:

    a. Click New Connection.

    b. Enter "**(local)**" in the server name combo box if you're running SQL Server on your local computer, or enter or select the name of a remote copy of SQL Server from the drop-down list.

    c. Choose the appropriate type of security for your server: Windows NT Integrated security or SQL Server username and password security. If you choose the latter, enter the appropriate user name and password.

    d. Select the pubs (or other) database on the target server.

    e. Test the connection to make sure that it has been properly set up.

    f. Click Next to move along in the wizard.

5. Leave the Query Type selection at "Use SQL Statements." This selection has no effect on the connection string created.

6. Enter any SQL `SELECT` statement appropriate for the chosen database, such as "`SELECT authors.* FROM authors`" for pubs. Again, the particular statement that you enter here has no effect on the connection string created. Click Next.

7. After the commands are generated, click Finish.

The `DataAdapter` creates both a `DataAdapter` object and a `Connection` object on your form; they appear in the Component Tray. Select the `SqlConnection1` object and open the Properties windows in the IDE, if it isn't already visible. Double-click on the words "Connection String" in the property windows to select the generated string. Copy it to the Windows Clipboard, and paste it anywhere you can take a

11

The `DataAdapter` **Object**

good look at it. This could be in a Notepad or Word file, or in the code behind the form. It doesn't matter where—you just need to be able to examine it.

Here's the connection string that results:

```
workstation id=DIM4300;packet size=4096;user id=sa;integrated security=SSPI; _
data source=DIM4300;persist security info=False;initial catalog=pubs
```

Note that the workstation ID (DIM4300) and the data source name (also DIM4300, in this case) are specific to the environment where you created the statement. You will get names appropriate to your configuration.

If you repeat the process starting with an `OleDbDataAdapter`, you should get a connection string similar to the following:

```
Integrated Security=SSPI;User ID=sa;Data Source=DIM4300;Tag with column
 collation when possible=False;Initial Catalog=pubs;Use Procedure for
Prepare=1;Auto Translate=True;Persist Security Info=False;Provider=
"SQLOLEDB.1";Workstation ID=DIM4300;Use Encryption for Data=False;
Packet Size=4096
```

If you're hand-coding your connection string, it needn't be as complicated as these two strings because many of the parameter values specified are actually defaults anyway. For more information on `ConnectionStrings`, search the MSDN help file for Visual Basic .NET using the search string "ConnectionString property." You'll find entries with lots of specifics for `SqlConnection`, `OleDb`, ODBC, and Oracle connection strings.

Concurrency Violations

Concurrency violations occur when the following scenario arises in a multiuser application:

1. User 1 (or process 1) reads record A.
2. User or process 2 reads record A.
3. User or process 1 changes record A and saves the changes to the database.
4. User or process 2 changes record A and attempts to save those changes to the database.

When this scenario occurs, ADO.NET, under default settings, does not save the second set of changes to the database. Instead, it sets the error flag for the record with the unsaved changes and throws an exception.

The `DataAdapter.Update()` method, which manages updates in batches, issues a single update, insert, or delete command for each record in its data source that represents a change from the records it loaded from the back-end database. By default, if one of those commands fails, it issues no further write commands. However, this default behavior can be overridden by setting the property ContinueUpdateOnError to True. The set of records that were not saved can then be obtained by calling the GetErrors method on the source DataTable or DataSet. The application ConcurrencyViolator, described in the next section, enables you to create your own concurrency violations and handles them by presenting you with both the local and server versions of each record that could not be saved because of them. With the information about what you'll be wiping out at your disposal, you then can decide which local versions you want to save.

Illustrative Applications on the Code Website

Three applications related to the material in this chapter are included on the code website. These are listed in Table 11.5.

TABLE 11.5

Illustrative Applications on the Code Website

Application Name	Description
TransactionsAndDataSets	Illustrates a number of behaviors of transactions, some related functionality of the DataSet, and interactions between the two
TransactionIsolationLevels	Illustrates the effect of IsolationLevel settings on the various read and write operations
ConcurrencyViolator	Demonstrates the creating and handling of concurrency violations.

The TransactionsAndDataSets Application

The TransactionsAndDataSets application illustrates various basic behaviors of a transaction, as well as the use of the DataSet.RejectChanges() method. The latter operates on pending changes to a DataSet rather than pending changes to the back-end database, but otherwise it functions in a manner somewhat similar to the Transaction.Rollback() method.

A series of experiments using this application are prescribed in its ReadMe form (accessible through the Help menu). These experiments illustrate

- ▶ the operation of the RejectChanges() method of the DataSet;

- ▶ the operation of the DataAdapter's Update() method, in the absence of an active transaction; and

- ▶ the consequences of wrapping the call to the DataAdapter.Update() method inside a transaction, then either rolling back that transaction, or committing it, or simply closing the connection on which is was initiated.

11

Illustrative Applications on the Code CD

The TransactionInteractionExplorer Application

In the TransactionInteractionExplorer application, shown in Figure 11.4, you can set in motion two independent operations: your choice of a read against a table or an edit, add, or delete of a record from that table. At your option, either or both operations can be wrapped inside transactions with independently selectable isolation levels. Any operations that involve writing to the data are performed on a `DataSet`; the changes are then optionally communicated to the back-end database. By experimenting with different settings, you can explore the interactions of operations that read and write to the same database table under different conditions.

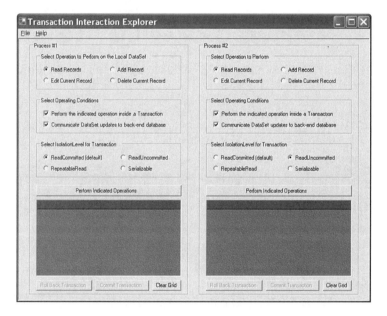

FIGURE 11.4
The TransactionInteractionExplorer Application

Table 11.6 lists a number of scenarios involving two interacting transactions, along with the results that can be observed in these scenarios. When you perform a simple read in process 1, a read in process 2 is successful regardless of the isolation level of either transaction. But if your process 1 operation is a write (add, edit, or delete of a record), the *only* read that will work for process 2 is one that takes place inside a transaction with an isolation level of `ReadUncommitted`. Read attempts under all other isolation levels will time out because the second transaction will encounter locks set by the first and will expire while waiting for them to be released (unless you release them by clicking process 1's Rollback or Commit button).

An attempt in process 2 to edit records read by process 1 will succeed only if the process 1 read took place inside a transaction with an isolation level of

ReadCommitted or ReadUncommitted. Neither of those isolation levels leaves locks on the records read when the read is completed. On the other hand, if the read operation in process 1 takes place inside a transaction with an isolation level of ReadRepeatable or Serializable, process 2 will be unable to edit or delete any of the records read by process 1. However, process 2 will be capable of adding a record to the table if the isolation level for the process 1 transaction was ReadRepeatable; this is because ReadRepeatable guarantees only that process 1 will be capable of reading the same set of records again (and with unchanged data) that it read the first time. It does not guarantee than no new records will be added between the reads (as Serializable does).

TABLE 11.6

Results for Interaction Transactions

Process 1		Process 2		
Operation Attempted	Transaction Isolation Level	Operation Attempted	Transaction Isolation Level	Result
Read	ReadCommitted	Read	ReadCommitted	Success
Read	ReadUncommitted	Read	ReadUncommitted	Success
Read	ReadRepeatable	Read	ReadRepeatable	Success
Read	Serializable	Read	Serializable	Success
Write	ReadCommitted	Read	ReadCommitted	Timeout
Write	ReadUncommitted	Read	ReadUncommitted	Success
Write	ReadRepeatable	Read	ReadRepeatable	Timeout
Write	Serializable	Read	Serializable	Timeout
Read	ReadCommitted	Edit	ReadCommitted	Success
Read	ReadUncommitted	Edit	ReadUncommitted	Success
Read	ReadRepeatable	Edit	ReadRepeatable	Timeout
Read	Serializable	Edit	Serializable	Timeout
Read	ReadCommitted	Add	ReadCommitted	Success
Read	ReadUncommitted	Add	ReadUncommitted	Success
Read	ReadRepeatable	Add	ReadRepeatable	Success
Read	Serializable	Add	Serializable	Timeout
Read	ReadCommitted	Delete	ReadCommitted	Success
Read	ReadUncommitted	Delete	ReadUncommitted	Success
Read	ReadRepeatable	Delete	ReadRepeatable	Timeout
Read	Serializable	Delete	Serializable	Timeout

11

Experiments

As for the TransactionsAndDataSets application, a series of experiments using the TransactionInteractionExplorer application are prescribed in the its ReadMe form, accessible through its Help menu. The experiments for this app are described in Table 11.7.

Illustrative Applications on the Code CD

TABLE 11.7

Suggested Experiments with TransactionInteractionExplorer

No.	What It Demonstrates
1	If the operation in transaction 1 is a read, read operations in transaction 2 will succeed, regardless of the isolation levels of either transaction.
2	If the operation in transaction 1 is a write, read operations in transaction 2 will succeed only when the isolation level of transaction 2 is `ReadUncommitted`.
3	If the operation in transaction 1 is a read, edits and deletes in transaction 2 will succeed only when the isolation level of transaction 1 is either `ReadUncommitted` or `ReadUncommitted`. Edits and deletes in transaction 2 will fail when the isolation level of transaction 1 is `ReadRepeatable` or `Serializable`.
4	If the operation in transaction 1 is a read, adds in transaction 2 will succeed for all transaction 1 isolation levels except `Serializable`.

The ConcurrencyViolator Application

The ConcurrencyViolator application demonstrates the creation and handling of concurrency violations.

A concurrency violation occurs when the following sequence of events occurs:

1. User 1 reads record A.

2. User 2 reads record A.

3. User 1 changes record A, and saves changes to the database.

4. User 2 changes record A, and attempts to save her changes to the database.

But ADO.NET knows that the data in record A has changed since User 2 read in from the database, and therefore that saving the changes made by User 2 may overwrite changes made by User 1. As a consequence, it issues a concurrency violation and refuses to save the second set of changes.

In this app, shown in Figure 11.5, two copies of a program called "Data Editor" are launched.

To create a concurrency violation, to the following:

1. Load products records into both copies;

2. Edit a few records in the first copy, then click <Update Database> to save the changes.

3. Edit some of the same records in the second copy, then click <Update Database>.

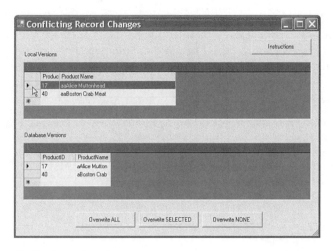

FIGURE 11.5   The `ConcurrencyViolator` Application.

Because the changes affect records that have changed in the back-end database since they were loaded for the second form, the saves will fail and the local copies of the records involved will be flagged as having a concurrency error. The Data Editor app uses that information to pass those records to another form, frmShowRecordVersions, where they are displayed in a `DataGrid`. Also displayed there are the corresponding server versions of the same records. You (playing the role of end user) then have a change to overwrite the server versions with the local copies whose changes were initially rejected.

Summary

Now that you've been through some of the details, take a moment to review, in brief, what you've learned:

- ▶ The `Connection` object establishes a connection to a specific data source, such as a SQL Server or Oracle database.

- ▶ `Transactions` are initiated on a `Connection` object and permit the programmer to abort (or "roll back") all changes executed from within the transaction if any errors occur during any part of the transaction process.

- ▶ The `Command` object houses the necessary settings and parameters, and possesses the capability to execute a command against a data source.

- ▶ A `DataReader` retrieves a forward-only, read-only stream of data from a data source.

11

Summary

- A `DataSet` (not a member of the set of provider-specific objects) is a kind of in-memory database engine that permits tables to be created, relationships between those tables to be defined and maintained, and data to be housed and manipulated. A `DataSet` has a collection of `DataTables`, which, in turn, have a collection of `DataColumns`, `DataRows`, `Constraints`, and `DataRelations`.

- A `DataView` provides a sorted and/or filtered view of the `DataRows` in a `DataTable`.

- A `DataAdapter` facilitates interactive data maintenance by mediating between an ADO.NET `DataSet` and a back-end data source.

Further Reading

Hamilton, Bill, and Matthew MacDonald. *ADO.NET in a Nutshell*. O'Reilly & Associates, 2003.

Balena, Francesco. *Programming Microsoft Visual Basic .NET* (specifically, the "Database Applications" section). Microsoft Press, 2002.

Petroutsos, Evangelos, and Asli Bilgin. *Mastering Visual Basic .NET Database Programming*. Sybex, 2002.

"Support WebCast: Microsoft ADO.NET Concurrency Using Visual Basic Windows Forms." http://support.microsoft.com/default.aspx?scid=kb;EN-US;817281.

"Concurrency Control in ADO.NET." http://msdn.microsoft.com/library/default.asp?url=/library/en-us/vbcon/html/vboridataupdatesconcurrency.asp.

"Connection Pooling for the .NET Framework Data Provider for SQL Server." http://msdn.microsoft.com/library/default.asp?url=/library/en-us/cpguide/html/cpconconnectionpoolingforsqlservernetdataprovider.asp.

"Connection Pooling for the .NET Framework Data Provider for OLE DB." http://msdn.microsoft.com/library/default.asp?url=/library/en-us/cpguide/html/cpconconnectionpoolingforsqlservernetdataprovider.asp.

"Connection Pooling for the .NET Framework Data Provider for Oracle." http://msdn.microsoft.com/library/default.asp?url=/library/en-us/cpguide/html/cpconconnectionpoolingforsqlservernetdataprovider.asp.

11

"Connection Pooling for the .NET Framework Data Provider for ODBC."
http://msdn.microsoft.com/library/default.asp?url=/library/en-
us/cpguide/html/cpconconnectionpoolingforsqlservernetdataprovider.asp.

"Programming for Garbage Collection." .NET Framework Developer's Guide,
http://msdn.microsoft.com/library/default.asp?url=/library/en-
us/cpguide/html/cpconprogrammingessentialsforgarbagecollection.asp.

11

IN BRIEF

This chapter is a primer on the basics of creating and working with databases from within the Visual Studio .NET Integrated Development Environment (IDE) using Server Explorer. Here you'll learn how to create a SQL Server database, but most of the material applies equally to working with other databases within Server Explorer.

> **TIP**
>
> Server Explorer is accessed through a panel by that name that appears in the Visual Studio Integrated Development Environment (IDE). If the panel is not already visible, you can open it by going to the main menu and choosing View, Server Explorer, or by pressing the shortcut key combination Ctrl+Alt+S.

Server Explorer is particularly well designed for work with MSDE, Microsoft's free but hobbled version of SQL Server. MSDE, which comes bundled with some version of Visual Studio .NET, and which you can also download from the Microsoft website, is just SQL Server with a governor added on that intentionally degrades performance when the database comes under concurrent use by more than five users. MSDE also lacks the SQL Server front-end tools, *Enterprise Manager* (which supports sophisticated import, export, backup, and restore operations on databases), and *Query Analyzer* (which provides facilities for detailed query-performance analysis and optimization). But what you *can* do with Visual Studio and MSDE is design, maintain, and write applications around databases that are purebred SQL Server in all their details and that can be moved to SQL Server without modification if you need to scale up.

> **TIP**
>
> In addition to providing the Enterprise Manager and Query Analyzer, SQL Server (unlike MSDE) provides abundant and helpful documentation related to both the database engine itself and SQL Server's Transact-SQL programming language. However, for some time, Microsoft has been making a 120-day evaluation version of SQL Server available for free download. (Look for the SQL Server trial software link on the Microsoft SQL Server home page at http://www.microsoft.com/sql/.) Although the database engine associated with the Evaluation Edition ceases to function after the trial period expiration date, currently the administrative tools and documentation remain available on your system without expiration.

In this chapter, you'll create a complete relational database, including tables, views, relationships defined in a database diagram, and stored procedures. The database will model an academic institution and will be designed to track information on students, instructors, courses, and enrollments. It's a simple scenario, but it includes both one-to-many and many-to-many relationships.

WHAT YOU NEED

SOFTWARE REQUIREMENTS	Windows 2000, Windows XP, or Windows Server 2003
	.NET Framework 1.1
	Visual Studio .NET 2003 with Visual Basic .NET installed
	SQL Server or Microsoft Desktop Database Engine (MSDE)

HARDWARE REQUIREMENTS	PC desktop or laptop
SKILL REQUIREMENTS	Intermediate knowledge of the .NET Framework
	Intermediate knowledge of Windows Forms
	Understanding of relational database concepts and applications

CREATING AND MAINTAINING A DATABASE IN VISUAL STUDIO AT A GLANCE

12

CREATING AND MAINTAINING A DATABASE IN VISUAL STUDIO AT A GLANCE

Creating a Database

To create a database, right-click the Data Connections node in Server Explorer and select Create New SQL Server Database. This launches the dialog box shown in Figure 12.1.

To create a new database, you must identify the instance of SQL Server that you want to use. If you're running SQL Server locally and have just a single instance of SQL Server running, you can simply enter ., (local), or localhost, as shown in the figure. Otherwise, enter the name of that instance of SQL Server that you want to target.

You must also give the new database a name; in this case, call it VbUnleashedSchool.

12

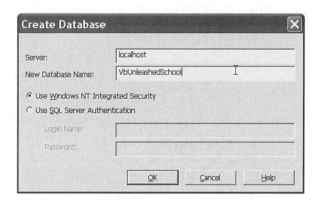

FIGURE 12.1   Create a database.

SQL Server gives you a choice of two security models:

▶ Use Windows NT Integrated Security

▶ Use SQL Server Authentication

If you choose Windows NT Integrated Security, SQL Server bases its security decisions on the privileges of the user whose credentials you have used to log into Windows. In other words, if you logged into Windows as Sue, SQL Server bases its security decisions on the rights of user Sue.

SQL Server has available its own authentication system, separate from the Windows authentication system. If you choose to use SQL Server Authentication, you are required to pass a SQL Server UserID and password to SQL Server for all secured operations and accesses. You can do this from code, but doing so means you have to either embed an ID and password in your code or retrieve it from a database or other persistent store, as needed. In either case, unless you also create a means of encrypting and decrypting these, your system will be quite vulnerable to password theft. Generally, Window NT Integrated Security offers both better security and greater convenience than using the SQL Server login.

For this exercise, choose Window NT Integrated Security. When you click OK, Visual Studio sets up a new database.

Creating and Updating Database Components

Figure 12.2 shows the new database displayed in Server Explorer. (The name of your database server will be different from the one shown.) Folders have been created in the new database for all of the following types of components:

12

Creating and Updating Database Components

- ▸ Database diagrams

- ▸ Tables

- ▸ Views

- ▸ Stored procedures

- ▸ Functions

In your newly created database, all of these folders are currently empty.

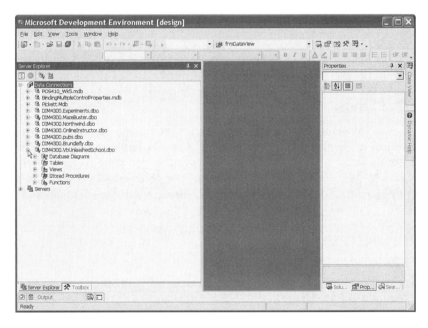

FIGURE 12.2   Database components.

12

Creating a New Table

Get started populating your database by creating some tables. To create a table, right-click the Tables node under the School database branch of the Data Connections tree. From the resulting shortcut menu, choose New Table (see Figure 12.3).

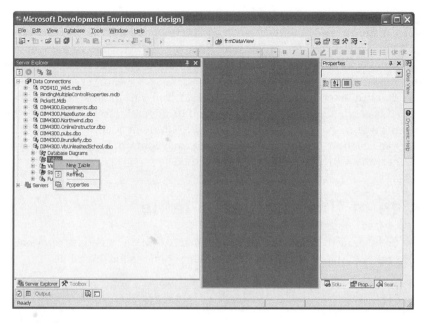

FIGURE 12.3   Create a new table.

This displays the table design grid, shown in Figure 12.4.

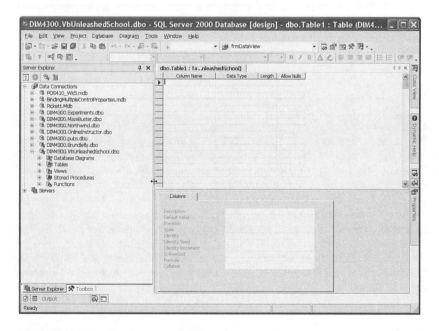

FIGURE 12.4   Table design grid.

12

Using this grid, you can define columns for your new table and specify many different properties of those columns. You can specify each column's name, data type, and length; whether it can contain null values (that is, whether it can be left empty at the time a new row is created); and whether it should be an Identity column (with unique values automatically supplied to it by SQL Server whenever a new row is created). You can describe the column's intended contents and assign a default value to be given to it whenever a new row is created in the table. You can specify whether it represents a primary key column, to be used in uniquely identifying a particular row. You can set additional property values for each column, but those already listed are the ones with which this chapter is concerned.

Design of the Instructor Table

The first table you will design for the School database is one to house information about the school's Instructors. You'll create eight columns for this table:

▶ `Inst_ID`   ▶ `Inst_LastName`

▶ `Inst_FirstName`   ▶ `Inst_SSN`

▶ `Inst_Email`   ▶ `Inst_Phone`

▶ `Inst_OfficeBldg`   ▶ `Inst_Office Number`

You'll use a naming convention that employs a four-character prefix for each column name that indicates the entity of which it is an attribute. This yields advantages in views and joins, when columns from many different tables are combined for display in a single grid. The prefixes make the source of each column in such displays instantly clear.

TIP

Some developers use other variants of this naming scheme used previously. For example, you could use the entire table name as a prefix (as in, `Instructor_`), you could use a two-character abbreviation (`IN`), or you could use no prefix. In the past, some developers used prefixes that indicated the data type of the column (as is still often done with private variables in code), but this convention has fallen out of favor, partly because the names and availability of specific data types vary from one database engine to another, and the schemes break down when data is ported between them (as from Access to SQL Server). However, the more important reason such schemes have fallen out of favor is that databases are often accessed by many different types of people, many of whom find names such as `strLastName`, `intID`, and `dtmBirthDate` rather forbidding. In this regard, the most widely adopted naming conventions for database columns are similar to those for public properties of objects, where the choice favors intelligibility by a wide cross-section of people over technical information content.

Defining a Primary Key

For starters, you define a primary key column for the table. Many different styles and systems for primary keys exist; the next section, "Considerations for Primary Key Styles," discusses some considerations for these. For now, select a simple identity column based on a Long integer value (for those familiar with Microsoft Access, this is similar to an incrementing Autonumber column). When you designate a column as an identity, SQL Server automatically generates a unique numeric value for it whenever a new row is created in the table (therefore, identity columns must always be given a numeric data type). By default, SQL Server uses 1 for the Identity Seed and 1 for the Increment, meaning that the first row created in the table is given a value of 1 in the identity column, and each subsequent row is given a value one unit higher. (The second row gets a 2, the third gets a 3, and so forth.) The counter is kept internally, and values are never reassigned; if you enter three rows and then delete the third, the next row entered receives an identity value of 4, even though 3 is unused at that point.

Figure 12.5 shows a column being designated as an autoincrementing primary key.

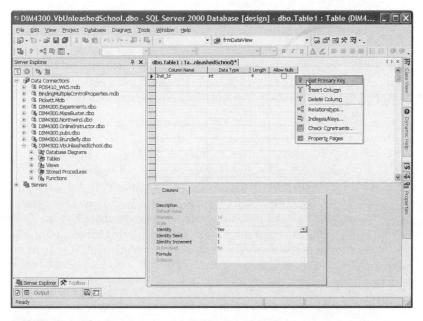

FIGURE 12.5   Create an AutoIncrement primary key.

12

After making the row an identity, you must separately designate it the row's primary key because there is no necessary correspondence between identity columns and primary keys. To make the Instructor_ID column a primary key, right-click anywhere in the row and, from the resulting shortcut menu, select Primary Key. The selected row is marked with a key icon.

Considerations for Primary Key Styles

Any column (or columns) designated as a primary key must, of course, be populated so that it contains a unique value for every row. However, many algorithms are used to create those unique values. This is not the place for an exhaustive discussion of the characteristics and benefits of different key-creation methods, but a short discussion seems in order.

Key types can be classified as follows:

- ▶ Natural keys
- ▶ Artificial keys
- ▶ Arbitrary identifier keys

Natural Keys

Natural keys are formed from attributes of the entity instance being represented in a row. For example, if the entity represented in a table is an employee, a natural key could be formed from the employee's last name combined with her first initial and social security number (as in BrownJ829838399). Natural keys have the advantage of containing identifiable information in and of themselves: You can look at the previously mentioned key and know immediately that it's for an employee named J. Brown. Adding the social security number provides a high assurance of uniqueness; on the other hand, it might cause the key value to violate privacy regulations—and those regulations might be imposed by your state or federal legislature a year from now!

The fundamental problem with natural keys is precisely *that* they have a basis in reality. J. Brown might be Jane Brown now, but she might get married next month or next year and change her name. Phone numbers and addresses change. Even employee ID numbers assigned by the company might be subject to change or reuse, depending on how they are arrived at and how coordinated all of the company's computer systems are. There are certainly situations in which natural keys can be used without problems. For example, the two-letter code mandated by the U.S. Postal Service for states in the United States has been stable since invented, and the Social Security Administration probably *should* use the social security number as the primary key in its own database.

Furthermore, because some databases (such as SQL Server and Access) support cascading updates that change foreign key values in linked tables automatically when a primary key value is changed, having to change a primary key now and again to reflect changed reality might be a perfectly supportable design.

Still, many database developers avoid natural keys because they've discovered through hard experience that things you don't expect to change sometimes do. By creating keys that have no identifiable relationship to the attributes of the entities they represent, you can guarantee that reality will never make obsolete one of your key values.

12

Artificial Keys

Artificial keys are not based on actual attributes of the entity being represented in a row and can't be checked against the values of other columns in that row, but they can contain some bits of categorical or sequential information meaningful to the system that created them. Examples are social security numbers and the ISBN number that publishers assign to books.

Arbitrary Identifier Keys

Arbitrary identifier keys are values generated by a software algorithm that have neither a relationship to the attributes of the entity being identified nor connection to any systematic numbering system based on outside considerations. Microsoft Access's `AutoNumber` keys are an example of these, as is the SQL Server's Identity key that you used earlier for the Instructor table. The algorithm used by both of those key generators is simple in the extreme: Increment the previously assigned integer key value by 1.

> **NOTE**
>
> Access actually supports another subflavor of the `Autonumber` key that generates 9- or 10-digit random numbers. In terms of the automatic key values that SQL Server supports, that key is some-where between an identity and a GUID. It's not as long as the latter, nor quite as guaranteed to be unique everywhere, but it's a lot closer to that than the simple integer-incrementing identity.

These integer-incrementing keys almost look like row numbers from the days when database application developers routinely concerned themselves with the physical row order of database tables—but they're not really because, as you can see by delet-ing a few rows at the "end" of your table and then adding more, it isn't hard to dislodge them from the role of reliable, sequential row numbers. It's really best to think of them as arbitrary numbers, with no relation to anything of any conse-quence, including the physical or even logical order of rows in the table.

A problem with identity keys arises when used in context of applications that do disconnected database access (a technology that is both critically important in distributed applications and central to .NET design goals. If two users download the same set of records from a database and then begin adding records simultaneously, it's virtually guaranteed that they will each generate in their copy of the data key values that conflict with key values in the other copy. When they attempt to communicate their local updates to the central database, whoever gets there second will be unable to insert the records with the locally generated key.

SQL Server has a solution for this problem in a different flavor of arbitrary identifier called the Globally Unique Identifier (GUID). The name is perhaps a slight oversell, but it's still a pretty good key—and nobody will ever mistake it for something indi-cating record order or intended for use by humans as a nickname for a particular record. It's a computer deal!

12

Design of the Instructor Table

GUID Keys

A GUID key is a 128-bit (or 16-byte) automatically generated random integer that has—to quote the MSDN Help file entry, whose authors were a bit more cautious than the guys who named the thing—"a very low probability of being duplicated." SQL Server's version of the GUID is its `uniqueidentifier` data type. The `uniqueidentifier` works slightly different than the identity key, and also different from Access's `Autonumber` data type set, to generate random keys. To make a `uniqueidentifier` column self-populating, you have to set its default value to the function `NewId()`, supplied by SQL Server. Alternatively, you can populate a `uniqueidentifier` from .NET code by calling the `System.Guid.NewGuid` method to return a GUID value.

When you view a populated `uniqueidentifier` column in a SQL Server table, the GUID appears as a 32-character string value, enclosed in curly braces and separated into shorter chunks by hyphens, as in `{7641EF9C-310C-4996-B0EC-BEE6E431F50B}`. Each character position can be occupied by a number from 0 to 9 or a capital letter from A to Z. But under the hood, remember that it's a 128-bit integer. You can specify 2^{128} different integers in 128 bits, and that's how many different `uniqueidentifier` values there are. The best way I know of speaking that number, other than to use scientific notation, comes out something like "340 billion octillion." Here's what it looks like in print (rounded off to the precision of Microsoft Excel):

340,282,366,920,938,000,000,000,000,000,000,000,000

With a reasonably robust number-generation algorithm that comes anywhere close to being random (therefore, giving as much probability to any one of those 340 billion octillion possibilities as to any other), you can see that the chances of the same key getting generated for two different records in the same database table are indeed small and probably not worth worrying about.

The `uniqueidentifier`, therefore, solves the disconnected problem: Two users can happily create new records locally for the same table, confident that their copy of the GUID-generated isn't going to produce values that conflict with the other user's.

Alas, however, there is no free lunch: GUIDs do have a downside. Because they're four times the size of an identity key, they result in larger clustered indexes, which can't get searched as quickly as the indexes created by identity keys. This isn't likely to be a problem except in very large databases with very high transaction rates. If you need to address that situation, you might have to come up with a different key scheme for that table. For example, you could generate GUIDs locally. Then when you update the central database, you could store the locally generated GUID value in a nonkey `uniqueidentifier` column and allow the table to generate an identity

12

key. (You would have to write some code to synchronize the key values between the central database and the local copies.) Another alternative would be to use a combination of a natural key and an identity value (the combination of the two would have a very low probability of being accidentally duplicated).

For the example database here, let's change the primary key to a uniqueidentifier and use that style of key henceforward as shown in Figure 12.6.

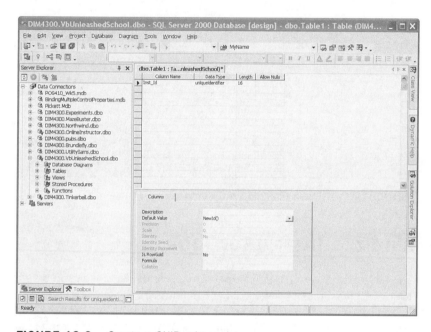

FIGURE 12.6   Create a GUID primary key.

The Completed Instructor Table Design

This section shows the complete table design. Most of the columns in this table are of the data type varchar, short for variable-length character. This is an appropriate data type for textual information whose exact length you cannot predict. SQL Server allocates only as much space for a varchar column as its content requires.

The Inst_SSN column for a social security number, on the other hand, is a predictable nine characters in length, so you make it a fixed-length char column.

Note that in Figure 12.7, the Instructor_ID column has been defined.

12

Design of the Instructor Table

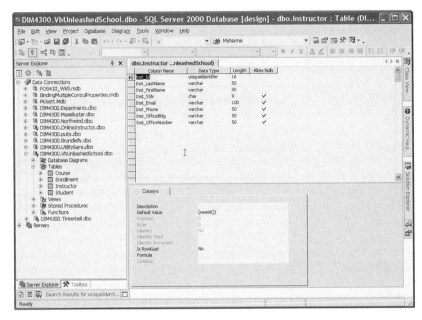

FIGURE 12.7   Column definitions for the Instructor table.

Naming the Instructor Table

When the table design is ready (or at any point along the way), you can save it to the database by choosing File, Save from the main menu, by clicking the Save icon from the toolbar, or by attempting to close it and responding Yes to the prompt about saving it. When you first save a table, SQL Server prompts you for a table name. If you're following along with this narrative by creating your own version of the School database, enter **Instructor** as the name for this table and click OK. Figure 12.8 shows the Instructor table being named.

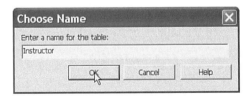

FIGURE 12.8   Naming the Instructor table.

Note that, in Figure 12.9, the Instructor table appears in the Server Explorer hierarchy with a + sign next to it, indicating that the node can be expanded. When you click the + sign, you will see a list of the table's columns. This list is simply for visual reference; you cannot initiate further design work directly at the level of a column node.

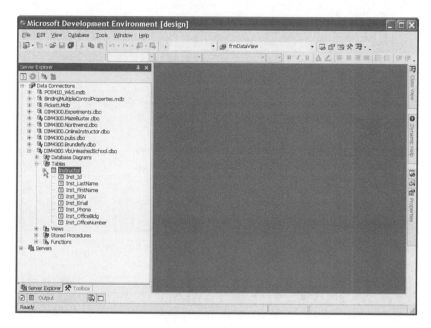

FIGURE 12.9   Instructor table expanded in Server Explorer.

Design of the Student Table

Figure 12.10 shows the design for the Student table. Note the column with a `bit` data type. That's SQL Server's equivalent of the Access Yes/No, or Boolean column, except that it supports values of `0` and `1` only (no `-1` values).

Design of the Student Table

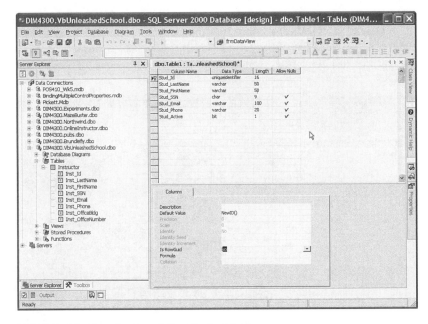

FIGURE 12.10   Design of the Student table.

Design of the Course Table

The third entity for the School database is the Course. The table design for it is shown in Figure 12.11.

The new element here is a foreign key: Inst_ID. This column will hold the primary key of whichever instructor teaches this particular course. In a real school, multiple instructors likely would teach any given course, and this would have to be covered in a many-to-many table design. But that base was covered with the Enrollment table (to be discussed next), so you can keep this one simple.

Note that the data type of the foreign key column matches that of the primary key column from which it draws its values.

12

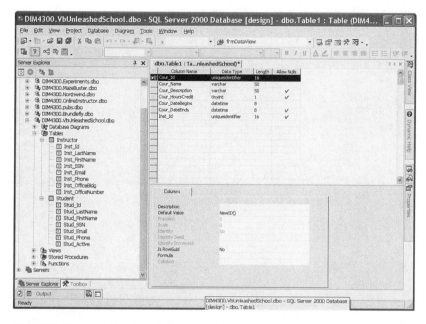

FIGURE 12.11   Design of Course table.

Design of the Enrollment Table

The Enrollment table places courses and students in a many-to-many relationship. Any given course naturally has multiple students enrolled; any given student is likely to be enrolled for multiple courses. The Enrollment table links a given course with a given student using foreign keys that link to the Course and Student tables. Its design is shown in Figure 12.12.

12

Design of the Enrollment Table

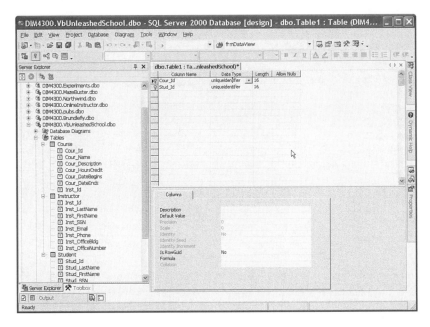

FIGURE 12.12   Design of Enrollment table.

Editing a Table Design

You can make adjustments to the design of a table at will, as long as you don't do something that violates existing relationships, constraints, or data content. To edit a table design, right-click the node for the desired table in the Data Connections tree and choose Design Table. This displays the table definition form with the existing settings, which you can then change. Figures 12.13–12.15 show how you can change the name of an existing SQL Server table in Server Explorer.

12

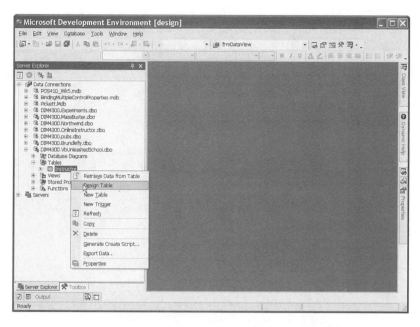

FIGURE 12.13   Return to design mode for the Instructor table.

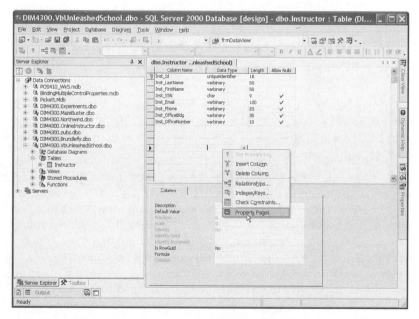

FIGURE 12.14   Selecting the property pages for the Instructor table.

12

Editing a Table Design

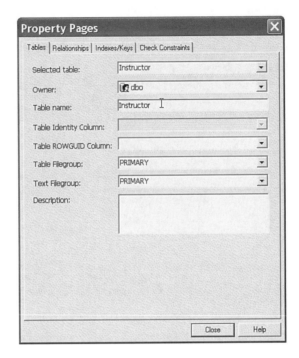

FIGURE 12.15   Changing the table name.

A Few Words on Data Types for Those with a Microsoft Access Background

This is not the place for an exhaustive discussion of SQL Server data types (look for that in the SQL help file or any good text on SQL server), but it's important to say a few words about them for those with backgrounds working with Microsoft Access and those who are new to SQL Server.

First, one of the easiest ways to get familiar with SQL Server data types is to use the Upsizing Wizard in Access to convert existing Access tables to SQL Server tables. From this, you can learn how the experts who designed this wizard thought that Access data types should map to SQL Server data types. Be aware, however, that because they were designing an automated process, and also because SQL Server offers more data types than Access, their conversions will not always be optimal. For example, Access offers only two types of text types, Text and Memo, whereas SQL Server has a whole slew of text types, including char, text, and varchar, as well as the related nchar, ntext, and nvarchar types (which accommodate text characters encoded in the Unicode system). The Upsizing Wizard always converts Access Text columns to SQL Server varchar columns, even though some of them (such as a nine-character social security number column) would be better converted to fixed-length char columns.

12

A Few Words on Data Types for Those with a Microsoft Access Background

This chapter already has discussed how to reproduce Access's `Autonumber` column type in SQL Server: by declaring an `int` type and designating it as an identity column. Access's integer types—`Byte`, `Integer`, and `Long Integer`—map to SQL Server's `TinyInt`, `SmallInt`, and `Int` types (however, the Upsizing Wizard converts an Access `Byte` column to a SQL Server `smallint` instead of `tinyint`, for some unknown reason). In addition, SQL Server offers the `BigInt` (a 64-bit integer) and `Bit` types, which have no exact analog in Access. However, the `Bit` type fulfills the same function as Access's `Yes/No` column.

Table 12.1 shows how the Upsizing Wizard mapped Access column types to SQL Server types in an Access table with one column of each data type offered by Access.

TABLE 12.1

Data Type Mappings: Access to SQL Server

Access Data Type	SQL Server Data Type
Autonumber	int
Text (30)	nvarchar(30)
Memo	text
Number—Byte	smallint
Number—Integer	smallint
Number—Long Integer	int
Number—Single	real
Number—Double	float
Number—Replication ID	uniqueidentifier
Number—Decimal	decimal
Date/Time	datetime
Currency	money
Yes/No	bit
OLEObject	image
Hyperlink	text

The Upsizing Wizard converted the `Autonumber` column to a 32-bit integer (SQL Server's `Int` type) that was marked as an Identity column with a Seed value of 1 and an Increment of 1. It was also marked as the primary key, as it had been in the source Access table.

Oddly enough, the `Byte` column in the Access table was converted to a `smallint` rather than `tinyint` type. The reason for that is not quite clear because the `tinyint` is the nearer equivalent.

Note that SQL Server converts the Access `Yes/No` type to a `bit` column. The SQL Server `bit` type stores data as a single bit, which can represent a value of 0 or 1.

12

A Few Words on Data Types for Those with a Microsoft Access Background

Interestingly, the Upsizing Wizard reported the Access data type for the `Hyperlink` field (which I defined as type `Hyperlink` in Access) to have been `memo` and converted it to the SQL Server data type of `text` (as it did with the other `memo` column).

Retrieve Data from Table

To view the data in an existing table, right-click the node for the desired table in the Data Connections tree and choose Retrieve Data from Table. The table's data content are displayed in a grid such as the one in Figure 12.16.

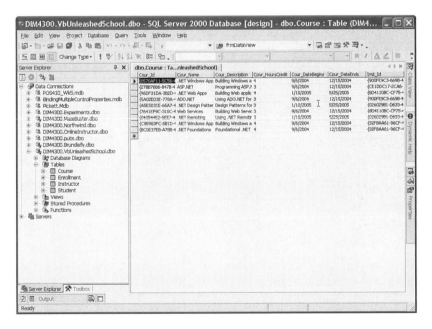

FIGURE 12.16   Retrieve data from a table.

School Database Diagram

Visual Studio provides a graphical means of defining relationships between tables in your database in its Database Diagram Designer. To create a database diagram, right-click the Database Diagrams node under the School database and select New Diagram (see Figure 12.17).

You will then be prompted to specify which tables to include in the diagram (see Figure 12.18).

12

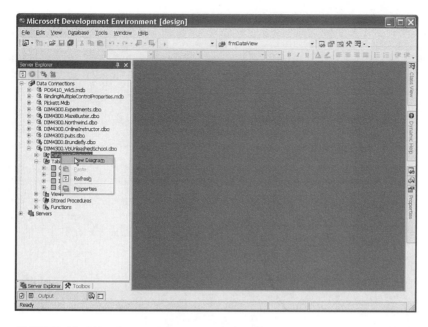

FIGURE 12.17   Create a database diagram.

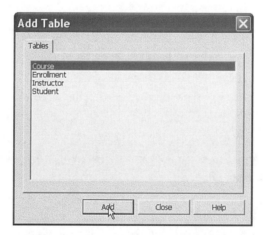

FIGURE 12.18   Add tables to the database diagram.

Select all four of the tables here because you want to establish relationships involving each of them.

With the tables added, the database diagram looks like Figure 12.19.

School Database Diagram

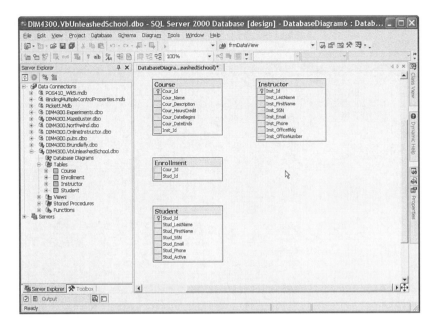

FIGURE 12.19   Tables added to database diagram.

Now you must define relationships among the tables.

Creating a New Relationship

To create a new relationship involving the Course table, right-click the Course table and select Relationships (see Figure 12.20).

The resulting screen looks similar to Figure 12.21.

Now click the New button (see Figure 12.22) to begin creating a relationship between the Course and Instructor tables.

Because you started the operation from the Course table, Visual Studio fills in some of the information for you. But you can override its suggested values for the relationship name, change the primary and foreign key tables, and, of course, change the settings for any of the properties defined using the check boxes.

12

TIP

What are called the primary and foreign key tables on the Relationships tab of the Database Diagram Properties dialog box are variously referred to as the parent and child tables, or the master and detail tables, in Visual Studio and in other database literature.

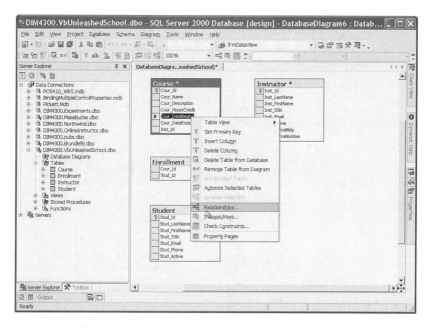

FIGURE 12.20   Enter relationship design mode.

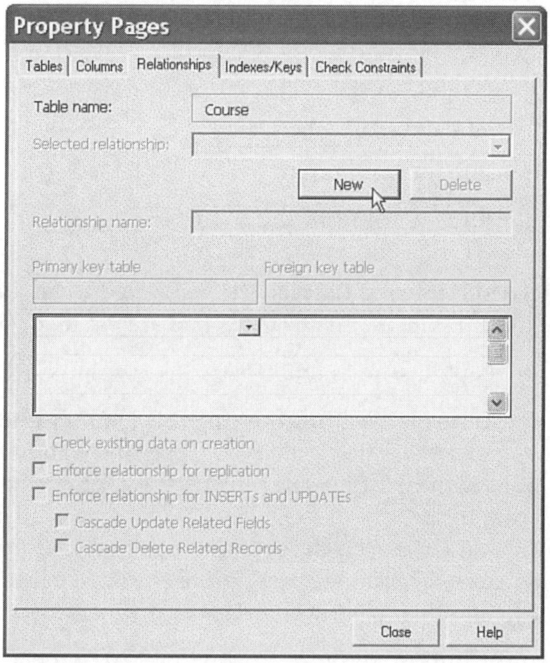

FIGURE 12.21   Create a new relationship.

Creating a New Relationship

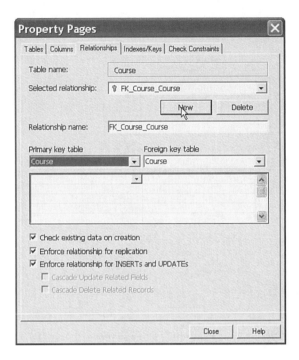

FIGURE 12.22   Relationship defaults.

These are the relationship defaults:

- ▶ Check Existing Data on Creation

- ▶ Enforce Relationship for Replication

- ▶ Enforce Relationship for INSERTs and UPDATEs

Cascade Update Related Fields and Cascade Delete Related Fields are suboptions of Enforce Relationship for INSERTs and UPDATEs and are *not* set by default.

The meanings of these options are as follows:

- ▶ **Check Existing Data on Creation**—Setting this option causes SQL Server to apply the constraint to existing data at the time the relationship is added to the foreign key table. If the existing data violates the relationship constraint at the time you attempt to save the diagram, SQL Server reports that it cannot create the relationship, and it cancels the save attempt. You can then change the relationship parameters (for example, to skip the check on existing data) or delete the relationship and then perform the Save again.

- ▶ **Enforce Relationship for Replication**—Setting this option causes SQL Server to apply the constraint when the foreign key table is copied to a different database.

12

▶ **Enforce Relationship for INSERTs and UPDATEs**—Setting this option causes SQL Server to apply the constraint to data that is inserted into, deleted from, or updated in the foreign key table. It also prevents a row in the primary key table from being deleted when a matching row exists in the foreign key table.

▶ **Cascade Update Related Fields**—(Not set by default.) Setting this option causes SQL Server to update foreign-key values of this relationship automatically whenever the primary key value is updated.

▶ **Cascade Delete Related Fields**—(Not set by default.) Setting this option causes SQL Server to delete rows of the foreign key table whenever the row of the primary key table to which they refer is deleted.

If you are not yet accustomed to working with these various constraints set, you might be surprised by how they seem to interfere with various data-manipulation activities that you want to carry out. Nevertheless, they can be very helpful in maintaining data integrity when you get used to working with them.

Course-Instructor Relationship

In this example, you want to use primary key values from the Instructor table in the `Inst_ID` column of the Course table, so set your values as shown in Figure 12.23.

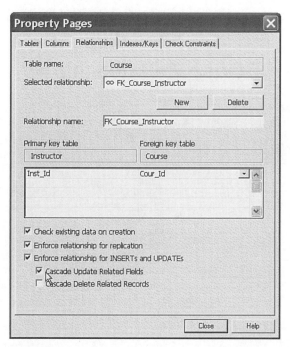

FIGURE 12.23   Course–Instructor relationship as desired.

Course-Instructor Relationship

Close the relationship design dialog box. You will see the new relationship depicted in the database diagram (see Figure 12.24).

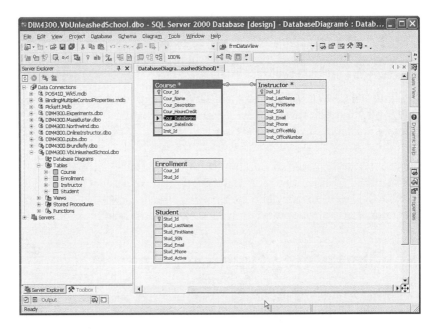

FIGURE 12.24   Completed relationship displayed in the database diagram.

Enrollment-Course Relationship

You need to create similar relationships between the Enrollment and Course tables, and the Enrollment and Student tables. These are shown in Figures 12.25 and 12.26.

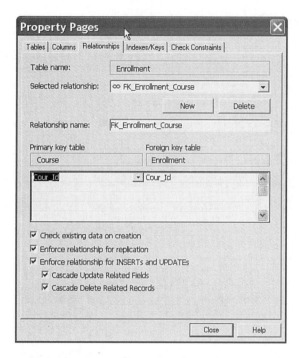

FIGURE 12.25 Enrollment-Course relationship.

Enrollment-Student Relationship

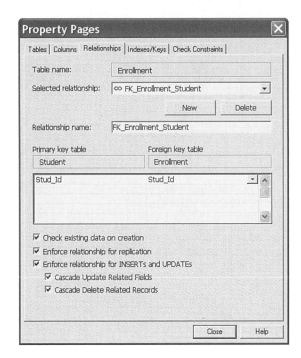

FIGURE 12.26   Enrollment-Student relationship.

The Completed Database Diagram

The completed database diagram for the School database looks like Figure 12.27 (after dragging the tables and relationships around a bit to line them up neatly in the upper-left corner of the diagram). Note the relationship lines, which identify the primary key tables with a key symbol.

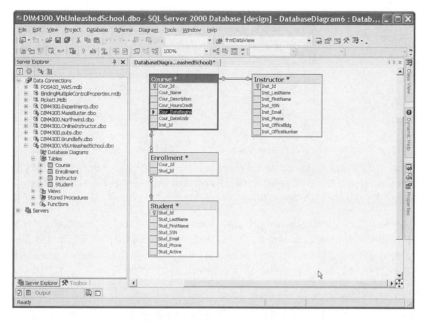

FIGURE 12.27   The completed database diagram.

Saving a Database Diagram

To save your database diagram, from the Main menu, choose File, Save, and then click the Save icon on the toolbar—or, simply attempt to close the database diagram design window and respond Yes to the prompt about saving changes (see Figure 12.28).

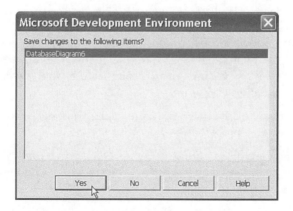

FIGURE 12.28   Saving a database diagram.

You'll see a response dialog box similar to the one in Figure 12.29.

Saving a Database Diagram

FIGURE 12.29   Saving a database diagram.

Note that attempting to save the diagram results in a message about saving tables to the database. That's because the relationships that you defined are stored as constraints on the tables themselves.

The Save Test File button simply prompts for a filename and location to store a text file with information about which tables were affected by the changes you made. The Warn About Tables Affected option controls whether this dialog box appears the next time you save a database diagram or selected tables.

Examining a Table's Properties

This section takes a look at the property pages for a table to see what got put there when you created the database diagram, as well as the other aspects of table design that you can work with there. Figure 12.30 shows the selection of Property Pages from the shortcut design menu for the Course table. Figure 12.31 shows the Relationships tab on the Property Pages dialog box for the same table.

Note that, on the Relationships page, you see described the relationship just defined in the Database Diagram between the Instructor and Course tables. The relationship has been set to enforce cascading for UPDATEs. If the primary key value for a given instructor changes, the corresponding value in the Inst_Id column of the Course table will be updated. Of course, because you're using uniqueidentifier keys here, it is unlikely that you'll have any reason to change the primary key for an instructor, so you might never use this particular feature. Still, it would be the right thing to do if the situation ever arose.

On the Tables property page, shown in Figure 12.32, you can see and change the settings for various table properties.

On the Indexes property page, shown in Figure 12.34, you'll find information about any indexes being maintained on your table. You can also create new indexes and change the settings of existing ones.

12

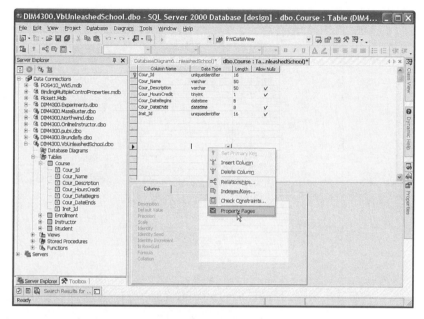

FIGURE 12.30   Check the property pages for a table.

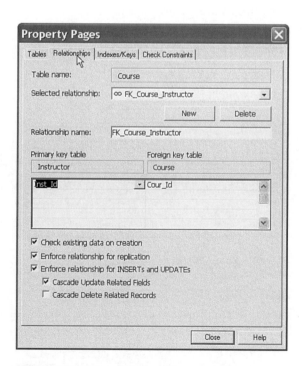

FIGURE 12.31   Relationships property page.

12

Examining a Table's Properties

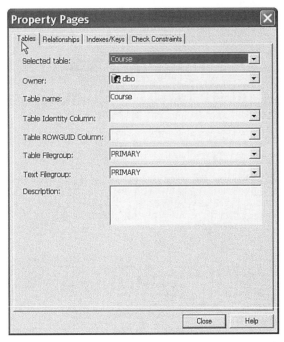

FIGURE 12.32   Tables property page.

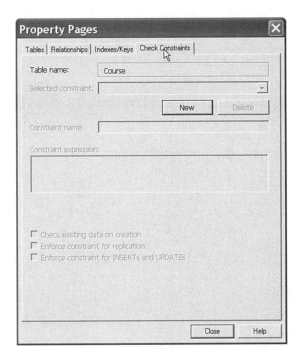

FIGURE 12.33   Constraints property page.

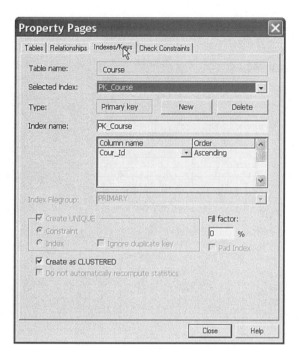

FIGURE 12.34 Indexes property page.

Creating a New View

You're done creating tables in this example, but with any well-normalized database, you'll need views of your data that draw columns from multiple related tables. Now you can create a view that expands the rather cryptic data stored in the Enrollment table into something a human could understand directly. You'll want to use the Stud_ID foreign key from the Enrollment table to look up a student name in the Student table, the Cour_ID foreign key from the Enrollment table to look up a course name in the Course Table, and the Inst_ID foreign key from the Course record to look up an instructor name in the Instructor table. So, you'll need all four tables for your view.

After you open the New View dialog box (see Figure 12.35), you must select tables to include in the view (see Figure 12.36).

Having selected the tables you want to include, you will notice that the relationships you defined when creating the database diagram are automatically reflected in the design pane (see Figure 12.37).

12

Creating a New View

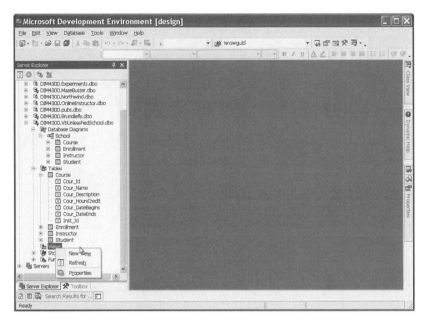

FIGURE 12.35   Creating a new view.

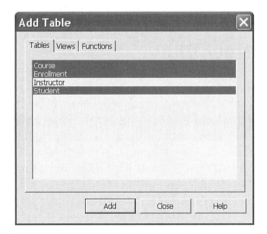

FIGURE 12.36   Adding tables to a view.

12

Figure 12.38 shows the completed view. The view designer depicts the data you've related in four different ways: as a table diagram, as a design grid, as a SQL statement, and as a data display grid. You can do design work in any of the first three depictions, and as long as you don't do anything that can't be displayed in the other depictions, all will be updated (if not immediately, upon saving your changes).

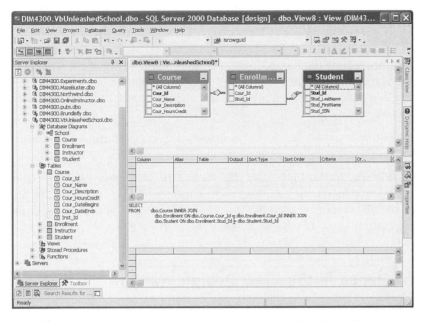

FIGURE 12.37   Predefined relationships automatically reflected in the view.

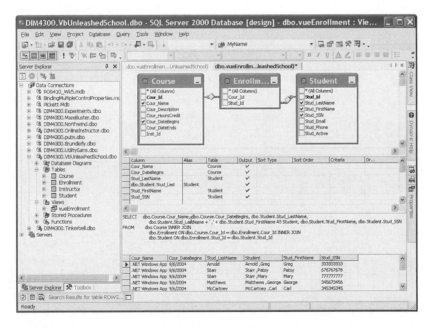

FIGURE 12.38   Completed design of the Enrollment view.

Creating a New View

In this example, the `Stud_FirstName` and `Stud_LastName` columns initially were added from the Student table to the view. This was a convenient way to get the column names written into the SQL statement, but the goal was to combine those columns into a single full name. To do this, the comma between the two column names in the SQL statement was replaced with the characters + and +, and `AS Student` was added after the `Stud_FirstName` reference. These changes resulted in this expression:

```
dbo.Student.Stud_LastName + ', ' + dbo.Student.Stud_FirstName AS Student
```

This displays the student's full name, last name first, as a single value in a column named Student. Upon saving these changes (made in the SQL pane), Visual Studio updates the diagram by unchecking the `Stud_FirstName` and `Stud_LastName` columns because they are now no longer directly included (as themselves) in the view.

Hiding Panes in the View Design Windows

You might have noticed that real estate is a bit scarce in the View Design window, with a Design pane, Grid pane, SQL pane, and Results pane stacked atop one another. Thoughtfully, the Visual Studio designers have given you toolbar buttons to hide and redisplay those panes easily and individually. These are shown in Figures 12.39–12.42.

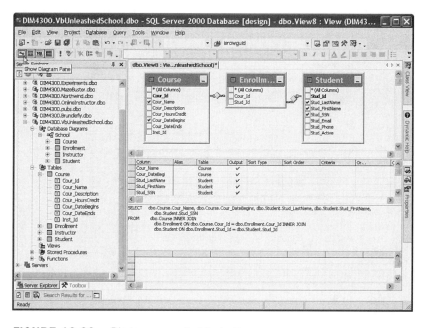

FIGURE 12.39   Diagram pane toggle button.

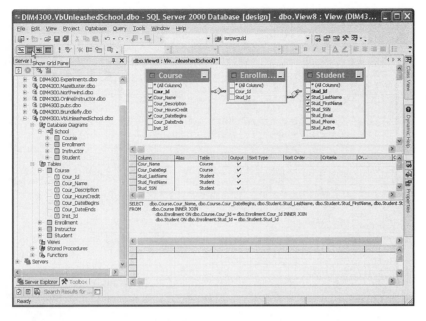

FIGURE 12.40   Grid pane toggle button.

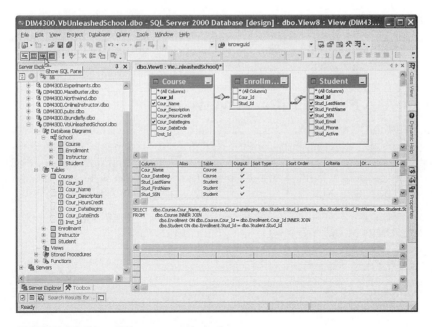

FIGURE 12.41   SQL pane toggle button.

12

Creating a New View

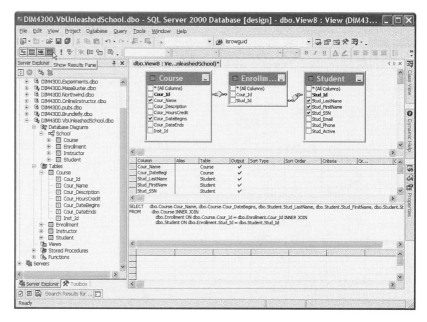

FIGURE 12.42   Results pane toggle button.

You can use two more handy toolbar buttons when working with your view. A Verify SQL Syntax button (see Figure 12.43) is provided to check the syntax of your SQL statement without actually executing it; a Run Query button (see Figure 12.44) is provided to do the latter.

Displaying Records from a View

With the Run Query toolbar button, or by right-clicking anywhere in the View design pane and selecting Run from the resulting shortcut menu, you can get Visual Studio to execute your query and display result in the bottommost pane (see Figure 12.45). Thus, you can verify that the view retrieves what you wanted, ordered and formatted as you desired.

By hiding the Design and Grid panes, you can see more of the results, together with the SQL statement that retrieved them, as in Figure 12.46.

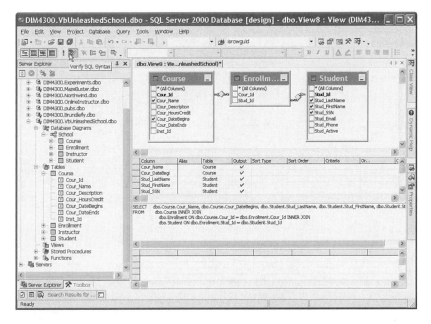

FIGURE 12.43   Verify the syntax of Your SQL statement.

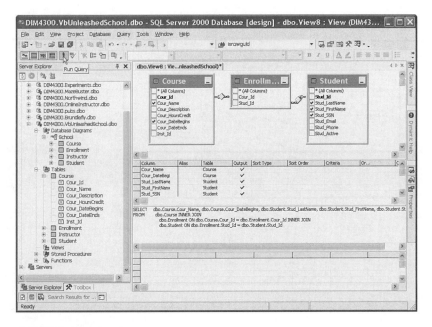

FIGURE 12.44   Run your query.

Creating a New View

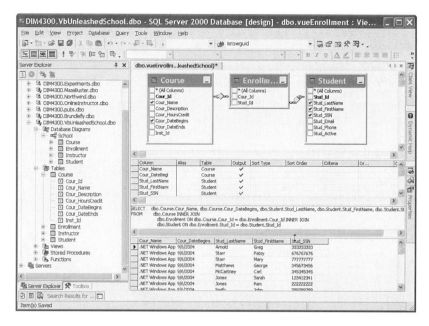

FIGURE 12.45 Displaying results in the Results pane.

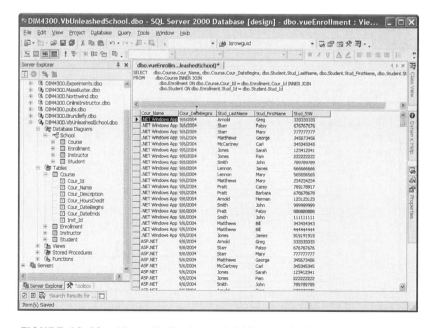

FIGURE 12.46 View with Design and Grid panes hidden.

Saving the View

You can save a view on which you're working in design view by selecting File, Save <View Name> from the Main menu, by clicking the disk icon in the toolbar, or simply by attempting to close a view with unsaved changes and answering Yes to the prompt about saving the view. When saving a view for the first time, you get a prompt like that shown in Figure 12.47.

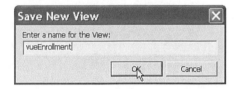

FIGURE 12.47   Saving the view.

Retrieving Data from a Closed View

To retrieve data from a view listed in Server Explorer but not open in design mode, right-click its node and select Retrieve Data from View from the resulting shortcut menu. This brings up the data associated with the view in a window the full size of the available pane on the Visual Studio design surface (see Figure 12.48).

12

Retrieving Data from a Closed View

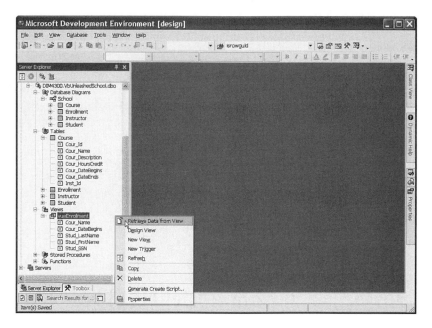

FIGURE 12.48   Retrieving the view.

Considerations with Respect to Ordering Views

Note that the records in the vueEnrollment view were not ordered. Whether you want to do that depends upon how you intend for (or expect) the view to be used. If it is to be used as the source for other views or for queries that will sort the records in a variety of different ways, it is probably best not to sort the records: If you do, you will incur the overhead of that initial sort in every operation that builds upon it (such as the one that sorts the records the way you *really* want to see them).

If you do order the records in a view (as shown in Figures 12.49 and 12.50, note that SQL Server automatically adds a TOP 100 PERCENT clause after the SELECT keyword in the query. The reasons are somewhat esoteric, but the addition of this clause can serve as a reminder to make sure that you really want to be ordering your view.

12

Considerations with Respect to Ordering Views

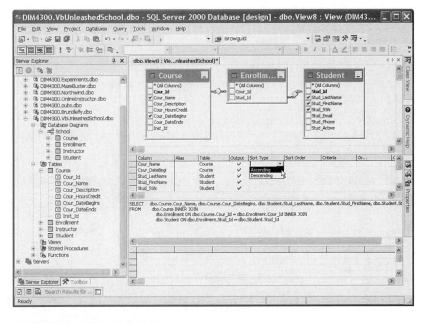

FIGURE 12.49   Ordering a view.

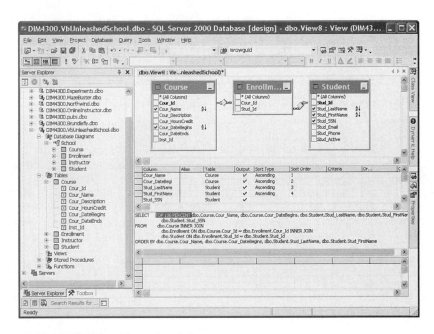

FIGURE 12.50   The ordered view.

12

Creating a Stored Procedure

If your database supports stored procedures, as SQL Server does, you can create them through Server Explorer. To create a new stored procedure, right-click the Stored Procedures node under your choice of database and select New Stored Procedure (see Figure 12.51).

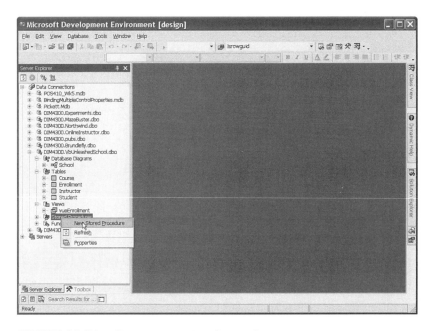

FIGURE 12.51   Create a new stored procedure.

When you create a new stored procedure, Visual Studio starts you out with a template, as shown in Figure 12.52. Note that this template is not the stored procedure itself, but a T-SQL script to create a procedure.

Figure 12.53 shows a completed script to create a stored procedure to select records from the Course table.

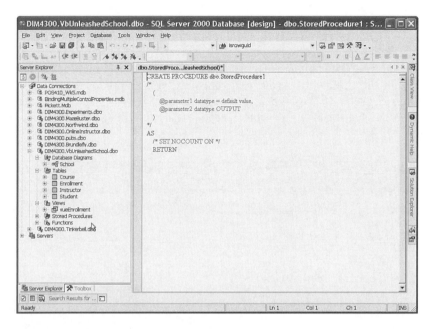

FIGURE 12.52   Stored procedure template.

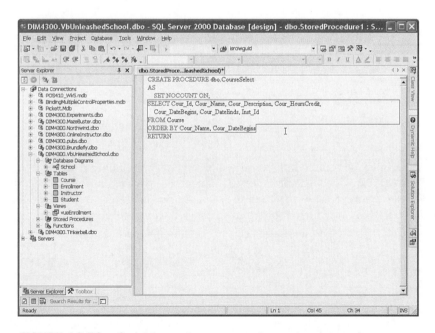

FIGURE 12.53   Script to create `CourseSelect` stored procedure.

12

Creating a Stored Procedure

Figure 12.54 shows the script to create a more complicated procedure, to update records in the Course table. This procedure uses eight parameters, which include two versions of the primary key value, `Cour_Id`. Therefore, it would permit the primary key value to be updated along with the other values (assuming that the database table would allow that). To remove that capability, you simply remove the first parameter (`@Cour_Id`) and the `Cour_Id = @Cour_Id` clause in the group of `SET` clauses. (Note that the `@` symbol must be the first character of SQL Server parameter names.)

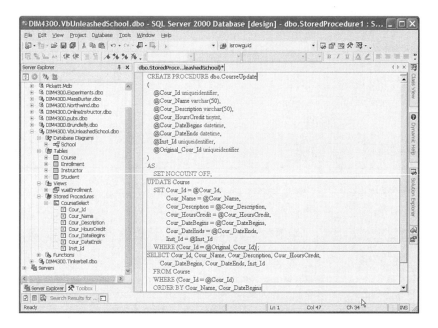

FIGURE 12.54   Script to create `CourseUpdate` stored procedure.

Note the display of your completed stored procedures in Server Explorer (see Figure 12.55). When expanded, the node for the parameterless stored procedure that does a simple select shows a list of the columns to be returned. The expanded node for the Update procedure shows both the input parameters and the output columns.

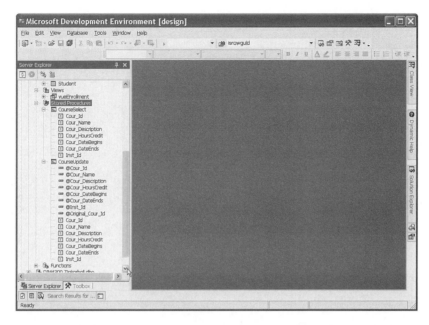

FIGURE 12.55   Stored procedure branches in the Server Explorer tree.

Editing a Stored Procedure

To edit an existing stored procedure, simply right-click its node in Server Explorer and select Edit Stored Procedure, as shown in Figure 12.56 This opens the editing window with a script such as the following:

```
ALTER PROCEDURE dbo.CourseSelect
AS
    SET NOCOUNT ON;
SELECT Cour_Id, Cour_Name, Cour_Description, Cour_HoursCredit,
    Cour_DateBegins, Cour_DateEnds, Inst_Id
FROM Course
ORDER BY Cour_Name, Cour_DateBegins
RETURN
```

Note that, again, this is a script based on the T-SQL statement ALTER PROCEDURE that, when saved, causes the existing procedure to be overwritten with the new statements that follow the AS keyword.

12

Editing a Stored Procedure

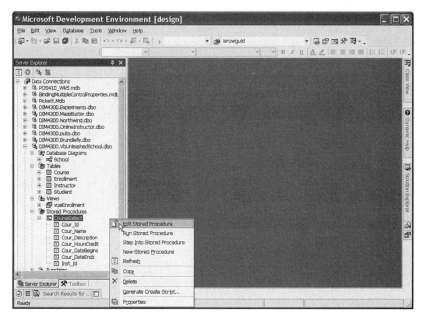

FIGURE 12.56   Edit a stored procedure.

Creating a Stored Procedure Using the `SqlDataAdapter`

Besides creating a stored procedure manually, you can let Visual Studio do it for you using the DataAdapter Configuration Wizard. `DataAdapters` were discussed in more detail in Chapter 11, "ADO.NET Classes," so for here, it will suffice to say that whenever you drag a `DataAdapter` control (such as a `SqlDataAdapter`) on to a Windows form, Visual Studio launches a wizard that, among other things, asks you whether you want it to generate SQL statements within your code, create new stored procedures, or use existing stored procedures.

The procedures generated by the DataAdapter wizards tend to be decidedly on the verbose side, often passing more parameters than you really need. Specifically, they tend to have very long and complex `WHERE` conditions to guarantee that they'll be operating on just the right record, when often a `WHERE` condition simply specifying the appropriate primary key would be sufficient. They also fail miserably in attempting to generate appropriate `DELETE` or `UPDATE` statements when the data source is a view rather than a simple table.

Nevertheless, they are a good way both of learning about stored procedures, and they can also be useful as a quick and dirty way to generate first drafts of procedures that you then whittle down and otherwise refine before use.

12

Creating a Stored Procedure Using the `SqlDataAdapter`

Figures 12.57 through 12.59 show screens of the SqlDataAdaptor Wizard that address the creation of stored procedures. See Chapter 11 for more detail.

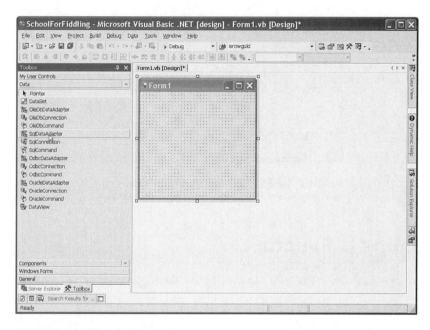

FIGURE 12.57   Selecting the `SqlDataAdapter` from the Visual Studio toolbox.

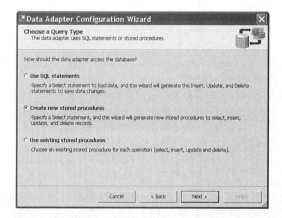

FIGURE 12.58   Selecting the Create New Stored Procedures option in the DataAdapter Configuration Wizard.

Creating a Stored Procedure Using the `SqlDataAdapter`

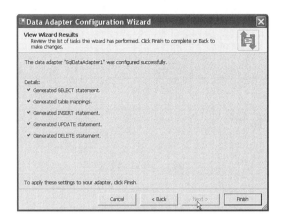

FIGURE 12.59   Wizard dialog box showing successful generation of the stored procedures.

Creating a Function

The final type of object that you can create for a database using Server Explorer (assuming that the connection you're working with is to a database that supports them) is a user-defined function. SQL Server supports three types of user-defined functions:

- Scalar functions

- Multistatement table-valued functions

- Inline table-valued functions

Scalar functions return a single value (like the functions you're used to creating and working with in Visual Basic). *Multistatement table-valued functions* return a table built from multiple T-SQL statements. They are similar to stored procedures but can be used as a data source in the FROM clause of a SELECT statement. *Inline table-valued functions* also return a table but do so with a single SELECT statement. Similar to the *multistatement table-valued functions*, they can be used in the FROM clause of a SELECT statement.

To create a user-defined function, right-click the Functions node in Server Explorer and then select the type of function you want to create. For this example, choose New Scalar-Valued Function, as shown in Figure 12.60.

The function editor is launched with a template. As with stored procedures, the template is for a script that creates the desired function (see Figure 12.61).

Figure 12.62 shows a completed user-defined function; Figure 12.63 shows the function used in a view.

12

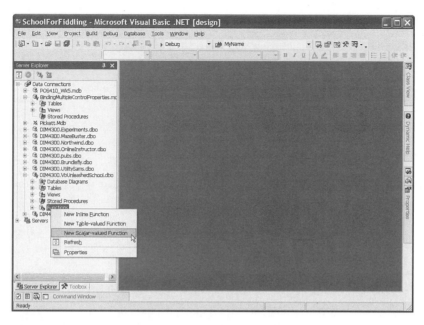

FIGURE 12.60   Create a new scalar-valued function.

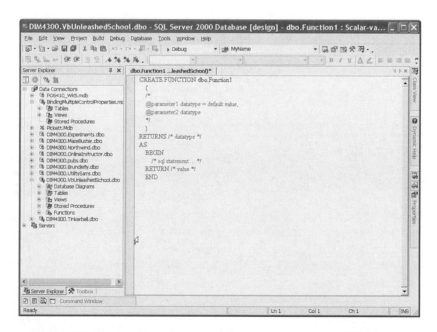

FIGURE 12.61   Template for new scalar-valued, user-defined T-SQL function.

12

Creating a Function

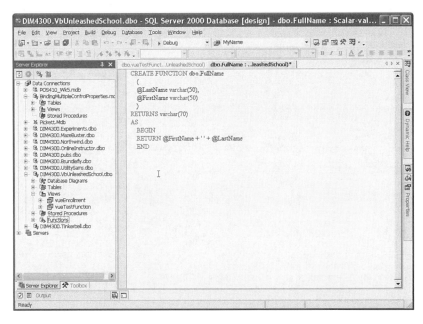

FIGURE 12.62   Completed scalar-valued, user-defined T-SQL function.

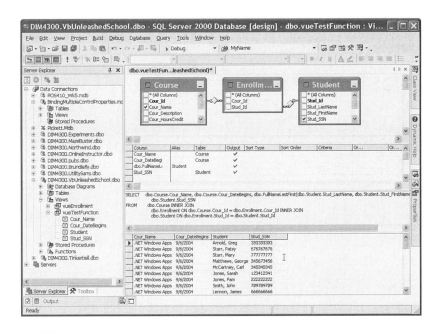

FIGURE 12.63   Scalar-valued user-defined, T-SQL function in use in a view definition.

Database Maintenance Operations You Can't Do with Visual Studio

As you have seen, you can do quite a bit of database design and maintenance without ever leaving Visual Studio. Thus, with just a copy of Visual Studio and MSDE, you can design and maintain databases—and applications that work with them—that can be moved to SQL Server without modification if you need to scale up.

Still, you can do some important additional things with SQL Server's Enterprise Explorer and Query Analyzer tools that you can't do with the Visual Studio Server Explorer, even with Enterprise Edition. SQL Server's Enterprise Manager, for example, gives you many sophisticated options for importing, exporting, backing up, and restoring data that you don't have in Server Explorer. With Enterprise Manager, you can create logins and users, change database security rights, set the locations of physical database files, and perform other tuning and management functions that aren't available from Server Explorer. You can copy objects (tables, views, stored procedures, functions, and so forth) from one database to another using Enterprise Manager, but not with Server Explorer. Query Analyzer provides sophisticated tools for examining and optimizing query performance that aren't available in Server Explorer.

The best case, of course, is to have all the tools available. If you're lucky enough to have that environment, you might find yourself doing most of your database maintenance from Server Explorer in Visual Studio and then jumping out to Enterprise Manager or Query Analyzer only when you need their special facilities.

Summary

In this chapter, you learned how to create and maintain a database using Server Explorer in Visual Studio. In the examples, you worked with SQL Server, but using Server Explorer you can do similar tasks on other database platforms such as Microsoft Access and Oracle. You created a simple, four-table database design; defined record structures for the tables; and designated their primary keys. Discussed in that context were the advantages and disadvantages of different types of primary keys, including natural keys, artificial keys, and arbitrary identifier keys, including the GUID keys provided by both SQL Server and the .NET Framework. You then defined relationships, including a one-to-many relationship and a many-to-many relationship, using a database diagram. You built views based on the tables, and you created stored procedures and user-defined functions. Finally, the chapter addressed the database-related operations that you *can't* do with Visual Studio and pointed you to the tools that will help you do them.

12

Further Reading

"Visual Studio Server Explorer." MSDN website, http://msdn.microsoft.com/library/default.asp?url=/library/en-us/vsintro7/html/vxurfserverexplorerwindow.asp.

"Microsoft SQL Server." MSDN website, http://msdn.microsoft.com/library/default.asp?url=/library/en-us/sql64/ht_sql64_2982.asp.

12

13

USING THE DATA FORM AND DATAADAPTER WIZARDS IN WINDOWS APPLICATIONS

IN BRIEF

Visual Studio's Data Form Wizard, available within Windows application projects, creates a database-connected form. Although the form the wizard generates is of only modest complexity, it encapsulates sufficient functionality to be an excellent vehicle for learning about ADO.NET and the construction and functioning of data-connected forms. When you fully understand it, you also can use it as a code-generation tool for starting more complex data-connected forms that this wizard can't produce on its own.

In this chapter, you will use the Data Form Wizard against SQL Server 2000's Pubs database to produce an end-user form for navigating and updating a database. You'll work with all of the following data-related object types: `Connection`, `Command`, `DataAdapter`, `DataSet`, `DataTable`, `DataRow`, `DataColumn`, `CurrencyManager`, `DataView`, and `DataGrid` objects. You will become thoroughly familiar with the code generated by the Data Form Wizard to see how it declares, initializes, and uses these objects to communicate with the database and display data for viewing and updating by the user. Finally, you will learn how to begin breaking away from the Data Form Wizard by creating your own `Connections`, `DataAdapters`, and `DataSets`.

WHAT YOU NEED

SOFTWARE RECOMMENDATIONS	Windows 2000, Windows XP, or Windows Server 2003 .NET Framework 1.1 Visual Studio .NET 2003 with Visual Basic .NET installed SQL Server 2000 or corresponding version of the Microsoft Desktop Database Engine (MSDE)
HARDWARE RECOMMENDATIONS	PC desktop or laptop, .NET-enabled server, desktop client
SKILLS REQUIRED	Intermediate knowledge of the .NET Framework Intermediate knowledge of Windows Forms Understanding of relational database concepts and applications Familiarity with error trapping using `Try-Catch` blocks Familiarity with SQL Server 2000

USING THE DATA FORM AND DATAADAPTER WIZARDS IN WINDOWS APPLICATIONS AT A GLANCE

USING THE DATA FORM AND DATAADAPTER WIZARDS IN WINDOWS APPLICATIONS AT A GLANCE

Wizard Overview

Among the items you can elect to add to a Windows application project is one called the Data Form Wizard. This wizard prompts you for various items of information that it needs to create a database-connected form. When the wizard has completed its survey, it generates a database-connected form that loads and saves data to a database under the full control of the end user, displaying (depending upon the options you selected) parent (or "Master") table records along with synchronized "Detail" records from a related child table. The Master data can be displayed in Form view or in a `DataGrid`; the Detail data is always displayed in a `DataGrid`. The displayed data can be edited, records can be added and deleted, and navigational controls are provided to permit the end user to move around in the data and keep up with where he is.

When you right-click a Windows application project in Solution Explorer and select Add followed by Add New Item, among the choices presented is one called a Data Form Wizard. When you select that item, Visual Studio launches a wizard that gathers the following information from you before generating a form:

Wizard Overview

13

- ▸ A `DataSet` name

- ▸ A `Connection`

- ▸ A selection of tables whose data will be accessible through controls on the form

- ▸ Information about relationships between the tables

- ▸ A selection of columns to display from each table

- ▸ Instructions about form layout

The wizard then creates a form that utilizes all the following object types:

- ▸ Text boxes, buttons, and labels

- ▸ A `DataGrid`

- ▸ A `DataGridTableStyle` and `DataGridColumnStyles`

- ▸ `Connection`, `DataSet`, `DataAdapter`, `Command`, and `Parameter` objects

- ▸ `CurrencyManagers`

Code generated by the wizard either creates these objects or gives them specific characteristics and capabilities. This code falls into the following categories:

- ▸ Variable declarations

- ▸ Instantiations and initializations

- ▸ Event handler methods

- ▸ Non–event handler methods

Now you'll create a data-connected form using the wizard so you can see all this in its gory detail.

Creating the Data Form

If you have an accessible copy of SQL Server 2000 (and the Pubs database that comes with it as a sample), you can follow the steps in this section to create your own version of the data form you'll be exploring. Otherwise, just read along.

As just discussed, the Data Form Wizard prompts you for the following pieces of information:

- ▸ It asks whether you want to use an existing `DataSet` or create a new one, and, if the latter, what you want to name it.

▶ It asks whether you want to use an existing `Connection` or create a new one. If you choose an existing `Connection`, you can select it from a list; otherwise, you are prompted for information sufficient to create the new one.

▶ When it has a `Connection` to work with, the wizard reads the data source's catalog and presents a list of tables and views. You must specify all items you want to access.

▶ If you have selected multiple tables, you are asked to describe the relationships between them, specifying which table is a parent and which a child, primary and foreign keys on which to link them, and relationship names.

▶ You must select the columns from each selected table that you want to display on the form.

▶ You must tell the wizard how you want data from the main table to be displayed and what additional controls you want placed on the form.

To begin the process of creating a data form using the wizard, right-click the project in Solution Explorer, select Add, and then select Add New Item. You will see the dialog box in Figure 13.1.

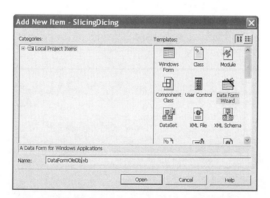

FIGURE 13.1 Add a form to be generated by the Data Form Wizard.

You are required to either accept the default name ("DataForm1.vb", if it's the first you've created this in the current project) or supply a new name. Name the form "DataFormOleDb.vb".

Next, the Data Form Wizard prompts you for a `DataSet`. Indicate a new `DataSet` and name the new `DataSet` dsPubs, as in Figure 13.2.

Creating the Data Form

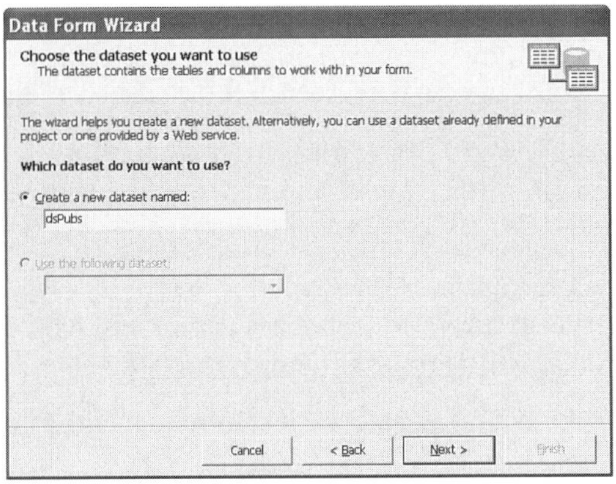

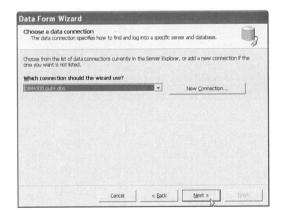

FIGURE 13.2   Name the `DataSet`.

As discussed in Chapter 11, "ADO.NET Classes," a `DataSet` is an in-memory database structure—something very central to the .NET key goal of supporting disconnected access to databases. Forms can use multiple `DataSets`, but, in most cases (and, certainly, this one), one is plenty.

Next, the Data Form Wizard needs a `Connection` to a database. You can either select an existing connection or create a new one. To select an existing connection, choose it from the drop-down list (see Figure 13.3).

FIGURE 13.3   Select an existing connection.

To create a new connection, click the New Connection button and fill in the resulting dialog box. (Note that the use of (local) for the server name assumes that you are running a single-instance SQL Server 2000 on the same machine where you are performing this exercise; if not, simply substitute the name of the SQL Server 2000 instance you want to use.)

13

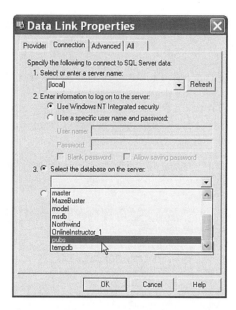

FIGURE 13.4   Create a new connection.

Visual Studio reads the database's catalog and presents a list of tables and views. Select the Publishers and Titles tables, as in Figure 13.5.

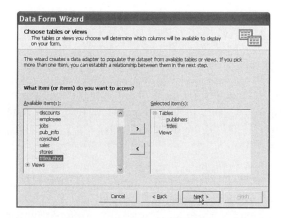

FIGURE 13.5   Select the tables whose data you want the form to be able to access.

Visual Studio needs to understand the relationship between the two tables selected. Create a relationship named `PublishersTitles`, as shown in Figure 13.6. That

Creating the Data Form

relationship links the two tables on the `pub_id` field (the publisher's ID in the database) and establishes the Publishers table as the parent (Master) table in the relationship and the Titles table as the child (Detail).

(Incidentally, when working with the Data Form Wizard, you are free to select more than two tables and define more than one relationship. However, no more than two of the tables will be displayed on the created form. For the others, the Data Form Wizard simply creates `DataAdapters` and leaves you to write the code to display or otherwise work with their data.)

Now you must define the relationship between the Publishers and Titles tables. Make selections as shown in Figure 13.6.

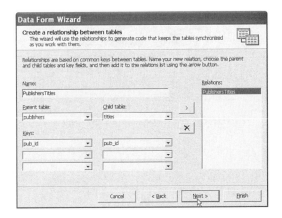

FIGURE 13.6   Define the relationship.

In the next panel, you must select the columns from each table that you want displayed on the resulting form (see Figure 13.7). To keep nonessential complication out of this example, choose just the pub_id and pub_name columns from the Publishers table. From the Titles table, select title id, title, type, and pubdate; you'll want the title column to clearly identify the book, and you'll need the other three columns on display in the `DataGrid` to add a record.

Note that the selection of columns in the previous step determines only which columns display on the form (either in text boxes or in the `DataGrid`). *The Data Form Wizard includes **all** columns from the selected table in the `DataSet` that it creates, regardless of your selections.* In this regard, it operates differently from the wizards that run when you drag a `DataAdapter` onto a form—something you'll explore in the section "Breaking Away from the Data Form Wizard," later in this chapter.

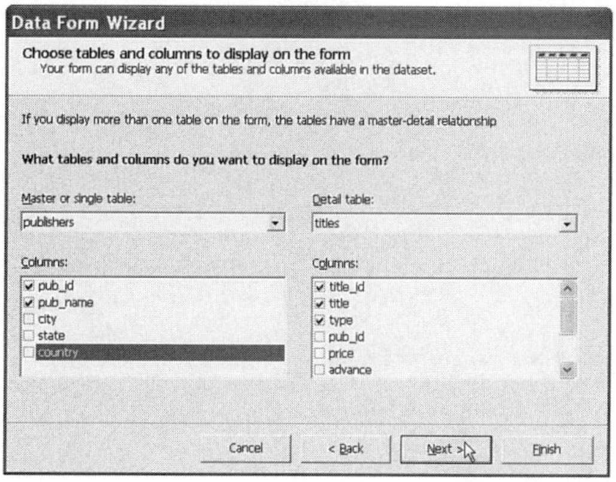

13

FIGURE 13.7   Select the data columns to appear on the form.

Finally, you need to tell the wizard how you want the data to be laid out on the form. Choose Single Record in Individual Controls, and accept all the default settings for additional controls. That causes the Data Form Wizard to add buttons for Cancel All, Add, Delete, Cancel, and record navigation (see Figure 13.8).

FIGURE 13.8   Choose the display style.

Having gathered the information it needs, the Data Form Wizard immediate generates a fully functional form that looks like Figure 13.9.

If you tidy the form's appearance a bit by relocating and resizing some of the controls, it appears as in Figure 13.10.

Creating the Data Form

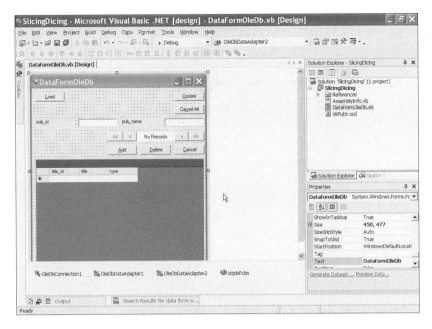

FIGURE 13.9   Completed form as produced by the Data Form Wizard.

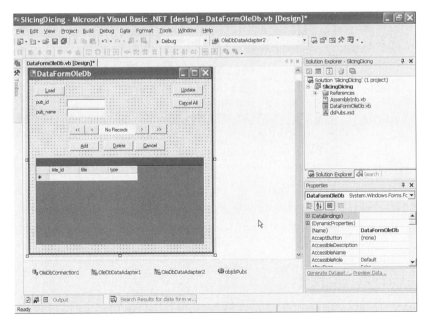

FIGURE 13.10   Completed form after minor makeover.

What the Wizard Creates

In addition to, or as part of, a Windows form, the Data Wizard creates all of the following:

- ▸ A `Connection` object
- ▸ Two `DataAdapter` objects (one for each table or view)
- ▸ An XML `DataSet` class (`.xsd` file, an XML schema)
- ▸ A `DataSet` object
- ▸ A `DataGridTableStyle`
- ▸ A number of `DataGridTextBoxColumns`
- ▸ Numerous buttons, labels, and text boxes
- ▸ Code to make all of these fully functional

The created form exhibits all of the following features:

- ▸ **Disconnected data access**—No data is loaded from the back-end database until the user says to load it (by clicking the Load button). No records are updated in the back-end database until the user says to update them (by clicking the Update button). In between those two actions, the user can do any desired amount of updating, inserting, and deleting of the displayed records. All of these changes are made only to the `DataSet`, the local, in-memory copy of the records downloaded from the back-end database. Because access to the `DataSet` is all local, changes get made at very high speed.

- ▸ **Synching of detail to master**—Master records are displayed in Form view at the top of the form; so-called Detail records are displayed in the `DataGrid`. The selection of records displayed in the Detail grid is automatically synched to the Master record displayed in Form view. When you move to a new Master record, the selection of records displayed in the detail `DataGrid` automatically changes to feature only those that are related by the `pub_id` to the currently displayed Master record.

- ▸ **Navigational controls**—Controls are provided to move forward and backward (or to the first or last records) in the set of records from the Master table. A label is automatically updated to indicate both the number of records in the Master table and the ordinal number of the current record in that set of records.

Examining the Generated Code

The code behind the form generated by the Data Form Wizard can be grouped into four main types:

- ▶ Variable declarations
- ▶ Instantiations and initializations
- ▶ Event handler methods
- ▶ Non–event handler methods

These are examined in order next.

Variable Declarations

Variable declarations are made in the Windows Form Designer Generated Code region. You'll see quite a bit of new code here, all associated with objects added by the Data Form Wizard. The declaration statements are listed here:

```
Friend WithEvents OleDbSelectCommand1 As System.Data.OleDb.OleDbCommand
Friend WithEvents OleDbInsertCommand1 As System.Data.OleDb.OleDbCommand
Friend WithEvents OleDbUpdateCommand1 As System.Data.OleDb.OleDbCommand
Friend WithEvents OleDbDeleteCommand1 As System.Data.OleDb.OleDbCommand
Friend WithEvents OleDbSelectCommand2 As System.Data.OleDb.OleDbCommand
Friend WithEvents OleDbInsertCommand2 As System.Data.OleDb.OleDbCommand
Friend WithEvents OleDbUpdateCommand2 As System.Data.OleDb.OleDbCommand
Friend WithEvents OleDbDeleteCommand2 As System.Data.OleDb.OleDbCommand
Friend WithEvents OleDbConnection1 As System.Data.OleDb.OleDbConnection
Friend WithEvents OleDbDataAdapter1 As System.Data.OleDb.OleDbDataAdapter
Friend WithEvents OleDbDataAdapter2 As System.Data.OleDb.OleDbDataAdapter
Friend WithEvents objdsPubs As 13_1.dsPubs
Friend WithEvents btnLoad As System.Windows.Forms.Button
Friend WithEvents btnUpdate As System.Windows.Forms.Button
Friend WithEvents btnCancelAll As System.Windows.Forms.Button
Friend WithEvents lblpub_id As System.Windows.Forms.Label
Friend WithEvents editpub_id As System.Windows.Forms.TextBox
Friend WithEvents lblpub_name As System.Windows.Forms.Label
Friend WithEvents editpub_name As System.Windows.Forms.TextBox
Friend WithEvents btnNavFirst As System.Windows.Forms.Button
Friend WithEvents btnNavPrev As System.Windows.Forms.Button
Friend WithEvents lblNavLocation As System.Windows.Forms.Label
Friend WithEvents btnNavNext As System.Windows.Forms.Button
Friend WithEvents btnLast As System.Windows.Forms.Button
Friend WithEvents btnAdd As System.Windows.Forms.Button
Friend WithEvents btnDelete As System.Windows.Forms.Button
```

13

```
    Friend WithEvents btnCancel As System.Windows.Forms.Button
    Friend WithEvents grdtitles As System.Windows.Forms.DataGrid
    Friend WithEvents objTableStylegrdtitlestitles As System.Windows.Forms.
➡DataGridTableStyle
    Friend WithEvents objColumnStylegrdtitlestitle_id As System.Windows.Forms.
➡DataGridTextBoxColumn
    Friend WithEvents objColumnStylegrdtitlestitle As System.Windows.Forms.
➡DataGridTextBoxColumn
    Friend WithEvents objColumnStylegrdtitlestype As System.Windows.Forms.
➡DataGridTextBoxColumn
    Friend WithEvents objColumnStylegrdtitlespubdate As
System.Windows.Forms.DataGridTextBoxColumn
```

Note that all objects are declared as friends, which, you might recall, gives them a
sort of semipublic scope: They're visible to all other objects within the same code
assembly (but not beyond, as a `Public` object would be). They're also declared
`WithEvents`, designating them to the compiler as objects that can raise events. Note
also that the data-oriented objects (`Commands`, `Connection`, and `DataAdapters`)
are of the OleDb persuasion. Unlike the DataAdapter Wizards, which you might be
familiar with, the Data Form Wizard does not offer a SqlClient flavor optimized for
SQL Server 2000. You can convert your form to that with some careful global edits,
but if you need a `SqlClient` version of your data form, you're probably better off
deleting and re-creating the `Connection`, `DataAdapter`, and `DataSet` objects
using the DataAdapter Wizard. That approach is described later in this chapter in the
section "Breaking Away from the Data Form Wizard."

Instantiations and Initializations

Instantiations and initializations are performed inside the
`InitializeComponents()` method. The following subsections look at a sampling
of those that get generated by the Data Form Wizard.

Simple Instantiations

Note that the following statements would not be likely to appear contiguously in the
generated code. A subset simply has been extracted to illustrate the range of objects
instantiated:

```
    Me.OleDbSelectCommand1 = New System.Data.OleDb.OleDbCommand
    Me.OleDbConnection1 = New System.Data.OleDb.OleDbConnection
    Me.OleDbDataAdapter1 = New System.Data.OleDb.OleDbDataAdapter
    Me.objdsPubs = New 13_1.dsPubs
    Me.btnLoad = New System.Windows.Forms.Button
    Me.lblpub_id = New System.Windows.Forms.Label
    Me.editpub_id = New System.Windows.Forms.TextBox
    Me.grdtitles = New System.Windows.Forms.DataGrid
```

Examining the Generated Code

```
        Me.objTableStylegrdtitlestitles = New System.Windows.Forms.
➥DataGridTableStyle
```

Properties also get set for various objects. Here are statements that set properties for two Command objects:

```
'OleDbSelectCommand1
'
Me.OleDbSelectCommand1.CommandText = "SELECT pub_id, pub_name, city, state,
➥country FROM publishers"
Me.OleDbSelectCommand1.Connection = Me.OleDbConnection1
'
'OleDbInsertCommand1
'
Me.OleDbInsertCommand1.CommandText = "INSERT INTO publishers(pub_id, pub_name,
city, state, country) VALUES (?, ?, ?, ?" & _
", ?); SELECT pub_id, pub_name, city, state, country FROM publishers WHERE (pub_i"
& _
"d = ?)"
        Me.OleDbInsertCommand1.Connection = Me.OleDbConnection1
        Me.OleDbInsertCommand1.Parameters.Add(New System.Data.OleDb.
➥OleDbParameter("pub_id", System.Data.OleDb.OleDbType.VarChar, 4, "pub_id"))
        Me.OleDbInsertCommand1.Parameters.Add( _
New System.Data.OleDb.OleDbParameter("pub_name", _
System.Data.OleDb.OleDbType.VarChar, 40, "pub_name"))
        Me.OleDbInsertCommand1.Parameters.Add(New System.Data.OleDb.
➥OleDbParameter("city", System.Data.OleDb.OleDbType.VarChar, 20, "city"))
        Me.OleDbInsertCommand1.Parameters.Add(New System.Data.OleDb.
➥OleDbParameter("state", System.Data.OleDb.OleDbType.VarChar, 2, "state"))
        Me.OleDbInsertCommand1.Parameters.Add(New System.Data.OleDb.
➥OleDbParameter("country", System.Data.OleDb.OleDbType.VarChar, 30, "country"))
        Me.OleDbInsertCommand1.Parameters.Add( _
New System.Data.OleDb.OleDbParameter("Select_pub_id", _
System.Data.OleDb.OleDbType.VarChar, 4, "pub_id"))
```

Note that, in the first line in the OleDbInsertCommand1 section, the wizard breaks out statements to multiple lines (using the Visual Basic line-continuation character of _ (space, underscore) when they exceed a certain modest length. If you're studying your own copy of the code generated by the wizard, you could edit that line to read as follows:

```
Me.OleDbInsertCommand1.CommandText = _
"INSERT INTO publishers(pub_id, pub_name, city, state, country) " & _
"VALUES (?, ?, ?, ?, ?); " & _
"SELECT pub_id, pub_name, city, state, country FROM publishers WHERE (pub_id = ?)"
```

Each of the six question marks in the SQL statement assigned to the `OleDbInsertCommand1` `CommandText` property requires a parameter value passed to it when the `DataAdapter` executes this update command. Each of these six parameters must be declared and added to the `Command` object's `Parameters` collection. In the statements generated by the wizard, a concise syntax is employed wherein each parameter object is declared and instantiated within a single statement passed as the argument to the `Add` method of the `Parameters` collection object.

The only property that has to be set for the `Connection` object is its `ConnectionString`. That's done in the statement repeated here. Note that the string assigned to the `ConnectionString` property in this statement is OleDb specific. It you were setting a `ConnectionString` value for a `SqlClientConnection` object, the value would look very different.

```
'
'OleDbConnection1
'
        Me.OleDbConnection1.ConnectionString = _
"Auto Translate=True;Integrated Security=SSPI;User ID=sa;Data Source=DIM4300;" & _
"Tag with column collation when possible=False;Initial Catalog=pubs;Use Procedure
➥for " & _
"Prepare=1;Provider=""SQLOLEDB.1"";Persist Security Info=False;Workstation
➥ID=DIM4300;" & _
"Use Encryption for Data=False;Packet Size=4096"
```

To set up a `DataAdapter` for useful work, you must assign the appropriate command objects to the corresponding properties of the adapter:

```
'
'OleDbDataAdapter1
'
        Me.OleDbDataAdapter1.DeleteCommand = Me.OleDbDeleteCommand1
        Me.OleDbDataAdapter1.InsertCommand = Me.OleDbInsertCommand1
        Me.OleDbDataAdapter1.SelectCommand = Me.OleDbSelectCommand1
        Me.OleDbDataAdapter1.UpdateCommand = Me.OleDbUpdateCommand1
```

Next, you must tell the adapter what table (or view) in the data source at the other end of the connection to access and what to call it locally. You do the same for columns of that table. This capability of the `DataAdapter` to map the back-end names into different local names enables you to vaccinate your code, as it were, from the threat of changes to table and column names in the back-end database. The statement that maps the names (shown shortly) would have to be updated, but the rest of your code can still use whatever names it always has when acting against data in the local `DataSet`. Note that the Data Form Wizard maps back-end names to front-end names that are exactly the same; in so doing, however, it creates a template that can easily be changed manually later if names in the database change.

Examining the Generated Code

```
        Me.OleDbDataAdapter1.TableMappings.AddRange( _
New System.Data.Common.DataTableMapping() _
{New System.Data.Common.DataTableMapping("Table", "publishers", New System.Data.
➥Common.
DataColumnMapping() _
{New System.Data.Common.DataColumnMapping("pub_id", "pub_id"), _
New System.Data.Common.DataColumnMapping("pub_name", "pub_name"), _
New System.Data.Common.DataColumnMapping("city", "city"), _
New System.Data.Common.DataColumnMapping("state", "state"), _
New System.Data.Common.DataColumnMapping("country", "country")})})
```

TIP

The statement that describes the `DataAdapter` table mappings employs a .NET syntax for populating an array that permits it to be populated in the same statement in which it is declared. Perhaps this can be most easily demystified by showing what a statement that declares and populates a simple string array in this style looks like:

```
dim EyeColor() as String {"Brown", "Green", "Blue"}
```

The array is declared without dimensions, but then a series of values is immediately passed to it in the same statement, inside curly braces. This results in a one-dimensional array with three elements:

```
        EyeColor(0) = "Brown"
        EyeColor(1) = "Green"
        EyeColor(2) = "Blue"
```

Thus, the table mappings statement shown earlier could be rewritten as follows:

```
        Dim columnMapping(4) As System.Data.Common.DataColumnMapping
        columnMapping(0) = New System.Data.Common.DataColumnMapping("pub_id", "pub_id")
        columnMapping(1) = New System.Data.Common.DataColumnMapping("pub_name",
    "pub_name")
        columnMapping(2) = New System.Data.Common.DataColumnMapping("city", "city")
        columnMapping(3) = New System.Data.Common.DataColumnMapping("state", "state")
        columnMapping(4) = New System.Data.Common.DataColumnMapping("country",
➥"country")
        Dim tableMapping(0) As System.Data.Common.DataTableMapping
        tableMapping(0) = _
New System.Data.Common.DataTableMapping("Table", "publishers", columnMapping)
        Me.OleDbDataAdapter1.TableMappings.AddRange(tableMapping)
```

This latter form is not quite as concise, but it is perhaps more readily understandable.

Initialization for the `DataSet` consists of assigning its name and locale. (The Locale setting determines how dates, times, currencies, and other culture-specific information are formatted for display.)

```
'
'
'objdsPubs
'
Me.objdsPubs.DataSetName = "dsPubs"
Me.objdsPubs.Locale = New System.Globalization.CultureInfo("en-US")
```

The code then undertakes the routine initialization of buttons, labels, and text boxes. (The following code snippet consists of excerpts. Many more, similar objects are initialized in the actual code.)

```
'
'btnLoad
'
Me.btnLoad.Location = New System.Drawing.Point(8, 8)
Me.btnLoad.Name = "btnLoad"
Me.btnLoad.TabIndex = 0
Me.btnLoad.Text = "&Load"
'
'lblpub_id
'
Me.lblpub_id.Location = New System.Drawing.Point(8, 48)
Me.lblpub_id.Name = "lblpub_id"
Me.lblpub_id.Size = New System.Drawing.Size(48, 23)
Me.lblpub_id.TabIndex = 3
Me.lblpub_id.Text = "pub_id"
'
'editpub_id
'
Me.editpub_id.DataBindings.Add( _
New System.Windows.Forms.Binding("Text", Me.objdsPubs, "publishers.pub_id"))
Me.editpub_id.Location = New System.Drawing.Point(72, 48)
Me.editpub_id.Name = "editpub_id"
Me.editpub_id.TabIndex = 4
Me.editpub_id.Text = ""
```

Next the `DataGrid` for the `Detail` records is initialized—it is sized, titled, colored, and located, and its place in the tabbing order is set. The grid's `DataSource` is set to the app's `DataSet`. But note that its DataMember is set, not to the Titles table, but

Examining the Generated Code

instead to the *relation* object, `publishers.PublishersTitles`, whose specifications you gave to the wizard. In ADO.NET, a relation can deliver rows of data to a data consumer just as a table might. When used in this way, a relation object keeps the selection of records in the child (Detail) table automatically synchronized to the current record in the parent (Master) table—Publishers, in our case.

A single-element array of `DataGridTableStyles` is also assigned to the grid's `TableStyles` collection. In the form generated by the wizard (as in many forms you are likely to design on your own), a single `DataGridTableStyle` is entirely sufficient to present the desired grid appearance (colors, headers, column widths, data mappings, and so forth). After the `DataGridTableStyle` object is added to the `DataGrid`'s `TableStyles` collection, the `DataGridTableStyle`'s own collection of `GridColumnStyles` is populated with the `DataGridcolumnStyle` objects that control the appearance of individual columns.

```
'
'grdtitles
'
Me.grdtitles.AllowNavigation = False
Me.grdtitles.DataMember = "publishers.PublishersTitles"
Me.grdtitles.DataSource = Me.objdsPubs
Me.grdtitles.HeaderForeColor = System.Drawing.SystemColors.ControlText
Me.grdtitles.Location = New System.Drawing.Point(16, 168)
Me.grdtitles.Name = "grdtitles"
Me.grdtitles.Size = New System.Drawing.Size(464, 232)
Me.grdtitles.TabIndex = 15
Me.grdtitles.TableStyles.AddRange(New System.Windows.Forms.
➥DataGridTableStyle() {Me.objTableStylegrdtitlestitles})


'
'objTableStylegrdtitlestitles
'
Me.objTableStylegrdtitlestitles.DataGrid = Me.grdtitles
Me.objTableStylegrdtitlestitles.GridColumnStyles.AddRange(New
➥System.Windows.Forms.DataGridColumnStyle() {Me.objColumnStylegrdtitlestitle_id,
➥Me.objColumnStylegrdtitlestitle, Me.objColumnStylegrdtitlestype,
➥Me.objColumnStylegrdtitlespubdate})
Me.objTableStylegrdtitlestitles.HeaderForeColor = _
System.Drawing.SystemColors.ControlText
Me.objTableStylegrdtitlestitles.MappingName = "titles"
'
'objColumnStylegrdtitlestitle_id
'
Me.objColumnStylegrdtitlestitle_id.Format = ""
Me.objColumnStylegrdtitlestitle_id.FormatInfo = Nothing
```

```
Me.objColumnStylegrdtitlestitle_id.HeaderText = "title_id"
Me.objColumnStylegrdtitlestitle_id.MappingName = "title_id"
Me.objColumnStylegrdtitlestitle_id.Width = 75
'
'objColumnStylegrdtitlestitle
'
Me.objColumnStylegrdtitlestitle.Format = ""
Me.objColumnStylegrdtitlestitle.FormatInfo = Nothing
Me.objColumnStylegrdtitlestitle.HeaderText = "title"
Me.objColumnStylegrdtitlestitle.MappingName = "title"
Me.objColumnStylegrdtitlestitle.Width = 75
'
'objColumnStylegrdtitlestype
'
Me.objColumnStylegrdtitlestype.Format = ""
Me.objColumnStylegrdtitlestype.FormatInfo = Nothing
Me.objColumnStylegrdtitlestype.HeaderText = "type"
Me.objColumnStylegrdtitlestype.MappingName = "type"
Me.objColumnStylegrdtitlestype.Width = 75
'
'objColumnStylegrdtitlespubdate
'
Me.objColumnStylegrdtitlespubdate.Format = ""
Me.objColumnStylegrdtitlespubdate.FormatInfo = Nothing
Me.objColumnStylegrdtitlespubdate.HeaderText = "pubdate"
Me.objColumnStylegrdtitlespubdate.MappingName = "pubdate"
Me.objColumnStylegrdtitlespubdate.Width = 75
```

Finally, various properties of the `Form` object itself are initialized. Note how all the buttons, labels, and text boxes on the form are added to its `Controls` collection, along with the `DataGrid` object.

```
'
'DataFormOleDb
'
Me.AutoScaleBaseSize = New System.Drawing.Size(5, 13)
Me.ClientSize = New System.Drawing.Size(496, 418)
Me.Controls.Add(Me.btnLoad)
Me.Controls.Add(Me.btnUpdate)
Me.Controls.Add(Me.btnCancelAll)
Me.Controls.Add(Me.lblpub_id)
Me.Controls.Add(Me.editpub_id)
Me.Controls.Add(Me.lblpub_name)
Me.Controls.Add(Me.editpub_name)
Me.Controls.Add(Me.btnNavFirst)
```

Examining the Generated Code

```
Me.Controls.Add(Me.btnNavPrev)
Me.Controls.Add(Me.lblNavLocation)
Me.Controls.Add(Me.btnNavNext)
Me.Controls.Add(Me.btnLast)
Me.Controls.Add(Me.btnAdd)
Me.Controls.Add(Me.btnDelete)
Me.Controls.Add(Me.btnCancel)
Me.Controls.Add(Me.grdtitles)
Me.Name = " DataFormOleDb"
Me.Text = "Wizard-Generated Form"
CType(Me.objdsPubs, System.ComponentModel.ISupportInitialize).EndInit()
CType(Me.grdtitles, System.ComponentModel.ISupportInitialize).EndInit()
Me.ResumeLayout(False)
```

Methods Created by the Data Form Wizard

Thus far, this chapter has covered the declarations, instantiations, and initializations performed by the Data Form Wizard's code. Now it's time to look at the methods it includes. These are the pieces of code you would normally code for yourself when creating a form, even after dragging smart controls onto its design surface.

About half of the methods generated are used as event handlers, making button clicks do useful things. The other half are called down the chain from those event handlers. The next subsections look at them by category.

Methods Used as Event Handlers

The methods used as event handlers are shown in Tables 13.1–13.3.

TABLE 13.1

Event Handlers for Loading and Updating Data from or in the Database

Sub	Event Handled	Header Statement	Purpose
btnLoad_Click	Click event of button btnLoad	Private Sub btnLoad_Click (ByVal sender As System.Object, ByVal e As System.EventArgs) Handles btnLoad.Click	Loads data from the Pubs database to the DataSet

Methods Created by the Data Form Wizard

TABLE 13.1

Continued

Sub	Event Handled	Header Statement	Purpose
btnUpdate_Click	Click event of button btnUpdate	Private Sub btnUpdate_Click (ByVal sender As System.Object, ByVal e As System.EventArgs) Handles btnUpdate.Click	Writes data changes made by the user to the database
btnCancelAll_Click	Click event of button btnCancelAll	Private Sub btnCancelAll_Click (ByVal sender As System.Object, ByVal e As System.EventArgs) Handles btnCancelAll.Click	Cancels all changes made by the user

TABLE 13.2

Event Handlers for Adding and Deleting Records in the Master Table

Sub	Event Handled	Header Statement	Purpose
btnAdd_Click	Click event of button btnAdd	Private Sub btnAdd_Click(ByVal sender As System.Object, ByVal e As System.EventArgs) Handles btnAdd.Click	Adds a master (or parent) record (for this example, a Publishers table record)
btnDelete_Click	Click event of button btnDelete	Private Sub btnDelete_Click (ByVal sender As System.Object, ByVal e As System.EventArgs) Handles btnDelete.Click	Deletes a master (or parent) record (for this example, a Publishers table record)
btnCancel_Click	Click event of button btnCancel	Private Sub btnCancel_Click (ByVal sender As System.Object, ByVal e As System.EventArgs) Handles btnCancel.Click	Cancels changes to the current master (or parent) record

Methods Created by the Data Form Wizard

TABLE 13.3

Event Handlers for Record-Navigation Buttons

Sub	Event Handled	Header Statement	Purpose
btnNavFirst_Click	Click event of button btnNavFirst	Private Sub btnNavFirst_Click (ByVal sender As System.Object, ByVal e As System.EventArgs) Handles btnNavFirst.Click	Fills form controls with data from the first record (in the current sort order) from the DataSet to which they are bound.
btnNavPrev_Click	Click event of button btnNavPrev	Private Sub btnNavPrev_Click (ByVal sender As System.Object, ByVal e As System.EventArgs) Handles btnNavPrev.Click	Fills form controls with data from the record immediately before the one currently displayed (based on the current sort order).
btnNavNext_Click	Click event of button btnNavNext	Private Sub btnNavNext_Click (ByVal sender As System.Object, ByVal e As System.EventArgs) Handles btnNavNext.Click	Fills form controls with data from the record immediately subsequent to the one currently display (based on the current sort order)
btnLast_Click	Click event of button btnLast	Private Sub btnLast_Click (ByVal sender As System.Object, ByVal e As System.EventArgs) Handles btnLast.Click	Fills form controls with data from the first record (in the current sort order) from the DataSet to which they are bound.

**Note that the name that the Data Form Wizard gives this button is not consistent in form with the names given the other navigational buttons. (This is called a micro-buglet.)

Non–Event Handler Methods

Table 13.4 lists the non–event handler methods.

TABLE 13.4

Non–Event Handler Methods

Sub	Header Statement	Purpose
New	Public Sub New()	Serves as the constructor for the form class.
Dispose	Protected Overloads Overrides Sub Dispose(ByVal disposing As Boolean)	Serves as the destructor for the form class.
objdsPubsForm_ PositionChanged()	Private Sub objdsPubsForm_ PositionChanged()	Updates the record position label associated with the Main table.
UpdateDataSet()	Public Sub UpdateDataSet() 'Create a new dataset to hold the changes that have been made to the main dataset.	Calls UpdateDataSource to update the DataSet from the database. Before doing so, UpdateDataSet() ends current edits and populates a temporary DataSet with those rows from the main DataSet that have changes (including newly inserted rows). UpdateDataSet() then merges the ChangedRows DataSet with the main DataSet and invokes the AcceptChanges method on the main DataSet to remove all change flags from its row. That prevents those rows from triggering database updates again (and redundantly) in the future.
LoadDataSet()	Public Sub LoadDataSet() 'Create a new dataset to hold the records returned from the call to FillDataSet. 'A temporary DataSet is used because filling the existing DataSet would require the data bindings to be rebound.	Calls FillDataSet to fill the DataSet that supplies controls on the form with data from the database. LoadDataSet creates a temporary instance of a DataSet with the same structure as that which supplies controls on the form. It fills this DataSet from the database and then merges it with the one that supplies the controls.

Methods Created by the Data Form Wizard

TABLE 13.4

Continued

Sub	Header Statement	Purpose
UpdateDataSource()	Public Sub UpdateDataSource (ByVal ChangedRows As DataFormWizard2.dsPubsForm)	Called by UpdateDataSet, UpdateDataSource actually executes the Update method of the form's DataAdapters to update the back-end database. It is passed an instance of the main DataSet class that contains only changed rows.
FillDataSet	Public Sub FillDataSet (ByVal dataSet As DataFormWizard2.dsPubsForm) 'Turn off constraint checking before the dataset is filled. This allows the adapters to fill the dataset without concern for dependencies between the tables.	Called by LoadDataSet, FillDataSet is a general-purpose method that actually executes the Fill method of the DataSet passed to it as a parameter. Before executing the fill, it opens the necessary connection and turns off enforcement of constraints on the target DataSet. After executing the fill, it reactivates the constraints and closes the connection.

Now you look at the code that uses these methods from a functional viewpoint.

Code Walkthrough for Various Functional Operations

In this section, you tour the code that performs the various key functions of the data form produced by the Data Form Wizard. These include methods that load and update data, add and delete records, cancel changes, and navigate the Master table.

Loading Data

When you first open the form that the Data Form Wizard creates, you see its controls unpopulated by data. To populate them, you click the Load button. The Click event handler for that button, as created by the Data Form Wizard, is as follows:

```
    Private Sub btnLoad_Click(ByVal sender As System.Object, ByVal e As
System.EventArgs) Handles btnLoad.Click
        Try
            'Attempt to load the dataset.
            Me.LoadDataSet()
        Catch eLoad As System.Exception
            'Add your error handling code here.
            'Display error message, if any.
            System.Windows.Forms.MessageBox.Show(eLoad.Message)
        End Try
        Me.objdsPubs_PositionChanged()

    End Sub
```

btnLoad_Click calls LoadDataSet() to do most of its work. That procedure's listing is as follows:

```
    Public Sub LoadDataSet()
        'Create a new dataset to hold the records returned from the call to
➥FillDataSet.
        'A temporary dataset is used because filling the existing dataset would
        'require the databindings to be rebound.
        Dim objDataSetTemp As SlicingAndDicing.dsPubs
        objDataSetTemp = New SlicingAndDicing.dsPubs
        Try
            'Attempt to fill the temporary dataset.
            Me.FillDataSet(objDataSetTemp)
        Catch eFillDataSet As System.Exception
            'Add your error handling code here.
            Throw eFillDataSet
        End Try
        Try
            grdtitles.DataSource = Nothing
            'Empty the old records from the dataset.
            objdsPubs.Clear()
            'Merge the records into the main dataset.
            objdsPubs.Merge(objDataSetTemp)
            grdtitles.SetDataBinding(objdsPubs, "publishers.PublishersTitles")
        Catch eLoadMerge As System.Exception
            'Add your error handling code here.
            Throw eLoadMerge
        End Try

    End Sub
```

Code Walkthrough for Various Functional Operations

Note the comment at the top of `LoadDataSet()`. It claims that "filling the existing `DataSet` would require the data bindings to be rebound," referring to the data bindings previously established for the form's controls. But is this really the case?

To answer the question, you have to continue tunneling through the code to the `FillDataSet()` procedure that `LoadDataSet()` calls to do the actual work of filling the `DataSet`. The `FillDataSet()` code is as follows:

```
Public Sub FillDataSet(ByVal dataSet As SlicingAndDicing.dsPubs)
    'Turn off constraint checking before the dataset is filled.
    'This allows the adapters to fill the dataset without concern
    'for dependencies between the tables.
    dataSet.EnforceConstraints = False
    Try
        'Open the connection.
        Me.OleDbConnection1.Open()
        'Attempt to fill the dataset through the OleDbDataAdapter1.
        Me.OleDbDataAdapter1.Fill(dataSet)
        Me.OleDbDataAdapter2.Fill(dataSet)
    Catch fillException As System.Exception
        'Add your error handling code here.
        Throw fillException
    Finally
        'Turn constraint checking back on.
        dataSet.EnforceConstraints = True
        'Close the connection whether or not the exception was thrown.
        Me.OleDbConnection1.Close()
    End Try

End Sub
```

`FillDataSet()` invokes the `Fill()` methods on the form's two `DataAdapters`. Remember, the Data Form Wizard created one `DataAdapter` for the Publishers table, acting as the Master table in this scenario, and also created a second `DataAdapter` for the Titles table, which serves as the Detail, or child, table and which populates the form's `DataGrid`.

The Data Form Wizard's code comment gives the impression that invoking a `DataAdapter Fill()` command destroys data bindings that reference existing tables in the `DataSet` targeted by the `Fill` operation. But this does not appear to be the case. Try modifying `LoadDataSet` to pass the main `DataSet`, `objdsPubs`, to `FillDataSet()` instead of passing a temporary `DataSet`. Then remove or

Code Walkthrough for Various Functional Operations

comment out the code that clears objdsPubs, merging the data from the temporary DataSet into it, and resets the grid bindings. That makes LoadDataSet() look like the following:

```
Public Sub LoadDataSet()
    Try
            'Attempt to fill the temporary dataset.
            Me.FillDataSet(Me.objdsPubs)
        Catch eFillDataSet As System.Exception
            'Add your error handling code here.
            Throw eFillDataSet
        End Try


    End Sub
```

With this version of LoadDataSet(), the loading of data works just as well as before.

The code that clears and resets the data bindings on the DataGrid control also appears to be unnecessary. Returning to the original version of LoadDataSet(), comment out the lines that clear and reset the grid bindings (marked 'DISABLED here):

```
            'DISABLED grdtitles.DataSource = Nothing
            'Empty the old records from the dataset.
            objdsPubs.Clear()
            'Merge the records into the main dataset.
            objdsPubs.Merge(objDataSetTemp)
            'DISABLED grdtitles.SetDataBinding(objdsPubs, "publishers.
➥PublishersTitles")
        Catch eLoadMerge As System.Exception
            'Add your error handling code here.
            Throw eLoadMerge
```

Again, loading of the data works just fine.

You can, in fact, completely bypass the LoadDataSet() procedure, calling FillDataSet() directly from the Click event handler for the form's Load button:

```
    Private Sub btnLoad_Click(ByVal sender As System.Object, ByVal e As
➥System.EventArgs)
 Handles btnLoad.Click
            Me.FillDataSet(Me.objdsPubs)
        Catch eLoad As System.Exception
            'Add your error handling code here.
            'Display error message, if any.
```

Code Walkthrough for Various Functional Operations

```
            System.Windows.Forms.MessageBox.Show(eLoad.Message)
        End Try
        Me.objdsPubs_PositionChanged()
    End Sub
```

This produces the same result as the original. Moral: Don't believe everything you read, even when it's in code generated by Visual Studio.

Updating Data

The user explicitly updates the database behind a Data Form Wizard form by clicking the Update button. The `Click` event handler for that button, `btnUpdate_Click`, calls `UpdateDataSet()` to perform the updates. It then calls the `objdsPubs_PositionChanged()` method to update the `lblNavLocation` label with the current record position and count.

`UpdateDataSet()` creates a temporary `DataSet` from the same XML schema used for the form's main `DataSet`. It puts copies of all changed `DataRows` into that temporary `DataSet`, which is then used to the back-end database. Before selecting the modified rows, however, `UpdateDataSet()` stops any edits in progress on any controls bound to either of the tables being used to supply data to the form. It does this by calling the `EndCurrentEdit()` method of the `CurrencyManager` for each of the two tables:

```
Me.BindingContext(objdsPubs, "authors").EndCurrentEdit()
Me.BindingContext(objdsPubs, "vueTitleAuthor").EndCurrentEdit()
```

Note that the form's `BindingContext` object returns a `CurrencyManager` object when passed parameters of a `DataSet` and a `DataTable`. Chapter 14, "Data Binding in Windows Applications," talks more about `BindingContexts`; for now, just be aware of the following points:

Every form automatically has a `BindingContext` object; it inherits it from the `System.Windows.Forms.Control` class.

When passed a list of items (such as a `DataTable` or an `ArrayList`), the form's `BindingContext` object returns a `CurrencyManager` object.

The job of that `CurrencyManager` object is to keep the values of all controls bound to its data source current. It maintains a record pointer for the data source and makes sure that all controls bound to that data source display values from the current record.

The CurrencyManager relieves ADO.NET applications of having to rely on the back-end data source to maintain a record pointer. Maintaining a record pointer is no problem for a back-end data source that is a database manager (such as SQL Server

13

2000, Oracle, or Access), but the ADO.NET developers wanted you to be able to use other, less intelligent data sources as well, such as text files that contain XML or even just comma-delimited rows. By moving the function of maintaining a record pointer into the .NET application, ADO.NET can support a broad spectrum of data sources in the same even-handed manner.

After ending all current edits, `UpdateDataSet()` calls the `GetChanges()` method on the main `DataSet` in the following statement:

```
objDataSetChanges = CType(objdsPubs.GetChanges, SlicingAndDicing.dsPubs)
```

This returns a set of all rows that have been modified since they were loaded. (Passing it through `Ctype()` simply converts the untyped `DataSet` returned by `GetChanges` to a strongly typed `dsPubs` `DataSet`.) The procedure then passes this `DataSet` of updated rows to the `UpdateDataSource()` method created by the Data Form Wizard:

```
Me.UpdateDataSource(objDataSetChanges)
```

Assuming that all goes well, the next thing done by the Data Form Wizard's code is curious. It invokes the `Merge()` method on the main `DataSet`, passing it the `DataSet` of changed rows.

```
objdsPubs.Merge(objDataSetChanges)
```

This is an apparently pointless operation because those rows came from the main `DataSet` to begin with. However, the possibility exists that some of those rows could be further modified by the user while the update operation is taking place. Because the next action of `UpdateDataSource()` is to accept changes on the main `DataSet`, any changes made on those rows during the update would never get committed to the database:

```
objdsPubs.AcceptChanges()
```

The `AcceptChanges()` method would mark them as unchanged. By merging the `DataSet` of changed rows, any changes made to rows in the `DataSet` in that (short) interim period would still get thrown away, but they would appear *immediately* as having been thrown away, instead of appearing that way only after a subsequent fresh load from the database (by which time the user would almost surely have forgotten them). Note that, in ordinary circumstances, it is quite unlikely that more than a tiny amount of data would be involved. For the user to have time to make a significant number of updates, the update operation would have to be very slow (for example, the result of a huge update combined with a very slow connection).

Canceling All Changes

If the user clicks the Cancel All button, its event handler simply invokes the DataSet RejectChanges() method:

```
Me.objdsPubs.RejectChanges()
```

This rolls back all the changes made to the DataSet since it was created or since the last time its AcceptChanges() method was called.

Adding a Record for a Publisher

The btnAdd_Click() event handler stops any current edits (to the Publishers table, in this example) and invokes the CurrencyManager's AddNew() method:

```
Try
    'Clear out the current edits
    Me.BindingContext(objdsPubs, "publishers").EndCurrentEdit()
    Me.BindingContext(objdsPubs, "publishers").AddNew()
    Catch eEndEdit As System.Exception
    System.Windows.Forms.MessageBox.Show(eEndEdit.Message)
  End Try
Me.objdsPubs_PositionChanged()
```

The procedure then calls objdsPubs_PositionChanged() to update the record position label.

Deleting a Publishers Record

After first making sure that the Publishers table has at least one record in it, the btnDelete_Click() event handler calls the CurrencyManager's RemoveAt() method to remove the current record from the list:

```
If (Me.BindingContext(objdsPubs, "publishers").Count > 0) Then
    ➥Me.BindingContext(objdsPubs, "publishers").RemoveAt
    ➥ (Me.BindingContext(objdsPubs, "publishers").Position)
    ➥Me.objdsPubs_PositionChanged()
End If
```

The procedure then calls objdsPubs_PositionChanged() to update the record position label.

Canceling Changes to a Publishers Record

The btnCancel_Click() event handler calls the CurrencyManager's
CancelCurrentEdit() method, which rolls back any changes made to the
current record:

```
Me.BindingContext(objdsPubs, "publishers").CancelCurrentEdit()
Me.objdsPubs_PositionChanged()
```

The procedure then calls objdsPubs_PositionChanged() to update the record
position label.

Navigating the Publishers Table

Four buttons are provided for navigating records in the Publishers table:
btnNavFirst, btnNavPrev, btnNavNext, and the inconsistently named
btnLast. These all change the value of the Position property of the
CurrencyManager in charge of the Publishers table. The statements they use to do
that are discussed next.

btnNavFirst

```
Me.BindingContext(objdsPubs, "publishers").Position = 0
```

btnNavPrev

```
Me.BindingContext(objdsPubs, "publishers").Position = _
(Me.BindingContext(objdsPubs, "publishers").Position - 1)
```

btnNavNext

```
Me.BindingContext(objdsPubs, "publishers").Position = _
(Me.BindingContext(objdsPubs, "publishers").Position + 1)
```

btnLast

```
Me.BindingContext(objdsPubs, "publishers").Position = _
(Me.objdsPubs.Tables("publishers").Rows.Count - 1)
```

The Click event handlers of each of these buttons then call the form's
objdsPubs_PositionChanged() method to update the label that displays the
record position and count.

```
objdsPubs_PositionChanged()
```

13

This concludes the code walkthrough for the code that the Data Form Wizard generates for a Master-Detail form with Master table records displayed in Form view, and Detail records in a `DataGrid`.

Breaking Away from the Data Form Wizard

If you were content to limit yourself to data forms such as those that can be generated by the Data Form Wizard, you probably would not have worked this hard studying the code it generates. You could just, well, *use* it. The point has been not so much to become an authority on the wizard's code as to learn the lessons of ADO.NET and data access that it had to teach.

So now it's time to begin breaking away. You could certainly take a shot at simply coding a similar form "from scratch" (actually, you'd probably still end up letting Visual Studio do a lot of the work for you, unless you're a *really* hard-core code cranker), but I'm going to suggest that you take a smaller step toward independence first.

You will begin by creating a data form using the wizard, exactly as you did earlier in this chapter. But instead of stopping there, you will delete the data provider objects it created: the `OleDbConnection`, the `DataAdapters` and their component parts, and the XML Schema that defines its strongly typed `DataSet`.

Having done that, you re-create them with the help of another wizard: the Data Adapter Configuration Wizard. The Data Adapter Configuration Wizard gives you many more choices than the Data Form Wizard over how you will do your data access. For example, you can get it to generate and use SQL Server 2000 stored procedures for you if you like, instead of putting SQL statements in your code. Unlike the Data Form Wizard, the Data Adapter Wizard also comes in a SqlClient flavor as well as an OleDb one. In the following exercise, you'll use the SqlClient version to create a data-connected form optimized for use with SQL Server 2000.

With this process, you'll still let the Data Form Wizard lay out the form, create the table style to show the appropriate columns in the `DataGrid`, create the navigational code, and write the methods to load and store the data. But you'll be taking control over many more aspects of the data access than previously.

Creating a SqlClient Data Form Using the Data Form Wizard and the SqlDataAdapter Wizard

Here are the steps to follow:

1. The first thing you need for this exercise is a data form exactly like the one you created for the project in the section "Creating the Data Form" (which you named `DataFormOleDb`). You can use that very form if you like—or if you prefer to leave that project intact, you can create a new project and repeat the

steps to create `DataFormOleDb`. Recall that the form you created referenced the Pubs database, created a `DataSet` that you named `dsPubs`, used the `Publishers` table as the master or parent and the `Titles` table as the detail or child, defined a relationship between the two tables that linked them on their `pub_id` columns (named `PublishersTitles`), and displayed records from the master table using individual controls rather than a `DataGrid`. You can repeat the steps shown in Figures 13.2–13.10 if you are re-creating the form.

TIP
If you want to perform surgery on a Visual Studio solution, but you want to be sure you can recover to a starting point if you clobber something, the best way is to use source code control with a tool such as Visual SourceSafe, which enables you to keep a trail of code versions. Short of that, you can also easily copy a complete Visual Studio solution and work on the copy, leaving the original intact.
Particularly when working on single-project solutions such as those in this chapter, copying the solution is as simple as closing it in Visual Studio and then using Windows Explorer to make a copy of the complete directory where the solution, project, class, and other files reside. You can place the copied directory wherever you like on your disk.
Note, however, that the solution and project name remain the same in the copy as in the original. If you want to change those as well, *open the solution in Visual Studio and make the changes there.* (You can select the solution or project name in the Solution Explorer object tree and press F2 to rename them.) Changing the project name outside Visual Studio causes the Solution to "lose" the project.
You can also add a `ReadMe` text file to the solution or project and keep notes on changes there.

2. When the form is complete, select its class file, named `DataFormOleDb.vb`, in Solution Explorer and press Ctrl+C followed by Ctrl+V to copy it and paste the copy into the project. Rename the copy `DataFormSqlClient.vb`.

3. Open `DataFormSqlClient.vb` in Code view and replace all occurrences of the string `DataFormOleDb` with the string `DataFormSqlClient`. That renames the class so that it does not conflict with the class name of the form from which you copied it. Note that until you change the class name, Visual Studio refuses to allow you to open the form in Design view because of the name conflict (see Figure 13.11).

4. Open the form `DataFormSqlClient` in Design view. Clear the Component Tray by deleting the `Command` object `OleDbConnection1`, the two `DataAdapters` `OleDbDataAdapter1` and `OleDbDataAdapter1`, and the `DataSet` `objdsPubs`. Note that when you delete the `DataAdapters` in this manner in Design view, all the code that creates their component `Command` and `Parameter` objects also gets deleted from the generated code region in the form's code. These objects literally cease to exist in the form. *However,*

Breaking Away from the Data Form Wizard

several of the methods that the wizard generates in the form code continue to refer to those objects. That's a problem you'll fix momentarily.

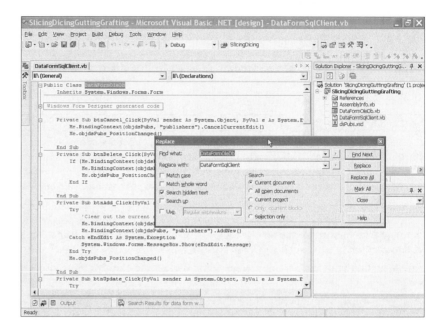

FIGURE 13.11   Renamed class for the copied form.

5. In the Solution Explorer, delete the schema file for the DataSet, dsPubs.xsd. This also deletes the correspondingly named class, dsPubs.vb, which sits in the Solution Explorer hierarchically below and connected with dsPubs.xsd (visible only when you have Show All Files toggled in Solution Explorer).

6. Drag a SqlDataAdapter from the Data section of the toolbox onto the data form. This launches the Data Adapter Configuration Wizard, shown in Figure 13.13, which you use to create a DataAdapter to handle data from the Publishers table. You will find the dialog forms in the Data Adapter Configuration Wizard similar in many respects to those presented by the Data Form Wizard.

7. Select all columns from the table. The easiest way to do this is simply to enter the SQL command string select * from publishers in the query window of the dialog box, without opening the Query Builder. If you like, you can define a sort order, too, by substituting the statement select * from publishers order by pub_name. Of course, you can always use the Query Builder, if you prefer.

Breaking Away from the Data Form Wizard

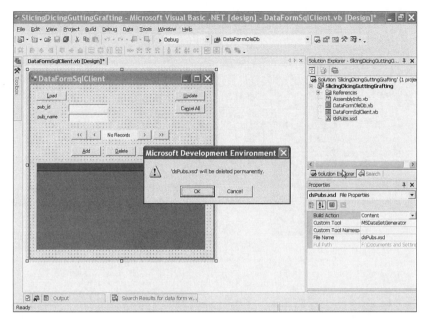

FIGURE 13.12   Deleting the schema file.

TIP

One significant difference of the Data Adapter Configuration Wizard compared to the Data Form Wizard is that when you pick table columns in the latter, you are picking *the columns you want displayed on the form*, not the columns to be included in the `SELECT` statement used by the resulting `DataAdapter`. The `DataAdapters` created by the Data Form Wizard automatically select *all* columns from the targeted table.

In the Data Adapter Configuration Wizard, the columns you select are those that are included in the resulting `SELECT` statement.

When you complete the SqlDataAdapter Wizard, a `SqlDataAdapter` for the Publishers table is created, along with an appropriate `SqlConnection` object.

8. Now drag a second `DataAdapter` from the `Data` section of the toolbox to the data form. Again indicate the Pubs database, but this time indicate that you want data from the `Titles` table by entering `select * from titles` (or `select * from titles order by title`) in the query window. This second `DataAdapter` automatically uses the Connection object created by the first because the Data Adapter Wizard recognizes that it is getting its data from the same database.

Breaking Away from the Data Form Wizard

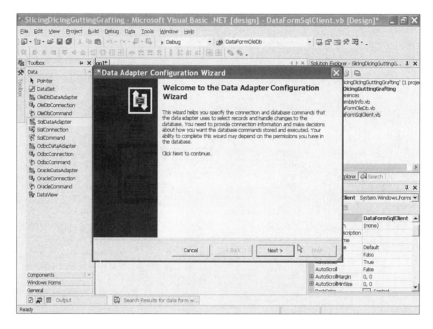

FIGURE 13.13   The Data Adapter Configuration Wizard.

9. Rename the `Connection` and `DataAdapter` objects as shown in Table 13.5. (This step isn't essential, but the suggested new names are rather more helpful than the originals.) To rename an object, select it in Design view and use the Properties window to change the value of the `(Name)` property.

TABLE 13.5

Names for the `Connection` and `SqlDataAdapter` Objects

Old Name	New Name
SqlConnection1	conPubs
SqlDataAdapter1	daPublishers
SqlDataAdapter2	daTitles

Your form should now appear as shown in Figure 13.14.

10. Select the `daPublishers DataAdapter` in the Component Tray, and then click the `Generate DataSet` link near the bottom of the Properties window. This launches the dialog box shown in Figure 13.15, which creates the `dsPubs` schema and the associated .NET class, and defines the schema for the Publishers table in both. It also places an icon for the `DataSet` in the Component Tray. Specify all options as shown in the figure.

Breaking Away from the Data Form Wizard

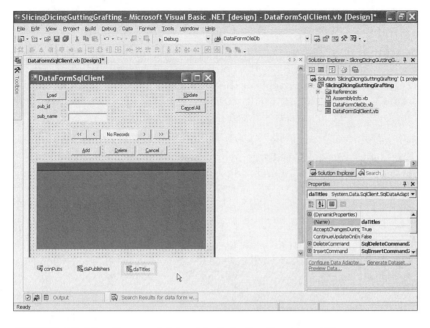

FIGURE 13.14   Renamed data objects in the Component Tray.

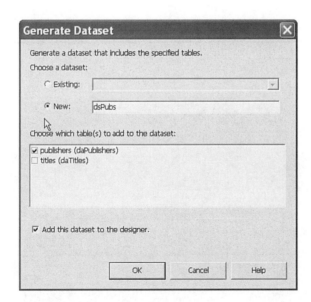

FIGURE 13.15   Generate the `DataSet`.

11. Rename the `DsPubs1` component to `objDsPubs` (the name that was given to the corresponding object created by the Data Form Wizard). Again, you can do

Breaking Away from the Data Form Wizard

this by selecting the DsPubs1 icon in the Component Tray and using the Properties window to change its (Name) property.

12. Select the daTitles DataAdapter in the Component Tray, and again click the Generate DataSet link at the bottom of the Properties window. This time accept all the default settings in the Generate DataSet dialog box, which should now indicate the dsPubs DataSet as its target. This defines the Titles DataTable in the dsPubs.xsd schema file.

13. The relation established by the Data Form Wizard between the Publishers and Titles tables was destroyed when you deleted the original version of the dsPubs schema. Because the code in the form still references that relation, you must re-create it.

TIP

To create a relation between two tables in an .xsd schema file, double-click the schema in the Solution Explorer. Right-click the child table in the intended relation and select Add, New Relation from the shortcut menus. In the EditRelation dialog box, name the relation and set other properties of it as desired.

---

14. Relate the two tables on their pub_id columns, with Publishers as the parent table and Titles as the child. Name the relation PublishersTitles because that's what you called it when you defined it using the Data Form Wizard, and that's how it is still referred to in the procedures the wizard generates. Your settings for the relation should be as those shown in Figure 13.16. After you create the new relation, save your changes and close the schema window.

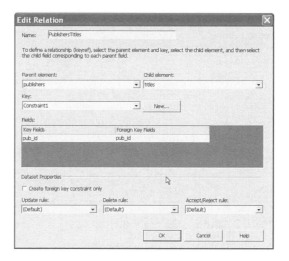

FIGURE 13.16 Specification for the relationship between the Publishers and Titles tables.

13

15. You are now ready to attempt to build the solution. Do so by choosing Build, Build Solution from the Visual Studio main menu. You should see errors like those shown in Figure 13.17. The errors exist in the code because several of the procedures originally generated by the Data Form Wizard still refer to the `Connection` and `DataAdapter` objects by the names they were originally given; you gave them new names in step 8.

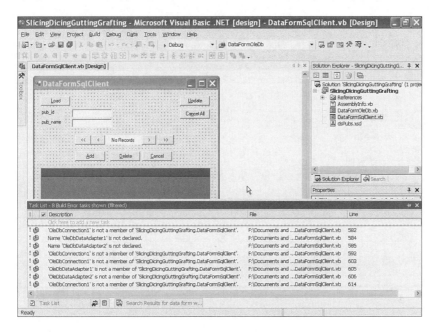

FIGURE 13.17 Build errors mismatch between the current names of data components and the references to them in the code by their old names.

16. The errors can be easily corrected by three simple global `Replace` operations to change the names in the code. Double-click on the first error, and Visual Studio jumps you right to the offending code line—probably a statement like this:

```
Me.OleDbConnection1.Open()
```

Replace all occurrences of `OleDbConnection1` with `conPubs`. Do the same to change all occurrences of `OleDbDataAdapter1` to `daPublishers`, and `OleDbDataAdapter2` to `daTitles`. That should clear the errors from the task list.

17. You're almost there, but you need to restore the data bindings for the two text boxes that display the `pub_id` and `pub_name` values from the Publishers

Breaking Away from the Data Form Wizard

table. These bindings got cleared when you regenerated the Publishers `DataTable` in the `DataSet`. Set the bindings to the appropriate columns from the Publishers table. (Figure 13.18 shows the binding for the `Text` property of the `editpub_id` TextBox being set to the `pub_id` column from the Publishers `DataTable` in the `objdsPubs` DataSet.)

TIP

To reset the data binding for a `TextBox`, select it in Design view and then expand the `(DataBindings)` entry in the Properties window. Select the `Text` property, then drop down the list of binding sources, expand the appropriate table, and select the appropriate column to be the data source.

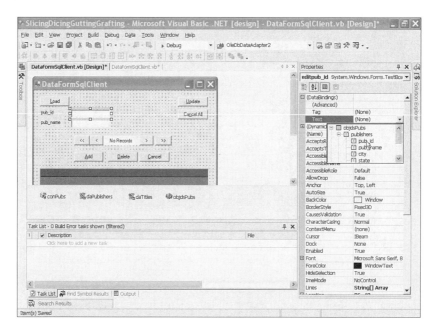

FIGURE 13.18   Setting the data binding for the `Text` property of the `editpub_id` TextBox.

18. Make `DataFormSql` the startup object for your project, and then click the Start button on the toolbar. Your data form should now be working, using SqlClient data providers to retrieve and update data from the Pubs database. Its appearance should resemble that of the running form shown in Figure 13.19.

> **TIP**
>
> To set the Startup Object for a project, right-click on the project in Solution Explorer and select Properties from the shortcut menu. Find the `ComboBox` for Startup Object in the main Project Properties, and select the desired object.

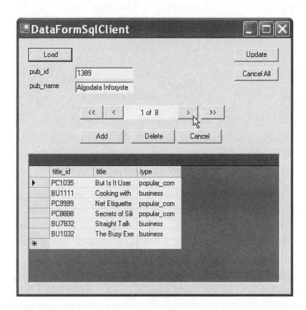

FIGURE 13.19 The completed SqlClient data form, displaying data from the Publishers table and related data from the Titles table.

The two versions of the pubs data form are included for reference in the app, SlicingDicingGuttingGrafting, included on the code website. If you want to run them, be sure to change the connection strings in the generated code section of the forms to point to your instance of SQL Server.

Next Steps

At this point, you're close to being completely independent of the Data Form Wizard. In the last exercise, you took greater control over creating the `Command`, `DataAdapter`, and `DataSet` objects; having studied the code generated by the Data Form Wizard, you should be able to hand-code methods similar to those, in a form of your own, that the wizard generated for navigation, data loading, and data updating. This would be a very good exercise at this point, to consolidate what you learned in this chapter. (By all means, use the wizard-generated code as a reference.)

Next Steps

A few more mysteries remain to be explored in the `dsPubs.xsd` schema file, but these are discussed in Chapter 15, "ADO.NET and XML." You could also explore using the SqlDataAdapter Wizard to generate stored procedures instead of SQL code statements. And You might also want to further explore working with `DataGridTableStyles` to control the appearance of `DataGrids`, working either through the Design view by using the Properties window, or by defining the table and column styles in code.

Summary

In this chapter, you studied the code that Visual Studio's Data Form Wizard generates, which combines most of the essential elements of an updateable data-connected form. You saw the declarations and initializations for form controls, data providers, and other data-related objects; became familiar with the methods that give the form its functionality; and walked through all the principle operations that the form facilitates.

You then looked at ways to grow into independence from the Data Form Wizard by using the DataAdapter Wizard to replace the `Connection`, `DataAdapters`, and `DataSet` in a form that the Data Form Wizard generates. You also reset data bindings on some of the form's controls and define a relationship directly in the XML schema. If you followed this up by creating a form from scratch with functionality similar to that provided by the one you created using the Data Form wizard, you should be starting to feel quite comfortable creating data-connected forms.

Further Reading

"Data Form Wizard." From the MSDN Help file for Visual Studio .NET, http://msdn.microsoft.com/library/default.asp?url=/library/en-us/vsintro7/html/vburfdataformwizard.asp.

"Data Form Wizard Generated Code." From the MSDN Help file for Visual Studio .NET, http://msdn.microsoft.com/library/default.asp?url=/library/en-us/vsintro7/html/vxconDataFormWizardGeneratedCode.asp.

"Data Adapter Configuration Wizard." From the MSDN Help file for Visual Studio .NET, http://msdn.microsoft.com/library/default.asp?url=/library/en-us/vsintro7/html/vburfADODataSetCommandConfigurationWizard.asp.

"Accessing Data with Data Adapters and Data Sets." From StartVbDotNet.com, www.startvbdotnet.com/ado/dataadapter.htm.

Beachemin, Bob. "Take Advantage of Oracle in .NET." *Visual Studio Magazine* July 2003. (See especially the section "Leverage the DataAdapter Wizard.") www.fawcette.com/vsm/2003_07/magazine/columns/databasedesign/default_pf.aspx.

13

14 DATA BINDING IN WINDOWS APPLICATIONS

IN BRIEF

In this chapter, you will learn about binding form controls and other objects to data sources so that the controls automatically receive (and, optionally, update) data from those sources. Data binding in .NET represents a complete paradigm shift from its implementation in previous versions of Visual Basic. Redesigned to fully support the .NET design objective of disconnected data access, it has freed itself from the performance problems associated with its use in the past. Because bound controls no longer require a continuous connection to a database, their use is entirely practical in enterprise applications, and even in applications with components that must collaborate over an Internet connection.

.NET support of data binding is far-reaching. The discussion in this chapter covers the most common type of data binding—in which the display property of a control on a form is bound to a column in a `DataTable`—but it does not stop there. You'll see form controls bound to properties of user-defined objects, multiple properties of a single object bound to multiple properties of another object, and examples of binding to many different kinds of collections. Finally, you'll learn how you can create your own bindable objects and collections.

WHAT YOU NEED

SOFTWARE RECOMMENDATIONS	Windows 2000, Windows XP, or Windows Server 2003 .NET Framework 1.1
	Visual Studio .NET 2003 with Visual Basic .NET installed SQL Server 2000 or corresponding version of the Microsoft Desktop Database Engine (MSDE)
HARDWARE RECOMMENDATIONS	PC desktop or laptop, .NET-enabled server, desktop client
SKILLS REQUIRED	Intermediate knowledge of the .NET Framework Intermediate knowledge of Windows Forms Understanding of relational database concepts and applications Familiarity with error trapping using `Try-Catch` block Familiarity with SQL Server 2000

DATA BINDING IN WINDOWS APPLICATIONS AT A GLANCE

DATA BINDING IN WINDOWS APPLICATIONS AT A GLANCE

14

Overview of Data Binding

14

Data binding is a technique for linking properties of one object to properties of a second object so that the properties of the first object automatically take on the values of linked properties in the second. Optionally, data binding can permit changes in the property values of the first object to be communicated back to the second.

Historically, data binding has been used to link the display values of controls on a form to columns in a record from a data table. The database-management system hosting the table kept track of a record pointer, or relative row position within the table; whenever the front-end application ordered a position change, the latter would retrieve values from the new current record to populate bound controls on a form or in a report.

Data binding was a popular application development shortcut for single-user desktop applications, but proved problematic for multiuser apps and inconceivable for web apps because it depended upon a constant and stateful connection to a database. But in .NET, data binding has reincarnated as a powerful and elegant development short-cut for data-maintenance forms—this time in the context of a disconnected data-access model that is very well-suited for enterprise and web-based applications.

.NET extends the scope of data binding in other new ways as well. Binding is no longer restricted to form or report controls; any property of any object, properly implemented, is potentially data-bindable. For those with data-binding experience, some aspects of data binding in .NET can be a bit off-putting initially because of new levels of abstraction associated with the ADO.NET goal of supporting a wide variety of data sources. Fortunately, it's much less forbidding when you understand what it's designed to do.

In the recent past (specifically, in the DAO and ADO object models that predated ADO.NET), the binding of controls directly to data sources required the data sources themselves to be capable of dealing successfully with the concept of a "current record." When the front-end application sent a request to the data source for values from the "next record" or "previous record," the data source had to know just which record it should move forward or back from to accommodate the request. That's not a problem for a brainy database engine such as SQL Server or Access or Oracle, but it most definitely is a problem for an ASCII text file or an XML data file, both of which are pure data sources with no intelligence of their own. Building in strong support for the use of XML data files was a particularly high priority because those have two properties that suit them uniquely for passing data around the Internet:

▶ They are encoded as plain-text files and so will pass through firewalls that don't like binaries.

▶ They are an external standard supported by innumerable proprietary vendors and disparate organizations.

To address this problem of accommodating vital but brainless data sources, the .NET architects decided to bring the maintenance of the record pointer in-house. "You supply the data, we'll supply the brain," you can almost hear them saying. So in ADO.NET, there is something called a *binding context*, which is the brain for the data source. When you want to populate a form's controls with data from some record other than the one they're currently using, instead of telling the data source, you tell the binding context.

But the .NET architects didn't stop there. In addition to providing developers with great flexibility in the choice of data sources, they wanted to support a variety of architectural styles, from the "fairly object oriented" to the "very object oriented indeed." So they built in support for binding not only to database-like objects such as the `DataSet`, but also to arrays and to objects of virtually any sort. Indirectly, they even built in support for binding to custom collections, although you have to go to a bit of extra work to tap that capability.

In this chapter, you'll learn how to bind to `DataSets`, objects, arrays, and collections. You'll also learn how to use data sources including databases, .NET collections, and custom collections. In addition, you'll learn how to bind multiple properties of a single control to different columns in a data source and to different properties of an object. Finally, you'll learn how to separate data-retrieval code from user interface code, laying the foundation for the multitier architectures discussed by Heinrich Gantenbein later in this book.

The discussions and code examples in this chapter are embedded within the context of Windows Forms apps; Chapter 17, "Data Binding in Web Applications," discusses specific techniques for data binding in the context of web apps. Nevertheless, you might find that much of the material in this chapter is applicable to your work even if you are exclusively a web applications developer. This will most definitely be true if your work with web apps grows to include "smart client" applications, in which a Windows Forms app on the client side communicates over the Internet with web servers. Those are a special interest of Microsoft these days, and they combine the rich, responsive front end of Windows apps with the effortless deployment and ubiquitous availability of web apps.

Data Binding Categories: Read-Only vs. Read-Write, and Simple vs. Complex

The realm of data binding can be meaningfully decomposed along a couple different classification lines. *Read-only* data binding does not provide for updating of the data in the data source; *read-write* data binding does so provide. *Simple* data binding occurs when you link a single property of a control to a data source; *complex* data binding occurs when you link multiple items associated with a control (for example, the items in a drop-down list) to a data source.

Overview of Data Binding

NOTE
In earlier versions of Visual Basic, data binding was effected through the medium of a `data control`, which also provided the normally obligatory navigational buttons (First, Previous, Next, and Last), along with a display of the record position. In Visual Basic .NET, the data control is no more, and you have to write your own navigational controls. Fortunately, it's easy to do the latter (and the Data Form Wizard, detailed in Chapter 13, "Using the Data Form and DataAdapter Wizards in Windows Applications," can deliver a coded example to you anytime you need one).

Potential Data Sources and Support for the `IList` Interface

The minimum requirement for any collection to function as a bindable .NET data source is that it must support .NET's `IList` interface. You might recall that an interface is simply an empty class that defines certain properties and methods for which code must be provided in any class that *implements* that interface. The `IList` interface from the `System.Collections` namespace defines the methods and properties listed in Table 14.1.

Potential Data Sources and Support for the IList Interface

TABLE 14.1

IList Interface Members

Methods

Name	Mandated Signature	Purpose for Which Member Is Intended	Return Values
Add	`Public Overridable Function Add(ByVal value As Object) As Integer`	Adding an item to `System.Collections.IList`	The position into which the new element was inserted
Clear	`Public Overridable Sub Clear()`	Removing all items from `System.Collections.IList`	
Contains	`Public Overridable Function Contains(ByVal value As Object) As Boolean`	Determining whether `System.Collections.IList` contains a specific value	`true` if the `System.Object` is found in `System.Collections.IList`—otherwise, `false`
IndexOf	`Public Overridable Function IndexOf(ByVal value As Object) As Integer`	Determining the index of a specific item in `System.Collections.IList`	The index of `value` if found in the list—otherwise, `-1`
Insert	`Public Overridable Sub Insert (ByVal index As Integer, ByVal value As Object)`	Inserting an item into `System.Collections.IList` at the specified position	
Remove	`Public Overridable Sub Remove (ByVal value As Object) Member of: System.Collections.IList`	Removing the first occurrence of a specific object from `System.Collections.IList`	
RemoveAt	`Public Overridable Sub RemoveAt (ByVal index As Integer) Member of: System.Collections.IList`	Removing the `System.Collections.IList` item at the specified index	

Properties

Name	Mandated Signature	Purpose for Which Member Is Intended	Return Values
IsFixedSize	`Public Overridable ReadOnly Property IsFixedSize() As Boolean`	Indicating whether `System.Collections.IList` has a fixed size	
IsReadOnly	`Public Overridable ReadOnly Property IsReadOnly() As Boolean`	Indicating whether `System.Collections.IList` is read-only	

14

Potential Data Sources and Support for the ILIst Interface

TABLE 14.1 Continued

Properties

Name	Mandated Signature	Purpose for Which Member Is Intended	Return Values
Item	`Public Overridable Default Property Item(ByVal index As Integer) As Object`	Getting or setting the element at the specified index	

Events

| ListChanged | | Occurs when the list changes or an item in the list changes | |

Source: MSDN Help file for Visual Studio 2003

.NET Classes That Implement the ILList Interface

More than 40 .NET classes implement the IList interface. Some of these are shown in Table 14.2; you can find the complete list, with descriptions, in the MSDN help file entry for the IList interface in your copy of Visual Studio. (The same help file entry is also available on the web; see the reference in "Further Reading" at the end of this chapter.)

TABLE 14.2

A Sample of the .NET Classes That Implement ILList

Array	LinkLabel.LinkCollection
ArrayList	ListBox.SelectedIndexCollection
CheckedListBox.CheckedItemCollection	ListView.SelectedIndexCollection
ComboBox.ObjectCollection	Menu.MenuItemCollection
Control.ControlCollection	OleDbParameterCollection
DataColumnMappingCollection	PropertyDescriptorCollection
DataTableMappingCollection	SchemaNameCollection
DataView	SqlParameterCollection
DataViewManager	StringCollection
EventDescriptorCollection	TabControl.TabPageCollection
GridColumnStylesCollection	TableCellCollection
GridTableStylesCollection	ToolBar.ToolBarButtonCollection
ImageList.ImageCollection	TreeNodeCollection

The code provided with this chapter includes an application, BindToIListCollections, that illustrates how several of the collection classes listed can, in fact, be used as data sources for bound controls. A bit more background is necessary to fully appreciate the app, however, so its discussion is deferred to the section "Using the CurrencyManager for Nontable Bindings," later in this chapter.

The BindingContext

Every class that inherits from Systems.Windows.Forms.Control (which, incidentally, includes System.Windows.Forms.Form) comes with a BindingContext property. The BindingContext object assigned to this property is provided to manage a collection of objects—typically, CurrencyManagers—which, in turn, manage individual binding objects. Every data source gets its own CurrencyManager, whose job it is to see that all controls with properties bound to that data source get updated properly when the position pointer in the data source is changed. The position pointer is maintained as the Position property of the CurrencyManager.

The `BindingContext`

Take the case of a simple Windows form with a few controls that correspond to columns in a data record. Because the form inherits from `System.Windows.Forms.Control`, it comes out of the box with a `BindingContext` property. Thus, you can put the following two statements inside any method of a Windows form:

```
Dim bc As BindingContext
bc = Me.BindingContext()
```

Usually, you won't do this, however, because what you typically want to work with is a `CurrencyManager` (which you get *from* a `BindingContext` object).

The `CurrencyManager` Object

When passed a `DataTable`, `ArrayList`, or other collection that implements the `IList` interface, the `BindingContext` for a Windows form returns a `CurrencyManager` object.

```
Dim cmAuthors As CurrencyManager
cmAuthors = Me.BindingContext(Me.objdsData.authors)
```

The `CurrencyManager`'s job is to maintain a notion of position within a set of objects and, when that position changes, to make sure all controls bound to that set get their values updated. The most typical situation is that the set of objects at issue is the collection of rows—or, more specifically, `DataRows`—comprising a `DataTable`. One row of that set is always considered the current one, and values for controls that are bound to different columns of the `DataTable` are drawn from their associated column in that current row. When the "record pointer" is moved to a different record, the bound controls get new values, drawn from the columns of that different record.

NOTE

It is actually not a `DataTable`, but a `DataView`—specifically, the `DataView` assigned to the `DefaultView` property of a `DataTable`—that supports data binding by virtue of implementing the `IBindingList` interface (an industrial-strength cousin of `IList` that is discussed in the section, "Read-Write Binding"). When you assign a `DataTable` as the data source for a control such as a `DataGrid`, `ComboBox`, or `ListBox`, the `DataTable` `DefaultView` is automatically used.

A `DataView`, you may recall, is a customized view of a `DataTable` that permits sorting, filtering, searching, editing, and navigation of that table.

Similarly, if you assign a `DataSet` as a data source, .NET actually creates the binding to the `DataViewManager` for that `DataSet`.

As noted, the set of objects do not have to be `DataRows`; they can be some other type of object, including a user-defined one. The container for that set also can be not just a `DataTable`, but any collection object that implements `IList`.

The `CurrencyManager` is discussed further in later sections in this chapter; first, you need an introduction to its sibling, the `PropertyManager`, and a discussion of the basics of creating data bindings.

14

The `PropertyManager` **Object**

When passed a simple object rather than a collection, the `BindingContext` for a Windows form returns a `PropertyManager` object (see Figure 14.1). The `PropertyManager`'s job is to manage bindings between the properties of that simple object and one or more data-bound properties of other objects. This contrasts with the `CurrencyManager`, which manages bindings between properties of objects *in a collection* and the data-bound properties of the targeted objects.

Because the `PropertyManager` does not manage a collection of objects—instead, it manages just a single object—it does not maintain any list pointer. Accordingly, there are no `Position` or `Count` properties associated with a `PropertyManager`. Similarly, the `AddNew` and `RemoveAt` methods are not supported.

The BindingContext application in the code for this chapter illustrates how to get the `BindingContext` to return a `CurrencyManager` or a `PropertyManager`. The application does little else, and is simply meant to emphasize the fact that the BindingContext returns two different types of objects, with different behaviors, depending upon the type of data source it is passed. Applications addressed later in this chapter build upon that knowledge, exercising the returned objects in more complex ways.

FIGURE 14.1 The BindingContext application explores the two different types of object that can be returned by a form's `BindingContext`.

The `PropertyManager` Object

14

NOTE

All applications included on the code website for this chapter include a description and instructions which are accessible via the Help option on the main menu (see Figure 14.2).

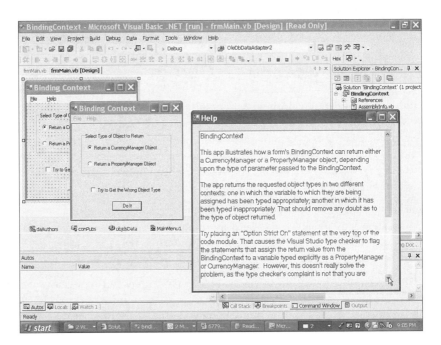

FIGURE 14.2   The BindingContext application with the help form displayed.

Data-Bound Objects

Bindable controls fall into two categories: simple and complex. Simple bindable controls, of which `TextBox` controls are the most obvious example, hold and display data from a single item (such as a column value from the current row of a `DataTable`).

Complex bindable controls house and display data from collections of items. Those collections can be the rows in a `DataTable`, the objects in an `ArrayList`, or other things. Examples of controls that accommodate complex binding are the `ComboBox` and `DataGrid` controls.

Even with simple controls, the picture can be more complex than with previous versions of Visual Basic. In the past, you bound *controls* (or, more generally, objects) to data sources; now you bind *properties* of controls or objects to data sources. ADO.NET supports binding to a much finer granularity than previous data access object models used with Visual Basic.

If you've done data binding in the past, the object you've undoubtedly bound most often is the TextBox control. In the past, when you bound a TextBox control to a data source, you were implicitly binding the TextBox's Text property. Like the original Model T cars, which a buyer could order in any color as long as it was black, you had no choice, at the property level, about what actually got bound.

Visual Basic .NET, by contrast, permits just about any runtime-assignable property of a TextBox (or other object) to be bound to a data source. One consequence of this greatly increased flexibility is that you must now specify explicitly what property you want targeted in a given binding. When you want to bind the Text property of a TextBox, you have to say so: the .NET architects aren't assuming anything about which property you want to work with. You could, for example, design a data source that would supply all the information your Windows form needed to specify not only the *values* to be displayed in the TextBox controls on a data entry form, but also numerous aspects of their appearance (such as typeface, font size, background and foreground colors, and so forth). In fact, you will find an application on the code website that does exactly that. That application is discussed later in this chapter in the section "Binding an Object Property to a Table Value."

But here you start with the basic types of bindings, which are also the ones you will likely create most frequently.

Simple Binding: The TextBox Control

The TextBox control is the most basic and most often used of the Windows form controls. To bind the Text property of a TextBox control named txtOrderNumber, use a statement such as the following:

```
Me.txtOrderNumber.DataBindings.Add("Text", Me.objdsDataBinding, "Orders.OrderId")
```

In this statement, the Text property is bound to the OrderId column of an Orders table in a DataSet named objdsDataBinding. Note that the TextBox object has a collection property called DataBindings and that you must add a member to that collection. The member that you add is a System.Windows.Forms.Binding object; thus, you could have written the earlier statement as follows:

```
Dim MyBinding As New System.Windows.Forms.Binding("Text", Me.objdsDataBinding,
➥"Orders.OrderId")
Me.txtOrderNumber.DataBindings.Add(MyBinding)
```

The DataBindings collection for the TextBox control clearly could contain other bindings (otherwise, why have a collection?). You'll look at a situation later in this chapter for a single control with multiple data bindings.

Complex Binding: The `ComboBox` Control

The `ComboBox` poses a somewhat more complicated binding problem, in that you might want to bind both the list of choices it displays to a collection of some sort; and the selected member of that list to a specific property of a specific item. Obviously, you cannot bind those to the same thing because one is a list and the other is a single value. Furthermore, the text displayed for the selected member of the list might not be the value you want to have stored or retrieved.

The code statements that follow bind the list displayed in `ComboBox cboCustomer` to rows in the Customers table from the `objdsDataBinding DataSet`. The `ComboBox`'s `DisplayMember` is set to the CompanyName column; its `ValueMember` is set to the CustomerID column. That means that the user will see company names, but upon selecting one, the value delivered by the `ComboBox` to the data source will be that from the `CustomerID` column.

In addition, a `Binding` object is added to the `ComboBox DataBindings` collection to bind its `SelectedValue` property to the CustomerID column in the data source. That means that, upon navigating to a new record, the member of the `ComboBox` list whose `CustomerId` value matches that of the row in the data source is automatically selected. It also means, conversely, that a change made by the user in the `SelectedValue` is communicated back to the source table.

```
Me.cboCustomer.DataSource = Me.objdsDataBinding
Me.cboCustomer.DisplayMember = "Customers.CompanyName"
Me.cboCustomer.ValueMember = "Customers.CustomerID"
Me.cboCustomer.DataBindings.Add( _
New System.Windows.Forms.Binding("SelectedValue", Me.objdsDataBinding, "Orders.
➥CustomerID"))
```

The `DataGrid` Control

The `DataGrid` control isn't part of ADO.NET, but it is an important form control for use with data-connected forms. The `DataGrid` control comes in two varieties: one for use on Windows forms and another for use in web forms. There are differences in functionality between the two. This chapter uses the Windows forms version; see the chapters on web applications for details on using the web forms version.

Basically, the `DataGrid` displays data from a `DataTable` or an array list of objects in a grid format (it can also be bound to a `DataSet`, in which case it displays icons for expanding and collapsing a hierarchy of related tables). Depending on your grid settings, this data can be edited. The most important property of the `DataGrid` with respect to data binding is its `DataSource` property. Simply assign a `DataTable` or `ArrayList` that will fill the grid with the appropriate data. The following statement sets the DataSource property of a DataGrid object, grdOrderDetails, to a DataTable Orders contained in a DataSet, objdsDataBinding:

```
Me.grdOrderDetails.DataSource = Me.objdsDataBinding.Tables("Orders")
```

You can also specify the DataSet and Table separately, as follows:

```
Me.grdOrderDetails.DataSource = Me.objdsDataBinding
Me.grdOrderDetails.DataMember = "Orders"
```

Alternatively, you can use the SetDataBinding() method of the grid control to do the same thing:

```
Me.grdOrderDetails.SetDataBinding(Me.objdsDataBinding, "Orders")
```

Here's another way of accomplishing the same thing. However, this version uses a syntax that works only with a strongly typed DataSet:

```
Me.grdOrderDetails.DataSource = Me.objdsDataBinding.Orders
```

If the DataSource is set to a DataSet that contains DataRelation objects, parent tables appear with a plus sign (+) in each row header. Clicking the plus sign causes a node to appear that contains links to child tables. For example, if a DataSet contains two DataTable objects named Orders and Order_Details_Extended and these have a parent-child relationship set, setting the DataMember to the Orders table causes the DataGrid to display the Orders table with a plus sign visible on each row header. When the plus sign is clicked, a link is displayed that says "Orders_Order_Details_Extended." When clicked, the link displays records from the Order_Details_Extended table that are linked to the record marked as current in the Orders table.

Using a DataRelation As the Data Member

You can bind a DataGrid not only to a DataTable, but also to a DataRelation:

```
Me.grdOrderDetails.SetDataBinding(Me.objdsDataBinding, "Orders.Orders_OrderDetails")
```

In the previous statement, Orders_OrderDetails is the name of a DataRelation in which the Orders table plays the role of the parent. Binding a DataGrid as shown causes it to display records from the child table in the specified DataRelation. The child records shown are those that are linked to whatever record is current in the parent table (Orders). To find out what record is current, ADO.NET consults the CurrencyManager for the parent table.

Matching the Data Source in Navigational Statements to the Data Source in a Data Binding

As you saw in the section "The DataGrid Control," it is possible to establish apparently equivalent data bindings using different syntaxes. But it is also possible to establish data bindings that appear to be equivalent but aren't—at least, for purposes of list navigation.

For example, you can bind the Text property of a TextBox control to the OrderId field of an Orders table using either of the following statements:

```
Me.txtOrderNumber.DataBindings.Add("Text", Me.objdsDataBinding, "Orders.OrderId")
Me.txtOrderNumber.DataBindings.Add("Text", Me.objdsDataBinding.Orders, "OrderID")
```

These statements are not equivalent, however, because the first passes a DataSet object (Me.objdsDataBinding) for the DataSource argument to the DataBindings.Add() method, whereas the second passes a DataTable object (Me.objdsDataBinding.Orders) for the datasource. ADO.NET considers those two objects to be different data sources, and it assigns different CurrencyManagers to manage their list pointers. Accordingly, if you set a binding using the first statement and then attempt to reposition to a new record within the Orders table using the following statement, you will find that the value displayed in your TextBox control does not get updated to reflect any change:

```
Me.BindingContext(Me.objdsDataBinding.Orders).Position =
Me.BindingContext(Me.objdsDataBinding.Orders).Position + 1
```

The application BindingAndNavigationSyntaxLinkage in the code for this chapter illustrates how mismatches between the syntax style used to establish data binding and that used for record navigation within a form's CurrencyManager can cause data binding to work improperly.

The application's main form uses a parent-child relationship between an Orders table and an Order_Details_Extended table that is established in the dsDataBinding schema. When working properly, navigational controls on the form change the record position in the CurrencyManager for the parent (Orders) table; a TextBox control and a ComboBox control bound to the current Orders record get their display values updated; and the DataGrid displays corresponding records from the child (Order_Details_Extended) table.

The help file for BindingAndNavigationSyntaxLinkage, available from its main menu, describes the operation and purpose of the application (see Figure 14.3). It also prescribes experiments that you can perform to see its main points and draws conclusions based on those experiments. See if you agree with the conclusions.

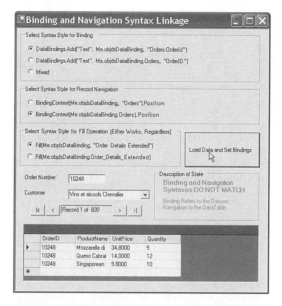

FIGURE 14.3   The BindingAndNavigation-
SyntaxLinkage application illustrates how navigational statements must reference a datasource
in the same way as did the statements that
established data bindings to that data source.

TIP

Make sure that your syntax is consistently either `DataSet`-focused or `DataTable`-focused, but not
a mix of these, for statements that set data bindings and statements that navigate within the
`CurrencyManager` that controls those data bindings. You can do as you please with other statements that refer to a data source (such as calls to a `DataAdapter`'s `Fill()` method), but you're
probably best served by using one consistent syntax within any given form for *all* statements that
refer to the same data source. This reinforces the use of the style in your mind and the minds of
other programmers who might work with the same code, avoiding downstream maintenance
problems.

Binding Form Controls to a `DataSet`

When you bind a control to a `DataTable`, .NET actually creates the binding to the
default `DataView` of that table. A `DataView`, you will recall, is a customized view of
a `DataTable` that permits sorting, filtering, searching, editing, and navigation of
that table. As it so happens, it is also the entity that supports data binding (which it
does by implementing the `IBindingList` interface).

Binding Form Controls to a `DataSet`

Similarly, if you bind a control to a `DataSet`, .NET actually creates the binding to the `DataViewManager` for that `DataSet`.

The application BindToADataTable illustrates both the basics of binding controls to tables in a `DataSet` and also the most basic type of separation of data-manipulation code from user interface code (see Figure 14.4). Data retrieval and updating is performed with the `Data` class (which resides in the `Data.vb` file), whereas `frmMain` provides the user interface functionality. This shows the beginnings of a two-tier architecture that isolates the user interface from details of the database structure.

The `TableMappings` method of `daProducts`, the `DataAdapter` used in the `Data.vb` class, can be used to remap any column name changes made in the database to the names that the UI expects. Because the `Fill` method of the `DataAdapter` specifies the name of the target table in the `DataSet`, a change to the name of the table in the back-end database can also be buffered.

NOTE

Because this app uses a strongly typed `DataSet` defined by the `dsNw.xsd` schema, the schema also would have to be updated to reflect the new names if any such changes were made.

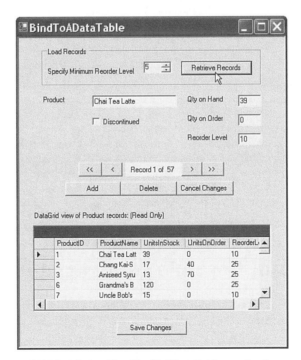

FIGURE 14.4   The BindToADataTable application illustrates conventional data binding to a DataTable, but with the beginnings of a separation between UI and data layers.

Binding an Object Property to a Table Value

As discussed in the section "Data-Bound Objects," it is now possible, using ADO.NET, to bind not just an object, but multiple specific properties of an object simultaneously. The application BindObjectPropertyToTableValue (see Figure 14.5), included on the code website, illustrates this capability.

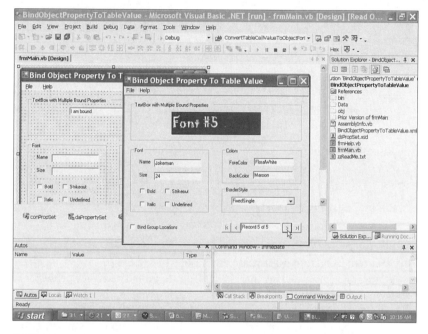

FIGURE 14.5   Using the application, BindObjectPropertyToTableValue.

The BindObjectPropertyToTableValue application illustrates two things: the simultaneous binding of multiple properties of a single TextBox control, and the conversion of simple type data from a database table into a complex object for assignment to a bound property that requires one.

The application also addresses a special problem that occurs when you want to bind to a table value a property that is itself a complex object rather than a simple data type. For example, the Font property of a TextBox requires nothing as simple as a text string containing "Times New Roman"; instead, it takes a System.Drawing.Font object, of which the font family designation is but one property.

But how do you store a System.Drawing.Font object in a relational database?

Binding an Object Property to a Table Value

No doubt, tricky methods could be devised, but it's much more straightforward just to store in the database the various pieces of information needed to specify a font and then at runtime declare and instantiate a font with those properties.

As it so happens, .NET provides an event defined on the binding object that permits exactly this sort of thing. The Format event fires when data is pushed from the data source into the bound property, and offers the opportunity to change the form of that data before it is delivered to the property.

In frmMain of BindObjectPropertyToTableValue, the variable m_tblPropSet is declared at the class level as a type DataTable. In the form's Load event, it is set to the PropertySet DataTable of the objdsPropSet DataSet:

```
Dim m_tblPropSet As DataTable
m_tblPropSet = Me.objdsPropSet.PropertySet
```

Later, the following statements are executed in the method SetPrimaryBindings():

```
Dim bindingFont As New Binding("Font", m_tblPropSet, "ID")
AddHandler bindingFont.Format, AddressOf ConvertDataToFont
Me.txtBound.DataBindings.Add(bindingFont)
```

The first statement declares and initializes an object of the type System.Windows.Forms.Binding, specifying Font as the target property to be bound to the ID column of the DataTable m_tblPropSet. Note that the binding object is instantiated quite independently of the *control* to which it will be applied (even though the name of the *property* to which it will be applied *is* specified when it is instantiated).

The second statement establishes the ConvertDataToFont() method as the handler for the Format event of the binding just instantiated. With that handler wired into the event, the ConvertDataToFont() method fires whenever data is pushed into the binding from table m_tblPropSet. ConvertDataToFont() then does whatever it has been trained to do (something you'll see in a moment). In the final statement, the instantiated binding object is added to the DataBindings collection of the TextBox control txtBound. Only then is the binding linked to a specific control.

Here's the code for the ConvertDataToFont method:

```
Private Sub ConvertDataToFont(ByVal sender As Object, ByVal e As ConvertEventArgs)
    Dim intCurrentRow As Int32 = Me.BindingContext(m_tblPropSet).Position
    Dim rowCurr As DataRow = m_tblPropSet.Rows(intCurrentRow)
    Dim fontstyleX As New System.Drawing.FontStyle
    If rowCurr("FontBold") Then fontstyleX = FontStyle.Bold
```

```
    If rowCurr("FontItalic") Then fontstyleX += FontStyle.Italic
    If rowCurr("FontStrikeout") Then fontstyleX += FontStyle.Strikeout
    If rowCurr("FontUnderlined") Then fontstyleX += FontStyle.Underline
    Dim strFontFamily As String = rowCurr("FontFamily")
    Dim sglFontSize As Single = rowCurr("FontSize")
    e.Value = New Font(strFontFamily, sglFontSize, fontstyleX)
End Sub
```

Note that the data source for the binding declared previously was the ID column of a record in the table m_tblPropSet. That value is passed into `ConvertDataToFont` as the `Value` property of the `ConvertEventArgs` parameter. Because that value just happens to be the row's primary key (and, therefore, guaranteed unique), you could use it to locate the exact row from m_tblPropSet from which you want to draw information to build a `Font` object.

To do so, you would sort the table on that column and then use the `Find` operation of the table's `DefaultView` to locate the desired record:

```
m_tblPropSet.DefaultView.Sort = "ID"
Dim rowCurr As DataRow = _
    m_tblPropSet.Rows(m_tblPropSet.DefaultView.Find(e.Value))
```

But in this case, there is an easier way to get the needed row. That is simply to observe that the binding is trying push a value from the row of m_tblPropSet to which its `CurrencyManager` currently points. You can therefore use the `Position` property of the `CurrencyManager` to get the index of the current row in m_tblPropSet:

```
Dim intCurrentRow As Int32 = Me.BindingContext(m_tblPropSet).Position
Dim rowCurr As DataRow = m_tblPropSet.Rows(intCurrentRow)
```

Regardless of which method you use to get the needed row, when you have it, you can retrieve any desired values from it. In `ConvertDataToFont()`, the values retrieved all represent different properties of a `FontStyle`, which is one of the primary pieces of information needed to create a `System.Drawing.Font` object. So the procedure instantiates a `FontStyle` object and sets its properties using values from the data row:

```
Dim fontstyleX As New System.Drawing.FontStyle
If rowCurr("FontBold") Then fontstyleX = FontStyle.Bold
If rowCurr("FontItalic") Then fontstyleX += FontStyle.Italic
If rowCurr("FontStrikeout") Then fontstyleX += FontStyle.Strikeout
If rowCurr("FontUnderlined") Then fontstyleX += FontStyle.Underline
```

Binding an Object Property to a Table Value

It then instantiates a new `Font` object, passing the `FontStyle`, a font family name, and a font size to the `Font` object's constructor, and then assigns the result to `e.Value`:

```
Dim strFontFamily As String = rowCurr("FontFamily")
Dim sglFontSize As Single = rowCurr("FontSize")
e.Value = New Font(strFontFamily, sglFontSize, fontstyleX)
```

But recall that `e.Value` is the value that is on its way from the data row to the bound property of the `txtBound` control. It came into `ConvertDataToFont()` as a record ID value, but it leaves as a `System.Drawing.Font` object. And that's what is delivered to the `Font` property of the bound `TextBox`!

Important `BindingContext` and `DataSet` Methods

Before proceeding further in this discussion of data binding, you must become familiar with a few key methods of both the `CurrencyManager` and the `DataSet`, summarized in Tables 14.3 and 14.4.

TABLE 14.3

Important Public Data Binding–Related Members of the `CurrencyManager` Class

Methods

Member Name	Overrides	Remarks
`EndCurrentEdit()`	`BindingManagerBase.EndCurrentEdit()`	Ends the current edit.
		This method is supported only if the data source implements the `IEditableObject` interface. In this case, changes are saved. If the object does not implement the `IEditableObject` interface, changes made to the data are not saved.
`CancelCurrentEdit()`	`BindingManagerBase.CancelCurrentEdit()`	Cancels the current edit.
		This method is supported only if the data source implements the `IEditableObject` interface. If the object does not implement the `IEditableObject` interface, changes made to the data are not discarded.

Important `BindingContext` and `DataSet` **Methods**

TABLE 14.3

Continued

Methods

Member Name	Overrides	Remarks
`AddNew()`	`IBindingList.` `AddNew()`	Adds a new item to the underlying list. This method is supported only if the data source implements
		`IBindingList` and the data source allows adding rows. This property was designed to allow complex-bound controls, such as the `DataGrid` control, to add new items to list.
		You typically use this property only if you are creating your own control that incorporates the `CurrencyManager`. Otherwise, to add items, if the data source is a `DataView`, use the `AddNew` method of the `DataView` class. If the data source is a `DataTable`, use the `NewRow` method and add the row to the `DataRowCollection`.
`RemoveAt()`	`IList.RemoveAt()`	Removes the item at the specified index.
		In collections of contiguous elements, such as lists, the elements that follow the removed element move up to occupy the vacated spot. If the collection is indexed, the indexes of the elements that are moved are also updated. This behavior does not apply to collections in which elements are conceptually grouped into buckets, such as a hashtable.
`SuspendBinding()`	`BindingManagerBase.` `SuspendBinding`	Suspends data binding. Use this when you need to allow the user to make several edits to data fields before validation occurs.
		`SuspendBinding` and `ResumeBinding` are two methods that allow the temporary suspension and resumption of data binding. You typically suspend data binding if the user must be allowed to make several edits to data fields before validation occurs—for example, if one field must be changed in accordance with a

14

Important `BindingContext` **and** `DataSet` **Methods**

TABLE 14.3

Continued

Methods

Member Name	Overrides	Remarks
		second, but validating the first field would cause the second field to be in error.
`ResumeBinding()`	`BindingManagerBase.ResumeBinding`	Resumes data binding. See the earlier entry for `SuspendBinding`.

Event Handlers

Member Name	Overrides	Remarks
`OnCurrentChanged`	`BindingManagerBase.OnCurrentChanged`	Fires when a bound value changes.

Events

Member Name	Overrides	Remarks
`OnItemChanged`	Nothing	Fires when an item that includes a bound value changes. The `ItemChanged` event occurs when the user calls the `ResumeBinding` or `SuspendBinding` methods. The `ItemChanged` event occurs only when the item itself has been changed in some manner. For example, if the value of an item is changed from `10` to `42`, the event will occur. This shouldn't be confused with the `PositionChanged` event, in which the item has been changed to a new item. The event also occurs if the underlying data changes. For example, if you change the value of a `DataRowView`, the `ItemChanged` event occurs. Note that if you are creating your own control that uses the `CurrencyManager`, you should use the `ListChanged` event of the `IBindingList` class instead of the `ItemChanged` event. The `ListChangedType` property of the `ListChangedEventArgs` object enables you to determine the type of action that has occurred.

14

Important `BindingContext` and `DataSet` Methods

TABLE 14.3

Continued

Properties

Member Name	Overrides	Remarks
Bindings	Inherited from BindingManagerBase. Bindings	The collection of bindings being managed by the CurrencyManager.
Count	BindingManagerBase. Count	The number of rows in the data source being managed by the CurrencyManager.
Position	BindingManagerBase. Position	Gets or sets the position in the underlying list managed by the CurrencyManager.

Use Position to iterate through the underlying list maintained by the BindingManagerBase. To go to the first item, set Position to 0. To go to the end of the list, set Position to the value of the Count property minus one. |

TABLE 14.4

Important Public Data Binding–Related Members of the `DataSet` Class

Methods

Member Name	Remarks
HasChanges()	Gets a value indicating whether the DataSet has changes, including new, deleted, or modified rows.

Both the DataRow and DataTable classes also have AcceptChanges methods. Calling AcceptChanges at the DataTable level causes the AcceptChanges method for each DataRow to be called. Similarly, invoking AcceptChanges on the DataSet causes AcceptChanges to be called on each table within the DataSet. In this manner, you have multiple levels at which the method can be invoked. Calling AcceptChanges of the DataSet enables you to invoke the method on all subordinate objects (for example, tables and rows) with one call.

When you call AcceptChanges on the DataSet, any DataRow objects still in edit mode successfully end their edits. The RowState property of each DataRow also changes; Added and Modified rows become Unchanged, and Deleted rows are removed.

If the DataSet contains ForeignKeyConstraint objects, invoking the AcceptChanges method also causes the AcceptRejectRule to be enforced. |

Important `BindingContext` **and** `DataSet` **Methods**

TABLE 14.4

Continued

Methods

Member Name	Remarks
`GetChanges()`	Gets a copy of the `DataSet` containing all changes made to it since it was last loaded or since `AcceptChanges` was called.
`AcceptChanges()`	Commits all the changes made to this `DataSet` since it was loaded or since `AcceptChanges` was called.
`Merge()`	The various overloads of this method merge a specified `DataSet`, `DataTable`, or array of `DataRow` objects into the current `DataSet` or `DataTable`.
`Clear()`	Clears the `DataSet` of any data by removing all rows in all tables.
	If the `DataSet` is bound to an `XmlDataDocument`, calling `DataSet.Clear` or `DataTable.Clear` raises `NotSupportedException`. To avoid this situation, traverse each table, removing each row one at a time.

Properties

`EnforceConstraints()`	Gets or sets a value indicating whether constraint rules are followed when attempting any update operation.
	Constraints are set at the `DataTable` level (`Constraints` property).

Table excerpted from the MSDN Help file for Visual Studio 2003

The `CurrencyManager` methods listed play a role in all types of list-oriented data binding; that is, they are used whether you bind to a `DataSet` object or, as discussed later in this chapter, to a custom collection class that implements the `IBindingList` interface.

The `DataSet` methods listed play critical roles in binding data to `DataSets`. Furthermore, if you intend to code a substitute for `DataSets` (for example, a custom collection object), it might be necessary to implement substitutes in that collection for several of the listed `DataSet` methods.

Using the `CurrencyManager` for Nontable Bindings

The application BindToIListCollections, shown in Figure 14.6 and first discussed in the section ".NET Classes That Implement the `IList` Interface," illustrates how various objects from `IList`-implementing classes return `CurrencyManager` objects if passed to the containing form's `BindingContext`. These objects can be used as the data source for bindings.

Using the `CurrencyManager` for Nontable Bindings

FIGURE 14.6   The BindToIListCollections application illustrates binding to a variety of .NET classes that implement `IList`.

In this application, the `Text` property of a `TextBox` control is bound, by your choice, to any of the following four things:

1. The `Text` property of a `TabPage` in a `TabPages` collection

2. The `ParameterName` property of a `SqlParameter` in `SqlParameters` collection

3. The `Text` property of a `MenuItem` in a `MenuItems` collection

4. The `Text` property of a `Control` in a `Form.Controls` collection

The code to clear existing bindings and then establish a new binding to the `ParameterName` property of the current object in a `SqlParameters` collection is as follows:

```
Me.txtBound.DataBindings.Clear()
m_colDataSource = Me.m_cmdUpdate.Parameters
m_strDataMember = "ParameterName"
m_CollectionDescription = "cmdUpdate.SqlParameters"
```

Using the `CurrencyManager` for Nontable Bindings

```
Dim MyBinding As New System.Windows.Forms.Binding("Text", m_colDataSource,
➥m_strDataMember)
Me.txtBound.DataBindings.Add(MyBinding)
```

With that binding established, the user can navigate among members of the
`SqlParameters` collection by using First, Previous, Next, and Last buttons, as he
might in a typical form with controls bound to a database table. Here, for example, is
the code for the Next button:

```
    Private Sub btnNavNext_Click(ByVal sender As System.Object, ByVal e As
➥System.EventArgs) Handles btnNavNext.Click
        Me.BindingContext(m_colDataSource).Position = Me.BindingContext
➥(m_colDataSource).Position + 1
        DataSource_PositionChanged()
    End Sub
```

Note that `m_colDataSource` is a member variable of the form class, so it is accessible inside all methods of that class. When the user clicks the Next button, the
TextBox `txtBound` displays the name of the next `SqlParameter` in the
`SqlParameters` collection.

Binding Multiple Form Controls to Different Properties of a Single Object

As previously discussed, it is possible to bind control properties not just to columns
of a `DataRow`, but equally to properties of a user-defined object. The application
BindToAnObject (see Figure 14.7) in this chapter's code illustrates this capability. In
the application, a `Product` object is instantiated from a `Product` class; then the
display properties of several `TextBoxes` and a `CheckBox` on a form are bound to
properties of that `Product` object. Finally, a message is displayed providing detail
about the bindings. The source for the information in the message is the `Bindings`
collection of the `PropertyManager` object associated with the `Product`.

The variables `m_objProduct` and `m_pmProduct` are declared at the class level with
the data types `Product` and `PropertyManager`, respectively.

```
Dim m_objProduct As Product
Dim m_pmProduct As PropertyManager
```

Binding Multiple Form Controls to Different Properties of a Single Object

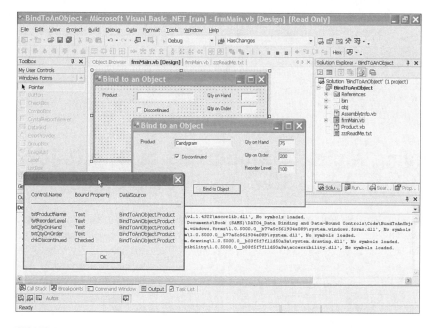

FIGURE 14.7 The BindToAnObject app illustrates the binding of multiple form controls to a user-defined object.

A `Product` object is then instantiated and given values for its properties. The statements that create the bindings to various properties of the object are as follows:

```
Me.txtProductName.DataBindings.Add("Text", m_objProduct, "ProductName")
Me.txtReorderLevel.DataBindings.Add("Text", m_objProduct, "ReorderLevel")
Me.txtQtyOnHand.DataBindings.Add("Text", m_objProduct, "UnitsInStock")
Me.txtQtyOnOrder.DataBindings.Add("Text", m_objProduct, "UnitsOnOrder")
Me.chkDiscontinued.DataBindings.Add("Checked", m_objProduct, "Discontinued")
```

The `PropertyManager` is used as a source for information in the sub `ShowBindings`:

```
    Private Sub ShowBindings()
        Dim strMsg As String
        Dim b As Binding
        strMsg += "Control.Name".PadRight(18) & ControlChars.Tab & "Bound
➥Property".PadRight(18) & ControlChars.Tab & "DataSource".PadRight(18)
➥ & ControlChars.NewLine
        strMsg += "".PadRight(54, "_") & ControlChars.NewLine &
➥ControlChars.NewLine
        For Each b In m_pmProduct.Bindings
            strMsg += b.Control.Name.PadRight(18) & ControlChars.Tab
```

Binding Multiple Form Controls to Different Properties of a Single Object

```
        strMsg += b.PropertyName.PadRight(18) & ControlChars.Tab
        strMsg += b.DataSource.ToString.PadRight(18) & ControlChars.NewLine
    Next
    MessageBox.Show(strMsg)

End Sub
```

Binding Multiple Properties of One Object to Multiple Properties of Another Object

The application PropertyManagerExplorations (see Figure 14.8) in this chapter's code explores the `PropertyManager` object by binding multiple properties of a `TextBox` control (`txtTargetNew`) to different properties of a source object (which is, in this case, another `TextBox` control, `txtSource`). The code that instantiates a `TextBox` and establishes its data bindings (placed in the event handler for the form's `Load` event) is as follows:

```
txtBound = New TextBox
Me.txtBound.Multiline = True
Me.txtBound.DataBindings.Add("Text", Me.txtSource, "Text")
Me.txtBound.DataBindings.Add("Width", Me.txtSource, "TextLength")
Me.txtBound.DataBindings.Add("Height", Me.txtSource, "TextLength")
Me.txtBound.DataBindings.Add("Top", Me.txtSource, "TextLength")
Me.txtBound.DataBindings.Add("Left", Me.txtSource, "TextLength")
Me.Controls.Add(txtBound)
```

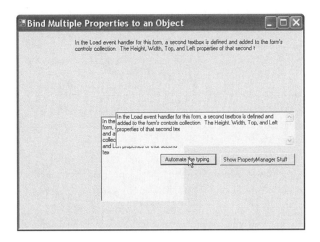

FIGURE 14.8   The BindMultiplePropertiesToAnObject app illustrates the binding of multiple properties of a *single* control to properties of another object.

Note that bindings are set for multiple properties of the TextBox, not simply the Text property. The latter is set to the Text property of another TextBox, txtSource, so that as characters are entered into txtSource, they are immediately echoed in txtBound. However, the Width, Height, Top, and Left properties for txtBound are bound to the TextLength property of txtSource. Each time you type a character into txtSource, not only is that character added to the end of the string displayed in txtBound, but the size and position of the txtBound control also change (ever so slightly). As you type more text, the txtBound control grows in size and moves diagonally across the form. A button is also provided to automate the process of typing in text so that you can simply sit back and contemplate what you're watching.

Binding Form Controls to an `ArrayList` of Objects

As previously noted, it is possible to bind controls to any collection that implements IList. The ArrayList object qualifies and also accommodates any type of member objects. This makes it a fine out-of-the-box candidate for use in a data-binding scheme that bypasses the use of the DataSet.

Before you get too excited about this alternative, however, you need to be aware that it provides adequate support only for *read-only* data binding. To get support for read-write binding, you need a collection class that implements IBindingList, and that narrows your choices considerably. In fact, the only .NET classes that support IBindingList are DataView and DataViewManager—and those are the media actually used when you bind to a DataTable or DataSet. Custom collection objects that implement IBindingList are discussed later in this chapter, in the section "Implementing Read-Write Binding to a Custom Collection of Objects." But for now, let's proceed stepwise from the simpler to the more complex.

The application BindingToArrayListOfObjects (see Figure 14.9) on the website illustrates the binding of form controls to business objects passed in from a separate data class. Although this application is single tier, data retrieval and packaging operations are cleanly separated from the front-end form, so it would be a short step to move that data-retrieval functionality into a separate software component. Multitier apps are discussed in Chapter 34, "Introduction to Enterprise Services."

BindToAnArrayListOfObjects contains three important classes: frmMain, the display form; Product, which defines the object from which controls in the form will take their values via data binding; and Data, which provides the functionality to retrieve data from the database, package it as Product objects in an ArrayList, and pass that ArrayList to the front-end form. The application retrieves its data from the Products table of the Northwind database (supplied by Microsoft with SQL Server 2000).

Binding Form Controls to an `ArrayList` of Objects

The `Product` class defines the following properties: `ProductId`, `ProductName`, `UnitsInStock`, `UnitsOnOrder`, and `ReorderLevel`. This is a subset of the columns defined in the Products table, quite adequate for the purpose of this discussion. It also defines two overloads of the constructor: one requiring no parameters and another that permits values for all properties to be passed in at instantiation.

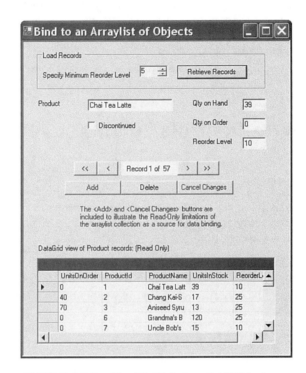

FIGURE 14.9 The BindToAnArraylistOfObjects sample app illustrates read-only binding using an `ArrayList` of user-defined objects as the data source.

The `Data` class includes a `GetProducts()` method that accepts a parameter defining the minimum `ReorderLevel` for products to be retrieved; and a `GetArrayListOfProducts()` method, called from `GetProducts`, that copies the data from a strongly typed `DataSet` to an `ArrayList`. `GetProducts()` returns that `ArrayList` to the calling procedure. Data also includes a read-only property, `NumberOfProducts`, that provides the current `Count` of the `ArrayList`. The constructor for `Data` declares and initializes a `Connection` object (you need to change the connection string to work on your machine), a `DataAdapter`, and a `Command` object used to retrieve the data.

In the form, the Retrieve Data button instantiates an object based on the `Data` class and then invokes its `GetProducts()` method to retrieve an `ArrayList` of products from the Northwind Products table. Bindings are then cleared (in case it's not the first time the retrieval has been performed) and reset. The navigational buttons First, Previous, Next, and Last are provided to reposition the list pointer within the `ArrayList`'s `CurrencyManager`. These are similar in code and in functionality to the navigational buttons produced by the DataForm Wizard, except, of course, that they reference the `ArrayList` as the data source rather than a `DataSet` or `DataTable`. Here, for example, is the event handler for the Next button:

```
    Private Sub btnNavNext_Click(ByVal sender As System.Object, ByVal e As
➡ System.EventArgs) Handles btnNavNext.Click
        Me.BindingContext(m_arlProducts).Position = Me.BindingContext
➡ (m_arlProducts).Position + 1
        UpdateRecordPositionDisplay()
    End Sub
```

Read-Only Limitations of the BindingToArrayListOfObjects Application

BindToAnArrayListOfObjects intentionally attempts to implement some aspects of read-write functionality so you can see where and how that breaks down with an `IList`-based collection object:

▶ The `AddNew()` method of the `ArrayList`'s `CurrencyManager` doesn't work because `AddNew` functionality requires implementation of `IBindingList` (which the `ArrayList` doesn't do).

▶ The `EndCurrentEdit()` and `CancelCurrentEdit()` methods of the `CurrencyManager` also require implementation of `IBindingList` for proper functioning.

For example, try adding a record to the list of products. You'll get the following message (also shown in Figure 14.10):

In a proper read-write implementation, you would invoke the `AddNew()` method of the `CurrencyManager` now. However, because the `ArrayList` object that contains your `Products` doesn't implement `IBindingList`, `AddNew()` isn't supported. Instead, you simply invoke the `Add()` method of the `ArrayList`. This results in a new product being added to the `ArrayList`, but the `CurrencyManager` doesn't know how to work with it. If you attempt to navigate to the added object (last in the list), you will find that the effort fails.

In a moment, you'll begin learning how to implement a collection that fully supports read-write operations. But first you must understand why you might want to do that.

14

Binding Form Controls to an `ArrayList` of Objects

In a proper read-write implementation, we would invoke the AddNew() method of the CurrencyManager now. However, since the arraylist object which contains our Products doesn't implement IBindingList, AddNew() isn't supported. So, instead, we simply invoke the Add() method of the arraylist. This results in a new product getting added to the arraylist, but the CurrencyManager doesn't know how to work with it. If you attempt to navigate to the added object (last in the list), you will find that the effort fails.

OK

FIGURE 14.10   The main form of the BindToAnArraylistOfObjects sample app, after a user has attempted to add an item.

Read-Write Binding

In .NET, there are only two collection types to which you can do read-write data binding. Strictly speaking, those two collection types are the `DataView` and `DataViewManager` classes, but practically speaking, that translates to `DataTables` and `DataSets`. This chapter has covered binding to many different types of objects, but for anything beyond read-only binding, the only data sources that work, among those discussed, have been the `DataTable` and the `DataSet`.

> **NOTE**
>
> When you bind the `Text` property of a control to a column in a `DataTable`, you actually do so through the intermediary of that `DataTable`'s `DefaultView`. The `DefaultView` is an object of type `DataView`; the `DataView` class, not the `DataSet`, actually supports binding and navigation.
>
> The `DataSet` and `DataViewManager` classes have a similar relationship. A `DataSet` has a `DefaultViewManager` property whose data type is a `DataViewManager`. When you tell .NET to set the data source for a `DataGrid` to a `DataSet`, it actually sets it to the `DataViewManager` that is automatically assigned to that `DataSet`'s `DefaultViewManager` property.

To support read-write data binding in .NET, a class must implement the `IBindingList` interface. The DataView and DataViewManager classes are the only .NET-supplied classes that do that; but the facilities are there to write your own read-write bindable classes.

But why would you *want* to do read-write binding to something besides `DataTables` and `DataSets`? Well, many developers don't. On the other hand, binding a data entry form to a `Products` collection instead of a `Products` `DataTable` does have a certain object-oriented appeal. `DataTables` are two-dimensional constructions, whereas the objects we work with in real life (and most of the objects we work with in code) are multidimensional. While highly normalized relational schemas are very efficient structures for persisting data, it's really more natural to think of things in an object-oriented way.

Multitier architectures in which data-access operations are segregated from other aspects of an application (notably, the presentation of a user interface and implementation of business rules) have become the standard for enterprise applications. Segregating the data-access operations has been found to be very useful because it buffers the rest of the application from the inevitable structural changes made to data stores in response to demands often entirely external to your application. Doing so can also give your application independence from particular brands of DBMS, enabling it to be deployed in more diverse environments, or simply to take advantage more easily of technological leapfrogging between competing DBMS vendors.

But the separation of application from database embodied in today's multitier architectures could be taken a step further with the replacement of bindings to `DataTables` and `DataSets` by bindings to custom collections. Your application could be freed not only from dependence upon specific DBMS vendors, but even from dependence on a relational view of data.

Implementing Read-Write Binding to a Custom Collection of Objects

To support read-write data binding, you need to implement two key interfaces: `IEditableObject` in the item class, and `IBindingList` in the collection that will contain instances of the item class. You also have to create additional properties and methods to provide the functionality you desire.

`IEditableObject` provides the functionality to commit or roll back changes to an object that is used as a data source. It exposes three public methods: `BeginEdit()`, `CancelEdit()`, and `EndEdit()`. Implementations of these must be included in the item class. Examples are provided and discussed later in the discussion of the sample app ReadWriteBindableCollection.

Implementing `IBindingList` in the collection class is a more complex affair. As with many programming jobs, there are many ways to do it. One approach is shown in the sample app. In addition to implementing IBindingList, you will want to inherit the `CollectionBase` class in your collection class. `CollectionBase` contributes important members such as a `Count` property to return the number of items in your collection; the `List` property, which is the collection of those items; an `Equals` method to compare objects in the collection; the `RemoveAt` method to remove an item from the collection; a `Clear` method to remove all objects from the collection; and a number of additional methods that can do custom processing after inserts, deletions, and other operations.

Table 14.5 lists members of `IEditableObject`. Table 14.6 lists members of `IBindingList`.

Read-Write Binding

TABLE 14.5

`IEditableObject` **Members**

Public Methods

Member Type	Name	Function
Public method	BeginEdit	Begins an edit on an object
Public method	CancelEdit	Discards changes since the last `BeginEdit` call
Public method	EndEdit	Pushes changes since the last `BeginEdit` or `IBindingList.AddNew` call into the underlying object

Source: MSDN Help file for Visual Studio 2003

TABLE 14.6

`IBindingList` **Members**

Public Properties

Name	Function
AllowEdit	Gets whether you can update items in the list
AllowNew	Gets whether you can add items to the list using `AddNew`
AllowRemove	Gets whether you can remove items from the list, using `Remove` or `RemoveAt`
IsSorted	Gets whether the items in the list are sorted
SortDirection	Gets the direction of the sort
SortProperty	Gets the `PropertyDescriptor` that is being used for sorting
SupportsChangeNotification	Gets whether a `ListChanged` event is raised when the list changes or an item in the list changes
SupportsSearchin	Gets whether the list supports searching using the `Find` method
SupportsSorting	Gets whether the list supports sorting

Public Methods

AddIndex	Adds the `PropertyDescriptor` to the indexes used for searching
AddNew	Adds a new item to the list
ApplySort	Sorts the list based on a `PropertyDescriptor` and a `ListSortDirection`
Find	Returns the index of the row that has the given `PropertyDescriptor`
RemoveIndex	Removes the `PropertyDescriptor` from the indexes used for searching
RemoveSort	Removes any sort applied using `ApplySort`

Public Events

ListChanged	Occurs when the list changes or an item in the list changes

Source: MSDN Help file for Visual Studio 2003

Sample Application: ReadWriteBindableCollection

The application ReadWriteBindableCollection (see Figure 14.11) illustrates read-write bindable objects housed in a custom collection class.

The objects are instantiated from a class named `Product` that implements the `System.ComponentModel.IEditableObject` interface; the custom collection named Products implements `System.ComponentModel.IBindingList` and inherits from the .NET class `System.Collections.CollectionBase`. In this app, the initial product data is hard-coded in the front-end form, but the application could be easily adapted to load `Product` data from the Products table of the Northwind database. The properties defined for a `Product` correspond to a subset of the columns from that table.

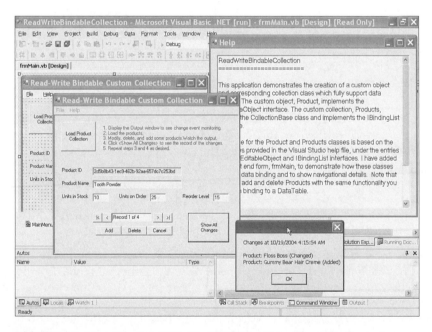

FIGURE 14.11   The ReadWriteBindableCollection app, which illustrates techniques for creating custom read-write bindable Objects and collections.

First you will learn about the basic operation of ReadWriteBindableCollection; then you'll learn about the two key classes and how they give the app its read-write bindable functionality.

How ReadWriteBindableCollection Works

When you first launch ReadWriteBindableCollection, note the instructions that appear on the main form.

Read-Write Binding

1. Display the Output window to see change event monitoring.

2. Load the products.

3. Modify, delete, and add some products. Watch the output.

4. Click Show All Changes to see the record of the changes.

5. Repeat steps 3 and 4 as desired.

You will want the Visual Studio Output window open in the foreground when you run ReadWriteBindableCollection because the application writes messages there as the `Products` collection captures change events on its member `Products`. Figure 14.11 shows the application after a user has done the following four things:

1. Loaded products by clicking the Load Product Collection button

2. Changed one record and added another

3. Opened the Help form using the Help option on the main menu

4. Clicked the `Show All Changes` button

At this point, you can simply change, delete, and add a few products to the list, noting the messages written to the Output window as you perform each of those actions. Then, at any point, you can click the Show All Changes button to see the accumulated changes. Show All Changes displays in a message box the `Product` name associated with each item that has been changed. It also displays the nature of the change: whether the item was changed, added, or deleted. If an item is changed and then deleted, it shows as deleted; if the added was added and then deleted in the same editing session, it does not show up in the list.

Although, for simplicity, ReadWriteBindableCollection does not connect to a database, it is written as if it did and were operating in disconnected mode. In other words, changes are made locally and affect the in-memory collection of objects. If it were connected to a database, an Update button would be provided that would commit changes to the database, synchronize the local copy of the data with the database, and clear the change flags for all products in the local collection. An AcceptChanges-type method in the `Products` class would perform the latter function. (Note that this method would not have to be called "AcceptChanges"—you would be writing it, so you could call it whatever you liked—but using this name here indicates that it would perform a function similar to the method of that name offered by the .NET `DataSet` object.)

ReadWriteBindableCollection includes `HasChanges` and `GetChanges` methods, which perform functions similar to the `DataSet` class's methods of that name. `HasChanges` returns a Boolean value if any product in the `Products` collection have been changed, added, or deleted during the current editing session. `GetChanges` returns a collection of `Products` consisting of the subset of the total list of `Products` representing `Products` that have been changed, added, or deleted during the current editing session.

```
Private Sub btnLoadProducts_Click(ByVal sender As System.Object, ByVal e As
➥System.EventArgs) Handles btnLoadProducts.Click

    Dim objProduct As Product
    objProduct = New Product(System.Guid.NewGuid)
    objProduct.ProductName = "Tooth Powder"
    objProduct.UnitsInStock = 10
    objProduct.UnitsOnOrder = 25
    objProduct.ReorderLevel = 15
    Products.Add(objProduct)

    objProduct = New Product(System.Guid.NewGuid)
    objProduct.ProductName = "Floss"
    objProduct.UnitsInStock = 200
    objProduct.UnitsOnOrder = 500
    objProduct.ReorderLevel = 300
    Products.Add(objProduct)

    objProduct = New Product(System.Guid.NewGuid)
    objProduct.ProductName = "Face Soap"
    objProduct.UnitsInStock = 200
    objProduct.UnitsOnOrder = 500
    objProduct.ReorderLevel = 300
    Products.Add(objProduct)

    'In a database-connected version of this app, you would replace all of
    'the above code with a call to a LoadData() method in Products that
    'would load Product data from the database, package it as a Products
    'collection of Product objects, and deliver it here to the front end.

    Clearbindings()
    SetBindings()
    Me.BindingContext(Products).Position = 0
    UpdatePositionDisplay()

End Sub
```

After the initial data (three products) is loaded, you can navigate through the collection using the provided navigational buttons, changing, adding, and deleting `Product` data as you like (except that you are not allowed to change the primary key value). Changes, additions, and deletions trigger events that keep the list and the individual objects in synch and permit a collection of altered `Products` to be

Read-Write Binding

obtained at any time (such as the set of changed rows that you get from the `DataSet` class's `GetChanges()` method). That collection of altered `Products` could be used to update a back-end database.

The following subsections examine the `Product` and `Products` classes in detail. With a little study of this material and some experimentation with the provided app, you should have a good beginning understanding of how to implement read-write bindable custom objects and collections in .NET.

The `Product` **Class**

The basic properties of a `Product` for this app include `ProductId`, `ProductName`, `UnitsInStock`, `UnitsOnOrder`, and `ReorderLevel`. Two additional properties (`Changed` and `Added`) are included to flag whether an instance has been changed or added since the data was loaded. The property `ChangedDuringThisEdit` keeps up with whether a `Product` has been changed during the current editing session. (If it has, the `OnProductChanged()` method is called to update information in the `Products` collection class of which the `Product` is a member.)

For convenience, a structure is defined to hold internal values for those seven properties:

```
Structure ProductData
    Friend ProductId As Guid
    Friend ProductName As String
    Friend UnitsInStock As Int16
    Friend UnitsOnOrder As Int16
    Friend ReorderLevel As Int16
    Friend Changed As Boolean
    Friend Added As Boolean
    Friend ChangedDuringThisEdit As Boolean
End Structure
```

Note that the `ProductId` is typed as a globally unique identifier (GUID). GUIDs are discussed in Chapter 12, "Creating and Maintaining a Database in Visual Studio," in the section "Primary Key Styles." But for a quick orientation, here is the definition of a GUID from the MSDN Help File:

> A GUID is a 128-bit integer (16 bytes) that can be used across all computers and networks wherever a unique identifier is required. Such an identifier has a very low probability of being duplicated.

The `System.Guid` structure in .NET provides a shared function, `NewGuid`, to generate random GUID values. You use that function here to initialize any new products you add to the collection.

In form `frmMain` of `ReadWriteBindableCollection`, the `Products` collection is declared and instantiated as a private member variable at the class level:

```
Dim Products As New Products
```

In the event handler for the form's `Load` event, three products are created and added to the list. Each product is added with code similar to that shown next. Notice how `System.Guid.NewGuid` is invoked to return a GUID value that is passed to the `Product` constructor to be used as the primary key value.

```
Dim objProduct As Product
objProduct = New Product(System.Guid.NewGuid)
objProduct.ProductName = "Tooth Powder"
objProduct.UnitsInStock = 10
objProduct.UnitsOnOrder = 25
objProduct.ReorderLevel = 15
Products.Add(objProduct)
```

The `Product` class defines a property, `ContainingCollection`, to keep a reference to the collection of which the current instance of `Product` is a member. As previously mentioned, `Product` implements the `BeginEdit()`, `CancelEdit()`, and `EndEdit()` methods mandated by `IEditableObject`. It also includes a method named `OnProductChanged()` that is called whenever editing is ended and it is determined that at least one of its properties has been given a new value.

Next you get a bit more detail on each of the key methods and properties of the `Product` class.

Persistable Properties of the `Product` Object

Persistable properties of the `Product` class—those you would save to a database—include `ProductId`, `ProductName`, `UnitsInStock`, `UnitsOnOrder`, and `ReorderLevel`. The `ProductId` property, representing the key value for the `Product`, is implemented as a `ReadOnly` property:

```
Public ReadOnly Property ProductID() As Guid
    Get
        Return Me.m_ProdData.ProductId
    End Get
End Property
```

Here is the definition for the `ProductName` property:

```
Public Property ProductName() As String
    Get
        ProductName = Me.m_ProdData.ProductName
    End Get
```

14

Read-Write Binding

```
      Set(ByVal Value As String)
          If Not Me.m_ProdData.ProductName.Equals(Value) Then
              Me.m_ProdData.ProductName = Value
              If Me.m_blnEditInProgress Then
                  Me.m_ProdData.ChangedDuringThisEdit = True
                  Me.m_ProdData.Changed = True
              End If
          End If
      End Set
End Property
```

Note that in the Set section, you check whether the current value of the ProductName matches the incoming value. If it does not, the code for the property not only changes the stored value, but also sets the Changed and ChangedDuringThisEdit flags for the instance.

The remaining persistable properties are all defined in a manner similar to ProductName. Any change in their values sets the two "changed" flags for the current instance of the Product. You will see in a moment that EndEdit checks the ChangedDuringThisEdit flag to determine whether to notify the Products collection that an item has been changed.

BeginEdit()

BeginEdit() implements the BeginEdit() method defined in IEditableObject. Its function is to back up data for the current item before it is changed. Because the editable product data is maintained in a structure, the backup is easy. A Boolean variable, m_blnEditInProgress, which is scoped at the class level, keeps track of whether a fresh backup is required.

```
Sub BeginEdit() Implements IEditableObject.BeginEdit
    If Not m_blnEditInProgress Then
        m_BackupData = m_ProdData
        m_blnEditInProgress = True
        m_ProdData.ChangedDuringThisEdit = False
    End If
End Sub
```

CancelEdit()

CancelEdit() implements the CancelEdit() method defined in IEditableObject. It restores attribute values from the backup copy of the item data to the primary copy and sets the m_blnEditInProgress flag so the next BeginEdit() call will create a fresh backup.

```
Sub CancelEdit() Implements IEditableObject.CancelEdit
    If m_blnEditInProgress Then
        Me.m_ProdData = m_BackupData
        m_blnEditInProgress = False
    End If
End Sub
```

EndEdit()

EndEdit() implements the EndEdit() method defined in IEditableObject. It sets the backup structure object to a new instance of the ProductData structure, preparing it for new values when editing is restarted on this instance or another one. EndEdit() also sets the m_blnEditInProgress flag to False so the next BeginEdit() call will create a fresh backup.

If any editable property of the current item was changed, the Changed property will have been set, and EndEdit() will invoke the OnProductChanged() method.

```
Sub EndEdit() Implements IEditableObject.EndEdit
    If m_blnEditInProgress Then
        m_BackupData = New ProductData
        m_blnEditInProgress = False
    End If

    If Me.m_ProdData.ChangedDuringThisEdit Then
        Me.OnProductChanged()
    End If
End Sub
```

ContainingCollection

The ContainingCollection property of Product is defined as follows:

```
Friend Property ContainingCollection() As Products
    Get
        Return m_colContainingCollection
    End Get
    Set(ByVal Value As Products)
        m_colContainingCollection = Value
    End Set
End Property
```

It simply contains a reference to the Products collection that contains the current Product instance.

Read-Write Binding

`OnProductChanged()`

`OnProductChanged()` calls the `ProductChanged` method of the containing collection (an instance of the `Products` class) to inform that collection that the current item has been changed:

```
Private Sub OnProductChanged()
    If Not m_blnEditInProgress And Not (m_colContainingCollection Is Nothing) Then
        m_colContainingCollection.ProductChanged(Me)
    End If
End Sub
```

The `Products` Class

The `Products` class inherits `CollectionBase` and implements `IBindingList`. It specifies the method `OnListChanged` as a `ListChangedEventHandler`, and `objResetEvent` as a `ListChangedEventArgs` object. An `ArrayList` is declared as a temporary repository for deleted products, and a `ChangedProducts` collection (itself of the data type `Products`) is declared to hold a collection of all products either updated, inserted, or deleted during an editing session. When populated, `ChangedProducts` is similar to the rowset you get when you invoke `GetChanges` on a `DataSet` object: It is structurally identical to the larger set but contains only modified items.

```
Imports System.ComponentModel
Public Class Products
    Inherits CollectionBase
    Implements IBindingList

    Private objResetEvent As New ListChangedEventArgs(ListChangedType.Reset, -1)
    Private arlDeletedItems As ArrayList
    Dim ChangedProducts As Products
```

Properties and methods in `Products` are segregated into four regions, whose themes are as follows:

- ▶ Noninherited, noninterface members
- ▶ Members that override inherited members
- ▶ Members that implement `IBindingList` members
- ▶ Members that implement `IBindingList` members nonsupportively

Noninherited, Noninterface Members

This region comprises properties and methods that neither override members inherited from `CollectionBase` nor implement members mandated by `IBindingList`.

The region includes a single property, `Item`, and six methods: `Add`, `Delete`, `ProductChanged`, `HasChanges()`, `GetChanges()`, and `GetDescriptionOfChanges()`.

The `Item` property is used for accessing a particular object in the collection and is designated as the default property for the class. The `Get` accessor returns the indicated item, retrieved from the `Products` collection's underlying list and cast to a `Product` type. Setting the item replaces the item at the indicated index in the underlying list with the object passed into the property.

```
Default Public Property Item(ByVal index As Integer) As Product
    Get
        Return CType(List(index), Product)
    End Get
    Set(ByVal Value As Product)
        List(index) = Value
    End Set
End Property
```

The `Add()` method adds an object to the `List` collection inherited by `Products` from the `CollectionBase` class. It then returns the index of the position in the list where the new item was inserted.

```
Public Function Add(ByVal value As Product) As Integer
    Return List.Add(value)
End Function
```

The functionality of the `Delete()` method will now be described, beginning with the last thing it does and working backward, because its operation is easier to understand that way. The most fundamental job of this method is the one it does last; as you back up from there, you handle ancillary functions and special-case actions in roughly decreasing order of importance.

`Delete()` calls the `RemoveAt` method (inherited from `CollectionBase`) to delete the indicated item from the list. Before doing that, it adds the deleted `Product` to an `ArrayList` of deleted products that can be used later by `GetChanges()`. Before that, it clears the `Changed` flag so that `GetChanges()` treats it as a deleted object rather than a changed one. (Deleting trumps changing: If you're ultimately going to delete the object—from the back-end database, let's say—there's not much point in first trying to update its property values there.) Finally (still backing up, at last arriving at the beginning), `Delete()` checks whether the object to be deleted is marked as having been added (since products were loaded). If so, it is simply allowed to vanish: It is removed from the collection without being added to the `ArrayList` of deleted objects. That's because if it didn't exist before and it's being deleted now, you really don't need to keep any record of it.

Read-Write Binding

```
Public Sub Delete(ByVal index As Integer)
    If Me.Item(index).Added Then
        'If item was added, then deleted, don't add it to the arraylist
        'of deleted items, since it doesn't yet exist in the database and
        'therefore doesn't need to be deleted.
    Else
        'Clear the Changed flag so that if the item was changed and then
        'deleted, the item state won't be misdiagnosed as Changed when
        'GetChanges examines it.
        Me.Item(index).Changed = False
        'Add item to the arraylist of deleted items.
        If arlDeletedItems Is Nothing Then
            arlDeletedItems = New ArrayList
            arlDeletedItems.Add(Me.Item(index))
        End If
    End If
    'Remove the item from the collection.
    Me.RemoveAt(index)

End Sub
```

`ProductChanged()` is designed to be called by a `Product` object when that object's data changes. `ProductChanged()` looks up the index of the incoming `Product` instance and then calls the `OnListChanged()` method, passing it that index and an enum value indicating the type of change that was made to the item. Information about the change is then communicated to the underlying list.

`OnClearComplete`, `OnInsertComplete`, `OnRemoveComplete`, and `OnSetComplete` are event handlers that override methods inherited from `CollectionBase`. They come prewired as the event handlers for the `Clear`, `Insert`, `Remove`, and `Set` events, and are called when those actions occur against items in the list. As with `ProductChanged()`, each of these event handlers calls `OnListChanged()`.

`OnListChanged()`, in this app, simply calls `WriteChangeInfoToConsole()`. Clearly, you could have simply placed the code in the latter method inside `OnListChanged()`, but `OnListChanged()` seems like it will be a useful gathering place for other functions one might want to perform in the future, in other applications; and since `WriteChangeInfoToConsole()` is entirely a tool for exploring how the custom collection class operates, it would likely be removed from those future apps. Keeping it discrete makes that cleaner and easier to do when the time comes.

```
Protected Overridable Sub OnListChanged(ByVal ev As ListChangedEventArgs)
    WriteChangeInfoToConsole(Me, ev)
End Sub
```

```
Private Sub WriteChangeInfoToConsole(ByVal ev As ListChangedEventArgs)
    'This sub writes a diagnostic line to the Console whenever an item is
    'changed, inserted, or deleted
    Dim strProductName As String
    Dim strActionTaken As String
    Select Case ev.ListChangedType
        Case ListChangedType.ItemMoved
            strActionTaken = "(moved)"
            strProductName = list.Item(ev.NewIndex).ProductName & " "
        Case ListChangedType.ItemAdded
            strActionTaken = "(added)"
            strProductName = list.Item(ev.NewIndex).ProductName & " "
        Case ListChangedType.ItemChanged
            strActionTaken = "(changed)"
            strProductName = list.Item(ev.NewIndex).ProductName & " "
        Case ListChangedType.ItemDeleted
            strActionTaken = "(deleted)"
            If ev.NewIndex <= list.Count - 1 Then
                strProductName = list.Item(ev.NewIndex).ProductName & " "
            Else
                'The list no longer contains this item.
                strProductName = "<Item added during this editing session>"
            End If
        Case ListChangedType.Reset
            strActionTaken = "(The list was reset)"
            strProductName = list.Item(ev.NewIndex).ProductName & " "
        Case Else
            strActionTaken = "(Error in ListChanged event handler.
            ➥Unexpected ListChangedType)"
    End Select
    If strProductName = " " Then
        strProductName = "<As yet unnamed product>"
    End If
    Console.WriteLine(strProductName & strActionTaken)
End Sub
```

You might note the special handling of deleted items. If the item deleted is the last one in the list (as happens with any item added and then deleted in the same session), the value of `ev.NewIndex` equals the highest-numbered index in the list *before* the current item was removed. But by the time execution finds its way to this method, the item has already been removed, so attempting to reference `Item(ev.NewIndex)` results in an error. Therefore, instead of doing so, you simply set the `strProductName` value to `Item` added during this editing session.

Read-Write Binding

`HasChanges()` mimics the `HasChanges()` method provided by the .NET `DataSet` class, which returns `True` or `False` based whether the collection includes at least one item that was deleted, inserted, or changed.

```
Public Function HasChanges() As Boolean
    If Not arlDeletedItems Is Nothing Then
        Return True
    End If

    Dim objProduct As Product
    For Each objProduct In Me
        If objProduct.Changed Or objProduct.Added Then
            Return True
        End If
    Next
End Function
```

`GetChanges()` mimics the `GetChanges()` method provided by the .NET `DataSet` class. Recall that `DataSet.GetChanges()` returns the set of `DataRows` from a table or `DataSet` that have changes. The set of changed rows can then be passed to the `Fill()` method of a `DataAdapter` object to update the back-end database in an efficient way. The `GetChanges()` method implemented in this `Products` class returns a typed collection of `Product` objects that represent the subset of the collection in `Products` that have had changes made to them.

The .NET `DataSet` class includes an overload of `GetChanges()` that permits you to get changes of a particular type (`Insert`, `Delete`, or `Update`). Products includes no corresponding overloaded implementation of `GetChanges()`—not because it wouldn't be useful in a production app, but simply because it seems an unnecessary complication for this teaching app. Writing it would be straightforward.

```
Public Function GetChanges() As Products
    'Return a typed collection containing all Products that have been
    'changed since loading.
    ChangedProducts = New Products

    Dim objProduct As Product
    For Each objProduct In Me
        If objProduct.Changed Or objProduct.Added Then
            ChangedProducts.Add(objProduct)
        End If
    Next
    If Not arlDeletedItems Is Nothing Then
        For Each objProduct In arlDeletedItems
            ChangedProducts.Add(objProduct)
        Next
```

```
    End If
    GetChanges = ChangedProducts
End Function
```

The front-end form calls `GetDescriptionOfChanges()` when the user clicks the Show All Changes button. `GetDescriptionOfChanges()` calls `GetChanges()` for a collection of changed `Product` objects. It then iterates through that collection, assembling an informational string that is returned to the form and displayed in a message box:

```
Public Function GetDescriptionOfChanges() As String
    'Return a string that describes all changes made to the collection
    'of products
    Dim ChangedProducts As Products = GetChanges()
    Dim objProduct As Product
    Dim strMsg As String

    strMsg = "Changes at " & Now.ToUniversalTime & ControlChars.NewLine &
    ➡ControlChars.NewLine
    For Each objProduct In ChangedProducts
        strMsg += "Product: " & objProduct.ProductName & " ("
        'Change types must be checked in this order: Added, then Changed.
        'Anything in Changed products that isn't marked as having been
        'Added or Changed must be there by virtue of having been deleted.
        If objProduct.Added Then
            strMsg += "Added"
        ElseIf objProduct.Changed Then
            strMsg += "Changed"
        Else
            strMsg += "Deleted"
        End If
        strMsg += ")" & ControlChars.NewLine
    Next

    GetDescriptionOfChanges = strMsg
End Function
```

Members That Override Inherited Members

This region of the `Products` class definition comprises methods that override event-handler methods inherited from the `CollectionBase` class. These include `OnClear`, `OnClearComplete`, `OnInsertComplete`, `OnRemoveComplete`, and `OnSetComplete`. These methods are specified in `CollectionBase` as the event handlers for the `Clear`, `Insert`, `Remove`, and `Set` events.

Read-Write Binding

`OnClear` clears the collection by setting the `ContainingCollection` property of each included item to `Nothing`.

```
Protected Overrides Sub OnClear()
    Dim objProduct As Product
    For Each objProduct In List
        objProduct.ContainingCollection = Nothing
    Next objProduct
End Sub
```

At the conclusion of `OnClear`'s operation, `OnClearComplete` calls `OnListChanged` with `objResetEvent`:

```
Protected Overrides Sub OnClearComplete()
    OnListChanged(objResetEvent)
End Sub
```

`OnInsertComplete` and `OnRemoveComplete` set the inserted object's `ContainingCollection` property to Me, the `Products` collection object.

```
Protected Overrides Sub OnInsertComplete(ByVal index As Integer, ByVal value As
➥Object)
    Dim objProduct As Product = CType(value, Product)
    objProduct.ContainingCollection = Me
    OnListChanged(New ListChangedEventArgs(ListChangedType.ItemAdded,
        ➥index))
End Sub
```

```
Protected Overrides Sub OnRemoveComplete(ByVal index As Integer, ByVal
➥value As Object)
    Dim objProduct As Product = CType(value, Product)
    objProduct.ContainingCollection = Me
    OnListChanged(New ListChangedEventArgs(ListChangedType.ItemDeleted,
        ➥index))
End Sub
```

`OnSetComplete()` banishes the `Product` that contains the old property values from the collection and adds the `Product` that contains the new property values:

```
Protected Overrides Sub OnSetComplete(ByVal index As Integer, ByVal
➥oldValue As Object, ByVal newValue As Object)
    If oldValue <> newValue Then
        Dim oldProduct As Product = CType(oldValue, Product)
        Dim newProduct As Product = CType(newValue, Product)
```

```
        oldProduct.ContainingCollection = Nothing
        newProduct.ContainingCollection = Me

        OnListChanged(New ListChangedEventArgs(ListChangedType.ItemAdded,
        ➥index))
    End If
End Sub
```

14

Members That Implement IBindingList Members

This region comprises properties and methods that implement members defined in
the IBindingList interface. Properties include AllowEdit, AllowNew,
AllowRemove, SupportsChangeNotification, SupportsSearching, and
SupportsSorting. One public event, ListChanged, is declared and implements
IBindingList.ListChanged. Finally, AddNew is implemented.

AllowEdit, AllowNew, AllowRemove, SupportsChangeNotification,
SupportsSearching, and SupportsSorting specify operations that the Products
collection will and will not permit:

```
'Properties
ReadOnly Property AllowEdit() As Boolean Implements IBindingList.AllowEdit
    Get
        Return True
    End Get
End Property


ReadOnly Property AllowNew() As Boolean Implements IBindingList.AllowNew
    Get
        Return True
    End Get
End Property


ReadOnly Property AllowRemove() As Boolean Implements
➥IBindingList.AllowRemove
    Get
        Return True
    End Get
End Property


ReadOnly Property SupportsChangeNotification() As Boolean Implements
➥IBindingList.SupportsChangeNotification
    Get
        Return True
    End Get
End Property
```

Read-Write Binding

```
ReadOnly Property SupportsSearching() As Boolean Implements
➡IBindingList.SupportsSearching
    Get
        Return False
    End Get
End Property

ReadOnly Property SupportsSorting() As Boolean Implements
➡IBindingList.SupportsSorting
    Get
        Return False
    End Get
End Property

' Events.
Public Event ListChanged As ListChangedEventHandler Implements
➡IBindingList.ListChanged
```

AddNew() creates a new product, adds it to the collection, and returns the product object to the calling procedure.

```
Function AddNew() As Object Implements IBindingList.AddNew
    Dim guiX As Guid = System.Guid.NewGuid
    Dim objProduct As New Product(guiX)
    List.Add(objProduct)
    Return objProduct
End Function
```

Members That Implement IBindingList Members Nonsupportively

This region comprises properties and methods that implement members defined in the IBindingList interface but, in doing so, don't provide any actual functionality other than to throw a NotSupportedException. Properties in this category include IsSorted, SortDirection, SortProperty, AddIndex, ApplySort, Find, RemoveIndex, and RemoveSort. These properties could be implemented in a more meaningful way to give increased richness of functionality to your custom class:

```
' Properties.
ReadOnly Property IsSorted() As Boolean Implements IBindingList.IsSorted
    Get
        Throw New NotSupportedException
    End Get
End Property

ReadOnly Property SortDirection() As ListSortDirection Implements
➡IBindingList.SortDirection
```

```
    Get
        Throw New NotSupportedException
    End Get
End Property


ReadOnly Property SortProperty() As PropertyDescriptor Implements
➥IBindingList.SortProperty
    Get
        Throw New NotSupportedException
    End Get
End Property


' Methods.
Sub AddIndex(ByVal prop As PropertyDescriptor) Implements IBindingList.AddIndex
    Throw New NotSupportedException
End Sub


Sub ApplySort(ByVal prop As PropertyDescriptor, ByVal direction As
➥ListSortDirection) Implements IBindingList.ApplySort
    Throw New NotSupportedException
End Sub


Function Find(ByVal prop As PropertyDescriptor, ByVal key As Object) As
➥Integer Implements IBindingList.Find
    Throw New NotSupportedException
End Function


Sub RemoveIndex(ByVal prop As PropertyDescriptor) Implements
➥IBindingList.RemoveIndex
    Throw New NotSupportedException
End Sub


Sub RemoveSort() Implements IBindingList.RemoveSort
    Throw New NotSupportedException
End Sub 'IBindingList.RemoveSort
```

Additional Work Required to Make the ReadWriteBindableCollection App Database Connectable

ReadWriteBindableCollection provides the foundation for an app that can read and write Product data to a database. Here's what you would have to do to make that happen:

Read-Write Binding

1. Provide functionality in the `Products` class (or accessible by way of the `Products` class) to load `Product` data from a database.

2. Package that data into a set of `Product` objects stored in a `Products` collection, and pass the collection to the application's front end.

3. Provide functionality in the `Products` class (or accessible by way of the `Products` class) to update data in the database. Note that `Products` already implements `HasChanges()` and `GetChanges()`, which provide functionality similar to that supplied by the corresponding methods in the `DataSet` class. You might want to enhance `GetChanges()` to accept an argument to specify the type of changes you want to retrieve.

You could, if you liked, leverage the `Fill` and `Update` functionality of a `DataAdapter` in satisfying the third previous requirement. You could use a `DataAdapter` to load a `DataSet` with the data necessary to populate the `Product` objects; populate the objects from that `DataSet`; and then keep that `DataSet` around (or write it to disk as XML) while a user-editing session takes place. Then, upon a request to update the database, the collection of products returned by `Products.GetChanges()` could be used to update the `DataSet`; and the changes there could then be communicated to the database the `DataAdapter`'s `Update()` method.

Applications on the Code Website

Table 14.7 lists all the applications associated with this chapter that are included on the code website. The applications are listed in the order in which they were discussed.

TABLE 14.7

Description of Sample Applications

App Name	Description and Notes
BindingContext	Illustrates how a form's `BindingContext` can return either a `CurrencyManager` or a `PropertyManager` object, depending upon the type of parameter passed to the `BindingContext`.
BindingAndNavigationSyntaxLinkage	Illustrates how mismatches between the syntax style used to establish data binding and that used for record navigation within a form's `CurrencyManager` can cause data binding to work improperly.
BindToADataTable	Illustrates the binding of control properties to columns in `DataTables`. It also separates data-manipulation code from user interface code. It remains a single-tier app, but because all data retrieval and storage occurs in a class that is separate from the form that constitutes the user interface, the app shows the beginnings of what could be converted to a multitier architecture that isolates the user interface from details of the database structure.

TABLE 14.7

Continued

App Name	Description and Notes
BindObjectPropertyToTableValue	Illustrates two techniques: 1. Binding a property that is a complex type to a single column in a database table 2. Using an `ArrayList` of items whose type is a user-defined class as the data source for a `ComboBox`, while binding the `SelectedValue` property of the `ComboBox` to a column in a database table
BindToIListCollections	Illustrates how a control's properties can be bound to a variety of collections that implement the `IList` interface, including a `TabPages` collection, a `SqlParameters` collection, a `MenuItems` collection, and the `Controls` collection of a `form`.
BindToAnObject	Binds the `Text` properties of multiple `TextBoxes` and binds the `Checked` property of a `CheckBox` control to different properties of a single object.
BindMultiplePropertiesToAnObject	(Another exploration of the Property Manager.) Binds multiple properties of a *single* control to different properties of the same object. Specifically, it binds the `Width`, `Height`, `Top`, and `Left` properties of one `TextBox` control to the `TextLength` property of another `TextBox`. It also binds the `Text` property of the first `TextBox` to the `Text` property of the second.
BindToAnArraylistOfObjects	As with BindToADataTable, separates data-manipulation code from user-interface code. Unlike that project, however, it passes the data between the data and UI "tiers" as an `ArrayList` of objects rather than as a `DataSet`. It also illustrates how a collection class that does not implement the `IBindingList` interface breaks down when used for read-write data binding.
ReadWriteBindableCollection	Demonstrates the creation of a custom object and corresponding collection class that fully support data binding. The custom object, `Product`, implements the `IEditableObject` interface. The custom collection, `Products`, inherits the `CollectionBase` class and implements the `IBindingList` interface.

Summary

This chapter covered a lot of material on data binding. You've seen how Visual Basic .NET accomodates a much wider variety of data sources than did previous versions of

14

Summary

Visual Basic. You explored the relationships and differences of the `BindingContext`, `CurrencyManager`, and `PropertyManager` objects, and you learned how bindings and navigational statements that use a `CurrencyManager` must be defined with consistent syntax. You saw how to bind the Windows form controls to `DataSets`, objects, and collections of objects; and we explored the difference between *simple* binding (such as what occurs when you bind the `Text` property of a `TextBox` control to a column in a table or property of an object) and *complex* binding (such as what occurs when you bind the list of items in a `ComboBox` or `DataGrid` to rows in a table or objects in a collection). Finally, you explored how to implement read-write bindable custom objects and collections using the `IEditableObject` and `IBindingList` interfaces and the `CollectionBase` class.

Further Reading

Lhotka, Rocky. "Windows Forms Data Binding and Objects." Available at the Microsoft Visual Basic Developer Center, http://msdn.microsoft.com/vbasic/using/building/windows/data/default.aspx?pull=/library/en-us/dnadvnet/html/vbnet02252003.asp.

Mackenzie, Duncan. "Data Binding Radio Buttons to a List." *MSDN Magazine*, July 2004. Available online at http://msdn.microsoft.com/vbasic/default.aspx?pull=/msdnmag/issues/04/07/advancedbasics/default.aspx.

Spencer, Ken. "Data Binding in Visual Basic .NET." *MSDN Magazine*, August 2003. Available online at http://msdn.microsoft.com/msdnmag/issues/03/08/AdvancedBasics/.

Jain, Tarum. "Data Binding Concepts in .NET Windows Forms." The Code Project, www.codeproject.com/vb/net/databindingconcepts.asp.

Shepherd, George. "Frequently Asked Questions on Windows Forms Data Binding." At George Shepherd's Windows Forms FAQ website, www.syncfusion.com/FAQ/WinForms/default.asp#43.

Fussell, Mark. "Data Access Support in Visual Studio.NET." Tutorial at Dot Net Junkies website, www.dotnetjunkies.com/Tutorial/B47B0E30-0C40-494A-8DF8-CDA4F824D9C3.dcik.

"INFO: Roadmap for Windows Forms Data Binding." Microsoft Knowledge Base article ID 313482, http://support.microsoft.com/default.aspx?scid=kb;en-us;313482.

15

ADO.NET AND XML

IN BRIEF

In this chapter, you will learn about ADO.NET support for and integration of XML. You will learn about these topics:

▶ The XML schema files used to persist the specifications for strongly-typed `DataSets`

▶ The `DataSet`'s facilities for reading and writing data in XML, inferring schemas from XML data, and reading and writing schemas as XML

▶ The `DataAdapter`'s `FillSchema` method, which reads schema information from a back-end database into a `DataSet`

WHAT YOU NEED

SOFTWARE RECOMMENDATIONS	Windows 2000, Windows XP, or Windows Server 2003 .NET Framework 1.1 Visual Studio .NET 2003 with Visual Basic .NET installed SQL Server 2000 or corresponding version of the Microsoft Desktop Database Engine (MSDE)
HARDWARE RECOMMENDATIONS	PC desktop or laptop, .NET-enabled server, desktop client
SKILL REQUIREMENTS	Intermediate knowledge of the .NET Framework Intermediate knowledge of Windows Forms Understanding of relational database concepts and applications Familiarity with error trapping using `Try-Catch` blocks Familiarity with SQL Server 2000

ADO.NET AND XML AT A GLANCE

ADO.NET AND XML AT A GLANCE

Introduction

According to the *.NET Framework Developer's Guide* that ships with Visual Studio, Microsoft had three primary goals for the design of ADO.NET:

- ▶ To leverage current ADO knowledge

- ▶ To support the *n*-tier programming model

- ▶ To integrate XML support

Earlier chapters discussed how the determination of the ADO.NET designers to support disconnected data access—the foundation block for *n*-tier programming—shaped the design of ADO.NET. To a considerable extent, the dissimilarities between ADO and ADO.NET that work against the first design objective contributed to the achievement of the second objective. The topic of this chapter is the third objective: the integration of and support for XML.

If you've ever used the Data Form Wizard or dragged a `DataAdapter` from the Toolbox onto a form, you've seen an important instance of that integration in the artifacts produced by either of those processes. Upon completing a session of the Data Form Wizard, you discover not only a new form in your project, but also a file with an unusual icon and an extension of `.xsd`. That file is an XML Schema Definition, the successor of the Document Type Definition (DTD) that predated it. If you started your process by dragging a `DataAdapter` onto your form, you have to generate the XSD file in a separate but simple step, by clicking on the Generate DataSet link at the bottom of the Properties window for the `DataAdapter`.

An XML Schema definition is an industry-standard document that describes the structure of data in an XML file. The .xsd files created by .NET describe databases. They include information about tables, columns, data types, primary and foreign keys, constraints, and relationships—everything you need to create a database (or an in-memory representation of a database, like ADO.NET's `DataSet` object). When you generate a `DataSet`, a second file gets created that is visible only if you toggle Show All Files in Solution Explorer. This second file is a class definition with the same name as that of the `.xsd` file but with the standard class file extension of `.vb`.

Introduction

It contains a class for the `DataSet` itself (which inherits from `System.Data.DataSet`), classes for each table in the `DataSet` (these inherit from `System.Data.DataTable`), classes that define the row structure for each table (these inherit from, you guessed it, `System.Data.DataRow`), and a RowChange event for each of those row structures (which inherits from `System.EventArgs`). When you declare a strongly-typed `DataSet` object in your code, it uses the class definitions in this module, and they learn everything they know about the structure your `DataSet` needs from the schema definition file (`.xsd`).

The `DataAdapter` object contains all the information Visual Studio needs to create that schema-definition file. From its `Connection` property, Visual Studio can learn how to connect to the database on the back end for detailed schema information. From its `SelectCommand` property, Visual Studio learns exactly what tables and columns are to be included in the `DataSet`. When you invoke a `DataAdapter`'s `Fill()` method to fill a `DataSet` (or one of its included `DataTables`) with data, the `DataAdapter` expects to find a schema in the target `DataSet` that matches the one from the `DataSource`.

XML-Related Methods of the `DataSet` Class

The integration of XML with .NET goes beyond the integration of XML with ADO.NET, but this chapter focuses on the latter. The integration of XML with ADO.NET manifests most directly and overtly through the several methods of the `DataSet` class listed in Table 15.1.

TABLE 15.1

XML-Related Methods of the `DataSet` Class

Method	Description	Number of Overloads
InferXmlSchema	Overloaded. Applies an XML schema to the `DataSet`.	3
ReadXmlSchema	Overloaded. Reads an XML schema into the `DataSet`.	3
WriteXml	Overloaded. Writes XML data and, optionally, the schema from the `DataSet`.	7
WriteXmlSchema	Overloaded. Writes the `DataSet` structure as an XML schema.	3
GetXml	Returns the XML representation of the data stored in the `DataSet`.	0
GetXmlSchema	Returns the XSD schema for the XML representation of the data stored in the `DataSet`.	0
ReadXml	Overloaded. Reads XML schema and data into the `DataSet`.	7

The code for this chapter includes several solutions that demonstrate or permit you to explore the various effects of these XML-related `DataSet` methods. These solutions are summarized in Table 15.2.

TABLE 15.2

Tutorial Applications That Illustrate the XML-Related `DataSet` Methods

Method	Description
ReadAndWriteXmlSchemas	Demonstrates the use of the `DataSet.ReadXmlSchema()` and `DataSet.WriteXmlSchema()` methods
ReadXmlWorkoutMachine	Demonstrates the use of the following `DataSet` methods: `ReadXml()` `InferXmlSchema()` `GetXmlSchema()` `GetXml()`
WriteXmlWorkoutMachine	Demonstrates the use of the `DataSet.WriteXml()` method

Reading and Writing XML Schemas

`ReadXmlSchema()` reads schema information from an XML file. `WriteXmlSchema()` writes schema information to an XML file using the XML Schema Definition (XSD) standard.

The application ReadAndWriteXmlSchemas, in Figure 15.1, illustrates the use and results from the `ReadXmlSchema()` and `WriteXmlSchema()` methods of the `DataSet` class.

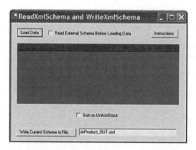

FIGURE 15.1   Main form of the ReadAndWriteXmlSchemas application.

The Load Data button calls a method that invokes `ReadXml()` to load data from an XML data file, `Products.XML`. Optionally, the method first calls

Reading and Writing XML Schemas

ReadXmlSchema() to load schema information from an XML schema-definition file, dsProduct.xsd.

```
Private Function LoadData() As Boolean
    objdsProduct = Nothing              'Clear any existing version
    objdsProduct = New DataSet     'Create a new DataSet

    'Optionally, load an external schema
    Try
        If Me.chkLoadSchema.Checked Then
            objdsProduct.ReadXmlSchema("..\dsProduct.xsd")
        End If
    Catch ex As Exception
        MessageBox.Show(ex.Message)
        Return False
    End Try

    'Fill the DataSet
    Try
        objdsProduct.ReadXml("Products.xml")
    Catch ex As Exception
        MessageBox.Show(ex.Message)
    End Try
    Return True

End Function
```

Products.XML does not contain schema information. Therefore, when ReadXml() is called to load the data, if the option to read schema information has not been selected, ReadXml() must infer the schema from the incoming data. Thus, in this circumstance, the ReadXml("Products.xml") call is equivalent to the more explicit ReadXml("Products.xml", XmlReadMode.InferSchema). You can see this if you click the Write Current Schema to File button. The Click event handler for that button executes the following statement:

```
objdsProduct.WriteXmlSchema(Me.txtOutputFile.Text)
```

If you then double-click the file dsProduct_OUT.xsd in Solution Explorer to open it, you will see that all columns have been typed as strings:

```
<xs:element name="ProductID" type="xs:string" minOccurs="0" />
<xs:element name="ProductName" type="xs:string" minOccurs="0" />
<xs:element name="UnitPrice" type="xs:string" minOccurs="0" />
<xs:element name="UnitsInStock" type="xs:string" minOccurs="0" />
<xs:element name="Discontinued" type="xs:string" minOccurs="0" />
```

On the other hand, if you check the Read External Schema Before Loading Data check box so that schema information gets loaded from dsProduct.xsd before the data is loaded and then you write the dsProduct_OUT.xsd file, you can observe that columns are typed as you find them in the Products table of the Northwind database:

```
<xs:element name="ProductID" msdata:DataType="System.Guid, mscorlib,
➥Version=1.0.5000.0, Culture=neutral, PublicKeyToken=b77a5c561934e089"
➥type="xs:string" minOccurs="0" />
<xs:element name="ProductName" type="xs:string" minOccurs="0" />
<xs:element name="UnitPrice" type="xs:decimal" minOccurs="0" />
<xs:element name="UnitsInStock" type="xs:integer" minOccurs="0" />
<xs:element name="Discontinued" type="xs:boolean" minOccurs="0" />
```

15

Effect of the Schema Information on the Data Displayed in the `DataGrid`

You can see the effect of loading the schema information by observing the loaded data as displayed in the `DataGrid`. When all columns are typed as strings, the Discontinued column (which is Boolean in the Northwind database and in the dsProduct.xsd schema definition) displays as the text strings "True" or "False". When schema information is loaded from dsProduct.xsd instead of being inferred, the Discontinued column displays as a check box, the `DataGrid`'s default display for Boolean columns.

Note also the differences in sorting behavior. Selecting the check box Sort on UnitsInStock runs a `SortData()` method that sorts data in the `DataGrid`'s `DataSource`, the `DefaultView` of the loaded table.

```
Private Sub SortData()
    If chkSortOnUnitsInStock.Checked Then
        objdsProduct.Tables("Product").DefaultView.Sort = "UnitsInStock"
    Else
        objdsProduct.Tables("Product").DefaultView.Sort = ""
    End If
End Sub
```

When the schema is inferred, `UnitsInStock` is typed as a string, and sorting follows the ASCII order of numeric characters. Thus, a product with 115 units in stock sorts ahead of one with 13 or 24. This is probably not what you really want to see!

On the other hand, when the schema is loaded from dsProduct.xsd, `UnitsInStock` is typed as an integer, and the sort order is the correct numeric one: 13, 24, and then 115.

The Help file for the application ReadAndWriteXmlSchemas, available from its main menu, prescribes a series of experiments that permit you to see the result of applying the external schema.

Reading XML Data

ADO.NET provides a ReadXml() method in the DataSet class. This versatile class reads XML-formatted data, but it can also read schema information in the source file, if it is present, or infer schema information, if it is absent. The application ReadXmlWorkoutMachine, in Figure 15.2, enables you to explore the various options of the ReadXml() method.

ReadXmlWorkoutMachine also demonstrates the InferXmlSchema(), GetXmlSchema(), and GetXml() methods of the DataSet class. InferXmlSchema() is used to create schema information in the calling DataSet by inferring it from an XML data file. Calling InferXmlSchema() creates the same schema information created by calling ReadXml(), with the mode parameter set to XmlReadMode.InferSchema. Unlike the latter, however, it does not load any data. In ReadXmlWorkoutMachine, InferXmlSchema() is invoked using the button Execute InferXmlSchema(). In the app, this button is enabled only when the InferSchema option is selected for XmlReadMode. The is not because it actually uses the XmlReadMode parameter (it doesn't), but simply to emphasize the fact that InferXmlSchema() returns the same XML (minus data) as ReadXml called with XmlReadMode.InferSchema.

GetXmlSchema() and GetXml() are similar to WriteXmlSchema() and WriteXml(), in that they retrieve schema information and data, respectively, from a DataSet object and in XML format. However, GetXmlSchema() and GetXml() write that data to a string instead of writing it out to a Stream, TextWriter, XmlWriter, or file. They are used in ReadXmlWorkoutMachine to provide an immediate XML display of the data and schema information read.

The ReadXmlWorkoutMachine Application

The ReadXmlWorkoutMachine application enables you to explore the results of using ReadXml() in different situations and with different XmlReadModes. You have four sets of choices to make in fixing the scenario for reading XML:

- Whether to use an untyped DataSet or a strongly-typed DataSet

- Whether to read from an XML file that includes schema information, that has no schema information, or that is a DiffGram

- Whether to use an overload of ReadXml() that specifies the read mode, or an overload that does not

- What XmlReadMode to use for the Mode parameter of the ReadXml() call (if you choose to specify the read mode)

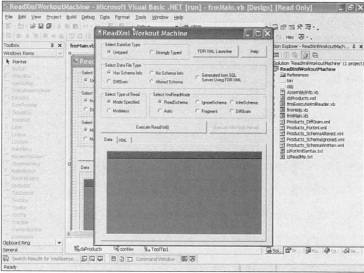

FIGURE 15.2 Main form of the ReadXmlWorkoutMachine application, with the XmlReader Executor opened in the background.

The application loads, from XML data files, product information that originated in the Northwind database's Products table. Four different data files are available:

▶ `Products_SchemaWritten.xml`

▶ `Products_SchemaIgnored.xml`

▶ `Products_DiffGram.xml`

▶ `Products_SchemaAltered.xml`

The first three data files were created using the WriteXmlWorkoutMachine application, using the modes `XmlWriteMode.WriteSchema`, `XmlWriteMode.IgnoreSchema`, and `XmlWriteMode.DiffGram`, respectively. The first includes both schema information and data; the second includes data only. The third file, `Products_DiffGram.xml`, contains no schema information, the same set of data as `Products_SchemaIgnored.xml`, and, in addition, data regarding changes that were made to the `DataSet` between the time it was filled and the time it was written. Those changes included an update to the ProductName column in one record, deletion of a second record, and insertion of a third record.

The final file, `Products_SchemaAltered.xml`, was produced by making a copy of `Products_SchemaWritten.xml` and then changing the data types on all of the `int16` ("short") columns to `int32` ("int"). This data file gives you a way of seeing "which schema wins" when you use a strongly-typed `DataSet` but also specify a read mode of `ReadXmlSchema`.

Reading XML Data

ReadXml() is an overloaded method with eight different versions. Four of the over-loads do not specify the read mode, and four do. The two sets of four overloads allow four different types of input: an XmlReader, a Stream, a TestReader, and a FileName. In this application, input always is read from a file.

If you choose to specify the read mode, you have six choices, corresponding to the members of the XmlReadMode enumeration:

- XmlReadMode.ReadSchema

- XmlReadMode.IgnoreSchema

- XmlReadMode.InferSchema

- XmlReadMode.Auto

- XmlReadMode.Fragment

- XmlReadMode.DiffGram

XmlReadMode.ReadSchema loads the schema information from the XML data file and then loads its data, interpreting it according to that schema.

XmlReadMode.IgnoreSchema bypasses the schema information in the XML data file (if present) and simply attempts to load its data. If ReadXml() is invoked from an untyped DataSet, no data is loaded.

XmlReadMode.InferSchema bypasses the schema information in the XML data file (if present) but attempts to infer a schema from the data it finds. Invoking ReadXml() from an untyped DataSet with this mode should result in a successful load. Note that when you select this option for XmlReadMode, the button Execute InferXmlSchema() is enabled and can be clicked as an alternative to the Execute ReadXml() button. The InferXmlSchema() method does not actually use the XmlReadMode parameter, but in the application its invocation is restricted to the situation in which that option is selected, simply to emphasize the fact that InferXmlSchema() returns the same XML (minus data) as ReadXml called with XmlReadMode.InferSchema.

XmlReadMode.Auto lets you leave the read mode decision to ADO.NET. It makes its choice according to the following rules:

- If the data is a DiffGram, it sets XmlReadMode to DiffGram.

- If the DataSet already has a schema or the document contains an in-line schema, it sets XmlReadMode to ReadSchema.

- If the DataSet does not already have a schema and the document does not contain an in-line schema, it sets XmlReadMode to InferSchema.

XmlReadMode.Fragment reads XML documents such as those generated by executing FOR XML queries against an instance of SQL Server. When XmlReadMode is set to Fragment, the default namespace is read as the inline schema.

XmlReadMode.DiffGram reads a DiffGram produced by a WriteXml() call and applies changes from the DiffGram to the DataSet. The DataSet must have the same schema as the DataSet on which WriteXml was called to produce the DiffGram, or the DiffGram operation will fail.

How to Use ReadXmlWorkoutMachine

The ReadXmlWorkoutMachine application permits you to experiment with different combinations of the four basic choices and see both the data that gets loaded, in a DataGrid, as a user might see it (on the Data tab); and an XML representation of the information in the DataSet (on the XML tab). The loaded DataSet produces the latter by calling the WriteXml() method with the XmlWriteMode.WriteSchema parameter. It writes the XML representation of the DataSet to a memory stream. It then is read by a StreamReader into a string, and the string is assigned to the Text property of the text box in which you see it displayed.

Experiments that guide you through the different scenarios are prescribed in the Help file for the application (available from its main menu).

Modeless Reads

If you use an untyped DataSet and select Modeless as your Type of Read, the ReadXml() method behaves as follows:

- ▶ It reads the schema from the data file, if there is one.

- ▶ It infers the schema otherwise.

If you use a strongly-typed DataSet and do a modeless read, the schema in the DataSet trumps any schema in the data file.

Writing XML Data

The DataSet's WriteXml() method outputs data and schema information from the DataSet to a Stream, TextWriter, XmlWriter, or file. The application WriteXmlWorkoutMachine, in Figure 15.3, illustrates the effect of the three different available settings of the mode parameter of the DataSet.WriteXml() method:

- ▶ XmlWriteMode.WriteSchema produces an output XML file, Products_WriteSchema.xml, that includes both data and schema metadata.

- ▶ XmlWriteMode.IgnoreSchema produces an output XML file, Products_IgnoreSchema.xml, that includes only data, no schema information.

Writing XML Data

▶ XmlWriteMode.DiffGram produces an output XML file,
Products_DiffGram.xml, that is similar to that produced by
XmlWriteMode.IgnoreSchema but that includes additional information
about changes made to the data since the DataSet was loaded (or since its
AcceptChanges() method was invoked).

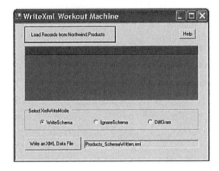

FIGURE 15.3   Main form of the
WriteXmlWorkoutMachine application.

Sample Outputs from `WriteXml()` Calls

The output from WriteXml() is simplest with the mode set to
XmlWriteMode.IgnoreSchema. In this mode, WriteXml() simply writes the
data from a DataSet in XML format. Here's what it produces from a DataSet
loaded with data from the Northwind database's Products table. (Most of the records
have been deleted in the following listing—for the purpose of illustration, a couple
of them are sufficient.)

```
<?xml version="1.0" standalone="yes"?>
<dsProducts xmlns="http://www.tempuri.org/dsProducts.xsd">
  <Products>
    <ProductID>4</ProductID>
    <ProductName>Chef Anton's Cajun Seasoning</ProductName>
    <SupplierID>2</SupplierID>
    <CategoryID>2</CategoryID>
    <QuantityPerUnit>48 - 6 oz jars</QuantityPerUnit>
    <UnitPrice>22.0000</UnitPrice>
    <UnitsInStock>53</UnitsInStock>
    <UnitsOnOrder>0</UnitsOnOrder>
    <ReorderLevel>0</ReorderLevel>
    <Discontinued>false</Discontinued>
  </Products>
  <Products>
    <ProductID>5</ProductID>
```

```
    <ProductName>Chef Anton's Gumbo Mix</ProductName>
    <SupplierID>2</SupplierID>
    <CategoryID>2</CategoryID>
    <QuantityPerUnit>36 boxes</QuantityPerUnit>
    <UnitPrice>21.3500</UnitPrice>
    <UnitsInStock>0</UnitsInStock>
    <UnitsOnOrder>0</UnitsOnOrder>
    <ReorderLevel>0</ReorderLevel>
    <Discontinued>true</Discontinued>
  </Products>

</dsProducts>
```

Here's the same table, written to XML using `XmlWriteMode.WriteSchema` for the mode (and with the same records omitted for brevity). Note the schema information at the beginning of the file:

```
<?xml version="1.0" standalone="yes"?>
<dsProducts xmlns="http://www.tempuri.org/dsProducts.xsd">
  <xs:schema id="dsProducts" targetNamespace="http://www.tempuri.org/dsProducts.xsd"
xmlns:mstns="http://www.tempuri.org/dsProducts.xsd"
xmlns="http://www.tempuri.org/dsProducts.xsd"
xmlns:xs="http://www.w3.org/2001/XMLSchema" xmlns:msdata="urn:schemas-microsoft-
➥com:xml-msdata"
attributeFormDefault="qualified" elementFormDefault="qualified">
    <xs:element name="dsProducts" msdata:IsDataSet="true"
➥msdata:EnforceConstraints="False">
      <xs:complexType>
        <xs:choice maxOccurs="unbounded">
          <xs:element name="Products">
            <xs:complexType>
              <xs:sequence>
                <xs:element name="ProductID" msdata:ReadOnly="true"
➥msdata:AutoIncrement="true" type="xs:int" />
                <xs:element name="ProductName" type="xs:string" />
                <xs:element name="SupplierID" type="xs:int" minOccurs="0" />
                <xs:element name="CategoryID" type="xs:int" minOccurs="0" />
                <xs:element name="QuantityPerUnit" type="xs:string" minOccurs="0" />
                <xs:element name="UnitPrice" type="xs:decimal" minOccurs="0" />
                <xs:element name="UnitsInStock" type="xs:short" minOccurs="0" />
                <xs:element name="UnitsOnOrder" type="xs:short" minOccurs="0" />
                <xs:element name="ReorderLevel" type="xs:short" minOccurs="0" />
                <xs:element name="Discontinued" type="xs:boolean" />
                <xs:element name="Photo" type="xs:base64Binary" minOccurs="0" />
              </xs:sequence>
```

15

Writing XML Data

```
        </xs:complexType>
      </xs:element>
    </xs:choice>
  </xs:complexType>
  <xs:unique name="Constraint1" msdata:PrimaryKey="true">
    <xs:selector xpath=".//mstns:Products" />
    <xs:field xpath="mstns:ProductID" />
  </xs:unique>
</xs:element>
</xs:schema>
<Products>
  <ProductID>4</ProductID>
  <ProductName>Chef Anton's Cajun Seasoning</ProductName>
  <SupplierID>2</SupplierID>
  <CategoryID>2</CategoryID>
  <QuantityPerUnit>48 - 6 oz jars</QuantityPerUnit>
  <UnitPrice>22.0000</UnitPrice>
  <UnitsInStock>53</UnitsInStock>
  <UnitsOnOrder>0</UnitsOnOrder>
  <ReorderLevel>0</ReorderLevel>
  <Discontinued>false</Discontinued>
</Products>
<Products>
  <ProductID>5</ProductID>
  <ProductName>Chef Anton's Gumbo Mix</ProductName>
  <SupplierID>2</SupplierID>
  <CategoryID>2</CategoryID>
  <QuantityPerUnit>36 boxes</QuantityPerUnit>
  <UnitPrice>21.3500</UnitPrice>
  <UnitsInStock>0</UnitsInStock>
  <UnitsOnOrder>0</UnitsOnOrder>
  <ReorderLevel>0</ReorderLevel>
  <Discontinued>truc</Discontinued>
</Products>

</dsProducts>
```

Now suppose that you edit the ProductName for the first record, delete the second record, add a record, and then write the XML using XmlWriteMode.DiffGram for the mode. (Again, for brevity, this omits the same set of about 80 records omitted in the previous two examples).

As with the XML produced with XmlWriteMode.IgnoreSchema, the resulting text includes no schema information. But there is new information at the end of the file: the complete contents of the inserted record (ProductID = 86; note that a value was supplied only for the ProductName, not for other columns), the data from the record with `ProductID = 4` as it existed before `ProductName` was edited, and the complete contents of the record with `ProductID = 5` that was deleted:

```
<?xml version="1.0" standalone="yes"?>
<diffgr:diffgram xmlns:msdata="urn:schemas-microsoft-com:xml-msdata"
➥xmlns:diffgr="urn:schemas-microsoft-com:xml-diffgram-v1">
  <dsProducts xmlns="http://www.tempuri.org/dsProducts.xsd">
    <Products diffgr:id="Products4" msdata:rowOrder="3" diffgr:hasChanges=
    ➥"modified">
      <ProductID>4</ProductID>
      <ProductName>Chef Anton's Bodacious Cajun Seasoning</ProductName>
      <SupplierID>2</SupplierID>
      <CategoryID>2</CategoryID>
      <QuantityPerUnit>48 - 6 oz jars</QuantityPerUnit>
      <UnitPrice>22.0000</UnitPrice>
      <UnitsInStock>53</UnitsInStock>
      <UnitsOnOrder>0</UnitsOnOrder>
      <ReorderLevel>0</ReorderLevel>
      <Discontinued>false</Discontinued>
    </Products>
    <Products diffgr:id="Products82" msdata:rowOrder="81"
➥diffgr:hasChanges="inserted">
      <ProductID>86</ProductID>
      <ProductName>Chef Anton's Four-Alarm Cherry Bomb Sauce</ProductName>
    </Products>
  </dsProducts>
  <diffgr:before>
    <Products diffgr:id="Products4" msdata:rowOrder="3"
➥xmlns="http://www.tempuri.org/dsProducts.xsd">
      <ProductID>4</ProductID>
      <ProductName>Chef Anton's Cajun Seasoning</ProductName>
      <SupplierID>2</SupplierID>
      <CategoryID>2</CategoryID>
      <QuantityPerUnit>48 - 6 oz jars</QuantityPerUnit>
      <UnitPrice>22.0000</UnitPrice>
      <UnitsInStock>53</UnitsInStock>
      <UnitsOnOrder>0</UnitsOnOrder>
      <ReorderLevel>0</ReorderLevel>
      <Discontinued>false</Discontinued>
    </Products>
    <Products diffgr:id="Products5" msdata:rowOrder="4"
➥xmlns="http://www.tempuri.org/dsProducts.xsd">
      <ProductID>5</ProductID>
      <ProductName>Chef Anton's Gumbo Mix</ProductName>
```

15

Writing XML Data

```
      <SupplierID>2</SupplierID>
      <CategoryID>2</CategoryID>
      <QuantityPerUnit>36 boxes</QuantityPerUnit>
      <UnitPrice>21.3500</UnitPrice>
      <UnitsInStock>0</UnitsInStock>
      <UnitsOnOrder>0</UnitsOnOrder>
      <ReorderLevel>0</ReorderLevel>
      <Discontinued>true</Discontinued>
    </Products>
  </diffgr:before>
</diffgr:diffgram>
```

This is an XML representation of the data maintained by ADO.NET inside a `DataSet` that permits such useful operations as those performed by the `DataSet`'s `HasChanges()`, `GetChanges()`, and `AcceptChanges()` methods.

Creating an `XmlReader` Using a `Command` Object

The `Command` class—or, rather, the implementation of the `Command` class supplied by the SqlClient provider (`SqlCommand`)—has one XML-specific method: `ExecuteXmlReader()`. The operation of this command is illustrated in the application ExecuteXmlReader (see Figure 15.4).

FIGURE 15.4 Main form of the ExecuteXmlReader application.

Creating an `XmlReader` Using a `Command` Object

This application assigns a user-specified `CommandText` string to a `SqlCommand` object that connects to the Northwind database. It then invokes the `ExecuteXmlReader()` method of that `Command` object to create an `XmlTextReader` object. Finally, it uses the `XmlTextReader` to walk through the XML representation of the retrieved data, assign that to a string variable, and display the contents of that string to the output window.

Here is the `Click` event handler for the button Run Query & Display Result:

```
Private Sub btnCreateReader_Click(ByVal sender As System.Object, ByVal
➡e As System.EventArgs) Handles btnCreateReader.Click

    Dim conNw As SqlConnection
    Dim cmdSelectProducts As SqlCommand
    Dim XmlReaderX As System.Xml.XmlTextReader
    Dim strMsg As String

    conNw = New SqlConnection
    conNw.ConnectionString = "data source=""(local)"";initial
➡catalog=Northwind;"
    conNw.ConnectionString += "integrated security=SSPI;persist security
➡info=False;"

    cmdSelectProducts = New SqlCommand
    cmdSelectProducts.Connection = conNw
    cmdSelectProducts.CommandText = Me.txtQuery.Text
    Try
        conNw.Open()
        XmlReaderX = cmdSelectProducts.ExecuteXmlReader()
        While XmlReaderX.Read
            XmlReaderX.MoveToContent()
            XmlReaderX.WhitespaceHandling = WhitespaceHandling.None
            If XmlReaderX.NodeType = XmlNodeType.Element Then
                strMsg += XmlReaderX.ReadInnerXml()
            End If
        End While
        XmlReaderX.Close()
    Catch ex As Exception
        MessageBox.Show(ex.Message)
    Finally
        conNw.Close()
    End Try
    Me.txtOutput.Text = strMsg
End Sub
```

15

Creating an XmlReader **Using a** Command **Object**

XmlTextReader is analogous to ADO.NET's DataReader class. It maintains an open connection to a data source and can traverse that data source in a forward-only fashion using a variety of methods (of which the Read method used in the previous code is but one).

Writing Schema Information to a DataSet Using the DataAdapter

Strictly speaking, the DataAdapter.FillSchema() method is not one of the XML-related methods, in that it reads schema information from a back-end database into a DataSet. Nevertheless, because it is so closely related to the other methods discussed in this chapter, it is included in this discussion. The application DataAdapter.FillSchema (see Figure 15.5) illustrates its use.

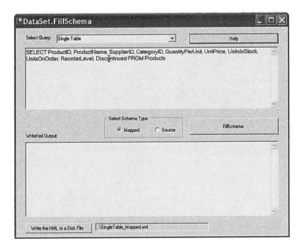

FIGURE 15.5   Main form of the DataAdapterFillSchema application.

This application illustrates the operations of the DataAdapter's FillSchema() method. That method loads a DataSet object with schema information from a database specified in the DataAdapter's Connection property and from tables referenced in its SelectCommand property.

The CommandText for the DataAdapter's SelectCommand is set at runtime and can be controlled by you, the user. You can type in your own command or select from preconstructed CommandText strings using the Select Query combo box. The three preconstructed queries in the supplied application are as follows:

- Single-table
- Parent-child
- Complex relationship

The single-table query selects columns from a single Northwind table, named Products:

```
SELECT ProductID, ProductName, SupplierID, CategoryID, QuantityPerUnit,
UnitPrice, UnitsInStock, UnitsOnOrder, ReorderLevel, Discontinued FROM Products
```

The parent-child query selects columns from an inner join of the Categories and Products tables:

```
SELECT Categories.CategoryID, Categories.CategoryName, Categories.Description,
Products.ProductID, Products.ProductName, Products.UnitPrice
FROM Categories INNER JOIN Products ON Categories.CategoryID = Products.CategoryID
```

The complex relationship query selects columns from a many-way join of the Categories, Products, Suppliers, Order Details, and Orders tables:

```
SELECT Orders.OrderID, Orders.OrderDate, Orders.RequiredDate, Orders.ShippedDate,
[Order Details].OrderID AS Expr1, [Order Details].ProductID,
[Order Details].UnitPrice,
[Order Details].Quantity, [Order Details].Discount, Products.ProductID AS Expr2,
Products.ProductName, Products.SupplierID, Suppliers.SupplierID AS Expr3,
Suppliers.CompanyName, Suppliers.ContactName, Suppliers.ContactTitle,
Categories.CategoryID, Categories.CategoryName, Categories.Description
FROM Categories INNER JOIN Products ON Categories.CategoryID = Products.CategoryID
INNER JOIN Suppliers ON Products.SupplierID = Suppliers.SupplierID
INNER JOIN [Order Details] ON Products.ProductID = [Order Details].ProductID
INNER JOIN Orders ON [Order Details].OrderID = Orders.OrderID
```

When you have specified the `CommandText` for the `SELECT` command, you can invoke the `FillSchema()` method by clicking the FillSchema button. The method is invoked with a schema type parameter value of either `SchemaType.Mapped` or `SchemaType.Source`, according to your selection on the form.

```
If Me.radSchemaType_Mapped.Checked Then
    daQuery.FillSchema(m_dsData, SchemaType.Mapped)
ElseIf Me.radSchemaType_Source.Checked Then
    daQuery.FillSchema(m_dsData, SchemaType.Source)
End If
```

Writing Schema Information to a `DataSet` Using the `DataAdapter`

The first mode setting incorporates any table mappings that have been applied to the `DataAdapter` when loading the schema; the second mode setting ignores table mappings. To illustrate the difference, the code includes a simple mapping of the name of the incoming table:

```
Select Case Me.cboQuery.SelectedIndex
    Case QueryType.SingleTable
        daQuery.TableMappings.Add("Table", "SimpleTable")
    Case QueryType.ParentChild
        daQuery.TableMappings.Add("Table", "ParentChild")
    Case QueryType.ComplexRelationship
        daQuery.TableMappings.Add("Table", "ComplexRelationship")
End Select
```

Note that ADO.NET treats the name of the source table (first) parameter as `Table` when the `CommandType` is `CommandText`, so you must map that name to something else. In the previous code, the table name is mapped to strings that reflect your query selection from the combo box.

If you select the Simple Table query and cause `FillSchema()` to be called with the `SchemaType.Mapped` schema type setting, the first few lines of the generated output will appear as follows:

```
<?xml version="1.0" encoding="utf-16"?>
<xs:schema id="NewDataSet" xmlns="" xmlns:xs="http://www.w3.org/2001/XMLSchema"
➥xmlns:msdata="urn:schemas-microsoft-com:xml-msdata">
  <xs:element name="NewDataSet" msdata:IsDataSet="true">
    <xs:complexType>
      <xs:choice maxOccurs="unbounded">
        <xs:element name="SimpleTable">
```

On the other hand, if you specify that `FillSchema()` should be called with the `SchemaType.Source` schema type setting, the same lines will appear like this:

```
<?xml version="1.0" encoding="utf-16"?>
<xs:schema id="NewDataSet" xmlns="" xmlns:xs="http://www.w3.org/2001/XMLSchema"
➥xmlns:msdata="urn:schemas-microsoft-com:xml-msdata">
  <xs:element name="NewDataSet" msdata:IsDataSet="true">
    <xs:complexType>
      <xs:choice maxOccurs="unbounded">
        <xs:element name="Table">
```

Only the line listed last differs between the two cases.

Applications on the Code Website

Table 15.3 lists the applications associated with this chapter that are included on the code website. The applications are listed in the order in which they were discussed.

TABLE 15.3

Description of Sample Applications

App Name	Description and Notes
ReadAndWriteXmlSchemas	Demonstrates the use of the `DataSet.ReadXmlSchema()` and `DataSet.WriteXmlSchema()` methods

ReadXmlWorkoutMachine	Demonstrates the use of the following `DataSet` methods:
	`ReadXml()`
	`InferXmlSchema()`
	`GetXmlSchema()`
	`GetXml()`

WriteXmlWorkoutMachine	Demonstrates the use of the `DataSet.WriteXml()` method
ExecuteXmlReader	Demonstrates the use of the `Command.ExecuteXmlReader` method
DataSetFillSchema	Demonstrates the use of the `DataSet.FillSchema` method

Other XML Support in the .NET Framework and in Visual Studio

As noted early in this chapter, the integration of XML with .NET goes beyond the integration of XML with ADO.NET. This chapter has focused on the latter, but if you work extensively with XML, you will almost certainly want to explore additional aspects of .NET's support for it. Those aspects include Visual Studio's XML Designer and the facilities of the XML-related namespaces listed in Table 15.4.

TABLE 15.4

XML-Related Namespaces in the .NET Framework

Namespace	Description
`System.Xml`	Provides standards-based support for processing XML.
`System.Xml.Schema`	Contains the XML classes that provide standards-based support for XML Schemas definition language (XSD) schemas.
`System.Xml.Serialization`	Contains classes that are used to serialize objects into XML-format documents or streams.
`System.Xml.Xpath`	Contains the XPath parser and evaluation engine.
`System.Xml.Xsl`	Provides support for Extensible Stylesheet Transformation (XSLT) transforms.

Source of descriptions: MSDN help file for Visual Studio

Summary

In this chapter, you learned about ADO.NET support for and integration of XML. You explored the XML schema files used to persist the specifications for strongly-typed `DataSet`s. You worked with methods of the `DataSet` that enable it to read and write XML schemas and data, and to infer schemas. You also learned about the `DataAdapter`'s `FillSchema` method, used to read schema information from a back-end database into a `DataSet`.

15

Sample applications included on the code website permit you to explore the behavior of each of these methods under different conditions and using different combinations of their options.

Further Reading

Markatos, Dimitrios. "Reading, Storing, and Transforming XML Data in .NET. Dot Net Junkies web site, www.dotnetjunkies.com/Tutorial/99B637B8-8559-4C3E-BFE6-9A7DC5D511A0.dcik.

Sprotty. "A Closer Look at XML Data Binding." MSDN Magazine August 2003. Available online at www.codeproject.com/soap/XML_Data_Binding.asp.

"XML and the DataSet." From the .NET Framework Developer's Guide, http://msdn.microsoft.com/library/default.asp?url=/library/en-us/cpguide/html/cpconxmldataset.asp.

van der Vlist, Eric. "Using W3C XML Schema." www.xml.com/pub/a/2000/11/29/schemas/part1.html.

"Introduction to XML Schema." W3Schools, www.w3schools.com/schema/schema_Intro.asp.

".NET XML XSD, XDR Schemas." TopXML, www.topxml.com/schema/default.asp.

Part IV

Web Applications (ASP.NET)

16 BASIC WEB APPLICATION

IN BRIEF

In this chapter, we get into the fundamentals of Active Server Pages .NET (ASP.NET)—how it works, what it means to create a web application, and how it's different from a traditional desktop-based application. Imagine it as a crash course with everything you need to know to build a basic website. To get a solid grasp of these basics, you'll create several rather rudimentary (although not necessarily simple) applications that can fully showcase the technologies involved, including web forms, controls, and events.

WHAT YOU NEED

SOFTWARE REQUIREMENTS	Windows 2000, Windows XP, or Windows Server 2003 .NET Framework 1.1 SDK Visual Studio .NET 2003 with Visual Basic .NET installed SQL Server or Microsoft Desktop Database Engine (MSDE) Internet Information Server (version 5 or later)
HARDWARE REQUIREMENTS	PC desktop or laptop system
SKILL REQUIREMENTS	Advanced knowledge in HTML Intermediate knowledge in the .NET Framework

BASIC WEB APPLICATION AT A GLANCE

Create a Simple Web Application

A web application—or, more specifically, an ASP.NET application—is simply a collection of files (ASP.NET source files, images, configuration files, and so on) that rely on a web server to execute any intended functionality. Without a web server, ASP.NET files are useless. Among other things, the web server enables you to serve ASP.NET pages over the Internet and let anyone with web access interact with the dynamic content generated by executing the ASP.NET files on the server. Therein lies the largest difference between desktop-based applications and web applications (although many smaller differences and headaches are also introduced by this paradigm, as you will see in this section and subsequent subsections).

Thankfully, ASP.NET tries to minimize these differences, which enables you to migrate fairly easily to web applications if you are a traditional desktop developer. In this section, you will create a minimal ASP.NET application that enables you to experience the fundamentals of ASP.NET.

Preparing the Web Server

This chapter doesn't go into the details of server set up, but you'll need to make sure that you have Internet Information Server version 5 or greater installed and running, and that you have at least one website running. Figure 16.1 shows an example of the IIS console, which you can find under the Administrative Tools control panel if you have it installed. From here, you can create websites, manage them, set security information, and more.

IIS MANAGEMENT IN .NET

Before ASP.NET, the IIS console was the sole way to administer a website, which often was not easy to do (especially when you didn't have direct access to the server). However, .NET has introduced XML configuration files that can do everything the IIS console can do and more. The largest benefit to these files is that they can be easily manipulated and transferred from one computer to another. These configuration files are discussed in Chapter 20, "Website Management."

If you have IIS properly configured, you should notice an inetpub directory in your C: drive. You place all your ASP.NET files in the `C:\inetpub\wwwroot` folder. This directory, known as a *virtual directory*, is exposed via IIS to the Internet for anyone to have access to. You can have multiple virtual directories physically represented by directories all over your computer, and IIS will work with them all.

You can access the website on your computer, through IIS, by going to http://127.0.0.1 in your browser. By default, you should see something like Figure 16.2, depending on your operating system and IIS version. Any subdirectories or virtual directories will be accessed from this root location. For example, the C:\inetpub\wwwroot\dotnet\examples folder can be accessed via http://127.0.0.1/dotnet/examples, and the D:\MyFiles\MyImages folder, if set up as a virtual directory, can be accessed via http://127.0.0.1/MyImages.

Create a Simple Web Application

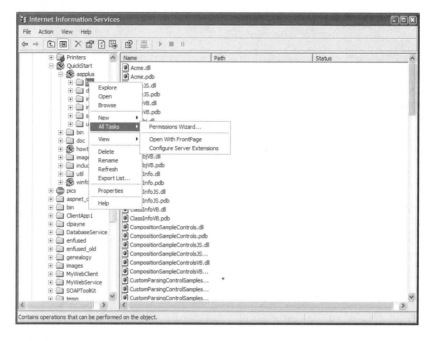

FIGURE 16.1   The IIS Console enables you to manage websites.

NOTE

Remember that ASP.NET files work only through IIS (the next section explains why). If you try to execute these files without going through IIS (in other words, without going through your website at http://127.0.0.1), they won't work properly.

Now that you know where everything is and how to get to it, you need to take one more step before moving to building your site.

Setting Up the Database

One of the most common tasks performed by web applications is to retrieve data from a database and present it to the user for display or modification. As such, you need to get one set up for the sites you'll be creating in subsequent sections.

This chapter doesn't cover the details of setting up your database (see Part III, "Database Programming,"), but you'll need to make sure that you have one set up (the examples use SQL Server). Figure 16.3 shows the created database in Enterprise Manager.

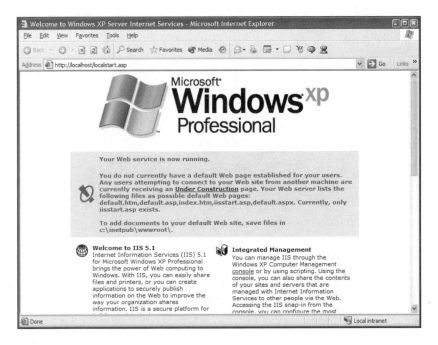

FIGURE 16.2   The IIS default start page.

16

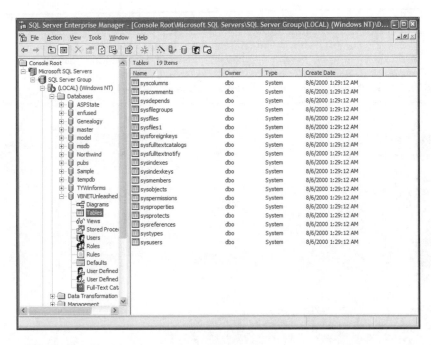

FIGURE 16.3   Make sure you have a database ready for your ASP.NET sites.

Create a Simple Web Application

For these examples, you'll need to create a single table, as described in Table 16.1. Save it as tblWebBlog (see the `tblWebBlog.sql` file for the SQL code to generate this table).

TABLE 16.1

tblWebBlog

Field Name	Data Type	Description
fldIdentity	Int	Primary key, identity
fldAuthor	Varchar(50)	Field to hold author name
fldBlurb	Varchar(1000)	Field to hold journal entries
fldDate	DateTime	Default (getdate()), date of entry

16

Creating Your Home Page Blog

The most common first web page that a person builds is a basic home page, so this example uses that to illustrate a basic ASP.NET site. On this home page, you will include basic welcoming information, blogging capabilities, and some links. When you understand the source code, you'll examine how the ASP.NET engine can deliver the page differently than you're used to with desktop-based applications. Listing 16.1 shows the code in its entirety; discussion follows.

NOTE

Because ASP.NET files are plain text, you can use any text editor that you want to create these files, from Notepad or Microsoft Word (be sure save the file as a plain text document and not a DOC file) to development tools such as Visual Studio or ASP.NET Web Matrix. Use whatever you are most comfortable with. All examples after this first one use Visual Studio .NET.

LISTING 16.1

Your Home Page Blog

1
```
<%@ Page Language="VB" %>
<%@ Import Namespace="System.Data" %>
<%@ Import Namespace="System.Data.SqlClient" %>
```

2
```
<script runat="server">
    sub Page_Load(Sender as Object, e as EventArgs)
        dim i as integer

        'set up connection
        dim conBlog as new SqlConnection _
            ("Data Source=localhost;user id=sa;" & _
```

LISTING 16.1
Continued

```
            "Initial Catalog=VBNETUnleashed;")

        'get data
        dim cmdBlog as new SqlDataAdapter _
            ("select * from tblWebBlog", conBlog)

        'fill dataset
        dim dsBlog as DataSet = new DataSet()
        cmdBlog.Fill(dsBlog)

        'display data
        for i = 0 to dsBlog.Tables(0).Rows.Count - 1
            lblBlurb.Text += dsBlog.Tables(0).Rows(i)("fldDate").ToString() & _
            "<BR>" & dsBlog.Tables(0).Rows(i)("fldBlurb").ToString() + "<p>"
        next i

        DataBind()
end sub
</script>
```

```
<html>
<head><title>My Blog</title></head>

<body>
<table bgcolor="#FFDD55" width=100%>
<tr>
    <td><font size=5>My First ASP.NET Site</font><p></td>
</table>
<p>
Welcome. You are user <%# Session.SessionID %>.<br>
It is currently <%# DateTime.Now %>.<br>
Your IP address is <%# Request.ServerVariables("Remote_Addr") %>.<p>
<hr>
<table>
<tr>
    <td width=200 valign=top align=right>
        <a href="">My Friend's site</a><br>
        <a href="">My Other Friend's site</a><br>
        <a href="http://www.asp.net">Official ASP.NET site</a><br>
    </td>
```

16

3

Create a Simple Web Application

LISTING 16.1
Continued

```
      <td>
          <asp:Label id="lblBlurb" runat="server"/>
      </td>
</tr>
</table>
```

Before you actually create the application, let's break this code into three sections: the page declaration block **1**, the code declaration block **2**, and the HTML portion **3**.

The first section **1** is responsible for providing your ASP.NET page and VB .NET compiler with information it needs to function properly. The @ Page directive on the first line really only tells you which language you're using here; it's VB. NET in this case, but you could use C# or any other .NET–compliant language. This directive is used more extensively in subsequent examples. The next couple of lines import other .NET namespaces using the Import keyword, just like any other VB .NET class. Note the use of brackets <% and %>; these are used to delimit code that can be compiled in many places outside the code declaration block in ASP.NET, so you'll get used to them quickly.

The code declaration block in the second section **2** is where most of the action happens. Most important, the VB .NET code that you write goes in here. There are three things to note: The entire block is enclosed in a <script runat="server"> tag, which might look somewhat familiar if you are versed in HTML, the single method called Page_Load, and code that retrieves data from the database you set up in the previous section. Most of all the code that you write in ASP.NET pages will be placed in the <script> block. The runat="server" attribute tells the ASP.NET engine that the enclosed code should be processed by the server instead of the regular client-side script, such as JavaScript. You'll see this more later. The last part of this block is fairly straightforward to understand (except the bits about lblBlurb and DataBind, which are discussed in the next two sections) if you've covered Part III.

Finally, the third section **3** contains mostly plain HTML. The parts to note are the lines with <%#...%> tags, which contain some more executable code, and the <asp:Label /> tags, which create an ASP.NET web control. Again, you'll learn more about these in a moment.

If you're using Visual Studio .NET, create a new ASP.NET application at http://localhost/VBNetUnleashed/listing1601. View the source code of the automatically generated WebForm1.aspx file (ignore the code-behind file, WebForm1.aspx.vb, for now) and replace the code with Listing 16.1. Press Ctrl+F8 to build the project and view it in your browser.

If you're using Notepad or something similar, save this code as `WebForm1.aspx` in the C:\inetpub\wwwroot\VBNetUnleashed\listing1601 directory (note that all ASP.NET pages end in the extension `.aspx`), and view it in your browser at http://127.0.0.1/ VBNetUnleashed/listing1601/WebForm1.aspx. You should see the page in Figure 16.4.

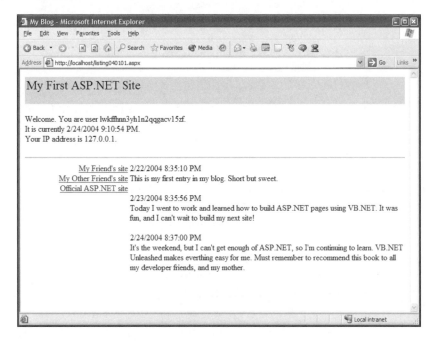

FIGURE 16.4   Your first website in ASP.NET.

Remember that ASP.NET applications are delivered over the Internet in a client/server relationship, also known as the request/response model. The server contains the source code and handles any processing, and the client requests the data, displays it to the user, and sends requests back to the server again, if necessary. The client (your web browser) is really just a display tool. When you request the page through http://127.0.0.1, your computer is acting as both the client and the server, but keep in mind that the typical setup will have at least two computers located apart from each other. Figure 16.5 illustrates this paradigm.

Back on the server, you might have guessed that the code in the code declaration block executed automatically and that any code enclosed in `<%` and `%>` was executed as it was reached. But what do each of these pieces mean and how does this all fit into the .NET Framework?

Create a Simple Web Application

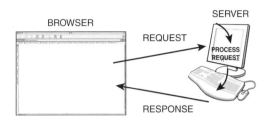

FIGURE 16.5   The request/response model of ASP.NET pages.

The first thing to know is that although it might not appear so at first, this file is compiled just like every other VB .NET application: The ASP.NET engine handles it automatically when you request the file through IIS at runtime. And because it is compiled, every piece of the file has some form of representation in the .NET Framework. In fact, an ASP.NET page is simply an extension of the `System.Web.UI.Page` class. Even the HTML portion of the file is compiled into an instance of the `System.Web.UI.LiteralControl` class. It is important to note the execution order of these objects after they are compiled, but that is covered in a moment.

Compiling the code is obviously a performance hit, so ASP.NET compiles it once and stores the results in its own cache. The compiled data then is executed; the source file remains untouched. If ASP.NET detects that you've made a change to the source file, it recompiles the source and begins again. Thus, you get the benefits of fully compiled code without having to worry about doing it yourself.

Table 16.2 illustrates the steps of execution for this page. Each step (with the exception of compilation) has an associated event that you can hook into to control page functionality. For example, the `Page_Load` method handles the event described in step 5.

TABLE 16.2

The Order of Execution for ASP.NET Files

Step	Description
1.	The ASP.NET file is processed and compiled just like any VB. NET application.
2.	Page initialization occurs.
3.	Viewstate is loaded (this is covered in Chapter 18, "State Management").
4.	Form postback data is processed (discussed in the next section and in Chapter 17, "Data Binding").
5.	The page, including any included objects and controls, is loaded and the state is restored. Generally, this is where a lot of your executable code will go.
6.	Events are raised, based on postback data.
7.	Any postback events are handled.

TABLE 16.2

Continued

Step	Description
8.	Prerendering occurs (sort of a last chance to make any changes before rendering).
9.	The viewstate is saved as form information.
10.	The ASP.NET page output is rendered to the browser (in other words, the output of the executed program is sent to the client).
11.	Dispose of any created objects (similar to the dispose procedure in any VB. NET application).
12.	Any last cleanup is performed.

Quite a few steps are involved, but with the exception of step 1, it happens for every ASP.NET page every time you request it in your browser. Knowing this process is key to being able to make your ASP.NET pages do everything you want them to. In essence, ASP.NET comes with a built-in execution engine that you would typically have to build yourself in a standalone desktop application.

> **TIP**
>
> At this point, it's probably a good idea to browse the documentation that came with the .NET Framework SDK, if you installed it, and take a look at the various events that can be handled. For most of these events, you can simply create a method with the name `Page_eventName` to handle it and perform additional functionality.

ASP.NET also automatically maps or "wires" (these wires can be thought of as event delegates) certain method names to the events listed in Table 16.2. For example, you can handle the event described in step 2 with the `Page_Init` method, step 5 with the `Page_Load` method, and step 12 with the `Page_Unload` method. In this way, you just need to decide where your code fits into the process and find the appropriate method to use.

Most events in ASP.NET also have the same signature; they pass two parameters: an instance of the `System.Object` class that represents the object that generated the event, and an instance of the `System.EventArgs` class that contains any extra information about the event. You'll see the same parameter list that you do here many times. The exceptions are discussed when the different types of events are covered.

After these steps are enumerated, the application can be put into the same process list, shown in Table 16.3.

16

Create a Simple Web Application

TABLE 16.3

Listing 16.1 Broken into ASP.NET Steps

Step	Description
1.	The compiler compiles the source code, references any necessary namespaces, translates the HTML portions into `LiteralControl` objects, and so on
2.	This step is not used here.
3.	Very little viewstate information must be loaded, so this step is ignored here.
4.	There is no form postback data to process.
5.	A database connection is made, and some data is retrieved and displayed.
6.	No postback data exists.
7.	No postback data exists.
8.	The page is being readied for rendering.
9.	The viewstate is saved as HTML data that will be rendered in the next step.
10.	The output of the execution is sent to the browser (which, at that point, is displayed in your window).
11.	This step is not used here.
12.	This step is not used here.

Although knowing the ASP.NET execution process is immensely helpful and enables you to do a lot of interesting things, the real power comes into play with web forms and web controls.

Building Web Forms

The web forms framework is the ASP.NET way of interacting with your web visitor. The stateless model of the request/response model is now simplified to one that is more familiar to desktop-based developers. It also works very similarly to Windows Forms, described in Part II, "Windows Forms Applications," so if you've covered that material, much of this will seem familiar.

This section expands on the web blog example from the previous section and adds interactivity to the page. This enables you to showcase the features of web forms and learn how to deal with user input in ASP.NET. Also, because you got a chance to write the code by hand in the last section, you'll use Visual Studio .NET's (VS .NET) rapid-deployment tools to build the next examples more quickly. But first, you need to understand the difference between request/response and web forms; it will help down the line.

Handling Data over the Web

If all you ever did with a website was request a simple web page and display it in your browser, things would be very simple. But the Web is much more powerful than that.

It enables users to exchange data with servers in many forms. Without sending information, you wouldn't be able to shop online, join any discussion groups, or do any of the other many things you've become accustomed to. A key point in any web technology such as ASP.NET is its capability to handle such sent data.

The problem arises in how to handle this data. You have to learn to deal with data as it comes from many different locations, in different types, and in unpredictable formats. That's not to mention that it is often not enough just to collect data from a user; you might also need to present that data *back* to the user to edit or verify. The Web is *stateless* and disconnected, which means that when a person requests one web page right after another, there is no way to maintain any data between the pages or the states of those pages, or even know that it is the same user who is hitting the different pages. When a person requests a page and renders it in the browser, the transaction is over, and any information about that user is immediately forgotten. Thus, you have to take special care that you find some way to present the user with a cohesive experience across different web pages or even on a single page.

This isn't to say that it can't be done. Through HTML forms and HTTP cookies, you can pass data back and forth, with or without the user's knowledge, to help you maintain state and cohesiveness. But again, the intricacies and uncertainties of doing so are often complex and end up getting in the way of the actual *raison d'être* for the application. You also still suffer from the limited knowledge that the server has when dealing with the data. Figure 16.6 illustrates the disconnected nature of the Web.

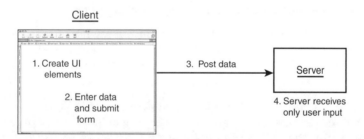

FIGURE 16.6   The server knows only the limited information that the client gives it.

Enter ASP.NET web forms. One of the main motivations for web forms and ASP.NET is to hide all of this complexity from you as the developer so that you can focus on building the meaningful parts of your application instead of handling the semantics of a request/response model. You can still deal with this nitty-gritty if you need to, but you'll find that it is often much simpler just to let the web forms framework handle it for you.

Another related hazard of web development is that you can never be sure what your users are running on their end. Many different browsers and operating systems are in use today, and creating a consistent interface across all of them can be a chore.

Web forms and the associated controls *automatically* adjust their output to suit the client's system. You can take advantage of browser-specific features to tailor and enhance your application, but all of the basics are handled for you.

Finally, through web controls, you can provide a very interactive and easy-to-use user interface (UI) with a minimum of effort. The following section takes a look at some of these web controls, but you'll see even more later in this section.

Using Code-Behind Forms

Before you get too far building ASP.NET pages, it's helpful to learn the different methods of building them. Listing 16.1 highlighted one way: a single .aspx file with all your code (UI and otherwise). A lot of people prefer this method because it is easy to manage and it mimics the Windows Forms development paradigm.

However, there are a couple drawbacks. First, there's no separation of user interface code and functional code. If you haven't had much web development experience this might not mean much to you, but being able to separate the UI from the functional code means that you can easily have different people working on the same application without one person having to know how to do everything. A VB .NET developer can focus on writing VB .NET code, while a design or HTML guru can create the UI separately. Second, when you distribute the application in the single-file model, you have to distribute your source code as well. Remember that ASP.NET source files are not compiled until runtime, which means that anyone who has your .aspx file has access to your code, a potential security and intellectual property issue.

Thus, ASP.NET enables you to use *code-behind* forms. In essence, a code-behind form simply allows you to separate the UI from the functional code (see Figure 16.7). To understand them more deeply, however, it's helpful to take a step back and look at how the ASP.NET engine treats ASP.NET pages.

Technically, an ASP.NET page is any object that derives, *directly or indirectly*, from the System.Web.UI.Page class. When you create a single-file ASP.NET page such as the one in Listing 16.1, the code is compiled and automatically inherits from the Page class. But this definition means that you can have any number of intermediate classes in between the Page class and your .aspx file; you just have to make sure that the inheritance chain from your .aspx file leads back to the Page class. Figure 16.8 illustrates this concept.

First, create your code-behind file; it is no different than a normal VB .NET source file, and it even ends in the .vb extension and goes in the same directory where your .aspx file would have been. In this file, you declare and instantiate all the UI controls and objects you'll use in your application, as well as write all the functional logic of your application.

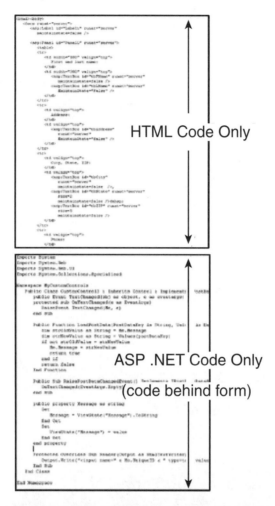

FIGURE 16.7 ASP.NET enables you to completely separate the UI from the logic with code-behind forms.

Then, in your `.aspx` file, you inherit from your newly created code-behind file and create the HTML portion of your application just like you've been doing. Any UI portions of this file that require interactivity should then derive from the objects you declared in the code-behind file. When you complete this section, you'll understand more fully how this works.

If this sounds more complicated than the single-file paradigm, that's because it is. However, a tool such as VS .NET actually handles much of the complexity for you. The code-behind is automatically created, and your `.aspx` file automatically inherits from the code-behind. The code-behind paradigm is actually the preferred method in VS .NET, so you should have no problem diving in.

16

Building Web Forms

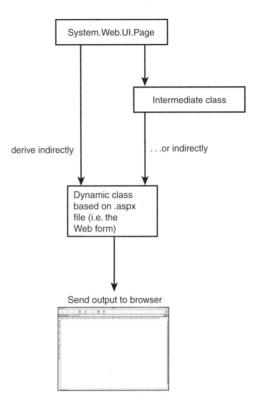

FIGURE 16.8   An ASP.NET page must derive directly or indirectly from the `System.Web.UI.Page` class.

Creating an Interactive Web Form

In this section, you create a data-entry system for the blog page developed in the previous section using web forms. You'll see exactly how the web forms processing model works and how it hides the complexities of dealing with the request/response model.

Create a new ASP.NET project in Visual Studio .NET at http://localhost/ VBNetUnleashed/listing1602. Make sure that the Show All Files option is checked in the Project menu. You'll notice a plus next to the default form: `WebForm1.aspx`. Expand it, and you'll notice a file called `WebForm1.aspx.vb`; this is your code-behind file, which is discussed in more detail in a moment. Expand the code-behind file, and you'll see a `WebForm1.aspx.resx` file, the automatically generated resource file similar to the one that VS .NET generated for your Windows Forms applications.

Because VS .NET is a visual tool, you'll create as much of this ASP.NET application as possible with the interactive wizards. You'll still be creating and writing code, but VS .NET handles a lot of work for you. Drag a `SqlConnection` object and a `SqlCommand` object onto the page, and rename them `conBlog` and `cmdBlog`, respectively. Use the wizard to generate your connection string for your `SqlConnection` object.

In the HTML portion of your `WebForm1.aspx` file, use the code from Listing 16.2. Note that you can either enter this code by hand or use VS .NET's visual tools to drag and drop these controls onto your page. The HTML code is presented in its entirety in this way to make things easier to discuss.

LISTING 16.2
An Interactive Web Form

```
<%@ Page Language="vb" AutoEventWireup="false" Codebehind="WebForm1.aspx.vb"    1
  Inherits="listing1602.WebForm1"%>
<html>
<head><title>My Blog</title></head>

<body>
<table bgcolor="#FFDD55" width=100%>
<tr>
    <td><font size=5>My First Web forms Page</font><p></td>
</tr>
</table>

<asp:Label id="lblMessage" runat="server" ForeColor="red" />            2

<form runat="server">
<table>
<tr>
    <td valign=top align=right>Author:</td>
    <td>
        <asp:TextBox id="txtAuthor" runat="server"/>                    3
    </td>
</tr>
<tr>
    <td valign=top align=right>Blurb:</td>
    <td>
        <asp:TextBox id="txtBlurb" runat="server"                      4
            Rows=5 Columns=50
            TextMode="Multiline"/>
    </td>
</tr>
```

16

Building Web Forms

LISTING 16.2
Continued

```
<tr>
    <td align=center colspan=2>
        <asp:Button id="btnSubmit" runat="server"
            Text="Save!"/>
    </td>
</tr>
</table>
</form>
</body></html>
```

Note that, unlike Listing 16.1, this file has no VB .NET code or script declaration block; it's all in the code-behind. The only real code is in the first line █**1**. Here is where you tell your `.aspx` file to inherit from the code-behind using the `Codebehind` and `Inherits` attributes. The first tells you the location of the source of the code-behind file (that VS .NET automatically generated for you). The latter is the name of the class in the code-behind file that derives from the `Page` class, which your `.aspx` file, in turn, derives from.

You've seen the HTML form tag with the attribute `runat="server"` before. Basically, it tells the ASP.NET engine that when the page is requested, the object in question should actually be created as a server-side object instead of as a regular HTML element. In this case, appending `runat="server"` to a regular HTML form tag causes the server to create an instance of the `System.Web.UI.HtmlControls.HtmlForm` class.

This `HtmlForm` instance is the web form itself. It contains all the functionality necessary to provide the benefits of web forms (more on that in a moment).

The next interesting bits of code are in the next four highlighted sections. Again, you see the `runat="server"` tag, but the rest of the code doesn't look like normal HTML. These are instances of ASP.NET web controls, which are just more classes in the `System.Web.UI.WebControls` namespace.

The code in these lines represents a different method of instantiating objects than you might be used to. You use the special `ASP:controlName` HTML tag to tell the ASP.NET engine to create an instance of an object and what object exactly you are trying to create: in this case, a label (`System.Web.UI.WebControls.Label` █**2**), two text boxes (`System.Web.UI.WebControls.TextBox` █**3** █**4**), and a button (`System.Web.UI.WebControls.Button` █**5**). The other attributes in these pieces of code are simply properties of these classes. This method of creating controls in ASP.NET is referred to here as the HTML syntax version, which differs from creating them programmatically as you've been used to. The two methods are functionally identical, and you can use either one. The HTML syntax way is sometimes easier for developers who migrate from plain-jane HTML pages, and it also enables you to easily separate UI from functionality. Creating web controls programmatically is covered later.

Next, view the code for the code-behind file `WebForm1.aspx.vb`, and add the code
in Listing 16.3 (alternatively, you can double-click the btnSubmit button in design
view of your `WebForm1.aspx` file and let VS .NET create the method for you—you
just enter the "meat" of the method yourself).

LISTING 16.3
Your Event Handler

```
Private Sub btnSubmit_Click(ByVal sender As System.Object, _
    ByVal e As System.EventArgs) Handles btnSubmit.Click
    conBlog.Open()

    'insert data
    cmdBlog.Connection = conBlog
    cmdBlog.CommandText = "INSERT INTO tblWebBlog (fldAuthor, fldBlurb) _
        VALUES (@Author, @Blurb)"
    cmdBlog.Parameters.Add(New SqlParameter("@Author", txtAuthor.Text))
    cmdBlog.Parameters.Add(New SqlParameter("@Blurb", txtBlurb.Text))

    cmdBlog.ExecuteNonQuery()
    conBlog.Close()

    lblMessage.Text = "Data saved!"
End Sub
```

Because VS .NET generated all the initialization code for you, all you have to do is
create the method that actually adds your data to the database, which is done simply
by using your `SqlCommand` object. Notice that this method uses the `Handles`
syntax to handle the button's `Click` event just like any other .NET application (also
note the same parameter list from Listing 16.1). ASP.NET also enables you to specify
the event handler in HTML syntax. You would modify the code in Listing 16.2 to add
the attribute:

```
OnClick="btnSubmit_Click"
```

Technically, the `OnClick` attribute is the event delegate for the button's `Click`
event. This is functionally identical to using the `Handles` syntax in Listing 16.3. You
can handle any object's events in this manner. You'll examine web controls further in
the next section.

Finally, you need to import the `System.Data.SqlClient` namespace at the top of
your code-behind file:

```
Imports System.Data.SqlClient
```

16

NOTE

The `runat="server"` tag is very important, especially when it comes to web controls. Without this attribute, the ASP.NET engine treats the code you've written, whether it looks like a web control or not, as plain HTML. This means that it doesn't provide any functionality and won't work the way you expect it to. Don't forget `runat="server"`.

Also note that all ASP.NET web controls require a closing HTML tag as well:

```
<asp:Label ...></asp:Label>
```

This can be shortened to the following:

```
<asp:Label ... />
```

Take a minute to examine what you now know so far. The page itself is represented by the Page class. Inside the page are a few web controls that are represented by the HtmlForm, TextBox, and Button classes. Finally, the rest of the HTML is represented by instances of the LiteralControl class. Figure 16.9 illustrates this relationship. Even though you haven't yet covered all of the different code and controls in an ASP.NET web form, you should be able to dissect the controls on a page.

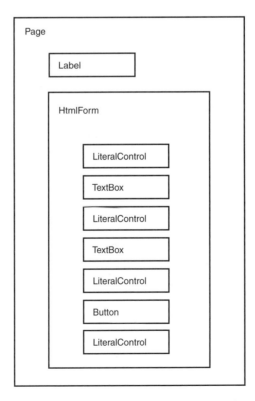

FIGURE 16.9 How the code translates into ASP.NET objects.

Now you're ready to execute the page. Right-click on your `WebForm1.aspx` file and select Build and Browse (alternatively, after your project is built, you can access it from your browser from http://127.0.0.1/VBNetUnleashed/listing1602/WebForm1.aspx). Enter some data in the text boxes and click the Save button. Figure 16.10 shows the results. If you then re-execute Listing 16.1, you'll see a new entry in the blog.

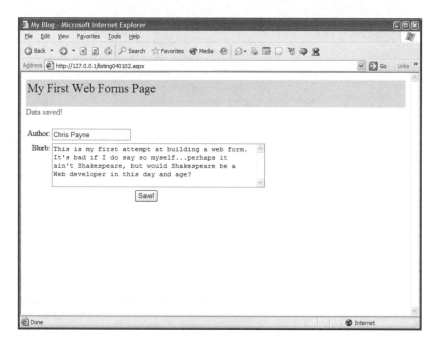

FIGURE 16.10   The output from your web forms page.

If you are familiar with traditional HTML development, it might help to know that the button click actually generates a form submission, also known as a *postback*. The ASP.NET page receives this postback and, via the various controls and parameters (and autogenerated hidden HTML form tags) in the page, knows to execute the `btnSubmit_Click` method. Much of the power of web forms becomes apparent in this postback.

You might notice something a bit odd: The text that you entered in the text boxes remains after you submitted the form. Typically, in an HTML form, the text would have disappeared. This feature is ASP.NET's viewstate management at work. It essentially remembers what a user has entered into the forms and repopulates the fields automatically (remember step 3 of the process described in Table 16.3). This feature can save a lot of headaches for the user when having to reenter data, and it makes things easier to manage for the developer as well. Viewstate is discussed further in Chapter 18.

Building Web Forms

The process covered so far should be very logical and familiar if you worked with Windows Forms applications in Part II. Web forms were designed to provide a common development experience to those familiar with other .NET development and to minimize the distractions of typical web development. Note that nowhere in this process did you have to worry about the request/response model or dealing with the transmission of HTML data back and forth from client to server. It actually appears like the event-driven model of desktop-based programming. To the developer, it appears that your application is interacting directly with the user rather than across the Internet, which makes it easier to visualize and create applications. Exactly how ASP.NET does this is covered in the next section on web controls.

So, to recap, a web form in code is simply an HTML form tag with a `runat="server"` attribute. But in execution, the web form becomes an instance of the `HtmlForm` class, which provides many built-in features that make web development easier. The simple addition of `runat="server"` might seem rather insignificant, but it enables you to participate in the viewstate management, hides the complexities of Internet transactions, and deals with the unknowns of client browsers. All of this serves to make development faster and more intuitive for the developer.

Code-behind forms use the object-oriented aspects of ASP.NET to enable you to separate UI from logic code. You'll be using them from now on in this book.

CODE-BEHINDS IN THE REAL WORLD

You might not actually find code-behinds used that often in the real world aside from examples. This is because they are a new paradigm that not many people have yet adopted (because they are used to doing it another way or because it introduces more complexity) and because, unfortunately, much typical development still requires a developer who is proficient in VB .NET to build the entire applications, including the UI. A designer who is not proficient in .NET doesn't often have room in building the applications, aside from creating graphical mockups.

Code-behinds are still very useful, however, and are suited for this book because they simplify the presentation.

Another benefit of web forms is the capability to use web controls, which enable you to develop rich, full-featured UIs with minimal effort. These controls are discussed next.

Using Web Controls to Add Functionality to Pages

You've already seen a few of the simplest web controls in action: `Label`, `TextBox`, and `Button`. But there are more than 25 more, and that's not including HTML controls. They range from simple to very complex, but, in the end, all are intended to represent various facets of traditional web user interfaces.

In this section, you'll further expand the web blog example, adding a plethora of web controls, and learn how easy it is to make full-featured UIs.

Getting to Know Web Controls

As mentioned previously, most web controls are simply classes in the `System.Web.UI.WebControls` namespace, and they all inherit from the base `Object` class. This means that they have certain features that you should already be familiar with. In addition, most inherit from the `System.Web.UI.WebControls.WebControl` class, which provides basic functionality that is common to normal HTML elements. In the simplest sense, they all represent some piece of HTML code, from an input text box to a table, to a hyperlink. The point is that none of these is difficult to use, and when you use one, you have a good understanding of how to use any other. Table 16.4 lists the various web controls for use in ASP.NET.

16

TABLE 16.4

The Web Controls

Class Name	Description
AdRotator	A component used to display images according to a percentage schedule
Button	Typically an HTML Submit button
Calendar	A calendar
CheckBox	An HTML check box
CheckBoxList	A group of CheckBoxes
CompareValidator	A control to ensure that a user-entered value matches a specified value or other control
CustomValidator	A control that enables you to validate user input with a custom-written function
DataList	A templated control to display data in a table format
DataGrid	A templated control to display data in a table format; more advanced than the DataList
DropDownList	A drop-down list of selectable items
HyperLink	An HTML hyperlink
Image	An HTML image
ImageButton	An HTML form image button
Label	A placeholder for text; represented in most browsers by the span HTML element
LinkButton	An HTML form submit button, but appears as a hyperlink instead of a button
ListBox	Similar to DropDownList, but allows multiple selections and can statically display more than one item at a time
Panel	A container for groups of other controls (for example, a group of check boxes)

Using Web Controls to Add Functionality to Pages

TABLE 16.4

Continued

Class Name	Description
PlaceHolder	A container for other controls; generally used to hold dynamically created controls instead of predefined groups
RadioButton	An HTML radio button
RadioButtonList	A group of RadioButtons
RangeValidator	A control to validate that a user entry is within a certain range of values
RegularExpressionValidator	A control to validate that a user entry matches a regular expression
Repeater	A templated control to display collections of data in a user-defined format; more flexible than DataList
RequiredFieldValidator	A control to ensure that a form field contains a user-entered value
Table	An HTML table
TableCell	An HTML table cell
TableRow	An HTML table row
TextBox	An HTML form text box
ValidationSummary	A summary of any user-entry validation errors on a page

Most of these, such as the RadioButton, Table, and HyperLink controls, are simply .NET representations of regular HTML elements. A few, such as the Calendar, are much more complex and render more than a simple HTML element. The Repeater, DataList, and DataGrid are known as *data-binding* controls, and are the most complex of the group. Because they provide so much functionality, discussion of these three is reserved until Chapter 17.

Remember that all of these control can be created in their simplest forms with the <asp:*controlName* runat="server"/> syntax. For example:

```
<asp:ListBox runat="server"/>
<asp:RadioButtonList runat="server"/>
```

Of course, you'll often want to do more with these controls than simply create them, but you get the point.

TIP

Your skill as a developer often relies on how well you know the various web controls. It is a good habit to examine the documentation for these controls because you'll often discover things about them that you didn't know could be done before (especially regarding their events).

In addition to the controls in Table 16.4, you can turn any regular HTML element into a web control—or, more precisely, into an HTML server control—simply by adding `runat="server"` in your HTML code. For example, this:

```
<input type="text" id="tbTest" value="Testing!">
```

can become a server-side object by adding `runat="server"`:

```
<input type="text" id="tbTest" value="Testing!" runat="server">
```

Now you can access this text box programmatically through VB .NET code and control its properties just as you would any other object:

```
<script runat="server">
sub Page_Load(Sender as Object, e as EventArgs)
    tbTest.Value = "This is a server control!"
end sub
</script>
```

16

The control now participates in viewstate management and has all the other benefits of web forms. In this case, the text box becomes an instance of the `System.Web.UI.HtmlControls.HtmlInputText` object, which is very similar to the `System.Web.UI.WebControls.TextBox` control that you've already used; they both do the same thing, but they have a few different properties.

You have the two sets of controls (HTML server controls and web controls) at your call. HTML server controls are a bit simpler, with less functionality, and you might want to use them if you're most comfortable with regular HTML. Web controls, on the other hand, have more functionality and adhere to the .NET document object model, so you should use these if you're familiar with any other .NET programming. The web controls are used in the examples here; the one notable exception is the web form object itself, which technically is an HTML server control (`System.Web.UI.HtmlControls.HtmlForm`).

NOTE

Just because you *can* turn everything in your HTML code into a server control doesn't mean that you *should*. Server controls require more processing and memory usage on the server; if you don't need to access the control programmatically, it's better to use a plain HTML element instead.

Now that you know a bit more about web controls, you will create a UI with them.

Using Web Controls to Add Functionality to Pages

Building a Full-Featured UI

The data entry tool from Listings 16.2 and 16.3 can be expanded with a few new web controls to make the page more interactive.

To do this, you can start with the visual aspects. Drag new `SqlConnection` and `SqlCommand` objects onto your `WebForm1.aspx` in design mode, and set them up like you did in the previous section. Also drag a `SqlDataAdapter` object and use the wizard to specify the following SQL statement:

```
select * from tblWebBlog WHERE fldDate BETWEEN @datStart AND @datEnd
```

In the Advanced options of the wizard, deselect Generate Insert, Update, and Delete Statements; they aren't necessary.

Next, you create the HTML portion of the file, as shown in Listing 16.4.

LISTING 16.4
Enhanced Data Entry with Web Controls

```
<%@ Page Language="vb" Codebehind="WebForm1.aspx.vb"
    Inherits="listing1604.WebForm1"%>
<html>
<head><title>My Blog</title></head>
<body>
<table bgcolor="#ffdd55" width="100%">
<tr>
    <td><font size="5">My First Web Controls</font><p></p>
    </td>
</tr>
</table>
<asp:Label id="lblMessage" runat="server" ForeColor="red" />
<form runat="server" ID="Form1">
<table>
<tr>
    <td valign="top" align="right">Author:</td>
    <td>
        <asp:TextBox id="txtAuthor" runat="server" />
        <asp:RequiredFieldValidator id="vdrAuthor"
            ControlToValidate="tbAuthor" Display="Dynamic"
            ErrorMessage="You forgot your name" runat="server" />
    </td>
    <td rowspan="3">
1       <asp:Calendar id="cdarDates" runat="server" />
    </td>
</tr>
<tr>
```

LISTING 16.4
Continued

```
        <td valign="top" align="right">Blurb:</td>
        <td>
            <asp:TextBox id="txtBlurb" runat="server" Rows="5"
                Columns="50" TextMode="Multiline" />
            <asp:RequiredFieldValidator id="vdrBlurb"
                ControlToValidate="tbBlurb" Display="Dynamic"
                ErrorMessage="You forgot your blurb" runat="server" />
        </td>
    </tr>
    <tr>
        <td align="middle" colspan="2">
            <asp:Button id="btnSubmit" runat="server" Text="Add Blurb!" />
        </td>
    </tr>
    </table>
    <asp:Label id="lblBlurb" runat="server" />                        2
    </form>
</body></html>
```

This code is very similar to Listing 16.3, but with quite a few new web controls here: Labels, TextBoxes, RequiredFieldValidators, a Calendar, and a Button. The first Label, the two TextBoxes, and the Button are identical to those in Listing 16.2; they enable the user to enter data into your tblWebBlog table.

RequiredFieldValidators are used to ensure that the user has actually entered something into an HTML form field, thus preventing any errors that might arise due to unpredictable user input. Validation controls can work client-side; if the user hasn't entered anything, submission of the form stops and an error message is displayed immediately, without having to make a trip to the server. Notice the ControlToValidate property. This tells the validator to watch the txtAuthor text box control and make sure that the user enters some data before allowing the form to be submitted. Through this property, you can tell the validator to watch any control anywhere on the page, no matter where it is located. You can even have multiple validation controls watching a single web control (but not the other way around). The ErrorMessage property is the message that appears to the user if this validation fails.

Finally, the Display="Dynamic" property tells the control to use dynamic HTML to insert the error message into the text when necessary. When the message is not present, your page layout appears just as if you didn't use the validator. If you set the Display property to Static, space is allocated on the page for your error message even when it isn't shown, which can alter the layout of your page. You might want to experiment with this property to get the desired look. The validator follows the exact same syntax; most validation controls will, in fact, look similar.

Using Web Controls to Add Functionality to Pages

VALIDATION ON THE CLIENT AND SERVER

Validation controls are not just client-side tools; you don't have to rely on them to perform all of their functionality on the client. They are server-side objects just like any other web control, which means that you can access them programmatically as you can a `TextBox` or `Label`. Each validation control has an `IsValid` property that tells you whether the validation for that particular control has passed. Therefore, you can handle all of the validation on the server if you want.

In addition, the **ASP.NET** `Page` object has an `IsValid` property, which tells you at once whether all validation controls on the page have passed muster. This way, you don't have to examine each validation control individually.

The `Calendar` control **1** appears very simple. When you get to the code-behind file, you'll see how to give it some more functionality. The last `Label` **2** on the page is used to display some additional output that you'll get to in a bit.

Now here's to handle the events. First, you need to create an identical `btnSubmit_Click` method from Listing 16.3, with three exceptions. The SQL statement should now read as follows:

```
INSERT INTO tblWebBlog (fldAuthor, fldBlurb, fldDate) VALUES
    (@Author, @Blurb, @Date)
```

You need to add a new parameter to the `SqlCommand` object:

```
cmdBlog.Parameters.Add(New SqlParameter("@Date", cdarDates.SelectedDate.Add( _
    DateTime.Now.TimeOfDay)))
```

Instead of using the database default of `GETDATE()` to populate the `fldDate` column in the tblWebBlog table when an entry is added, you use the selected date of the calendar. This way, you can change the date in the calendar and enter a new blog entry for that date. Finally, add the following bit of code near the end of the method:

```
cdarDates SelectionChanged(Nothing, Nothing)
```

Call the `cdarDates_SelectionChanged` method (shown in Listing 16.5) to retrieve the newly entered entry and display it. The data isn't automatically displayed after you enter a new blurb because the code to display such entries executes only when the calendar date is changed. When you click the Add Blurb button, the calendar date stays the same and `cdarDates_SelectionChanged` doesn't execute. It can be common to call a control's event handler method from another method. In this case, you pass in two `Nothing` values into the method because those parameters are never used anyway.

Next, create the method shown in Listing 16.5 (you can double-click on the `Calendar` control in the design view of your `WebForm1.aspx` to autogenerate the method).

LISTING 16.5

Handling the `Calendar`'s Events

```
Private Sub cdarDates_SelectionChanged(ByVal sender As System.Object, _
    ByVal e As System.EventArgs) Handles cdarDates.SelectionChanged
    Dim i As Integer
    Dim dsBlog As New DataSet()
    lblBlurb.Text = ""

    'get data and fill dataset
    daBlog.SelectCommand.Parameters("@datStart").Value = _
    cdarDates.SelectedDate
    daBlog.SelectCommand.Parameters("@datEnd").Value = _
    cdarDates.SelectedDate.AddDays(1)
    daBlog.Fill(dsBlog)

    'display data
    For i = 0 To dsBlog.Tables(0).Rows.Count - 1
        lblBlurb.Text += dsBlog.Tables(0).Rows(i)("fldDate").ToString() & _
        "<BR>" & dsBlog.Tables(0).Rows(i)("fldBlurb").ToString() + "<p>"
    Next i

    DataBind()

End Sub
```

When you click a date on the calendar, the `SelectionChanged` event fires, and this method is there to handle it. Using the `SqlDataAdapter` that you created visually earlier, it retrieves any blog entries in your database for the selected date on the calendar. It is essentially the same code from Listing 16.1, except that a calendar is used to specify the date range of blogs to read. This gives it sort of a journal feel; you can flip to any date and see the blog entries for that date.

Finally, you need to add a little bit of code to the `Page_Load` event:

```
if not Page.IsPostBack then
    cdarDates.SelectedDate = DateTime.Now.Date
end if
```

This tells ASP.NET to set the selected date of the calendar control to today. The `IsPostBack` code is covered a bit later in the "Handling Web Events" section, but know for now that it is necessary for this page to work correctly.

Don't forget to import the `System.Data.SqlClient` namespace in your code-behind file as well. Figure 16.11 shows an example of using this interface.

16

Using Web Controls to Add Functionality to Pages

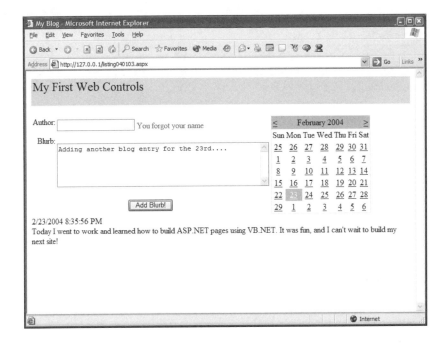

FIGURE 16.11   Testing the validation and calendar controls.

If you are familiar with HTML development or earlier versions of Active Server Pages, you might be a bit confounded right about now. Recall that the main problem with web development is that the server and client are separated and communicate only through infrequent sparse messages. Because of this, it makes it hard for the developer to predict or the web server to know what exactly is going on in the application at any given moment. Therefore, this makes it harder to control.

One of ASP.NET's big secrets is that it gets around the hurdles of client/server development by automatically creating a lot of behind-the-scenes JavaScript code for you. This JavaScript code does mainly two things: It handles some processing (that would normally be handled on the server) on the client's browser, and it can generate form submissions to stealthily transmit data back to the server without the user's knowledge (or, rather, without the user's explicitly telling it to do so). Therefore, more processing is automatically done on the client's side, and the server has a better stream of communication with the client to maintain control over the application. These two factors make the application appear to you, the developer, as if you are interacting more directly with the client, and it enables you to perform things that were more difficult before, such as validating user input.

Now that you know how web forms and web controls work, there's one last thing to understand about the basics of ASP.NET: web events. These have been covered briefly so far, but you get an in-depth look next.

Handling Web Events

An event is simply something that happens in an application: The user clicks a button, enters some text in a box, selects an entry from a list. The event-driven model tells us that whenever an event happens, the application should respond and execute some functionality. This concept is fairly straightforward when dealing with traditional desktop-based applications, but the introduction of the Internet in the middle of it all makes things a bit more complex.

The next few sections examine how exactly web events are different than regular events, and how ASP.NET enables you to handle them. This is often the most confusing aspect of ASP.NET, but it is necessary to grasp fully if you intend to build anything more than very simple applications.

ASP.NET Events Revisited

You've already seen how to handle ASP.NET events. Simply assign a method to the control's event that you want to handle (or, more precisely, the event delegate). For example, when you want to execute a method on a button click, you can use the following VB .NET syntax:

```
Sub MyMethod(parameters) Handles btnTest.Event
```

Or the HTML syntax code:

```
<asp:Button id="btnTest" runat="server" OnClick="MyMethod"/>
```

The OnClick property is the event delegate for the Click event of the button. A delegate just maps an event to a method that will handle that event.

You might have seen a third way to do this elsewhere in this book, in the programmatic form:

```
dim btnTest as new Button()
AddHandler btnTest.Click, AddressOf MyMethod
```

16

Handling Web Events

The problems arise when the Internet jumps in the middle and causes a disconnection between the objects that generate the events (on the client) and the code that is supposed to execute when the event fires (on the server). You've seen how ASP.NET tries to hide this complexity from the developer through the use of client-side JavaScript and other techniques, but sometimes these methods are not enough and the complexities shine through anyway.

The only way for the client to communicate with the server is through an HTML form submission, known as a POST operation (actually, the client can communicate with a GET operation as well, but this method isn't used in web forms, so you can ignore it for now). That means every time an event happens that needs to be handled, the form is submitted and data is sent back to the server.

So what limitations are there when every event that happens is accompanied by a form post? First, and probably most apparent to the user, is that anything that was entered in the form is lost after the form is submitted. ASP.NET gets around that by maintaining viewstate (see "Creating an Interactive Web Form," earlier in the chapter, or Chapter 18 for more information). Second, and more important to the developer, just as with any web page, an ASP.NET page does not run constantly on the server. When it has finished sending any data to the client, it stops. This means that every time you access the page (whether via a regular browser request or through a form post), the page has to start up and run from scratch again. This is why the procedure in Table 16.3 has to run for every ASP.NET page every time it is requested. These two issues are enough to make things very complicated. Although the first issue is handled well via the viewstate management, the second needs to be taken carefully into consideration when building an application.

GENERATING FORM POSTS

By default, not all events that can occur generate form posts for the server to handle. If this were the case, there would be a constant back-and-forth between the client and server, which would drastically reduce the performance of your application due to the inherent nature of the Internet. (The client's bandwidth, Internet traffic, the server hardware, and so on all affect performance of a web application.)

Some events, such as a button click or a link click, do and should generate posts. These are things that the user expects to cause a form submission, so ASP.NET automatically generates them.

However, it is possible in ASP.NET to have nearly any event generate a form post simply by adding `AutoPostBack="true"` to any web control. For example, if you want to examine what a user entered into a text box before clicking the Submit button, you can use this:

```
<asp:TextBox id="tbTest" OnTextChanged="MyMethod" AutoPostBack="true"/>
```

Now, not only will the event be handled on the server with the `MyMethod` method, but the form also will be posted as soon as the event happens.

Detecting Form Posts

Just because an ASP.NET page has to start from scratch every time it is requested doesn't mean that every part of that application has to execute every time. For example, suppose that you retrieve information from a database when a person first comes to your page, and you fill several HTML elements with the data. When the page is submitted via a form post, ASP.NET automatically remembers the data and prefills the fields for you again, thanks to viewstate management. Therefore, you don't need to re-execute the code that retrieves the information from the database; it would be a waste of time and processing effort. (Not only is it unnecessary to do so, but it might actually render your application useless if you do, as you'll learn in the next section.)

In situations such as this, you want to be able to detect whether the page is being submitted via a form post (when viewstate management kicks in), and conditionally execute or not execute some code.

The `Page.IsPostBack` property tells you exactly this. You saw it working in the previous task's `Page_Load` method. When you first came to that page (meaning that `Page.IsPostBack` returns `false`), you want to select the current date in the calendar. Imagine that the user then clicks on a different date, which causes a form post and `Page.IsPostBack` to be set to `true`. When the user submits the form then, without the check to `Page.IsPostBack`, your code would reset the selected date to today's date, and the user's selection would be lost. Thus, you don't want to execute the code every time the page loads; you want to do so only when the page does not load due to a form post, and when viewstate management doesn't automatically prefill the data.

> **TIP**
>
> Often the most puzzling conundrums in ASP.NET development occur when your code overrides the viewstate management in some way, which causes your application to function differently than you would expect it to. Always check to make sure you are using `Page.IsPostBack` properly.

The Order of Events

Another related problem arises from the order of ASP.NET page processing. Table 16.3 really comes in handy in these situations.

You can see that handling of events doesn't occur until step 7, but the loading of the page (the `Page_Load` event) occurs at step 5. Often an event that is raised depends on certain information, and you'll notice that it becomes all too easy to accidentally override that information in your `Page_Load` or `Page_Init` methods, just as with the viewstate discussed in the last section.

Another more devious example is illustrated in Figure 16.12. It occurs when you try to retrieve data from a database in your `Page_Load` method. The data is displayed in a form for the user to modify and then saved back in the database with a Save button click. Because the Save button click won't be handled until step 7, the `Page_Load` method again retrieves the original data from the database and prefills the fields.

Handling Web Events

When the `Save` method executes, it sees the original values instead of the user-modified ones. Endless amounts of frustration can be caused by this scenario, so make sure you remember the order in which events are handled in your page.

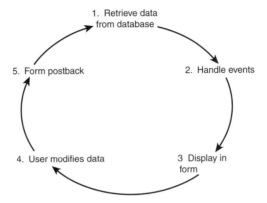

FIGURE 16.12   Don't forget the ASP.NET processing loop.

Mastering Event Handling

In this section, you build a calculator such as the one built into Windows. The functionality isn't complex, but it enables you to see many different events in action and learn how to handle them all efficiently. You'll also see viewstate management in action and use it to your advantage.

You don't need any database objects for this task, so you can jump straight into the UI HTML, shown in Listing 16.6.

LISTING 16.6

A Calculator

```
<%@ Page Language="vb" AutoEventWireup="false"
    Codebehind="WebForm1.aspx.vb" Inherits="listing1606.WebForm1"%>
<html><body>
<form runat="server" ID="Form1">
<table width="250">
<tr>
    <td width="100%" colspan="5">
        <asp:Textbox id="txtNumber" runat=server text="0"
            enabled="false" width="100%" />
    </td>
</tr>
<tr>
    <td align="right" width="100%" colspan="5">
```

LISTING 16.6
Continued

```
        <asp:Button id="btnBS" Text="Backspace" runat=server width="75"/>
        <asp:Button id="btnClear" Text="C" runat=server width="35"/>
    </td>
</tr>
<tr>
    <td width="32">
        <asp:Button id="btn7" Text="7" runat=server width="35"/><p>
    </td>
    <td width="32">
        <asp:Button id="btn8" Text="8" runat=server width="35"/><p>
    </td>
    <td width="32">
        <asp:Button id="btn9" Text="9" runat=server width="35"/><p>
    </td>
    <td width="32">
        <asp:Button id="btnDivide" Text="/" runat=server width="35"/><p>
    </td>
    <td width="32">
        <asp:Button id="btnSqrt" Text="sqrt" runat=server width="35"/><p>
    </td>
</tr>
<tr>
    <td width="32">
        <asp:Button id="btn4" Text="4" runat=server width="35"/><p>
    </td>
    <td width="32">
        <asp:Button id="btn5" Text="5" runat=server width="35"/><p>
    </td>
    <td width="32">
        <asp:Button id="btn6" Text="6" runat=server width="35"/><p>
    </td>
    <td width="32">
        <asp:Button id="btnMultiply" Text="*" runat=server width="35"/><p>
    </td>
    <td width="32">
        <asp:Button id="btnPercent" Text="%" runat=server width="35"/><p>
    </td>
</tr>
<tr>
    <td width="32">
        <asp:Button id="btn1" Text="1" runat=server width="35"/><p>
    </td>
```

16

Handling Web Events

LISTING 16.6
Continued

```
        <td width="32">
            <asp:Button id="btn2" Text="2" runat=server width="35"/><p>
        </td>
        <td width="32">
            <asp:Button id="btn3" Text="3" runat=server width="35"/><p>
        </td>
        <td width="32">
            <asp:Button id="btnSubtract" Text="-" runat=server width="35"/><p>
        </td>
        <td width="32">
            <asp:Button id="btnOneOver" Text="1/x" runat=server width="35"/><p>
        </td>
    </tr>
    <tr>
        <td width="32">
            <asp:Button id="btn0" Text="0" runat=server width="35"/><p>
        </td>
        <td width="32">
            <asp:Button id="btnNegate" Text="+/-" runat=server width="35"/><p>
        </td>
        <td width="32">
            <asp:Button id="btnDot" Text="." runat=server width="35"/><p>
        </td>
        <td width="32">
            <asp:Button id="btnAdd" Text="+" runat=server width="35"/><p>
        </td>
        <td width="32">
            <asp:Button id="btnEqual" Text="=" runat=server width="35"/><p>
        </td>
    </tr>
    </table>
    <input type="hidden" id="hiddenvalue" value="" runat="server"
        NAME="hiddenvalue">
    <input type="hidden" id="hiddenoperator" value="" runat="server"
        NAME="hiddenoperator">
    </form>
    </body></html>
```

Quite a few web controls have been created here: one TextBox (txtNumber), 22 Buttons, and two HtmlInputHidden controls. The text box control is simply the display output of the calculator. The Enabled property is set to false so that the user can't directly enter text into the box without going through the event handlers.

Each of the buttons represents either a number in the calculator, a backspace, a clear, or one of the arithmetic operations (divide, multiply, subtract, add, square root, percentage, inverse, or equals). Each of the number buttons uses the same event handler for the `Click` event: `btNumber_Click`. The operator buttons point to similar methods; you'll learn about all these in a moment.

The two `HtmlInputHidden` controls **1** are the secret weapon in making this calculator work properly. They are used to store values or operations temporarily while the user finishes the input.

Listing 16.7 shows the methods to add to the code-behind file.

LISTING 16.7
The Calculator Logic

```
Sub btnOperator_Click(ByVal Sender As Object, ByVal e As EventArgs) _
    Handles btnMultiply.Click, btnDivide.Click, btnPercent.Click,
    btnSubtract.Click, btnAdd.Click
    If (hiddenvalue.Value <> "" And hiddenvalue.Value <> "0") Then
        hiddenvalue.Value = Operate(Sender.Text, hiddenvalue.Value, _
        txtNumber.Text)
        hiddenoperator.Value = Sender.Text
        txtNumber.Text = "0"
    Else
        'save old number as hidden input field
        ' and clear text box
        hiddenvalue.Value = txtNumber.Text
        hiddenoperator.Value = Sender.Text
        txtNumber.Text = "0"
    End If
End Sub


Sub btnSpecOperator_Click(ByVal Sender As Object, ByVal e As EventArgs) _
    Handles btnSqrt.Click, btnOneOver.Click, btnNegate.Click
    txtNumber.Text = Operate(Sender.Text, hiddenvalue.Value, txtNumber.Text)
    hiddenvalue.Value = ""
    hiddenoperator.Value = ""
End Sub


Private Sub btnNumber_Click(ByVal sender As System.Object, _
    ByVal e As System.EventArgs) Handles btnDot.Click, btn0.Click, _
    btn1.Click, btn2.Click, btn3.Click, btn4.Click, btn5.Click, _
    btn6.Click, btn7.Click, btn8.Click, btn9.Click
    If txtNumber.Text <> "0" Then
        txtNumber.Text = txtNumber.Text & sender.Text
    Else
        txtNumber.Text = sender.Text
```

16

Handling Web Events

LISTING 16.7
Continued

```
        End If
End Sub

Sub btnClear_Click(ByVal Sender As Object, ByVal e As EventArgs) _
    Handles btnClear.Click
    txtNumber.Text = "0"
    hiddenoperator.Value = ""
    hiddenvalue.Value = ""
End Sub

Sub btnBS_Click(ByVal Sender As Object, ByVal e As EventArgs) _
    Handles btnBS.Click
    If txtNumber.Text <> "0" Then
        txtNumber.Text = Left(txtNumber.Text, Len(txtNumber.Text) - 1)
    End If
End Sub

Sub btnEqual_Click(ByVal Sender As Object, ByVal e As EventArgs) _
    Handles btnEqual.Click
    If hiddenvalue.Value <> "" And hiddenoperator.Value <> "" Then
        'operate numbers
        txtNumber.Text = Operate(hiddenoperator.Value, hiddenvalue.Value, _
            txtNumber.Text)
        hiddenvalue.Value = ""
        hiddenoperator.Value = ""
    Else
        'do nothing
    End If
End Sub

Private Function Operate(ByVal operator As String, ByVal number1 As String, _
    Optional ByVal number2 As String = "1") As Double
    Select Case operator
        Case "+"
            Operate = CDbl(number1) + CDbl(number2)
        Case "-"
            Operate = CDbl(number1) - CDbl(number2)
        Case "*"
            Operate = CDbl(number1) * CDbl(number2)
        Case "/"
            Operate = CDbl(number1) / CDbl(number2)
        Case "sqrt"
```

16

LISTING 16.7
Continued

```
            Operate = CDbl(Math.Sqrt(number2))
        Case "1/x"
            Operate = CDbl(1 / CDbl(number2))
        Case "+/-"
            Operate = CDbl(-CDbl(number2))
    End Select
End Function
```

Consider the btnNumber_Click method. This code is rather simple. If there is nothing yet entered in the calculator, it puts the number that was just clicked in txtNumber. If there is something already in the calculator, it appends the incoming number to whatever's there; the user is entering a multidigit number. Note how the Sender parameter was used to retrieve the number that was clicked. Recall that this parameter represents the object that generated the event—in this case, the number button.

Next, consider the btnOperator_Click method. This code is a bit more complex. After a user enters the first number (multidigit or otherwise), he or she clicks an operator button. When that happens, you need to clear the text box so that the user can enter the second number of the operation. The problem is that if you clear the text box, you lose track of the first number. This is where the hidden fields of Listing 16.6 come into play. If there is no value in these hidden fields, this is the first time that the user has clicked an operator button, so you need to store the value in the text box and the operator in the hidden fields. If there already is a value in the hidden fields, it means that the user has clicked an operator a second time, and you need to perform a calculation (the call to the Operate method which is discussed in a moment), store the results, and then clear the text box for the next number. In this way, the user can enter a number, followed by an operation, followed by a number, followed by an operation, followed by a number (for example, $9 \times 9 \times 9$), and the result will be the cumulative operation (729).

The btnSpecOperator_Click method is similar, but these operations (square root, negate, and inverse) don't require multiple operands; they require only one number to function. Therefore, you don't need to store any of the values in the hidden fields.

btnClear_Click is very simple: It only clears any stored hidden values and resets the text box. btnBS_Click uses some string manipulation to remove the last-entered (in other words, the rightmost) digit from the text box.

Next is btnEqual_Click. This method is very similar to btnOperator_Click because they really should do the same thing; whether you click on the equals button or another operator, a result should be calculated. The only difference is that when you click the equals button, you're expecting a final answer, so nothing needs to be stored in hidden fields. However, if you immediately follow with another operator, the btnOperator_Click method handles everything properly.

16

Handling Web Events

Finally, consider the `Operate` method. This method takes in an operator and two numbers (the second is optional) to perform a calculation. The `select case` statement contains functions for every operator on the calculator, so all math calculation is combined into one function. Note that the second number is optional because of the operators handled by the `btnSpecOperator_Click` method that require only one number to function.

Figure 16.13 shows the output of this example.

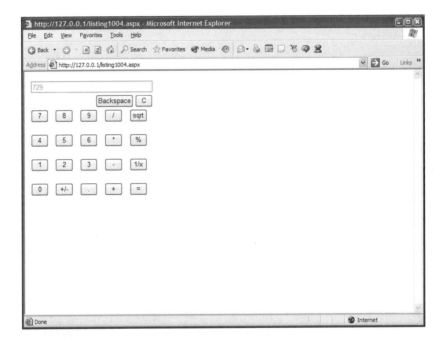

FIGURE 16.13   The calculator in action ($9 \times 9 \times 9 = 729$).

There are two things to note in this page. First, you could have easily created a separate event-handler method for each button on the page (all 22 of them). But because you can handle multiple events with a single method, why create 22 separate ones? With some forethought and planning, you can craft a few multipurpose methods that streamline the code. In this way, web forms and web controls enable you to make the code and development tighter.

Second, and you might even miss this aspect if you're not paying attention, is that the viewstate management handled the form submissions invisibly, without your having to worry about it. Remember that every time you clicked a button, the form was submitted to the server. You didn't have to worry at all about repopulating the `txtNumber` text box or the hidden fields, or about dealing with the mechanics of the form submissions. In fact, working with this page is almost the same as working with a Windows application.

After dealing with all the events in this calculator, you should have a strong understanding of how to control your ASP.NET pages and the controls on them.

REAL-WORLD ASP.NET DEVELOPMENT

As an ASP.NET developer, you'll find that most of everything that you develop will be related to something discussed in this chapter. Creating UIs is a major part of any web application, and web forms are there to help you do so. The better you learn this stuff, the stronger a developer you will be.

That said, the subsequent chapters in this section address more advanced topics that will help in dealing with sets of data and help your application to perform better and more securely. Every ASP.NET developer should keep these in mind when building his or her applications.

16

Summary

This chapter was a crash course on the basics of ASP.NET, but by the end, you were developing full applications and handling events like a professional. Two of the most important parts to remember are the ASP.NET process model in Table 16.2 and the various web controls available to you in Table 16.4. Armed with this knowledge, you can build almost any type of web application.

Be sure to check out the .NET Framework SDK documentation if you haven't yet. This is an invaluable source of information, especially when you're trying to find that obscure web control event to take advantage of.

Microsoft's ASP.NET site, conveniently located at http://www.asp.net, also has a wealth of information. It has quickstart examples to help you along, as well as tutorials, code submitted by developers from around the world, and various downloadable goodies.

You might also check out Part II, on Windows development, if you haven't already. The knowledge in this chapter can be easily applied to Windows application development, thanks to the familiar document object model of the .NET Framework (in fact, ASP.NET development might be even easier).

Further Reading

Microsoft ASP.NET site, http://www.asp.net.

Payne, Chris. *Sam's Teach Yourself ASP.NET in 21 Days, Second Edition.* Pearson Education, 2002.

17 DATA BINDING IN WEB APPLICATIONS

IN BRIEF

You might have already learned about data binding in a previous chapter on Windows database programming (see Chapter 14, "Data-Aware Controls and Data Binding"), but it is an almost entirely different beast in ASP.NET. Much of the fundamentals stay the same, but the implementation and details can be very different because of the way web controls are structured. In this chapter, you'll learn how exactly data binding is different in ASP.NET. Then you move on to some more detailed analysis of the controls and their uses.

WHAT YOU NEED

SOFTWARE REQUIREMENTS	Windows 2000, Windows XP, or Windows Server 2003 .NET Framework 1.1 SDK Visual Studio .NET 2003 with Visual Basic .NET installed SQL Server or Microsoft Desktop Database Engine (MSDE) Internet Information Server (version 5 or later)
HARDWARE REQUIREMENTS	PC desktop or laptop system
SKILL REQUIREMENTS	Advanced knowledge in HTML Intermediate knowledge in the .NET Framework

DATA BINDING AT A GLANCE

Binding Data to Simple Controls

In this section, you quickly review data binding and then examine how it can be used in ASP.NET with the web controls that you learned about in Chapter 16, "Basic Web Application." Because ASP.NET controls can be written in plain HTML as well as in VB .NET code, you have to learn a few new techniques. But don't worry—ASP.NET makes it easy.

Typical data binding is used to tie a source of data (which can be a DataSet, an array, even a simple variable) to the display of an object. This enables you to view, edit, and update the original data source easily. You typically bind data only to some property of the object that provides a user display.

Data binding in web forms is quite different. First, there's no limitation of having to bind only to display properties; you can bind any piece of data to any property of a web control, which makes for very flexible applications. Second, web forms data binding does not provide inherent capabilities to edit or update data. This is because an assumption is made (and rightly so) that most information on a web page is going to be static and not editable. To streamline things for the web, such functionality has been stripped out, requiring you to build it yourself if you need it. Finally, a few implementation details are different. For example, there are no BindingContexts or DataBindings, but the DataSource property is still available.

Whether you're data binding in Windows forms or web forms, it is a powerful mechanism that only gets better as you deal with more complex sources of data.

Next you build a simplistic example that highlights the way data binding in ASP.NET works. This is something that you might actually come across in the real world. Create a new VS .NET application at http://localhost/VBNetUnleashed/listing1701. Listing 17.1 shows the HTML portion of the WebForm1.aspx file.

LISTING 17.1
Simple Data Binding

```
<%@ Page Language="vb" AutoEventWireup="false" Codebehind="WebForm1.aspx.vb"
    Inherits="listing1701.WebForm1"%>
<html>
<head><title>Simple Data Binding</title></head>

<body bgcolor="<%# Color %>">                                        1
<table bgcolor="#FFDD55" width=100%>
<tr>
    <td><font size=5>Simple Data Binding</font><p></td>
</td>
</table>
```

Binding Data to Simple Controls

LISTING 17.1
Continued

```
<form id="Form1" method="post" runat="server">
```

2   `Today is: <%# DateTime.Now.ToString("MMM, dd, yyyy") %><p>`

```
    Choose a background color for the page and textarea:
```
3
```
    <asp:ListBox ID="lbxColors" Runat="server" rows=1 AutoPostBack=true />
    <br>
    <asp:TextBox id="txtColors" runat="server" TextMode="MultiLine" Rows=5
        BackColor="<%# System.Drawing.Color.FromName(Color) %>">
        Hi there
    </asp:TextBox>
```

```
</form>
</body></html>
```

Data binding in ASP.NET looks differently than in Windows Forms; you bind data by using the <%# and %> tags in your HTML code. These tags are known simply enough as data-binding tags. The first highlighted portion **1** shows an example of binding the page's Color property (that is discussed in a moment) to the bgcolor attribute of the body tag. Note that the body tag did not have to be a web control. In this case, data binding serves to simply write the data out to the HTML code.

The second highlighted portion **2** shows another example, but in the <%#...%> tags this time is a method call, ToString(). You can use nearly any statement inside your data-binding tags, as long as it evaluates to a value that the context can use. This code simply displays static text.

The last portion **3** contains a ListBox control that will contain an array of colors that will be used to set the Color property that you saw earlier in the code. Note that the AutoPostBack=true attribute means that every time a selection is changed in the ListBox, the web form submits itself for processing.

The TextBox control shows the final example of data binding. Here, the code is binding to a property of a web control, using another method and the Color property.

Take a look at the portion of the code-behind file that you'll have to write, shown in Listing 17.2.

LISTING 17.2
Data Binding Logic

```
Dim m_color As String
Dim m_colors As String() = New String() {"Red", "Orange", "Yellow", _
    "Green", "Blue", "Indigo", "Violet"}
```

LISTING 17.2
Continued

```
Property Color()
    Get
        Return m_color
    End Get
    Set(ByVal Value)
        m_color = Value
    End Set
End Property

Private Sub Page_Load(ByVal sender As System.Object, ByVal e As _
    System.EventArgs) Handles MyBase.Load
    'Put user code to initialize the page here
    If Not Page.IsPostBack Then                                         1
        m_color = "White"

        lbxColors.DataSource = m_colors
        DataBind()
    End If
End Sub

Private Sub lbxColors_SelectedIndexChanged(ByVal sender As System.Object, _
    ByVal e As System.EventArgs) Handles lbxColors.SelectedIndexChanged
    m_color = lbxColors.SelectedValue                                  2
    DataBind()
End Sub
```

The first two lines declare two member variables, m_color and m_colors. The first is the private representation of the public Color property. The latter contains an array of colors that you'll use.

In the Page_Load method, you check if the page has been posted back on itself via a form post **1**, set an initial color, and then bind your array to the ListBox that you created in Listing 17.1. The DataSource property takes any collection of data that implements the IEnumerable interface, which includes DataSets, DataTables, arrays, and other collections. When you specify the DataSource property, the ListBox knows to iterate through the data collection and populate itself. (The DataSource property is implemented on other web controls as well, which you'll get to later in this chapter.)

Finally, you call the DataBind method **2**. This method is very important: Without it, no data binding would occur, even though you specify such properties as DataSource.

17

Binding Data to Simple Controls

> **NOTE**
>
> This is different than with Windows Forms, when you didn't need to call such a command.

In sum, upon first viewing the `Page_Load` method causes your page's background to appear in white and populates the `ListBox` with the values from you `m_colors` array.

The `lbxColors_SelectedIndexChanged` method is fired when you make a selection change in the `ListBox`. It causes the page and `TextBox` to change background colors. This is done simply by retrieving the newly selected value from the `ListBox` and then calling the `DataBind` method again to rebind the controls on the page with the new data.

To reiterate the importance of the `DataBind` method, you must call `DataBind`, or no binding will occur on your page. In addition, any time you change a data source, you typically have to rebind it.

> **NOTE**
>
> The order of execution of ASP.NET pages (see Table 16.2 in Chapter 16) can cause problems with your data binding. It is important to pay close attention to when and where you call the `DataBind` method. Because data binding occurs only when you call `DataBind`, and because events are not handled until after the `Page_Load` method executes, you must make sure that you don't rebind old data when you expect to see new data.
>
> For example, in Listing 17.2, if you did not do the `IsPostBack` to check the `Page_Load` method **1**, your color would always be reset to white and the changes to the `ListBox` would do nothing.

Every web control inherits the `DataBind` method from the `Control` class. So, you can individually bind controls if you want to. However, the `Page` class's `DataBind` method is a one-stop shop; calling it subsequently calls the `DataBind` method for all controls on that page. Generally, it's just easier to make one `Page.DataBind` call than to bind individually the controls, although it might incur some overhead because every control has to be data bound, even if it doesn't require it.

Figure 17.1 shows the output of this application after changing the color to yellow (the figure might actually be in black and white, but trust us—it's yellow).

Data binding is a fundamental aspect of .NET applications and is very important to ASP.NET, in particular. You'll come across simple binding like this task so often that it will eventually become second nature to you. In subsequent sections in this chapter, you'll learn more advanced techniques and controls.

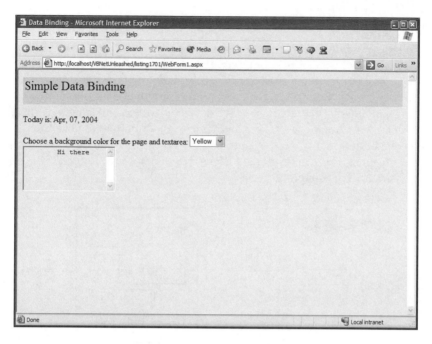

FIGURE 17.1   Data binding in action.

Using Templated Controls to Display Data

A class of web controls known as templated controls provides the capability to apply a
data source, typically a collection of data, to a template for display. The ListBox is a
very simple example; each item in the data source is displayed as a ListItem object
with a certain look and feel. The ListBox technically isn't a templated control,
however, because the developer can't fully control its display, nor does it implement
the System.Web.UI.INamingContainer interface, a requirement. Another
example is the DataGrid that you might have seen in the Windows Forms sections.

In addition to being able to display collections of data, templated controls let you
easily handle events that pertain to each individual item of your data collection. For
example, if your data source was a DataTable and you displayed it with the
DataGrid templated control, you could allow the user to modify each DataRow of
your table individually and handle the events all from one place.

In this section, you examine the three main templated controls for use with ASP.NET
applications. These range from the very flexible and simplistic Repeater to the rigid
and fully functional DataGrid.

Using Templated Controls to Display Data

Event Bubbling

Most container controls support a process known as *event bubbling*. This process allows any control inside of the container to pass its events to the container for handling instead of handling them itself. This is useful if you would rather handle one control's events (specifically, the container) rather than a multitude (the controls inside the container). This can often make development easier. Figure 17.2 illustrates event bubbling. An analogy is having all members of a household make their requests of a butler (such as grocery shopping), who carries them out as their representative. At times, this can be more efficient than having each household member do their own grocery shopping.

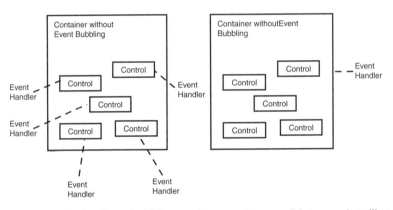

FIGURE 17.2   Event bubbling enables you to consolidate your handling.

Event bubbling becomes especially useful with templated controls. Because these controls can automatically loop through your data source, it can potentially create hundreds of contained controls. Allowing all of these contained controls to bubble their events up to the templated control can save some time and headache.

> **NOTE**
>
> Just because event bubbling is available doesn't mean that you have to use it. You can still handle each contained control's events just as you would a noncontained control.

When you bubble an event, the container control enables you to pass optional parameters with each event. The three templated controls that you'll see here have specialized parameters that can be used to perform certain tasks. You'll get to them first in the section on the `DataList`.

The Repeater

The Repeater is the simplest of the templated data-binding controls in ASP.NET. It leaves all display details up to you, the developer. This means that you can have the data be output in an HTML table, as plain text, or in whatever other layout you choose.

Open a new VS. NET ASP.NET project and call it listing1703. Add a SqlDataConnection and SqlDataAdapter to your page, as you did for the tasks in Chapter 16. Specify the following SQL statement for your SELECT command of your DataAdapter:

```
SELECT fldIdentity, fldAuthor, fldBlurb, fldDate FROM tblWebBlog
ORDER BY fldDate DESC
```

You'll return all of the data from your blog table and display it automatically using a Repeater. Listing 17.3 shows the HTML source code for this page.

LISTING 17.3
Using a Repeater

```
<%@ Page Language="vb" AutoEventWireup="false" Codebehind="WebForm1.aspx.vb"
    Inherits="listing1703.WebForm1"%>
<html>
<head><title> The Repeater Control </title></head>
<body>
<table bgcolor="#FFDD55" width=100%>
<tr>
    <td><font size=5>The Repeater Control</font><p></td>
</td>
</table>

<form id="Form1" method="post" runat="server">

<asp:Repeater id="rptBlog" runat="server">
    <HeaderTemplate>
        <table width=600>
    </HeaderTemplate>
    <ItemTemplate>
        <tr>
            <td>Posted by:</td>
            <td><%# DataBinder.Eval(Container.DataItem, "fldAuthor") %></td>
            <td align=right><%# DataBinder.Eval(Container.DataItem,"fldDate")%>
            </td>
        </tr>
```

17

Using Templated Controls to Display Data

LISTING 17.3
Continued

```
            <tr>
                <td colspan=3><%# DataBinder.Eval(Container.DataItem, "fldBlurb")%>
                </td>
            </tr>
        </ItemTemplate>
        <FooterTemplate>
            </table>
        </FooterTemplate>
</asp:Repeater>
</form>
</body></html>
```

This HTML page is very simple. In the highlighted portion ■ **1** ■, you see the beginning of your `Repeater`. It contains three types of templates: `HeaderTemplate`, which defines any applicable header to your data output; `ItemTemplate`, which defines the way each individual item in your data source will look; and `FooterTemplate`, which naturally defines the footer. In this example, you can see that the header and footer templates simply open and close a table; this could also have been done outside the `Repeater`.

The `ItemTemplate` is where all the interesting stuff happens. For each blog entry, you want to display two table rows: one for the author and date entered data fields, and one for the text of the blog entry. These are done using regular HTML syntax. To then instruct the `Repeater` of which fields to actually display, you use the `DataBinder.Eval` method.

TIP

It is helpful to realize that each template element in the `Repeater` is represented programmatically by a `RepeaterItem` object, which has its own set of properties and methods that you might find useful. In this case, if your data source had five rows (in other words, five blog entries), you would end up with seven `RepeaterItem` objects: one each for the header and footer, and five from the `ItemTemplates`.

The `DataBinder` class enables you to easily reference a bound control's data source and bind an individual data field. It was designed specifically for use in visual design tools such as VS .NET, but, in general, it simplifies the code syntax needed to bind items in a templated control. The `Eval` method takes two parameters: the data source and the field in that data source to bind. In this case, `Container.DataItem` refers to the `Repeater`'s data source, which, as you'll see in Listing 17.4, is a `DataSet`.

17

> **NOTE**
>
> You don't have to use the `DataBinder` if you prefer not to. You could have referenced the data source directly and then built some custom code to make sure that the `Repeater` row matches the data source row. More often than not, you don't need to bother with that and can just implement the easy-to-use `DataBinder`.

So you see the `fldAuthor`, `fldDate`, and `fldBlurb` data fields bound to the page (in other words, displayed as plain text).

You can use two other templates with the `Repeater`: `AlternatingItemTemplate`, which is exactly the same as `ItemTemplate`, except that it is used on every other row, which enables you to perhaps display the row in a different color to make differentiation easier; and `SeparatorTemplate`, which is displayed in between rows, which can also make differentiation easier.

Take a look at the VB. NET code in the code-behind file next, shown in Listing 17.4.

LISTING 17.4
Binding Your `Repeater`

```vbnet
Private Sub Page_Load(ByVal sender As System.Object, _
    ByVal e As System.EventArgs) Handles MyBase.Load
    'Put user code to initialize the page here
    Dim dsBlog As New DataSet()

    'use a SqlDataAdapter to fill the dataset
    daBlog.Fill(dsBlog)

    'bind the repeater
    rptBlog.DataSource = dsBlog
    rptBlog.DataBind()
End Sub
```

In this case, you only need to add code to the `Page_Load` method. It simply fills a `DataSet` using the `SqlDataAdapter` that you created earlier and then binds it to the `Repeater` control from Listing 17.3. Remember to call the `DataBind` method. Figure 17.3 shows the output from this application.

Recall the blog applications from Chapter 16. You used a loop to iterate through the data source and display the entries. Here, you use a `Repeater` to automatically perform the work for you. This is a great tool for quick and easy display of data, and it is endlessly customizable. However, it doesn't provide much other functionality. You'll look at the `DataList` and `DataGrid` controls next, which provide less display customizability but offer more built-in features.

Using Templated Controls to Display Data

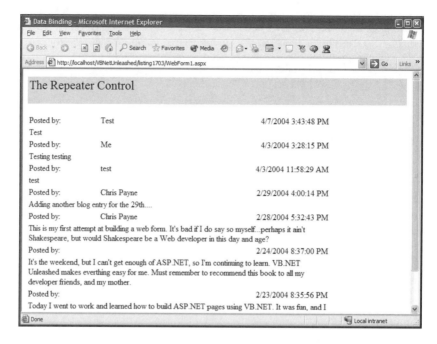

FIGURE 17.3   The `Repeater` automatically loops through your data source to display rows.

The `DataList`

The `DataList` is essentially a more advanced version of the `Repeater`. Its advantages are the capabilities to edit and delete rows in your template through inherent functionality. The drawback is that the display is more rigid; the `DataList` always displays data rows in a single HTML row, which makes what you did in Listing 17.3 much harder to accomplish (but not impossible). Because you're familiar with the `Repeater`, you can jump straight into an example that utilizes the enhanced features of the `DataList`.

Create a new VS .NET project named `listing1705`, and add your usual `SqlConnection` and `SqlDataAdapter` objects. Use the same SQL statement that you used for the previous task.

Listing 17.5 shows the HTML portion of this page.

LISTING 17.5
Creating a `DataList` Control

```
<%@ Page Language="vb" AutoEventWireup="false" Codebehind="WebForm1.aspx.vb"
    Inherits="listing1705.WebForm1"%>
<html>
<head><title> The DataList Control </title></head>
```

LISTING 17.5
Continued

```
<body>
<table bgcolor="#ffdd55" width="100%">
<tr>
    <td><font size="5">The DataList Control</font><p></p>
</td>
</tr>
</table>
<form id="Form1" method="post" runat="server">
<asp:DataList id="dltBlog" runat="server">
    <ItemTemplate>
        <table width="600">
        <tr>
            <td>Posted by:</td>
            <td>
               <%# DataBinder.Eval(Container.DataItem, "fldAuthor")%>
            </td>
            <td align="right">
               <%# DataBinder.Eval(Container.DataItem, "fldDate") %>
            </td>
            <td align="right">
                <asp:LinkButton ID="lbnEdit" runat="server"
                    Text="Edit" CommandName="Edit" />
            </td>
        </tr>
        <tr>
            <td colspan="4">
               <%# DataBinder.Eval(Container.DataItem, "fldBlurb") %>
            </td>
        </tr>
        </table>
    </ItemTemplate>
    <EditItemTemplate>
        <table width=600>
        <tr>
            <td>Posted by:</td>
            <td>
                <asp:TextBox ID="txtAuthor"
                    Text='<%# DataBinder.Eval _
                    (Container.DataItem, "fldAuthor") %>' runat="server"/>
            </td>
            <td align="right">
                <asp:TextBox ID="txtDate"
```

17

Using Templated Controls to Display Data

LISTING 17.5
Continued

```
                         Text='<%# DataBinder.Eval _
                         (Container.DataItem, "fldDate") %>' runat="server"/>
                    </td>
                    <td align="right">
                        <asp:LinkButton ID="lbnUpdate" runat="server"
                            Text="Update" CommandName="Update" />
                        <asp:LinkButton ID="lbnCancel" runat="server"
                            Text="Cancel" CommandName="Cancel" />
                    </td>
                </tr>
                <tr>
                    <td colspan="4">
                        <input type="hidden" ID="txtIdentity" Runat="server"
                            Value='<%# DataBinder.Eval _
                            (Container.DataItem, "fldIdentity") %>'/>
                        <asp:TextBox ID="txtBlurb"
                            Text='<%# DataBinder.Eval _
                            (Container.DataItem, "fldBlurb") %>' runat="server"
                            Columns=50 TextMode="Multiline"/>
                    </td>
                </tr>
                </table>
            </EditItemTemplate>
    </asp:DataList>
    </form>
    </body></html>
```

As you can see, the DataList is already much more complex than the Repeater.
First, two new additional template types are available with the DataList:
SelectedItemTemplate and EditItemTemplate. The former is typically used to
display additional information about a selected item in the DataList. The latter, of
course, is used to edit the data contained in a particular row. Note that the exact
layout of these new templates is still up to you, so you can make any field that you
want editable.

ItemTemplate works exactly as with the Repeater, except that you should
remember that a DataList automatically puts your content in an HTML table: You
have to take special precautions to make sure that everything displays as you want it
to. This is why you've added the surrounding table.

EditItemTemplate in Listing 17.5 is nearly identical to ItemTemplate, with the
exception that all fields that were simply bound to the page as plain text are now
bound to TextBox controls for editing.

The next question is, how do you get the edit and selected item templates to display?
Note the LinkButtons; these are integral to the procedure, examined in Listing 17.6.

LISTING 17.6
Editing DataList Items

```
Private Sub Page_Load(ByVal sender As System.Object, _
    ByVal e As System.EventArgs) _
    Handles MyBase.Load
    'Put user code to initialize the page here
    GetData()

    If Not Page.IsPostBack Then
        dltBlog.DataBind()
    End If
End Sub


Sub GetData()
    Dim dsBlog As New DataSet()

    daBlog.Fill(dsBlog)
    dltBlog.DataSource = dsBlog
End Sub


Sub dltBlog_EditCommand(ByVal Sender As Object, _
    ByVal e As DataListCommandEventArgs) Handles dltBlog.EditCommand
    dltBlog.EditItemIndex = e.Item.ItemIndex
    dltBlog.DataBind()
End Sub


Sub dltBlog_UpdateCommand(ByVal Sender As Object, _
    ByVal e As DataListCommandEventArgs) Handles dltBlog.UpdateCommand
    '
    'SqlUpdateCommand1
    '
    Me.SqlUpdateCommand1.CommandText = "UPDATE tblWebBlog SET fldAuthor = " & _
        @fldAuthor, fldBlurb = @fldBlurb, fldDate = @fl" & _
        "dDate WHERE fldIdentity = @fldIdentity"
    Me.SqlUpdateCommand1.Connection = Me.conBlog
    Me.SqlUpdateCommand1.Parameters.Add(New System.Data.SqlClient.SqlParameter _
        ("@fldAuthor", System.Data.SqlDbType.VarChar, 50, "fldAuthor"))
    Me.SqlUpdateCommand1.Parameters.Add(New System.Data.SqlClient.SqlParameter _
        ("@fldBlurb", System.Data.SqlDbType.VarChar, 1000, "fldBlurb"))
    Me.SqlUpdateCommand1.Parameters.Add(New System.Data.SqlClient.SqlParameter _
        ("@fldDate", System.Data.SqlDbType.DateTime, 8, "fldDate"))
```

17

Using Templated Controls to Display Data

LISTING 17.6
Continued

```
    Me.SqlUpdateCommand1.Parameters.Add(New System.Data.SqlClient.SqlParameter _
        ("@fldIdentity", System.Data.SqlDbType.Int, 4, "fldIdentity"))

    SqlUpdateCommand1.Parameters("@fldAuthor").Value = _
        CType(e.Item.FindControl("txtAuthor"), TextBox).Text
    SqlUpdateCommand1.Parameters("@fldBlurb").Value = _
        CType(e.Item.FindControl("txtBlurb"), TextBox).Text
    SqlUpdateCommand1.Parameters("@fldDate").Value = _
        CType(e.Item.FindControl("txtDate"), TextBox).Text
    SqlUpdateCommand1.Parameters("@fldIdentity").Value = _
        CType(e.Item.FindControl("txtIdentity"), HtmlInputHidden).Value
    SqlUpdateCommand1.Connection.Open()
    SqlUpdateCommand1.ExecuteNonQuery()

    GetData()

    dltBlog.EditItemIndex = -1
    dltBlog.DataBind()
End Sub

Sub dltBlog_CancelCommand(ByVal Sender As Object, _
    ByVal e As DataListCommandEventArgs) Handles dltBlog.CancelCommand
    dltBlog.EditItemIndex = -1
    dltBlog.DataBind()
End Sub
```

Our discussion starts with the Page_Load method beginning in the first line. It simply retrieves data from the database and conditionally binds it to the DataList. Note that you've separated the actual database call into a separate function because it will be called from multiple locations later; this increases code reuse.

The dltBlog_EditCommand method instructs the DataList to go into edit mode and display the EditItemTemplate from Listing 17.5. You simply set the EditItemIndex property to the selected index of the DataList, which tells the DataList which row should be edited, to the index returned in the DataListCommandEventArgs parameter. Then you rebind the DataList, and your EditItemTemplate shows up magically, as shown in Figure 17.4.

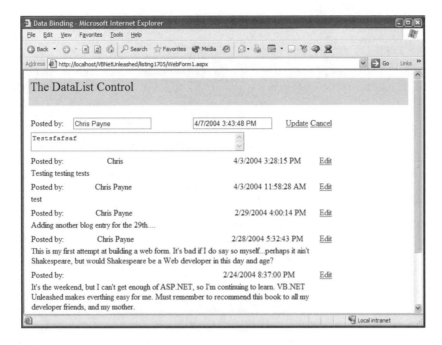

FIGURE 17.4   To edit an item in a `DataList` simply, set the `EditItemIndex` property.

This event obviously handles the `DataList.EditCommand` event, but when did that event fire? Recall that earlier you learned that templated controls use event bubbling. In particular, the `Repeater`, `DataList`, and `DataGrid` have specific parameters that you can use to trigger certain events. In this example, the `LinkButton` bubbles its `Click` event to the `DataList`, passing the parameter `Edit` in the `CommandName` attribute. This instructs the template control to generate the `EditCommand` event, which is then handled by your `dltBlog_EditCommand` method. Likewise, when you pass the `CommandName` values of `Select`, `Update`, `Delete`, and `Cancel`, the `DataList` generates the `SelectIndexChanged`, `UpdateCommand`, `DeleteCommand`, and `CancelCommand` events, respectively.

Applying this knowledge, the `LinkButton` in Listing 17.5 generates the `CancelCommand` event, which is handled by the `dltBlog_CancelCommand` method of Listing 17.6. This method simply returns the `DataList` to a default state (no rows selected for editing).

You aren't limited to passing only these five commands; you can pass any value in the `CommandName` property that you want. For values that don't generate one of the predefined events, the `DataList` generates a generic `ItemCommand` event for bubbled events. Just make sure that if you bubble multiple events, your `ItemCommand` event handler can distinguish the events (the `DataListCommandEventArgs.CommandName` property can help you in this regard).

17

Back to the code, the `dltBlog_UpdateCommand` method is mostly self-explanatory. It simply updates the database with newly entered values, retrieves the new data, and binds it to the `DataList`. The one thing to note is the use of the `DataListItem`. `FindControl` method. This method searches the selected row's control hierarchy for a specified control, which saves you from having to know any details about the hierarchy itself.

Using this example, you can do nearly any kind of manipulation with a set of data in a `DataList`. In the next section, you examine some features that the `DataGrid` has above and beyond the `DataList`.

The `DataGrid`

If you covered Part III, "Database Programming," you might be familiar with the Windows Forms version of the `DataGrid`. Just as the `DataList` is a more functional version of the `Repeater`, the `DataGrid` is a more functional form of the `DataList`. But this extra functionality comes at the cost of less flexibility in layout control.

The `DataGrid` relegates the various templates (such as `ItemTemplate` and `EditItemTemplate`) of the previous templated controls, to the background, in favor of column definitions (the templates are still available but aren't used typically). You are limited to a strict table display and have the flexibility only to define what goes in which column. Five types of columns exist:

- ▸ **Bound columns**—Enable you to specify which data columns to display and in what order, and allow you to format style attributes.

- ▸ **Button columns**—Display buttons for items on the grid, for which you can define custom functionality.

- ▸ **Edit command columns**—Enable you to edit a row in the `DataGrid`. These essentially replace all bound columns with modifiable fields (such as a `TextBox`).

- ▸ **Hyperlink columns**—Display data as a hyperlink.

- ▸ **Templated columns**—Enable you to use the templates as you did with the `Repeater` and `DataList` controls.

Earlier sections discussed handling event bubbling and edit and update commands with the `DataList`, so now you can look at an example that implements only the new features of the `DataGrid`.

Create a new VS .NET project and add your usual `SqlConnection` and `SqlDataAdapter` objects, using the SQL statements from earlier in this chapter. Listing 17.7 shows the HTML for this page.

LISTING 17.7
Defining a DataGrid

```
<%@ Page Language="vb" AutoEventWireup="false" Codebehind="WebForm1.aspx.vb"
    Inherits="listing1707.WebForm1"%>
<html>
<head><title>The DataGrid Control</title></head>
<body>
<table bgcolor="#ffdd55" width="100%">
<tr>
    <td><font size="5">The DataGrid Control</font><p></p>
    </td>
</tr>
</table>
<form id="Form1" method="post" runat="server">
    <asp:DataGrid id="dgBlog" runat="server"
        AutoGenerateColumns=false
        AllowSorting="True"
        AllowPaging="True"
        PageSize="5">
        <Columns>                                                    1
            <asp:BoundColumn HeaderText="ID" DataField="fldIdentity"
                SortExpression="fldIdentity" />
            <asp:BoundColumn HeaderText="Author" DataField="fldAuthor"
                SortExpression="fldAuthor" />
            <asp:BoundColumn HeaderText="Date" DataField="fldDate"
                SortExpression="fldDate"  />
            <asp:ButtonColumn HeaderText="Edit" Text="Edit"
                CommandName="Edit" />
        </Columns>
    </asp:DataGrid>
</form>
</body></html>
```

17

The HTML for the DataGrid is much simpler because all of the format and layout is
defined for you; the DataGrid displays everything in a grid table, and you have to
define only the columns, as shown in the highlighted portion **1**. These columns
are all types that we outlined earlier, and they have standard HeaderText,
DataField, and SortExpression properties. The first is the text that will display
in the table header for that column, the second is the field in your data source to
bind, and the third is the field to sort by when the column header is clicked. The
ButtonColumn is just like LinkButtons from Listing 17.6, and it can be handled
in the exact same way, so you can ignore it for now.

Using Templated Controls to Display Data

A few other properties to note are in the `DataGrid` declaration. By default, the `DataGrid` automatically generates one column for each of the columns in your data source. You turn off that feature using the `AutoGenerateColumns` property to display our own columns as defined in the `<Columns>` element (if you left `AutoGenerateColumns` to `true` and also defined your own columns, the `DataGrid` would display both sets). `AllowSorting` and `AllowPaging` simply turn on the sorting and paging features for the `DataGrid`. `PageSize` dictates how many rows to display on each page of the `DataGrid`.

Take a look at the VB .NET code for this page, shown in Listing 17.8, which is equally simple.

LISTING 17.8

Controlling a `DataGrid`

```
Private Sub Page_Load(ByVal sender As System.Object, _
    ByVal e As System.EventArgs) Handles MyBase.Load
    'Put user code to initialize the page here
    Dim dsBlog As New DataSet()

    daBlog.Fill(dsBlog)

    dgBlog.DataSource = dsBlog
    If Not Page.IsPostBack Then
        dgBlog.DataBind()
    End If
End Sub

Sub dgBlog_SortCommand(ByVal Sender As Object, _
    ByVal e As DataGridSortCommandEventArgs) Handles dgBlog.SortCommand
    Dim dsBlog As New DataSet()
    Dim dvSorted As DataView

    daBlog.Fill(dsBlog)

    dvSorted = dsBlog.Tables(0).DefaultView
    dvSorted.Sort = e.SortExpression

    dgBlog.DataSource = dvSorted
    dgBlog.DataBind()
End Sub

Sub dgBlog_PageIndexChanged(ByVal Sender As Object, _
    ByVal e As DataGridPageChangedEventArgs) Handles dgBlog.PageIndexChanged
    dgBlog.CurrentPageIndex = e.NewPageIndex
    dgBlog.DataBind()
End Sub
```

17

The Page_Load method here is standard and should be familiar at this point. The
dgBlog_SortCommand method is executed when a column header is clicked in the
DataGrid to sort that column. The DataGridSortCommandEventArgs parameter
passes the name of the field to sort by (as defined by the SortExpression attributes in Listing 17.7). This method essentially retrieves the data from the database
again, uses a DataView to sort appropriately, and then rebinds the DataGrid.

The final method, dgBlog_PageIndexChanged, simply sets the
DataList.CurrentPageIndex value to the number passed in from the
DataGridPageChangedEventArgs parameter and rebinds the DataGrid to
change the page. The output is shown in Figure 17.5.

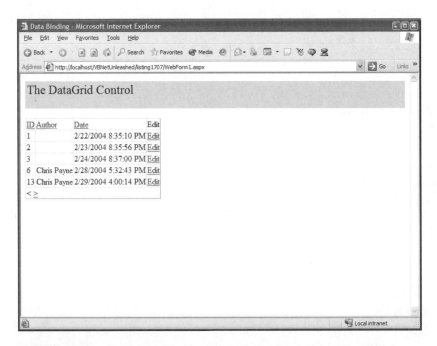

FIGURE 17.5   Sorting and paging a DataGrid is easily accomplished.

The DataGrid does provide some more properties that enable you to customize its
appearance, although you're still stuck with a basic table layout. Using various
TableItemStyle properties (AlternatingItemStyle, EditItemStyle,
ItemStyle, and so on), you can specify typical CSS/HTML properties. For example,
when put inside your DataGrid control, the following code would display every
other row in yellow:

```
<AlternatingItemStyle BackColor="Yellow" />
```

These types of properties also apply to the DataList, but not the Repeater.

> **TIP**
>
> It might often seem like a good idea to start with a `DataGrid`, but you might find that its additional features do not make up for its rigidity. Many web pages require more customized output than the `DataGrid` can easily deliver. You could spend time fiddling with the `DataGrid`, or you can just take a step back and use the `Repeater` and build any additional features, such as paging, sorting, or editing in, yourself.

Writing "Bindable" Web Controls

To create a web control, you simply create a new class that inherits (directly or indirectly) from the `System.Web.UI.Control` class and then override the `Render` method. `Control` provides all of the properties and functionality that will get you started in participating in ASP.NET web forms. The `Render` method is called by the ASP.NET engine to do the actual writing of HTML code to the client browser. In addition, every web control has a `Controls` property to which you can easily and efficiently add other controls to enhance your functionality.

A very simple control could look like Listing 17.9.

LISTING 17.9
A Simple Web Control

```
Imports System
Imports System.Web.UI
Imports System.Web.UI.WebControls


Namespace VBNetUnleashed
    Public Class MyControl
        Inherits Control

        Protected Overrides Sub Render(output As HtmlTextWriter)
            output.Write("Hello")
        End Sub
    End Class
End Namespace
```

When compiled and used in your application, this control simply writes `Hello` to the browser. That, in particular, isn't very useful, but this simple framework applies to all web controls. In the `Render` method, you can incorporate other controls and classes to fill out your control. `HtmlTextWriter` is a form of `StringWriter` that sends HTML content to the browser; anything that you write to this `StringWriter` is displayed to the user.

Also recall that, earlier, you learned that you can bind any data to any property of a web control. Custom controls that you build are no exception.

Now you examine a more real-world scenario: You'll create a custom web control that contains bindable properties. First create a new Web Control Library VS .NET project called LoginForm. VS .NET autogenerates a few properties and methods for you. Listing 17.10 shows the code for your control.

LISTING 17.10
Custom Login Form Control

```
Imports System.ComponentModel
Imports System.Web.UI
Imports System.Web.UI.WebControls


Public Class LoginForm                                                    1
Inherits System.Web.UI.WebControls.WebControl

    Dim m_username As String
    Dim m_password As String
    Dim txtUsername As New TextBox()
    Dim txtPassword As New TextBox()

    <Bindable(True), Category("Appearance"), DefaultValue("")> Public Property
        Username() As String
        Get
            Return m_username
        End Get
        Set(ByVal Value As String)
            m_username = Value
        End Set
    End Property

    <Bindable(True), Category("Appearance"), DefaultValue("")> Public Property
        Password() As String
        Get
            Return m_password
        End Get
        Set(ByVal Value As String)
            m_password = Value
        End Set
    End Property
```

17

Writing "Bindable" Web Controls

LISTING 17.10
Continued

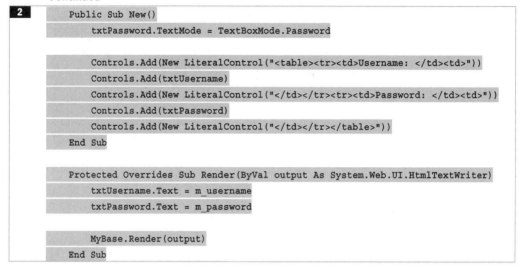

```
Public Sub New()
    txtPassword.TextMode = TextBoxMode.Password

    Controls.Add(New LiteralControl("<table><tr><td>Username: </td><td>"))
    Controls.Add(txtUsername)
    Controls.Add(New LiteralControl("</td></tr><tr><td>Password: </td><td>"))
    Controls.Add(txtPassword)
    Controls.Add(New LiteralControl("</td></tr></table>"))
End Sub

Protected Overrides Sub Render(ByVal output As System.Web.UI.HtmlTextWriter)
    txtUsername.Text = m_username
    txtPassword.Text = m_password

    MyBase.Render(output)
End Sub
```

```
End Class
```

This shouldn't look much different than any other .NET class you've created. The first thing to note is that your class inherits from the WebControl class **1** (which, in turn, inherits from the Control class). A couple of properties and private member variables are then declared; this is standard stuff.

The constructor **2** adds a few controls to your control's Control collection (try saying that three times fast). Recall that LiteralControls are rendered as plain HTML. The two TextBoxes, txtUsername and txtPassword, are parts of your login form.

Finally, the Render **2** method assigns properties to your TextBoxes and then, because you don't need to do any other custom functionality, calls the parent's Render method to spit out everything as HTML.

NOTE

Instead of creating two TextBox controls to display your output, you could have just as easily written the HTML by hand in the Render method. This method is actually more optimal because it involves less overhead, but it requires you to build more functionality by hand, whereas TextBox controls do them by nature.

For example, the following code would have accomplished the same thing for the `txtUsername` control:

```
output.Write("<input type=text name='" & Me.UniqueID & "_txtUsername' " & _
"value='" & Username & "'>")
```

Recall that the `HtmlTextWriter.Write` method sends whatever you ask it to the browser. The `Me.UniqueID` property enables you to give your control a unique name that can be used to control processing. You'll learn about this and the additional functionality that you have to create in the next section.

Build this project and add a new ASP.NET web application project to the existing solution. Call it `listing1710`. This web form will use your newly created control, but first you need to add that control to your project. The easiest way to do this is visually. Right-click on the toolbox in VS .NET and click Add/Remove Items (or Customize Toolbox, depending on your version of VS .NET). Click the Browse button to find the newly created control, `LoginForm.dll`. This adds the DLL to the list of references for your project, and you should now see the `LoginForm` control in the toolbox. Drag an instance of this control onto your form (you must be in design mode to do this). Listing 17.11 shows the HTML code for the `.aspx` file.

LISTING 17.11

Using a Custom Control in an `.aspx` page.

```
<%@ Register TagPrefix="VBNetUnleashed" Namespace="VBNetUnleashed"        1
    Assembly="LoginForm" %>
<%@ Page Language="vb" Codebehind="WebForm1.aspx.vb"
    Inherits="listing1710.WebForm1"%>
<html>
<head><title>Data Binding</title></head>
<body>
<table bgcolor="#ffdd55" width="100%">
<tr>
    <td><font size="5">The DataGrid Control</font><p></p></td>
</tr>
</table>
<form id="Form1" method="post" runat="server">
    <vbnetunleashed:LoginForm id="LoginForm1" runat="server"        2
        Username="<%# Username %>"
        Password="<%# Password %>"/>
</form>
</body></html>
```

17

Writing "Bindable" Web Controls

First things first: You need to tell your ASP.NET how to use the new control. Because it's not part of the existing ASP.NET framework, you need to be able to reference it somehow. The first line **1** uses the @ Register directive to define a friendly name for the control (the TagPrefix attribute), and it instructs the file of what namespace and assembly to look in for the class. This is a typical way of getting access to custom controls.

Then, in the next portion **2**, you instantiate the control using the TagPrefix you specified previously, and the class you built in Listing 17.10. The Username and Password properties are data bound with values that are created in your code-behind file, shown in Listing 17.12.

LISTING 17.12
The Logic for Your Custom Web Control

```
Public Class WebForm1
    Inherits System.Web.UI.Page
    Protected WithEvents LoginForm1 As VBNetUnleashed.LoginForm
    Public Username As String = "clpayne"
    Public Password As String = "TESTING"


    #Region " Web Form Designer Generated Code "
        ...
    #End Region

    Private Sub Page_Load(ByVal sender As System.Object, _
        ByVal e As System.EventArgs) Handles MyBase.Load
        'Put user code to initialize the page here
        DataBind()
    End Sub

End Class
```

This code-behind is about as simple as you can get. Your custom control is declared early on **1**, two properties are defined (note that in a more realistic application, such values would probably be retrieved from a database), and then the DataBind method is called **2**. This causes the values clpayne and TESTING to display in the control, as shown in Figure 17.6.

This particular example is rather simplistic, but it highlights everything that is needed to create custom controls and bind data to them. In the next section, you examine how to more fully take part in web forms functionality.

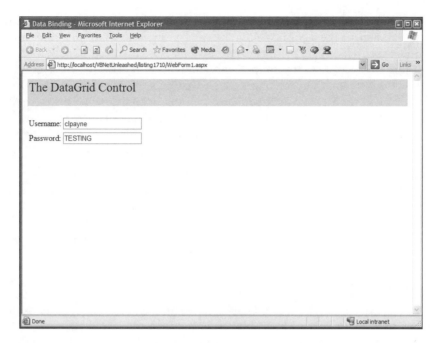

FIGURE 17.6   You can easily data-bind properties of custom web controls.

Retrieving Data During Postback

Most web controls have inherent functionality to retrieve postback data and raise events. For example, when you change the value in a `TextBox` and submit a form, the modified value is rendered when the page comes back, and the `TextChanged` event is raised. When you incorporate existing web controls in your custom controls, they maintain that capability, enabling you to concentrate on other functionality.

However, as mentioned earlier, incorporating existing web controls can involve additional overhead. It is thus faster if, instead of using web controls, you directly write the HTML output. The drawback to this is that you lose the postback and event-raising capabilities inherently provided by web controls. But do not worry—you can write that functionality yourself and take full advantage of web forms processing.

The Postback Processing Model

Processing postback data is a multistep process. ASP.NET logically divides each step to ensure that every control on a page can do its own thing without interfering with other controls. These three steps are important to know if you plan to create your own custom controls.

Retrieving Data During Postback

When a form post is first generated, ASP.NET finds all of the web controls on that page that implement the IPostBackDataHandler interface. This interface provides the contract that tells ASP.NET that a control wants to be involved in postback; without this interface, a control simply ignores any form processing. For every control that implements this interface, ASP.NET collects the respective posted data and calls the LoadPostData method, passing in the collected data. This method, required by IPostBackDataHandler, is where you process any data and, optionally, update the display of your control. After processing, if you decide that the state of your control has changed, you return true; otherwise, you return false.

Second, after all controls on a page have had LoadPostData called and returned true, ASP.NET calls the RaisePostDataChangedEvent method, also required by IPostBackDataHandler. This is where you can raise other events in response to the new data in your control. For example, when the text in a TextBox control changes, LoadPostData returns true, and RaisePostDataChangedEvent is called; it then raises the TextChanged event. The handling of these events can be done anywhere, but it is typically left to the web form developer to handle in an .aspx or code-behind file.

Finally, if your control plans to handle its own postback events (such as a button click), you need to implement the IPostBackEventHandler interface and tell the page that you expect to handle events. After the first two steps, ASP.NET calls the RaisePostBackEvent method, required by IPostBackEventHandler, for any control that is registered to raise events, and where you can then raise any necessary events. For example, when the Button control is clicked, it raises the Click event in the RaisePostBackEvent method.

Table 17.1 outlines this process and Figure 17.7 illustrates the three steps.

TABLE 17.1

The ASP.NET Postback Life Cycle

Step	Process
1.	Collect data and call LoadPostData
2.	If necessary, call RaisePostDataChangedEvent
3.	If necessary, call RaisePostBackEvent

One requirement must be met in all of this: Your control must have created unique names for any HTML form elements that you have created. This is easily done using the Control.UniqueID property. ASP.NET looks for controls with the proper name to pass data to and call methods from. Without the unique name, nothing is mapped correctly and your control can't function properly. If you have multiple HTML elements in your control, one of them must bear the exact UniqueID name for ASP.NET to route your events properly.

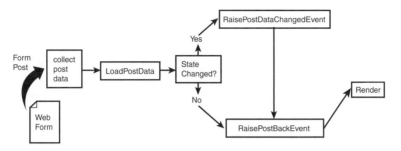

FIGURE 17.7   The postback life cycle of a control.

Modifying the `LoginForm` Control

It's time to jump straight into the code. Set up a new Web Controls Library VS .NET project, as you did for the last task, and name it `LoginForm2`. Use the code in Listing 17.13 to build your control; it is nearly identical to the one from the previous task, but instead of using a `TextBox` control, you render your own HTML.

LISTING 17.13
Rendering Your Custom Control

```
Imports System.ComponentModel
Imports System.Web.UI
Imports System.Collections.Specialized

Public Class LoginForm2                                                    1
    Inherits System.Web.UI.WebControls.WebControl
    Implements IPostBackDataHandler, IPostBackEventHandler

    Dim m_username As String
    Dim m_password As String

    'set up Username and Password properties here
    ...

    Public Event Submit As EventHandler                                    2

    Public Overridable Sub OnSubmit(ByVal e As EventArgs)
        RaiseEvent Submit(Me, e)
    End Sub

    Public Function LoadPostData(ByVal postDataKey As String, _
        ByVal postCollection As NameValueCollection) As Boolean _
        Implements IPostBackDataHandler.LoadPostData
        m_username = postCollection(Me.UniqueID + "_Username")
```

Retrieving Data During Postback

LISTING 17.13
Continued

```
        m_password = postCollection(Me.UniqueID + "_Password")
3       Page.RegisterRequiresRaiseEvent(Me)
        Return False
    End Function


    Public Sub RaisePostDataChangedEvent() _
        Implements IPostBackDataHandler.RaisePostDataChangedEvent
        'do nothing
    End Sub


    Public Sub RaisePostBackEvent(ByVal eventArgument As String) _
        Implements IPostBackEventHandler.RaisePostBackEvent
        OnSubmit(EventArgs.Empty)
    End Sub


    Protected Overrides Sub Render(ByVal output As System.Web.UI.HtmlTextWriter)
        output.Write("<table><tr><td>Username: </td><td>")
4       output.Write("<input type=text name=""" & Me.UniqueID & _
            "_Username"" Value=""" & m_username & """>")
        output.Write("</td></tr><tr><td>Password: </td><td>")
        output.Write("<input type=password name=""" & Me.UniqueID & _
            "_Password"" value=""" & m_password & """>")
        output.Write("</td></tr><tr><td colspan=2>")
        output.Write("<input type=""submit"" name=""" & Me.UniqueID & """ " & _
            "value=""Submit"">")
        output.Write("</td></tr></table>")
    End Sub


End Class
```

The first portion **1** implements the two interfaces that you learned about in the last section. The next highlighted section **2** declares an event that your control will raise when the form is submitted the OnSubmit method that invokes the delegate for that event (see Part I, "Fundamentals," for more information on creating events and delegates).

The rest of the code then defines the three methods that are required by the IPostBackDataHandler and IPostBackEventHandler interfaces: LoadPostData, RaisePostDataChangedEvent, and RaisePostBackEvent.

The first method takes in a `NameValueCollection` object that contains the values passed in from the form submission. The key of that `NameValueCollection` is the name of the element in the control, which you'll define in a moment. In this case, `LoadPostData` retrieves the posted values and populates the member variables with the data. You call the `Page.RegisterRequiresRaiseEvent` **3** , passing in the current control. This method tells ASP.NET that you expect your control to handle events (the third step from Table 17.2) and that the `RaisePostBackEvent` method should be called later.

The `RaisePostDataChangedEvent` does nothing here; in fact, this method will never even be called in the example. It is here only because `IPostBackDataHandler` requires it. Had you returned `true` from `LoadPostData`, this method would have been called. You could raise any necessary events here.

The `RaisePostBackEvent` method simply calls the `OnSubmit` event, which generates the `Submit` event. The handling of that event is left to the web form. In this case, the `eventArgument` parameter holds nothing, but it could be used to pass a parameter (more on that in a moment).

Finally, the `Render` method outputs the HTML that the control should spit out to the browser. It should look similar to Listing 17.10, except that, instead of using web controls, you are creating your own output. Notice the assignment of the `UniqueID` property to the `name` attribute of the various elements **4** . Each of the `name` attributes should be different, but at least one should have the `UniqueID` property as its name, or nothing will work correctly.

You're going to generate just a simple web forms page to use this control. Create a new ASP.NET web forms project in VS .NET, and import your custom control into the toolbox, as you did in the previous task. Add your control to the page, and add the method shown in Listing 17.14 to your code-behind file.

LISTING 17.14
Handling the Control's Event

```
Sub LoginForm_Click(ByVal Sender As Object, ByVal e As EventArgs) _
    Handles LoginForm21.Submit
    lblOutput.Text = "Form Submitted!"
End Sub
```

When you click the button displayed by your custom control, you should see something similar to Figure 17.8.

Retrieving Data During Postback

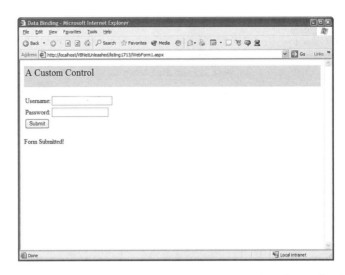

FIGURE 17.8   Your custom control can now handle postback data and events.

There is another way to generate postback events. Instead of relying on the automatic submission that an HTML button element generates, you can use client-side JavaScript to generate a postback. For example, you could have replaced the button in Listing 17.13 with the following:

```
output.Write("<input type=""button"" OnClick=""jscript:" & _
   Page.GetPostBackEventReference(Me, "Submit") & """ value=""Submit"">")
```

The GetPostBackEventReference method automatically generates the necessary client-side JavaScript code to cause a postback. The two parameters are the control itself and a value that is passed as the eventArgument parameter of the RaisePostBackEvent method.

The GetPostBackEventReference method gives you more control than the method you used in Listing 17.13, and it also enables you to generate postbacks for HTML elements that might not normally do so (such as a link tag or text box). Finally, when you use this method, you no longer have to call the RegisterRequiresRaiseEvent method, as in Listing 17.13; ASP.NET generates the JavaScript code that makes it understood that RaisePostBackEvent should be called.

Summary

In this chapter, you learned everything from simple data binding to complex custom control postback and data binding handling. You'll encounter the three templated controls (`Repeater`, `DataList`, and `DataGrid`) everywhere you go; they are very useful and, consequently, should be examined further through your own applications. Custom web controls are also very common, and you saw how to enhance their performance by building your own postback-handling methods.

As always, be sure to check out the .NET Framework SDK documentation, if you haven't yet. Also, http://www.gotdotnet.com houses some great visitor-submitted web controls that go into advanced data-binding techniques.

Part III discusses the Windows Forms equivalent of the `DataGrid` control. It might be helpful to examine the differences and understand the similarities.

Further Reading

17

GotDotNet User Samples, http://www.gotdotnet.com/community/usersamples/.

IBuySpy Portal, http://www.asp.net/IBS_Portal/DesktopDefault.aspx.

"Roadmap for Web Forms Data Binding." MSDN website, http://support. microsoft.com/default.aspx?scid=kb;en-us;313481.

18 STATE MANAGEMENT

IN BRIEF

Maintaining state in a web application is very important. With traditional desktop applications, it is assumed that the same person who initiated the application is following through with the use of the application; in other words, you typically have a one user/one application installation paradigm. You can keep track of what the user does, where the user has been, and any settings that the user has applied. This isn't so in web applications.

The Web is a stateless medium because everything works on a disconnected model. A client makes a request of a server, receives the response, and then disconnects. If it wasn't this way, Internet traffic would be impossible to handle, and bandwidth would be certainly an issue—especially for those over dial-up connections. That's not to mention that the server would have to maintain a separate application for each client request.

So you've come to learn that you don't interact with web applications the way you do with traditional desktop-based ones. From the client perspective, you can't be guaranteed that your information will be saved if you browse to a different site or submit a form. From the server perspective, you have to take extra steps just to make sure that you can present a cohesive experience to the user, as well as to perform any kind of traffic logging.

However, that doesn't mean it can't be done. Many supplemental technologies have been developed to address this issue, some more complicated than others. ASP.NET makes it very easy to maintain state in several different forms and to keep track of your users as if each was the only user of your application.

WHAT YOU NEED

SOFTWARE REQUIREMENTS	Windows 2000, XP, or 2003 .NET Framework 1.1 SDK Visual Studio .NET 2003 with Visual Basic .NET installed SQL Server or Microsoft Desktop Database Engine (MSDE) Internet Information Server (version 5 or later)
HARDWARE REQUIREMENTS	PC desktop or laptop system
SKILL REQUIREMENTS	Advanced knowledge in HTML Intermediate knowledge in the .NET Framework and ASP.NET

STATE MANAGEMENT AT A GLANCE

Storing Application-Level Data

Recall that an ASP.NET application is the collection of all files within a virtual directory, including images, HTML files, and application files (.aspx, .ascx, .asmx, web.config, global.asax, .dll). Application state, then, is a collection of data that applies to your application as a whole, regardless of how many users or visitors you have.

Managing application state is very easy to do in ASP.NET, but a few precautions must be taken. This section shows you how to become adept at doing so.

Every time an ASP.NET application is started, a pool of instances of the System.Web.HttpApplicationState class is created. This class is like any other collection or dictionary object: It contains key-value pairs of information that you can insert, update, or delete from.

You can access this instance from your code in one of two ways: through the Page.Application property or through the HttpContext.Application property (the HttpContext class encapsulates all information about an HTTP client request). The latter is useful when you might not have an instance of the Page class available, but your code is running as part of an HTTP request, such as in a custom web control or DLL.

Listing 18.1 shows a use of application state. With a few exceptions, it doesn't get any more complicated than this.

LISTING 18.1
Using Application State

```
<%@ Page Language="vb" %>
<script runat=server>
    sub Page_Load(Sender as object, e as EventArgs)      1
        Application("MyVariable") = "Hello World!"

        DataBind()
    end sub
</script>
<html>
<head>
    <title>Maintaining State</title>
</head>
<body>
    <table bgcolor="#ffdd55" width="100%">
    <tr>
        <td><font size="5">Application state</font><p></p>
        </td></tr>
    </table>
```

18

Storing Application-Level Data

LISTING 18.1
Continued

```
<form id="Form2" method="post" runat="server">
    <%# Application("MyVariable").ToString() %>
</form>
</body>
</html>
```

In the `Page_Load` method early in the code ▮1▮, you insert a value into application state (or update it if it is there already). Then you output that value on your page through data binding. That's all there is to it. As a collection type object, the `HttpApplicationState` object has typical properties and methods, such as `AllKeys`, `Count`, `Add`, `Clear`, and `Remove` (the usage of collection objects is beyond the scope of this chapter—see Part 1, "Fundamentals," for more information). You can also store any type of object, including custom web controls, in application state. These objects can be inserted just as you've done in Listing 18.1, or inserted at the initialization of the application (see Chapter 20, "Website Management," for more information).

> **TIP**
>
> In the real world, application state isn't used very often; there are often better mechanisms (such as cache or session state) to do whatever you need to do. Perhaps even less frequently seen are objects inserted during application initialization. Also, threading issues (which are beyond the scope of this chapter) can affect your usage of application state.
>
> That doesn't mean that application state isn't useful, but you should be sure to weigh your options when you need to store data in a state mechanism.

You can now access the `MyVariable` application value from anywhere in your application, from any `.aspx` file or code-behind. This value has become global to your entire application. That said, there are certain usage guidelines for application state.

First, the data you store here should be appropriate for the context. For example, you should store global data such as total website visits instead of data specific to a single request, such as a user's personal information. The latter belongs to a specific user, not the entire application, so it should be stored in session state instead (which you'll see in the next section).

Second, you must keep in mind the volatility of application state, or any type of state in a web application. The application state is tied to an application, so any time the application is restarted (due to a crash, a maintenance recycling, and so on), the application-state data is lost. Anything that you need to persist should be stored in a more permanent medium, such as a database. Application state then could become a great cache location to store data retrieved from a database.

Third, remember that data stored in application state is stored in the machine's memory. Most web servers nowadays have plenty of memory to spare, but even so, storing a seldom-used 100MB `DataSet` in application state isn't exactly the best use of resources, and it can affect application performance even if you have 4GB of RAM to spare.

Finally, as with any multithreaded application, you need to be aware of concurrency issues. Because multiple threads could be accessing the same value at the same time, you should ensure that no data is lost or overwritten in these situations. You can do this by placing locks on the application state using the `HttpApplicationState.Lock` and `HttpApplicationState.UnLock` methods to synchronize access. Figure 18.1 shows an example of locking; see Part V, "Advanced Programming," for more information about thread synchronization.

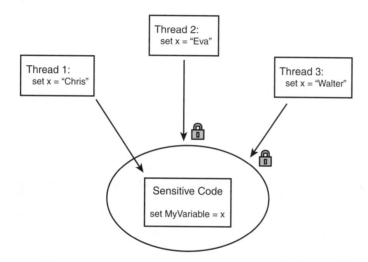

FIGURE 18.1   With synchronization, only one thread is allowed in at a time; all others are locked out.

Storing Session-Specific Data

As with application state, session state represents a collection of data that can be used to provide cohesiveness for visitors to an application. Session state, however, is user-specific, meaning that every visitor to your site has his or her own session store. As such, session state is a bit more complicated to handle and more strenuous to the server.

A Refresher on Web Sessions

If the Web is stateless, how do you know when one visit to your site is from the same visitor as 5 minutes ago? How do you keep track of a single user? The answer is to use some type of unique identifying information for each user and somehow make sure that that data is communicated across every web request.

Storing Session-Specific Data

ASP.NET has two ways of doing this: via HTTP cookies and via the HTTP query string. Either way, a globally unique identifier (GUID) is created for every user upon first hitting your application. In the cookie scenario, that value is then written to the client's computer as a cookie, which is then passed back and forth on subsequent requests to keep track of that user. This is the most common scenario and the easiest to implement, but the drawback is that users can easily disable cookie usage on their computers, thereby rendering your session control useless.

In the other method, known as cookieless session state, or sometimes as cookie-munging, every link that the user follows must contain the GUID in the URL. ASP.NET can automatically and dynamically modify every link on your site to contain this GUID so that when a user clicks on a link, you can retrieve this value and identify the user. This method is more versatile than cookies because it doesn't depend on the client, but the user session GUID is exposed to the user (which could be a security issue) and some rare browsers actually don't work properly with this method. You can usually discern when cookieless session state is being used simply from the URL of a website. For example:

```
http://localhost/VBNetUnleashed/listing1801/(por3ki45tbwkvp45lazhpfyy)/WebForm1.aspx
```

Here you can see the GUID (`por3ki45tbwkvp45lazhpfyy`) embedded in the URL. Either way, you can access and modify session data in the same manner.

One other concern about session state is knowing how long a session can remain valid. This is a subjective matter and can vary from one site to another. For example, if you receive one request at 1 p.m., then a second request with the same GUID at 10 p.m., and nothing in between, is that the same user? Or, more specifically, is that the same session from the same user? Also recall that session-state data is stored in memory like application state. Is it a good idea to hold one person's information in memory for 9 hours or longer?

Typically, a web session is defined to "end," or time out, after 20 minutes of inactivity. In the previous example, the two requests would constitute two separate sessions. This is usually an appropriate amount of time to monitor user visits and keep your server memory tied up.

See Chapter 20 for more information on configuring how session state works on your server, including adjusting the timeout and cookie values.

Working with Sessions

You use session state exactly as you do application state. Every time a user visits your site and is determined to be a new user (in other words, no identifying information is passed that can match that user to an existing session), an `HttpSessionState` object is created. As with `HttpApplicationState`, this object is a key-value collection of data that can be referenced either through the `Page.Session` or the `HttpContext.Session` properties.

You can easily modify Listing 18.1 to use session state by simply replacing the word `Application` with `Session`:

```
Session("MyVariable") = "Hello World!"
```

The collections work identically. The main difference is that session data is accessible only by the user identified by that session GUID; no one else can access it. This makes it a nice place to store user-specific information.

You should be aware of a few additional properties and methods. `HttpSessionState.SessionID` returns the GUID for the current session. This can be useful if you need to track or store this information in a database. The `Abandon` method immediately ends a session and deletes any stored session data. This is useful for users who would like to "log out" of the application.

All of the guidelines for using application state apply to session state, except for the concurrency issue. It is assumed that because a single session represents a single user and, therefore, a single thread, concurrency does not need to be maintained; no more than one thread should ever access a single session store.

TIP

ASP.NET enables you make session data less volatile by storing it in places other than in-process memory. The data can be stored in out-of-process memory (so that application restarts won't affect session store), in a database, or on an entirely different server. Each of these involves performance hits but provides extra insurance if your session data is critical. Chapter 20 provides more information on how to set this up.

Finally, you can turn off session state storage for a given page using the `@ Page` directive:

```
<%@ Page Language="VB" ... EnableSessionState="value" %>
```

`value` can be `true`, `readonly`, or `false`. Turning off session state (the default for ASP.NET is on) nets you a small performance gain because ASP.NET doesn't have to manage that extra data. See Chapter 20 for information on how to disable it for your entire application.

Store Viewstate

A control's viewstate is its current condition: What color is it? What text is contained within it? What font size does it use? Is it visible? Every ASP.NET control (including the `Page` class) provides its own viewstate management so that it can restore its look and feel upon form postbacks.

Store Viewstate

You can also use viewstate to store temporary data, as you would with application and session states. The difference is that data stored in viewstate persists only for a form post—a single page—instead of over the entire application or user session. Control over viewstate can be useful when designing user interfaces.

Recall from Table 16.2 in Chapter 16, "Basic Web Application," that viewstate management happens automatically in an ASP.NET page lifecycle (steps 3 and 9). When a page is rendered, any viewstate information is encoded and output in HTML hidden elements. Then when the form is submitted, the encoded viewstate data is decoded and the page reinstates any necessary values when the page is displayed again.

For example, open Listing 18.1 in a browser and view the HTML source. You should see something similar to Listing 18.2 in your form.

LISTING 18.2
Encoded Viewstate Information

```
<form name="Form2" method="post" action="WebForm1.aspx" id="Form2">
    <input type="hidden" name="__VIEWSTATE"
    value="dDwxNDEzNDIyOTIxO3Q8O2w8aTwxPjs+O2w8dDw7bDxpPDA+Oz47bDx0PEA8SGVsbG8g
        V29ybGQhOz47Oz47Pj47Pj47PsdTQRSlfRCZajFTuGzjpEOJTC/8" />
```

The long string in lines 3 and 4 contains data regarding the appearance and properties of any controls on your page. This string is submitted upon a form post, is used by ASP.NET to restore values, and then is rewritten (with any changes) back to the page as a hidden element.

You can add data to the viewstate just as you do with application and session stores. In fact, the class behind viewstate, `System.Web.UI.StateBag`, is just another type of name-value pair collection object and can be accessed via the `ViewState` property of any control. Listing 18.1 can therefore be modified to use viewstate by replacing the word `Application` with `ViewState`. In such a case, you would be accessing the `Page` control's viewstate.

Let's examine a more useful scenario: developing a tab control similar to the one available in Windows Forms, albeit much simpler. Listing 18.3 shows the code for the custom control. You will create a new Web Control Library project in VS .NET and use the code here.

LISTING 18.3
Using ViewState in a Custom Control

```
Imports System.ComponentModel
Imports System.Web.UI

Public Class TabControl
    Inherits System.Web.UI.WebControls.WebControl
    Implements IPostBackEventHandler
```

LISTING 18.3
Continued

```
<Bindable(True), Category("Appearance"), DefaultValue("")> _
Property SelectedTab() As Integer                                        1
    Get
        Return CType(ViewState("TabIndex"), Integer)
    End Get
    Set(ByVal Value As Integer)
        ViewState("TabIndex") = CType(Value, Integer)
    End Set
End Property

Public Sub RaisePostBackEvent(ByVal eventArgument As String) _
Implements IPostBackEventHandler.RaisePostBackEvent
    ViewState("TabIndex") = CType(eventArgument, Int32)
End Sub

Protected Overrides Sub Render(ByVal output As System.Web.UI.HtmlTextWriter)
    output.Write("<table border=1 width=300><tr>")
    output.Write("<td><a id=""" & Me.UniqueID & """ href=""javascript:" & _
        Page.GetPostBackEventReference(Me, 1) & """>A</a></td>")
    output.Write("<td><a id=""" & Me.UniqueID & """ href=""javascript:" & _
        Page.GetPostBackEventReference(Me, 2) & """>B</a></td>")
    output.Write("<td><a id=""" & Me.UniqueID & """ href=""javascript:" & _
        Page.GetPostBackEventReference(Me, 3) & """>C</a></td>")
    output.Write("</tr><tr><td colspan=3>")

    Select Case ViewState("TabIndex")
        Case 1
            output.Write("<input type=submit value='A'>")
        Case 2
            output.Write("<input type=submit value='B'>")
        Case 3
            output.Write("<input type=submit value='C'>")
    End Select

    output.Write("</td></tr></table>")
End Sub

End Class
```

In this example, you would like the currently selected tab to persist no matter what happens elsewhere on the page. For this reason, you store data in the viewstate.

Store Viewstate

The `SelectedTab` property 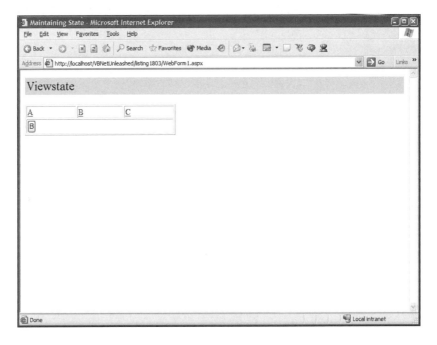 that the user can use to manually set the selected tab is then defined. Note that the value is stored and retrieved from viewstate; if you didn't do this, the selected tab value would be lost on every form post. This will make more sense when you compile this control and use it.

The `RaisePostBackEvent` method is then defined so that your control can participate in form postback processing (which is needed if you plan to allow users to select tabs). This method simply retrieves the `eventArgument` parameter and stores it in the viewstate. The `Render` method then conditionally writes some HTML code, depending on which tab was selected (note that the use of HTML submit buttons here is trivial, but it gets the point across).

NOTE

See "Write Your Own 'Bindable' Web Controls" in Chapter 17, "Data Binding in Web Applications," for more information on handling postback in a custom control and on using custom controls in an ASP.NET page.

Compile and drop this new custom control on an `.aspx` page and view it in your browser. Figure 18.2 shows an example output.

FIGURE 18.2   Viewstate allows your control to maintain state across form posts.

When you click on one of the tab headings, the button that is displayed changes appropriately. When you then click on one of the buttons (and thus generate a form post), the selected tab remains selected. If in Listing 18.3 you did not save the `SelectedTab` property in viewstate, the control would have no way to remember which tab was selected before the form post; it would revert to the initial value every time.

If you were to re-create this example using three `Panel` or `PlaceHolder` controls and their `Visible` properties, for example, it could work without any code to explicitly manage viewstate. This is because every web control already manages its own viewstate. Each control remembers whether it was visible thanks to viewstate and hidden HTML elements.

You can store any object in viewstate that can be serialized or that has a `TypeConverter` class defined for it. Here you simply stored an integer, but that opens up access to a lot of different types of data (including `DataSets`, using the `WriteXml` method to serialize the data). As with anything in programming, just because you can store anything doesn't mean that you should.

Remember that viewstate management happens at two steps in the ASP.NET page lifecycle, and that data is encoded and written to the client and transmitted back and forth. If you have a lot of viewstate information, all of this can add up to quite a performance hit. If you have a lot of data to store, try putting it elsewhere, such as in application or session stores, or in cache (which you learn about in Chapter 19, "Caching").

You can also disable viewstate management for any existing control in ASP.NET to enhance performance through the `Control.EnableViewState` property. For example, if you used the following code (where `TabControl1` is the instance of the tab control from Listing 18.3), you would effectively render the control useless:

```
TabControl1.EnableViewState = false
```

The control wouldn't be capable of remembering which tabs were selected and, therefore, wouldn't function correctly.

Similarly, you can turn off viewstate storage for all controls on a page using the @ Page directive:

```
<%@ Page Language="vb" ... EnableViewState="false" %>
```

Doing this enables you to squeeze more performance out of your pages, but be aware that you might lose a lot of functionality that you didn't realize depended on viewstate.

Store Viewstate

VIEWSTATE ON SERVER FARMS

Viewstate can get tricky to manage on server farms (where a website is hosted by more than one machine). Viewstate data is encoded when it is written to the page, and part of this encoding contains identifying information about the machine the code was generated on. When viewstate is decoded, this identifying information is matched against the currently executing code to ensure that no breach of security has occurred—in other words, that the form postback was not arbitrarily generated from another machine that might be trying to gain access to your application.

This is obviously a problem on server farms, where one particular user can be bounced from one machine to another at any point. In this case, the foreign machine can be trusted, but the viewstate security still prevents execution with the error message "The View State is invalid for this page and might be corrupted." This is known as session-state migration.

You can get around this issue by using the `EnableViewStateMac` property:

```
<%@ Page Language="VB" ... EnableViewStateMac="false" %>
```

When set to `false` (the default is `true`), a machine authentication check (MAC) is not performed, and your application will work across a server farm.

Be aware, though, that now you have no defense against a client-tampered viewstate value. This is a very rare problem anyway, but it is still one that should be observed in today's security-conscious world.

Managing Cookies

An HTTP cookie is simply a file issued from a web server that is stored on a client's computer. Cookies are typically used to store identifying information about a user or personal preferences. They've gotten a bad rap over the years and are still misunderstood by a large percentage of the Internet-going population. Cookies are actually very useful tools that can enhance the performance and usability of your application.

This section shows you how to read, write, and otherwise control cookies on a client's computer.

A Refresher on Cookies

Technically, a web server does not create or write cookies to a client's computer; that would be an incredible security issue. Instead, a server can issue certain HTTP commands that instruct a client's browser to write the cookie file for it. The HTTP commands are well known and must be supported (and accepted) by the browser; they are written in limited security contexts and are limited to very simple data types.

Likewise, cookies are sent back to the server via data streams and command in HTTP commands and headers. The server does not read from the client's computer, nor does the server tell the client to surrender its cookies; clients voluntarily provide them to the server.

Furthermore, cookies are domain specific, meaning that one site cannot, in theory, read cookies issued by another site—or even sometimes by the same site. For example, http://127.0.0.1 and http://localhost both represent the web server on your own local computer, but cookies issued at one URL would not be accessible from the other. In reality, these security measures can by bypassed as well, but that is beyond the scope of this book.

Cookies also have expiration dates, dictated by the web server. They can be any time from when the user closes his browser to 100 years in the future.

All that said, cookies are actually secure and should not be feared. As a developer, you're probably already aware of that. They do provide a great way to extend functionality on your website. For example, as previously mentioned, session IDs are often written to cookies so that you can track a user. Cookies can also be used as a cache of information that might be otherwise time consuming to get, such as website preferences stored in a database. Many sites actually depend on cookies to allow users to "log in" and view more personal or secure information.

Even with all this power, cookies are very easy to manage. You'll find there's not much difference between them than application or session states.

Working with Cookies

Cookies are very simple to work with, but there are a few things to note about them. For example, when you want to read cookies from the client, you use the intrinsic Request object (an instance of the HttpRequest class). When you want to write cookies, you use the intrinsic Response object (an instance of the HttpResponse class). These two classes control and provide data about the requests issued from clients and the responses sent back to them.

Create a new web forms project in VS .NET, and use Listing 18.4 as the HTML portion of your page.

LISTING 18.4
Viewing and Adding Cookies

```
<%@ Page Language="vb" AutoEventWireup="false" Codebehind="WebForm1.aspx.vb"
    Inherits="listing1804.WebForm1"%>
<html>
<head><title>Maintaining State</title></head>
<body>
    <table bgcolor="#ffdd55" width="100%">
    <tr><td><font size="5">Cookies</font></td></tr>
    </table>
    <form id="Form1" method="post" runat="server">
        <table border="1">
        <tr>
```

18

Managing Cookies

LISTING 18.4
Continued

```
                <td><b>Name</b></td>
                <td><b>Value</b></td>
                <td><b>Domain</b></td>
                <td><b>Expires</b></td>
                <td><b>Path</b></td>
                <td><b>Secure</b></td>
            </tr>
            <asp:Repeater ID="rptCookies" Runat="server">
                <ItemTemplate>
                    <tr>
                        <td><%# Request.Cookies(Container.DataItem).Name %></td>
                        <td><%# Request.Cookies(Container.DataItem).Value %></td>
                        <td><%# Request.Cookies(Container.DataItem).Domain %></td>
                        <td><%# Request.Cookies(Container.DataItem).Expires %></td>
                        <td><%# Request.Cookies(Container.DataItem).Path %></td>
                        <td><%# Request.Cookies(Container.DataItem).Secure %></td>
                    </tr>
                </ItemTemplate>
            </asp:Repeater>
            <tr>
                <td><asp:TextBox ID="txtName" Runat="server" /></td>
                <td><asp:TextBox ID="txtValue" Runat="server" /></td>
                <td> </td>
                <td><asp:TextBox ID="txtExpires" Runat="server" /></td>
                <td> </td>
                <td><asp:TextBox ID="txtSecure" Runat="server" /></td>
            </tr>
            <tr>
                <td colspan="6"><asp:Button ID="btnSubmit" Text="Submit"
                    Runat="server" /></td>
            </tr>
            </table>
        </form>
        </body>
</html>
```

Here a simple `Repeater` control binds the properties of any existing cookies **1**. In this case, `Container.DataItem` evaluates to the name of the cookie, so you use that as your index value to retrieve said cookie from the `Request.Cookies` collection (which returns an `HttpCookieCollection` object, another type of dictionary object). The properties in the `ItemTemplate` are the various properties of the `HttpCookie` object, which represents a cookie on the client's system.

In the rest of the code, you create some `TextBox` controls so that you can add new cookies.

Listing 18.5 shows the applicable code-behind code for this page.

LISTING 18.5
Managing Cookies

```
Private Sub Page_Load(ByVal sender As System.Object, ByVal e As System.EventArgs) _
    Handles MyBase.Load
        'Put user code to initialize the page here
        If (Not Page.IsPostBack) Then
        rptCookies.DataSource = Request.Cookies
        rptCookies.DataBind()
    End If
End Sub


Sub AddCookie(ByVal Sender As Object, ByVal e As EventArgs) _
    Handles btnSubmit.Click
    'create cookie and set values
    Dim myCookie As New HttpCookie(txtName.Text)
    myCookie.Expires = txtExpires.Text
    myCookie.Value = txtValue.Text
    myCookie.Secure = txtSecure.Text
```

`Response.Cookies.Add(myCookie)`   **1**

```
    'bind cookie collection
    rptCookies.DataSource = Request.Cookies
    rptCookies.DataBind()
End Sub
```

18

In the `Page_Load` method, you bind your `Repeater` control to the `Request.Cookies` collection (again, remember that `Request` is used to collect information from the client and, in this case, all issued cookies). The `AddCookie` method takes the values entered into the `TextBox` controls in Listing 18.4, creates a new cookie, and then rebinds the `Repeater`. The code `Response.Cookies.Add(myCookie)` **1** is very important; if you don't add your newly created cookie to the `Response.Cookies` collection (and, therefore, to the response sent back to the client), the cookie will never be set on the client's computer and the data will be lost when the page is done executing.

Fire up this application in your browser and experiment with adding cookies. Figure 18.3 shows an example. If you create a cookie and then create another cookie with the same name, you overwrite the first cookie. When you first hit the page, you might see two cookies right away: `ASP.NET_SessionId`, which holds the session GUID that ASP.NET generated automatically; and `.ASPXAUTH`, a cookie used for ASP.NET authentication (see Chapter 21, "Security," for more information on authentication).

Managing Cookies

You might also note that Listing 18.4 didn't include `TextBox` controls to set values for the `Domain` and `Path` properties (the issuing website and application path). Although it's perfectly legal to do so, you'll find that if you set these properties to anything other than their default values, the cookies aren't actually set. This is because these two properties are security features. If you try to set the domain or path to something that doesn't exist on your website, or perhaps to another website, you violate the security and the cookie simply isn't written.

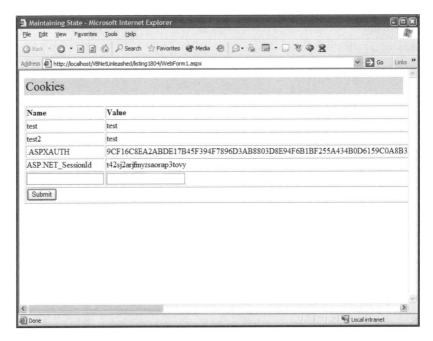

FIGURE 18.3   Cookies are easy to read and set on a client computer.

NOTE

If you try to retrieve a cookie that doesn't exist, ASP.NET returns `Nothing`. For example, the following code breaks if the cookie doesn't exist:

```
Dim i As Integer = Request.Cookies("Testing").Value
```

If the `Testing` cookie does not exist, it returns `Nothing`. Trying to access the `Value` property causes you to receive a `NullReferenceException`.

The expiration date should be set to some time in the future; if it is set to the past, the cookie won't actually be set. In fact, this is how you destroy existing cookies: You set the `Expires` property to a date in the page. If you don't set an expiration date, the cookie simply expires automatically when the user closes his or her browser.

One last interesting thing should be noted. Because cookies are strictly client side and are set and read via HTTP commands, a cookie isn't set on the client's computer until the page has rendered its output (and all HTTP commands have been interpreted and executed). In other words, you can't be sure that a cookie has been written until the next time that the user hits your page and sends back the cookie via HTTP (and if the client has cookies disabled in the browser, you'll never be sure). This is key to being able to work with cookies.

That said, try setting a cookie with an expiration date in the past (or even with explicit values for the `Domain` or `Path` properties); in other words, a cookie that won't be written. When you click the submit button, the newly created cookie will appear in your `Repeater`. Knowing that cookies aren't created until after the page is finished rendering and that this is an invalid cookie, theoretically, the cookie should not appear in the list.

The reason is simple: The `Response.Cookies` and `Request.Cookies` properties point to the *same* cookie collection. The `Response` and `Request` objects are responsible for either populating that collection or passing it to the client (see Figure 18.4). Therefore, because you added a cookie in Listing 18.5, that cookie is still there by the time the `Repeater` binds its data; at this point, the cookie is still an object in the server's memory. When the page is done rendering, however, and the HTTP commands are sent, the cookie isn't actually written to the client. The next time the user hits the page, that cookie isn't returned in `Request.Cookies`.

18

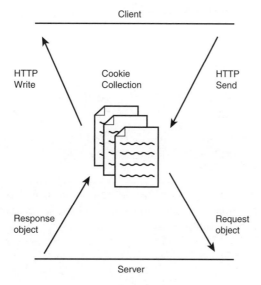

FIGURE 18.4   Cookies are sent and written via HTTP commands and are handled with the `Request` and `Response` objects.

Managing Cookies

This is a confusing issue that many beginners trip over, distinguishing between a cookie that the client has returned and a cookie that has only been created on the server computer. The former actually exists and is stored on the client's computer; the latter is only ephemeral. Just remember that your code must not try to read a cookie unless you are sure of its condition, or your application might do unexpected things.

DETECTING COOKIE USAGE

A client can choose to disable cookie usage on his or her computer, but because of the delayed writing/retrieval discussed in this task, it is difficult to know whether the cookie will actually be written or whether the user has disabled usage. This can severely interfere with any applications you've written that depend perhaps on identifying information in a cookie (such as session IDs).

The only sure way to detect whether a client allows cookies is a three-step process: Issue the cookie, wait for the user to request your page again (or if you can't wait, manually redirect the user to another page), and then try to retrieve that cookie. If it isn't there, you know that the user doesn't accept cookies.

Although this isn't an ideal solution and won't work for many applications, unfortunately, it is your only option if you need to determine cookie usage.

18

Summary

Not only is state management helpful in keeping track of users, but it also can be used to enhance performance. Making sure that you are properly using (or not using) state management requires intimate knowledge of your application and how it is supposed to function. Cookies are also an integral web technology that have gotten a bad rap; they are incredibly useful for preserving user state and ensuring cohesiveness.

The next chapter discusses a similar technology: ASP.NET caching. Properly using caching and state management can greatly enhance the performance of any application.

Further Reading

"Underpinnings of the Session State Implementation in ASP.NET." MSDN website, http://msdn.microsoft.com/library/default.asp?url=/library/en-us/dnaspp/html/aspnetsessionstate.asp.

"Taking a Bite Out of ASP.NET ViewState." MSDN website, http://msdn. microsoft.com/library/default.asp?url=/library/en-us/dnaspnet/html/ asp11222001.asp.

"How to Share Session State Between Classic ASP and ASP.NET." MSDN website, http://msdn.microsoft.com/library/default.asp?url=/library/en-us/dnaspp/ html/converttoaspnet.asp.

18

19 CACHING

IN BRIEF

By definition, a cache is a store that is easily accessible. People (or animals) put things in caches so that they can return to one place and spare the trouble of having to gather their belongings again from different locations. Caching in ASP.NET is no different; it is a buffer from which it is easier to retrieve processed data than go the long route of accessing the disk. You can put anything you want in ASP.NET's cache (which, in actuality, is the server's memory) and easily access it whenever and from wherever you want. For instance, you could store a commonly used `DataSet` in cache to avoid having to make costly database calls.

You'll find that caching is a powerful mechanism that can enhance the performance of web applications by orders of magnitude.

WHAT YOU NEED

SOFTWARE REQUIREMENTS	Windows 2000, XP, or 2003 .NET Framework 1.1 SDK Visual Studio .NET 2003 with Visual Basic .NET installed SQL Server or Microsoft Desktop Database Engine (MSDE) Internet Information Server (version 5 or later)
HARDWARE REQUIREMENTS	PC desktop or laptop system
SKILL REQUIREMENTS	Advanced knowledge in HTML Intermediate knowledge in the .NET Framework and ASP.NET

CACHING AT A GLANCE

Caching Static Elements

Caching static elements in ASP.NET is almost no different than using the application state store (see Chapter 18, "State Management"); both use a key-value-based dictionary paradigm. You can cache any object, from a simple string to a complex custom web control.

In this section, you'll see how to cache database queries to increase performance and how to manipulate that cache from creation to expiration.

Caching in ASP.NET is handled through the `System.Web.Caching.Cache` class, which is instantiated at the start of your application and available through the `Page.Cache` or `Context.Cache` properties. This class has various overridden methods to allow you to fine-tune your caching, but at its simplest, you use it just like a dictionary object:

```
Cache("MyCachedItem") = "Hey ya!"
```

or

```
txtFirstName.Text = Cache("MyFirstName").ToString()
```

Although this by itself is still very useful, it doesn't provide you with a lot of options. More useful are the `Add` and `Insert` methods, which look similar but have some fundamental differences. Primarily, the `Add` method will break (raise an exception) if you are trying to add a key a to cache that already exists; `Insert` will not. Also, `Add` provides only one implementation, whereas `Insert` has four overridden signatures. `Add` returns an object representing the item you added to the cache, and `Insert` returns nothing.

Take a look at the one signature that the two methods share. Its usage is as follows:

```
Cache.Insert(Key as string, Value as object, dependency as CacheDependency, _
    expiration as DateTime, slidingExpiration as TimeSpan, priority as
    CacheItemPriority,_removedCallback as CacheItemRemovedCallback)
```

Obviously, the `Key` and `Value` parameters are the key and value of the item you are inserting into the cache.

The `CacheDependency` object accepts a file or directory name (or array of names), other cache keys, or other `CacheDependency` objects to monitor. When the dependency changes, the cache in question automatically expires (it is then up to you to insert the updated data into the cache, if necessary). A common scenario is to monitor an XML file for changes.

The `expiration` parameter gives you an absolute time at which the cached item should expire itself (so that you can be sure your cached data never goes out of date, like milk).

19

Caching Static Elements

slidingExpiration is similar, but it defines a time period at which the item should expire, starting from the last time the cached item was accessed. For example, you can use this parameter to tell ASP.NET that a given item should expire if it is not accessed in 20 minutes. This is useful if the data itself never really goes out of date, but you don't need to keep the item in cache indefinitely. You cannot set both absolute and sliding expirations on a single cache item.

The priority parameter tells ASP.NET how important this particular item is in relation to other cached items. ASP.NET uses this information in case it ever needs to remove items from the cache based on server limitations. For example, if your server is running out of memory, ASP.NET will start to drop items from cache automatically based on the priority.

Finally, the removedCallback parameter enables you to execute a method upon expiration or removal. This can be useful, for example, if you have cached a database query and would like to send an email to an administrator when it has been removed, perhaps for monitoring purposes.

Create a new VS .NET web forms application based on Listing 17.3 (which has simple data-retrieval and binding operations). Add a Label control named lblTime to your web form; this keeps track of the time it takes to build your page, before and after caching. Listing 19.1 shows the code-behind file for this application.

LISTING 19.1
Implementing Caching

```
Private Sub Page_Load(ByVal sender As System.Object, ByVal e As System.EventArgs) _
    Handles MyBase.Load
    'Put user code to initialize the page here
    Dim startTime As DateTime = DateTime.Now
    Dim dsBlog As DataSet

    dsBlog = CType(Cache("BlogData"), DataSet)
    If (dsBlog Is Nothing) Then
        dsBlog = New DataSet()


        daBlog.Fill(dsBlog)


        Cache.Insert("BlogData", dsBlog, Nothing, DateTime.Now.AddSeconds(5), _
            TimeSpan.Zero, Caching.CacheItemPriority.Default, AddressOf onRemove)
    End If
```

LISTING 19.1
Continued

```
    rptBlog.DataSource = dsBlog
    rptBlog.DataBind()
    lblTime.Text = (DateTime.Now.Subtract(startTime)).ToString()
End Sub

Sub onRemove(ByVal key As String, ByVal value As Object, ByVal _          2
    reason As CacheItemRemovedReason)
    'do something
End Sub
```

This is very simple code. After the declarations, it tries to retrieve a `DataSet` from cache and then inserts one into cache **1**. Upon first execution, the data has to be pulled from the database. Subsequently, it is pulled from cache (at least for the next 5 seconds—you might want to adjust the absolute expiration for your applications).

The `onRemove` method **2** here does nothing, but you can use it to execute some code when the item is removed from cache. The method signature is standard, and each parameter should be self-explanatory.

NOTE

Note that the code in the remove callback executes at the appropriate time, *whether or not your ASP.NET page is being requested.*

However, to do this in the previous example, an instance of your page would have to be kept in memory so that ASP.NET can access the callback method without first receiving a user request. This can be a waste of resources.

To get around this issue, declare your `onRemove` method as `Shared` (`static` in C#). That way, ASP.NET can access this method without having to keep your page class in memory.

Also be sure that any code you execute here does something that is useful. For example, it would be useless to write a message to a `Label` control because no one would ever see it.

Figure 19.1 shows an example of pulling the data from the database. You'll notice that even in this simple example, you save 10–20 milliseconds of processing time, depending on your configuration, by using cache. With more complex applications, the savings can be orders of magnitude greater.

Caching Static Elements

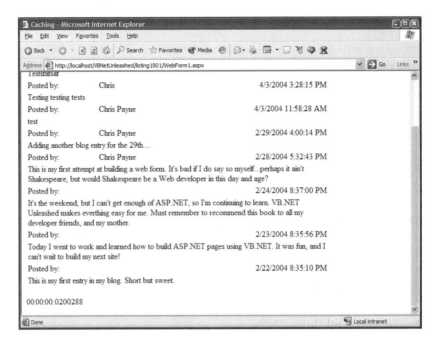

FIGURE 19.1 You can see the difference caching makes.

Caching Entire Pages

Sometimes it's more beneficial to cache the entire output of a page than to cache a piece of data here or there. ASP.NET lets you easily do so, while taking into account the various ways that an ASP.NET page can be called.

To cache the output of an entire page (that is, the HTML output), you need to use the @ OutputCache page directive or the Response.Cache property. The former is the declarative way of caching pages, and the latter is used for programmatic caching. The syntax is simple:

```
<%@ OutputCache Duration="xx" VaryByParam="none" VaryByControl="xxx"
   VaryByCustom="xxx" VaryByHeader="xxx" Location="any" %>
```

Duration is the amount of time to hold the page in the cache, in seconds. Each of the VaryBy attributes enables you to cache multiple versions of the page, depending on various parameters. VaryByParam is used to take into account querystring and form post values. For example, for the following @ OutputCache directive:

```
<%@ OutputCache Duration="60" VaryByParam="item" %>
```

the following two URLs would produce three different pages in the cache:

```
http://localhost/VBNetUnleashed/listing1901/WebForm1.aspx
http://localhost/VBNetUnleashed/listing1901/WebForm1.aspx?item=1
http://localhost/VBNetUnleashed/listing1901/WebForm1.aspx?item=2
```

The following two URLs, however, would produce only one version of the page in cache:

```
http://localhost/VBNetUnleashed/listing1901/WebForm1.aspx?item=1
http://localhost/VBNetUnleashed/listing1901/WebForm1.aspx?item=1&name=b
http://localhost/VBNetUnleashed/listing1901/WebForm1.aspx?item=1&value=63
```

Only the *item* querystring value is used to vary the versions in the cache. You can place multiple values in the VaryByParam attribute, separated by semicolons.

VaryByControl enables you to do the same as VaryByParam, this time using property names of controls on your page. VaryByCustom can be set to *browser* or another custom string. If *browser* is used, the cache is varied by the browser name and major version. If another string is entered, you must override the HttpApplication.GetVaryByCustomString method in the global.asax file (more on this in Chapter 21, "Security"). VaryByHeader takes into account the names of any HTTP headers sent by the client.

19

> **NOTE**
>
> This has some interesting side effects. For instance, one of the problems that a developer faces is that a page requested by IE 6.0 might also be requested by Netscape Navigator 4.0; the same page from cache would be served to both browsers, which might not be ideal. In essence, you would be overriding ASP.NET automatic down-level rendering of HTML. If VaryByCustom is set to browser, and if the cached page is requested by NN 4.0, the page is executed again and the appropriate down-level client HTML is buffered separately and sent to the client.

Finally, Location sets the *cacheability* of the page—in other words, where in the HTTP pipeline this page can be cached. The OutputCacheLocation enumeration (Any, Client, Downstream, Server, None) contains the applicable values.

Only the Duration and VaryByParam attributes are required in ASP.NET pages. If you don't want to vary by querystring or post values, set this attribute to none.

You can also set these values with the HttpCachePolicy object, returned by the HttpResponse.Cache property (using the Response.Cache syntax), as shown in Listing 19.2.

Caching Entire Pages

LISTING 19.2
Setting Cache Options Programmatically

```
sub Page_Load(Sender as Object, e as EventArgs)
    Response.Cache.SetExpires(DateTime.Now.AddSeconds(60)
    Response.Cache.VaryByParams("item") = true
    ...
end sub
```

The `HttpCachePolicy` class has quite a few other methods that deal with various HTTP headers that control caching. Most of the time, you'll never use them, but it might be useful to explore them on your own.

Caching the entire output of a page can be very useful if the entire page has the same volatility. If one component on your page needs to remain dynamic—changing output on every request, for example—page output caching doesn't suit the situation. It might be more useful to cache pieces of data or individual controls.

Caching Controls

Caching controls in ASP.NET, also known as fragment caching, is typically done declaratively, in a very similar manner to page caching. This section examines the methods to do so in both the `.aspx` and code-behind files, as well as a third, more programmatic method.

Declarative Caching

Custom controls (both user controls and custom server controls) can be cached individually if you'd rather have higher-level caching than data caching, but page caching is too restrictive. In a user control `.ascx` file, this is done in the exact same manner as page caching: by using the `@ OutputCache` directive (see the earlier section "Caching Entire Pages" for more information). You can set durations, vary by parameters, and set the location of caching.

You can also manage caching in code using the `PartialCachingAttribute` class (for custom server controls, this is the only method available). Simply place this attribute in front of your class declaration in your class file:

```
<PartialCaching(10)> Public Class MyCachedControl
```

This attribute has two overloaded methods that you can use to set only the duration in seconds to cache the control, or to also specify `VaryBy` parameters:

```
<PartialCaching(10, "item", Nothing, Nothing)> Public Class CachedControl
```

The additional three parameters are the `VaryByParam`, `VaryByControls`, and `VaryByCustom` values.

When you specify caching attributes on a control, whether via the @ `OutputCache` directive or via `PartialCachingAttribute`, ASP.NET creates an instance of the `PartialCachingControl` class to take your control's place. This `PartialCachingControl` is placed in the page hierarchy where your control would have been and contains a reference to your original control.

The reasoning for this is a bit tricky. When you cache a control, you are technically caching its output (rendered HTML). Subsequent requests, then, should not access the control itself any longer; they should access only the cached output. The `PartialCachingControl` class contains the necessary logic to render the cached output, if it is available, or the control itself, if it isn't (and then put it into cache after rendering). Think of `PartialCachingControl` as a wrapper around your control. Figure 19.2 illustrates this logic.

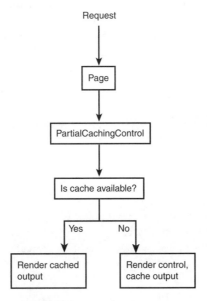

FIGURE 19.2   `PartialCachingControl`
contains logic to render your control or its output cache.

A side effect of this is that you lose the capability to manipulate your control programmatically. This is understandable, though. HTML has no programmatic capabilities, so why would you be able to manipulate a cached control? Any manipulation that you do should be performed when your control instantiates or renders itself.

Caching Controls

This includes any postback event or data handling. Additionally, if you ever need to reference your control, you need to verify its existence before you do so:

```
If not MyCachedControl is nothing then
    'do something with MyCachedControl
end if
```

If your control has been cached, `MyCachedControl` is not an instantiated variable, so you need to check its existence before you do anything with it.

Programmatic Caching

You can also cache the output of your controls without using the `@ OutputCache` or `PartialCachingAttribute` classes, thanks to the framework of ASP.NET controls.

Recall that every control is responsible for creating and sending its output to the client in the `Render` method. `Render` simply sends any HTML to a `StringWriter` object (technically, an `HtmlTextWriter` object) that then sends that output to the client. Thus, you can easily add code to the `Render` method of your controls to intercept and cache this output. Listing 19.3 shows a sample `Render` method.

LISTING 19.3
Caching Output Programmatically

```
protected Overrides Sub Render(ByVal output as HtmlTextWriter)
    Dim tempWriter = New StringWriter()
    dim cachedOutput as string

    if (Cache("MyKey") is nothing) then
        MyBase.Render(New HtmlTextWriter(tempWriter))
        cachedOutput = tempWriter.ToString()
        Cache.Insert("MyKey", cachedOutput, nothing, DateTime.Now.AddSeconds(60), _
        TimeSpan.Zero)
    else
        cachedOutput = Cache("MyKey")
    end if

    output.Write(cachedOutput)
end sub
```

This method performs any rendering necessary and passes the output to a `StringWriter`. You can then cache the resulting string using the techniques described in the "Caching Static Elements" section in this chapter. Then either the cached output or the freshly created output is sent to the browser.

This method enables you to get around the `PartialCachingControl` restrictions from the previous section, but it does require an additional step: In the previous method, the instantiation of the control itself could be skipped (thanks to the `PartialCachingControl` object), but that step must be performed here. Depending on your control, this might or might not involve additional processing overhead. The benefits, however, are that you can more finely tune the caching mechanism used in your controls (for example, dynamically setting the duration).

Summary

Whatever method you use, caching can almost always speed up your applications. Proper implementation, however, can require carefully analysis of the way your application functions and what exactly can be cached. It is common in web applications to have several different types of data cached and mechanisms of caching used.

One last thing to note: A cache is application specific. You can't access one application's cache from another, nor can you save cache in an out-of-process store such as SQL Server, as you can with session data.

Further Reading

IBuySpy Portal application documentation, http://www.ibuyspy.com

19

20 WEBSITE MANAGEMENT

IN BRIEF

One of the more advanced aspects of ASP.NET applications—or any web application, for that matter—is website management. Many web developers never touch on this issue, but it is an important one to make sure that you get the most out of your applications, from performance to security.

ASP.NET provides an extensible, easy-to-manage configuration system through the `global.asax` and XML `web.config` files. This chapter covers the most common configuration scenarios; Chapter 21, "Security," and Chapter 22, "Extending ASP.NET," cover additional topics specific to security and extending ASP.NET.

WHAT YOU NEED

SOFTWARE REQUIREMENTS	Windows 2000, XP, or 2003 .NET Framework 1.1 SDK Visual Studio .NET 2003 with Visual Basic .NET installed Internet Information Server (version 5 or later)
HARDWARE REQUIREMENTS	PC desktop or laptop system
SKILL REQUIREMENTS	Advanced knowledge in HTML Intermediate knowledge in the .NET Framework and ASP.NET

WEBSITE MANAGEMENT AT A GLANCE

Configuring a Site

You should be familiar with two main configuration files in ASP.NET: `global.asax` and `web.config`. The former is used to hook into events raised by your application; the latter contains settings that are used to control various aspects of your application. Both are optional files and are often ignored in smaller applications, but you'd be hard-pressed to build a medium- to enterprise-level site without understanding how these work.

Aside from the role these two files play, ASP.NET treats them specially. First, you cannot access these files from a web browser, and rightfully so. ASP.NET prevents access to them from any clients for security issues; any requests to them result in a "This type of page is not served" error.

Second, because these two files control how an application is supposed to run, changes in them must affect the application, and the only way to affect those changes is to restart the application. So, when ASP.NET detects a change in one of these files, it creates a new instance of the application, gracefully siphons off any pending requests from the old application, and then kills the old application. This means that your users won't ever lack access to your site, but restarting can be rather intensive, so it's best not to change these files often.

global.asax

There isn't much to the `global.asax` file itself, but because it represents an integral part of the way ASP.NET functions, it is important to know where this file fits into the framework. This file is typically located in the root directory of your website.

In a typical ASP.NET application, when a request is first made, a new `AppDomain` is created (one per virtual directory), and a pool of `HttpApplication` objects is instantiated. For every request that comes in, an `HttpApplication` object is pulled out of the pool to handle that entire request. `HttpApplication` is responsible for every aspect of that request, from sending output back to the client to calling any additional handlers or assemblies for functionality. When it is finished, it goes back into the pool. (Chapter 22 contains more information on the ASP.NET pipeline that handles a web request.)

You can have one `global.asax` file per application. When present, it is compiled and derived from the `HttpApplication` class. In essence, when you create a `global.asax` file, you are creating a custom `HttpApplication` object for use with your site (just as every `.aspx` file you create is a dynamically generated `Page`-derived class). Your custom `HttpApplication` object is then used to service all requests instead of the regular `HttpApplication` object. In `global.asax`, then, you can hook into any event of the `HttpApplication` object to control specific behaviors. If you do not create a `global.asax` file, ASP.NET simply uses the built-in `HttpApplication` object for your application (although VS .NET always autogenerates an empty `global.asax` file for you).

20

Configuring a Site

In addition to the `HttpApplication` class's events, ASP.NET makes available events raised from HTTP modules. These include events such as `Session_Start` and `Session_End`, which fire when a new ASP.NET session is created and destroyed, respectively. In Chapter 22, you'll examine more details regarding HTTP modules and their events.

Finally, two more events can be hooked into in `global.asax`: `Application_OnStart` and `Application_OnEnd`. These fire when the first `HttpApplication` object is instantiated and when the last one is destroyed. Note that these two events are raised only once per application. This differs from the `BeginRequest` method, which fires once per request that the `HttpApplication` object handles (remember that `HttpApplication` objects are recycled in a pool). Because of this, any code that you execute in the `Application_OnStart` method applies only to the first `HttpApplication` created (unless you use static members). This makes these two methods rather limited, but they can still be useful.

If you create a new web forms project in VS .NET and take a look at the auto-generated `global.asax` file, you'll see the most common events that ASP.NET uses. By default, they are empty. Listing 20.1 shows a simple example of tapping into the `Application_Error` event.

LISTING 20.1
Using `global.asax` to Handle Errors

```
Imports System.Web
Imports System.Web.SessionState
Imports System.Web.Mail


Public Class Global
Inherits System.Web.HttpApplication


#Region " Component Designer Generated Code "

      ...
#End Region


    Sub Application_Error(ByVal sender As Object, ByVal e As EventArgs)
        Dim mail As New MailMessage()
        mail.To = "Admin@MySite.com"
        mail.From = "The Website <admin@MySite.com>"
        mail.Subject = "ERROR!"
        mail.Body = "There was an error in the application."
        SmtpMail.Send(mail)
    End Sub
End Class
```

This simple example sends an email to the administrator of the site any time an unhandled error occurs anywhere on the site (a very useful tool if you have a very large site).

By implementing the various methods in your `global.asax` file, you can see more clearly the order of execution in an ASP.NET application. In general, the methods execute in the following order on first request:

1. `Application_OnStart`

2. `Application_BeginRequest`

3. `Application_AuthenticateRequest`

4. `Application_AuthorizeRequest`

5. `Application_ResolveRequestCache`

6. `Session_Start`

7. `Application_AcquireRequestState`

8. `Application_PreRequestHandlerExecute`

9. The `Page_Load` method inside your `.aspx` or code-behind file, followed by any other page outputs

10. `Application_PostRequestHandlerExecute`

11. `Application_ReleaseRequestState`

12. `Application_UpdateRequestCache`

13. `Application_EndRequest`

14. `Application_PreSendRequestHeaders`

Other methods might execute conditionally in this chain (for example, the `Error` method runs only when an error occurs).

`global.asax` is a useful tool for controlling your applications, doesn't require much knowledge of the inner workings of ASP.NET, and is much easier to implement than HTTP handlers or modules.

web.config

Simply put, `web.config` is an XML file that contains settings to be used on your website—everything from security to error page settings. It has predefined sections that ASP.NET parses out and instantiates classes to handle, but you can easily add new sections and build functionality to handle them (more on that in a moment).

20

Configuring a Site

ASP.NET configuration settings are hierarchical in nature, by directory structure. In other words, settings in the `web.config` file in your root directory apply to all ASP.NET files in your entire site, but settings in the `web.config` file in the `chapter20` subdirectory apply only to files in the `chapter20` folder and its subdirectories. Additionally, if there are matching settings in each file, the deepest directory settings apply—in this case, the `chapter20\web.config` file. This way, you can configure each directory in your application separately but maintain an overriding set of rules, if needed. Both of these features—setting inheritance and directory applicability—can be overridden, however.

`web.config` Sections

Table 20.1 lists the various configuration sections available in the `web.config` file. Covering all of these sections in detail is beyond the scope of this book (and could take up an entire book of its own), but you will examine a few of them in this chapter and subsequent chapters. These `b.config` elements are in camel case (first letter of the first word is lowercase, and subsequent first letters are uppercase) and are case sensitive.

TABLE 20.1

`web.config` Configuration Settings

Section	Description
`<appSettings>`	Used to store your own custom application settings.
`<authentication>`	Governs authentication settings used by your application (more in Chapter 21, "Security").
`<authorization>`	Controls access to ASP.NET resources.
`<browserCaps>`	Controls settings regarding client browser capabilities.
`<clientTarget>`	Used to provide aliases to client types.
`<compilation>`	Responsible for all compilation settings used by ASP.NET.
`<customErrors>`	Tells ASP.NET how to display errors in the browser.
`<globalization>`	Has the responsibility of configuring the globalization settings of an application.
`<httpHandlers>`	Has the responsibility of mapping incoming URLs to `IHttpHandler` classes. Subdirectories do not inherit these settings. It is also responsible for mapping incoming URLs to `IHttpHandlerFactory` classes. Data represented in `<httpHandlerFactories>` sections are hierarchically inherited by subdirectories.
`<httpModules>`	Has the responsibility of configuring HTTP modules within an application. HTTP modules participate in the processing of every request into an application. Common uses include security and logging.
`<httpRuntime>`	Governs ASP.NET HTTP runtime settings.
`<identity>`	Controls how ASP.NET accesses its resources (which identity it uses to access those resources).

20

TABLE 20.1

Continued

Section	Description
`<location>`	Acts as a special tag that controls how settings apply to a directory in your application.
`<machineKey>`	Contains keys to use for encryption/description of forms authentication cookie data. It cannot be used in subdirectories.
`<pages>`	Controls page-specific configuration settings typically found in the @ Page directive (viewstate, session state, and so on).
`<processModel>`	Configures the ASP.NET process model settings on IIS web server systems.
`<securityPolicy>`	Maps security levels to policy files.
`<sessionState>`	Configures session state.
`<trace>`	Configures the trace service.
`<trust>`	Codes access security levels for an application.
`<webServices>`	Governs settings for web services.

The format of a typical web.config file is shown in Listing 20.2. With a few exceptions, all of the sections described in Table 20.2 are placed under the `<system.web>` element—the ASP.NET section. Numerous other sections can be placed in a web.config file, but most either are not used by ASP.NET or are obscure.

LISTING 20.2

A Typical web.config File

```
<?xml version="1.0" encoding="utf-8" ?>
<configuration>

    <system.web>
        <compilation defaultLanguage="vb" debug="true" />       1
        <customErrors mode="RemoteOnly" />

        <authentication mode="Windows" />
        <authorization>
            <allow users="*" /> <!-- Allow all users -->
        </authorization>

        <trace enabled="false" requestLimit="10" pageOutput="false"
            traceMode="SortByTime" localOnly="true" />

        <sessionState
            mode="InProc"
            stateConnectionString="tcpip=127.0.0.1:42424"
            sqlConnectionString="data source=127.0.0.1;user id=sa;password="
```

20

Configuring a Site

LISTING 20.2
Continued

```
            cookieless="false"
            timeout="20"
        />

        <globalization requestEncoding="utf-8" responseEncoding="utf-8" />

    </system.web>
</configuration>
```

In Listing 20.2, the ASP.NET application is configured to use VB .NET as its default language and to output debug symbols. The `<customErrors>` section **1** allows local testers/developers to see detailed ASP.NET compiler errors; any remote clients will be redirected to a custom error page. Here's another example:

```
<customErrors defaultRedirect="error.htm" mode="on">
    <error statusCode="404" redirect="error404.htm" />
</customErrrors>
```

Here, for all errors except 404 errors, users are redirected to `error.htm`; 404 errors are sent to `error404.htm`. When custom error handling is on, ASP.NET passes a querystring parameter, `aspxerrorpath`, to the redirection page that contains the virtual path of the file that generated the error. For example, if a user requested a nonexistent `helloworld.aspx` file, he would be redirected to this URL:

```
http://localhost/VBNetUnleashed/listing2003/error404.htm?
    aspxerrorpath=/VBNetUnleashed/helloworld.aspx
```

This can be useful in capturing and debugging errors.

The `<authentication>` and `<authorization>` sections are discussed in Chapter 21; `Trace` is discussed later in this chapter. The `<sessionState>` element configures an in-process session store (see Chapter 18, "State Management"). Finally, `<globalization>` sets some encoding properties.

Two other elements are important to note: `<location>` and `<appSettings>`. Both can be used in Windows Forms application and, as such, aren't particular to ASP.NET. They are placed outside of the `<system.web>` elements. The first is used to apply other settings and elements to only specific directories; it is most commonly used for security settings. For example:

```
<configuration>
    <location path="members.aspx">
        <system.web>
```

```
            <authorization>
                <deny users="?"/>
            </authorization>
        </system.web>
    </location>
</configuration>
```

This `web.config` file denies access to the `members.aspx` file from any anonymous users.

The `<location>` element has one more useful application: It can be used to lock settings on a particular directory so that they cannot be overridden by other `web.config` files. If you're running only your own site on a server, this isn't much help, but if you're hosting several sites, all run by different administrators, this is a good way to set certain settings and make sure that no one else can change them. Simply add the `allowOverride` attribute and set it to `false`:

```
<configuration>
    <location path="WebSite1" allowOverride="false">
        <system.web>
            <authorization>
                <deny users="?"/>
            </authorization>
        </system.web>
    </location>
</configuration>
```

Now any `web.config` files in the `WebSite1` directory and its subdirectories cannot modify the authorization settings.

ASP.NET itself doesn't use the `<appSettings>` section, but any values contained in this section are returned in a dictionary object to your application for use. This is a great place for application-wide settings (such as connection strings). For example:

```
<appSettings>
    <add key="ApplicationName" value="MyApp" />
</appSettings>
```

From any ASP.NET file, you can retrieve the `ApplicationName` variable using the following code:

```
ConfigurationSettings.AppSettings("ApplicationName")
```

20

Custom `web.config` Sections

To define a custom section, you first need to define a section handler, a class that is used to parse and return your custom section and data from the `web.config` file. These handlers are defined in the `<configSections>` element. The machine-level `machine.config` file (typically located at `C:\Windows\Microsoft.NET\Framework\vXXXX\config`) contains quite a few predefined handlers.

To create a handler section, you need to specify only the section name and type of class (and the assembly that contains that class) to handle the section:

```
<configuration>
   <configSections>
      <section name="customSection"
         type="System.Configuration.NameValueFileSectionHandler, System" />
   </configSections>
   ...
   <system.web>
      <customSection>

         ...

      </customSection>
   </system.web>
</configuration>
```

The class that you use to handle your custom section must implement the `IConfigurationSectionHandler` interface, which requires only one method: `Create`. This method's signature is shown in Listing 20.3. It retrieves the data and places it in an `XmlNode` object, which reads directly from the `web.config` file.

LISTING 20.3
`IConfigurationSectionHandler.Create`

```
public function Create(ByVal parent as Object, ByVal configContent as Object, _
   ByVal section as XmlNode) as Object
```

To now retrieve these values from your ASP.NET files, use the `ConfigurationSettings.GetConfig` method, passing in the qualified name of your section:

```
dim oSection as NameValueCollection
oSection = CType(ConfigurationSettings.GetConfig("system.web/customSection"), _
   NameValueCollection)
```

Using the Assembly Cache for Application Files

.NET uses the assembly cache to hold compiled resources that will be loaded at application startup. In most cases, it is the \bin directory in your application folder; VS .NET always creates one for you automatically and places compiled code-behind files there.

The Global Assembly Cache (GAC) also typically is located at C:\Windows\ Microsoft.NET\Framework\vXXXX. The assemblies here, such as System.dll and System.web.dll, are loaded by the common language runtime to enable .NET applications to function on your computer.

There isn't much to the assembly cache, aside from knowing that it's there. If you weren't using VS .NET to build your applications, you would need to make sure that any compiled libraries are placed in the \bin directory. ASP.NET then automatically would load anything in this directory into memory so that your code could programmatically access any classes, methods, and variables.

One other thing to note is that ASP.NET monitors this directory for changes. As with the web.config and global.asax files, when this directory changes, ASP.NET gracefully restarts the application to effect any changes. Technically, shadow copies are made of the assemblies in this folder during application startup (which are typically located in C:\Windows\Microsoft.NET\<version>\Temporary ASP.NET Files). These copies are loaded into memory, leaving the actual files free to be modified or deleted. Then when ASP.NET detects a change, a new AppDomain is created with shadow copies of the new files, requests are siphoned off the old application in favor of the new one, and eventually the old one is destroyed.

In the end, this boils down to the fact that, to deploy your application, all you need to do is copy the necessary files to your server. All settings are contained in web.config, compiled resources are in the assembly cache, and ASP.NET handles everything else.

20

Tracing an ASP.NET Application

Before any application is deployed, diagnostics should be run against it to make sure that it performs optimally and as expected. This can be done in multitudes of ways, including using the web application stress tool in VS .NET) but ASP.NET has a built-in, easy-to-use method called tracing that provides information on memory usage, response times, custom debug information, and numerous other categories of information.

Tracing an ASP.NET Application

Tracing a page on your site is easy: Simply add `Trace="true"` in your `@ Page` directive:

```
<%# Page Language="VB" Trace="true" %>
```

When you turn on tracing for a page, ASP.NET automatically appends a number of tables containing trace information to the end of your output, as shown in Figure 20.1. This information includes details on the client request (session IDs, encodings, times, and so on), execution times for your page, a breakdown of the controls on your page (including the amount of memory it takes to maintain them), and HTTP cookie, header, and server variable information. Especially useful is the execution timing section, which can help you identify any rough spots in your code that need to be optimized.

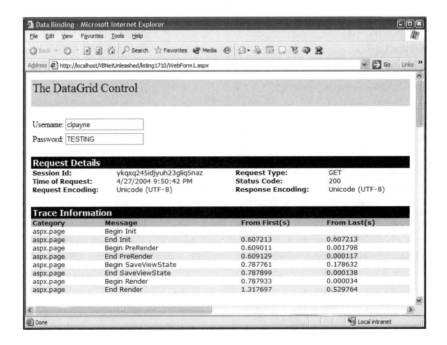

FIGURE 20.1   Tracing appends debug information to your pages.

You can also enable tracing for an entire application in the `web.config` file:

```
<system.web>
    <trace enabled="true" requestLimit="10" pageOutput="false"
        traceMode="SortByTime" localOnly="true" />
</system.web>
```

The application logs the trace output for every page up to the limit specified in the `requestLimit` attribute. You can then view this information from a central location via the trace viewer. This viewer is a special URL created by ASP.NET to collect the information: Simply go to `/trace.axd` from the root directory of your application (for example, `http://localhost/VBNetUnleashed/listing1710/trace.axd`). This application holds the trace information for each page requested in your application. You can view basic summary information, as well as the same detailed view provided in page-level tracing. Figure 20.2 shows a sample output from the trace viewer.

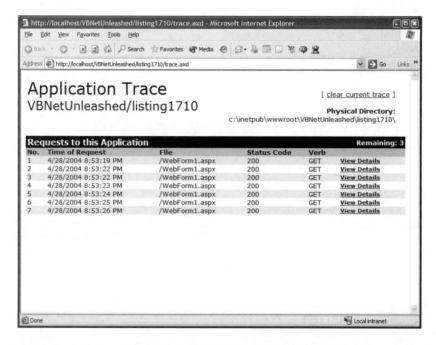

FIGURE 20.2   You can view application-level tracing from the trace viewer.

TIP

`trace.axd` is actually an HTTP handler; it is a special type of .NET class that handles incoming requests. You'll revisit HTTP handlers in Chapter 22, "Extending ASP.NET."

By default, enabling tracing for an entire application causes each page to append the debug information to its output, as in Figure 20.1. You can override this behavior by setting `trace=false` on individual pages or setting the `pageOutput` attribute to `false` in your `web.config` file, as shown here.

Tracing an ASP.NET Application

The ASP.NET tracing mechanism also enables you to output custom messages that will appear in any trace output. These messages can be left in your application when you deploy it, unlike typical debug messages. If tracing is disabled, the application simply ignores them, and the end user never sees the messages.

Two methods do this: `Trace.Write` and `Trace.Warn`. The only difference between the two is that the `Warn` method outputs the messages in red. Both enable you to group your output messages by categories and provide error information to go along with your messages. For example:

```
Trace.Warn("My message")
Trace.Warn("My Category", "My Message")
Trace.Warn("My Category", "My Message", new Exception())
```

The first call displays your message in the default aspx.page category. The second creates a custom category named My Category and displays your message under that. The third call is the same as the second call, but it also outputs the text "Exception of type System.Exception was thrown." along with your message.

These two methods are useful for testing conditional pieces of code and determining the exact order of execution in your application.

NOTE

Remember that tracing is purely a debugging tool. For one thing, you obviously don't want the tables of output shown in Figure 20.1 displayed to end users for user interface and security purposes. Second, tracing adds overhead to your application because your application has to keep track of additional information. Although there's not much, there's no real reason to leave tracing enabled on a production site.

Having said that, you can still leave the `Trace.Write` and `Trace.Warn` methods in your code because they won't affect the site. If you do decide to turn tracing back on, you'll still have these messages to refer to.

20

Summary

The application control, configuration, deployment, and debugging aspects of ASP.NET are all easy to set up and modify, when necessary. These features enable you to remotely administer and test a site without having to worry about fiddling with the IIS management console or manually restarting the application to effect change.

The number of ways to configure your site with `global.asax` and `web.config` are nearly limitless. There are often multiple ways to do a single thing, and there isn't always a better choice. Unfortunately, there isn't a definitive resource, either, on the proper ways to do things; the best way to learn more advanced topics is by example. IBuySpy is a good place to start, and GotDotNet contains excellent resources for delving deeper.

Further Reading

IBuySpy Portal application documentation, http://www.ibuyspy.com

GotDotNet user forums, http://www.gotdotnet.com

20

21 SECURITY

IN BRIEF

Security is a very important topic—and very complicated one—in ASP.NET. You can implement security aspects in numerous ways, and you can take advantage of various layers available to .NET, from Windows to IIS to ASP.NET, to SQL, to IP, and combinations thereof. All of this can lead to some very complex choices that leave novice—and even advanced—developers in a daze. This chapter sorts through all the available options and discusses more thoroughly the most common ones for ASP.NET development. Part VII, "Remoting," goes into further detail about the various types of security available in .NET applications as a whole.

WHAT YOU NEED

SOFTWARE REQUIREMENTS	Windows 2000, XP, or 2003
	.NET Framework 1.1 SDK
	Visual Studio .NET 2003 with Visual Basic .NET installed
	Internet Information Server (version 5 or later)
HARDWARE REQUIREMENTS	PC desktop or laptop system
SKILL REQUIREMENTS	Advanced Knowledge in HTML
	Intermediate Knowledge in the .NET Framework
	Intermediate Knowledge of Security Concepts

SECURITY AT A GLANCE

Overview of ASP.NET Security

Before you actually attempt to secure your applications, it's a good idea to learn what options are available and what various notions mean in .NET. This section brings you up to speed with .NET security concepts; subsequent sections put into practice the topics discussed here.

The two main concepts of nearly any security implementation are authentication and authorization. Authentication is used to determine who a user is: the username, the password, from where the user came, and so on. In ASP.NET, this is especially important because any of the millions of people in the world who have access to the Internet can access your application. Authorization is the process by which, based on a user's identity (often supplied from the authentication step), that user is denied or granted access to resources. Does user A have permissions to read file X? Does user B have permission to view page Y? When a user gets passed authentication, he or she still needs to be checked for security clearance to have access to various parts of your application. Figure 21.1 shows a typical security flow of an ASP.NET application.

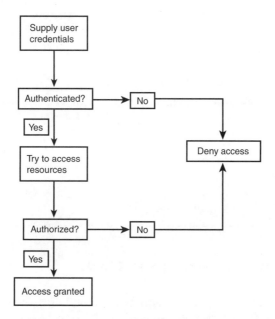

FIGURE 21.1   ASP.NET Application Security Flow

Authentication and authorization can each be performed in many different methods, and they are not always correlated. Before looking at these methods, it is helpful to know about a couple fundamental .NET security topics: principals and identities. You can implement ASP.NET security without having any knowledge of these concepts, but more advanced security topics require understanding them.

Overview of ASP.NET Security

Identities are fairly easy to understand. A user's identity just tells you who he or she is. The actual form of the identity can vary, depending on how you obtained that identity; regardless, it gives you certain unique identifying information about a user. In .NET, identities are represented by instances of classes that implement the `IIdentity` interface, which has three self-explanatory properties: `Name`, `IsAuthenticated`, and `AuthenticationType`.

A principal, on the other hand, is more abstract. It represents a security context that a user is working within; it contains a set of permissions that a user has. For example, a principal will tell you that a user has administrative privileges on this computer. All principals in .NET are defined by the `IPrincipal` interface.

In .NET, there are two main types of principals: `WindowsPrincipal` and `GenericPrincipal`. The former is applicable when the operating system's (Windows) authentication and security schemes are used, and the latter applies for just about everything else. In ASP.NET, you can use either. In addition, certain identities can be associated with each type of principal, but you'll get to those in subsequent sections.

To recap, authentication provides you with the `IPrincipal` and `IIdentity` objects, which can then be used for authorization to determine whether a user can access whatever he or she is requesting. A user is represented by the `GenericPrincipal` and `GenericIdentity` objects until he or she is authenticated.

NOTE

For all intents and purposes, in ASP.NET, you can disable authentication, meaning that all users are granted access to your application under the default Windows ASP.NET identity, IUSR_*MACHINENAME* (where *MACHINENAME* is the NetBIOS name of your computer). This is known as anonymous authentication. Authorization still takes place without your explicit implementations, using permissions associated with IUSR_*MACHINENAME*. Naturally, this identity is rather restricted in its security permissions—you don't want random users roaming freely in your application.

Anonymous authentication is not covered in this chapter simply because it is not a security implementation, per se, but rather an assumed access paradigm.

Authenticating the Web User

In general, there are two routes to authentication in ASP.NET. The first is to rely on the operating system to provide your security checks for you (Windows security). The second is to simply build your own method using various ASP.NET technologies. Each has several well-defined subpaths for you to choose, or you can even go your own way there as well.

This section covers the different types of authentication available to ASP.NET applications. The topics in this section are applicable in a later section, "Authorize Users and Roles." Choices that you make here also might dictate the methods available to you later in the security implementation.

To turn on authentication in your application, you need to add the
<authentication> element in your web.config file (see Chapter 20, "Website
Management," for more information about web.config). For example:

```
<configuration>
   <system.web>
      <authentication mode="Mode" />
   </system.web>
</configuration>
```

The *Mode* attribute can be Windows, Forms, Passport, or None, to indicate the
type of authentication used. The first three are covered here; the latter indicates
either that no authentication is used or that you're going to build your own custom
routines, which aren't discussed here.

The <authentication> element has additional attributes as well, but you'll see
those as you come across them in their specific sections.

Windows Authentication

Windows authentication is a simple way to implement this security step because most
of the work has already been done for you. When a user accesses your application, typically the first step is to encounter the web server application itself, Internet Information
Server (IIS). With Windows authentication, IIS stops users and asks for a username and
password. IIS can work with the operating system to authenticate these credentials and
assign privileges. Thus, all identities must be existing users of the operating system.

To view or modify the list of users for your computer in Windows 2000, go to Start,
Settings, Control Panel, Users and Passwords. In Windows XP, go to Start, Control
Panel, User Accounts. Figure 21.2 shows a typical list.

Because all authenticated users must be users of the machine itself, Windows authentication can get tedious to manage, especially if you have more than a dozen or so
users. The advantage is that it requires little or no code to be written for your application.

IIS can authenticate users through Windows in three ways: basic, digest, and NTLM
(also known as integrated Windows authentication). Each relies on interrogating
users as they encounter IIS, but they vary in the credential transference details.

To enable any of these forms of authentication, open the IIS Manager (ISM) by going
to Start, Settings, Control Panel, Administrative Tools, Internet Services Manager (or
Internet Information Services in Windows XP). Expand the default website, right-
click on the directory or file you would like to secure (or the entire website, for that
matter), and click Properties. Select the Directory Security tab and click Edit under
the Authentication Control section. You should see the dialog box in Figure 21.3.

21

Authenticating the Web User

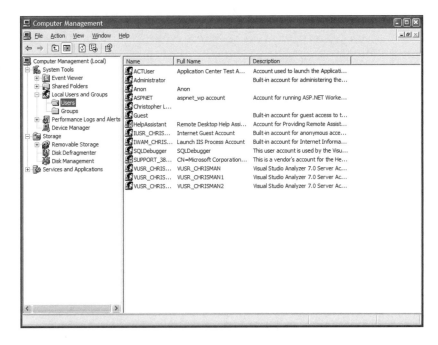

FIGURE 21.2   A list of users and groups in Windows XP.

FIGURE 21.3   Make sure that Anonymous Access
is deselected if you enable any of the other methods.

Basic is the simplest method and is an industry-standard method of authentication. The
user is prompted with a box (shown in Figure 21.4) to enter the username and password.
These credentials are sent from the client to the server in plain text and then are used by
IIS and Windows for authentication. The problem is that, because the credentials are
sent as plain text, anyone can read these values with network-snooping tools.

FIGURE 21.4   When basic authentication is enabled, the browser asks for credentials.

Digest authentication is similar, but the username and password that are passed back to the server are encrypted using a one-way hash that cannot be decrypted. Digest authentication works only with Internet Explorer, and the server must be part of a domain.

NTLM also encrypts the credentials before it sends them, but it does not prompt the user for them. Instead, the client's operating system automatically sends the logged-in user's identity to the server, encrypted. Thus, the user is never prompted to enter the username and password. This method also requires Internet Explorer and Windows (on both client and server) to function properly.

After a user's credentials have been verified, a `WindowsIdentity` and a `WindowsPrincipal` (which implement `IIdentity` and `IPrincipal`, respectively) are created for the user. The `WindowsPrincipal` object stores the roles that the current user belongs to, as defined by the operating system. The `WindowsIdentity` object contains information about the current user. You'll examine these two objects further in the "Authorizing Users and Roles" section in this chapter.

Forms Authentication

Forms authentication is also very common in ASP.NET applications. Essentially, when users try to access a restricted resource (see "Authorizing Users and Roles" later in this chapter for information on how to restrict resources in this manner), they are redirected to a page in your site that performs some type of custom authentication (usually with a username and password verified against a database).

The user credentials are sent across the network as plain text. After they are verified, ASP.NET sets an authentication cookie (loosely represented as a `FormsAuthenticationTicket` object) on the client's computer (assuming the client has enabled and accepts cookies) containing the user's identity. Subsequent requests use this value to identify the user so that he or she isn't forced to reauthenticate. Figure 21.5 illustrates this process.

21

Authenticating the Web User

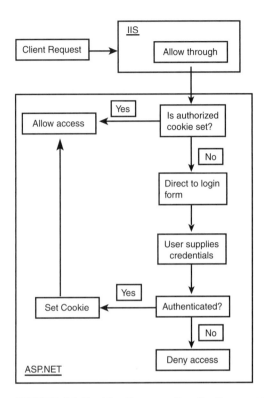

FIGURE 21.5   The Forms authentication workflow.

To enable Forms authentication, set the Mode attribute in your `<authentication>` web.config element to Forms. You then need to specify the authentication gateway in your site. Listing 21.1 shows an example.

21

LISTING 21.1
Using Forms Authentication

```
<configuration>
    <system.web>
        <authentication mode="Forms">

            <forms name="MyCustomForm" loginUrl="/login.aspx"
                protection="None" timeout="20" />

        </authentication>
    </system.web>
</configuration>
```

The `<forms>` element specifies details that ASP.NET will use in the forms authentication scenario. The `name` attribute specifies the name of the cookie set on the client's computer (the default is `.ASPXAUTH`). The `loginUrl` attribute **1** contains the URL of the ASP.NET page that contains your authentication logic. Typically, this is just a simple page with username and password text boxes that verify supplied information against a database. (More on this page in a moment.)

The `protection` attribute indicates how the cookie data should be handled. Specifying `None` means that the value written in the cookie is both unencrypted and nonvalidated, which is perhaps less intensive to perform but also not very secure; it should be used only when the identity information is not used for authorization later. This attribute can also be specified as `Encryption`, `Validation`, and `All`.

A few additional properties of the `<forms>` element exist: `timeout` specifies the lifetime of the cookie. `path` specifies the cookie's path value. There is also a `credentials` subelement, against which you can hard-code usernames and passwords. This method is not recommended because it is inflexible and can be insecure; validate against a stronger store, such as a database.

ASP.NET provides the `FormsAuthentication` class, which contains a few useful shared (static) methods that you can use in your application. Table 21.1 shows these methods.

TABLE 21.1

`FormsAuthentication` Class Methods

Name	Description
Authenticate	Attempts to validate supplied information against the `<credentials>` section in `web.config`.
Decrypt	Decrypts the authentication information in the user cookie and returns a `FormsAuthenticationTicket` object.
Encrypt	Returns an encrypted string created from a `FormsAuthenticationTicket` object.
GetAuthCookie	Enables you to create an authentication cookie based on a supplied username. Returns an `HttpCookie` object.
GetRedirectUrl	Returns the restricted URL that initiated the authentication procedure.
HashPasswordForStoringInConfigFile	Returns an encrypted string based on a supplied hash algorithm (such as sha1 or md5).
RedirectFromLoginPage	Redirects an authenticated user back to the originally requested URL.
RenewTicketIfOld	Updates the expiration time for an authentication cookie.

21

Authenticating the Web User

TABLE 21.1

Continued

Name	Description
SetAuthCookie	Does the same as GetAuthCookie, except that the cookie is automatically added to the response stream.
SignOut	Removes the authentication cookie.

Using these methods, you can customize the manner in which your user is handled after being authenticated. For example, you could call GetAuthCookie to retrieve a cookie, add a custom value to it, add it to the response output, and then redirect to wherever the user came from. Or, more simply, call SetAuthCookie and provide a "Successfully logged in" message, with a link back to wherever the user came from:

```
'is user valid?
if Username = "XXXX" and Password = "XXXX" then
1
    Dim authCookie As new HttpCookie _
        FormsAuthentication.GetAuthCookie("CHRIS", False)

    Response.Cookies.Add(authCookie)

    Response.Redirect(FormsAuthentication.GetRedirectUrl("CHRIS", False))
end if
```

When the user hits another page, the authentication cookie **1** is sent to the server, and ASP.NET can use the identifying information to authenticate the user. This ensures that the user doesn't need to keep being redirected to the login page.

By default, ASP.NET creates GenericPrincipal and FormsIdentity objects when a user is authenticated via forms authentication. You can retrieve these values in your application from the HttpContext.User property, which returns an IPrincipal object (make sure you cast it to a GenericPrincipal). For example:

```
Response.Write(CType(Context.User, GenericPrincipal).ToString() & "<BR>")
Response.Write(CType(Context.User.Identity, FormsIdentity).Name.ToString() & "<BR>")
```

If you need to do any role-based authorization, however, a few additional steps might be necessary. Specifically, it's helpful at this point to also retrieve a list of custom-defined roles that the authenticated user belongs to; these roles could be stored in a database or any other storage mechanism you've used. When you obtain the roles, you need to add them to the authentication ticket. Unfortunately, you can't do so using the built-in FormsAuthentication methods; you need to create the FormsAuthenticationTicket object on your own:

21

```
'retrieve roles in string
' for example, "Administrator,User,Power User"
dim strRoles as string = GetRoleList()

'create new authentication ticket with constructor
' (version, username, issue date, expire date, persistent, user data)
dim authTicket as new FormsAuthenticationTicket _
    (1, "CHRIS", DateTime.Now, DateTime.Now.AddMinutes(20), false, strRoles)

'encrypt ticket
dim strEncryptedTicket = FormsAuthentication.Encrypt(authTicket)

'create authentication cookie with encrypted ticket
dim authCookie as new HttpCookie(FormsAuthentication.FormsCookieName, _
    strEncryptedTicket)

'add authentication cookie to response output
Response.Cookies.Add(authCookie)
```

Now the roles are stored with your authentication cookie for role-based authorization later.

TIP
Forms authentication is often used to personalize websites for users. After a user's identity has been verified with this method, you can tailor the site accordingly and need not implement any authorization scenarios.

Passport Authentication

Passport authentication is a centralized authentication server that Microsoft provides. It works very similarly to Forms authentication, except that you don't need to build any custom functionality yourself. Both create authentication cookies that reside on the client and are used for authorization. When users encounter passport authentication on your site, they are redirected to the Passport login page (see http://www.passport.com for more details), which provides a very simple form to fill out. This form then checks user credentials against Microsoft's Passport service and determines whether a user is valid. If so, the Passport site redirects the user back to your site, passing an encrypted authentication ticket in the query string. Your site then sets the authentication cookie, similarly to Forms authentication.

We don't examine this service much further because your site must be a member of Microsoft's Passport service to use this authentication method. Additionally, you need to pay a fee to become a member. For more information, check out the Passport documentation at http://www.passport.com/business. When you've become a member, you need to download the Passport SDK and configure your application accordingly.

21

Authenticating the Web User

The final step in setting up Passport authentication is to set up your web.config file properly by setting the Mode attribute to Passport.

The Passport service is a very useful and easy way to implement security that you can trust on your site. Many existing websites, including nearly all of Microsoft's sites, use the Passport service. When a user has a valid Passport identity, he or she can log in to any Passport site with the same username and password. Thus, if you plan to team up with other sites or to build a family of different sites, the Passport service might be a good security measure to look into.

On the other hand, there may be drawbacks to using Passport as well. For instance, not everyone is comfortable with the idea of entrusting a commercial entity with his or her personal information. Also, you lose control of your users' information. For these and other reasons, the Passport service has not become a huge player in the authentication game.

Authorizing Users and Roles

Two general approaches to authorization exist: role-based authorization, in which you use the user's identity and role membership to programmatically determine his or her access; and resource (or file)–based authorization, in which you use the underlying security mechanisms in Windows to control access to file-based resources. The main difference between the two approaches lies in the way in which resources (code, files, databases, and so on) are accessed. This section covers the various methods available and how they apply in various authentication scenarios.

Role-Based Authorization

Role-based authorization is the most common type of authorization in web applications. Essentially, you rely on one of the authentication methods described earlier in this chapter to determine who your user is and then programmatically to allow or deny access to that user based on his or her permissions—or, more specifically, the user's role membership. All access to specific resources, then, is done through another set of predefined identities that are more trusted.

In other words, imagine your ASP.NET application as a library with top-secret information. Just to walk in the door; you need to have clearance (in other words, you must be authenticated). Your security badge tells the librarian what top-secret materials you have access to—what levels of permission. But the librarian is the only one with access to everything. If you ask her for document X, she checks your permissions and, if you are eligible, brings the document to you. If not, she refuses you.

In the same way, a user must be authenticated into an ASP.NET application. The ASP.NET code (which you've written and which runs in a privileged context) acts as the librarian. It checks the user's permissions and accesses certain resources on the user's behalf.

These could be files and databases or even methods or procedures you've written. In this way, the code is the only entity that needs to be trusted with access to resources. Figure 21.6 illustrates this concept.

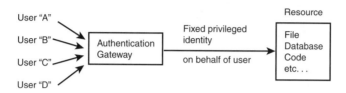

FIGURE 21.6   Role-based authentication relies on the trusted subsystem model.

This paradigm is known as the trusted subsystem model because the code (the librarian), which has very powerful access permissions, must trust the authentication gateway to properly identify users. After this assumption is made, you can programmatically control user access.

With Windows and Forms Authentication

If you used Windows authentication to identify your users, again, most of the work is done for you. The identity and role membership of a user have already been determined and created for you. It is then up to you to perform role-based checks in your application. Let's move on to authorization with Forms authentication.

Recall that ASP.NET automatically creates `GenericPrincipal` and `GenericIdentity` objects for you when a user is authenticated using Forms authentication. If you use the built-in `FormsAuthentication` methods, an authentication cookie (and a ticket) are created for you and associated with the user. The problem is that none of these automatic procedures takes into account role information. During authentication, you had to take additional steps to manually create an authentication ticket with role information. Similarly, during authorization, you need to take an additional step to retrieve that role information: retrieve the custom authentication ticket and create new `IPrincipal` and `IIdentity` objects with the roles. You need to do this every time the user is authenticated, which is essentially every time the user hits a page in your site. The `global.asax` file comes into play here (see Chapter 20 for more information).

The application-level event `Application_AuthenticateRequest` occurs every time the application identifies a user (and because the Web is stateless, this happens every time the user hits a page on your site). You take advantage of this method to complete the procedure with Forms authentication:

Authorizing Users and Roles

```
Sub Application_AuthenticateRequest(sender As Object, e As EventArgs)
    if (not HttpContext.Current.User is nothing) then
        if (HttpContext.Current.User.Identity.IsAuthenticated) then
            if (TypeOf HttpContext.Current.User.Identity is FormsIdentity) then
                dim id as FormsIdentity = CType(HttpContext.Current.User.Identity, _
                    FormsIdentity)
                dim authTicket as FormsAuthenticationTicket = id.Ticket

                'get user roles, split up delimited string if necessary
                dim userData as string = authTicket.UserData
                dim roles as string() = userData.Split(",")

                HttpContext.Current.User = new GenericPrincipal(id, roles)
            end if
        end if
    end if
end sub
```

This simple method checks to see whether there is a currently authenticated user and whether that user was authenticated via Forms authentication. Then it retrieves the authentication ticket of that user. Recall that the role information was stored as a comma-separated string in the UserData property of the ticket; this is retrieved and parsed into a string array. Finally, a new GenericPrincipal object is created and associated with the current identity and roles. Now you have roles associated with your Forms authentication user.

URL Authorization

URL role-based authorization is very simple to implement and is configured entirely by your web.config file. This enables you to restrict access to certain paths in your application, based on a user's identity. For example, the following web.config code snippet stops all unauthenticated (in other words, anonymous) users from hitting any page in your site:

```
<configuration>
    <system.web>
        <authorization>
            <deny users="?"/>
        </authorization>
    </system.web>
</configuration>
```

The <authorization> element has two subelements: <deny> and <allow>. Both can accept either a comma-separated list of usernames, roles, or HTTP verbs (such as GET and POST). The ? and * wildcards can be used to control anonymous and all users, respectively. The following snippet allows all administrators access but denies everyone else:

```
<configuration>
   <system.web>
      <authorization>
         <allow roles="Administrators" />
         <deny users="*"/>
      </authorization>
   </system.web>
</configuration>
```

In conjunction with the `<location></location>` element tags in `web.config` (see Chapter 20, "Website Management"), you can control access to specific files or folders as well:

```
<configuration>
   <location path="private">
      <system.web>
         <authorization>
            <allow roles="Administrators" />
            <deny users="*"/>
         </authorization>
      </system.web>
   </location>

   <location path="public">
      <system.web>
         <authorization>
            <allow users="*"/>
         </authorization>
      </system.web>
   </location>
</configuration>
```

This snippet allows only administrators into the `private` folder but allows all users into `public`.

NOTE

ASP.NET URL authorization protects only files that are mapped to ASP.NET, such as `.aspx` files. Excluded types include `.html`, `.txt`, `.gif`, `.jpg`, `.asp`, and others. IIS and the operating system, however, still maintain secure checks on these other files. Keep this in mind when you are securing your site.

21

Programmatic Authorization

Programmatic authorization enables you to check in your code if a user is authorized to access whatever he or she is trying to access. Chapter 30, "User- and Role-Based Permissions," goes into this type of authorization in more detail, so this section only skims the topic.

With these methods, you can secure objects, methods, properties, or entire blocks of code in your application. You can do this via a direct test of the user's identity:

```
if (Context.User.Identity.Name = "CHRIS") then
    ... 'your code here
end if
```

A role check:

```
if (Context.User.IsInRole("Administrators")) then
    .... 'your code here
end if
```

An imperative check:

```
dim objPermission as new PrincipalPermission("CHRIS", "Administrators")
objPermission.Demand()
```

Or a declarative check:

```
<PrincipalPermission(SecurityAction.Demand, Role:="Administrators")> _

    Sub MySecureMethod()
```

The exact method that you use depends on what exactly you're trying to secure and how you expect to handle failed permission checks. For example, a role check using the IPrincipal.IsInRole method simply moves on if the role check fails, but the declarative check throws a security exception and possibly halts your application if the check fails.

Resource-Based Authorization

Unlike role-based authorization, resource-based authorization does not rely on the trusted subsystem model; no fixed set of identities acts on behalf of users. Instead, a user's identity is used directly to determine his or her access to resources (see Figure 21.7). There is no librarian from the previous analogy, and the top-secret materials themselves must have secure locks on them. These secure locks translate into operating system security features, such as Windows Access Control Lists (ACLs).

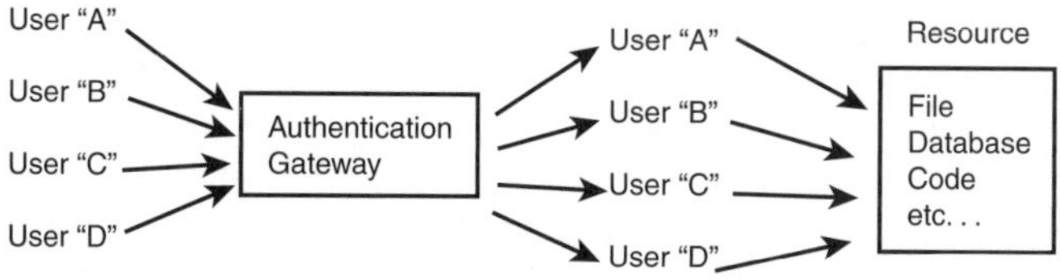

FIGURE 21.7 Resource-based authorization relies on a user's identity for security access.

This means that you need to ensure that all resources that a particular user might request have the appropriate permissions for that user defined directly on the object, usually in the form of an ACL. This can actually get quite tedious because ACLs are relatively complex to manage. For that reason, resource-based authorization is typically used only in intranet (or other small) environments where the user base is small and maybe static and where the number of files is small.

To use resource-based authorization, you must use Windows authentication. Simply set the Mode attribute in your web.config file to Windows:

```
<configuration>
   <system.web>
      <authentication mode="Windows" />
   </system.web>
</configuration>
```

An additional topic of concern arises with resource-based authorization: impersonation. Impersonation allows ASP.NET to act as the authenticated user. This means that all resource security authorizations are checked against the incoming user's identity. In other words, if the authenticated user Bob is trying to access the file default.aspx, Bob needs to have the proper Windows OS permission (via an ACL on default.aspx).

This sounds exactly like Windows authentication and resource-based authorization *without* impersonation. What is the difference? The distinction is made between resources that users request directly and those that they don't (those used by your code). For example, if a Windows authenticated user requests default.aspx, regardless of impersonation, that user's identity and role is checked against ACLs to determine access privileges, as described earlier. Subsequently, without impersonation, if in default.aspx you access a database via Windows security, ASP.NET uses its own process identity for authorization. With impersonation, however, the user's identity is used. In the former case, you only need the database to have permissions for the fixed ASP.NET account; in the latter, you need a set of permissions for every user who could access your application. This is known as *flowing identity* to access downstream resources—resources that aren't directly accessed by a user.

Authorizing Users and Roles

The same concept applies if, instead of accessing a database in code, you access a text file, a graphic image, a network shared folder, or whatever else. Without impersonation, ASP.NET itself is checked for permissions; with impersonation, the user is checked.

> **NOTE**
>
> If the user accessed those resources directly (without going through your ASP.NET application), impersonation wouldn't matter. For directly requested resources, regular resource-based authorization is used.

The advantage that impersonation gives you is the capability to flow the user's identity to all resources, not just those requested directly. This can mean additional security for your application because now each user can be held accountable for his or her actions. By performing an audit, you can see exactly who accessed what resource and when. In contrast, without impersonation, you can see only ASP.NET access.

The drawback, however, is that because each user uses his or her own identity, ASP.NET cannot use any sort of pooling to conserve resources and improve performance. For example, ASP.NET typically pools database connections based on user identity. Without impersonation, all accesses are through one account, and pooling can be used. With impersonation, each access is through a separate user account, so pooling would do no good. Additionally, managing permissions in the form of ACLs and database users in this manner can get very tedious.

In general, it is a good idea to stay away from impersonation, unless you have a very specific reason to use it (such as security auditing).

Preventing Injection Attacks

An injection attack is one in which a user enters some cleverly written text in an otherwise innocuous input field. This user-entered text can sometimes trick your application into doing unexpected things and could potentially wreak havoc on your system. This section takes a look at a few examples and how to prevent them.

The most common type of injection attack is an SQL injection. Imagine that you've created a login form for use with Forms authentication. Your code compares a user-entered username and password to values in a database and returns `true` or `false` via the following VB .NET code:

```
dim strSQL as string = "SELECT 1 FROM Users WHERE UserName = '" & txtUsername.Text
➥& _
    "' AND Password = '" & txtPassword.Text & "'"
```

This statement by itself seems harmless. Now imagine that the user enters the following text into the `txtUsername` text box:

```
'; DELETE FROM Users --
```

Your original code would then construct the following SQL statement:

```
SELECT 1 FROM Users WHERE UserName = ''; DELETE FROM Users --' AND Password = ''
```

MSSQL interprets this as two separate statements, and suddenly all of your user data is deleted.

There are a few ways around this issue. First, if you can, *always* used parameterized stored procedures instead of dynamically constructed SQL statements. For example:

```
dim cmdAuth as new SqlCommand("qryUserAuthenticate")
cmdAuth.CommandType = CommandType.StoredProcedure
cmdAuth.Parameters.Add(new SqlParameter("@Username", txtUsername.Text))
cmdAuth.Parameters.Add(new SqlParameter("@Password", txtPassword.Text))
cmdAuth.Parameters.Add(new SqlParameter("@Result", DBNull.Value))
cmdAuth.Parameters("Result").Direction = ParameterDirection.Output
cmdAuth.ExecuteNonQuery()
```

In this case, no matter what the user enters in the text boxes, the data is interpreted as literal content and no SQL statements can be injected.

If you can't use a stored procedure, you can still use a parameterized dynamic SQL statement:

```
dim strSQL as string = "SELECT @Result = 1 FROM Users WHERE UserName = @Username "
➥& _
    "AND Password = @Password"
dim cmdAuth as new SqlCommand(strSQL)
cmdAuth.Parameters.Add(new SqlParameter("@Username", txtUsername.Text))
...
cmdAuth.ExecuteNonQuery()
```

A third method is to parse out any potentially damaging user-entered data. This can be rather daunting, but often a simple check of apostrophes does the trick:

```
dim strSQL as string = "SELECT 1 FROM Users WHERE UserName = '" & _
    txtUsername.Text.Replace("'", "''") & "' AND Password = '" & _
    txtPassword.Text.Replace("'", "''") & "'"
```

21

Preventing Injection Attacks

MSSQL considers double quotes as an escape character, so by replacing any single quotes with double quotes, the previous harmful statement becomes not only harmless, but meaningless:

```
SELECT 1 FROM Users WHERE UserName = '''; DELETE FROM Users --' AND Password = ''
```

You can also parse user-input strings to ensure that they meet the length criteria of your SQL queries. For example, if you know that the username field can be a maximum of 10 characters, restrict or truncate the user input so that it is only 10 characters. This step also solves the previous issue.

Finally, a more brute-force approach is to limit the permissions of the database account that is executing your SQL code. Without delete privileges, the previous SQL injection statement doesn't work. Depending on the application, this sometimes isn't possible, but it is a very good option to consider.

Securing Connection Strings and Other Keys

All of the previous security topics deal with preventing users from getting unauthorized access to your system. But what happens if a rogue user gets access? You can take steps to diminish the risk associated with this situation, such as ensuring that any sensitive information such as passwords is inaccessible even then.

To be as secure as possible, sensitive data should never be exposed to anyone, authorized or not. This is a tall order and is not always feasible, but it is the only way to ensure complete security. For example, if you store your application's user passwords in plain text in a database, a rogue administrator with database privileges could steal those passwords and potentially get a lot of private information. A better way would be to encrypt those passwords in a way that they cannot be decrypted.

Another example is storing database connection strings (with credential information) in the `web.config` file—a common occurrence, but a potentially unsafe one.

One easy method that helps mitigate risk is to ensure that all of the proper ACL permissions are set and that every user has the minimum permissions and strongest password possible (don't leave your `sa` user account in MSSQL without a password, the default setting). If you store passwords plainly in a text file, make sure that very few people have access to that file via a tight ACL. Additionally, make sure that files that aren't directly requested by users live outside of your web application's directory structure. This ensures that a web user won't get access to those files.

As for the content within files, Windows comes with a built-in technology called the Data Protection API (DPAPI) that you can use to encrypt sensitive information. This is a Win32 function, not a .NET component, so the details aren't covered here. For more information, try one of the following web links:

21

▶ For an overview of DPAPI, see http://msdn.microsoft.com/library
/default.asp?url=/library/en-us/dnsecure/html/windataprotection-dpapi.asp.

▶ For more on using DPAPI in ASP.NET, see http://msdn.microsoft.com/library/
default.asp?url=/library/en-us/dnnetsec/html/SecNetHT08.asp.

DPAPI can be used to encrypt connection strings in your `web.config` file so that
they aren't stored as plain text for any user to see.

Finally, if you are prepared to encrypt data so that there is no way to ever decrypt it
(meaning that you would need to change the data entirely if you needed to retrieve
it), you can perform a one-way hash encryption. For example, the following code
snippet shows how to encrypt a string using a random salt value and a hash (a salt
value is a cryptographically strong random number, which just makes it that much
harder to break):

```
'get random salt value
dim rng as new RNGCryptoServiceProvider()
dim buff as byte() = new byte(10)
ng.GetBytes(buff)
dim salt as string = Convert.ToBase64String(buff)

'concatenate salt value and sensitive string
dim saltAndPwd as string = string.Concat("MyPassword", salt)

'hash encrypt it
dim hashedPwd as string = FormsAuthentication.HashPasswordForStoringInConfigFile _
    (saltAndPwd, "SHA1")
```

With this method, you can never retrieve the original value, so make sure that you
are willing to take this step.

21

Summary

Unfortunately, the only secure computer is one that has been dropped into a black
hole (and maybe not even then). It is nearly impossible to prevent some type of security breach when someone has direct access to your machine. With the proper steps
mentioned in this chapter, however, you can stop most malicious users in their
tracks.

Keep the topics in the last two sections of this chapter constantly in mind, and integrate them into all applications as habit. If nothing else, they are good coding practices for all developers to consider.

Summary

The majority of ASP.NET applications don't require any specific authentication or authorization scheme; anonymous access with default permissions is typically good enough. However, when you do need a security scheme, you should carefully weigh your options. Table 21.2 shows some guidelines.

Finally, one consideration that was not covered in this chapter is secure communications. Technologies such as SSL or IPSec should definitely be considered when a user is transmitting any sensitive data. The only options that we discussed here that transmit secure data are digest and NTLM authentication, which aren't supported by all platforms and browsers.

TABLE 21.2

Security Guidelines in ASP.NET

Authentication	Authorization	When to Use
Windows	Resource based without impersonation	Your number of users is small or is increasing either slowly or not at all, and you don't need to flow identities. You also have a small set of resources to manage.
Windows	Resource based with impersonation	You have a small number of users and need to flow identities (for example, for security auditing). You also have a small set of resources to manage.
Windows	Role based with URL authorization	You have a small number of users, and you want to deny access to entire files or directory structures.
Windows	Role based with programmatic authorization	You have a small number of users, and you want to deny access to specific pieces of functionality (for example, conditionally displaying an Edit button on a data form).
Windows	None	You have a small number of users, but you don't need to identify users for security reasons (you intend to perform only basic personalization).
Forms	Resource based	Not available.
Forms	Role based with URL authorization	You have a larger, ever-increasing, or non–administrator-maintained number of users that should be custom authenticated (that is, against a database), and you want to deny access to entire files or directory structures.
Forms	Role based with programmatic authorization	You have a larger number of users, and you want to deny access to specific pieces of functionality.
Forms	None	You have a larger number of users, but you don't need to identify users for security reasons (that is, you intend to perform only basic personalization).

21

Further Reading

"Building Secure ASP.NET Applications: Authentication, Authorization, and Secure Communication." MSDN website, http://msdn.microsoft.com/library/default.asp?url=/library/en-us/dnnetsec/html/secnetlpMSDN.asp.

"Windows Data Protection." MSDN website, http://msdn.microsoft.com/library/default.asp?url=/library/en-us/dnsecure/html/windataprotection-dpapi.asp.

"How to Use DPAPI (Machine Store) from ASP.NET." MSDN website, http://msdn.microsoft.com/library/default.asp?url=/library/en-us/dnnetsec/html/SecNetHT08.asp.

21

22 EXTENDING ASP.NET

IN BRIEF

ASP.NET provides many powerful capabilities that you can use to build your applications, but sometimes they aren't enough. Thankfully, ASP.NET is easily extensible, meaning that you can add new functionality that directly interfaces with the underlying engine. Thus, you can build a complete ASP.NET custom application, from handling low-level requests/responses to dealing with visual interfaces.

WHAT YOU NEED

SOFTWARE REQUIREMENTS	Windows 2000, XP, or 2003 .NET Framework 1.1 SDK Visual Studio .NET 2003 with Visual Basic .NET installed Internet Information Server (version 5 or later)
HARDWARE REQUIREMENTS	PC desktop or laptop system
SKILL REQUIREMENTS	Advanced knowledge in HTML Advanced knowledge in the .NET Framework and ASP.NET

EXTENDING ASP.NET AT A GLANCE

Understanding the ASP.NET HTTP Pipeline

Before we get to the specifics of extending ASP.NET, it is helpful to understand the out-of-the-box processing model. This section briefly outlines the HTTP pipeline scheme that ASP.NET uses and will greatly help you understand subsequent sections in this chapter.

When a request from a client comes into an ASP.NET application, a procedure is followed to make sure that everything is handled properly. Using the same technology that you will use to extend ASP.NET, ASP.NET handles requests and sends responses back to the client.

IIS is the first stop for any and all requests to your application. IIS uses a technology called ISAPI extensions, which allows it to handle incoming requests. Think of an ISAPI extension as a mini-application that handles a certain type of request. Figure 22.1 shows a typical list of ISAPI extensions that IIS uses. In this case, when a request comes in for any ASP.NET–related item (for example, requests for `.aspx`, `.asmx`, `web. config` files, and so on), IIS looks to the `ASPNET_ISAPI.dll` ISAPI extension. The only thing that `ASPNET_ISAPI.dll` does is forward the request directly onto the ASP.NET worker process, `aspnet_wp.exe`. This executable file represents your web application and handles things such as your pool of `HttpApplication` instances (see Chapter 20, "Website Management," for more information on `HttpApplication`).

> **NOTE**
>
> In IIS version 6.0 and above, included in Windows Server 2003 and later, the `ASPNET_ISAPI.dll` ISAPI extension is done away with. ASP.NET is integrated directly into the operating system with IIS, which means greater performance and scalability.
>
> More specifically, these processes have been integrated into the kernel, so instead of having to execute to run partly in user space and partly in privileged kernel space, all the IIS service code now runs in kernel space. This makes the system run faster primarily because the context switches involved in migrating between user space and kernel address spaces is done away with.

22

When the ASP.NET worker process has the request, it sends it through a number of processors, known as HTTP handlers. These handlers can modify or tweak the request (and the outgoing response) as necessary to perform whatever functionality is needed. For example, session state handling, authentication, and output caching are all functionalities enabled through HTTP modules. ASP.NET defines a set of modules for you, by default, but you can add as many as necessary.

> **NOTE**
>
> HTTP modules are discussed further in the next section, "Using `HttpModules` to Alter Output."

Understanding the ASP.NET HTTP Pipeline

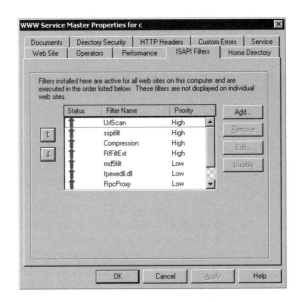

FIGURE 22.1   ISAPI extensions allow IIS to handle incoming requests.

After all of the HTTP modules have had their turns, the request is sent to an HTTP handler. A handler is responsible for servicing a request, performing functionality, and spitting out results. The Page class that you've been working with all this time (every ASP.NET page inherits from Page) is an example of an HTTP handler; it is the endpoint for an incoming request. ASP.NET determines which handler should be used for a given request by examining the requested file type and type of request. Thus, all requests to .aspx files ultimately go to the Page class, all requests to .asmx files go to a web service handler, all requests to .config files go to a forbidden request handler, and so on. Table 22.1 lists the various ASP.NET file types and their handlers.

22

TABLE 22.1

ASP.NET File Types and Handlers

File Extension	Handler Class	Description
.aspx	PageHandlerFactory	ASP.NET file
.ashx	SimpleHandlerFactory	HTTP handler file
.asmx	WebServiceHandlerFactory	Web service file
.rem	HttpRemotingHandlerFactory	Remoting file
.soap	HttpRemotingHandlerFactory	Web service SOAP file
.asax	HttpForbiddenHandler	Application file
.ascx	HttpForbiddenHandler	User control file

TABLE 22.1

Continued

File Extension	Handler Class	Description
.config	HttpForbiddenHandler	Configuration file
.axd	TraceHandler	Trace viewer file
.cs, .csproj	HttpForbiddenHandler	C# code file
.vb, .vbproj	HttpForbiddenHandler	VB .NET code file
.webinfo	HttpForbiddenHandler	.NET project file
.asp	HttpForbiddenHandler	Classic ASP file
.licx	HttpForbiddenHandler	Licensed control file
.resx	HttpForbiddenHandler	XML resource file
.resources	HttpForbiddenHandler	Globalization resource file

Finally, the handler sends any output back through any applicable HTTP modules and to the client through IIS. This gives you one last chance to use a module to alter any response data. Figure 22.2 illustrates this pipeline.

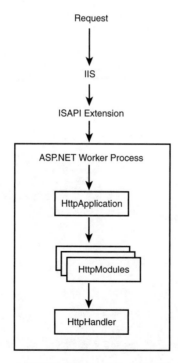

FIGURE 22.2 The ASP.NET pipeline provides logical and extensible steps.

You can see the default modules and handlers in the system `machine.config` file under the `HttpModules` and `HttpHandlers` sections. In subsequent sections in this chapter, you will learn how to create custom modules and handlers and how to tie them into the HTTP pipeline.

Using `HttpModules` to Alter Output

As described in the previous section, an HTTP module is used to alter incoming and outgoing requests in the ASP.NET HTTP pipeline. In this section, you create a custom HTTP module, insert it into the pipeline, and filter content.

An `HttpModule` is just a class that implements the `IHttpModule` interface. This interface defines only two requirements: the `Dispose` and `Init` methods. The former is a typical `Dispose` method that is used to clean up any used resources; the latter is where you initialize your module.

Typically, your HTTP modules tap into an existing event in your application to perform its processing. For example, if you wanted to authenticate incoming requests, you would handle the `Application_AuthenticateRequest` event in your module. You use the `Init` method to hook into these events. You can also create and raise your own custom events in a module, which can then be handled in your `global.asax` file.

Listing 22.1 shows an example of an HTTP module that provides debug output if the request is coming from the local machine.

LISTING 22.1
Sending Debug Output to Administrators

```
Imports System
Imports System.Web
Imports System.IO


Public Class RequestFilterModule
    Implements IHttpModule

    Overloads Sub Dispose() Implements IHttpModule.Dispose
    End Sub


    Overloads Sub Init(ByVal context As HttpApplication) Implements _
        IHttpModule.Init
        AddHandler context.BeginRequest, AddressOf Me.Application_BeginRequest
    End Sub


    Private Sub Application_BeginRequest(Sender As Object, e As EventArgs)
        Dim strTemp As String
```

LISTING 22.1
Continued

```
    Dim response As HttpResponse = CType(Sender, HttpApplication).Response    2
    Dim request As HttpRequest = CType(Sender, HttpApplication).Request

        If request.ServerVariables("REMOTE_ADDR") = "127.0.0.1" Then
            response.Write("<table border=1>")
            For Each strTemp In request.ServerVariables.AllKeys
                response.Write("<tr><td>" & strTemp & "</td><td>")
                response.Write(request.ServerVariables(strTemp))
                response.Write("</td></tr>")
            Next
            response.Write("</table>")
        End If
    End Sub
End Class
```

Your `Dispose` method here does nothing. The `Init` method simply attaches a handler—`Application_BeginRequest`—to the `HttpApplication`. `BeginRequest` event **1**, which, as you'll recall, executes every time that the server receives a request.

The `Application_BeginRequest` method then gets local references to the `HttpRequest` and `HttpResponse` objects **2** from the `Sender` parameter, which is essentially an `HttpApplication` object. If the requesting IP address is the local loopback address, it writes out a table with all of the server variables.

Compile and place this file into your application's `bin` directory. The next step is to modify your `web.config` file to include this new HTTP module, as shown in Listing 22.2.

LISTING 22.2
Including HTTP Modules in Your Application

```
<configuration>
   <system.web>
      <httpModules>
         <add type="VBNetUnleashed.RequestFilterModule, RequestFilterModule"
            name="RequestFilterModule"/>
      </httpModules>
   </system.web>
</configuration>
```

22

Using `HttpModules` to Alter Output

The `type` attribute tells the application what namespace, class name, and assembly to find the module in. The `name` attribute is used mostly in case you have created custom events that need to be handled elsewhere. In this case, the event handler for any events must take the signature `RequestFilterModule_EventName`.

Finally, create a web forms page and request it. If your computer is both the server and the client, you should see something similar to Figure 22.3. If the machines are separate, you won't see the debug output.

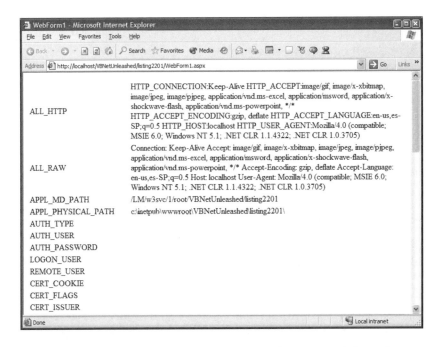

FIGURE 22.3   Outputting different output based on request information.

HTTP modules are very simple to create and implement, but the possibilities are endless. You have access to all of the ASP.NET intrinsic objects (`HttpRequest`, `HttpResponse`, `ServerUtility`, and so on) and events, which enable you to alter the content as you see fit. Table 22.2 shows the typical events that execute during a request and at what point you can use them to alter the behavior of your application.

TABLE 22.2

Application Event Ordering

Event	Executes When
Before the Application Executes	
`BeginRequest`	The request is first received.
`AuthenticateRequest`	The request is about to be authenticated.

TABLE 22.2

Continued

Event	Executes When
Before the Application Executes	
AuthorizeRequest	The request is about to be authorized.
ResolveRequestCache	The application determines whether it should serve output-cache stored data or serve dynamically.
AcquireRequestState	State is about to be obtained.
PreRequestHandlerExecute	The HTTP handler is about to take over.
After the Application Returns	
PostRequestHandlerExecute	The HTTP handler finishes execution.
ReleaseRequestState	State is about to be stored.
UpdateRequestCache	The output data is ready to be cached.
EndRequest	All processing ends; this is the final event that you can participate in.
Nondeterministic Order	
PreSendRequestHeaders	HTTP headers are ready to be sent to the client.
PreSendRequestContent	Content is ready to be sent to the client.
Error	An unhandled exception occurs.

TIP

If you need to filter the content of the output, you're better off using the `HttpResponse.Filter` property than trying to intercept output using an **HTTP** module. It's difficult to alter the output due to the write-only nature of the output stream, but the `Filter` property is used for this exact purpose.

Creating Custom `HttpHandlers`

As mentioned in a previous section, an HTTP handler is used to actually process a request. It is the last stop of a request on a server, after which response is returned. Common ASP.NET handlers are the `Page` class, the private `HttpForbiddenHandler` class, and the `WebServiceHandlerFactory` class.

An HTTP handler class must implement the `IHttpHandler` interface. This interface defines two members: `IsReusable` and `ProcessRequest`. The former is used to tell ASP.NET whether any subsequent client requests can reuse the current instance of the module—in other words, should a pool of handlers be used? This property returns `true` or `false`. It's generally a good idea to allow pooling, in this case. The second member, `ProcessRequest`, is where you actually the processing of the request.

22

Creating Custom `HttpHandlers`

More than just implementing these methods, with an HTTP handler, you have to make decisions about what kind of requests to handle. For instance, will you handle requests for all `.aspx` files? For all requests for a custom file type? For only GET or only POST requests for a particular file? The handling is fairly customizable; the needs of your application often determine what types of requests you need to handle. Listing 22.3 shows an example of modifying your `web.config` file to handle different types of requests.

LISTING 22.3
Implementing Custom HTTP Handlers

```
<configuration>
  <system.web>
    <httpHandlers>
      <add verb="*" path="*.unleashed"
        type="VBNetUnleashed.CustomHandler, CustomHandler" />
    </httpHandlers>
  </system.web>
</configuration>
```

This configuration instructs that all requests to any files with the extension `.unleashed` will be handled by the `CustomHandler` class, shown in Listing 22.4.

LISTING 22.4
A Custom HTTP Handler to Handle `.unleashed` Files

```
Imports System.Web
Imports System.IO

Public Class CustomHandler
    Implements IHttpHandler

    ReadOnly Property IsReusable() As Boolean Implements IHttpHandler.IsReusable
        Get
            Return True
        End Get
    End Property

    Sub ProcessRequest(ByVal context As HttpContext)
     Implements IHttpHandler.ProcessRequest
        Dim strFileName As String
        strFileName = context.Request.ServerVariables("PATH_TRANSLATED")
        Dim sr As StreamReader = File.OpenText(strFileName)
        context.Response.Write(sr.ReadToEnd)
        sr.Close()
    End Sub
End Class
```

This custom handler very simply uses a `StreamReader` to open the requested file and output the contents **1**. Create a file with the extension `.unleashed`, and the custom handler, together with the `web.config` file from Listing 22.3, outputs everything in that file. In fact, this custom handler is very similar to what ASP.NET can do for simple HTML files.

NOTE

If you need to access session state values in your handler, you also need to implement the `IRequiresSessionState` interface. This interface defines no required members; it is simply a marker.

In addition, you can create an HTTP handler *factory*. A factory is used to dynamically generate new handler objects. For instance, ASP.NET uses the `PageHandlerFactory` class to handle incoming requests for `.aspx` files. This factory finds the compiled version of the requested page and generates the handler (a `Page` class) for you.

To create a factory, you must implement the `IHttpHandlerFactory` interface, which defines only the `GetHandler` and `ReleaseHandler` methods, which are responsible for creating and destroying your handler (in most cases, the handler is destroyed through .NET's garbage collection, so your `ReleaseHandler` method often remains empty). In `GetHandler`, you can dynamically determine what type of handler to create. For example, Listing 22.5 shows a typical implementation of this method.

TIP

Don't entirely disregard the `ReleaseHandler` method, however. It can still be useful—and sometimes might be essential—especially when you are dealing with unmanaged objects such as older COM components.

LISTING 22.5
Using a Handler Factory

```
Public Overridable Function GetHandler(context As HttpContext, _
    requestType As String, url As String, pathTranslated As String) _
    As IHttpHandler _
    Implements IHttpHandlerFactory.GetHandler

    Dim h As Object = Nothing

    if requestType = "GET" then
        h = Activator.CreateInstance(Type.GetType("GETHandler"))
```

22

Creating Custom HttpHandlers

LISTING 22.5
Continued

```
    else
        h = Activator.CreateInstance(Type.GetType("POSTHandler"))
    end if

    Return CType(h, IHttpHandler)
End Function
```

The method is fairly self-explanatory. This factory creates a different type of handler, based on the type of request that the client sent (GET or POST). You implement the factory in web.config the same as with a regular handler.

With HTTP handler factories, you can maintain greater control over the request than by implementing several separate handlers in your web.config file.

TIP

You can see from Table 22.1 that .NET itself uses many handler factories. It's often a good idea to use a factory to provide you with more flexibility.

Summary

ASP.NET enables you to participate in the inner workings of processing requests by creating HTTP modules and handlers. This is a very powerful yet easy way to build a completely customized engine for running your site, or to simply perform validation checks. The possibilities are nearly endless: custom authentication and authorization, URL rewriting, content filtering, image usage tracking, customized page building, and so on. Many examples of custom modules and handlers exist across the Web.

Remember, however, that HTTP modules and handlers work only for requests that the ASP.NET engine handles. This means that static files, such as HTML and image files, are not affected by any custom objects that you create unless you map those objects to the ASP.NET engine. This can create performance issues, and is beyond the scope of this chapter, but it can be a very valuable tip to keep in mind.

22

Further Reading

"Serving Dynamic Content with HTTP Handlers." MSDN website, http://msdn.microsoft.com/library/default.asp?url=/library/en-us/dnaspp/html/httphandl.asp.

"Implementing Intercepting Filter in ASP.NET Using HTTP Module." MSDN website, http://msdn.microsoft.com/library/default.asp?url=/library/en-us/dnpatterns/html/ImpInterceptingFilterInASP.asp.

"Securely Implement Request Processing, Filtering, and Content Redirection with HTTP Pipelines in ASP.NET." MSDN website, http://msdn.microsoft.com/msdnmag/issues/02/09/httppipelines/.

Part V

Advanced Programming

23 VERSIONING AND THE GLOBAL ASSEMBLY CACHE

IN BRIEF

This chapter discusses how .NET versioning works for private assemblies and shared assemblies. You will learn how you can take advantage of the .NET Framework to overcome the deployment problems associated with the old WIN32 and COM application.

The .NET Framework assemblies can be deployed in two different ways: as private assemblies or as shared assemblies. This chapter covers various assembly-related topics, including strong names and the Global Assembly Cache.

Finally, the chapter explains how the common language runtime locates assemblies and how you can control assembly binding by creating an application, publisher, or administrator policy.

WHAT YOU NEED

SOFTWARE REQUIREMENTS	Windows 2000, XP, or 2003
	Visual Studio .NET 2003 with Visual Basic .NET installed
	.NET Framework SDK v1.1
HARDWARE RECOMMENDATIONS	PC desktop or laptop
SKILL REQUIREMENTS	Familiarity with Visual Basic .NET
	Familiarity with assemblies

VERSIONING AND THE GLOBAL ASSEMBLY CACHE AT A GLANCE

Introduction to .NET Framework Versioning

Before the .NET Framework, the deployment and versioning model for Windows applications was the source of a problem commonly referred to as DLL hell. In the Win32 and COM era, every time an installation program copied a dynamic link library (DLL) to the Windows system directory or registered a COM component in the Windows Registry, all applications that shared that component automatically started using the newly installed version. This situation potentially caused one or more applications that were previously working fine to stop working. The nasty name "DLL hell" reflects the frustration of users and support professionals who tried to identify and resolve these problems.

The key reason for DLL hell was the component-sharing model used by Win32 and COM applications. One of the design goals for the .NET Framework is to eliminate DLL hell by using a new strategy for versioning and deployment. The .NET Framework enables you to version and deploy application components (assemblies) in two different ways:

▶ Private assemblies

▶ Shared assemblies

Private Assemblies

A private assembly is local to the application that uses it and is deployed within the application's directory structure. Any changes to a private assembly cannot possibly affect any other installed application on the same machine. The .NET Framework does not impose any special versioning or naming requirements for a private assembly.

For example, consider an application, MyApp.exe, that uses a private assembly, MyComponent.dll. In version 1 of the application, you can deploy both the files to a directory such as C:\Program Files\MyApp\v1.0. When you release a second version of the application, you can choose to deploy all of its files into a different directory structure, such as C:\Program Files\MyApp\v2.0. In this case, both the versions are independent of each other and also of any other application on the same machine. As you can see in this example, versioning of a private assembly is mostly the responsibility of the developer.

To minimize problems that might result from code sharing, by default, all assemblies in the .NET Framework are created as private assemblies.

23

Private Assemblies

> **TIP**
>
> The .NET Framework does not require assemblies to be registered in the Windows Registry. Applications that use private assemblies can be simply deployed by using the XCOPY command.

> **NOTE**
>
> You can specify a version for an assembly by using the assembly-level AssemblyVersion attribute. For a private assembly, this version information is only for informational purpose; the common language runtime does not use it to bind to a specific version of the assembly.

Shared Assemblies

A shared assembly can be referenced by more than one application. To avoid deployment issues, the .NET Framework allows multiple versions of a shared assembly to coexist. The .NET Framework also protects assemblies from different publishers from overwriting each other.

An assembly must meet the following requirements to be deployed as a shared assembly:

- A shared assembly must have an associated strong name.

- A shared assembly must be installed in the Global Assembly Cache (GAC).

Strong Name Signing

If shared assemblies are identified by just their names—as the private assemblies are—two software publishers theoretically could use the same name for an assembly. This would overwrite files and cause applications using those assemblies to behave abnormally.

To resolve this problem, the .NET Framework requires all shared assemblies to have a strong name. A strong name uses four attributes to identify an assembly:

- Simple name

- Version number

- Culture identity (optional)

- Public key token

Global Assembly Cache

A regular Windows folder can differentiate files based on just their simple names, not their strong names. Therefore, you need a special type of storage to store strongly named assemblies in a well-known shared location. The .NET Framework provides this storage in the form of the Global Assembly Cache (GAC). In addition to providing a shared location, the GAC provides the following benefits for shared assemblies:

▶ **Integrity check**—When assemblies are installed in the GAC, the GAC applies a strong integrity check on the assembly. This check guarantees that the contents of the assembly have not been changed since it was built.

▶ **Security**—The GAC enables only users with administrator privileges to modify its contents.

▶ **Side-by-side versioning**—Multiple assemblies with the same name but different version numbers can be maintained in the Global Assembly Cache.

Working with Shared Assemblies

In this section, you'll learn the following about shared assemblies:

▶ How to assign a strong name to an assembly

▶ How to add and remove an assembly from the GAC

▶ How to delay-sign an assembly

▶ What the binding policy is for shared assemblies

▶ How the common language runtime binds to an assembly

Assigning a Strong Name to an Assembly

To create a strong name, you need an assembly's simple name, its version number, an optional culture identity, and a key pair. The key pair consists of two related pieces of binary data: a public key and a private key.

The *public key* represents the identity of a software publisher. When you create a strongly named assembly, the public key is stored in the assembly manifest, along with other identification information, such as name, version number, and culture. This scheme does not look foolproof because the public key is easily available from the assembly manifest, and an assembly identity easily can be faked with some other company's public key. To verify that only the legitimate owner of the public key has created the assembly, an assembly is signed with the publisher's *private key*. The

23

Working with Shared Assemblies

private key is assumed to be known only to the assembly's publisher. The process of signing an assembly and verifying its signature works like this:

▶ **Signing an assembly**—When you sign an assembly, a cryptographic hash of the assembly's contents is computed. The hash is then encoded with the private key and is stored within the assembly. The public key is stored in the assembly manifest.

▶ **Verifying the signature**—When the common language runtime verifies an assembly's identity, it reads the public key from the assembly manifest and uses it to decrypt the cryptographic hash that is stored in the assembly. It then recalculates the hash for the current contents of the assembly. If the two hashes match, this ensures two things: The contents of the assembly were not tampered with after the assembly was signed, and only the party that has a private key associated with the public key stored in the assembly has signed the assembly.

You can easily generate public/private key pairs by using the command-line Strong Name tool (sn.exe). For example, you can use this command to create both the public and private keys and store them in a file named VbNetBook.snk:

```
sn -k VBNetBook.snk
```

TIP

You can easily run the .NET Framework command-line tool by using the Visual Studio .NET 2003 command prompt. A shortcut for this is available inside the Visual Studio .NET 2003 program group in the Windows Start menu.

When you have the key file, you can use the AssemblyKeyFile attribute to specify the name of a key file, which will then use it to generate the strong name.

The AssemblyKeyFile attribute can be applied for an assembly by modifying the AssemblyInfo.vb file of the Visual Studio .NET project. For example, the following code modifies the AssemblyVersion and AssemblyKeyFile attributes to specify a version and a key file for an assembly:

```
<assembly: AssemblyVersion("1.0")>
<assembly: AssemblyKeyFile("VBNetBook.snk")>
```

After you apply these attributes to the project and build the project, the project assembly is signed with a strong name that uniquely identifies its version number and identity.

23

> **TIP**
>
> If you want to assign a strong name to an assembly by using a command-line tool, you can use the Assembly Linker tool (`al.exe`) with the `-keyfile` option.

If an assembly consists of multiple files, just the file that contains the assembly manifest needs to be signed. The assembly manifest already contains file hashes for all the files that constitute the assembly implementation. The common language runtime can easily determine whether a file has been tampered with by matching its actual hash with what is stored in the assembly manifest.

The assembly's version in the `AssemblyVersion` attribute consists of up to four parts:

```
<major>.<minor>.<build>.<revision>
```

If you want to use a fixed version value, you can hard-code it. On the other hand, you can use an asterisk in place of build and revision numbers; this automatically updates the build and revision when you build the project for the first time in Visual Studio .NET. The version number remains constant for subsequent rebuilds within the same instance of Visual Studio .NET.

For strongly named assemblies, you should generally avoid the use of an asterisk in the `AssemblyVersion` attribute so that multiple builds of the same assembly are not inadvertently installed in the GAC as you test your application.

Adding an Assembly to the GAC

After you have associated a strong name with an assembly, you can place the assembly in the GAC. You can add an assembly to the GAC in several ways. Using the Windows Installer is the recommended approach for installing assemblies on the end user's computer. However, some quick alternatives are available for development purposes, too.

Using Windows Installer to Add an Assembly to the GAC

Using Microsoft Windows Installer is the preferred way of adding assemblies to the GAC. Windows Installer maintains a reference count for assemblies in the GAC and provides uninstallation support. You learned how to add assemblies using Windows Installer technology through the setup and deployment projects of Visual Studio .NET in Chapter 8, "Deploying Your Application."

Using Windows Explorer to Add an Assembly to the GAC

The Assembly Cache Viewer Shell Extension (`shfusion.dll`) is installed as a part of the .NET Framework. This extension enables you to view the complex structure of

23

Working with Shared Assemblies

the GAC using Windows Explorer and enables administrators to install and uninstall assemblies using drag-and-drop and menu operations.

The GAC is stored in the Assembly folder of the Windows installation directory (usually C:\Windows), as shown in Figure 23.1.

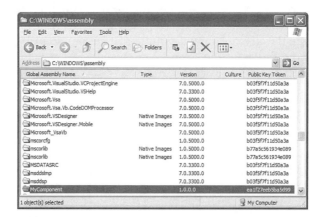

FIGURE 23.1   The Assembly Cache Viewer Shell Extension enables you to view and manage the contents of the assembly cache by using Windows Explorer.

NOTE

The assembly cache folder contains two caches: the GAC and the native image cache. Native image cache is for storing the processor-specific native code image of a managed assembly. To add an assembly to the native image cache, you need to use the .NET Framework Native Image Generation tool (ngen.exe).

In the assembly cache folder, you can right-click on an assembly and select Properties from the shortcut menu. The Properties dialog box appears, as shown in Figure 23.2.

If you want to remove a file from the GAC, you just delete it from Windows Explorer by selecting File, Delete, or by selecting Delete from the assembly's shortcut menu.

Using the .NET Framework Configuration Tool to Add an Assembly to the GAC

You can also use the .NET Framework Configuration tool (mscorcfg.msc) to manage an assembly in the GAC. The Microsoft .NET Framework Configuration tool can be started from the Administrative Tools section of Windows Control Panel.

FIGURE 23.2 You can view the properties of an assembly that is installed in the GAC.

To install a strongly named assembly by using the .NET Framework Configuration Tool, you click the hyperlink Add an Assembly to the Assembly Cache, as shown in Figure 23.3.

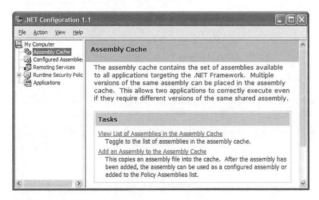

FIGURE 23.3 You can add assemblies in the GAC by using the .NET Framework Configuration tool.

To uninstall an assembly by using the .NET Framework Configuration tool, you click the other hyperlink, View List of Assemblies in the Assembly Cache. When you see a list of installed assemblies, you just select Action, Delete, or select Delete from the assembly's shortcut menu.

In addition to helping you add or remove assemblies, the .NET Framework Configuration tool helps you configure assemblies and manage their runtime

23

Working with Shared Assemblies

security policies; you will learn more about this in Chapter 29, "Code Access Security (CAS)."

Using the Global Assembly Cache Tool (`gacutil.exe`) to Add an Assembly to the GAC

`GacUtil.exe` is a command-line tool that is especially useful for adding and removing assemblies from the GAC via a program script or a batch file.

To install an assembly to the GAC, you can use the `/i` option of the tool:

```
gacutil /i MyComponent.dll
```

You can list all the assemblies in the GAC by using the `gacutil.exe` tool with the `/l` option.

You can use the `/u` option with the name of the assembly (without the file extension) to uninstall the assembly from the GAC:

```
gacutil /u MyComponent
```

You can also choose to uninstall an assembly of a specific version and specific culture from the GAC by specifying its version, culture, and public key, along with the name of the assembly:

```
gacutil /u MyComponent,Version=1.0.0.0,
➥Culture=neutral,PublicKeyToken=ea1f27eeb5ba5d99
```

Delay-Signing an Assembly

When you generate a key file by using the –k option, the output key file contains both the public key and a private key for a company. As discussed earlier in the chapter, the private key ensures that the assembly is signed only by its advertised publisher. Thus, in most companies, the private key is stored securely, and only a few people have access to it.

If the key is highly protected, it might be difficult to frequently access the key when multiple developers of a company are building assemblies several times a day. To solve this problem, the .NET Framework uses the delay signing technique for assemblies.

When you use delay signing, you use only the public key to build an assembly. Associating public keys with an assembly enables you to place the assembly in the GAC and complete most of the development and testing tasks with the assembly. Later, when you are ready to package the assembly, someone who is authorized signs the assembly with the private key. Signing with the private key ensures that the

23

common language runtime will provide tamper protection for the assembly. The following list summarizes the steps involved with delay signing:

1. **Extract a public key from the public/private key pair**—To extract the public key from a file that is storing the public/private key pair, you use the –p switch of the Strong Name tool:

   ```
   sn.exe -p VBNetBook.snk VBNetBookPublicKey.snk
   ```

   At this stage, the VBNetBookPublicKey.snk file can be freely distributed to the development team, and the VBNetBook.snk file that contains both the private and public keys can be stored securely, possibly on a hardware device such as a smart card or USB drive.

2. **Use Visual Studio .NET to delay-sign an assembly**—To use delay signing in a Visual Studio .NET project, you need to modify the following two attributes of the project's AssemblyInfo.vb file and build the assembly:

   ```
   <assembly: AssemblyDelaySign(true)>
   <assembly: AssemblyKeyFile("VBNetBookPublicKey.snk")>
   ```

3. **Turn off verification for an assembly in the GAC**—By default, the GAC verifies the strong name of each assembly. If the private key is not used to sign the assembly, this verification fails. For development and testing purposes, you can relax this verification for an assembly by issuing the following command:

   ```
   sn.exe -Vr MyComponent.dll
   ```

4. **Sign a delay-signed assembly with the private key**—When you are ready to deploy a delay-signed assembly, you need to sign it with the company's private key:

   ```
   sn.exe -R MyComponent.dll VBNetBook.snk
   ```

5. **Turn on verification for an assembly in the GAC**—Finally, you can instruct the GAC to turn on verification for an assembly by issuing the following command:

   ```
   sn.exe -Vu MyComponent.dll
   ```

23

Using the Assembly Linker Tool for Delay Signing

The Assembly Linker tool (al.exe) generates an assembly with an assembly manifest from the given modules or resource files. A module is a Microsoft Intermediate Language (MSIL) file without an assembly manifest.

Working with Shared Assemblies

While generating an assembly, you can also instruct the Assembly Linker tool to sign or delay-sign an assembly with the given public/private key file. When you use `al.exe` for delay signing, you also use the arguments listed in Table 23.1.

TABLE 23.1

Arguments Passed to `al.exe` for Delay Signing

Argument	Description
`<sourcefiles>`	You replace `<sourcefiles>` with the names of one or more complied modules that will be the parts of the resulting assembly.
`/delay[sign] [+|-]`	You can use either the `delay` argument or the `delay[sign]` argument for delay signing. The option + is used to delay-sign the assembly by storing just the public key manifest in the assembly manifest. The – option is used to fully sign an assembly with both public and private keys. If you do not use either + or -, the default value of – is assumed.
`/keyf[ile]:<filename>`	You can use either `keyf` or `keyfile` to specify the key file. You replace `<filename>` with the name of the file that stores the key(s).
`/out:<filename>`	You replace `<filename>` with the desired name of the output assembly file.

Assume that you want to create an assembly by linking two modules, Sample1.netmodule and Sample2.netmodule. The public key file is SamplePublicKey.snk, and the desired output assembly is SignedSample.exe. You would use the `al.exe` command, as follows:

```
al.exe Sample1.netmodule,Sample2.netmodule
➥/delaysign+ /keyfile:SamplePublicKey.snk /out:SignedSample.exe
```

Binding Policy for Assemblies

The binding policy for assemblies identifies a set of rules that specify the following:

- ► The directories in which the common language runtime should search for an assembly

- ► The version of an assembly for which the common language runtime should search

When the common language runtime searches an assembly, it goes through three stages of binding policy resolution, as shown in Figure 23.4.

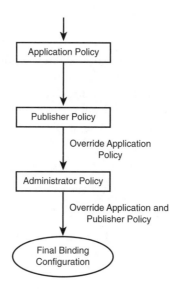

FIGURE 23.4   The common language runtime resolves the binding policy in three stages.

By default, an application binds to only an assembly with the same identity with which the application was originally compiled. So if you release a new version of the assembly and remove the old one, existing applications will break because they still will be looking for an older version of the assembly.

Fortunately, the application, the machine, and the publisher configuration files give you a mechanism to redirect the binding requests to a different version of the assembly, without needing to recompile already deployed applications.

Application Policy Resolution

At this stage, the common language runtime looks for an application configuration file for the binding rules. This configuration file can be used to specify additional search paths for an assembly. In addition, you can use this file to redirect the common language runtime to a specific version of an assembly. The application-specific binding rules are usually set either by the application developer or by an administrator.

Consider a scenario in which you have an application named MyApplication that uses version 1.0 of a shared component named MyComponent. When a new version 1.1 of the MyComponent component is released, you install it in the GAC. Some of the applications on your computer still use version 1.0 of the component. You want the already deployed MyApplication to start using version 1.1 of the component.

23

Binding Policy for Assemblies

You do not want to recompile MyApplication or affect the installation of other applications on the computer.

The best policy in this scenario is to modify the application configuration file of MyApplication to redirect any request for version 1.0 of MyComponent to version 1.1 of that assembly. Modifying configuration files does not require the application to be recompiled, and if you modify the application configuration file, it affects only the application to which it belongs.

All you need to do to configure application-level binding policy for an assembly is to open the .NET Framework Configuration tool and take the following steps:

1. Click the Applications node in tree view.

2. Click the Add an Application to Configure link.

3. In the Configure an Application dialog box, click the Other button and browse to the application folder to select the name of application (such as MyApplication.exe), and click OK.

4. Expand the new node in tree view and click the Configured Assemblies child node.

5. Click the Configure an Assembly link.

6. In the Configure an Assembly dialog box, select the option button to choose an assembly from the list of assemblies that this application uses. Click the Choose Assembly button. Select the MyComponent assembly and click Select, and then click Finish.

7. In the MyComponent Properties dialog box, select the Binding Policy tab. Enter 1.0.0.0 as the requested version and 1.1.0.0 as the new version, as shown in Figure 23.5.

8. Click OK to save the configured assembly information.

CAUTION

The .NET Framework Configuration tool performs no validation to determine whether the specified new version of the assembly even exists.

23

The previous steps modify the application's configuration file (such as MyApplication.exe.config). The new file will look something like this:

```
<?xml version="1.0"?>
<configuration>
  <runtime>
    <assemblyBinding
        xmlns="urn:schemas-microsoft-com:asm.v1">
      <dependentAssembly>
```

```
        <assemblyIdentity
            name="MyComponent"
            publicKeyToken="ea1f27eeb5ba5d99" />
        <bindingRedirect oldVersion="1.0.0.0"
            newVersion="1.1.0.0" />
      </dependentAssembly>
    </assemblyBinding>
  </runtime>
</configuration>
```

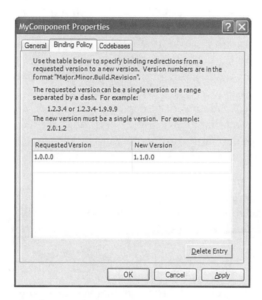

FIGURE 23.5   You can create a configured assembly and set its binding policy and
other settings with the help of the Microsoft
.NET Framework Configuration tool.

You can also create the application configuration file manually, although, in that
case, you need to know that you have to use the `<assemblyBinding>` element and
its subelements to redirect the version numbers.

Note that in the `<bindingRedirect>` element, the values for the attributes
`oldVersion` and `newVersion` need not be an old version and a new version,
respectively. In fact, you can redirect an application using a newer version of an
assembly to an older version also (provided, of course, that the changes are
nonbreaking).

As a result of the changes in the application configuration file, when you run the
`MyApplication.exe` application, it will now bind to version 1.1 of the
MyComponent assembly instead of version 1.0.

23

Binding Policy for Assemblies

Publisher Policy Resolution

The stage after application policy resolution is publisher policy resolution. The publisher of a shared assembly sets publisher policy to distribute service pack–like updates to customers. The publisher policy is specified in an XML file just as the application configuration file is. But unlike the application configuration file, the publisher policy is compiled into an assembly. In addition, the publisher policy contains information only about redirecting the common language runtime to a different version of the assembly.

Consider a scenario in which you might end up with multiple versions of an assembly in the GAC. In this scenario, you are the company that publishes the MyComponent component. You release version 1.0 of the component. Your customers develop applications, such as MyApplication, that use the component. The customers report that there is a bug in the component that needs to be fixed at high priority. You plan to release a service pack of the component. The new version of the component is version 1.1. You want to deploy the component on the customers' computers in such a way that all existing applications that refer to version 1.0 of the MyComponent component are redirected to version 1.1. You do not want customers' administrators to have to perform extra configuration steps.

The .NET Framework provides publisher policy for these very scenarios. To configure a publisher policy, use the publisher policy configuration file, which uses a format similar to that of the application configuration files. But unlike the application configuration file, a publisher policy file needs to be compiled into an assembly and placed in the GAC.

To create a publisher policy, follow these steps:

1. Create a publisher policy file. For example, you might create a new file named policy.1.0.MyComponent.config in the folder where the original MyComponent.dll assembly resides, and write the following code:

```
<configuration>
    <runtime>
        <assemblyBinding
          xmlns="urn:schemas-microsoft-com:asm.v1">
        <dependentAssembly>
          <assemblyIdentity
            name="MyComponent"
            publicKeyToken="ea1f27eeb5ba5d99" />
          <bindingRedirect oldVersion="1.0.0.0"
            newVersion="1.1.0.0"/>
        </dependentAssembly>
        </assemblyBinding>
    </runtime>
</configuration>
```

23

Of course, you'll need to change the `publicKeyToken` attribute to the appropriate public key for your assembly.

2. Use the Assembly Linker tool (`al.exe`) to convert the publisher policy file into a strongly named assembly. The name of the assembly should be of the format `policy.`*`majorNumber`*`.`*`minorNumber`*`.`*`AssemblyName`*`.dll`. Here, *`majorNumber`* and *`minorNumber`* are the major and minor version numbers of the existing assembly for which you want to redirect the binding requests. *`AssemblyName`* is the name of the assembly. For example, you can use the following command on the Visual Studio .NET 2003 command prompt:

```
al /link:policy.1.0.MyComponent.config
➥/out:policy.1.0.MyComponent.dll
➥/keyfile:VBNetBook.snk
```

3. Install the publisher policy assembly to the GAC just as you would install a strongly named assembly.

The publisher policy overrides the setting specified in the application configuration file. However, an application can ignore the publisher policy altogether if you set the `apply` attribute of the `<publisherPolicy>` element to `no` in the `<assemblyBinding>` element of the application configuration file:

```
<publisherPolicy apply="no"/>
```

Administrator Policy Resolution

This stage is the final stage for applying the binding rules. The binding rules at this stage are specified by the administrator in the machine-wide configuration file named `machine.config`. This file is stored in the Config subdirectory under the .NET Framework installation directory on a machine.

The settings specified in the machine configuration file override any settings specified in the application policy and the publisher policy.

To configure the machine-level binding policy for an assembly, open the .NET Framework Configuration tool and follow these steps:

1. Right-click the Configured Assemblies node in tree view, and select Add from its context menu.

2. In the Configure an Assembly dialog box, select the option button to choose an assembly from the assembly cache. Click the Choose Assembly button. Select the `MyComponent` assembly version 1.0.0.0, and click Select and then Finish.

23

Binding Policy for Assemblies

3. In the MyComponent Properties dialog box, select the Binding Policy tab. Enter **1.0.0.0** as the requested version and **1.1.0.0** as the new version.

4. Click OK to save the configured assembly information.

Now open the `machine.config` file and navigate to the `<assemblyBinding>` element. You will see the following binding information:

```
<configuration>
...
  <runtime>
    <assemblyBinding
        xmlns="urn:schemas-microsoft-com:asm.v1">
      ...
      <dependentAssembly>
        <assemblyIdentity name="MyComponent"
          publicKeyToken="ea1f27eeb5ba5d99 " />
        <bindingRedirect oldVersion="1.0.0.0"
            newVersion="1.1.0.0" />
      </dependentAssembly>
    </assemblyBinding>
  </runtime>
</configuration>
```

The changes in this example configure all the applications on a machine that uses the old version of `MyComponent` to use its new version.

How the Common Language Runtime Binds to an Assembly

The common language runtime uses the following steps to locate an assembly:

1. It determines the correct version of the assembly by examining the application configuration file, the publisher policy file, and the machine configuration file in the order mentioned in the preceding section.

2. It checks whether the assembly is already loaded. If the requested assembly has been loaded in one of the previous calls, it binds to the already loaded assembly and stops searching any further.

3. It checks the GAC. If the assembly is in the GAC, it loads the assembly from there, binds to it, and stops searching any further.

4. If a `<codebase>` element is specified in the configuration files, the common language runtime locates the assembly by using the paths specified in the `<codebase>` element. If the common language runtime finds the assembly,

23

the binding is successful; otherwise, the binding request fails and the common language runtime stops searching any further.

5. The common language runtime reads the configuration files to check whether any private path entries are in the `<probing>` element. If there are private path entries, the common language runtime uses these paths to search the assembly.

For example, with the following `<probing>` element:

```
<assemblyBinding xmlns="urn:schemas-microsoft-com:asm.v1">
      <probing privatePath="path1;path2"/>
</assemblyBinding>
```

the common language runtime uses the following locations in the given order to find the assembly:

- ▶ *AppBase*

- ▶ *AppBase\AssemblyName*

- ▶ *AppBase\path1*

- ▶ *AppBase\path1\AssemblyName*

- ▶ *AppBase\path2*

- ▶ *AppBase\path2\AssemblyName*

Note that the assembly name does not contain the extension; therefore, the common language runtime first attempts to find the assembly in a DLL file. If that fails, it searches these locations again for an EXE file. Here, *AppBase* is the directory where the requesting application is installed.

If the referenced assembly has culture information, the following culture-specific directories are also searched for the requested assembly:

- ▶ *AppBase\Culture*

- ▶ *AppBase\Culture\AssemblyName*

- ▶ *AppBase\path1\Culture*

- ▶ *AppBase\path1\Culture\AssemblyName*

- ▶ *AppBase\path2\Culture*

- ▶ *AppBase\path2\Culture\AssemblyName*

Here, *Culture* is a culture code that corresponds to the assembly. If the assembly is found in any of these locations, the common language runtime binds to the assembly and does not search any further.

23

6. If the common language runtime cannot locate the assembly after following the preceding steps, assembly binding fails.

You can modify appropriate elements in the configuration files to gain finer control over how the common language runtime locates your assembly. You can use the previously mentioned steps to debug your programs, in case a wrong assembly is being used or an assembly cannot be located.

Summary

This chapter explains how the components are versioned in the .NET Framework. Assemblies are the smallest unit of versioning in the .NET Framework. Two types of assemblies exist, characterized by how they are deployed: private assemblies and shared assemblies. The common language runtime provide no direct support for the versioning of private assemblies. On the other hand, specific rules and techniques apply to shared assemblies.

Shared assemblies must be installed in the Global Assembly cache (GAC), a common storage area that protects shared assemblies from version and name collisions. Each assembly installed in GAC must be signed with a strong name that clearly identifies its version and identity. In this chapter, you learned how to add and remove components from the GAC. You also learned how the common language runtime fulfills the request for assemblies that are installed in GAC.

Further Reading

Burton, Kevin. *.NET Common Language Runtime Unleashed.* Pearson Education, 2002.

Box, Don, with Chris Sells. *Essential .NET, Volume I: The Common Language Runtime.* Pearson Education, 2002.

23

24 IO AND PERSISTENCE

IN BRIEF

This chapter explores the .NET Framework support for file-based input/output operations and object persistence. In doing so, it introduces an array of classes from the System.IO, System.Xml.Serialization, and System.Runtime.Serialization namespaces.

This chapter introduces the concept of streams and files, and then goes into the details of *serialization*, a technology that allows objects to be persisted on disk for later revival.

The chapter also discusses how to customize the process of serialization to extend the built-in functionality provided by the .NET Framework.

WHAT YOU NEED

SOFTWARE REQUIREMENTS	Windows 2000, XP, or 2003 .NET Framework SDK v1.1 Visual Studio .NET 2003 with Visual Basic .NET installed
HARDWARE REQUIREMENTS	PC desktop or laptop
SKILL REQUIREMENTS	Familiarity with Visual Basic .NET Familiarity with developing console applications

IO AND PERSISTENCE AT A GLANCE

File Input and Output

In Part III, "Database Programming," you learned how to store and manage data by using a relational database. The .NET Framework also provides classes for working directly with disk files. File-based input and output in the .NET Framework use the concepts of backing stores and streams. A backing store is the storage medium for the data. This can be a disk file, an area in memory, or a network connection. A stream, on the other hand, represents the flow of data from or to a backing store.

The classes for working with streams and backing stores are part of the System.IO namespace. In this section, you'll learn how to use some of the important classes from this namespace. The File class enables you to perform file-level operations such as copy, move, and delete. The FileStream class gives you a generic stream-oriented view of a disk file. If you are familiar with the storage format of a file, you can use the BinaryReader and BinaryWriter classes to manipulate a file that stores binary data, or the StreamReader and StreamWriter classes to manipulate a file that uses standard text data.

Using the File Class

The File class is used for manipulating disk files. The File class contains shared methods that enable you to create, open, move, copy, and delete files. For example, the following code creates a backup copy of a file:

```
Dim sourceFile As String = "MyFile.txt"
Dim targetFile As String = "MyFile.Bak"

If System.IO.File.Exists(targetFile) Then
    Console.WriteLine("Target file already exists")
Else
    System.IO.File.Copy(sourceFile, targetFile)
End If
```

The Exists() method of the File class verifies whether a file already exists. The Copy() method creates a backup copy of the file.

The System.IO namespace also provides the FileInfo class for working with files. You can do almost everything with the FileInfo class that you can do with the File class, but unlike the File class, the FileInfo class does not contain shared methods. Therefore, you need to create an instance of FileInfo class before using it.

24

> **TIP**
>
> The `File` class performs security checks whenever a shared method is called. This certainly involves additional overhead. However, in the case of the `FileInfo` class, these security checks are performed once when the object is created and are not repeated with each method call. If you will reuse an object several times in your program, it is advisable to use the `FileInfo` class instead of the `File` class.

As with the `File` and `FileInfo` classes, the .NET Framework provides `Directory` and `DirectoryInfo` classes that enable you to access directories. The `Directory` class provides static methods, and the `DirectoryInfo` class provides instance methods.

Using the `FileStream` Class

The `FileStream` class is useful when you are not aware of—or when you don't care about—the format of the data stored in file. That's because the `FileStream` class treats a file as a generic stream of bytes. The code in Listing 24.1 (`UsingFileStream.vb`) shows an alternate way of making a copy of a file by using the `FileStream` class.

LISTING 24.1
`FileStream` Accessing the File Data as a Stream of Bytes

```vb
Imports System.IO
Module UsingFileStream

    Sub Main()
        ' Open the file for reading as a stream
        Dim fsIn As FileStream = File.OpenRead("UsingFileStream.exe ")
        ' Open the file for writing as a stream
        Dim fsOut As FileStream = File.OpenWrite("UsingFileStream.exe.bak")
        ' Copy all data from in to out, byte-by-byte
        Dim byt As Byte
        Dim bytesRead As Long = 0
        While (bytesRead < fsIn.Length)
            byt = fsIn.ReadByte()
            fsOut.WriteByte(byt)
            bytesRead = bytesRead + 1
        End While
```

1

2

24

LISTING 24.1
Continued

```
' Clean up                                                    3
        fsOut.Flush()
        fsOut.Close()
        fsIn.Close()
    End Sub
End Module
```

The code creates two `FileStream` objects, one each for the input and output files, by using static methods of the `File` class. **1** It then reads bytes from the input file by using the `ReadByte()` method and writes those bytes to the output file by using the `WriteByte()` method. **2** The number of bytes to read in the source file can be determined by calling the `Length()` method.

When the code is done writing, it calls the `Flush()` method of the output stream. **3** This is necessary to be sure that all the data has actually been written to the disk. Then the code closes both the input and output streams.

Table 24.1 shows some of the methods and properties of the `FileStream` class that you should be familiar with.

TABLE 24.1

Important Members of the `FileStream` Class

Member	Type	Description
CanRead	Property	Indicates whether you can read from this `FileStream` object
CanSeek	Property	Indicates whether you can seek to a particular location in this `FileStream` object
CanWrite	Property	Indicates whether you can write to this `FileStream` object
Close()	Method	Closes the `FileStream` object and releases the associated resources
Flush()	Method	Writes any buffered data to the backing store
Length	Property	Specifies the length of the `FileStream` object, in bytes
Position	Property	Gets the position within the `FileStream` object
Read()	Method	Reads a sequence of bytes
ReadByte()	Method	Reads a single byte
Seek()	Method	Sets the `FileStream` object to a specified position
Write()	Method	Writes a sequence of bytes
WriteByte()	Method	Writes a single byte

24

> **TIP**
>
> Listing 24.1 uses as many read and write operations as the number of bytes. You can improve performance by reading and writing chunks of bytes. You can achieve this by using the `Read()` and `Write()` methods of the `FileStream` class.

Using the `StreamReader` and `StreamWriter` Classes

The `StreamReader` and `StreamWriter` classes are designed for input and output of text data in a particular encoding. Encoding specifies how characters are internally represented. The `StreamReader` and `StreamwriTer` classes support a number of encoding formats, including ASCII, Unicode, UTF-7, and UTF-8 (the default encoding format).

> **TIP**
>
> The .NET Framework internally stores all characters encoded in the Unicode format. Because of its larger size, the Unicode format might be inefficient when transferring data over a slow network. To optimize the speed, you can use one of the different encoding classes, such as `UTF8Encoding` or `ASCIIEncoding`, available as part of the `System.Text` namespace.

Listing 24.2 (`UsingStreamReaderWriter.vb`) shows how to write to and read from a text file by using the `StreamReader` and `StreamWriter` classes.

LISTING 24.2

Reading and Writing to a File By Using the `StreamReader` and `StreamWriter` Objects

```
Imports System.IO
Module UsingStreamReaderWriter
    Sub Main()
        ' Create a new file to work with
        Dim fsOut As FileStream = File.Create("TextFile.txt")
        ' Create a StreamWriter to handle writing
        Dim sw As StreamWriter = New StreamWriter(fsOut)
        ' And write some data to the output file
        sw.WriteLine("Sample Text Line 1")
        sw.WriteLine("Sample Text Line 2")
        sw.WriteLine("Sample Text Line 3")
        sw.WriteLine("Sample Text Line 4")
        ' Cleanup objects that are no longer needed
```

1

2

LISTING 24.2
Continued

```
        sw.Flush()
        sw.Close()
        fsOut.Close()

        ' Now open the file for reading
        Dim fsIn As FileStream = File.OpenRead("TextFile.txt")
        ' Create a StreamReader to handle reading                    3
        Dim sr As StreamReader = New StreamReader(fsIn)
        ' And read the data
        While (sr.Peek() > -1)
            Console.WriteLine(sr.ReadLine())                         4
        End While
        ' Cleanup objects that are no longer needed
        sr.Close()
        fsIn.Close()
    End Sub
End Module
```

You can think of the StreamWriter and StreamReader classes as forming an additional layer of functionality on top of the FileStream class. The FileStream object handles opening a particular disk file, and it serves as a parameter to the constructor of the StreamWriter or StreamReader objects. Listing 24.2 first opens a StreamWriter object **1** and calls its WriteLine() method **2** multiple times to write lines of text to the file. It then creates a StreamReader object **3** that uses the same text file. The code makes use of the Peek() method **4** of the StreamReader object to watch for the end of the file. This method returns the next byte in the file without actually reading it, or it returns -1 if there is no more data to be read. As long as there is data to read, the ReadLine() method of the StreamReader object can read it to place it in the list box.

In addition to the methods that you see in Listing 24.2, the StreamWriter object has a Write() method, which writes output without adding a newline character. The StreamReader class implements the Read() and ReadToEnd() methods, which offer additional functionality for reading data. The Read() method reads a specified number of characters. The ReadToEnd() method reads all the remaining characters to the end of the stream.

The StreamReader and StreamWriter **classes inherit from the** TextReader **and**

24

File Input and Output

NOTE

`TextWriter` classes, respectively. Two other classes that inherit from the `TextReader` and `TextWriter` classes are the `StringReader` and the `StringWriter` classes, respectively. The `StringReader` and `StringWriter` classes enable you to work with strings, just as the `StreamReader` and `StreamWriter` classes enable you to work with file streams.

Using the `BinaryReader` and `BinaryWriter` Classes

For files with known internal structures, the `BinaryReader` and `BinaryWriter` classes offer streaming functionality that's oriented toward particular data types. Listing 24.3 (`UsingBinaryReaderWriter.vb`) shows how to write to and read from a text file by using the `BinaryReader` and `BinaryWriter` classes.

LISTING 24.3

Reading and Writing to a File By Using the `BinaryReader` and the `BinaryWriter` Objects

```
Imports System.IO
Module BinaryReaderWriter

    Sub Main()
        ' Test data
        Dim data1 As Integer = -47
        Dim data2 As Double = 101.6541
        Dim data3 As String = "Test String"

        ' Create a new file stream to work with
        Dim fsOut As FileStream
        fsOut = File.Create("test.dat")

        ' Create a BinaryWriter to handle writing
        Dim bw As BinaryWriter
        bw = New BinaryWriter(fsOut)

        ' Write the data to the stream
        bw.Write(data1)
        bw.Write(data2)
        bw.Write(data3)

        ' Clean up
        bw.Flush()
        bw.Close()
        fsOut.Close()
```

1

24

LISTING 24.3
Continued

```
        ' Now open the file for reading
        Dim fsIn As FileStream
        fsIn = File.OpenRead("test.dat")

        ' Create a BinaryReader to handle reading                2
        Dim br As BinaryReader
        br = New BinaryReader(fsIn)

        ' Read the data
        Console.WriteLine("Int32: {0}", br.ReadInt32())
        Console.WriteLine("Decimal: {0} ", br.ReadDouble())
        Console.WriteLine("String: {0}", br.ReadString())
        ' Clean up
        br.Close()
        fsIn.Close()
    End Sub
End Module
```

As with the `StreamWriter` and `StreamReader` classes, the `BinaryWriter` and `BinaryReader` classes provide a layer on top of the basic `FileStream` class. `BinaryWriter` and `BinaryReader` are oriented toward writing and reading particular types of data. The `BinaryWriter.Write()` **1** method has overloads for many data types, so it can handle writing almost anything to a file. The `BinaryReader` class **2** has methods for reading all those different data types; the code in Listing 24.3 shows the `ReadInt32()`, `ReadDouble()`, and `ReadString()` methods in action.

CAUTION
You must read exactly the same data types with the `BinaryReader` object that you originally wrote with the `BinaryWriter` object.

Serialization

When a .NET application is executing, the objects are created in memory. An object can refer to other objects, which might be stored at different memory addresses. A snapshot of the memory might look like a complex graph of objects referring to each other.

Serialization is the process of converting the state of an object into a sequence of bytes. Once serialized, it's easy to store the object's state on disk or send the bytes

24

Serialization

over the network to another program. Deserialization, by contrast, is a process of converting the sequence of bytes and re-creating the object in memory.

For example, ASP.NET uses serialization to save out-of-process session state. .NET Remoting also uses serialization to pass objects from one application domain to another.

> **NOTE**
>
> The process of serialization saves only the data for an object, not the code (such as methods). It is assumed that the code of the object is always available and will remain unchanged. Therefore, data is the only thing required to re-create the state of an object.

Traditionally, you would create your own routines for object serialization and deserialization. With the .NET Framework's built-in support, however, you can serialize and deserialize objects by writing only a few lines of code. In fact, the .NET Framework provides various ways to serialize an object. In this section, you will learn about two different ways, by using the classes in these namespaces:

- `System.Xml.Serialization`
- `System.Runtime.Serialization`

In many of the examples in this section, you will use a `Customer` object to demostrate the process of serialization and deserialization. Listing 24.4 shows the code for the `Customer` class (`Customer.vb`).

LISTING 24.4
The `Customer` Class

```vb
Public Class Customer
    Private _id As Integer
    Private _name As String
    Private _creditLimit As Double

    Public Sub New()
        _id = -1
        _name = ""
        _creditLimit = 0.0
    End Sub
    Public Sub New(ByVal Id As Integer, ByVal Name As String)
        _id = Id
        _name = Name
        _creditLimit = 0.0
    End Sub
```

24

LISTING 24.4
Continued

```
    Public Property Id() As Integer
        Get
            Return _id
        End Get
        Set(ByVal Value As Integer)
            _id = Value
        End Set
    End Property

    Public Property Name() As String
        Get
            Return _name
        End Get
        Set(ByVal Value As String)
            _name = Value
        End Set
    End Property

    Public Property CreditLimit() As Double
        Get
            Return _creditLimit
        End Get
        Set(ByVal Value As Double)
            _creditLimit = Value
        End Set
    End Property
End Class
```

XML Serialization

XML serialization is the process of converting the public fields and property values of an object into an XML stream. XML serialization is performed by using the XmlSerializer class of the System.Xml.Serialization namespace. The two key methods of this class are the Serialize() and Deserialize() methods, which perform all the hard work of serialization and deserialization, respectively.

24

> **NOTE**
>
> To serialize public as well as private fields and properties of an object, use the BinaryFormatter class. You will learn about this class later in this chapter.

Serialization

Listing 24.5 (XmlSerialization.vb) shows how to serialize and deserialize a Customer object by using the XMLSerializer class.

LISTING 24.5

Using XMLSerializer to Serialize and Deserialize a Customer Object

```vb
Imports System.IO
Imports System.Xml
Imports System.Xml.Serialization
Module XMLSerialization
    Sub Main()
        ' Create a Customer object
        Dim cus As Customer
        cus = New Customer(10, "John Doe")
        cus.CreditLimit = 1000.0
        ' Create an XmlSerializer for the Customer type
        Dim ser As XmlSerializer
        ser = New XmlSerializer(cus.GetType())
        ' Open a file to serialize to
        Dim fs As FileStream
        fs = File.Create("Customer.xml")

        ' Create a stream for writing XML data
        Dim xtw As XmlTextWriter
        xtw = New XmlTextWriter(fs, System.Text.Encoding.UTF8)
        xtw.Formatting = Formatting.Indented

        ' Serialize the object
        ser.Serialize(xtw, cus)
        ' Clean up
        cus = Nothing
        xtw.Close()
        fs.Close()

        ' Deserialize the Customer object
        fs = File.OpenRead("Customer.xml")
        cus = ser.Deserialize(fs)
        ' Clean up
        fs.Close()
        ' Print the Customer contents
        Console.WriteLine("ID          : {0}", cus.Id)
        Console.WriteLine("Name        : {0}", cus.Name)
        Console.WriteLine("Credit Limit: {0}", cus.CreditLimit)
    End Sub
End Module
```

1
2
3
4
5
24

In Listing 24.5, after a `Customer` object is created, the next order of business is to create an `XmlSerializer` object that is capable of serializing or deserializing the `Customer` object. **1** Next, you need an `XMLTextWriter` object to write the serialized XML to a disk file in a formatted manner. **2** You invoke the `Serialize()` method of the `XmlSerializer` object to serialize an object. **3** Similarly, when you deserialize the `Customer` object, you invoke the `Deserialize()` method of the `XmlSerializer` object. **4** Finally, when the object's state is restored, you can access its properties as usual. **5**

The contents of the persisted `Customer` object in Customer.xml looks as shown here:

```
<?xml version="1.0" encoding="utf-8"?>
<Customer xmlns:xsd="http://www.w3.org/2001/XMLSchema"
          xmlns:xsi="http://www.w3.org/2001/XMLSchema-instance">
  <Id xsi:type="xsd:int">10</Id>
  <Name xsi:type="xsd:string">John Doe</Name>
  <CreditLimit xsi:type="xsd:double">1000</CreditLimit>
</Customer>
```

As you can see, only public properties of the objects were persisted as part of the XML data.

TIP

When the objects are serialized to be stored on disk or to be transmitted over the network, they escape the security framework of your application. It is highly recommended that you encrypt the data before you serialize it.

Customizing XML Serialization

The `System.Xml.Serialization` namespace contains a number of attribute classes that you can use to customize the format of the XML generated in the process of serialization. For example, you might want one property to be serialized as an XML attribute and another property to be serialized as an XML element. To achieve this, all you need to do is mark type members with specific attributes. The following code exposes the `Id` property of the `Customer` class as an attribute using the `XmlAttribute` attribute.

```
<System.Xml.Serialization. _
  XmlAttribute(AttributeName:="CustomerId")> _
Public Property Id() As Integer
    Get
        Return _id
    End Get
```

24

Serialization

```
    Set(ByVal Value As Integer)
        _id = Value
    End Set
End Property
```

Here you customize the serialization for the `Id` property by using the `XmlAttribute` attribute. The output XML file generated by Listing 24.5 changes to this:

```
<?xml version="1.0" encoding="utf-8"?>
<Customer xmlns:xsd="http://www.w3.org/2001/XMLSchema"
          xmlns:xsi="http://www.w3.org/2001/XMLSchema-instance"
          CustomerId="10">
  <Name>John Doe</Name>
  <CreditLimit>1000</CreditLimit>
</Customer>
```

Here the `Id` property is persisted as `CustomerId` and is stored as an XML attribute rather than an XML element.

Refer to the documentation of the `System.Xml.Serialization` namespace to learn about other attributes that you can use for customizing XML serialization.

Evaluating XML Serialization

This section discusses various techniques for serialization. You should use XML serialization after considering the benefits and contraints listed in Table 24.2.

TABLE 24.2

Evaluating XML Serialization

Benefits	Constraints
XML output is human readable.	Only public properties and fields are persisted.
Customization to serialization can be performed without changing any serialization code.	Read-only properties are not persisted.
No special configuration is required for the objects that are serialized.	The class to be serialized must have a default public constructor.

24

DataSet SERIALIZATION

The ADO.NET `DataSet` object provides built-in methods for serialization and deserialization of its contents into an XML file.

You can save the contents of a `DataSet` object to an XML file by calling its `WriteXml()` method. To deserialize the `DataSet` object from an XML file, you invoke the `ReadXml()` method. Both these methods also provide the support for reading and writing the XML Schema.

Runtime Serialization

This technique for serialization uses formatter types, which do the actual hard work of serialization and deserialization. Two formatter types are included in the .NET Framework:

▶ The `BinaryFormatter` (part of the `System.Runtime.Serialization.Formatters.Binary` namespace) type serializes the objects in binary format.

▶ The `SoapFormatter` (part of the `System.Runtime.Serialization.Formatters.Soap` namespace) type serializes the objects in XML format.

TIP

The classes of the `System.Runtime.Serialization.Formatters.Soap` namespace are included in a separate library: `System.Runtime.Serialization.Formatters.Soap.dll`. To have the classes in this library available to your programs, you need to add a reference to this library in your projects (one way to do this is to select Project, Add Reference).

A formatter type implements the `System.Runtime.Serialization.IFormatter` interface. Although the `BinaryFormatter` and the `SoapFormatter` should meet most of your serialization requirements, it is possible to create custom formatters by implementing `IFormatter`. Listing 24.6 (`SoapSerialization.vb`) shows how to use a `SoapFormatter` class.

LISTING 24.6
Serialization by Using a `SoapFormatter` Class

```
Imports System.IO
Imports System.Runtime.Serialization.Formatters.Soap
Imports System.Runtime.Serialization.Formatters.Binary
Module SimpleSerialization
    Sub Main()
        Dim numList As New ArrayList
        Dim i As Integer
        For i = 1 To 10
            numList.Add(i)
        Next

        ' Open a stream                                                    1
        Dim stream As FileStream = File.Create("numList.xml")

        ' Create a SoapFormatter                                          2
        Dim soapFmt As New SoapFormatter
        soapFmt.Serialize(stream, numList)
```

24

Serialization

LISTING 24.6
Continued

```
          ' Clean up
          stream.Close()
          numList = Nothing
```
```
          ' Open a stream
          stream = File.Open("numList.xml", FileMode.Open)
```
```
          ' Deserialize the ArrayList
          numList = soapFmt.Deserialize(stream)
          ' Clean up
          stream.Close()
```
```
          ' Print the ArrayList contents
          For i = 1 To numList.Count
              Console.WriteLine(numList(i - 1))
          Next
      End Sub
  End Module
```

In Listing 24.6, first you create a `FileStream` object to a disk file. ▮**1** Next, you create a `SoapFormatter` object and invoke its `Serialize()` method to serialize the contents of an `ArrayList` object to the disk file. ▮**2** To deserialize the object, you follow the reverse path: First open the data file in read mode, ▮**3** and then invoke the `Deserialize()` method on the `SoapFormatter` object to deserialize the `ArrayList` object. ▮**4** After this is deserialized, you can access the `ArrayList` object in the usual way. ▮**5**

The `SoapFormatter` object serialize the objects in XML-based SOAP format. The contents of the `numList.xml` file created in Listing 24.6 resemble the following:

```
<SOAP-ENV:Envelope xmlns:xsi="http://www.w3.org/2001/XMLSchema-instance"
                   xmlns:xsd="http://www.w3.org/2001/XMLSchema"
                   xmlns:SOAP-ENC="http://schemas.xmlsoap.org/soap/
➥encoding/"
                   xmlns:SOAP-ENV="http://schemas.xmlsoap.org/soap/
➥envelope/"

xmlns:clr="http://schemas.microsoft.com/soap/encoding/clr/1.0"
SOAP-ENV:encodingStyle="http://schemas.xmlsoap.org/soap/encoding/">
<SOAP-ENV:Body>
<a1:ArrayList id="ref-1"
        xmlns:a1="http://schemas.microsoft.com/clr/ns/System.Collections">
<_items href="#ref-2"/>
<_size>10</_size>
<_version>10</_version>
```

```
</a1:ArrayList>
<SOAP-ENC:Array id="ref-2" SOAP-ENC:arrayType="xsd:anyType[16]">
<item xsi:type="xsd:int">1</item>
<item xsi:type="xsd:int">2</item>
<item xsi:type="xsd:int">3</item>
<item xsi:type="xsd:int">4</item>
<item xsi:type="xsd:int">5</item>
<item xsi:type="xsd:int">6</item>
<item xsi:type="xsd:int">7</item>
<item xsi:type="xsd:int">8</item>
<item xsi:type="xsd:int">9</item>
<item xsi:type="xsd:int">10</item>
</SOAP-ENC:Array>
</SOAP-ENV:Body>
</SOAP-ENV:Envelope>
```

NOTE

The `Serialize()` and `Deserialize()` methods of a formatter type use reflection to find information about an object and its members. You will learn more about reflection in Chapter 28, "Reflection to Extend the Framework."

Listing 24.6 can be modified for binary serialization by replacing the code in ▄**2** with the following:

```
' Create a BinaryFormatter
Dim binFmt As New BinaryFormatter
binFmt.Serialize(stream, numList)
```

And the code in ▄**4** with the following:

```
' Deserialize the ArrayList
numList = binFmt.Deserialize(stream)
```

The output of binary serialization is a compact binary format that is only machine readable.

CAUTION

You should use the same formatter type to serialize and deserialize an object. For example, if you serialize an object with `BinaryFormatter` and then try to deserialize the object with `SoapFormatter`, the `SoapFormatter` won't be capable of understanding the underlying format of bytes. A `System.Runtime.Serialization.SerializationException` will be thrown in such situations.

24

Serialization

Serialization Attributes

Runtime serialization worked very well with the `ArrayList` objects in Listing 24.6. However, if you modify this listing to serialize a `Customer` object, it fails. The common language runtime assumes that a type is not serializable unless it is specifically marked as serializable. To mark a type as serializable, you use the `Serializable` attribute.

In some cases, you might not want to serialize a field in a class. In these cases, you can mark the specific field with the `NonSerialized` attribute.

Listing 24.7 (`Customer.vb`) shows a modified version of the `Customer` class that is serializable but does not serializes its `CreditLimit` field.

LISTING 24.7
The `Customer` Class with Serialization Attributes

```
<Serializable()> _
Public Class Customer
    Private _id As Integer
    Private _name As String

    <NonSerialized()> _
1   Public CreditLimit As Double

    Public Sub New(ByVal Id As Integer, ByVal Name As String)
        _id = Id
        _name = Name
        CreditLimit = 0.0
    End Sub

2   Public ReadOnly Property Id() As Integer
        Get
            Return _id
        End Get
    End Property

3   Public ReadOnly Property Name() As String
        Get
            Return _name
        End Get
    End Property
End Class
```

Listing 24.7 removes the default constructor and changes the properties Id **2** and Name **3** to ReadOnly properties. It also changes CreditLimit **1** to a public field rather than a property, to access the _creditLimit private field. Note that runtime serialization by using formatter type does not require a type to have a default constructor and serializes private as well as public fields. Listing 24.8 (TypeSerialization.vb) serializes a Customer object.

LISTING 24.8
Serializing a Customer Object

```vb
Imports System.IO
Imports System.Runtime.Serialization.Formatters.Soap
Imports System.Runtime.Serialization.Formatters.Binary
Module TypeSerialization
    Sub Main()
        ' Open a stream
        Dim stream As FileStream = File.Create("customer.xml")
        Dim cus As Customer
        cus = New Customer(10, "John Doe")
        cus.CreditLimit = 1000.0
        ' Create a SoapFormatter                                          1
        Dim soapFmt As New SoapFormatter
        soapFmt.Serialize(stream, cus)
        ' Clean up
        cus = Nothing
        stream.Close()
        ' Open a stream                                                   2
        stream = File.Open("customer.xml", FileMode.Open)
        cus = soapFmt.Deserialize(stream)
        ' Clean up
        stream.Close()

        ' Print the Customer contents
        Console.WriteLine("ID          : {0}", cus.Id)
        Console.WriteLine("Name        : {0}", cus.Name)
        Console.WriteLine("Credit Limit: {0}", cus.CreditLimit)
    End Sub
End Module
```

The first part of this program serializes the Customer object, **1** and the later part deserializes the Customer object. **2** Looking at the data file that this program creates, you will note that the CreditLimit field is not serialized:

```
<SOAP-ENV:Envelope xmlns:xsi="http://www.w3.org/2001/XMLSchema-instance"
    xmlns:xsd="http://www.w3.org/2001/XMLSchema"
    xmlns:SOAP-ENC="http://schemas.xmlsoap.org/soap/encoding/"
    xmlns:SOAP-ENV="http://schemas.xmlsoap.org/soap/envelope/"
```

24

Serialization

```
    xmlns:clr="http://schemas.microsoft.com/soap/encoding/clr/1.0" S
    OAP-ENV:encodingStyle="http://schemas.xmlsoap.org/soap/encoding/">
<SOAP-ENV:Body>
<a1:Customer id="ref-1"
    xmlns:a1="http://schemas.microsoft.com/clr/nsassem/TypeSerialization/
    TypeSerialization%2C%20Version%3D1.0.1708.15197%2C%20Culture%3Dneutral
    %2C%20PublicKeyToken%3Dnull">
<_id>10</_id>
<_name id="ref-3">John Doe</_name>
</a1:Customer>
</SOAP-ENV:Body>
</SOAP-ENV:Envelope>
```

CAUTION

When you deserialize an object, although the object state is re-created in the memory, its constructor is not invoked. This constraint is placed on deserialization for performance reasons. You must consider the implication of this constraint when marking a type as serializable.

Evaluating SOAP and Binary Serialization

Although serialization by using the `SoapFormatter` class produces an XML-formatted file, internally it uses a completely different mechanism when compared to the `XmlSerializer` class.

You should use SOAP serialization only after considering the benefits and contraints listed in Table 24.3.

TABLE 24.3

Evaluating SOAP Serialization

Benefits	Constraints
XML output is human readable.	The types to be serialized either must implement the `ISerializable` interface or must be marked with the `Serializable` attribute.
Greater flexibility of object sharing and usage exists. The output can be processed by any program that understands SOAP.	This cannot work with arbitrary XML schema.
Deep serialization is provided. That is, all public as well as private member variables of an object are serialized.	

Table 24.4 lists the benefits and constraints of binary serialization.

TABLE 24.4

Evaluating Binary Serialization

Benefits	Constraints
This is the fastest serialization method.	The types to be serialized either must implement the ISerializable interface or must be marked with the Serializable attribute.
The size of the resulting binary data is very compact when compared to the XML or SOAP format.	Output is not human readable.
Deep serialization is provided. That is, all public as well as private member variables of an object are serialized.	Less interoperability is offered between different systems and platforms.

Custom Serialization

You can gain some degree of control over the default serialization process by letting the type that you want to serialize implement the ISerializable interface.

To implement ISerializable interface, a type must do the following:

▶ Implement the GetObjectData() method on your object. This method takes a SerializationInfo object and a StreamingContext object as its parameters.

▶ Add a constructor that takes a SerializationInfo object and a StreamingContext object as its parameters.

When you invoke the Serialize() method on the formatter type, the GetObjectData() method is called to handle the serialization of an object. Similarly, when you invoke the Deserialize() method on the formatter type, the new constructor is called to handle the deserialization of an object. You can write custom code in these two methods to impact the serialization or deserialization of an object. The code in Listing 24.9 (Customer.vb) shows how to implement the ISerializable interface.

LISTING 24.9
Custom Serialization

```
Imports System.Runtime.Serialization
<Serializable()> _
Public Class Customer
    Implements ISerializable
    Private _id As Integer
    Private _name As String
    Public CreditLimit As Double
```

24

Serialization

LISTING 24.9
Continued

```
Public Sub New(ByVal Id As Integer, ByVal Name As String)
    _id = Id
    _name = Name
    CreditLimit = 0.0
End Sub
```

1
```
Public Sub New(ByVal info As SerializationInfo, _
               ByVal context As StreamingContext)
    _id = info.GetInt32("_id")
    _name = info.GetString("_name")
    CreditLimit = info.GetDouble("CreditLimit")
End Sub
```

2
```
Public Sub GetObjectData(ByVal info As SerializationInfo, _
               ByVal context As StreamingContext) _
               Implements ISerializable.GetObjectData
    info.AddValue("_id", _id)
    info.AddValue("_name", _name)
    info.AddValue("CreditLimit", CreditLimit)
End Sub
```

```
Public ReadOnly Property Id() As Integer
    Get
        Return _id
    End Get
End Property

Public ReadOnly Property Name() As String
    Get
        Return _name
    End Get
End Property
End Class
```

The SerializationInfo object acts as a property bag that holds all the data needed to serialize and deserialize an object. In the GetObjectData() method, you can add each data item that needs to be serialized in this property bag as a name/value pair **2**. When you need to re-create the object, you need to extract the same name/value pair from the property bag in the constructor that receives SerializationInfo as a parameter **1**.

You are free to serialize any combination of fields, but you must make sure that the deserialization process will have enough data to re-create the state of an object.

24

Summary

The .NET Framework includes classes for manipulating disk files as part of the `System.IO` namespace. These classes treat data as streams that are supplied by backing stores, such as disk files.

This chapter also covered serialization, the process of converting object state in a sequence of bytes that can be persisted on a disk file or passed to another process.

You learned about three ways to serialize an object: XML serialization, SOAP serialization, and binary serialization. You also learned how to customize the process of serialization to extend the default functionality offered by the .NET Framework.

Further Reading

"Runtime Serialization, Part 1": www.msdn.com/msdnmag/issues/02/04/net.

"Runtime Serialization, Part 2": www.msdn.com/msdnmag/issues/02/07/net.

"Runtime Serialization, Part 3": www.msdn.com/msdnmag/issues/02/09/net.

25 INTEROPERABILITY WITH COM

IN BRIEF

This chapter discusses how you can make use of the .NET Framework interoperability features to integrate your code with the legacy code. You will learn how to invoke a component developed by using Visual Basic 6.0 in your Visual Basic .NET applications, and vice versa.

WHAT YOU NEED

SOFTWARE REQUIREMENTS	Windows 2000, XP, or 2003 .NET Framework SDK v1.1 Visual Studio .NET 2003 with Visual Basic .NET installed
HARDWARE REQUIREMENTS	PC that meets .NET SDK minimum requirements
SKILL REQUIREMENTS	Ability to create an assembly and install it in the Global Assembly Cache Ability to develop and consume a COM component by using Visual Basic 6.0

INTEROPERABILITY WITH COM AT A GLANCE

Introduction to .NET Framework COM Interoperability

The .NET Framework changes the way the code is compiled and executed. The .NET Framework code is targeted for execution in a managed execution environment provided by the common language runtime. This execution environment automatically provides services such as memory management, security, and version control. Therefore, the code targeting the .NET Framework is also known as managed code.

On the other hand, the previous-generation code was written based on Win32 library or the Component Object Model (COM) specification, in which programmers are mostly responsible for many of the services that the common language runtime now provides. By contrast, this code is also known as the unmanaged code.

As of now, most of the code for the applications targeting the Windows platform is unmanaged. Moving forward, however, most programmers and organizations would like to invest in the .NET Framework to reap its benefits.

Managed code and unmanaged code target different execution environments and cannot directly interoperate with each other. Fortunately, the .NET Framework provides interoperability support that enables you to call COM components from the .NET Framework applications and also call .NET Framework components from the COM application. This two-way interoperability support provides an easy migration path for organizations that want to move forward to .NET while taking advantage of the existing investment on the unmanaged code.

How the .NET Framework Interoperates with COM

How would you make two people who speak different languages understand each other? Of course, wit the help of the language interpreters. The .NET Framework uses the same concept to achieve interoperability between managed and unmanaged code. The .NET Framework uses a special set of objects called wrapper objects, which work as shown in Figure 25.1.

The wrapper objects work as a *bridge* that accepts commands and messages from one component, modifies them, and passes them to another component. The Runtime Callable Wrapper (RCW) exposes a COM component to the .NET Framework as if it is a .NET Framework component. On the other hand, a COM Callable Wrapper (CCW) exposes a .NET Framework component to COM as if it is a COM component.

The .NET Framework gives you tools for generating the RCW and CCW. Visual Studio .NET takes a step further and even automates the process of generating these wrappers for you.

How the .NET Framework Interoperates with COM

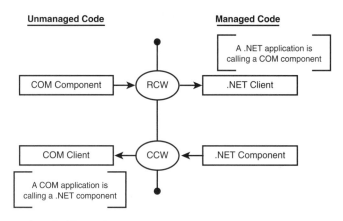

FIGURE 25.1   The wrapper objects enable interoperability between the managed and unmanaged code.

NOTE

The interoperability wrappers (RCW and CCW) work based on a specific set of predefined rules. However, you can use attributes to adjust the way these wrappers behave. For a list of attributes that you can use, refer to msdn.com/library/en-us/cpguide/html/cpconapplyinginteropattributes.asp.

CAUTION

Code that uses the interoperability will run slower because of an additional RCW or CCW layer.

Calling a COM Component from .NET Framework Applications

In this section, you see one facet of COM interoperability: how to call a COM component from a .NET Framework application. You'll learn how to do the following:

- Build and register a COM component
- Create a Runtime Callable Wrapper for the COM component
- Invoke the COM component from the .NET Framework

Creating and Registering a COM Component

To create a COM component, you can use an ActiveX DLL project in Visual Basic 6.0. If you type the code in Listing 25.1 and build the project, Visual Basic 6.0 creates a COM DLL. The name of the DLL file depends on the name of the project. For this example, it is assumed that the name of the output DLL file is `invCOM.dll`.

LISTING 25.1
Visual Basic 6.0 Code That Is Compiled into a COM DLL

```
Option Explicit
' Create a CalculateInventoryValue method
Public Function CalculateInventoryValue() As Currency
    CalculateInventoryValue = Int(Rnd() * 100000)
End Function
```

A COM DLL must be registered in the Windows Registry of a computer before it can be used. When you build a COM DLL by using Visual Basic 6, the COM DLL is automatically registered in the Windows Registry of that computer. If you want to register the COM DLL on a different machine, you can do so by using the `regsvr32.exe` command, shown here:

```
regsvr32 invCOM.dll
```

Creating a Runtime Callable Wrapper for a COM Component

The .NET Framework includes a command-line tool, the Type Library Importer tool (`tlbimp.exe`), that can create an RCW for a COM component. The Type Library Importer tool supports the command-line options listed in Table 25.1.

TABLE 25.1
Command-Line Options for the Type Library Importer Tool

Option	Meaning
`/asmversion:`*versionNumber*	Specifies the version number for the created assembly
`/delaysign`	Prepares the assembly for delay signing
`/help`	Displays help for command-line options
`/keycontainer:`*containerName*	Signs the assembly with the strong name from the specified key container
`/keyfile:`*filename*	Specifies a file containing public/private key pairs that is used to sign the resulting file

25

Calling a COM Component from .NET Framework Applications

TABLE 25.1

Continued

Option	Meaning
/namespace:*namespace*	Specifies the namespace for the created assembly
/out:*filename*	Specifies the name of the created assembly
/primary	Produces a primary interop assembly
/publickey:*filename*	Specifies the file containing a public key that is used to sign the resulting file
/reference:*filename*	Specifies a file to be used to resolve references from the file being imported
/silent	Suppresses information that would otherwise be displayed on the command line during conversion
/strictref	Refuses to create the assembly if one or more references cannot be resolved
/sysarray	Imports COM SAFEARRAY as instances of the System.Array type
/unsafe	Creates interfaces without the .NET Framework security checks
/verbose	Displays additional information on the command line during conversion
/?	Displays help about command-line options

A typical usage of the Type Library Importer tool is as follows:

```
tlbimp.exe invCOM.dll /out:RCWinvCOM.dll
```

The output of `tlbimp.exe` (RCWinvCOM.dll, in this case) is the Runtime Callable Wrapper that you can add to your Visual Studio .NET projects as a reference. After you do that, the classes in the COM component can be used just like any other .NET Framework classes. When you use a class from the COM component, .NET makes the call to the RCW, which, in turn, forwards the call to the original COM component and returns the results to your .NET managed code.

NOTE

The RCW is just a wrapper around the original COM component; it does not contain the functionality of the COM component. Instead, RCW just forwards the call to the original COM component for further execution. The COM component must still be registered and available to provide the functionality.

When you have an RCW, you can use it to invoke COM components in your Visual Basic .NET programs, as shown in Listing 25.2.

Calling a COM Component from .NET Framework Applications

LISTING 25.2

Using Visual Basic .NET Code to Invoke a COM Component Via an RCW

```
Private Sub btnGet_Click(ByVal sender As System.Object, _
        ByVal e As System.EventArgs) Handles btnGet.Click
    Dim inv As invCOM.InventoryClass
    inv = New invCOM.InventoryClass
    MessageBox.Show(inv.CalculateInventoryValue(), _
                    "Inventory Value")
End Sub
```

Note that, in this case, invCOM **1** is the name of the Visual Basic 6.0 DLL, and InventoryClass **1** is the name of the class in that DLL.

Creating a Runtime Callable Wrapper Automatically

You can use Visual Studio .NET to automatically generate the RCW for a COM DLL. All you need to do is follow these steps:

1. Right-click on the References node of a Visual Studio .NET project and select Add Reference from the shortcut menu.

2. In the Add Reference dialog box, select the COM tab and browse to the COM DLL, shown in Figure 25.2.

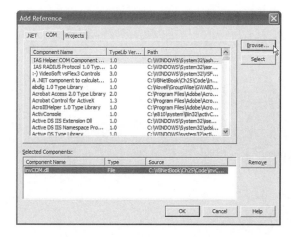

FIGURE 25.2   You can automatically generate an RCW for a COM component by adding a reference to the COM component.

As you take these steps, Visual Studio .NET automatically generates the RCW for the selected COM component. For example, if the COM component is invCOM.dll, the RCW is automatically generated in the interop.invCOM.dll file.

25

USING TLBIMP.EXE WITH SHARED COM COMPONENTS

If a component is shared by multiple clients, you need to sign the component with a strong name by using the `/keyfile` switch of the `tlbimp.exe` command.

Strong name signing establishes a unique identity for an assembly, which helps the common language runtime locate the correct assembly. You can learn more about code signing in Chapter 23, "Versioning and the Global Assembly Cache."

You should not generate RCW for the COM library that you have not written (for example, components bought from a vendor). For these components, you should obtain a Primary Interop Assembly (PIA) from the component vendor. PIA is signed with the vendor's strong name and serves as the official type definition for COM interoperability.

Calling a .NET Framework Component from COM Applications

In this section, you'll see another facet of COM interoperability: how to call a .NET component from a COM application. You'll learn how to do the following:

▶ Create a COM-consumable class by using Visual Basic .NET

▶ Create a COM Callable Wrapper (CCW) for the .NET Framework component

▶ Invoke the .NET Framework component from COM

Creating a COM-Consumable Class by Using Visual Basic .NET

Listing 25.3 shows a Visual Basic .NET class that follows the .NET Framework guidelines for creating a COM-consumable class.

LISTING 25.3

Creating a COM-Consumable Class That Follows the Guidelines

```
Option Explicit On
Option Strict On

Imports System.Runtime.InteropServices

<Guid("8739E231-849B-4a39-B6DE-9F40AA701476")> _
Public Interface IInventory
    Function CalculateInventoryValue() As Single
End Interface
```

Calling a .NET Framework Component from COM Applications

25

LISTING 25.3
Continued

```
                                                                          2
<ClassInterface(ClassInterfaceType.None), _
  Guid("DEE20588-0194-49f6-9A0B-07C1B2123400")> _
```

```
Public Class Inventory                                                    3
    Implements IInventory
    Public Function CalculateInventoryValue() As Single _
        Implements IInventory.CalculateInventoryValue

        Randomize()
        CalculateInventoryValue = Int(Rnd() * 100000)
    End Function
End Class
```

The code in Listing 25.3 follows these guidelines:

▶ A class and all of its members that should be visible to COM must be marked as public. **3**

▶ Assign a globally unique identifier (GUID) to the class. **2** When a .NET component is exposed to COM, it is identified by a GUID in the Windows Registry. When you explicitly assign a GUID to a class, the same GUID is used in the Windows Registry.

▶ You should define a public interface **1** and have the class implement that interface. **3** An interface separates the view of a class from its implementation. By using an interface, you avoid breaking any of the COM clients that use the component, as long as you keep your interface consistent in future versions. You should also assign a GUID to the public interface.

▶ Apply the `ClassInterface` attribute on the public class, and set its value to `ClassInterfaceType.None`. **2** This setting prevents any automatic interface generation in the COM type library and ensures that the interfaces that you explicitly defined are the only available ones.

▶ Sign the assembly with a strong name. This enables you to deploy an assembly to the Global Assembly Cache (GAC). Installing a component to the GAC ensures that the assembly can be located regardless of the location of the COM application.

Additionally, you should use the following assembly-level attributes:

```
<Assembly: AssemblyDescription("A .NET component to calculate inventory value")>
<Assembly: AssemblyVersion("1.0")>
<assembly: AssemblyKeyFile("VBNetBook.snk")>
```

25

The `AssemblyDescription` attribute assigns a description to the assembly, the `AssemblyVersion` attribute specifies a version number, and the `AssemblyKeyFile` atribute specifies the strong name key file.

When you build the project, Visual Studio .NET creates a strongly named assembly. To install an assembly to the GAC, you use the Global Assembly Cache tool (`gacutil.exe`), as follows:

```
gacutil.exe -i InvNET.dll
```

For more details about the strongly named assemblies and Global Assembly Cache tool, refer to Chapter 23.

Creating a COM Callable Wrapper (CCW)

The Assembly Registration tool (`regasm.exe`) is a command-line tool that reads a .NET assembly and adds the necessary entries to the Windows Registry to create a COM Callable Wrapper (CCW). After this tool registers an assembly, any COM client can use classes from that assembly as though the classes were from a COM class. A typical use of `regasm.exe` is shown here:

```
regasm.exe InvNET.dll
```

Table 25.2 lists all the options that are available with the `regasm.exe` tool.

TABLE 25.2

Command-Line Options for the Assembly Registration Tool

Option	Meaning
`/Codebase`	Specifies the version number for the created assembly.
`/help`	Displays help for command-line options.
`/nologo`	Prevents the tool from displaying the logo.
`/regfile:filename`	Generates the specified `.reg` file for the assembly, which contains the needed Registry entries. This option does not actually change the Registry. This option cannot be combined with the `/u` or `/tlb` options.
`/silent`	Suppresses information that would otherwise be displayed on the command line during conversion.
`/tlb:filename`	Generates a type library file that contains the definitions of the types defined within the assembly.
`/unregister` or `/u`	Unregisters the specified class. If this option is not specified, the tool always attempts to register a class.
`/verbose`	Displays additional information on the command line during conversion.
`/?`	Displays help about command-line options.

Calling a .NET Framework Component from COM Applications

If you use Visual Studio .NET, you can automate the generation of CCW. All you need to do is select the project's properties and check the Register for COM Interop option, as shown in Figure 25.3.

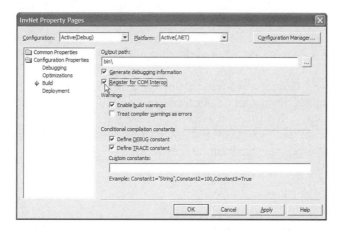

FIGURE 25.3   You can automatically generate a CCW for a .NET component by using the Register for COM Interop option.

If you check the Register for COM Interop option, Visual Studio .NET generates a CCW when the project is compiled. What Visual Studio .NET does automatically is the equivalent of using the /tlb option with the Assembly Linker tool. Using the /tlb option, a COM type library is generated in addition to CCW registration. As you will learn in the next section, this COM type library can be used for early binding with the COM client.

Invoking a .NET Component from a COM Application

You can invoke a .NET component from a COM application in the following ways:

▶ **Late binding**—With late binding, type resolution is delayed until the execution of the program. This is desirable when writing quick programs using a scripting language such as VBScript.

▶ **Early binding**—With early binding, the compiler resolves types at the time of compilation. Early binding improves the performance and reliability of applications.

Invoking a .NET Component from COM by Using Late Binding

A quick and easy way to invoke a COM object is to use an ActiveX scripting language such as VBScript. Listing 25.4 shows VBScript code to invoke the .NET component.

Calling a .NET Framework Component from COM Applications

LISTING 25.4
VBScript Code That Invokes a .NET Component Via Late Binding

```
Set obj = CreateObject("InvNet.Inventory")
MsgBox(obj.CalculateInventoryValue())
```

You can write the VBScript code in Listing 25.4 to a text file with a `.vbs` extension. To execute the code, you just need to double-click on the `.vbs` file.

Invoking a .NET Component from COM by Using Early Binding

To use early binding on the COM platform, you should use a compiled language such as Visual Basic 6.0 rather than VBScript. To expose the types in the .NET Framework assembly to Visual Basic 6.0, you need a COM type library, which can be generated by using the Assembly Registration tool, as shown:

```
regasm.exe InvNET.dll /tlb:InvNET.tlb
```

This command does two things. First, it exports the public types in the .NET assembly to a COM-compatible type library (`InvNET.tlb`, in this case). Second, it registers the .NET component and the type library in the Windows Registry. Registration of the .NET component in Windows Registry is needed to create a CCW. Registration of the type library in Windows Registry is needed so that programming tools such as Visual Basic 6.0 can display that type library in the References dialog box.

Alternatively, you can generate a type library by using the Register for COM Interop option in Visual Studio, shown in the previous section.

THE TYPE LIBRARY EXPORTER TOOL

Although the Assembly Registration tool (`regasm.exe`) enables you to generate a COM type library by using the `/tlb` option, as a side effect, it also registers the CCW for the assembly.

If you want to generate a type library but you don't want the CCW registration, you can use a different command-line tool, known as the Type Library Exporter tool (`tlbexp.exe`). A typical use of `tlbexp.exe` is shown here:

```
tlbexp InvNET.dll /out:InvNET.tlb
```

When you have the type library, you can create a Visual Basic 6.0 project and use the Project, References menu to add a reference to the type library in your project, as shown in Figure 25.4

With the references set, you can add the Visual Basic 6.0 code shown in Listing 25.5 to invoke a .NET component via early binding.

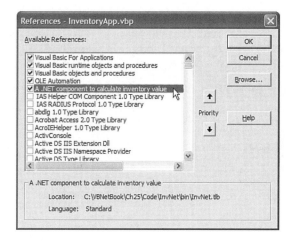

FIGURE 25.4   A type library enables you to take
advantage of early binding in COM applications.

LISTING 25.5
Visual Basic 6.0 Code That Invokes a .NET Object Via Early Binding

```
Private Sub cmdCalculate_Click()
    Dim inv As InvNet.Inventory
    Set inv = New InvNet.Inventory
    MsgBox (inv.CalculateInventoryValue())
End Sub
```

As you program in the Visual Basic 6.0 environment, you'll note that the methods
and properties of the component are available through IntelliSense, as with any other
COM component.

Summary

The .NET Framework includes a variety of tools that enable you to interoperate
managed code with unmanaged code. In this chapter, you learned the following:

> ▶ How to call a COM component from a .NET Framework application by using a
> Runtime Callable Wrapper (RCW)

> ▶ How to call a .NET Framework component from a COM application by using a
> COM Callable Wrapper (CCW)

Summary

25

An RCW or CCW is a proxy that sends data back and forth between the COM component and .NET components to make them look compatible with each other. You can create an RCW with the Type Library Importer tool (`tlbimp.exe`). You can create a CCW with the Assembly Registration tool (`regasm.exe`).

You also learned how to invoke a .NET component from COM by using early binding and late binding.

Further Reading

Nathan, Adam. *.NET and COM: The Complete Interoperability Guide*. Pearson Education, 2002.

26 EVENTS AND DELEGATES

IN BRIEF

In the previous chapters, you handled various events to create functional user interface. In this chapter, you will learn how to create and raise your own events.

Events in the .NET Framework are based on the concept of delegates. This chapter also introduces how to define, instantiate, and invoke a delegate object to add callback functionality in your programs. Finally, you will learn about multicast delegates.

WHAT YOU NEED

SOFTWARE REQUIREMENTS	Windows 2000, XP, 2003 .NET Framework SDK v1.1 Visual Studio .NET 2003 with Visual Basic .NET installed
HARDWARE REQUIREMENTS	PC that meets .NET SDK minimum requirements
SKILL REQUIREMENTS	Familiarity with Visual Basic .NET Familiarity with Windows Forms

EVENTS AND DELEGATES AT A GLANCE

Introduction to Events

An event occurs when something specific happens in a program. An event can be triggered by a user action, such as the click of a button, or can be a result of other activities in the environment, such as arrival of a new email.

Most modern applications, including those written in Visual Basic .NET, are event driven. An event-driven application constantly monitors for events and then responds by taking specific actions. In an event-driven application, you write sections of code that are executed only when a specific event occurs.

Three parts make up an event-driven Visual Basic .NET program design:

1. **Define the events**—Write code to define the specific events that a class is interested in raising.

2. **Raise the events**—Write code that raises an event when something specific happens.

3. **Handle the events**—Write code that takes specific actions when an event is raised.

In this chapter, you start working with events to develop an odometer application, shown in Figure 26.1. This application uses three instances of the `Digit` user control, each representing an odometer digit. When you click the Add Mile button, a mile is added to the rightmost digit. However, when the digit in the unit's position exceeds `9`, it generates an event that the Windows form handles to add a mile to the digit in the tens position and resets itself. The same rollover happens from the tens position to the hundreds position.

FIGURE 26.1   The `Odometer` form handles events raised by the individual digit user controls.

Defining and Raising the Events

Events are defined as class members by using the `Event` keyword. For example, consider a user control class, shown in Listing 26.1, that works as a single digit of odometer. The design of the user control itself consists of a single `TextBox` control (`txtDigit`).

Introduction to Events

LISTING 26.1
Defining and Raising Events

```
Public Class Digits
    Inherits System.Windows.Forms.UserControl
' Windows Form Designer generated code removed for brevity
    Private _value As Integer
```
1   `Public Event RollOver()`
```
    Public Sub Increment()
        If _value >= 9 Then
            _value = 0
```
2   `            RaiseEvent RollOver()`
```
        Else
            _value = _value + 1
        End If
        txtDigit.Text = CStr(_value)
    End Sub
End Class
```

In Listing 26.1, the Event keyword defines a RollOver event. **1** It is also possible to pass event-related data to an event in form of *event arguments*:

```
Public Event Changed(ByVal Value as Integer)
```

The Changed event, in this case, receives event-related data, Value.

NOTE

If you do not specify an access modifier with the Event keyword, the event is declared as Public by default.

NOTE

The event members of a class cannot have return values.

When something specific happens in your program, an event is raised by using the RaiseEvent statement. **2**

The RaiseEvent statement has syntax similar to that of a method invocation. If the event receives event-related data, you can pass that as shown:

```
RaiseEvent Changed(value)
```

The `RaiseEvent` statement notifies event handlers that a particular event has occurred.

Handling the Events

Event handlers are methods that are executed when an event is raised. The event handlers can be associated with an event in two ways: declaratively and dynamically.

Declarative Event Handling

With declarative event handling, a type can declare what event it handles and what methods will be invoked when an event is raised. Declarative event handling leads to code that is easy to read, understand, and debug.

Declarative event handling is done with the help of the `WithEvents` modifier and the `Handles` clause. In the odometer example, the code for the Windows Form that handles the events is shown in Listing 26.2.

LISTING 26.2
Declarative Event Handling

```
Public Class Form1
    Inherits System.Windows.Forms.Form

    'Windows Form Designer generated code removed for brevity
    Friend WithEvents Tens As Digits.Digits                            1
    Friend WithEvents Units As Digits.Digits
    Friend WithEvents Hundreds As Digits.Digits

    Private Sub Units_RollOver() Handles Units.RollOver                 2
        Tens.Increment()
    End Sub

    Private Sub Tens_RollOver() Handles Tens.RollOver                   3
        Hundreds.Increment()
    End Sub
    Private Sub btnAddMile_Click(ByVal sender As System.Object, _
            ByVal e As System.EventArgs) Handles btnAddMile.Click
        Units.Increment()
    End Sub
End Class
```

The `WithEvents` modifier **1** is applied to fields that can raise events. The `Handles` clause **2** specifies the method that needs to be invoked when a specific event is raised for a specific object. For example, in Listing 26.2, the `Units_RollOver` method **3** handles the `RollOver` event when the event is raised for the `Units` object.

Introduction to Events

TIP

You can use the `Handles` clause to allow a single event handler to handle one or more kind of events:

```
Private Sub Tens_RollOver() Handles Tens.RollOver, Tens.Changed
    Hundreds.Increment()
End Sub
```

Although declarative event handling is easy to use, it has several limitations:

- You cannot add or remove event handlers associated with an event at runtime.

- You cannot invoke multiple event handlers when an event is raised on an object.

- You cannot handle shared events because the shared events are not tied to an instance variable.

- The objects that raise events cannot be local variables in a procedure.

- You cannot create arrays of variables with the `WithEvents` modifier.

You can overcome these shortcomings by using dynamic event-handling techniques.

Dynamic Event Handling

Dynamic event handling enables you to add or remove event handlers with an event raised by an object programmatically at runtime. Dynamic event handling is made possible with the `AddHandler` and the `RemoveHandler` statements.

The `AddHandler` statement takes two arguments:

- The name of the object and the specific event that needs to be handled.

- The address of the method that handles the event. You use the `AddressOf` statement to retrieve the address of the event handler.

The following example associates an event handler with an event raised by an object:

```
AddHandler Object1.Event1, AddressOf Me.EventHandler1
```

To handle events using `AddHandler`, you follow these steps:

1. Declare an object variable of the class that raises the events you want to handle. For example:

```
Dim Object1 As New Class1()
```

2. Use the `AddHandler` statement to specify the name of the object and the specific event that you want to handle, as well as the `AddressOf` statement to provide the address of the event handler. For example:

```
AddHandler Object1.Event1, AddressOf Me.EventHandler1
```

3. Write code to handle the event, as in the following example:

```
Public Sub EventHandler1()
    MessageBox.Show("Event Handled")
End Sub
```

The `RemoveHandler` statement uses the same syntax as `AddHandler`, but it disconnects an event from an event handler:

```
RemoveHandler Object1.Event1, AddressOf Me.EventHandler1
```

CAUTION
You can use either declarative event handling or dynamic event handling, but you should not to use both techniques with the same event.

Introduction to Delegates

A delegate is a reference type whose object is capable of storing references of methods of a particular signature (parameters and return type).

If a delegate stores a reference to a method, you can use the delegate to indirectly invoke the referenced method. Why would you need to use an indirect reference to a method when you can call a method directly by its name? It's true that you can directly write the code to invoke a method, but what if you cannot determine which method to invoke until runtime? Delegates come in handy for such dynamic invocations.

The concept of delegates is new to Visual Basic, but this concept has been around for quite some time in programming languages such as C and C++ in the form of function pointers.

Delegates are used extensively in the .NET Framework to implement features such as event handling and asynchronous invocation.

Three steps are involved in defining and using a delegate in a Visual Basic .NET program:

1. Define the delegate.

2. Instantiate the delegate.

3. Call the delegate.

Introduction to Delegates

You now develop a Windows application that works with delegates, shown in Figure 26.2. This application writes a message to the selected destination: a message box or the application event log.

FIGURE 26.2   The `DelegateTest` form invokes a method dynamically by using delegates.

You can write the following methods to write messages to the message box and the application event log, respectively:

```
Public Sub SendToMessageBox(ByVal Message As String)
    MessageBox.Show(Message, Me.Text)
End Sub

Public Sub SendToEventLog(ByVal Message As String)
    Dim ApplicationLog As New EventLog
    ApplicationLog.Source = Me.Text
    ApplicationLog.WriteEntry(Message)
End Sub
```

> **NOTE**
>
> To use the `EventLog` class in your program, you might need to import the `System.Diagnostics` namespace.

To display the message, you might want to invoke either the `SendToMessageBox` or the `SendToEventLog` methods, but you want to delay this decision until runtime. Notably, both methods have the same signature; they accept a string parameter and have no return value.

Defining a Delegate

Delegates are declared by using the `Delegate` keyword. For example:

```
Delegate Sub MessageDelegate(ByVal Message As String)
```

This code declares a delegate type `MessageDelegate`, whose objects are capable of storing references to the methods that accept a string parameter and have no return value. An object of this `MessageDelegate` is capable of storing references to the `SendToMessageBox` and the `SendToEventLog` methods.

Instantiating a Delegate

A delegate is a reference type just like a class. Before you can use a delegate, you need to create a delegate object and assign a value to it.

To create an object of the `MessageDelegate` type, you use the following statement:

```
Dim SendMessage As MessageDelegate
```

When the user checks the radio buttons, you assign an appropriate method reference to the delegate type, as shown in the following code:

```
Private Sub rbMessageBox_CheckedChanged(ByVal sender As Object, _
        ByVal e As System.EventArgs) Handles rbMessageBox.CheckedChanged
    If (rbMessageBox.Checked) Then
        SendMessage = New MessageDelegate(AddressOf SendToMessageBox)      1
    End If
End Sub
```

Here, you create a new instance of the `MessageDelegate` type by passing it the reference to the `SendToMessageBox` method **1**. The `SendMessage` delegate object is now storing a reference to the `SendToMessageBox` method.

Similarly, if the user checks the Application Event Log check box, you can store the reference of `SendToEventLog` to the `SendMessage` delegate object **1**.

```
Private Sub rbEventLog_CheckedChanged1(ByVal sender As Object, _
        ByVal e As System.EventArgs) Handles rbEventLog.CheckedChanged
    If (rbEventLog.Checked) Then
        SendMessage = New MessageDelegate(AddressOf SendToEventLog)        1
    End If
End Sub
```

Invoking Delegates

Delegates can be invoked by using the name of the delegate object followed by the list of parameters that are accepted by the method that it references. For example:

```
Private Sub btnSend_Click(ByVal sender As Object, _
        ByVal e As System.EventArgs) Handles btnSend.Click
```

Introduction to Delegates

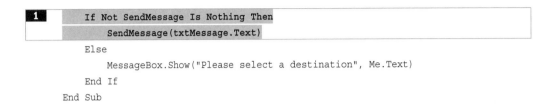

```
        If Not SendMessage Is Nothing Then
            SendMessage(txtMessage.Text)
        Else
            MessageBox.Show("Please select a destination", Me.Text)
        End If
    End Sub
```

When you invoke the `SendMessage` delegate object, 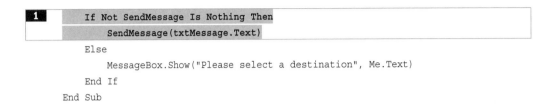 it invokes the method that it currently holds a reference to. It is recommended that you check that the object holds a valid reference before you invoke the delegate, as in this case.

The interesting thing to note here is that if you decide to add one more destination for the message, the code to invoke the delegate remains the same.

Multicast Delegates

A multicast delegate is just a regular delegate object, but it stores references to multiple methods. As a result, when you invoke a multicast delegate, you can cause multiple methods to be invoked concurrently.

Multicast delegates are made possible because internally the delegate stores the method references as a linked list. When you add a reference, it gets added to the end of the link list. When a delegate is invoked, it calls all the methods that are part of the internal linked list.

The application in Figure 26.3 is a variation of the earlier example, in which check boxes have replaced the radio buttons. In this example, users can select multiple destinations for sending the message.

FIGURE 26.3 The MulticastDelegateTest form invokes a multiple method dynamically by using multicast delegates.

With multicast delegates, the only piece of code that you need to change in this application is that for instantiating the delegates. The definition and the invocation of the delegate remain the same. Look at the following listing to see how multicast delegates are invoked:

```
Private Sub chkMessageBox_CheckedChanged(ByVal sender As Object, _
        ByVal e As System.EventArgs) Handles chkMessageBox.CheckedChanged
    Dim messageBoxDelegate = New MessageDelegate(AddressOf SendToMessageBox)
    If (chkMessageBox.Checked) Then
        SendMessage = SendMessage.Combine(SendMessage, messageBoxDelegate)    1
    Else
        SendMessage = MessageDelegate.Remove(SendMessage, messageBoxDelegate)  2
    End If
End Sub
```

In this code, rather than using a destructive assignment, the Combine method **1** of the Delegate class is used to add a new method reference to an already existing list of references that a delegate object might already have.

In this example, you are calling the Combine instance method that is available for a delegate object. The Delegate class also provides a shared version of Combine method, which can be used as follows:

```
SendMessage = [Delegate].Combine(SendMessage, messageBoxDelegate)
```

Delegate is also a keyword, so the Delegate class must be referred to using brackets to avoid any naming clash.

If you need to remove a method reference from the delegate's chain of method, you need to use the Remove method of the delegate object **2**. You can also invoke the shared version of the Remove method, as shown here:

```
SendMessage = [Delegate].Remove(SendMessage, messageBoxDelegate)
```

You write the code to instantiate the delegate object for the SendToEventLog method on the same lines:

```
Private Sub chkEventLog_CheckedChanged(ByVal sender As Object, _
        ByVal e As System.EventArgs) Handles chkEventLog.CheckedChanged
    Dim eventLogDelegate = New MessageDelegate(AddressOf SendToEventLog)
    If (chkEventLog.Checked) Then
        SendMessage = SendMessage.Combine(SendMessage, eventLogDelegate)
    Else
        SendMessage = MessageDelegate.Remove(SendMessage, eventLogDelegate)
    End If
End Sub
```

Events and Delegates

To make the event handling as simple as possible, Visual Basic .NET hides many of the implementation details from you. However, if you look closely, the .NET Framework implements events with the help of multicast delegates. For example, when you write the following

```
AddHandler Object1.Event1, AddressOf EventHandler1
```

it's actually a shorter way to say this:

```
AddHandler Object1.Event1, New EventHandler (AddressOf EventHandler1)
```

`EventHandler` is a predefined delegate class in the .NET Framework, defined as follows:

```
Public Delegate Sub EventHandler (ByVal sender as Object, ByVal e as EventArgs)
```

According to this declaration, this event handler is capable of storing references to methods that have nothing to return but receive two arguments:

> ▸ The first argument, of type `Object`, is the object that raised the event.

> ▸ The second argument, of type `EventArgs`, contains event-related data. The .NET Framework design guidelines recommend that any class that holds the event data derive from the base class `EventArgs`.

If you look at the default event handlers that Visual Studio .NET generates for the controls, you will see that Visual Studio .NET follows the guidelines for event handling.

Summary

Event handling plays a key role in user interface–based programming; through event handling, you respond to various events that are raised from user actions and that make programs interactive. This chapter discussed how you can define your own events and different ways to handle them.

A delegate is a reference type whose object is capable of storing references of methods of a particular signature. You can use a delegate to invoke the referenced methods. Delegates are used extensively in the .NET Framework to implement features such as event handling and asynchronous invocation.

Further Reading

26

Vick, Paul. *The Visual Basic .NET Programming Language*. Addison-Wesley, 2004.

27 MULTITHREADING

IN BRIEF

In this chapter, you will learn about the Microsoft .NET Framework support for working with multithreaded applications and asynchronous programming.

The first part of the chapter covers multithreaded applications, in which you divide the processor time among multiple pieces of simultaneously executing code, also known as threads. Even if you don't plan to create your own threads, it is important to understand multithreading because other developers might invoke the code that you write in a multithreaded environment.

The second part of the chapter covers how to develop responsive client applications by using multithreading and asynchronous programming techniques. Asynchronous programming refers to the programming technique that avoids blocking the main thread of an application while the application is processing a time-consuming task.

WHAT YOU NEED

SOFTWARE REQUIREMENTS	Windows 2000, XP, or 2003 .NET Framework SDK v1.1 Visual Studio .NET 2003 with Visual Basic .NET installed
HARDWARE RECOMMENDATIONS	PC that meets .NET SDK minimum requirements
SKILL REQUIREMENTS	Familiarity with Visual Basic .NET Familiarity with Windows Forms and console applications

MULTITHREADING AT A GLANCE

Introduction to Threading

Microsoft Windows is a preemptive multitasking operating system. In general terms, this means that Windows can execute multiple applications simultaneously.

In more technical terms, each application executes as a set of one or more processes. When Windows creates a process, it assigns a virtual address space and various system resources (such as handles to system objects and environment variables) to the process.

Each process is started with a single thread (known as a primary thread), but it can create additional threads. All threads in a process share its virtual address space and assigned system resources. A thread is an operating system construct that the common language runtime uses to execute code. A thread is also the smallest entity that can be scheduled for execution.

27

Windows can simultaneously execute as many threads as the number of processors on a machine. But even on a single-processor machine, Windows can allocate a processor time slice to each thread that it executes. The allocated time slice is so small that multiple threads appear to execute at the same time.

> **NOTE**
>
> The .NET Framework provides another level of isolation for managed code in the form of application domains. An application domain is considered a lightweight managed subprocess. A process may contain one or more application domains, but a thread is not confined to a single application domain and can run in any number of application domains within the same process.

Advantages of Multithreaded Processing

The main advantage of multithreaded processing is better utilization of CPU resources. For example, by virtue of multithreading, the user interface of a Windows Forms application can remain active while the application waits to complete other time-consuming tasks in a separate thread in the background.

Similarly, a thread that needs a lot of processing time periodically might yield the processor to other waiting threads. It is also possible to prioritize threads. For example, a time-critical thread can be assigned high priority while noncritical tasks execute under low-priority threads.

Disadvantages of Multithreaded Processing

A multithreaded application performs well when a mix of threads want to use the processor and the threads want to wait for an input/output/network operation to complete before demanding the next CPU cycle. If all threads are processor intensive and only a single processor is available, the overall performance of the application might, in fact, be slower because of the overhead involved in thread switching.

Introduction to Threading

Multithreading applications must be carefully designed. A poorly designed multi-threaded application can introduce bugs that are difficult to resolve, including dead-locks, race conditions, and data corruption. You will learn more about developing safe multithreading applications later, in the section "Thread Synchronization."

Working with Threads

Previous versions for Visual Basic provided little support, if any, for developing multi-threaded applications. Visual Basic .NET, however, can use the elaborate support for multithreading provided by the .NET Framework.

The types for multithreaded programming in the .NET Framework are part of the `System.Threading` namespace. In this section, you will start using the simple classes for starting, stopping, managing, and terminating threads.

Creating and Starting Threads

Unless you create threads explicitly, each .NET application starts as a single-threaded application. Listing 27.1 (`StartingThreads.vb`) shows a console application that creates an additional thread that executes in parallel with the primary thread.

LISTING 27.1
Creating and Starting Threads

```vb
Imports System.Threading
Class StartingThreads
    Public Value As Integer = 0

    Public Shared Sub Main()
        Dim instance As StartingThreads
        instance = New StartingThreads
        Thread.CurrentThread.Name = "Primary Thread"      ' 1
        ' Create a secondary thread
        Dim SecThread As Thread                            ' 2
        SecThread = New Thread(AddressOf instance.SomeTask)
        SecThread.Name = "Secondary Thread"
        ' Start secondary thread
        SecThread.Start()                                  ' 3
        ' Do some processing in the primary thread
        instance.SomeTask()
    End Sub
    Public Sub SomeTask()
        For i As Integer = 1 To 5
            Console.WriteLine("Message {0} from {1}", i, Thread.CurrentThread.Name)
            Thread.Sleep(100)                              ' 4
```

LISTING 27.1
Continued

```
        Next
    End Sub
End Class
```

You work with two threads in Listing 27.1. The first thread is the primary thread of the application and can be accessed through the `CurrentThread` shared property of the `Thread` class. The `CurrentThread` property returns a reference to the currently executing thread and, at this point of the program, the primary thread is the only executing thread. You assign a custom name to the thread by modifying its `Name` property. With a distinct name, it is easy to differentiate this thread from other threads in the application. **1**

A thread can be created by instantiating a new object of the `Thread` class. When you do so, you must specify which piece of code you want to associate with the thread. **2** On a single-processor machine, when the `Start()` method is invoked on a thread, **3** that thread does not start executing until the current thread yields or is preempted by the operating system. The `Start()` method submits an asynchronous request to the system and then returns the control to the next statement in the primary thread.

The `Thread.Sleep()` method **4** causes the currently executing thread to block its execution for the specified number of milliseconds. When you invoke the `Sleep()` method on a thread, the processor loads another waiting thread for execution.

When you execute this program, both the primary thread and second threads will yield for each other, causing an output similar to the following:

```
Message 1 from Primary Thread
Message 1 from Secondary Thread
Message 2 from Primary Thread
Message 2 from Secondary Thread
Message 3 from Primary Thread
Message 3 from Secondary Thread
Message 4 from Primary Thread
Message 4 from Secondary Thread
Message 5 from Primary Thread
Message 5 from Secondary Thread
```

> **NOTE**
>
> If you call the `Start()` method more than once on the same thread, the common language runtime throws a `ThreadStateException`.

Thread Properties

You already learned about two properties of the Thread class in Listing 27.1: Name and CurrentThread.

You can use the Thread.Priority property to get or set a thread's priority. The allowed values for Priority are one of the following values of the ThreadPriority enumeration:

- ▶ Highest
- ▶ AboveNormal
- ▶ Normal
- ▶ BelowNormal
- ▶ Lowest

For example, you can increase the priority of the secondary thread in Listing 27.1 by writing this:

```
secThread.Priority = ThreadPriority.AboveNormal
```

> **NOTE**
>
> The value of the Priority property is just an indication for the operating system. Windows is not required to honor the specified priority of a thread.

Another interesting property of the Thread class is the IsBackGround property. A thread can execute as either a foreground thread or a background thread. A managed process is kept alive until there is at least one foreground thread. When all the foreground threads have finished executing, the common language runtime terminates any background threads that are still alive and shuts down the program. To set a thread as a background thread, you write this:

```
secThread.IsBackGround = true
```

The Thread.ThreadState property of a thread provides the current state of a thread. For example, you can determine whether a thread is Unstarted, Running, Stopped, or Aborted. You can use the values of the ThreadState enumeration to specify the ThreadState, as shown in the following example:

```
If (secThread.ThreadState = ThreadState.Unstarted) Then
    ' Thread is not yet started
Else
    ' Thread is started
End If
```

Thread Methods

You have already seen the `Thread.Sleep()` method in Listing 27.1. You can use this method to immediately pause the execution of the current thread for the specified number of milliseconds:

```
' Sleep for 100 milliseconds
Thread.Sleep(100)
```

You can also write this:

```
Thread.Sleep(Timeout.Infinite)
```

In this case, execution of the current thread is paused until it is interrupted by another thread as a result of the `Thread.Interrupt()` method or is aborted as a result of the `Thread.Abort()` method.

TIP

A thread cannot invoke the `Sleep()` method on another thread. If a thread wants to pause the execution of another thread, it should invoke the `Thread.Suspend()` method.

You can also pause the execution of a thread by calling the `Thread.Suspend()` method. This method blocks the execution of the thread until a `Thread.Resume()` method is invoked on the thread. Unlike the `Thread.Sleep()` method, the `Thread.Suspend()` method does not cause a thread to stop immediately. The `Thread.Suspend()` method merely sends a request to the common language runtime to suspend the thread's execution when it is safe to do so.

CAUTION

Because a call to `Thread.Suspend()` waits for the CLR to release the resources before pausing its execution, application deadlocks are possible. In this situation, multiple threads wait indefinitely for each other to release the needed resources. A better way to synchronize threads is to use the `Monitor.Wait()` method.

The `Thread.Interrupt()` method wakes a thread from the paused state and also throws a `ThreadInterruptedException` in the destination thread. The destination thread should catch this exception and execute the appropriate code to continue working.

If you need to permanently terminate a thread, you should use the `Thread.Abort()` method. After a thread is terminated, you cannot restart it by calling the `Start()` method. Doing so results in a `ThreadStateException`.

27

Thread Synchronization

In a multithreaded application, multiple threads simultaneously might request the same data or other computer resources. This leads to two common problems: race conditions and deadlocks.

Race Condition

Consider a banking application, in which thread 1 is updating an account. At the same time, thread 2 is trying to find the balance of the bank account. In the case of simultaneous access, thread 2 can never be sure that the account balance that it read was for before or after the updates. In case more than one value is being updated, thread 2 can perform a *dirty read*—that is, a read in which part of the data comes from before the update and part of the data comes from after the update. This situation is called a *race condition*.

One possible solution to the race condition is for a thread to acquire a lock on the object before it attempts to update the object. If an object is locked, no other thread can access it at the same time. When the update is completed, the thread releases the lock so that other threads can access the object. This solution might work well when just one object might be accessed, but when multiple objects are involved in the same transaction, this solution could lead to another problematic situation: deadlock.

Deadlocks

Consider another banking transaction in which money is being transferred from account A to account B. This transaction involves the following steps:

1. Subtract the transfer amount from account A.

2. Add the transfer amount to account B.

To avoid a race condition, a thread must acquire a lock on both the account objects before the transfer operation can be completed. Imagine that thread 1 obtains the lock on account A, but before it can lock account B, thread 2 locks account B. Now if both the threads are doing the transfer between the same accounts, they are waiting indefinitely for the other to release its lock. This situation is known as a *deadlock*.

Synchronization Strategies

An ideal solution is to write code that does not require data to be shared by multiple threads. Alternatively, you can use the following synchronization strategies that the .NET Framework offers to provide synchronous access to an object's data members:

- Synchronized contexts
- Synchronized code regions
- Manual synchronization

Synchronized Contexts

A synchronized context is a special environment in which multiple objects share the same lock. Within a synchronized context, multiple threads are allowed to access the instance methods and fields, but only one at a time.

To create a synchronized context, you need to mark the class with the Synchronization attribute. The class also must inherit from the ContextBoundObject base class.

> **NOTE**
>
> The .NET Framework provides two Synchronization attributes. One is part of the System.EnterpriseServices namespace. This attribute can be used only with serviced components. This chapter discusses the other Synchronization attribute, which is part of the System.Runtime.Remoting namespace and can be used only with context-bound objects.

Listing 27.2 (SynchronizationContexts.vb) shows how to create a synchronized context by using the Synchronization attribute **1**.

LISTING 27.2

Creating a Synchronized Context

```vb
Imports System.Threading
Imports System.Runtime.Remoting.Contexts                          1


<Synchronization()> _
Class SynchronizedContext
    Inherits ContextBoundObject
    Public Value As Integer = 0

    Public Sub AddValue()
        For i As Integer = 1 To 5
            Value = Value + 1
            Console.WriteLine("Thread {0} increment the value to {1}", _
                Thread.CurrentThread.Name, Value)
            Thread.Sleep(100)
        Next
    End Sub

    Public Shared Sub Main()
        Dim instance As SynchronizedContext
        instance = New SynchronizedContext
```

Thread Synchronization

LISTING 27.2
Continued

```
        Thread.CurrentThread.Name = "Primary Thread"
        ' Create a secondary thread
        Dim SecThread As Thread
        SecThread = New Thread(AddressOf instance.AddValue)
        SecThread.Name = "Secondary Thread"

        ' Start secondary thread
        SecThread.Start()

        ' Do some processing in the primary thread
        instance.AddValue()
    End Sub
End Class
```

In Listing 27.2, after you mark the class with the `Synchronization` attribute, the runtime automatically synchronizes access to all of its instance members. That is, after the primary thread acquires the lock on the instance object, the secondary thread that attempts to use the methods and fields of the `SynchronizedContext` class must wait for the lock to be released.

CAUTION

A synchronized context does not protect shared fields and methods from concurrent access by multiple threads.

Synchronized Code Regions

An alternative synchronization technique is to synchronize only selected portions of the code. Visual Basic .NET provides three ways to create synchronized code regions:

▸ Using the `MethodImplAttribute` class

▸ Using the `Monitor` class

▸ Using the `SyncLock` keyword

`MethodImplAttribute` (part of the `System.Runtime.CompilerServices` namespace) is useful when you want to synchronize the code in a shared method or an instance method. All you need to do is mark the method with the `MethodImplAttribute` attribute with its `MethodImplOptions.Synchronized` parameter:

```
<MethodImplAttribute(MethodImplOptions.Synchronized)> _
Public Sub TransferFunds(ByVal amount As Double)
    'Thread safe code executes here
End Sub
```

or

```
<MethodImplAttribute(MethodImplOptions.Synchronized)> _
Public Shared Sub TransferFunds(ByVal amount As Double)
    'Thread safe code executes here
End Sub
```

Using the `Monitor` class or using the `SyncLock` keyword is more complex then using the `MethodImplAttribute`, but these approaches provide you more flexibility by enabling you to lock specific regions of a code instead of the complete method.

The following code segment shows how to use the `Monitor` class to synchronize code regions:

```
Class MonitorSample
    Public Sub SomeTask()
        ' Acquire the lock on the current object
        Monitor.Enter(Me)
        ' Do some processing here
        ' Release the lock
        Monitor.Exit(Me)
    End Sub
End Class
```

The `Monitor.Enter()` method acquires the lock, and the `Monitor.Exit()` method releases the lock on the given object. To acquire locks within a shared member, you need to use the expression `GetType(ClassName)`, as shown in the following code segment:

```
Class MonitorSample
    Public Shared Sub SomeTask()
        ' Acquire the lock on the current object
        Monitor.Enter(GetType(MonitorSample))
        ' Do some processing here
        ' Release the lock
        Monitor.Exit(GetType(MonitorSample))
    End Sub
End Class
```

Thread Synchronization

The Visual Basic .NET keyword SyncLock internally uses the Monitor.Enter()
and Monitor.Exit() methods to acquire and release the locks. For example, for
instance methods, you write this:

```
Class MonitorSample
    Public Sub SomeTask()
        ' Acquire the lock on the current object
        SyncLock Me
        ' Do some processing here
        ' Release the lock
        End SyncLock
    End Sub
End Class
```

For shared methods, you write this:

```
Class MonitorSample
    Public Shared Sub SomeTask()
        ' Acquire the lock on the current object
        SyncLock GetType(MonitorSample)
        ' Do some processing here
        ' Release the lock
        End SyncLock
    End Sub
End Class
```

The SyncLock method is equivalent to calling the Monitor.Enter() method; the
End SyncLock statement is equivalent to calling the Monitor.Exit() method on
the same object.

Manual Synchronization

In addition to the synchronization features just discussed, the .NET Framework
provide other classes that you can use to create your own thread-synchronization
mechanism:

- ▶ **The Interlocked Class**—This class provides atomic operations for incrementing (the Increment() method), decrementing (the Decrement() method),
  and swapping (the Exchange() method) the values of variables shared among
  multiple threads. The fourth method, CompareExchange(), combines two
  operations: comparing two values and storing a third value in one of the variables, based on the outcome of the comparison.

- ▶ **The Mutex Class**—You can use a Mutex object to synchronize among threads
  and across processes. A thread requests ownership of a Mutex by calling the
  WaitOne(), WaitAll(), or WaitAny() methods and releases the ownership
  by the ReleaseMutex() method.

▶ **The** `ReaderWriterLock` **Class**—The `ReaderWriterLock` class allows either concurrent read access for multiple threads or write access for a single thread. If an object will be changed infrequently, a `ReaderWriterLock` provides better performance than other locking strategies, such as using the `Monitor` class.

Asynchronous Programming

By now, you are familiar with the `Thread` class and the various synchronization strategies. In a synchronous method call, the thread that executes the method call waits until the called method finishes execution.

Such types of synchronous calls can make the user interface unresponsive if the client program is waiting for a long process to finish execution. The .NET Framework has a solution for this in the form of asynchronous methods. An asynchronous method calls the method and returns immediately, leaving the invoked method to complete its execution.

The .NET Framework Asynchronous Programming Model

In the .NET Framework, asynchronous programming is implemented with the help of delegate types. Delegates are types that are capable of storing references to methods of a specific signature. A delegate declared as follows is capable of invoking methods that take a string parameter and return a string type.

```
Delegate Function LongProcessDelegate(ByVal param As String) as String
```

If there is a method definition such as this:

```
Function LongProcess(ByVal param as String) As String
...
End Function
```

The `LongProcessDelegate` can hold references to this method like this:

```
Dim delLongProcess As LongProcessDelegate
delLongProcess = New LongProcessDelegate(AddressOf LongProcess)
```

Once you have the delegate object available, you can call its `BeginInvoke()` method to call the `LongProcess()` method asynchronously, such as:

```
Dim ar As IAsyncResult
ar = delLongProcess.BeginInvoke("Test", Nothing, Nothing)
```

Asynchronous Programming

Here, the IAsyncResult interface is used to monitor an asynchronous call and relate the beginning and the end of an asynchronous method call. When you use BeginInvoke() method, the control immediately comes back to the next statement, while the LongProcess() method still might be executing.

Getting Results from Asynchronous Method Calls

To return the value of an asynchronous method call, you can call the EndInvoke() method on the same delegate:

```
Dim result As String
result = delLongProcess.EndInvoke(ar)
```

However, it is important to know where to place this method call because when you call EndInvoke(), if the LongProcess() method has not yet completed execution, EndInvoke() causes the current thread to wait for the completion of the LongProcess() method. Poorly using EndInvoke(), such as placing it in the next statement after BeginInvoke(), might cause an asynchronous method call to result into a synchronous method call.

One of the alternatives to this problem is to use the IsCompleted property of the IAsyncResult object to check whether the method has completed the execution and call the EndInvoke() method only in such case.

```
Dim result As String
If (ar.IsCompleted) Then
    result = delLongProcess.EndInvoke(ar)
End If
```

Regular polling of ar.IsCompleted property requires additional work at the client side; there is a better way to do this, in the form of the callback methods.

Asynchronous Callbacks

In this technique, you can register a method that is automatically invoked as soon as the remote method finishes execution. You can then place a call to EndInvoke() method inside the callback method to collect the result of method execution.

Listing 27.3 shows how to implement the callback technique with an asynchronous method invocation in a Windows Forms application.

LISTING 27.3
Implementing Asynchronous Callbacks

```
Imports System.Threading

Public Class Form1
    Inherits System.Windows.Forms.Form

#Region " Windows Form Designer generated code "
   ' Windows Form Generated Code, trimmed for brevity
#End Region

    Delegate Function LongProcessDelegate(ByVal param As String) As String
    Delegate Sub CallbackDelegate(ByVal ar As IAsyncResult)          1
    Function LongProcess(ByVal param As String) As String
        Thread.Sleep(5000)
        Return param
    End Function

    Sub EndNotification(ByVal ar As IAsyncResult)                    2
        MessageBox.Show("Long Process Completed")
    End Sub
    Private Sub Form1_Load(ByVal sender As System.Object, _
             ByVal e As System.EventArgs) Handles MyBase.Load
        Dim delLongProcess As LongProcessDelegate
        delLongProcess = New LongProcessDelegate(AddressOf LongProcess)
        delLongProcess.BeginInvoke("Test", AddressOf EndNotification, Nothing)   3
    End Sub
End Class
```

When the application in Listing 27.3 is executed, it executes the LongProcess()
method in a secondary thread. The primary thread still displays the fully responsive
user interface. When the call to LongProcess() is completed, a notification is sent
back to the primary thread.

The key to this asynchronous operation is the asynchronous callback delegate,
CallbackDelegate. **1** The method EndNotification() is based on the
signature of the CallbackDelegate. **2** The LongProcess() method is invoked
asynchronously by invoking BeginInvoke() on its delegate, but this time a reference to the callback method is passed as a parameter to the BeginInvoke()
method. **3**

As a result, when the LongProcess() method is completed, the runtime takes the
responsibility of invoking the EndNotification() method.

Summary

In this chapter, you learned how to develop multithreaded applications. You also learned about issues such as race condition and dead locks, which can be introduced when multiple threads share data and resources. The chapter also covered various synchronization strategies to eliminate common issues with multithreading.

Finally, the chapter discussed the technique of asynchronous method invocation with the help of delegates. Asynchronous method classes make a user interface–based application such as a Windows Forms application responsive to user input even when a separate thread is busy doing another task.

27

Further Reading

Vick, Paul. *The Visual Basic .NET Programming Language*. Addison-Wesley, 2004.

28 REFLECTION TO EXTEND THE FRAMEWORK

IN BRIEF

Earlier in this book, you learned that a .NET assembly stores metadata in addition to the Microsoft Intermediate Language (MSIL) code. Reflection is a process by which you can read an assembly's metadata to dynamically obtain type information at runtime.

In this chapter, you will learn how to view an assembly's metadata and obtain type information from an assembly. You also will learn how to invoke properties and methods on dynamically instantiated objects.

WHAT YOU NEED

SOFTWARE REQUIREMENTS	Windows 2000, XP, or 2003 .NET Framework SDK v1.1 Visual Studio .NET 2003 with Visual Basic .NET installed
HARDWARE REQUIREMENTS	PC that meets .NET SDK minimum requirements
SKILL REQUIREMENTS	Familiarity with Visual Basic .NET Familiarity with assemblies

REFLECTION TO EXTEND THE FRAMEWORK AT A GLANCE

Metadata

Metadata is the information that defines each program element to the common language runtime. Metadata includes information such as the following:

- ▶ Information about the assembly (name, version, culture, public key)
- ▶ Information about the types defined in the assembly (classes, interfaces, methods, properties, and so on)
- ▶ Information about attributes that are applied to types and its members
- ▶ References to other assemblies

When you compile a program, the metadata is stored in the executable file along with the Microsoft Intermediate Language (MSIL) code. At runtime, the CLR loads the metadata to find information about the classes stored in the assembly.

You can use the .NET Framework MSIL Disassembler tool (`ildasm.exe`) to view the metadata for an assembly. To see the metadata of an assembly, you must first create one that you will use throughout this chapter. Create a Visual Basic .NET Class Library project (`Employee`) and add code to the `Employee.cs` class file, as shown in Listing 28.1.

LISTING 28.1
Defining an `Employee` Class

```
Public Class Employee
    Private _id As Long
    Private _name As String
    Private _salary As Double

    Public Sub New(ByVal Id As Long, ByVal Name As String)
        _id = Id
        _name = Name
    End Sub

    Public Property Salary()
        Get
            Return _salary
        End Get
        Set(ByVal Value)
            _salary = Value
        End Set
    End Property
```

Metadata

LISTING 28.1
Continued

```
    Public Function RaiseSalary(ByVal percent As Single)
        _salary = _salary + (_salary * percent / 100)
        Return _salary
    End Function
End Class
```

Build the project to create an assembly (`Employee.dll`). Now open the Visual Studio .NET command prompt and type the following command:

```
ildasm.exe Employee.dll
```

The MSIL Disassembler tool displays the metadata, as shown in Figure 28.1.

FIGURE 28.1   The MSIL Disassembler
tool displays the metadata for an assembly.

Introduction to Reflection

Reflection in the .NET Framework is made possible by the classes in the `System.Reflection` namespace. These classes enable you to get information about loaded types, methods, and fields. They also provide the capability to dynamically create and invoke types at runtime.

In addition to these classes, you need to use the `System.Type` class. The `Type` class represents the declarations for class types, interface types, array types, value types, and the enumeration types.

> **NOTE**
>
> The .NET Framework also provides a `System.Reflection.Emit` namespace whose classes enable you to create an assembly in memory dynamically at runtime. This namespace is mostly of interest to the language tool developers and is not covered in this chapter.

Reflecting on an Assembly

The `System.Reflection.Assembly` class defines an assembly. It provides methods and properties that enable you to gather all information about an assembly. The code in Listing 28.2 is a console application that displays selected information for an assembly and then prints the names of all assemblies that it references.

LISTING 28.2

Reflecting on an Assembly

```
Imports System.Reflection
Module AssemblyReflection
    Sub Main()
        Dim asm As [Assembly]                                              1

asm = [Assembly].LoadFrom( _                                              2
            "c:\VbNetBook\Chapter28\Employee\bin\Employee.dll")
        Console.WriteLine("Assembly.FullName = {0}", asm.FullName)
        Console.WriteLine("Assembly.Location = {0}", asm.Location)

        Console.WriteLine(vbCrLf + "Referenced Assemblies: ")
        Dim asmArray() As AssemblyName
        asmArray = asm.GetReferencedAssemblies()
        For Each asmName As AssemblyName In asmArray
            Console.WriteLine(asmName.Name)
        Next
    End Sub
End Module
```

Note that `Assembly` is a Visual Basic .NET keyword, so if you want to refer to the `Assembly` class, you might want to qualify it with the namespace, such as here:

```
Dim asm As System.Reflection.Assembly
```

Otherwise, you'll need to enclose the class name in square brackets. **1**

The code invokes the `LoadFrom()` method **2** to get a reference to the `Employee` assembly. Interestingly, the `Assembly` class provides no constructor.

Reflecting on an Assembly

That's because you will never need to create an assembly from scratch. Instead, you can get an already created `Assembly` object in any of the following ways:

▶ From the currently running code:

```
asm = [Assembly].GetExecutingAssembly()
```

▶ From the given filename:

```
asm = [Assembly].LoadFrom( _
   "c:\VbNetBook\Chapter28\Employee\bin\Employee.dll")
```

▶ From the assembly's display name:

```
asm = [Assembly].Load("mscorlib")
```

▶ From the assembly's partial name:

```
asm = [Assembly].LoadWithPartialName("System.Data")
```

▶ From an assembly that contains the given type

```
asm = [Assembly].GetAssembly(GetType(Integer))
```

Reflecting on a Type

Reflection typically is used for dynamic type discovery. That is, you can load an assembly at runtime and then determine the different available types and find information about type members. The code in Listing 28.3 (`TypeReflection.vb`) shows how to reflect on a type by using a Visual Basic .NET console application project.

LISTING 28.3
Reflecting on a Type

```
Imports System.Reflection
Module TypeReflection
    Sub Main()

        Dim asm As [Assembly]
        asm = [Assembly].LoadFrom( _
          "c:\VbNetBook\Chapter28\Employee\bin\Employee.dll")
```

LISTING 28.3
Continued

```
        For Each typ As Type In asm.GetTypes()                              1
            Console.WriteLine("Type Name: {0}", typ.FullName)
            Console.WriteLine("Number of Constructors: {0}", _
                    typ.GetConstructors().Length)
            Console.WriteLine("Number of Methods: {0}", _
                    typ.GetMethods().Length)
            Console.WriteLine("Number of Properties: {0}", _
                    typ.GetProperties().Length)
            Console.WriteLine(vbCrLf + "Methods: ")
            For Each minfo As MethodInfo In typ.GetMethods()               2
                Console.WriteLine(minfo.Name)
            Next
            Console.WriteLine(vbCrLf + "Properties: ")
            For Each pinfo As PropertyInfo In typ.GetProperties()         3
                Console.WriteLine(pinfo.Name)
            Next
        Next
    End Sub
End Module
```

If you run the project, the output will be this:

```
Type Name: Employee.Employee
Number of Constructors: 1
Number of Methods: 7
Number of Properties: 1

Methods:
GetHashCode
Equals
ToString
get_Salary
set_Salary
RaiseSalary
GetType

Properties:
Salary
```

28

Reflecting on a Type

The interesting thing to note here is that you defined only one method (RaiseSalary) in the Employee class, but the output of the program shows there are seven, including the one that you defined. Four of these methods (GetHashCode, Equals, ToString, and GetType) are being inherited from the Object class; the other two methods (get_Salary and set_Salary) are created as the accessor methods for the Salary property.

Listing 28.3 uses the Assembly.GetTypes() method to retrieve all the types in the Employee assembly. **1** This method returns an array of System.Type objects. The System.Type class provides properties to retrieve type information.

Next, this listing uses the System.Type.GetMethods() method to iterate over each method of the given class. **2** The GetMethods() method returns an array of the System.Reflection.MethodInfo objects. You can use the MethodInfo object to retrieve information about each method such as the following:

- ▸ Name (MethodInfo.Name)

- ▸ Return type (MethodInfo.ReturnType)

- ▸ Attributes (MethodInfo.Attributes)

- ▸ Accessibility Modifiers (MethodInfo.IsPrivate, MethodInfo.IsPublic, MethodInfo.IsStatic, and so on)

You can even find information about each parameter of a method by calling the MethodInfo.GetParameters() method, as shown in the following code segment:

```
For Each parinfo As ParameterInfo In minfo.GetParameters()
    Console.WriteLine("Parameter Name: {0}", parinfo.Name)
    Console.WriteLine("Parameter Type: {0}", parinfo.ParameterType)
    Console.WriteLine("Parameter Position: {0}", parinfo.Position)
Next
```

When you run this code, you will note that reflection will even return the exact parameter names used in your source code.

The final part of the code in Listing 28.3 retrieves information about the properties of a given class. **3** The Type.GetProperties() method returns an array of the System.Reflection.PropertyInfo objects. You can use the PropertyInfo object to retrieve information about each property:

- ▸ Name (PropertyInfo.Name)

- ▸ Property type (PropertyInfo.PropertyType)

- ▸ Attributes (PropertyInfo.Attributes)

- ▸ Whether a property can be read (PropertyInfo.CanRead) or written to (PropertyInfo.CanWrite)

> **NOTE**
>
> You can retrieve a lot of information from the `System.Type` class in addition to what is covered in this section. For example, if you want to find more information about the constructors of a class, you can call the `Type.GetConstructors()` method. This method returns an array of the `ConstructorInfo` objects. You should refer to the documentation of the `System.Type` class to see a complete list of available properties and methods.

CONTROLLING HOW THE TYPE MEMBERS ARE SEARCHED

Reflection also enables you to access the private or protected members of a class. You can use the `BindingFlags` enumeration values to create a filter that defines which members to include in a search. For example, if you wanted to include all nonpublic members in addition to the public members, you would create a filter like this:

```
Dim filter as BindingFlags
filter =  BindingFlags.Instance Or BindingFlags.Public _
        Or BindingFlags.NonPublic
```

The `BindingFlags.Instance` is included in the filter because you must specify either `BindingFlags.Instance` or `BindingFlags.Static` for the search to work.

After you have created a filter, you can specify it to the methods that retrieve members from a type:

```
Console.WriteLine("Number of Methods: {0}", _
        typ.GetMethods(filter).Length)
Console.WriteLine("Number of Properties: {0}", _
        typ.GetProperties(filter).Length)
```

These statements now return the count of all public and nonpublic instance methods and properties, respectively, for the given class.

Late Binding

Binding is a process that assigns an object to an object variable. When binding is performed at the time of program compilation, it's called early binding. By contrast, when the binding is performed at runtime, it's called late binding. The main advantage of late binding is the flexibility of delaying the binding decision until the runtime.

> **TIP**
>
> When performance is critical, prefer early binding over late binding. Early binding enables the language compiler to allocate memory and make optimization decisions before an application executes.

Late Binding

Reflection not only enables you to discover type information at runtime, it also enables you to invoke a method at runtime, thereby making late binding possible.

Listing 28.4 (LateBinding.vb) shows a Visual Basic .NET Console Application project (LateBinding) that uses late binding to invoke properties and methods of the Employee class.

LISTING 28.4
Late Binding by Using Reflection

```
Imports System.Reflection
Module LateBinding
    Sub Main()
        Dim asm As [Assembly]
        asm = [Assembly].LoadFrom( _
          "c:\VbNetBook\Chapter28\Employee\bin\Employee.dll")
        Dim typEmployee As Type
        typEmployee = asm.GetType("Employee.Employee")
        Dim argsC As Object() = {20, "Joe"}
        Dim objEmployee As Object
        objEmployee = Activator.CreateInstance(typEmployee, argsC)

        Dim mInfo As MethodInfo
        mInfo = typEmployee.GetProperty("Salary").GetSetMethod()
        Dim argsP As Object() = {1000}
        mInfo.Invoke(objEmployee, argsP)

        mInfo = typEmployee.GetMethod("RaiseSalary")
        argsP(0) = 15
        Dim retVal As Object = mInfo.Invoke(objEmployee, argsP)
        Console.WriteLine("Modified Salary: {0}", retVal)
    End Sub
End Module
```

As you can see from Listing 28.4, when you have information for a type, you can instantiate the type by using the `Activator.CreateInstance()` method. **1** This method invokes the constructor of the type with the given set of arguments and returns the created object.

Next, the program sets the `Salary` property. **2** Setting a property is a two-step process:

1. Retrieve the `MethodInfo` object corresponding to the `Set` accessor of the property. This can be done by invoking the `GetSetMethod()` on the `PropertyInfo` object.

2. Invoke the `Set` method referenced by the `MethodInfo` object by using the `MethodInfo.Invoke()` method.

The Invoke() method uses the following two parameters:

▶ The object on which this method needs to be invoked.

▶ An array of objects to pass, as the parameters to the method to be invoked. If no parameters are required to be passed, you can pass Nothing. If the parameters are optional, you need to pass Type.Missing field.

Finally, the program invokes the RaiseSalary() method dynamically to increase the salary by 15% and displays the return value. **3** In this case, too, you use the MethodInfo.Invoke() method for dynamic method invocation.

All the work done in this example to invoke a property and a method might seem like overkill when you can create a much more concise and efficient program by using early binding. The technique presented in this example proves to be much powerful when you have no prior information about the types at the time of program compilation.

28

Summary

Reflection enables you to get information about types, methods, and fields, and also provides the capability to dynamically create and invoke types at runtime. Reflection is made possible by the classes in the System.Reflection namespace and the System.Type class. In this chapter, you learned how to inspect the assembly's metadata and how to dynamically obtain type information from an assembly. You also learned how to invoke properties or methods on dynamically instantiated objects.

Further Reading

Burton, Kevin. *.NET Common Language Runtime*. Pearson Education, 2003.

Part VI

Securing Applications

29 CODE ACCESS SECURITY (CAS)

IN BRIEF

This chapter on code access security (CAS) explains how .NET improves on Windows security. CAS limits what an assembly is permitted to do. This does not eliminate the need to restrict the actions that a user is allowed to perform; it complements it. You will learn here how to secure computer systems with CAS and how to take advantage of CAS in your own code.

The security subsystem in .NET calculates a permission set for each loaded assembly at load time, based on the evidence provided by the assembly, the policies, and any additional restrictions the assembly requested. The .NET Framework (and your own code) issues security permission demands at load time, link time, and execution time. If the demand is not satisfied by the granted permission set, an exception is thrown. Additionally, so-called stack-walk modifiers can influence the security demand processing.

The principle of this is that both operations and resources are protected through security policies. Using CAS, you can restrict what your code can do, restrict which code can call your code, vouch for low-privileged code, and identify code.

WHAT YOU NEED

SOFTWARE REQUIREMENTS	Windows 2000, XP, or 2003 .NET Framework 1.1 SDK Visual Studio .NET 2003 with Visual Basic .NET installed
HARDWARE REQUIREMENTS	PC desktop or laptop
SKILL REQUIREMENTS	Advanced knowledge of Visual Basic .NET Advanced knowledge of the .NET Framework

CODE ACCESS SECURITY (CAS) AT A GLANCE

Administrating Code Access Security (CAS)

This section explores the default CAS configuration and explains the terms and concepts. Finally, it shows how to improve security for client and server machines.

Exploring the Default Security with the .NET Framework Configuration Tool

You can find the Microsoft .NET Framework 1.1 Configuration menu choice in the Administrative Tools menu. This menu is located in the Control Panel (for all versions of Windows with .NET support), in the Windows XP or Windows Server 2003 Start menu.

29

TIP
The command-line utility `caspol` can be used to script all the operations possible with the Windows tool. System administrators mostly use this tool. However, it can produce a short and concise listing of all the administratively configured items in CAS with the command `caspol -all -listgroups`.

After `Microsoft .NET Framework 1.1 Configuration` is started, expand the entire tree under Runtime Security Policy (see Figure 29.1).

To understand CAS, you must understand the following terms first:

- **Permission**—A right to do something or use a resource.

- **Permission set**—A collection of permissions to simplify the handling of permissions.

- **Code group**—An association of a permission set with a membership condition.

- **Evidence**—An authentication of the assembly at runtime to satisfy membership conditions in code groups.

- **Policy**—A collection of code groups. The rules in a code group use a membership condition. An assembly must present evidence.

Policies define complete sets of permissions granted to all assemblies used by a specific entity (enterprise, machine, user, or application domain). The permissions granted are the intersection of all policies; therefore, the most restrictive policy determines the permissions. The Enterprise policy should be maintained by corporate IT through Active Directory and should be used to set a maximum setting allowed by anyone in the company. The Machine policy is maintained by the local system administrator or in a corporate setting by corporate IT through Active Directory; this restricts an individual PC's capability to run .NET code further. The User policy

Administrating Code Access Security (CAS)

is maintained by the individual user or in a corporate setting by corporate IT through Active Directory; this restricts an individual user's capability to run .NET code further. This feature is rarely used. Application domains define a fourth policy. ASP.NET supports this with a notation in the `machine.config` or `web.config` file. The default policy for application domains is FullTrust for all assemblies.

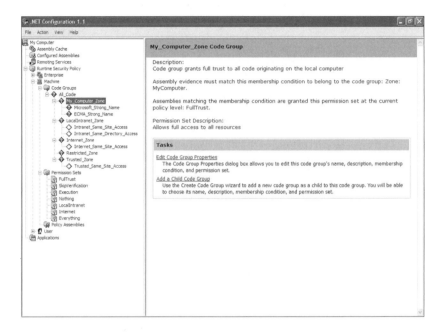

FIGURE 29.1   .NET Configuration Tool with Machine Policy expanded.

TIP

It is possible to define your own application domain policy. This requires you to write a hosting program that creates a new application domain (`AppDomain.CreateDomain`). You can set the application domain's security policy with AppDomain.SetAppDomainPolicy. However, this is considered esoteric and is mainly used by Microsoft.

Code groups define the permissions that a .NET assembly is granted by combining a member condition with a permission set. An assembly receives the union of the permission sets in all code groups for which it qualifies based on the evidence it presents to satisfy the membership condition. Nested child code groups can give additional permissions to an assembly if all of the conditions in the tree are true.

Membership condition and the runtime evidence are based on either location or content. Location-based evidence uses the assembly's origination information (where it is loaded from) as the reason to grant permission. Examples of location-based evidence are the directory on the local disk, anywhere on the local disk, any URL on the intranet, any URL on the Internet, and a specific URL. Content-based evidence uses the assembly's data as the reason to grant permissions. Examples of content-based evidence are the hash value of the assembly file; it is signed with a specific strong name or is signed with a publisher's certificate.

A permission set is a combination of any number of specific permissions. .NET predefines six and a half named permission sets. Unfortunately, two are named after the evidence that they are associated with, by default. `LocalIntranet` should really be called `PartialTrust`, and Internet should be called `MinimalTrust`. `SkipVerification` is not really a set, but a single permission (this explains the statement about half a set). Also, Everything is not everything in C# or Managed C++. It is everything in VB .NET, and this is where its name comes from. All possible permissions are `FullTrust`. `SkipVerification` is the difference between `Everything` and `FullTrust`. You need `SkipVerfification` for unsafe code. Unsafe code can be written only with C# or C++. Examples of unsafe code include accessing some native API calls (most APIs can be accessed with safe code) or resources such as external memory addresses outside the boundaries defined by the .NET Framework.

Spend some time looking at all permission sets in detail (they are the same in each policy). Next, look at each of the code groups, their evidence, and their permission sets.

29

TIP

Do not use the `.NET Wizards` menu `Adjust .NET Security` from `Administrative Tools`. The wizards hide the actual meaning of the permission sets granted behind the terms Low, Medium, and High. You need to guess which permission set each one of them maps to. Guessing is a bad strategy for security-related work.

Configure Your System for Maximum Security

The only truly secure computer is one without power, connections or data on its disks; unfortunately, this computer is not very useful. For the truly paranoid (sometimes called smart users or administrators), this section covers how to secure end-user systems (PC), as well as data center servers.

TIP

These are the rules for code access security settings: Make the settings very tight to start, and then relax them based on specific user complaints and actual needs. In other words, deny all permissions to all assemblies, and selectively enable them for specific assemblies or sets of assemblies.

Administrating Code Access Security (CAS)

TIP

Right-clicking on a policy shows a menu item to reset the policy to its default. This helps you correct serious mistakes.

Configuring an End-User System (PC)

For companies, the following changes should be applied at the Enterprise policy level and should be distributed through SMS or Active Directory. For individual computers (not managed by a corporate IT department), these should be applied to the Machine level locally. The following example uses the Machine-level policies.

First, deny all permissions to non-Microsoft assemblies.

1. Select `My_Computer_Zone`.

2. Click on Edit Code Group Properties.

3. In the `My_Computer_Zone` Property dialog box, select the Permission Set tab.

4. Select the permission set `Nothing` (see Figure 29.2).

5. Select the General tab and erase the comment. This comment no longer applies, and the default description generated is good enough.

6. Click OK.

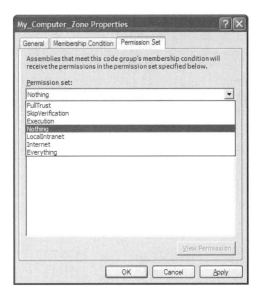

FIGURE 29.2   Setting CAS rights to Nothing.

Administrating Code Access Security (CAS)

You must never change the permission set for the child code groups
`Microsoft_Strong_Name` and `ECMA_Strong_Name` because they are required for
.NET to operate. Modifying or deleting either of them renders all of .NET, including
this configuration tool, inoperable.

Repeat the previous steps for `LocalIntranet_Zone`, `Internet_Zone`,
`Trusted_Zone`, and `Restricted_Zone`. Do not modify or delete any child code
groups.

Your computer is secure and can run only the .NET Framework runtime. To make it
useful, you need to grant permissions to other software. It is best to use a strong
name as the evidence. This example uses a strong name for all assemblies created by
Sams Publishing.

TIP

Your organization could use a single strong name for your entire corporation, a division, an individual
project, or even an individual component. However, the more strong names you use, the harder it is
to manage the security policies correctly. The sample that follows is one of many possible
approaches that works well.

29

Next, you add a new child code group with your entity's name to `All_Code`. You
may add this child code group below `My_Computer_Zone` instead, to trust only
your own code, if it is loaded from the local hard disk. This code group serves as a
container only and grants the permission set `Nothing`.

1. Select the code group `All_Code` and click on the task Add a Child Code Group.

2. In the Create Code Group Wizard, you name the code group after your organization (`Sams_Publishing`) and, optionally, provide a useful description (see
   Figure 29.3).

3. Click Next.

4. Select All Code for the membership condition type or evidence (see Figure 29.4).

5. Click Next.

6. Select Use Existing Permission Set and `Nothing` from the drop-down list (see
   Figure 29.5).

7. Click Next.

8. Click Finish.

Administrating Code Access Security (CAS)

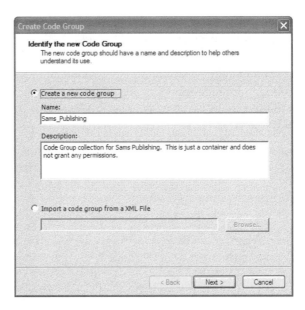

FIGURE 29.3 Adding the `Sams_Publishing` code group: name and description.

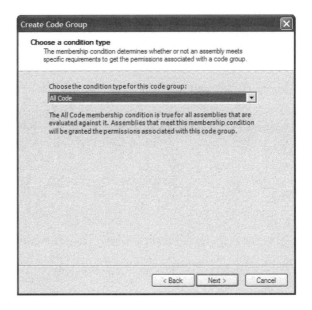

FIGURE 29.4 Adding the `Sams_Publishing` code group: membership condition.

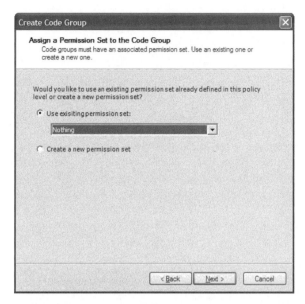

FIGURE 29.5 Adding the `Sams_Publishing` code group: permission set.

Next, add a child code group to the just-added child code group (`Sams_Publishing`) for each of your strong name/key pairs (one per organization or product).

1. Select the code group `Sams_Publishing`.

2. Click on the task Add a Child Code Group.

3. In the Create Code Group Wizard, name the code group after your organization and purpose (for example, `Sams_SmartClients`) and, optionally, provide a useful description (see Figure 29.6).

4. Click Next.

5. Select `Strong Name` for the membership condition type or evidence (see Figure 29.7).

6. Either type the public key of your strong name (it's very long) or click on Import and navigate to an assembly that is already signed.

7. Click Next.

Administrating Code Access Security (CAS)

8. Select Create a New Permission Set (see Figure 29.8).

9. Click Next.

10. Name the permission set with a useful name (such as `Sams_SmartClientPermissions`) and, optionally, provide a description (see Figure 29.9).

11. Click Next.

12. Select a very restrictive set of permissions. However, you must add the user interface, printing, assembly execution, and all the permissions required to communicate with your middle-tier servers. You might need to add file-related permissions and message queue permissions (see Figure 29.10).

13. Click Next.

14. Click Finish.

FIGURE 29.6   Adding the `Sams_SmartClients` code group: name and description.

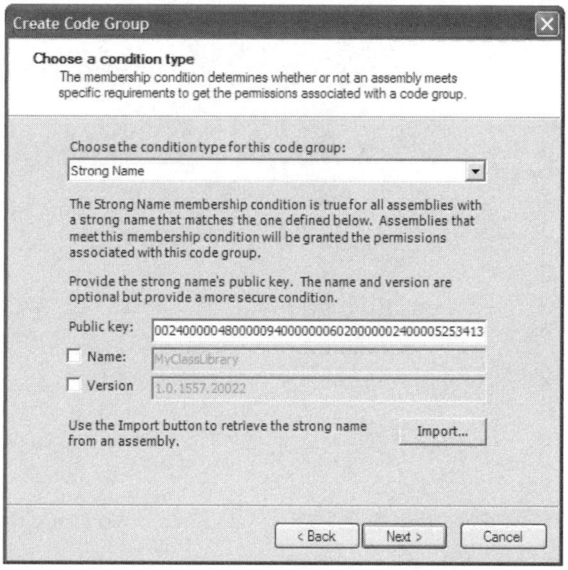

Administrating Code Access Security (CAS)

FIGURE 29.7   Adding the `Sams_SmartClients` code group: membership condition.

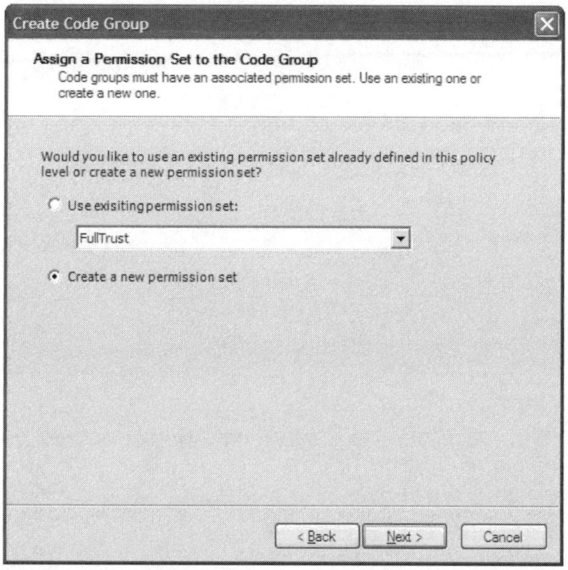

FIGURE 29.8   Adding the `Sams_SmartClients` code group: assign permission set.

Administrating Code Access Security (CAS)

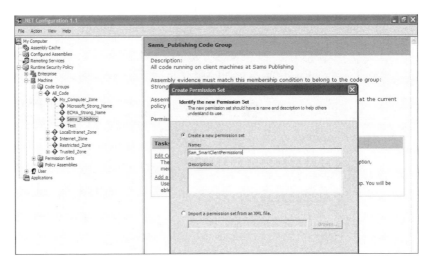

FIGURE 29.9 Adding the `Sams_SmartClients` code group: permission set name and description.

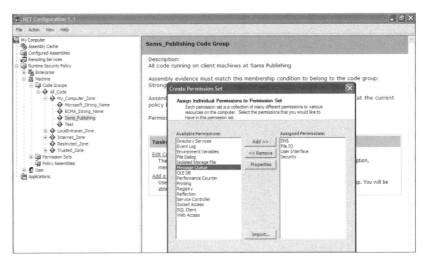

FIGURE 29.10 Adding the `Sams_SmartClients` code group: permission set.

Finally, add a code group for each of your other Organizational Units or products and your trusted vendors, with their strong names, by repeating the steps used to add your own strong name.

Configuring a Server System

The following changes should be applied at the Machine policy level and distributed through SMS, MOM, or Active Directory.

First, deny all permissions to non-Microsoft assemblies.

1. Select My_Computer_Zone.

2. Click on Edit Code Group Properties.

3. In the My_Computer_Zone Property dialog box, select the Permission Set tab.

4. Select the permission set Nothing (refer to Figure 29.3).

5. Select the General tab.

6. Erase the comment. This comment no longer applies, and the default description generated is good enough.

7. Click OK.

You must never change the permission set for the child code groups Microsoft_Strong_Name and ECMA_Strong_Name: They are required for .NET to operate. Modifying or deleting either of them renders all of .NET, including this configuration tool, inoperable.

Next, delete the code groups LocalIntranet_Zone, Internet_Zone, Trusted_Zone, and Restricted_Zone. They should never be used on a server.

Your computer is now secure and can run only software from Microsoft (the actual .NET Framework). To make it useful, you need to grant permissions to other server software. It is best to use a strong name as the evidence. This example uses a strong name for all assemblies created by Sams Publishing.

TIP
Your organization could use a single strong name for your entire corporation, a division, an individual project, or even an individual component. However, the more strong names you use, the harder it is to manage the security policies correctly. The sample that follows is one of many possible approaches that works well.

First, you add a new child code group with your entity's name to My_Computer_Zone. This code group serves as a container only and grants the permission set Nothing.

Administrating Code Access Security (CAS)

1. Select the code group `My_Computer_Zone`.

2. Click on the task Add a Child Code Group.

3. In the Create Code Group Wizard, you name the code group after your organization (`Sams_Publishing`) and, optionally, provide a useful description.

4. Click Next.

5. Select `All_Code` for the membership condition type (evidence).

6. Click Next.

7. Select Use Existing Permission Set and `Nothing` from the drop-down list.

8. Click Next.

9. Click Finish

Next, add a child code group to the just-added child code group (`Sams_Publishing`) for each of your strong name/key pairs (one per organization or product) that will be installed on this server.

1. Select the code group `Sams_Publishing`.

2. Click on the task Add a Child Code Group.

3. In the Create Code Group Wizard, you name the code group after your organization (`Sams_BookContentServers`) and, optionally, provide a useful description.

4. Click Next.

5. Select Strong Name for the membership condition type (evidence).

6. Either type the public key of your strong name (it's very long) or click on Import and navigate to an assembly that is already signed.

7. Click Next.

8. Select Use Existing Permission Set.

9. Select `Full_Trust` from the drop-down list.

10. Click Next.

11. Click Finish.

Add a code group for each of your trusted vendors (used in connection with your server code) with their strong names by repeating the steps used earlier to add your own strong name.

Relax Security for Software Development

You should always develop with the same restrictions as the target environment. Use delayed signing for your projects (see later section). For sample or test applications, use a development-specific personal strong name/key pair stored in the `C:\Keyfiles` directory (you must copy this file into each bin directory for web applications and web services), and secure the directory with an Access Control List (ACL). Add this key (strong name) to the trusted publishers on your machine only (see the preceding sections).

Deploying CAS Policies

You can produce a deployment package for CAS policies by right-clicking on Runtime Security Policy and selecting Create Deployment Package. Next, you select the policy level to deploy and enter a filename (see Figure 29.11). This creates an MSI file that can be deployed manually (double-click it) or through standard system administration tools.

29

> Microsoft Installer files end with the extension `.msi`. These are essentially databases and are executed by the Microsoft Installer Service included in Windows 2000, XP, and 2003.

FIGURE 29.11   Deployment Package Wizard.

Administrating Code Access Security (CAS)

Security policies in .NET are at four levels: Enterprise, Machine, User, and AppDomain. The Enterprise, Machine, and User security policy configurations are loaded from XML-based configuration files. The AppDomain policy level is not enabled by default. It must be explicitly specified programmatically. The User security policy is specific to an individual user on a specific machine. The Machine security policy is applied to all users on a machine. The Enterprise security policy applies to a family of machines that are part of an Active Directory installation. The AppDomain security policy is specific to an application running in an operating system process.

How the CLR Calculates the Permission Set Granted to an Assembly

Permissions for an assembly are calculated when an assembly is loaded into an application domain.

Calculating the Permissions Granted to an Assembly by the Policies

In each policy, calculate the union of all permissions based on the evidence. The system recursively examines the entire tree of code groups (see Figure 29.12).

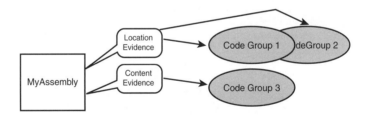

FIGURE 29.12   Union of all code groups for which assembly qualifies based on evidence.

The actual algorithm is best shown in the pseudocode of Listing 29.1.

LISTING 29.1
CAS Algorithm Pseudo Code

```
Public IsExclusive As Boolean = False
Public IsLevelFinal As Boolean = False

Public Function CalculatePermissions( _
   ByRef thisAssembly As AssemblyDescription, _
   ByRef thisCodeGroup As CodeGroup) As PermissionsCollection
```

LISTING 29.1
Continued

```
Dim permissionsGranted As PermissionsCollection
If thisAssembly.EvidenceMatches(thisCodeGroup.MembershipCondition) Then
    'We have a match
    permissionsGranted = thisCodeGroup.PermissionsGranted
    If thisCodeGroup.ThisPolicyLevelWillOnlyHaveThePermissionsFromThis Then
        'First checkbox in General tab of Code Group Property dialog
        'We are done, set flag and return through all levels
        IsExclusive = True
        Return permissionsGranted
    End If
    If thisCodeGroup.PolicyLevelsBelowThisLevelwillNotBeEvaluated Then
        'Second checkbox in General tab of Code Group Property dialog
        'After this policy level, we are done: set flag and continue
        IsLevelFinal = True
    End If
    For Each child As CodeGroup In thisCodeGroup.GetChildren()
        'Retrieve the PermissionsCollection for each child code group
        Dim childPermissions As PermissionsCollection
        childPermissions = CalculatePermissions(thisAssembly, child)
        If IsExclusive Then
            'Child code group has first checkbox in General tab of Code
            'Group Property dialog set
            'We are done, set flag and return through all levels
            Return childPermissions
        End If
        'Calculate the union of the already collected permissions and
        'the child code groups permissions
        CaclculateUnionOf(permissionsGranted, childPermissions)
    Next
End If

'Return the collected union of permissions at the code group and
'all the child code groups (recursively); maybe Nothing
Return permissionsGranted

End Function
```

The system executes this algorithm for the four policies in this order: Enterprise, Machine, User, and Application Domain. If the flag IsLevelFinal is set when calculating the Enterprise-level policy, the Machine- and User-level policies are skipped (set to FullTrust). If the flag IsLevelFinal is set when calculating the Machine-level policy, the User-level policy is skipped (set to FullTrust). The Application Domain–level policy is always calculated. Its default is Full_Trust.

How the CLR Calculates the Permission Set Granted to an Assembly

The system now has four sets of permissions. It calculates the intersection of these sets of permissions as the actual set of permissions possibly granted (see Figure 29.13).

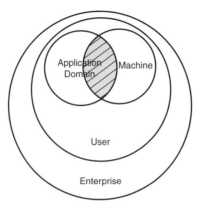

FIGURE 29.13   Intersection of the actual permissions granted at each policy level.

Applying Assembly-Level Attributes to Modify the Permissions Granted

Each assembly can ask for a minimal set of permissions. It can ask for an optional set of permissions or reject granted permissions. This is done through assembly-level attributes; they are usually added in `AssemblyInfo.vb`. Listing 29.2 shows how to add a minimal and optional set of permissions for the assembly.

> `AssemblyInfo.vb` is created automatically when coding in Visual Studio .NET. Otherwise, the file has to be created manually. Using `AssemblyInfo.vb` for assembly-level attributes is just a convention; you could add assembly-level attributes to any source file. However, this is considered bad programming style.

LISTING 29.2
Specifying Minimum and Optional Permissions in `AssemblyInfo.vb`

```
<Assembly: UIPermission(SecurityAction.RequestMinimum, _
                        Window:=UIPermissionWindow.SafeSubWindows)>
<Assembly: SecurityPermission(SecurityAction.RequestMinimum, _
                        Execution:=True, UnmanagedCode:=True, _
                        Assertion:=True)>
<Assembly: UIPermission(SecurityAction.RequestOptional, _
                        Window:=UIPermissionWindow.AllWindows)>
```

If the assembly is not granted the minimal permissions by the policies, it is not loaded.

The formula for the actual permission granted (if the minimum is contained in Policies) is as follows:

Granted = Policies ∩ (Minimal U Optional) − Rejected

You should always ask for a minimal set of permissions. Never combine optional permissions and reject permissions. This is legal but does not make sense. Simplified, you should specify one of the following:

▶ **Passable**—Specify permissions that you do not need as rejected permissions (see Figure 29.14)

▶ **Good**—The minimum set required

▶ **Excellent**—The minimum set required and the optional permissions desired (see Figure 29.15)

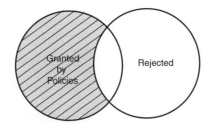

FIGURE 29.14   Rejected permissions subtract from originally granted permissions.

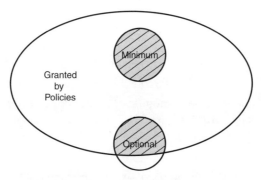

FIGURE 29.15   The minimum permissions and optional permission are granted.

How to Use Security Demands

.NET Framework classes make extensive use of permission demands (also called security demands). User code can use the same methods to further enhance code security. The security system contains three types of permission demands. Simple demands require that every caller who calls your code (directly or indirectly) be granted the demanded permission. This is accomplished by performing a stack walk.

How to Use Security Demands

The second type is a link demand, which requires only that the immediate caller be granted the demanded permission. The third type is an inheritance demand, which requires that all derived classes be granted the demanded permission.

TIP

You can extend the permissions with custom permissions. However, this is mostly esoteric and exceeds the scope of this book. You can find more detail in the .NET help files.

Simple Demands and Stack Walks

The most common security demand (`SecurityAction.Demand`) is used to ensure that every caller who calls your code (directly or indirectly) has been granted the demanded permission. This is accomplished by performing a stack walk. When demanded for a permission, the runtime's security system walks the call stack, comparing the granted permissions of each caller to the permission being demanded. If any caller in the call stack is found without the demanded permission, a security exception is thrown. The exception thrown is called `SecurityException` and is an instance of the `SecurityException` class from the `System.Security` namespace.

NOTE

Stack walks are not propagated across `Remoting` and `DCOM` (Enterprise Services) boundaries.

This prevents luring attacks. The framework classes protect all resources with a simple demand. Because stack walks are expensive, the framework tries to balance security with performance. An example is `FileIO`; the permission is demanded only on Open, not for every Read and Write operation.

Stack walk demands and stack walk modifications are done declaratively with attributes or programmatically with `IStackWalk`. Individual permission objects (actually, the base class `CodeAccessPermission`) and `PermissionSet` implement `IStackWalk`.

Stack walk modifiers assert permissions, deny permissions, or permit only a set of permissions.

Declaratively Initiating Stack Walks

Declarative demands should be used whenever the decision is static. Simply add an attribute (you can stack multiple demands) to your class or method (see Listing 29.3).

LISTING 29.3
Specifying a Simple Demand for a Class

```
<UIPermission(SecurityAction.Demand, _
            Window:=UIPermissionWindow.SafeSubWindows)> _
Public Class TestClass
```

Declarative demands can also be issued for named permission sets (from the configuration tool), for a file containing an XML description of the set, or for a string containing an XML description of the set (see Listing 29.4). This is rarely used.

LISTING 29.4
Specifying a `PermissionSet` Inheritance Demand for a Class

```
<PermissionSet(SecurityAction.Demand, Name:="FullTrust")> _
Public Sub UltraSecureMethod()
End Sub
```

Programmatically Initiating Stack Walks

Creating demands programmatically allows for greater flexibility (see Listing 29.5). It is a necessity for runtime decisions (for example, a filename is passed). You can ask for a single permission or a `PermissionSet`. It is possible to call multiple single permission demands, but because this causes multiple expensive stack walks, you should build a `PermissionSet` instead.

LISTING 29.5
Programmatic Stack Walk Demand for a Single Permission

```
Public Sub ShowMessageBoxProgrammatic(ByRef parent As Control)
    Dim demander As IStackWalk
    demander = New UIPermission(UIPermissionWindow.SafeSubWindows)
    demander.Demand()
    Win32MessageBox(parent.Handle, "Unmanaged Code Call", _
                "Programmatic Security: MessageBox", 0)
End Sub
```

How to Assert a Permission

The permission attribute action `SecurityAction.Assert` and the programmatic `IStackWalk.Assert` terminate the stack walk with a successful outcome. The assembly must have the asserted permission granted and must have the security permission to assert (assert permission does not initiate a stack walk—it is a link demand on the current assembly). This is often used to assert unmanaged code permissions.

How to Use Security Demands

Only one `Assert` stack walk modifier can be installed at any time per stack frame. Use the stacked declarative `Assert` (it causes a permission set) or a `PermissionSet` to assert multiple permissions. When using a programmatic assert, you must use a `Try-Finally-End Try` to revert the asserted permission or permission set with `CodeAccessPermision.RevertAssert` or `CodeAccessPermision.RevertAll`.

TIP

Microsoft explicitly warns that if asserts are not handled carefully, it can lead into luring attacks in which malicious code can call your code through trusted code. A class or method that asserts a permission signs an implied contract guaranteeing that it is well written and tested against luring attacks.

Declarative asserts should be used whenever the decision is static. Simply add an attribute (you can stack multiple asserts) to your class or method (see Listing 29.6).

LISTING 29.6

Specifying a Simple Assert for a Method

```
<SecurityPermission(SecurityAction.Assert, UnmanagedCode:=True)> _
Public Sub ShowMessageBoxDeclarative(ByRef parent As Control)
   Win32MessageBox(parent.Handle, "Unmanaged Code Call", _
      "Declarative Security: MessageBox", 0)
End Sub
```

Declarative asserts can also be issued for named permission sets (from the configuration tool), for a file containing an XML description of the set, or for a string containing an XML description of the set. This is rarely used.

Creating asserts programmatically allows for greater flexibility (see Listing 29.7). It is a necessity for runtime decisions (for example, a filename is passed). You can ask for a single permission or a permission set. It is not possible to call multiple single-permission asserts without calling `CodeAccessSecurity.RevertAssert`.

LISTING 29.7

Programmatic Stack Walk Assert for a Single Permission

```
Public Sub ShowMessageBoxProgrammatic(ByRef parent As Control)
   'assert unmanaged code
   Dim asserter As IStackWalk
   asserter = New SecurityPermission(SecurityPermissionFlag.UnmanagedCode)
   asserter.Assert()
   Win32MessageBox(parent.Handle, "Unmanaged Code Call", _
                "Programmatic Security: MessageBox", 0)
End Sub
```

The Assert-Demand Pattern to Protect Resources

Assert and Demand are useful as a combination pattern to "sandbox" privileged code. This is a necessity for any code that calls unmanaged code. You should assert unmanaged code and demand permissions to protect the resource exposed through the unmanaged code. This can be done declaratively (see Listing 29.8) or programmatically (see Listing 29.9).

LISTING 29.8

Declarative Assert Demand Pattern for a Single Permission

```
<UIPermission(SecurityAction.Demand, _
    Window:=UIPermissionWindow.SafeSubWindows), _
  SecurityPermission(SecurityAction.Assert, UnmanagedCode:=True)> _
Public Sub ShowMessageBoxDeclarative(ByRef parent As Control)
    Win32MessageBox(parent.Handle, "Unmanaged Code Call", _
                "Declarative Security: MessageBox", 0)
End Sub
```

LISTING 29.9

Programmatic Assert Demand Pattern for a Single Permission

```
Public Sub ShowMessageBoxProgrammatic(ByRef parent As Control)
    'assert unmanaged code
    Dim asserter As IStackWalk
    asserter = New SecurityPermission(SecurityPermissionFlag.UnmanagedCode)
    asserter.Assert()
    'immediately demand the real permission
    Dim demander As IStackWalk
    demander = New UIPermission(UIPermissionWindow.SafeSubWindows)
    demander.Demand()
    Win32MessageBox(parent.Handle, "Unmanaged Code Call", _
                "Programmatic Security: MessageBox", 0)
End Sub
```

Denying Granted Permissions

The permission attribute action SecurityAction.Deny and the programmatic IStackWalk.Deny terminate the stack walk with a security exception if the denied permission is the cause of the current demand stack walk. Only one Deny stack walk modifier can be installed at any time per stack frame. Use the stacked declarative Deny (it causes a permission set) or a permission set to deny multiple permissions. When using programmatic Deny, you must use a Try-Finally-End Try to revert the denied permission or permission set with CodeAccessPermision. RevertDeny or CodeAccessPermision.RevertAll. This is equivalent to using SecurityAction.RequestRefuse at the assembly level.

29

How to Use Security Demands

The permission attribute action `SecurityAction.PermitOnly` and the programmatic `IStackWalk.PermitOnly` limit the granted permission(s) to the ones specified. Only one `PermitOnly` stack walk modifier can be installed at any time per stack frame. Use the stacked declarative `PermitOnly` (it causes a permission set) or a permission set to `PermitOnly` multiple permissions. When using programmatic `PermitOnly`, you must use a `Try-Finally-End Try` to revert the denied permission or permission set with `CodeAccessPermision.RevertPermitOnly` or `CodeAccessPermision.RevertAll`. This is equivalent to using the `SecurityAction.RequestMinimal` and `SecurityAction.RequestOptional` actions at the assembly level.

Link Demands

Classes and methods can issue link demands. They are resolved when the JIT compiler links a class or method. A link demand only checks the immediate caller (direct caller) of your code. That means that it doesn't perform a stack walk. Linking occurs when your code is bound to a type reference, including delegate references and method calls.

If the assembly of the immediate caller does not have the demanded permission set, it is not linked and a security exception is thrown. The exception thrown is called `SecurityException` and is an instance of the `SecurityException` class from the `System.Security` namespace.

NOTE

This does not protect static constructors because they are called by the framework. The framework has `FullTrust`, so any demand always succeeds.

Link demands can be applied to classes and methods. They are most often applied to a class. A common one is to demand that the calling assembly have a specific strong name (see Listing 29.10).

LISTING 29.10
Specifying a Link Demand for a Class

```
<StrongNameIdentityPermissionAttribute(SecurityAction.LinkDemand, _
  PublicKey:="00240000048000009400000006020000002400005253413100040000010" & _
  "00100538a4a19382e9429cf516dcf1399facdccca092a06442efaf9ecaca33457be26ee0" & _
  "073c6bde51fe0873666a62459581669b510ae1e84bef6bcb1aff7957237279d8b7e0e25b" & _
  "71ad39df36845b7db60382c8eb73f289823578d33c09e48d0d2f90ed4541e1438008142e" & _
  "f714bfe604c41a4957a4f6e6ab36b9715ec57625904c6")> _
Public Class TestClass
```

Listing 29.11 shows how to apply a link demand to a method.

LISTING 29.11
Specifying a Link Demand for a Method

```
<UIPermission(SecurityAction.LinkDemand, _
            Window:=UIPermissionWindow.SafeSubWindows)> _
Public Sub MyMethod
```

Some link demands are executed automatically:

▸ Enable assembly execution (every assembly receives this)

▸ Skip verification (assembly with unsafe C# or C++ code at load time)

▸ FullTrust (see in later section) for assemblies calling strong named assemblies

Inheritance Demands

Classes and methods can issue inheritance demands. They are resolved when assemblies with derived classes are loaded into the application domain. An inheritance demand checks all directly or indirectly derived classes. That means that it doesn't perform a stack walk.

If the assembly of the derived class does not have the demanded permission set, it is not loaded and a security exception is thrown. The exception thrown is called `SecurityException` and is an instance of the `SecurityException` class from the `System.Security` namespace.

Listing 29.12 shows how to issue an inheritance demand for a class.

LISTING 29.12
Specifying an Inheritance Demand for a Base Class

```
<UIPermission(SecurityAction.InheritanceDemand, _
            Window:=UIPermissionWindow.SafeSubWindows)> _
Public Class MyBaseClass
```

Inheritance demands can be applied to classes and methods. They are most often applied to a class. This prevents abuses through protected members and reflection. Common scenarios include classes dealing with security.

TIP

You should seal such classes if no extensibility is required.

29

How to Use Security Demands

Automatic Link Demand for `FullTrust` and `AllowPartiallyTrustedCallersAttribute` (APTCA)

All strongly named assemblies issue a link demand to assemblies referencing them to have the `FullTrust` permission set associated with them. This behavior can be turned off by adding the `AllowPartiallyTrustedCallersAttribute` assembly attribute to `AssemblyInfo.vb`. Microsoft reasons that only security tested assemblies should specify `AllowPartiallyTrustedCallersAttribute` (see Listing 29.13), and this feature enforces that behavior.

TIP

The author views Microsoft's reasoning as flawed and believes that this "feature" has an unintended side effect. It is the cause of administrators granting `FullTrust` to code that does not need or deserve `FullTrust`; therefore, it reduces security instead of increasing it. This illustrates the classic security problem of balancing usability against security.

Therefore, the author recommends that all assemblies be signed with a strong name and that all class libraries specify `AllowPartiallyTrustedCallersAttribute` (APTCA).

Be warned that an assembly that specifies APTCA signs an implied contract guaranteeing that it is well written (of high quality) and tested against luring attacks.

LISTING 29.13
Specifying APTCA in `AssemblyInfo.vb`

```
<Assembly: AllowPartiallyTrustedCallers()>
```

Signing Assemblies

Signing an assembly requires at least two steps: creating a key pair and using `AssemblyInfo.vb` to instruct the compiler to sign the application. Most signed assemblies are also added to the Global Assembly Cache (GAC); however, private signed assemblies are possible to improve security. Only DLLs belong in the GAC; signed executables are handled like regular executables. Creating keys and strong name–related activities are initiated with the strong name command-line tool called sn.

Immediate Signing

First create a strong name/key pair, as shown in Listing 29.14.

LISTING 29.14
Creating a Strong Name Key Pair

```
sn -k keyfile.snk
```

Next, add the following two lines (see Listing 29.15) to `AssemblyInfo.vb` (assuming that you created your keys in `\KeyFiles`):

LISTING 29.15
Instructing Compiler to Sign the Assembly

```
<Assembly: AssemblyKeyFile("\KeyFiles\keyfile.snk")>
<Assembly: AssemblyDelaySign(False)>
```

Compile and, optionally, add to the GAC with `gacutil`, as shown in Listing 29.16.

LISTING 29.16
Using `gacutil` to Add an Assembly to the GAC

```
Gacutil -i MyAssembly.dll
```

29

Delayed Signing

Delayed-signing enables you to keep your private key(s) very secure. The security of the private key is vital to maintaining a trust relationship with your customers.

TIP

Physically secure files containing both the private and the public key with very restricted physical access (a CD-ROM in a bank vault with backup locations). Think of this key as your version of the Coca-Cola formula. Additionally, have a physically secured computer (ideally, in a vault or guarded room) with very restricted physical and Windows access to perform the delayed signing with the public key. This computer should not be connected to a network and should allow a blind signing only (no one can view the private key) and restrict code access to Microsoft code only.

Additionally, make sure that the CD itself is encrypted with the strongest possible cryptographic system. If possible, add several decoys within the vault itself—you do not want to trust the bank's security itself. Then place the key within steganographically embedded files. This system is being followed by at least one company. This might seem like paranoia, but, considering what can happen if an application is compromised, you can never be careful enough.

Signing Assemblies

The following steps should be done on a secure standalone computer (see the accompanying Tip).

1. Create a strong name/key pair (see the first line in Listing 29.17).

2. Extract the public portion of the key (see the second line in Listing 29.17).

3. Save `keyfile.snk` to removable media (see the accompanying Smart Tip for safe-keeping guidelines). Make multiple backups.

4. Save `publickeyfile.snk` to removable media (make multiple copies). This key file can be checked into a central location or source-control system because it contains the public key only.

LISTING 29.17

Creating a Strong Name/Key Pair and Extracting the Public Key

```
sn -k keyfile.snk
sn -p keyfile.snk publickeyfile.snk
```

Next, each developer references `publickeyfile.snk` in `AssemblyInfo.vb` and requests preparation for delayed signing (see Listing 29.18).

LISTING 29.18

Instructing Compiler to Sign the Assembly

```
<Assembly: AssemblyKeyFile("\KeyFiles\publckeyfile.snk")>
<Assembly: AssemblyDelaySign(True)>
```

Trying to run this code for testing is rejected because the code is not signed. Use the sn tool to instruct your computer to skip verifying the signature. This should be done only on developer and test machines.

Extract the public key token from `publickeyfile.snk`, and enable the public key token for your development or test computers by registering it for skip signature verification (see Listing 29.19).

LISTING 29.19

Registering the Local Framework to Skip the Signature Verification

```
sn -t publickeyfile.snk
sn -Vr *,<token-from-previous-command>
```

You can unregister this token when you are done with development using the commands, as shown in Listing 29.20.

LISTING 29.20

Unregistering the Local Framework to Skip the Signature Verification

```
sn -t publickeyfile.snk
sn -Vu *,<token-from-previous-command>
```

Releasing your code requires an actual signature. Retrieve your secured keyfile.snk (containing the key pair), and resign the assembly or assemblies on your secure computer (see Listing 29.21).

LISTING 29.21

Sign a Delayed-Signed Assembly (or Resign a Previously Signed One)

```
Sn -R <assemblyname> keyfile.snk
```

Putting It All Together

29

The preceding sections of this chapter explained each aspect of CAS and introduced code fragments showing its use. The included solution CAS.sln contains sample code illustrating the most useful practices in CAS. Project CasTest contains a Windows test client. Use it locally and deploy it through the Internet with No-Touch-Deployment, and observe the different behaviors. MyClassLibrary is using both declarative and programmatic security features, and is signed with the delayed signing method. It also includes batch files to execute multiples of the previously explained steps. StrongNameDelayed.cmd creates a strong name/key pair named <name-from-first-parameter>.snk, extracts the public key file Public<name-from-first-parameter>.snk, and displays the public key token. RegisterDelayedToken.cmd registers the public key token for delayed signing. UnregisterDelayedToken.cmd unregisters the public key token.

Summary

This chapter introduced you to code access security. It showed you how to configure a secure system and how to use CAS to improve the security of your own code. It also provided you with information on code signing with a strong name/key pair.

Much of the complexity of Code Access Security is not relevant for the developer. The developer can specifically request or deny permissions at the level of the assembly, with these being considered at assembly load time. At runtime, further demands can be made, in addition to temporary denials that restrict permissions before calling untrusted code. The .NET class libraries make demands, with each demand ensuring that all items on the call stack contain the requested permission. A developer can also request that the libraries linking to or inheriting from their code possess a certain permission set.

Further Reading

".NET Security." MSDN website, http://msdn.microsoft.com/library/
default.asp?url=/library/en-us/dnnetsec/html/secnetlpMSDN.asp.

"Microsoft Security Developer Center", MSDN website,
http://msdn.microsoft.com/security/.

29

30 USER- AND ROLE-BASED PERMISSIONS

IN BRIEF

The previous chapter on code access security (CAS) explained how .NET improves on Windows security. CAS limits what an assembly is permitted to do. This does not eliminate the need to restrict the actions that a user is allowed to perform; it complements it. Windows prevents users from accessing restricted system resources, such as files, executables, websites, the Registry, and databases. .NET adds further granularity to user-based security called .NET role-based security. It restricts execution of code sections based on the user's identity and role membership. This chapter shows how to authenticate users, deal with users and roles, and shows how to apply role-based security.

WHAT YOU NEED

SOFTWARE REQUIREMENTS	Windows 2000, XP, or 2003 .NET Framework 1.1 SDK Visual Studio .NET 2003 with Visual Basic .NET installed
HARDWARE REQUIREMENTS	PC desktop or laptop system
SKILL REQUIREMENTS	Advanced knowledge of Visual Basic .NET Advanced knowledge of the .NET Framework

USER AND ROLE BASED PERMISSIONS AT A GLANCE

Authorization and Authentication

User-based and role-based security allow access to sections of code (assemblies, classes, methods, or a block of code) based on the identity of a user.

Establishing the identity of a user is called authentication. The user must submit proof of identity. .NET can take advantage of built-in Windows authentication or a number of custom methods, including ASP.NET form and Microsoft Passport authentication. Custom authentication can be provided as well.

The user's identity often associates him or her with roles or groups. A Windows identity implies group membership(s). Custom authentication often assigns roles for every identity.

Authorization is the limitation of operations allowed, based on the user's authenticated identity and/or the identity's role memberships.

Authorization without authentication is meaningless because anybody could pretend to be a valid user of the system. It is equivalent to disabling all security while pretending that the program is secure.

Authenticated Users in .NET

Authentication manifests itself as an `IIdentity` (see Listing 30.1). `IIdentity` has four prebuilt concrete implementations: `GenericIdentity`, `FormsIdentity`, `PassportIdentity`, and `WindowsIdentity`. They know the user's name (login) and the type of authentication. Anonymous users are possible in ASP.NET, remoting, and Enterprise services. The absence of an authentication in these cases is indicated with a Boolean flag in `IIdentity`.

LISTING 30.1
`IIdentity` **Interface**

```
Public Interface IIdentity
    ReadOnly Property AuthenticationType() As String
    ReadOnly Property IsAuthenticated() As Boolean
    ReadOnly Property Name() As String
End Interface
```

`IPrincipal` encapsulate an identity's roles. `IPrincipal` (see Listing 30.2) has a property to retrieve the `IIdentity` and a function to query `IsInRole`. `IPrincipal` has two prebuilt implementations: `WindowsPrincipal` and `GenericPrincipal`.

Authenticated Users in .NET

LISTING 30.2
IPrincipal Interface

```
Public Interface IPrincipal
   ReadOnly Property Identity() As IIdentity
   Function IsInRole(ByVal role As String) As Boolean
End Interface
```

Windows authentication uses `WindowsIdentity` (representing the local or domain user) and `WindowsPrincipal` (representing local or domain groups). .NET retrieves this information automatically from the user's login information.

Forms authentication uses `FormsIdentity` and `GenericPrincipal`. The exact mechanics of how to authenticate the user and what to use for role assignments are left to the implementer. The use of custom databases or Active Directory Application Mode (ADAM) is common. For more information on forms authentication, see Chapter 21, "Security."

Each thread has an `IPrincipal` if user authentication has been enabled. The thread's `IPrincipal` is used for declarative and programmatic role-based security.

`WindowsIdentity` represents a Windows user (domain or local). This is always used for Windows clients and ASP.NET when identifying intranet clients with their Windows domain accounts.

ASP.NET sets the security policy automatically based on the authentication settings in `web.config`. WinForm clients must set the application domain's principal policy to enable authentication. You must set the policy to `PrincipalPolicy.WindowsPrincipal` even if you use a generic or custom principal (see Listing 30.3).

1. Include the imports before your main Windows Form ▪**1**▪ .

2. Add the form's load handler with the policy settings ▪**2**▪. `Thread.GetDomain` should really be called `Thread.GetAppDomain`; however, the designer of the `Thread` class decided to save typing.

LISTING 30.3
Enabling Authentication and Authorization in a Windows Program

```
Imports System.Threading
Imports System.Security.Principal

Private Sub TestMain_Load(ByVal sender As System.Object, _
                          ByVal e As System.EventArgs) Handles MyBase.Load
    Dim currentDomain As AppDomain = Thread.GetDomain()
    currentDomain.SetPrincipalPolicy(PrincipalPolicy.WindowsPrincipal)
End Sub
```

Role-Based Security

Role-based security can allow the authorization of users and/or roles, or authorize all authenticated users. Practically, user-based authorization is rarely used because hard-coding a user in your application is very limiting. Therefore, user-based authorization is not covered in this book. Users are normally mapped to roles (in Windows groups, a custom database or the COM+ catalog) and are authorized based on those roles.

As with code access security, role-based security can be done declaratively (with attributes) or programmatically (with code).

Declarative Role-Based Security

Declarative role-based security is very similar to declarative code access security. It should be used for static decisions, and it can be applied to classes and methods. Anyone can use classes and methods without security demands.

Class-level requirements are applied to all methods (including constructors), but you can change these selections for individual methods. The test class `MyTestClass` (see Listing 30.4) illustrates this behavior. The class attribute **1** requires that all methods without a different requirement (constructor `New` and method `RegularMethod`) be executable by authenticated users assigned to the role member (`HG_TABLET\ TestUser`. `HG-TABLET` is the name of my computer—you should change this to the name of your computer or domain. `TestUser` (as well as `PrivilegedTestUser`, later) is a Windows group on my computer; you should create these groups on your computer or domain.

The method attribute for `PrivilegedMethodDeclarative` **2** requires that this method is executable by authenticated users assigned to the role `HG-TABLET\ PrivilegedTestUser`.

It is also possible to specify any user, as long as that user is authenticated with `<PrincipalPermission(SecurityAction.Demand, Authenticated:=True>`.

LISTING 30.4
Test Class Demonstrating Declarative Role-Based Security

```
Imports System.Security
Imports System.Security.Permissions
Imports System.Security.Principal
Imports System.Threading
```

```
<PrincipalPermission(SecurityAction.Demand, _                          1
                  Role:="HG-TABLET\TestUser")>
Public Class MyTestClass

    Public Sub New()
    End Sub
```

30

Role-Based Security

LISTING 30.4
Continued

```
Public Sub RegularMethod()
End Sub
```

2

```
<PrincipalPermission(SecurityAction.Demand, _
                Role:="HG-TABLET\PrivilegedTestUser")> _
Public Sub PrivilegedMethodDeclarative()
    MessageBox.Show("Declarative", "PrivilegedMethod")
End Sub


End Class
```

Programmatic Role-Based Security

Programmatic role-based security can use method parameters to require different roles for different runtime values. The commonly used example is a banking system in which a manager is required to transfer $10,000 or more. `PrivilegedMethodProgrammatic` illustrates the use of two possible approaches (see Listing 30.5).

Programmatic security can be achieved by using the `IPrincipal` object retrieved from the current thread's `IIdentity` object. `IPrincipal` has a method named `IsInRole` that can be used to disable user interface objects that are not allowed based on the current user or that affect regular flow based on the user's identity **1**.

Alternatively, you can construct a `PrincipalPermission` object and issuing a demand for this permission **2**.

The first approach should be used to influence regular program flow (for example, hiding a button). The second method is preferred for defensive checking on the server side because it provides a consistent and secure exception generation and uses less code.

TIP

`SecurityException` should not reveal details about the violation. Keep the error message generic.

LISTING 30.5
Test Class Demonstrating Programmatic Role-Based Security

```
Imports System.Security
Imports System.Security.Permissions
Imports System.Security.Principal
Imports System.Threading


Public Class MyTestClass
    Public Sub PrivilegedMethodProgrammatic(ByVal value As Integer)
```

LISTING 30.5
Continued

```
    If value >= 20 Then                                                    1
        Dim authorized As Boolean
        Dim principal As IPrincipal = Thread.CurrentPrincipal()
        authorized = principal.IsInRole("HG-TABLET\SuperTestUser")
        If Not authorized Then
            Throw New SecurityException("Not authorized for this operation")
        End If

    ElseIf value >= 10 Then                                                2
        Dim permission As IPermission = New PrincipalPermission(Nothing, _
                              "HG-TABLET\PrivilegedTestUser")
        permission.Demand()
    End If
    MessageBox.Show("Programatic: Value = " + value.ToString(), _
                    "PrivilegedMethod")
  End Sub
End Class
```

30

Creating Custom Principal and Identity Objects

Custom identities are rarely used because the built-in ones provide all known useful implementations. However, it is useful to create custom principals. Reading the group membership from a database, Active Directory Application Mode (ADAM), or a COM+ application's role mapping are good examples of their usefulness. It is also useful to unify roles across different technologies (examples: Windows and ASP.NET forms authentication, or Windows applications and Enterprise Services [COM+] components).

Your custom principal class must implement IPrincipal. After you create a custom principal, you assign it to the current thread. Additionally, you can set the default principal for all threads in this application domain. You can do this only once per application domain.

TIP
Do not set the default principal for all threads in ASP.NET. Other threads will handle different users. This is useful only for multithreaded Windows applications.

Listing 30.6 uses the same test class from Listing 30.4. Instead of mapping the Windows groups that the user belongs to as roles, this custom principal **1** uses a custom mapping of the username to a set of roles. In this example, the mapping is hard-coded the same for any user; you normally use a database to store the mapping relationships.

Creating Custom Principal and Identity Objects

This project is easier to test than the `WindowsPrincipal` version because you do not need to log out to change the role mapping to your username.

LISTING 30.6

Custom Principal Class `UnleashedPrincipal` Implementing Mapping Between Usernames and Roles

```
Imports System.Security.Principal

Public Class UnleashedPrincipal
    Implements IPrincipal

    Private m_Identity As IIdentity

    Public Sub New(ByRef identity As IIdentity)
        m_Identity = identity
    End Sub

    Public Overridable ReadOnly Property Identity() As IIdentity _
        Implements IPrincipal.Identity
        Get
            Return m_Identity
        End Get
    End Property

    Public Overridable Function IsInRole(ByVal role As String) As Boolean _
        Implements IPrincipal.IsInRole
        If m_Identity.IsAuthenticated Then
            Dim userName As String = m_Identity.Name
            'lookup in database or for this exercise hard code it
            Select Case role
                Case "TestUser"
                    Return True
                Case "PrivilegedTestUser"
                    Return True
                Case "SuperTestUser"
                    Return False
                Case Else
                    Return False
            End Select
        Else
            Return False
        End If
    End Function
End Class
```

The test class (see Listing 30.7) and test client (see Listing 30.8) are similar to the previous ones for role-based security. In Sub TestMain_Load, UnleashedPrincipal is created and assigned to the current thread and is set as the default security principal for all threads in this application domain.

LISTING 30.7

Test Class for Custom Principal Class UnleashedPrincipal

```
Imports System.Security
Imports System.Security.Permissions
Imports System.Security.Principal
Imports System.Threading


<PrincipalPermission(SecurityAction.Demand, _
                    Role:="TestUser")> _
Public Class MyTestClass

    Public Sub New()
    End Sub


    Public Sub RegularMethod()
    End Sub


    <PrincipalPermission(SecurityAction.Demand, _
                        Role:="PrivilegedTestUser")> _
    Public Sub PrivilegedMethodDeclarative()
        MessageBox.Show("Declarative", "PrivilegedMethod")
    End Sub


    Public Sub PrivilegedMethodProgrammatic(ByVal value As Integer)
        If value >= 20 Then
            Dim authorized As Boolean
            Dim principal As IPrincipal = Thread.CurrentPrincipal()
            authorized = principal.IsInRole("SuperTestUser")
            If Not authorized Then
                Throw New SecurityException("Not authorized for this operation")
            End If
        ElseIf value >= 10 Then
            Dim permission As IPermission = New PrincipalPermission(Nothing, _
                                            "PrivilegedTestUser")
            permission.Demand()
        End If
        MessageBox.Show("Programatic: Value = " + value.ToString(), _
                    "PrivilegedMethod")
    End Sub

End Class
```

30

Creating Custom Principal and Identity Objects

LISTING 30.8
Test Client for Custom Principal Class `UnleashedPrincipal`

```vb
Imports System.Threading
Imports System.Security.Principal

Public Class TestMain
    Inherits System.Windows.Forms.Form

    Private m_TestClass As MyTestClass

#Region " Windows Form Designer generated code "

    Public Sub New()
        MyBase.New()

        'This call is required by the Windows Form Designer.
        InitializeComponent()

        'Add any initialization after the InitializeComponent() call

    End Sub

    'Form overrides dispose to clean up the component list.
    Protected Overloads Overrides Sub Dispose(ByVal disposing As Boolean)
        If disposing Then
            If Not (components Is Nothing) Then
                components.Dispose()
            End If
        End If
        MyBase.Dispose(disposing)
    End Sub

    'Required by the Windows Form Designer
    Private components As System.ComponentModel.IContainer

    'NOTE: The following procedure is required by the Windows Form Designer
    'It can be modified using the Windows Form Designer.
    'Do not modify it using the code editor.
    Friend WithEvents m_btnRegular As System.Windows.Forms.Button
    Friend WithEvents m_btnValue As System.Windows.Forms.Button
    Friend WithEvents m_btnPrivileged As System.Windows.Forms.Button
    Friend WithEvents m_lblExplanation As System.Windows.Forms.Label
    Friend WithEvents m_txtValue As System.Windows.Forms.TextBox
    Friend WithEvents Label1 As System.Windows.Forms.Label
    Friend WithEvents Label2 As System.Windows.Forms.Label
```

Creating Custom Principal and Identity Objects

LISTING 30.8
Continued

```vb
<System.Diagnostics.DebuggerStepThrough()> Private Sub InitializeComponent()
    Me.m_btnRegular = New System.Windows.Forms.Button
    Me.m_btnValue = New System.Windows.Forms.Button
    Me.m_btnPrivileged = New System.Windows.Forms.Button
    Me.m_lblExplanation = New System.Windows.Forms.Label
    Me.m_txtValue = New System.Windows.Forms.TextBox
    Me.Label1 = New System.Windows.Forms.Label
    Me.Label2 = New System.Windows.Forms.Label
    Me.SuspendLayout()
    '
    'm_btnRegular
    '
    Me.m_btnRegular.Location = New System.Drawing.Point(16, 16)
    Me.m_btnRegular.Name = "m_btnRegular"
    Me.m_btnRegular.TabIndex = 0
    Me.m_btnRegular.Text = "Regular"
    '
    'm_btnValue
    '
    Me.m_btnValue.Location = New System.Drawing.Point(16, 80)
    Me.m_btnValue.Name = "m_btnValue"
    Me.m_btnValue.TabIndex = 1
    Me.m_btnValue.Text = "Value"
    '
    'm_btnPrivileged
    '
    Me.m_btnPrivileged.Location = New System.Drawing.Point(16, 48)
    Me.m_btnPrivileged.Name = "m_btnPrivileged"
    Me.m_btnPrivileged.TabIndex = 2
    Me.m_btnPrivileged.Text = "Privileged"
    '
    'm_lblExplanation
    '
    Me.m_lblExplanation.Location = New System.Drawing.Point(16, 112)
    Me.m_lblExplanation.Name = "m_lblExplanation"
    Me.m_lblExplanation.Size = New System.Drawing.Size(200, 23)
    Me.m_lblExplanation.TabIndex = 3
    Me.m_lblExplanation.Text = "Value < 10: TestUser"
    '
    'm_txtValue
    '
```

30

Creating Custom Principal and Identity Objects

LISTING 30.8
Continued

```
        Me.m_txtValue.Location = New System.Drawing.Point(104, 80)
        Me.m_txtValue.Name = "m_txtValue"
        Me.m_txtValue.Size = New System.Drawing.Size(72, 20)
        Me.m_txtValue.TabIndex = 4
        Me.m_txtValue.Text = "1"
        '
        'Label1
        '
        Me.Label1.Location = New System.Drawing.Point(16, 144)
        Me.Label1.Name = "Label1"
        Me.Label1.Size = New System.Drawing.Size(176, 23)
        Me.Label1.TabIndex = 5
        Me.Label1.Text = "Value > 20: SuperTestUser"
        '
        'Label2
        '
        Me.Label2.Location = New System.Drawing.Point(16, 128)
        Me.Label2.Name = "Label2"
        Me.Label2.Size = New System.Drawing.Size(200, 23)
        Me.Label2.TabIndex = 6
        Me.Label2.Text = "Value < 20: PrivilegedTestUser"
        '
        'TestMain
        '
        Me.AutoScaleBaseSize = New System.Drawing.Size(5, 13)
        Me.ClientSize = New System.Drawing.Size(184, 166)
        Me.Controls.Add(Me.Label1)
        Me.Controls.Add(Me.Label2)
        Me.Controls.Add(Me.m_txtValue)
        Me.Controls.Add(Me.m_lblExplanation)
        Me.Controls.Add(Me.m_btnPrivileged)
        Me.Controls.Add(Me.m_btnValue)
        Me.Controls.Add(Me.m_btnRegular)
        Me.MaximizeBox = False
        Me.MinimizeBox = False
        Me.Name = "TestMain"
        Me.Text = "Custom Principal"
        Me.ResumeLayout(False)

    End Sub
```

Creating Custom Principal and Identity Objects

LISTING 30.8
Continued

```vbnet
#End Region

    Private Sub TestMain_Load(ByVal sender As System.Object, _
                                ByVal e As System.EventArgs) Handles MyBase.Load
        'Required to initialize security:
        '  sets the policy for this application domain to authenticated
        Dim currentDomain As AppDomain = Thread.GetDomain()
        currentDomain.SetPrincipalPolicy(PrincipalPolicy.WindowsPrincipal)
        'Create the new principal and pass the current Windows identity to it
        Dim newPrincipal As IPrincipal
        newPrincipal = New UnleashedPrincipal(Thread.CurrentPrincipal.Identity)
        'Set the current threads principal to the newly created one
        Thread.CurrentPrincipal = newPrincipal
        'Optional: set this principal as the default principal for all threads
        'in this application domain.  this can only be done once per application
        'domain.  It is unnecessary in this example since we are not creating
        'additional threads
        currentDomain.SetThreadPrincipal(newPrincipal)

        m_TestClass = New MyTestClass
    End Sub

    Private Sub OnRegular(ByVal sender As System.Object, _
                    ByVal e As System.EventArgs) Handles m_btnRegular.Click
        m_TestClass.RegularMethod()
    End Sub

    Private Sub OnPrivileged(ByVal sender As System.Object, _
                    ByVal e As System.EventArgs) Handles m_btnPrivileged.Click
        m_TestClass.PrivilegedMethodDeclarative()
    End Sub

    Private Sub OnValue(ByVal sender As System.Object, _
                    ByVal e As System.EventArgs) Handles m_btnValue.Click
        Dim value As Integer
        value = Convert.ToInt32(m_txtValue.Text)
        m_TestClass.PrivilegedMethodProgrammatic(value)
    End Sub
End Class
```

30

Summary

This chapter showed how to use built-in user-based and role-based security. It introduced the interfaces IIdentity and IPrincipal and their concrete implementations.

Next, you learned how to use roles to improve software security at a granular level.

Finally, you extended the built-in features with your own custom mapping of roles in a custom principal class implementing IPrincipal.

Further Reading

"Building Secure ASP.NET Applications: Authentication, Authorization, and Secure Communication." MSDN website, http://msdn.microsoft.com/library/default.asp?url=/library/en-us/dnnetsec/html/secnetlpMSDN.asp.

"Unified Security Principal Sample Code." IDesign website, http://idesign.net/idesign/uploads/UnifiedSecurity.zip.

".NET Security." MSDN website, http://msdn.microsoft.com/library/default.asp?url=/library/en-us/dnnetsec/html/secnetlpMSDN.asp.

"Microsoft Security Developer Center." MSDN website, http://msdn.microsoft.com/security/.

Part VII

Remoting

CHAPTER 31 Practical .NET Remoting

Remoting is the process of accessing a .NET component in a separate application domain, in a separate process on the same machine, or in a remote computer. All Remoting-related classes are defined in `System.Runtime.Remoting`.

This chapter starts with the basic concepts and terminology. This is followed by an introduction to application domains and, after that, the practical aspects of .NET Remoting. Finally, `ContexTboundObjects` are covered as a special case of Remoting.

WHAT YOU NEED

SOFTWARE REQUIREMENTS	Windows 2000, XP, or 2003 .NET Framework 1.1 SDK Visual Studio .NET 2003 with Visual Basic .NET installed
HARDWARE REQUIREMENTS	PC desktop or laptop
SKILL REQUIREMENTS	Advanced knowledge of Visual Basic .NET Advanced knowledge of the .NET Framework

PRACTICAL .NET REMOTING AT A GLANCE

PRACTICAL .NET REMOTING AT A GLANCE

Introduction to Remoting

This section introduces the basic building blocks of Remoting (application domains, marshalling, and serialization) and explains the Remoting architecture.

Windows Processes and .NET Application Domains

Windows 32 protects applications from each other by running them in separate processes. This keeps faulty code in one process from damaging the execution code in other processes. Processes use their own address space. Therefore, it is quite complex to call code in another process.

The process of calling code from one process to another is known as cross-process marshalling. Apart from IO and process creation, process context switching is one of the costliest steps in operating system execution.

In the managed world of .NET, processes contain one or more application domains (see Figure 31.1). You might think of them as lightweight logical processes. Application domains (and contexts) provide isolation and security without the expense of a Windows process. Contexts and context-bound objects are covered later.

31

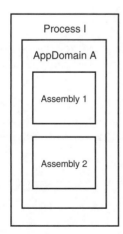
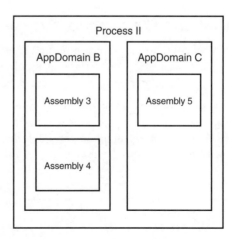

FIGURE 31.1 Processes and application domains.

Introduction to Remoting

Each Windows process hosts the .NET runtime, which includes the assembly loader, the JIT compiler, the managed heap, the garbage collector, and the security system (see Figure 31.2). Application domains with a process can start up and shut down independently. .NET threads are orthogonal to application domains. They can cross application domains. Shutting down an application domain also shuts down all threads currently executing in that application domain.

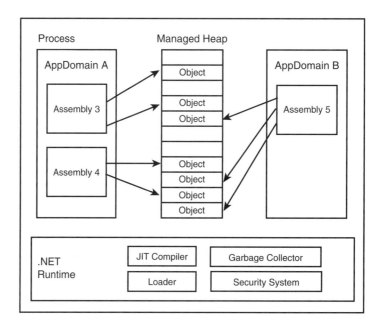

FIGURE 31.2   Process contents.

Remoting and Marshalling Explained

Machines, processes, and application domains (as well as contexts) define isolation boundaries. Crossing isolation boundaries requires the use of Remoting. Remoting is the act of marshalling an object or an object reference across boundaries.

Remoting is performed by serializing the parameters at one end and deserializing them at the other end. This process is reversed for out parameters, return values, and exceptions. The process of serializing and deserializing is called marshalling and is achieved with an interception architecture.

NOTE

Remoting is one of .NET's alternatives to DCOM interapplication development. The other is XML Web Services.

Marshall by Value

Objects that are not derived (directly or indirectly) from `MarshalByRefObject` and that are serializable are marshaled by value. An object is serializable if it has the attribute `<Serializable>` or if it implements the interface `ISerializable`. An actual copy is created in the target application domain. Any changes alter the copy only. The object might be marshaled back and a new object might be created, replacing the existing object in the source application domain. Marshall by value is available only for passing parameters.

Marshall by Reference

Objects derived (directly or indirectly) from `MarshallByRefObject` are always marshaled by reference. The object stays in the application domain that it was created in, and a proxy is created in the application domain using it. Therefore, only one object exists.

`ContextBoundObjects` **are derived from** `MarshalByRefObject` **and can be accessed across all boundaries.** `System.EnterpriseServices.ServicedComponent` **is derived from** `ContextBoundObject`. **This hierarchy is used to enable serviced components to act as remote objects. The transport mechanism is different (DCOM), but the rest of the architecture stays the same.**

Remoting Architecture

Remoting works by encoding data for transport using various transport protocols. These protocols are exposed in the form of channels. The different aspects of Remoting are achieved with an interception architecture (see Figure 31.3).

31

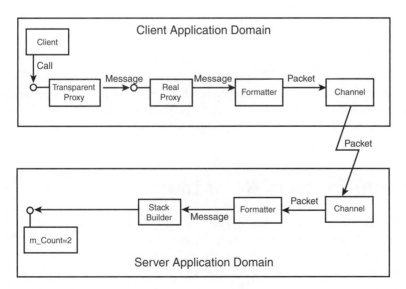

FIGURE 31.3   Remoting architecture basics.

Introduction to Remoting

A transparent proxy on the client side has the same signature as the actual remoted method. It creates a message (IMessage) from the stack frame and calls the real proxy. The real proxy might do more work and finally invokes a formatter. The formatter serializes the message into a packet suitable for transport. This packet is handed to a channel handler for transport to the remote application domain's channel handler. The remote channel handler at the remote application domain hands the packet to a formatter. The formatter deserializes the packet into a message and hands it to the stack builder. The stack builder might process the message further and calls the real object. This process is reversed for any output parameters, return values, and exceptions.

Crossing machine and process boundaries requires a cross-machine or cross-process channel, a serialization formatter, and explicit Remoting setup. .NET defines two formatters: binary and SOAP. .NET defines two explicit channels: TCP and HTTP. By default, the TCP channel uses binary formatting and the HTTP channel uses SOAP formatting.

> **NOTE**
>
> It is possible to use SOAP formatting with a TCP channel, as well as to use binary formatting with an HTTP channel. However, it is not a good practice.

31

.NET handles in-process cross–application domain (and cross-context) calls implicitly (without additional code).

> **TIP**
>
> .NET optimizes in-process cross–application domain (and cross-context) calls by skipping the formatter step and using a special highly efficient channel.

Explicit remote objects need to be hosted by a Remoting host. Choices for Remoting hosts are a custom process or IIS (5.0 or later) with ASP.NET 1.1. It is recommended that you use a custom host (you will learn how to write a universal custom Remoting host with two lines of code). IIS is more useful for web services, which are a different type of Remoting.

Simple In-Process Remoting

The CLR automatically handles cross–application domain Remoting within the same process. Automatic cross-context and cross–application domain Remoting (within the same process) follow the standard call semantics: One object is created for every instantiation requested by a client. You will create a console application that demonstrates this.

In Visual Studio, create an empty solution CrossAppDomain and add a new VB console application CrossAppDomain. Rename `Module1.vb` to `MyMain.vb`, and rename the module name in the source code from `Module1` to `MyMain` (see Listing 31.1) **1**. Next, change the startup object in the project's property dialog box to `MyMain`.

LISTING 31.1
Module MyMain

```
Module MyMain                                                        1
    Sub Main()
    End Sub
End Module
```

Now add a class `TestClass` that has a constructor and one method, each writing its name and the application domain name to the console (see Listing 31.2). This class is derived from `MarshalByRefObject`, which makes the class remotable.

LISTING 31.2
Class TestClass

```
Imports System.Threading

Public Class TestClass
    Inherits MarshalByRefObject
    Private m_Name As String
    Public Sub New()
        Dim app As AppDomain = AppDomain.CurrentDomain
        Console.WriteLine("TestClass.New in application domain {0}", _
            app.FriendlyName)
    End Sub
    Public Property Name() As String
        Get
            Return m_Name
        End Get
        Set(ByVal Value As String)
            m_Name = Value
        End Set
    End Property
    Public Sub TestMethod()
        Dim app As AppDomain = AppDomain.CurrentDomain
        Console.WriteLine("{1}.TestMethod called in application domain {0}", _
            app.FriendlyName, m_Name)
    End Sub
End Class
```

31

Simple In-Process Remoting

Next, extend Main to test this class as a regular local object (see Listing 31.3) **1** . The Console.ReadLine keeps the command window open until Enter is pressed.

LISTING 31.3
Test Main

```
Sub Main()
    Dim app As AppDomain = AppDomain.CurrentDomain
    Console.WriteLine("Main in application domain {0}", app.FriendlyName)
    Dim test As New TestClass
    test.Name = "test"
    test.TestMethod()
    Console.ReadLine()
End Sub
```

Test the application. Set a breakpoint on the line test.TestMethod, and hover your cursor over test; it should display a ToolTip test={CrossAppDomain. TestClass}.

Next, create a new application domain, app2, with a friendly name, SecondAppDomain, and create a second test object, test2, in it (see Listing 31.4) **1**.

LISTING 31.4
Extended Test Main

```
Sub Main()
    Dim app As AppDomain = AppDomain.CurrentDomain
    Console.WriteLine("Main in application domain {0}", app.FriendlyName)
    Dim test As New TestClass
    test.Name = "test"
    test.TestMethod()
    Dim app2 As AppDomain
    app2 = AppDomain.CreateDomain("SecondAppDomain")
    Dim test2 As TestClass
    test2 = CType(app2.CreateInstanceAndUnwrap("CrossAppDomain", _
        "CrossAppDomain.TestClass"), TestClass)
    test2.Name = "test2"
    test2.TestMethod()
    Console.ReadLine()
End Sub
```

Test the application. Set a breakpoint on the line test2.TestMethod, and hover your cursor over test; it should display a ToolTip test={CrossAppDomain. TestClass};, the same as before. Now hover your cursor over test2; it displays test2={System.Runtime.Remoting.Proxies.__TransparentProxy}. This indicates that a Remoting call through a proxy is involved.

Now add a method called `DoCallBack`, taking a `TestClass` object as a reference parameter (see Listing 31.5). By passing first `test` and then `test2` to `test2.DoCallBack` (see Listing 31.6) **1**, you can show how the system uses proxies when appropriate and does a direct call when no isolation boundary (such as an application domain boundary) is involved. To show this, you should set a break-point in `TestClass.DoCallBack` and over `testObject`, and observe the chang-ing behavior between the first call and the second call.

LISTING 31.5
DoCallBack Method in TestClass

```
Public Sub DoCallBack(ByRef testObject As TestClass)
    Dim app As AppDomain = AppDomain.CurrentDomain
    Console.WriteLine("{1}.DoCallBack({2}) called in application domain {0}", _
        app.FriendlyName, m_Name, testObject.Name)
    testObject.TestMethod()
End Sub
```

LISTING 31.6
Completed Test Main

```
Sub Main()
    Dim app As AppDomain = AppDomain.CurrentDomain
    Console.WriteLine("Main in application domain {0}", app.FriendlyName)
    Dim test As New TestClass
    test.Name = "test"
    test.TestMethod()
    Dim app2 As AppDomain
    app2 = AppDomain.CreateDomain("SecondAppDomain")
    Dim test2 As TestClass
    test2 = CType(app2.CreateInstanceAndUnwrap("CrossAppDomain", _
        "CrossAppDomain.TestClass"), TestClass)
    test2.Name = "test2"
    test2.TestMethod()
    test2.DoCallBack(test)                                              1
    test2.DoCallBack(test2)
    Console.ReadLine()
End Sub
```

31

Explicit Remoting

Explicit Remoting is required between application domains across process and machine boundaries. It can be used within a process as well. Explicit Remoting provides for three types of call semantics: client-activated, server-activated singleton, and server-activated single-call semantics. It requires programmatic or declarative configuration.

After learning about call semantics, you'll configure Remoting programmatically to see the actual process. Later you will use the much simpler and better declarative configuration with an XML configuration file.

Remote Object Activation Types

Explicit Remoting offers two main versions of call semantics: client activated and server activated. The client determines whether it wants to use client- or server-activated calls; however, the server must support the desired activation mode.

Client-activated objects create a new object for every client (see Figure 31.4). This mimics the semantics of a traditional local object. However, this model does not scale well for large numbers of clients.

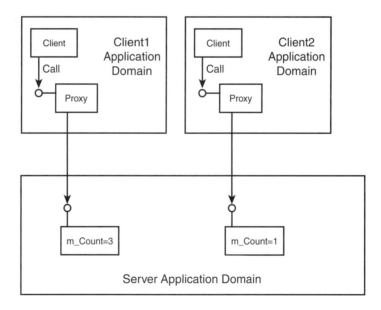

FIGURE 31.4   Client-activated object(s).

Server-activated objects are subdivided into two semantic models, single call and singleton. The server determines which semantic it supports. The client is unaware of this choice.

Server-activated single-call objects create a new remote object for every call, issue the method, and destroy the object (see Figure 31.5). The proxy is created only once. This scales very well, as long as the object creation is inexpensive. Additionally, any state required needs to be explicitly persisted between calls.

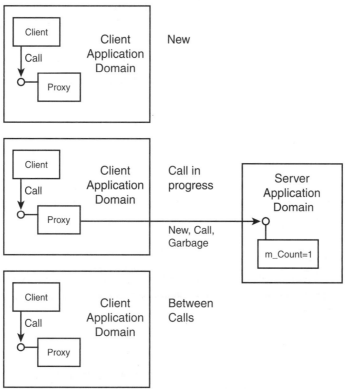

FIGURE 31.5   Server-activated single-call object.

Server-activated singleton objects are created once for all clients (see Figure 31.6). In other words, they are shared among multiple clients and, therefore, contain shared state, which requires them to be coded thread safe. They scale even less than client-activated objects.

TIP
Server-activated singleton objects should not handle client-specific state. Objects that maintain client state should be implemented as client-activated or single-call objects.

31

Explicit Remoting

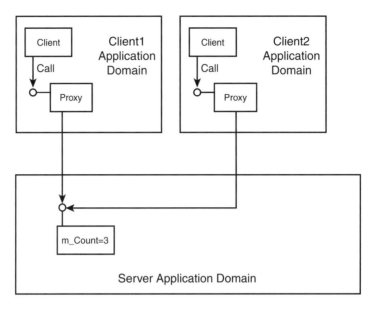

FIGURE 31.6   Server-activated singleton object.

NOTE

In practice, servers generally support only one of the three activation modes. The different semantics demand different object implementations, and the choice has architectural implications.

31

Remoting with Programmatic Configuration

This example shows all possible permutations of channel types and activation modes. You will develop the following:

- ▸ A class library (TestLibrary) containing a remotable class `TestClass`

- ▸ A Remoting host (`RemoteHostProgrammatic`) to select and register the channel (TCP or HTTP) and the activation mode (client, server-singleton, or server-single call)

- ▸ A client (ClientProgrammatic) to select and register the channel (TCP or HTTP) and the activation mode (client or server), as well as a call to a remote `TestMethod`

First, create an empty solution named Remoting.

Creating the TestLibrary

Create a library project named TestLibrary for the remote object example class:

1. Add a VB class library project named TestLibrary to the solution.

2. Delete `Class1.vb` from the solution.

3. Add a class `TestClass`.

4. Add the code in Listing 31.7  .

LISTING 31.7
Remotable `TestClass`

```
Imports System.Windows.Forms                                                    1
Public Class TestClass
    Inherits MarshalByRefObject                                                 2
    Private m_Counter As Integer
    Public Sub New()
        m_Counter = 0
        Dim app As AppDomain = AppDomain.CurrentDomain
        MessageBox.Show("New", "TestClass(" + app.FriendlyName + ")")
    End Sub
    Public Sub TestMethod()
        m_Counter += 1
        Dim app As AppDomain = AppDomain.CurrentDomain
        MessageBox.Show("TestMethod: Counter=" + m_Counter.ToString(), _
            "TestClass(" + app.FriendlyName + ")")
    End Sub
End Class
```

This code displays a `MessageBox` with the application domain name and the internal counter variable in the constructor and in `TestMethod`. This enables you to view the effect of the different activation methods.

Creating the Remoting Host RemoteHostProgrammatic
Create a new Windows application named RemoteHostProgrammatic to contain the Remoting host code for the solution.

1. Add a VB Windows application project named RemoteHostProgrammatic to the solution.

2. Rename `Form1.vb` to `MainWindow.vb`.

3. Rename the `Form1` class to `MainWindow`.

4. Change the startup object in the project's Property dialog box.

5. Add a reference to the TestLibrary project.

6. Add the code in Listing 31.8 to create two radio button groups and a Register button. Switch to designer mode (see Figure 31.7).

31

Explicit Remoting

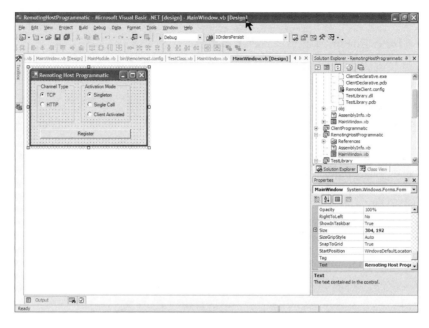

FIGURE 31.7   Programmatic Remoting host UI.

LISTING 31.8
Programmatic Remoting Host

```vb
Imports System.Runtime.Remoting
Imports System.Runtime.Remoting.Channels
Imports System.Runtime.Remoting.Channels.Tcp
Imports System.Runtime.Remoting.Channels.Http


Public Class MainWindow
    Inherits System.Windows.Forms.Form

#Region " Windows Form Designer generated code "
    Public Sub New()
        MyBase.New()
        'This call is required by the Windows Form Designer.
        InitializeComponent()
        'Add any initialization after the InitializeComponent() call
    End Sub
    'Form overrides dispose to clean up the component list.
    Protected Overloads Overrides Sub Dispose(ByVal disposing As Boolean)
        If disposing Then
            If Not (components Is Nothing) Then
                components.Dispose()
```

LISTING 31.8
Continued

```
      End If
    End If
    MyBase.Dispose(disposing)
End Sub
'Required by the Windows Form Designer
Private components As System.ComponentModel.IContainer
'NOTE: The following procedure is required by the Windows Form Designer
'It can be modified using the Windows Form Designer.
'Do not modify it using the code editor.
Friend WithEvents m_rbSingleton As System.Windows.Forms.RadioButton
Friend WithEvents m_rbSingleCall As System.Windows.Forms.RadioButton
Friend WithEvents m_btnRegister As System.Windows.Forms.Button
Friend WithEvents m_rbClientActivated As System.Windows.Forms.RadioButton
Friend WithEvents m_grpActivationMode As System.Windows.Forms.GroupBox
Friend WithEvents m_grpChannelType As System.Windows.Forms.GroupBox
Friend WithEvents m_rbTCP As System.Windows.Forms.RadioButton
Friend WithEvents m_rbHTTP As System.Windows.Forms.RadioButton
<System.Diagnostics.DebuggerStepThrough()> Private Sub InitializeComponent()
    Me.m_rbSingleton = New System.Windows.Forms.RadioButton
    Me.m_rbSingleCall = New System.Windows.Forms.RadioButton
    Me.m_btnRegister = New System.Windows.Forms.Button
    Me.m_rbClientActivated = New System.Windows.Forms.RadioButton
    Me.m_grpActivationMode = New System.Windows.Forms.GroupBox
    Me.m_grpChannelType = New System.Windows.Forms.GroupBox
    Me.m_rbTCP = New System.Windows.Forms.RadioButton
    Me.m_rbHTTP = New System.Windows.Forms.RadioButton
    Me.m_grpChannelType.SuspendLayout()
    Me.SuspendLayout()
    '
    'm_rbSingleton
    '
    Me.m_rbSingleton.Checked = True
    Me.m_rbSingleton.Location = New System.Drawing.Point(144, 24)
    Me.m_rbSingleton.Name = "m_rbSingleton"
    Me.m_rbSingleton.TabIndex = 2
    Me.m_rbSingleton.TabStop = True
    Me.m_rbSingleton.Text = "Singleton"
    '
    'm_rbSingleCall
    '
    Me.m_rbSingleCall.Location = New System.Drawing.Point(144, 48)
    Me.m_rbSingleCall.Name = "m_rbSingleCall"
```

31

Explicit Remoting

LISTING 31.8
Continued

```
Me.m_rbSingleCall.TabIndex = 3
Me.m_rbSingleCall.Text = "Single Call"
'
'm_btnRegister
'
Me.m_btnRegister.DialogResult = System.Windows.Forms.DialogResult.OK
Me.m_btnRegister.Location = New System.Drawing.Point(24, 120)
Me.m_btnRegister.Name = "m_btnRegister"
Me.m_btnRegister.Size = New System.Drawing.Size(232, 23)
Me.m_btnRegister.TabIndex = 5
Me.m_btnRegister.Text = "Register"
'
'm_rbClientActivated
'
Me.m_rbClientActivated.Location = New System.Drawing.Point(144, 72)
Me.m_rbClientActivated.Name = "m_rbClientActivated"
Me.m_rbClientActivated.TabIndex = 4
Me.m_rbClientActivated.Text = "Client Activated"
'
'm_grpActivationMode
'
Me.m_grpActivationMode.Location = New System.Drawing.Point(128, 8)
Me.m_grpActivationMode.Name = "m_grpActivationMode"
Me.m_grpActivationMode.Size = New System.Drawing.Size(128, 96)
Me.m_grpActivationMode.TabIndex = 4
Me.m_grpActivationMode.TabStop = False
Me.m_grpActivationMode.Text = "Activation Mode"
'
'm_grpChannelType
'
Me.m_grpChannelType.Controls.Add(Me.m_rbTCP)
Me.m_grpChannelType.Controls.Add(Me.m_rbHTTP)
Me.m_grpChannelType.Location = New System.Drawing.Point(16, 8)
Me.m_grpChannelType.Name = "m_grpChannelType"
Me.m_grpChannelType.Size = New System.Drawing.Size(96, 96)
Me.m_grpChannelType.TabIndex = 6
Me.m_grpChannelType.TabStop = False
Me.m_grpChannelType.Text = "Channel Type"
'
'm_rbTCP
'
Me.m_rbTCP.Checked = True
Me.m_rbTCP.Location = New System.Drawing.Point(8, 16)
```

31

LISTING 31.8
Continued

```
    Me.m_rbTCP.Name = "m_rbTCP"
    Me.m_rbTCP.Size = New System.Drawing.Size(64, 24)
    Me.m_rbTCP.TabIndex = 0
    Me.m_rbTCP.TabStop = True
    Me.m_rbTCP.Text = "TCP"
    '
    'm_rbHTTP
    '
    Me.m_rbHTTP.Location = New System.Drawing.Point(8, 40)
    Me.m_rbHTTP.Name = "m_rbHTTP"
    Me.m_rbHTTP.Size = New System.Drawing.Size(64, 24)
    Me.m_rbHTTP.TabIndex = 1
    Me.m_rbHTTP.Text = "HTTP"
    '
    'MainWindow
    '
    Me.AutoScaleBaseSize = New System.Drawing.Size(5, 13)
    Me.ClientSize = New System.Drawing.Size(296, 158)
    Me.Controls.Add(Me.m_grpChannelType)
    Me.Controls.Add(Me.m_rbClientActivated)
    Me.Controls.Add(Me.m_btnRegister)
    Me.Controls.Add(Me.m_rbSingleton)
    Me.Controls.Add(Me.m_rbSingleCall)
    Me.Controls.Add(Me.m_grpActivationMode)
    Me.Name = "MainWindow"
    Me.Text = "Remoting Host Programmatic"
    Me.m_grpChannelType.ResumeLayout(False)
    Me.ResumeLayout(False)
  End Sub
#End Region
End Class
```

Next, add the code to register the channel and to unregister the channel on exit.
Each channel that receives a call needs to listen on a well-known port. Port 8015
(parameter for constructor) was chosen arbitrarily for this example.

1. Double-click on the Registration button.

2. Add the code in Listing 31.9 in the handler ▆1▆. This code registers either a TCP
   channel or an HTTP channel. It is possible to support both in the same host.
   However, this reduces security by increasing the attack surface and should be
   avoided. Also, the code must remember the channel registered in m_Channel.

3. Unregister the channel in the closing handler (see Listing 31.10).

Explicit Remoting

TIP
If the chosen port number is already used by another application, the call to `RegisterChannel` throws an exception of type `System.Runtime.Remoting.RemotingException`. You must use a specific port only once per machine.

LISTING 31.9
Adding Channel-Registration Code

```
Private m_Channel As IChannel
Private Sub btnRegister_Click(ByVal sender As System.Object, _
    ByVal e As System.EventArgs) Handles m_btnRegister.Click
1       If m_rbTCP.Checked Then
            m_Channel = New TcpChannel(8015)
            ChannelServices.RegisterChannel(m_Channel)
        Else
            m_Channel = New HttpChannel(8015)
            ChannelServices.RegisterChannel(m_Channel)
        End If
End Sub
```

LISTING 31.10
Adding Channel Unregistration When Closing the Application

```
Private Sub MainWindow_Closing(ByVal sender As Object, ByVal e As _
    System.ComponentModel.CancelEventArgs) Handles MyBase.Closing
    If Not m_Channel Is Nothing Then
        ChannelServices.UnregisterChannel(m_Channel)
    End If
End Sub
```

Next you need to add the code in Listing 31.11 to register the service and type of activation (after the channel registration). You should also disable the UI elements for registration (see shaded area **5** in Listing 31.11).

For server-activated calls, `RemotingConfiguration.RegisterWellKnownServiceType` registers the class (see shaded areas **2** and **3** in Listing 31.11). It takes the type of the class to create (see shaded area **1** in Listing 31.11), a universal resource identifier (URI), and the type of server activation (singleton or single call) as parameters. The URI is a string that the client uses to identify this server object.

For client-activated calls, `RemotingConfiguration.RegisterActivatedServiceType` registers the class being available for client activation (see shaded area **4** in Listing 31.11). It takes the type of the class to create (see shaded area **1** in Listing 31.11) as its parameter.

> **TIP**
>
> A Remoting host can support multiple channels, activation modes and classes. Multiple classes for server-activated objects require a new registration with a unique URI for each supported class. Multiple classes for client-activated objects require a new registration for each supported class.

LISTING 31.11
Adding Activation Mode Registration to `btnRegister_Click`

```
Dim serverType As Type                                                    1
serverType = GetType(TestLibrary.TestClass)
If m_rbSingleton.Checked Then
    RemotingConfiguration.RegisterWellKnownServiceType(serverType, _      2
        "TestService", WellKnownObjectMode.Singleton)
ElseIf m_rbSingleCall.Checked Then
    RemotingConfiguration.RegisterWellKnownServiceType(serverType, _      3
        "TestService", WellKnownObjectMode.SingleCall)
Else
    RemotingConfiguration.RegisterActivatedServiceType(serverType)        4
End If
m_rbTCP.Enabled = False                                                   5
m_rbHTTP.Enabled = False
m_rbSingleCall.Enabled = False
m_rbSingleton.Enabled = False
m_rbClientActivated.Enabled = False
m_btnRegister.Enabled = False
```

Creating the Client ClientProgrammatic
Create a new Windows application named ClientProgrammatic to contain the client code for the solution.

1. Add a new VB Windows application project named ClientProgrammatic.

2. Rename `Form1.vb` to `MainWindow.vb`.

3. Rename the `Form1` class to `MainWindow`.

4. Change the startup object in the project's Property dialog box.

5. Add a reference to the TestLibrary project.

6. Add the code in Listing 31.12 to create two radio button groups, a Register button, and a Test button. Switch to designer mode (see Figure 31.8).

31

Explicit Remoting

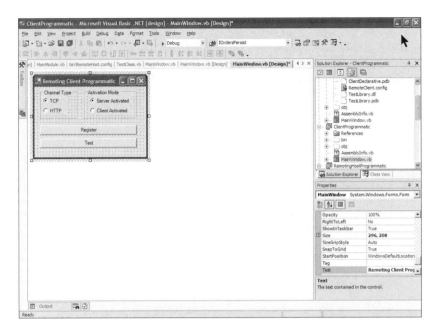

FIGURE 31.8   Programmatic Remoting client UI.

LISTING 31.12
Programmatic Remoting Client

```vb
Imports System.Runtime.Remoting
Imports System.Runtime.Remoting.Channels
Imports System.Runtime.Remoting.Channels.Tcp
Imports System.Runtime.Remoting.Channels.Http
Imports TestLibrary

Public Class MainWindow
    Inherits System.Windows.Forms.Form

#Region " Windows Form Designer generated code "
    Public Sub New()
        MyBase.New()
        'This call is required by the Windows Form Designer.
        InitializeComponent()
        'Add any initialization after the InitializeComponent() call
    End Sub
    'Form overrides dispose to clean up the component list.
    Protected Overloads Overrides Sub Dispose(ByVal disposing As Boolean)
        If disposing Then
            If Not (components Is Nothing) Then
```

LISTING 31.12
Continued

```vb
        components.Dispose()
      End If
    End If
    MyBase.Dispose(disposing)
  End Sub
  'Required by the Windows Form Designer
  Private components As System.ComponentModel.IContainer
  'NOTE: The following procedure is required by the Windows Form Designer
  'It can be modified using the Windows Form Designer.
  'Do not modify it using the code editor.
  Friend WithEvents m_grpChannelType As System.Windows.Forms.GroupBox
  Friend WithEvents m_rbTCP As System.Windows.Forms.RadioButton
  Friend WithEvents m_rbHTTP As System.Windows.Forms.RadioButton
  Friend WithEvents m_rbClientActivated As System.Windows.Forms.RadioButton
  Friend WithEvents m_btnRegister As System.Windows.Forms.Button
  Friend WithEvents m_rbServerActivated As System.Windows.Forms.RadioButton
  Friend WithEvents m_grpActivationMode As System.Windows.Forms.GroupBox
  Friend WithEvents m_btnTest As System.Windows.Forms.Button
  <System.Diagnostics.DebuggerStepThrough()> Private Sub InitializeComponent()
    Me.m_grpChannelType = New System.Windows.Forms.GroupBox
    Me.m_rbTCP = New System.Windows.Forms.RadioButton
    Me.m_rbHTTP = New System.Windows.Forms.RadioButton
    Me.m_rbClientActivated = New System.Windows.Forms.RadioButton
    Me.m_btnRegister = New System.Windows.Forms.Button
    Me.m_rbServerActivated = New System.Windows.Forms.RadioButton
    Me.m_grpActivationMode = New System.Windows.Forms.GroupBox
    Me.m_btnTest = New System.Windows.Forms.Button
    Me.m_grpChannelType.SuspendLayout()
    Me.SuspendLayout()
    '
    'm_grpChannelType
    '
    Me.m_grpChannelType.Controls.Add(Me.m_rbTCP)
    Me.m_grpChannelType.Controls.Add(Me.m_rbHTTP)
    Me.m_grpChannelType.Location = New System.Drawing.Point(16, 8)
    Me.m_grpChannelType.Name = "m_grpChannelType"
    Me.m_grpChannelType.Size = New System.Drawing.Size(96, 72)
    Me.m_grpChannelType.TabIndex = 12
    Me.m_grpChannelType.TabStop = False
    Me.m_grpChannelType.Text = "Channel Type"
    '
    'm_rbTCP
    '
```

31

Explicit Remoting

LISTING 31.12
Continued

```
Me.m_rbTCP.Checked = True
Me.m_rbTCP.Location = New System.Drawing.Point(8, 16)
Me.m_rbTCP.Name = "m_rbTCP"
Me.m_rbTCP.Size = New System.Drawing.Size(64, 24)
Me.m_rbTCP.TabIndex = 0
Me.m_rbTCP.TabStop = True
Me.m_rbTCP.Text = "TCP"
'
'm_rbHTTP
'
Me.m_rbHTTP.Location = New System.Drawing.Point(8, 40)
Me.m_rbHTTP.Name = "m_rbHTTP"
Me.m_rbHTTP.Size = New System.Drawing.Size(64, 24)
Me.m_rbHTTP.TabIndex = 1
Me.m_rbHTTP.Text = "HTTP"
'
'm_rbClientActivated
'
Me.m_rbClientActivated.Location = New System.Drawing.Point(144, 48)
Me.m_rbClientActivated.Name = "m_rbClientActivated"
Me.m_rbClientActivated.TabIndex = 10
Me.m_rbClientActivated.Text = "Client Activated"
'
'm_btnRegister
'
Me.m_btnRegister.DialogResult = System.Windows.Forms.DialogResult.OK
Me.m_btnRegister.Location = New System.Drawing.Point(16, 96)
Me.m_btnRegister.Name = "m_btnRegister"
Me.m_btnRegister.Size = New System.Drawing.Size(248, 23)
Me.m_btnRegister.TabIndex = 11
Me.m_btnRegister.Text = "Register"
'
'm_rbServerActivated
'
Me.m_rbServerActivated.Checked = True
Me.m_rbServerActivated.Location = New System.Drawing.Point(144, 24)
Me.m_rbServerActivated.Name = "m_rbServerActivated"
Me.m_rbServerActivated.Size = New System.Drawing.Size(112, 24)
Me.m_rbServerActivated.TabIndex = 7
Me.m_rbServerActivated.TabStop = True
Me.m_rbServerActivated.Text = "Server Activated"
'
```

LISTING 31.12
Continued

```
    'm_grpActivationMode
    '
    Me.m_grpActivationMode.Location = New System.Drawing.Point(128, 8)
    Me.m_grpActivationMode.Name = "m_grpActivationMode"
    Me.m_grpActivationMode.Size = New System.Drawing.Size(136, 72)
    Me.m_grpActivationMode.TabIndex = 9
    Me.m_grpActivationMode.TabStop = False
    Me.m_grpActivationMode.Text = "Activation Mode"
    '
    'm_btnTest
    '
    Me.m_btnTest.Enabled = False
    Me.m_btnTest.Location = New System.Drawing.Point(16, 128)
    Me.m_btnTest.Name = "m_btnTest"
    Me.m_btnTest.Size = New System.Drawing.Size(248, 23)
    Me.m_btnTest.TabIndex = 13
    Me.m_btnTest.Text = "Test"
    '
    'MainWindow
    '
    Me.AutoScaleBaseSize = New System.Drawing.Size(5, 13)
    Me.ClientSize = New System.Drawing.Size(286, 172)
    Me.Controls.Add(Me.m_btnTest)
    Me.Controls.Add(Me.m_grpChannelType)
    Me.Controls.Add(Me.m_rbClientActivated)
    Me.Controls.Add(Me.m_btnRegister)
    Me.Controls.Add(Me.m_rbServerActivated)
    Me.Controls.Add(Me.m_grpActivationMode)
    Me.Name = "MainWindow"
    Me.Text = "Remoting Client Programmatic"
    Me.m_grpChannelType.ResumeLayout(False)
    Me.ResumeLayout(False)
  End Sub
#End Region
End Class
```

Next, add the code to register the channel and to unregister the channel on exit. Each channel receiving callbacks or events needs to listen on a port. Specifying port 0 causes the framework to pick a port. Alternatively, you can pick a specific port to deal with firewalls.

31

Explicit Remoting

1. Double-click the Registration button.

2. Add the code in Listing 31.13 in the handler **1**. This code registers either a TCP channel or an HTTP channel. Also remember the channel registered in m_Channel. The code starts building a URL to register the object desired (8015 is the port the server has set up).

3. Add the code in Listing 31.14 to unregister the channel in the closing handler.

LISTING 31.13
Adding Channel-Registration Code

```
Private m_Channel As IChannel


Private Sub btnRegister_Click(ByVal sender As System.Object, _
    ByVal e As System.EventArgs) Handles m_btnRegister.Click
    Dim url As String
    If m_rbTCP.Checked Then
        m_Channel = New TcpChannel(0)
        ChannelServices.RegisterChannel(m_Channel)
        url = "tcp://localhost:8015"
    Else
        m_Channel = New HttpChannel(0)
        ChannelServices.RegisterChannel(m_Channel)
        url = "http://localhost:8015"
    End If
End Sub
```

LISTING 31.14
Adding Channel Unregistration When Closing the Application

```
Private Sub MainWindow_Closing(ByVal sender As Object, ByVal e As _
    System.ComponentModel.CancelEventArgs) Handles MyBase.Closing
    If Not m_Channel Is Nothing Then
        ChannelServices.UnregisterChannel(m_Channel)
    End If
End Sub
```

Next you need to add the code in Listing 31.15 to register the class and the activation type of service to create when instantiating the remote object. The activation mode must match the server's activation mode. You should also disable the UI elements for registration (see shaded area **4** in Listing 31.11).

For server-activated calls, RemotingConfiguration.
RegisterWellKnownClientType registers the class (see shaded area **2** in
Listing 31.15). It takes the type of the class to instantiate (see shaded area **1** in
Listing 31.15) and a URL as parameters. The URL consists of the base URL
(tcp://localhost:8015/) and the URI specified by the Remoting host
(TestService). The client cannot vote in the server's activation subtype (single call
or singleton) selection.

For client-activated calls, RemotingConfiguration
RegisterActivatedClientType registers the class being available for client-
activation. It takes the type of the class to instantiate (see shaded area **1** in
Listing 31.15) and a URL as its parameter. The URL is just the base URL (tcp://
localhost:8015/).

LISTING 31.15
Adding Activation Mode Registration to btnRegister_Click

```
Dim serverType As Type                                                    1
serverType = GetType(TestClass)
If m_rbServerActivated.Checked Then
    url += "/TestService"                                                 2
    RemotingConfiguration.RegisterWellKnownClientType(serverType, url)
Else
    RemotingConfiguration.RegisterActivatedClientType(serverType, url)    3
End If
m_rbTCP.Enabled = False                                                   4
m_rbHTTP.Enabled = False
m_rbServerActivated.Enabled = False
m_rbClientActivated.Enabled = False
m_btnRegister.Enabled = False
End Sub
```

Finally, you need to add code to use the remote object.

1. Double-click the Test button to add a handler.

2. Add the code in Listing 31.16 to test the remote class.

LISTING 31.16
Adding Test Calls

```
Private Sub btnTest_Click(ByVal sender As System.Object, _
    ByVal e As System.EventArgs) Handles m_btnTest.Click
    Dim test As TestClass
    test = New TestClass
```

Explicit Remoting

LISTING 31.16
Continued

```
        test.TestMethod()
        test.TestMethod()
    End Sub
End Class
```

Test the Created Solution

Test the solution by starting two Remoting clients and one Remoting host. Try all combinations of channel and activation modes. The channel selection does not change the behavior because it deals only with the transport and serialization behavior.

The activation modes cause the behaviors in Table 31.1. Test that you experience the desired behavior.

TABLE 31.1

Programmatic Remoting Test Results Based on Activation Mode

Clients	Server	Result
Client	Server (any)	Fails
Server	Client	Fails
Client	Client	Counter per client
Server	Server single-call	Counter per call (1)
Server	Server singleton	Shared counter

Remoting with Declarative Configuration

You have learned what is involved with Remoting by calling each registration step manually. This has drawbacks:

▶ Remoting hosts must be written for each remotable object. This causes lots of extra code to be written.

▶ The client is aware of the remote object's location. A core principle of well-designed Remoting is location transparency.

Now you'll learn know how to write Remoting hosts and clients configured with an XML configuration file. This solves both of the drawbacks from the programmatic approach. You will develop the following executables and reuse the solution and test class from the programmatic example.

▶ A Remoting host (UniversalRemoteHost) that loads a configuration file to select and register the channel (TCP or HTTP) and the activation mode (client, server singleton, or server single call)

▶ A client (ClientDeclarative) that loads a configuration file to select and register the channel (TCP or HTTP) and the activation mode (client or server), as well as calls a remote `TestMethod`

TIP

Programmatic as well as declarative Remoting clients can call programmatic or declarative Remoting hosts. This enables you to develop a declarative client first and test it against the programmatic Remoting host.

Creating the Client ClientDeclarative

Create a new Windows application named ClientDeclarative to contain the client code for the solution.

1. Add a new VB Windows application project named ClientDeclarative.

2. Rename `Form1.vb` to `MainWindow.vb`.

3. Rename the `Form1` class to `MainWindow`.

4. Change the startup object in the project's Property dialog box.

5. Add a reference to the TestLibrary project.

6. Add the code in Listing 31.17 to create a Test button. Switch to designer mode (see Figure 31.9).

31

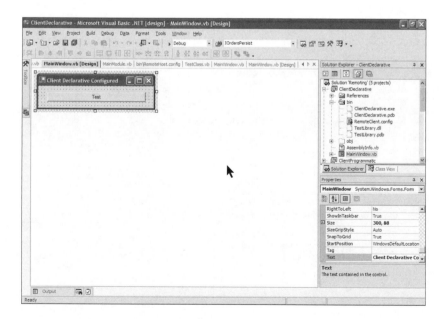

FIGURE 31.9 Declarative Remoting client UI.

Explicit Remoting

LISTING 31.17
Declarative Remoting Client

```vb
Imports System.Runtime.Remoting
Imports TestLibrary

Public Class MainWindow
    Inherits System.Windows.Forms.Form

#Region " Windows Form Designer generated code "
    Public Sub New()
        MyBase.New()
        'This call is required by the Windows Form Designer.
        InitializeComponent()
        'Add any initialization after the InitializeComponent() call
    End Sub
    'Form overrides dispose to clean up the component list.
    Protected Overloads Overrides Sub Dispose(ByVal disposing As Boolean)
        If disposing Then
            If Not (components Is Nothing) Then
                components.Dispose()
            End If
        End If
        MyBase.Dispose(disposing)
    End Sub
    'Required by the Windows Form Designer
    Private components As System.ComponentModel.IContainer
    'NOTE: The following procedure is required by the Windows Form Designer
    'It can be modified using the Windows Form Designer.
    'Do not modify it using the code editor.
    Friend WithEvents m_btnTest As System.Windows.Forms.Button
    <System.Diagnostics.DebuggerStepThrough()> Private Sub InitializeComponent()
        Me.m_btnTest = New System.Windows.Forms.Button
        Me.SuspendLayout()
        '
        'm_btnTest
        '
        Me.m_btnTest.Location = New System.Drawing.Point(24, 16)
        Me.m_btnTest.Name = "m_btnTest"
        Me.m_btnTest.Size = New System.Drawing.Size(248, 23)
        Me.m_btnTest.TabIndex = 15
        Me.m_btnTest.Text = "Test"
        '
        'MainWindow
        '
```

LISTING 31.17
Continued

```
        Me.AutoScaleBaseSize = New System.Drawing.Size(5, 13)
        Me.ClientSize = New System.Drawing.Size(292, 54)
        Me.Controls.Add(Me.m_btnTest)
        Me.Name = "MainWindow"
        Me.Text = "Client Declarative Configured"
        Me.ResumeLayout(False)
    End Sub
#End Region
End Class
```

This next step is the key to using a configuration file. A call to
RemotingConfiguration.Configure with the name of the configuration file
reads the configuration file and essentially executes the same steps previously done
programmatically. The actual configuration file is added to the bin directory.

1. Add the code in Listing 31.18 to use the configuration file
   RemoteClient.config.

2. Click Show All Files for the project ClientDeclarative in Solution Explorer.

3. Right-click on the bin directory and select Add, then Add New Item.

4. Select Application Configuration File.

5. Enter **RemoteClient.config** as the filename.

6. Add the XML in Listing 31.19. This file has configurations for all four combinations of channels and activation modes. Only one should not be commented out at any time. In Listing 31.19, Server-Activated with TCP Channel is active (not in an XML comment) **1**.

LISTING 31.18
Adding Registration Code

```
    Private Sub MainWindow_Load(ByVal sender As System.Object, _
        ByVal e As System.EventArgs) Handles MyBase.Load
      RemotingConfiguration.Configure("RemoteClient.config")
    End Sub
```

LISTING 31.19
Client Configuration File

```
<?xml version="1.0" encoding="utf-8" ?>
<configuration>
  <system.runtime.remoting>
```

Explicit Remoting

LISTING 31.19
Continued

```xml
<application>
  <!-- Client Activated TCP
  <client url="tcp://localhost:8015">
    <activated  type="TestLibrary.TestClass,TestLibrary"/>
  </client>
  <channels>
    <channel ref="tcp" port="0"/>
  </channels>
  -->
  <!-- Server Activated TCP -->
  <client>
    <wellknown  type="TestLibrary.TestClass,TestLibrary"
    url="tcp://localhost:8015/TestService"/>
  </client>
  <channels>
    <channel ref="tcp" port="0"/>
  </channels>
  <!-- -->
  <!-- Client Activated HTTP
  <client url="http://localhost:8015">
    <activated  type="TestLibrary.TestClass,TestLibrary"/>
  </client>
  <channels>
    <channel ref="http" port="0"/>
  </channels>
  -->
  <!-- Server Activated HTTP
  <client>
    <wellknown  type="TestLibrary.TestClass,TestLibrary"
    url="http://localhost:8015/TestService"/>
  </client>
  <channels>
    <channel ref="http" port="0"/>
  </channels>
  -->
</application>
</system.runtime.remoting>
</configuration>
```

1

31

The values are the same as in the previous programmatic configuration. Using the expression `type="TestLibrary.TestClass,TestLibray"` is the same as specifying `serverType` programmatically. `TestLibrary.TestClass` is the fully qualified class name composed of the namespace (`TestLibrary`) and the class name (`TestClass`). `TestLibrary` after the comma is the base name of the assembly containing the class.

Finally, add the same test handler as in the programmatic configuration example.

1. Double-click the Test button to add a handler.

2. Add the code in Listing 31.20. Test this code with the programmatic remote host **1** .

LISTING 31.20
Client Configuration File

```
Private Sub btnTest_Click(ByVal sender As System.Object, _
    ByVal e As System.EventArgs) Handles m_btnTest.Click
    Dim test As TestClass                                    1
    test = New TestClass
    test.TestMethod()
    test.TestMethod()
End Sub
```

Test this client against the previously written Remoting host RemoteHostProgrammatic using the same testing scenarios used with ClientProgrammatic. Instead of selecting a radio button and clicking the Register button, you change which section is commented out in the configuration file `RemoteClient.config`.

Creating the Remoting Host UniversalRemotingHostWin
Now you create a universal Remoting host. The code will always be the same, and configuration is done through a file. You will use a Windows application, for ease of testing.

TIP

For deployment, you should create a service application. The bundled code contains a universal Remoting host UniversalRemotingHostService written as a Service application. You install services with the `installutils.exe` tool included in the .NET Framework.

31

Explicit Remoting

Create a new Windows application named UniversalRemotingHostWin to contain the Remoting host code for the solution.

1. Add a new VB Windows application project named UniversalRemotingHostWin.

2. Rename `Form1.vb` to `MainWindow.vb`.

3. Rename the `Form1` class to `MainWindow`.

4. Change the startup object in the project's Property dialog box.

5. Add a reference to the TestLibrary project.

6. Change the form's `Text` property to Universal Remoting Host.

7. Double-click on the form to create a load handler.

8. Add a line to consume the configuration file RemoteHost.config (see Listing 31.21) ∎**1**. For a service application, add this line in the method `OnStart`.

9. Click Show All Files for the project UniversalRemotingHostWin in Solution Explorer.

10. Right-click on the bin directory and select Add, Add New Item.

11. Select Application Configuration File and enter **RemoteHost.config** as the filename.

12. Add the XML in Listing 31.22. This file has configurations for two channels and three activation modes. Only one of each should be commented out at any time. In Listing 31.22, Server-Activated Singleton ∎**1** with TCP Channel ∎**2** is active (not in an XML comment).

LISTING 31.21
Finishing `UniversalRemotingHostWin`

```
Private Sub MainWindow_Load(ByVal sender As System.Object, _
     ByVal e As System.EventArgs) Handles MyBase.Load
```

1   `RemotingConfiguration.Configure("RemoteHost.config")`

```
End Sub
```

The values are the same as in the previous programmatic configuration. Using the expression `type="TestLibrary.TestClass,TestLibrary"` is the same as specifying `serverType` programmatically. `TestLibrary.TestClass` is the fully qualified class name, composed of the namespace (`TestLibrary`) and the class name (`TestClass`). `TestLibrary` after the comma is the base name of the assembly containing the class.

LISTING 31.22
Server Configuration File

```xml
<?xml version="1.0" encoding="utf-8" ?>
<configuration>
    <system.runtime.Remoting>
        <application>
            <service>
                <!-- Client Activated
                <activated  type="TestLibrary.TestClass,TestLibrary"/>
                -->
                <!-- Server Activated Singleton -->                          1
                <wellknown  type="TestLibrary.TestClass,TestLibrary"
                            mode="Singleton" objectUri="TestService"/>
                <!-- -->
                <!-- Server Activated Single Call
                <wellknown  type="TestLibrary.TestClass,TestLibrary"
                            mode="SingleCall" objectUri="TestService"/>
                -->
            </service>
            <channels>
                <!-- TCP (can support both) -->                              2
                <channel ref="tcp" port="8015"/>
                <!-- -->
                <!-- HTTP (can support both)
                <channel ref="http" port="8015"/>
                -->
            </channels>
        </application>
    </system.runtime.Remoting>
</configuration>
```

Test the Created Solution
Test the solution by starting two Remoting clients and one Remoting host. Try all combinations of channel and activation modes through changes in the configuration files. The channel selection does not change the behavior because it deals with only the transport and serialization behavior.

The activation modes cause the behaviors in Table 31.2. Test that you experience the desired behavior.

31

Explicit Remoting

TABLE 31.2

Declarative Remoting Test Results Based on Activation Mode

Clients	Server	Result
Client	Server (any)	Fails
Server	Client	Fails
Client	Client	Counter per client
Server	Server single-call	Counter per call (1)
Server	Server singleton	Shared counter

> **TIP**
>
> You can also use the Activator class to create objects. This adds flexibility at runtime, at the cost of complexity, and at the loss of location transparency, a key requirement for any good Remoting architecture. Therefore, using New is the preferred method.

Remoting Security Features

Remoting is inherently insecure. The channels provided by default have no way of authenticating (and, therefore, authorizing) the caller, signing the content for message integrity, or encrypting the content for privacy. Furthermore, code access security does not continue the stack walk across a Remoting boundary. Microsoft provides sample code for a secure Remoting channel. However, for fine-grained enterprise-class security in a Remoting situation, Enterprise Services provides a better solution.

Disabling Restrictions on Remote Parameters

As a result of Microsoft's drive to improve security, a filter-level configuration was introduced in .NET 1.1. This prevents complex objects (any object except primitive types and strings) from being marshaled, under the assumption that they might contain malicious code. Unfortunately, this also prevents Remoting from being useful. Therefore, you need to change the channel specifications as in Listings 31.23 **1** **2** and 31.24 **1** **2** **3** **4**.

LISTING 31.23
Filter Level in Server Configuration File

```
<channels>
    <!-- TCP (can support both) -->
    <channel ref="tcp" port="8015">
```

LISTING 31.23
Continued

```
            <serverProviders>                                               1
                <formatter ref="soap"   typeFilterLevel="Full"/>
                <formatter ref="binary" typeFilterLevel="Full"/>
            </serverProviders>
        </channel>
        <!-- -->
        <!-- HTTP (can support both)
        <channel ref="http" port="8015">
            <serverProviders>                                               2
                <formatter ref="soap"   typeFilterLevel="Full"/>
                <formatter ref="binary" typeFilterLevel="Full"/>
            </serverProviders>
        </channel>
        -->
    </channels>
```

LISTING 31.24
Filter Level in Client Configuration File

```
<?xml version="1.0" encoding="utf-8" ?>
<configuration>
    <system.runtime.Remoting>
        <application>
            <!-- Client Activated TCP
            <client url="tcp://localhost:8015">
                <activated  type="TestLibrary.TestClass,TestLibrary"/>
            </client>
            <channels>
                <channel ref="tcp" port="0">
                    <serverProviders>                                       1
                        <formatter ref="soap"   typeFilterLevel="Full"/>
                        <formatter ref="binary" typeFilterLevel="Full"/>
                    </serverProviders>
                </channel>
            </channels>
            -->
            <!-- Server Activated TCP -->
            <client>
                <wellknown  type="TestLibrary.TestClass,TestLibrary"
                url="tcp://localhost:8015/TestService"/>
            </client>
            <channels>
```

31

Remoting Security Features

LISTING 31.24
Continued

```xml
            <channel ref="tcp" port="0">
                <serverProviders>
                    <formatter ref="soap"    typeFilterLevel="Full"/>
                    <formatter ref="binary" typeFilterLevel="Full"/>
                </serverProviders>
            </channel>
        </channels>
        <!-- -->
        <!-- Client Activated HTTP
        <client url="http://localhost:8015">
            <activated  type="TestLibrary.TestClass,TestLibrary"/>
        </client>
        <channels>
            <channel ref="http" port="0">
                <serverProviders>
                    <formatter ref="soap"    typeFilterLevel="Full"/>
                    <formatter ref="binary" typeFilterLevel="Full"/>
                </serverProviders>
            </channel>
        </channels>
        -->
        <!-- Server Activated HTTP
        <client>
            <wellknown  type="TestLibrary.TestClass,TestLibrary"
            url="http://localhost:8015/TestService"/>
        </client>
        <channels>
            <channel ref="http" port="0">
                <serverProviders>
                    <formatter ref="soap"    typeFilterLevel="Full"/>
                    <formatter ref="binary" typeFilterLevel="Full"/>
                </serverProviders>
            </channel>
        </channels>
        -->
    </application>
  </system.runtime.Remoting>
</configuration>
```

Managing a Remote Object's Life Cycle

Local objects have simple life cycles. They are instantiated by the client. Eventually, all references to it go out of scope or are explicitly set to Nothing, which makes them eligible for garbage collection during the next collection cycle.

The situation for remote objects is much more complicated. .NET provides a garbage collector for each Windows process. Therefore, the garbage collector in the remote host's process has no way of knowing when the client releases the object (and collects the proxy as garbage), terminates abnormally, or loses connectivity (temporarily or permanently). Additionally, who keeps the remote object alive?

> **NOTE**
>
> Server-activated single-call objects have simple life cycles. They are created for each call, are kept alive while the call is in progress, and are garbage-collected when the call returns. Therefore, they have no need for life-cycle management, and the rest of this chapter does not apply to them. Unfortunately, this behavior requires clients to be aware of the server-activation mode (singleton or single-call), which is really an internal server-side decision.

DCOM solved these problems with a complex handshake between remote objects that adds unnecessary overhead for the normal case.

31

.NET Remoting solves it with a less expensive method. The Remoting infrastructure provides a lease manager per application domain. Each exposed remote object is associated with a lease object. The lease manager keeps track of all leases in the system. The lease object holds a reference to the remote object that keeps it alive. Passing the object reference outside the process creates a lease. Leases are used for client-activated and server-activated singleton remote objects. Each lease has a lease timeout (default 5 minutes). When this timeout expires, the lease removes itself and the remote object is available for garbage collection. The lease timeout can be controlled by both the client and the remote object.

The lease class implements the interface ILease (see Listing 31.25), which is used to control the lease and is defined in System.Runtime.Remoting.Lifetime. CurrentLeaseTime returns the time left on the lease. CurrentState returns a LeaseState as Initial, Active, Expired, or Renewing. InitialLeaseTime is the time initially set; RenewalOnCall auto renews the lease for this time on every call. Renew allows for explicit renewal of the lease. Do not use explicit renewal. You'll learn about sponsorship (SponsorshipTimeout, Register, and Unregister) later.

Managing a Remote Object's Life Cycle

LISTING 31.25
`ILease` Definition

```
Public Interface ILease
    ReadOnly Property CurrentLeaseTime() As TimeSpan
    ReadOnly Property CurrentState() As LeaseState
    Property InitialLeaseTime() As TimeSpan
    Property RenewOnCallTime() As TimeSpan
    Property SponsorshipTimeout() As TimeSpan

    Function Renew(ByVal renewalTime As TimeSpan) As TimeSpan
    Sub Register(ByVal obj As ISponsor)
    Sub Register(ByVal obj As ISponsor, ByVal renewalTime As TimeSpan)
    Sub Unregister(ByVal obj As ISponsor)
End Interface
```

You will learn this information:

▶ How the remote object can control its own lease. This is very useful for single-ton objects, which should run independently of the clients.

▶ How the client can use explicit lease renewal. This is useful for client-activated remote objects. Its use is discouraged because it increases network traffic in a similar way to DCOM's solution.

▶ How to use a lease sponsor and a sponsorship manager to keep client-activated objects alive without incurring the overhead of explicit lease renewal.

How a Remote Object Controls Its Own Lease

The remote object can control its own lease parameters. They override `MarshalByRefObject.InitializeLifetimeService`, call the base class `InitializeLifetimeService`, and modify the lease object before returning it. This method is called when an object is created remotely, and after object construction but before the first call is handled. Trying to modify these values later is not valid and throws an exception of type `System.Runtime.Remoting.RemotingException`.

Client-activated objects should set `InitialLeaseTime` and `RenewOnCallTime` to the same value and should use a shorter timeout for sponsorship (see Listing 31.26).

LISTING 31.26
`InitializeLifetimeService` for a Client-Activated Object

```
Public Overrides Function InitializeLifetimeService() As Object
    Dim lease As ILease
    lease = CType(MyBase.InitializeLifetimeService(), ILease)
```

LISTING 31.26
Continued

```
        lease.InitialLeaseTime = TimeSpan.FromMinutes(10)
        lease.RenewOnCallTime = lease.InitialLeaseTime
        lease.SponsorshipTimeout = TimeSpan.FromSeconds(10)
        Return lease
    End Function
```

Server-activated single-call objects do not require a lease.

Server-activated singleton objects should live forever. The default lease time is 5 minutes, but even setting a very long time is not forever. The solution is to return Nothing **1** from `InitializeLifetimeService` to indicate an indefinite lease (see Listing 31.27).

LISTING 31.27
`InitializeLifetimeService` for a Server-Activated Singleton Object

```
    Public Overrides Function InitializeLifetimeService() As Object
        Return Nothing                                               1
    End Function
```

Renewing Leases with Explicit Lease Renewal

Server objects and clients can explicitly renew a lease (see Listings 31.28 and 31.29). This is bad way of keeping leases alive. The correct way is to provide a sponsor.

LISTING 31.28
Explicit Lease Renewal in the Remote Object

```
    Dim lease As ILease
    lease = CType(RemotingServices.GetLifetimeService(Me), ILease)
    lease.Renew(lease.InitialLeaseTime) 'initial time is a good choice
```

LISTING 31.29
Explicit Lease Renewal in the Client

```
    Dim obj as New TestClass
    ... more code
    Dim lease As ILease
    lease = CType(RemotingServices.GetLifetimeService(obj), ILease)
    lease.Renew(lease.InitialLeaseTime) 'initial time is a good choice
```

31

Managing a Remote Object's Life Cycle

Using a Sponsor to Manage a Remote Object's Lease

A sponsor is a third party that is asked to renew the lease on behalf of the client when the lease expires (see Figure 31.10). A lease can have multiple sponsors; each one is asked by the lease manager, in turn, until one renews the lease or all of them decide not to renew. If no one renews the lease, the lease expires and the remote object is garbage collected. If the sponsor is not reachable, the lease manager waits for, at most, the sponsorship timeout. The sponsor is a remotable object that implements ISponsor, and the client must keep a reference to the sponsor to keep it alive.

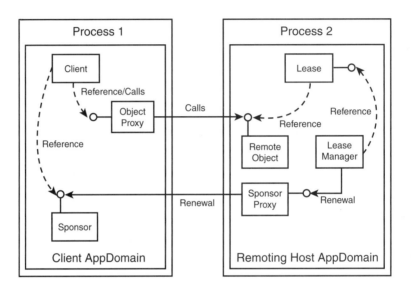

FIGURE 31.10   Sponsorship architecture.

ISponsor has one method, Renewal. Sponsors should always renew for the InitialTimeout duration. A simple sponsor looks like the one in Listing 31.30.

LISTING 31.30
Simple Sponsor

```
Imports System.Runtime.Remoting.Lifetime

Public Class SimpleSponsor
    Inherits MarshalByRefObject
    Implements ISponsor

    Public Function Renewal(ByVal lease As _
        System.Runtime.Remoting.Lifetime.ILease) As System.TimeSpan _
        Implements System.Runtime.Remoting.Lifetime.ISponsor.Renewal
```

LISTING 31.30
Continued

```
        Return lease.InitialLeaseTime
    End Function
End Class


Public Class SampleClient
    Public m_Object As TestObject
    Public m_Sponsor As Sponsor

    Public Sub New()
        m_Object = New TestObject
        m_Sponsor = New Sponsor
        Dim lease As ILease
        lease = CType(m_Object.GetLifetimeService(), ILease)
        lease.Register(m_Sponsor)
    End Sub
    'more code
End Class
```

The simple sponsor leaves a lot of housekeeping to the application code (the sample is actually incomplete).

This housekeeping can be abstracted into a universal sponsor. You can use it for every client-activated remote object. .NET provides a prebuilt universal sponsor, ClientSponsor, which does not handle renewal times correctly or implement cleanup code.

You will now develop your own universal sponsor as a class library named UniversalSponsor. You can reuse this sponsor whenever you need a sponsor for any project.

1. Add a new VB class library project named UniversalSponsor.

2. Delete Class1.vb.

3. Add a new class, Sponsor, to the project.

4. Replace the code with Listing 31.31.

LISTING 31.31
Universal Sponsor

```
Imports System.Runtime.Remoting.Contexts
Imports System.Runtime.Remoting.Lifetime
```

31

Managing a Remote Object's Life Cycle

LISTING 31.31
Continued

```vbnet
<Synchronization(SynchronizationAttribute.REQUIRES_NEW)> _
Public Class Sponsor
    Inherits ContextBoundObject
    Implements ISponsor, IDisposable

    Private m_LeaseList As Hashtable
    Private m_Disposed As Boolean

    Public Sub New()
        m_Disposed = False
        m_LeaseList = New Hashtable(8)
        Dim s As New ClientSponsor
    End Sub

    Public Function Renewal(ByVal lease As _
            System.Runtime.Remoting.Lifetime.ILease) As System.TimeSpan _
            Implements ISponsor.Renewal
        Return lease.InitialLeaseTime
    End Function

    Public Sub Register(ByVal obj As MarshalByRefObject)
        If Not m_Disposed Then
            'Use object only if not disposed
            Dim lease As ILease
            lease = CType(obj.GetLifetimeService(), ILease)
            If Not lease Is Nothing Then
                'object has a lease associated with it
                If Not m_LeaseList.Contains(lease) Then
                    'register only once
                    lease.Register(Me)
                    m_LeaseList.Add(obj, Nothing)
                End If
            End If
        End If
    End Sub

    Public Sub Unregister(ByVal obj As MarshalByRefObject)
        If Not m_Disposed Then
            'Use object only if not disposed
            Try
                Dim lease As ILease
                lease = CType(obj.GetLifetimeService(), ILease)
```

31

LISTING 31.31
Continued

```vb
            If Not lease Is Nothing Then
                'object has a lease associated with it
                If m_LeaseList.Contains(obj) Then
                    'unregister only once
                    lease.Unregister(Me)
                    m_LeaseList.Remove(obj)
                End If
            End If
        Catch ex As Exception
            'remote object no longer exists
        Finally
            If m_LeaseList.Contains(obj) Then
                'remove from list
                m_LeaseList.Remove(obj)
            End If
        End Try
    End If
End Sub


Public Sub Dispose() Implements System.IDisposable.Dispose
    Dispose(True)
End Sub


Protected Overrides Sub Finalize()
    Dispose(False)
End Sub


Private Sub Dispose(ByVal disposing As Boolean)
    If Not m_Disposed Then
        'Do not dispose twice
        Try
            For Each leaseObject As Object In m_LeaseList
                'unregister every lease sponsor
                Dim lease As ILease = CType(leaseObject, ILease)
                If Not lease Is Nothing Then
                    lease.Unregister(Me)
                End If
            Next
        Catch ex As Exception
            'remote object no longer exists
        Finally
            m_LeaseList.Clear()
```

31

Managing a Remote Object's Life Cycle

LISTING 31.31
Continued

```
            'prevent duplicate dispose
            m_Disposed = True
            If disposing Then
                'suppress finalization since Dispose cleaned up already
                GC.SuppressFinalize(Me)
            End If
        End Try
    End If
   End Sub
End Class
```

This class keeps a hash table with a list of leases registered and implements a
`Renewal` method, a `Register` method that registers this object as the sponsor for
the object passed, an `Unregister` method, and a `Dispose` method for cleanup.
Access to the hash table must be protected from concurrent access; the context-
bound attribute `Synchronization` was used for this. Please note the defensive code
to protect from crossing `Unregister` and `Dispose` with `Renewal`. Additionally,
the class protects itself from being used after `Dispose` has been called; it suppresses
finalization after `Dispose` has been called.

31

> **TIP**
>
> .NET 1.1 provides a built-in universal sponsor, `ClientSponsor`. Unfortunately, it does not provide
> the correct behavior for `Renewal`. It always returns its own property, `RenewalTime`. The universal
> sponsor in this chapter returns the lease's own `InitialLeaseTime`. Additionally, this lease manger
> cleans up its registration when it is disposed of or finalized.

Next, modify ClientDeclarative to use the new universal sponsor (see Listing 31.32).

1. Add a reference to the project UniversalSponsor.

2. Change the configuration files in both the client and the
   UniversalRemotingHost to use client activation over TCP.

3. Add a button m_btnNew with text New.

4. Add a button m_btnCall with text Call.

5. Add a button m_btnRelease with text Release.

6. Create handlers for the three new buttons and the form window by double-
   clicking on all of them.

7. Rename the button handlers as shown in Listing 31.32.

8. Add private member fields m_Object and m_Sponsor (see shaded area **1** in Listing 31.32).

9. Instantiate object m_Sponsor before the Remoting configuration in MainWindow_Load, as well as hooking the OnExit method to the event Application.Exit (this wires the cleanup correctly when exiting the application) (see shaded area **2** Listing 31.32).

10. Add a handler OnExit for the event Application.Exit to dispose of m_Sponsor (see shaded area **3** in Listing 31.32).

11. Instantiate object m_Object in the handler for m_btnNew, and register it with m_Sponsor (see shaded area **4** in Listing 31.32).

12. Call TestMethod in the handler for m_btnCall (see shaded area **5** in Listing 31.32).

13. Unregister m_Object with m_Sponsor, and set m_Object to Nothing in the handler for m_btnRelease **6**.

LISTING 31.32
Revised ClientDeclarative

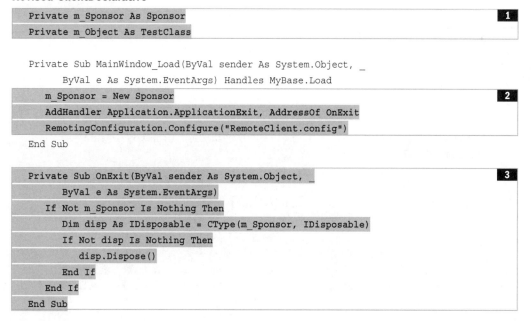

```
Private m_Sponsor As Sponsor                                            1
Private m_Object As TestClass

Private Sub MainWindow_Load(ByVal sender As System.Object, _
    ByVal e As System.EventArgs) Handles MyBase.Load
    m_Sponsor = New Sponsor                                             2
    AddHandler Application.ApplicationExit, AddressOf OnExit
    RemotingConfiguration.Configure("RemoteClient.config")
End Sub

Private Sub OnExit(ByVal sender As System.Object, _                     3
    ByVal e As System.EventArgs)
    If Not m_Sponsor Is Nothing Then
        Dim disp As IDisposable = CType(m_Sponsor, IDisposable)
        If Not disp Is Nothing Then
            disp.Dispose()
        End If
    End If
End Sub
```

31

Managing a Remote Object's Life Cycle

LISTING 31.32
Continued

```vb
Private Sub btnTest_Click(ByVal sender As System.Object, _
    ByVal e As System.EventArgs) Handles m_btnTest.Click
  Dim test As TestClass
  test = New TestClass
  test.TestMethod()
  test.TestMethod()
End Sub

Private Sub btnNew_Click(ByVal sender As System.Object, _
    ByVal e As System.EventArgs) Handles m_btnNew.Click
```
```vb
  If m_Object Is Nothing Then
      m_Object = New TestClass
      m_Sponsor.Register(m_Object)
  End If
```
```vb
End Sub

Private Sub btnCall_Click(ByVal sender As System.Object, _
    ByVal e As System.EventArgs) Handles m_btnCall.Click
```
```vb
  m_Object.TestMethod()
```
```vb
End Sub

Private Sub btnRelease_Click(ByVal sender As System.Object, _
    ByVal e As System.EventArgs) Handles m_btnRelease.Click
```
```vb
  m_Sponsor.Unregister(m_Object)
  m_Object = Nothing
```
```vb
End Sub
```

Next, add `InitializeLifetimeService` with short timeouts to the `TestClass`
(see Listing 31.33).

LISTING 31.33
Add `InitializeLifetimeService` to `TestClass`

```vb
'use for client activated objects
Public Overrides Function InitializeLifetimeService() As Object
  Dim lease As ILease
  lease = CType(MyBase.InitializeLifetimeService(), ILease)
  lease.InitialLeaseTime = TimeSpan.FromSeconds(20) 'test: short time
```

LISTING 31.33
Continued

```
    lease.RenewOnCallTime = lease.InitialLeaseTime
    lease.SponsorshipTimeout = TimeSpan.FromSeconds(10)
    Return lease
End Function
```

You are ready to explore the sponsorship behavior.

1. Set ClientDeclarative as the startup project.

2. Set a breakpoint in `UniversalSponsor.Sponsor.Renewal`.

3. Start ClientDeclarative (F5).

4. Start UniversalRemotingHostWin (right-click, Debug, Start New Instance).

5. In the client, click New (click OK on all message boxes).

6. After 20 seconds, the lease timeout expires and your breakpoint is reached.

7. Click Continue.

8. Click Test; after another 20 seconds, the lease timeout expires again, and your breakpoint is reached.

9. This time, wait more than 10 seconds before clicking Continue.

10. Click Test again. You encounter an exception. The sponsorship timeout (set to 10 seconds) expires and causes the lease to terminate.

11. Continue testing with different timing scenarios until you understand the behavior completely.

Life Cycle Best Practices

Client-activated remote objects should set acceptable timeout values in `InitializeLifetimeService`. Clients using client-activated remote objects should use `UniversalSponsor.Sponsor` to keep the object alive and dispose of the sponsor before exiting.

Server-activated single-call remote objects do not require any life cycle management on the client or the server.

Server-activated singleton remote object should return a `Nothing` lease from `InitializeLifetimeService`. They require no life-cycle management from the client.

31

One-Way Calls and Remote Events

Methods tagged with the attribute <OneWay> may not return any parameters or throw any exceptions. Remotely invoking one-way methods makes them asynchronous because the stub returns after starting the actual call. This is most useful for remote events. Events should always be one-way and asynchronous.

Remote event handlers must reside in a remotable class. You will add a class to your declarative client to receive the counter value after it has been updated in TestLibrary.TestClass. In the project ClientDeclarative, add the class TestEventHandler (see Listing 31.34).

LISTING 31.34
TestEventHandler

```
Imports System.Runtime.Remoting.Messaging
Imports System.Windows.Forms

Public Class TestEventHandler
    Inherits MarshalByRefObject

    <OneWay()> _
    Public Sub UpdateHandler(ByVal counter As Integer)
        MessageBox.Show("counter=" + counter.ToString(), "TestEventHandler")
    End Sub
End Class
```

Add an event UpdateEvent to the class TestClass, and add a RaiseEvent after incrementing m_Counter in TestLibrary.TestMethod (see Listing 31.35).

LISTING 31.35
Expanded TestLibrary

```
    Public Event UpdateEvent(ByVal counter As Integer)
'in TestMethod:
        RaiseEvent UpdateEvent(m_Counter)
```

Finally, you need to hook up the event in the client code. Add an event handler after creating the object, and remove the handler before releasing the object (see Listing 31.36).

LISTING 31.36
Revised Code for `btnNew_Click` **and** `btnRelease_Click`

```
Private Sub btnNew_Click(ByVal sender As System.Object,_
    ByVal e As System.EventArgs) Handles m_btnNew.Click
  If m_Object Is Nothing Then
    m_Object = New TestClass
    m_Sponsor.Register(m_Object)
      AddHandler m_Object.UpdateEvent, _                       ▮1
        AddressOf m_UpdateHandler.UpdateHandler
    End If
End Sub
Private Sub btnRelease_Click(ByVal sender As System.Object, _
    ByVal e As System.EventArgs) Handles m_btnRelease.Click
    RemoveHandler m_Object.UpdateEvent, _                      ▮2
      AddressOf m_UpdateHandler.UpdateHandler
  m_Sponsor.Unregister(m_Object)
  m_Object = Nothing
End Sub
```

Contexts and Services

Contexts provide an extensive environment for objects with "special" needs. Calls
into contexts are intercepted, and the interceptors can provide services. For example,
.NET uses contexts to provide high-level synchronization in a multithreaded application. The context architecture is potentially extensible with context attributes. Unlike
regular attributes, .NET is fully aware of context attributes, and it consults them
when creating a context-bound object. They can accept the existing context, demand
a new context, and install interceptors to provide services. However, this feature is
undocumented and will potentially be deprecated in Indigo.

31

> Indigo is Microsoft's next-generation messaging and Remoting infrastructure. It
> provides a unification of Remoting, web services, and Enterprise Services. It will provide
> the extensibility from `ContextBoundObjects`, the interoperability through web
> services, and the richness of services from Enterprise Service. Indigo is assumed to be
> available in the Longhorn (Microsoft's next major version of Windows) time frame.

Object, MarshalByRefObject, **and** ContextBoundObject

All objects are subdivided into regular context-agile (derived from Object), remotable context-agile (derived from MarshalByRefObject), and context-bound (derived from ContextBoundObject, which is derived from MarshalByRefObject) objects. Every object executes in a context (each application domain has a default context). Basic objects are context agile and execute in the context of the calling object. Context-bound objects are assigned to a context at instantiation. During construction, their attributes are asked whether the context of the creating object is acceptable. If it is not, they are created in their own context. When they are created, they always execute in this context. Context-bound objects are always called through a proxy, even if they are called from the same context.

Cross-context calls (between two context-bound objects) are implicitly remoted with a highly efficient Remoting channel. No user work is required because a ContextBoundObject is also a MarshallByRefObject.

Services

.NET provides one service: synchronization. The attribute <Synchronization> assigns an object to a synchronization domain. All calls are synchronized when entering the synchronization domain. Only one physical thread can execute in a synchronization domain at any time (see Chapter 27, "Multithreading"). We used this method of synchronization for our universal sponsor (see Listing 31.31).

31

Summary

You learned about Remoting, the interception architecture, activation modes, channels, distributed garbage collection, and remote events.

Remoting is location transparent and requires the assembly (or at least a metadata assembly created with soapsuds.exe) to be distributed with the clients. For remote events, the clients need to submit the assembly or a metadata data assembly to the server. This does not qualify as loosely coupled systems. Furthermore, Remoting does not offer a secure channel. It is recommended that you use Enterprise Services or web services for Remoting and multitier architectures.

Further Reading

Lowy, Juval. "Decouple Components by Injecting Custom Services into Your Object's Interception Chain." MSDN website, http://www.msdn.microsoft.com/msdnmag/issues/03/03/ContextsinNET/default.aspx.

Lowy, Juval. "Managing the Lifetime of Remote .NET Objects with Leasing and Sponsorship." MSDN website, http://msdn.microsoft.com/msdnmag/issues/03/12/LeaseManager/default.aspx.

31

Part VIII

Web Services

Web services provide a means of interacting with objects over a network. By using web services, applications running on different operating systems can interact with each other over a distributed network such as the Internet. Web services open a host of possibilities by which business organizations can interact with their customers and partners to share data and functionality.

Historically, several programming frameworks have been developed to enable two objects on different computers to interact with each other. What makes web services attractive is that fact that they use widely adopted standards for communication and data storage.

In this chapter, you will learn how to use Visual Studio .NET to create and consume a web service. The chapter discusses how to call publicly available web services in addition to those that you developed for internal use.

You also learn how to customize the behavior of a web service, such as caching and state management, by using the `WebService` and `WebMethod` attributes.

Finally, the chapter explains how you can extend the capabilities of a web service by passing information as part of the web service's SOAP header.

WHAT YOU NEED

SOFTWARE REQUIREMENTS	Windows 2000, XP, or 2003 .NET Framework SDK v1.1 Visual Studio .NET 2003 with Visual Basic .NET installed Internet Information Services 5.0 or above
HARDWARE RECOMMENDATION	PC that meets .NET SDK minimum requirements
SKILL REQUIREMENTS	Familiarity with Visual Basic .NET Knowledge of how to develop a Windows application Knowledge of how to develop a web application

BASIC WEB SERVICES AT A GLANCE

BASIC WEB SERVICES AT A GLANCE

Web Services Protocols

The key to understanding web services is to know about the following protocols that make web services possible:

▶ **DISCO and Universal Description, Discovery, and Integration (UDDI)**—Before you can access a web service, you need to know where to find one. Web services can be published through Microsoft's DISCO (short for Discovery) or the industry-wide OASIS UDDI Initiative (http://www.uddi.org).

▶ **Web Services Description Language (WSDL)**—WSDL describes the characteristics of a web service. With the help of WSDL, a web service can tell its client about the messages it accepts and the result it returns.

▶ **Simple Object Access Protocol (SOAP)**—SOAP specifies how messages are transported from one computer to another via the networks such as the Internet. To support multiple platforms, SOAP relies on widely adopted standards such as the Extensible Markup Language (XML) and the Hypertext Transfer Protocol (HTTP) to enable message transport. SOAP messages are encapsulated in an XML packet and then are transmitted over an HTTP channel.

32

> **NOTE**
>
> The SOAP specification allows for messages to be sent by using Internet transport protocols such as HTTP, the Simple Mail Transfer Protocol (SMTP), or the File Transfer Protocol (FTP). However, most SOAP implementations, including the .NET Framework, use HTTP as the transport protocol.

Creating a Web Service

Visual Studio .NET simplifies the process of creating and using web services. The details of the underlying protocols are made completely transparent so that you can focus on the business logic.

In this section, you will create a simple web service that calculates the area and perimeter of a rectangle. To create a web service, you need to create a new Visual Basic project based on the ASP.NET web service template, as shown in Figure 32.1.

Creating a Web Service

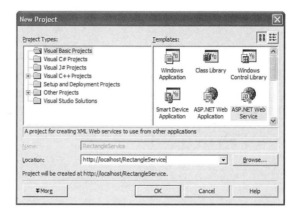

FIGURE 32.1   The ASP.NET web service template enables you to create a web service.

After the web service project is created, you might want to change the name of the default web service file from `Service1.asmx` to `RectangleService.asmx`. Change the code of the `RectangleService.asmx` file as shown in Listing 32.1.

LISTING 32.1

Creating a Simple Web Service: RectangleService.asmx

```
Imports System.Web.Services

<System.Web.Services.WebService(Namespace:= _
    "http://RectangleService/RectangleService")> _
Public Class RectangleService
    Inherits System.Web.Services.WebService

    'Web Services Designer Generated Code

    <WebMethod()> _
    Public Function Area(ByVal Length As Double, _
        ByVal Width As Double) As Double
        Return Length * Width
    End Function

    <WebMethod()> _
    Public Function Perimeter(ByVal Length As Double, _
        ByVal Width As Double) As Double
        Return 2 * (Length + Width)
    End Function
End Class
```

32

Defining a web service class is very similar to defining a class, except for the following main distinctions:

▶ The web service class inherits from the `System.Web.Services.WebService` class.

▶ The `WebService` attribute is applied on the web service class.

▶ The `WebMethod` attribute is applied on each public method that is exposed via the web service.

You just created a web service named `RectangleService` on your local web server that is ready for use. The URL of your web service is http://localhost/RectangleService/RectangleService.asmx.

Testing a Web Service

The .NET Framework enables you to test simple web services just by using a web browser. When you run the project or type the URL of the `RectangleService` in a web browser, you will see a screen like the one in Figure 32.2.

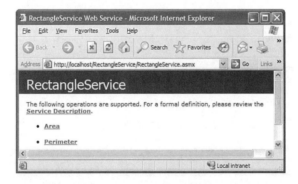

FIGURE 32.2   Testing an ASP.NET web service by using a web browser.

The web service lists only the public methods that are marked with the `WebMethod` attribute. These methods are also known as *web methods*.

When you click on a web method (such as `Area`), you will see a test page that enables you to invoke the method by passing the input parameters, as shown in Figure 32.3.

> **NOTE**
>
> A web service can be invoked in different ways, such as sending a SOAP message, sending an HTTP POST message, or sending an HTTP GET message. When you test the web service in a web browser, as shown in Figure 32.3, you are invoking the web service by sending an HTTP GET message.

32

Creating a Web Service

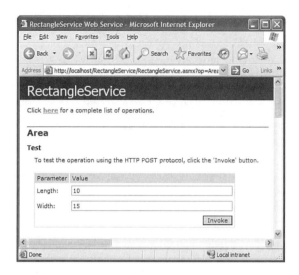

FIGURE 32.3   All public methods marked with the `WebMethod` attributes are exposed by the web service.

Enter values for `Length` and `Width`, and click the Invoke button. You will see the response from the web service in a separate window, as shown in Figure 32.4.

FIGURE 32.4   The web service response is returned in XML format.

You can also access the interface of an ASP.NET web service by appending the `WSDL` query string to the web service URL. For example, to retrieve the interface for the `RectangleService` web service, you use the following URL, as shown in Figure 32.5: http://localhost/RectangleService/RectangleService.asmx?WSDL.

The output of this command is XML data that explains the messages understood by the RectangleService, its parameters, and its return type.

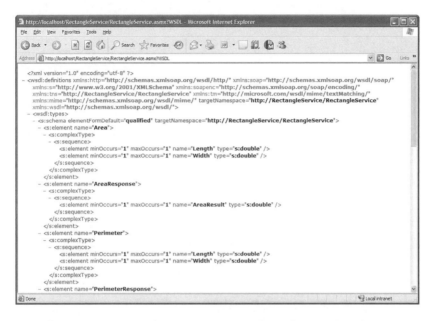

FIGURE 32.5   The WSDL describes the interface of the web service.

TESTING WEB SERVICES

One of the limitations of testing web services using a web browser is that complex parameters cannot be passed to the web service. This is because HTTP GET and HTTP POST protocols pass information to web methods in name-value pairs.

Many tools are available that enable you to test a web service with a finer level of control using a SOAP protocol that allows you to pass complex parameters to the web methods. One such tool is .NET Web Service Studio, which can be downloaded from http://www.gotdotnet.com/team/tools/web_svc.

Figure 32.6 shows how the RectangleService is invoked by using the .NET Web Service Studio tool.

This tool can be especially helpful in testing web services that are not written by using the .NET Framework and, therefore, do not provide a web browser test page.

32

Creating a Web Service

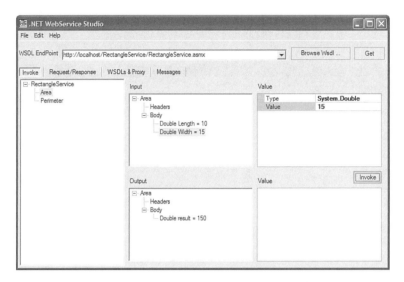

FIGURE 32.6   .NET Web Service Studio provides advanced options for testing a web service using a SOAP protocol.

Invoking a Web Service

In this section, you'll learn how to invoke a web service from a .NET application. You can invoke a web service by using different types of applications, such as a console application, a Windows application, or a web application. A Windows application is used in this section, but the process remains the same for other types of applications.

First, you need to create a new Visual Basic project based on the Windows Application template. Name the project `RectangleClient`. Create a Windows Form interface similar to that shown in Figure 32.7

To invoke a web Service, you'll need to add a web reference to the web service in the project. To do this, select the Project, Add Web Reference menu item. In the Add Web Reference dialog box, type the URL of the web service and click the Go button. Visual Studio .NET finds the web service, as shown in Figure 32.8. To add a reference to this web service in your project, click the Add Reference button.

TIP

The Web Reference name enables you to access the web service in your program. For example, the web service in Figure 32.8 will be identified as `localhost.RectangleService` in the client application. You can also use the Add Web Reference dialog box to assign a more useful name to your web reference.

FIGURE 32.7 Interface of a Windows application that you will use to invoke the RectangleService web service.

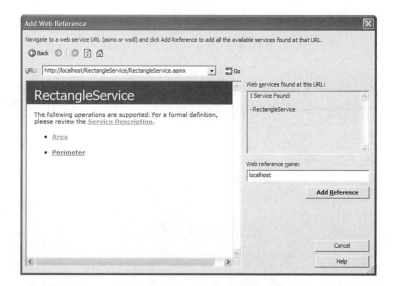

FIGURE 32.8 The Add Web Reference dialog box enables you to add a reference to a web service in your project.

To invoke the web service, you write an event handler for the Button object, as shown in Listing 32.2.

Invoking a Web Service

LISTING 32.2
Invoking a Web Service

```
Private Sub btnCalculate_Click(ByVal sender As System.Object, _
    ByVal e As System.EventArgs) Handles btnCalculate.Click
    Dim dblLength As Double
    Dim dblWidth As Double

    dblLength = Convert.ToDouble(txtLength.Text)
    dblWidth = Convert.ToDouble(txtWidth.Text)

    Dim rectService As localhost.RectangleService
    rectService = New localhost.RectangleService
    If (rbArea.Checked) Then
        txtResult.Text = rectService.Area( _
            dblLength, dblWidth).ToString()
    Else
        txtResult.Text = rectService.Perimeter( _
            dblLength, dblWidth).ToString()
    End If
End Sub
```

The code first creates a new instance of the web service object. **1** Depending on the user's selection, either the Area method **2** or the Perimeter method **3** of the web service is invoked.

To test your project, build and run it. Type the values for length and width, select the calculation you want to perform (area or perimeter), and click the Calculate button. The application invokes the web service behind the scene and displays the results shown in Figure 32.9.

FIGURE 32.9 A Windows application that invokes the RectangleService web service.

You can see in this exercise that after you add a web reference to a web service in your application, you can use it just like any other component.

TIP
If the web service is updated, you need not go through the complete exercise of removing and adding a web reference. Instead, you can just select **Project, Update Web Reference**.

Although it looks so simple, a lot of things are happening in the background:

▸ When you create the web reference, Visual Studio .NET reads the web service WSDL to determine what web services and methods are available from the web server.

▸ Visual Studio .NET then creates a `Reference.vb` file from the information contained in the WSDL file. The `Reference.vb` file is also called the web server proxy. The proxy contains the declaration for the web service class and its member (but contains no functionality). This proxy enables Visual Studio .NET to display IntelliSense when you are using the web services objects in your program. You can see the web services proxy shown in Figure 32.10 by selecting Project, Show All Files.

▸ When you call a method on a remote object, your call is translated into a SOAP message using the SOAP protocol and is transmitted to the web server.

▸ The application waits for the web server to process the message and generate the response. When the response is generated, the XML is parsed and the results are available in the application for further processing.

32

FIGURE 32.10   The `Reference.vb` file acts as a proxy for the web service.

TIP

The process of communicating with a web service suffers from overhead required for network communication. You can optimize the performance of the web service and the client program by minimizing the number of network requests needed to accomplish a task.

One way to achieve better performance is to have the methods return related information together. For example, instead of having separate methods that return the name, address, city, and state for a customer, you could design a method that returns all the information combined together.

Creating a Web Service That Uses Complex Parameters

The `RectangleService` web service created earlier in this chapter uses only primitive parameters. Because the data is formatted into XML, it is possible to pass complex types to and from a web service. These complex parameters can be predefined .NET Framework types such as `DataSet` or `DataView`, or they can be custom-defined types such as `Customer` or `Order`, as long as the complex parameters can be serialized to XML. For more information on serializing objects, see Chapter 24, "IO and Persistence."

In this section, you will create a web service that receives and returns a strongly typed `DataSet` object. For more information on strongly typed `DataSets`, see Chapter 11, "Working with ADO.NET Classes." The strongly typed `DataSet` object will contain customer information from the Northwind sample database provided with SQL Server 2000.

Begin by creating a new Visual Basic project based on the ASP.NET web service template. Call this web service `CustomersService`.

To create a strongly typed `DataSet`, drag the Customers table from Server Explorer and drop it onto the design surface of the web service. This creates `SqlConnection` and `SqlDataAdapter` objects. Right-click the `SqlDataAdapter` object and select Generate DataSet. In the Generate DataSet dialog box, name the strongly typed `DataSet` object `CustomersDataSet`, as shown in Figure 32.11.

Modify the web service name to `CustomersService.asmx`, and add the following two web methods: `RetrieveCustomers` and `UpdateCustomers`. These are shown in Listing 32.3.

LISTING 32.3
Creating a Web Service That Uses Complex Parameters: CustomersService.asmx

```
Imports System.Web.Services

<System.Web.Services.WebService(Namespace:= _
    "http://CustomersService/CustomersService")> _
```

32

LISTING 32.3
Continued

```vb
Public Class CustomersService
    Inherits System.Web.Services.WebService

    ' Web Services Designer Generated Code
```

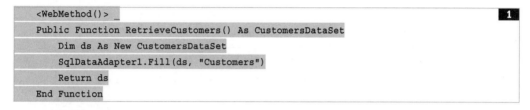
```vb
    <WebMethod()> _
    Public Function RetrieveCustomers() As CustomersDataSet
        Dim ds As New CustomersDataSet
        SqlDataAdapter1.Fill(ds, "Customers")
        Return ds
    End Function
```

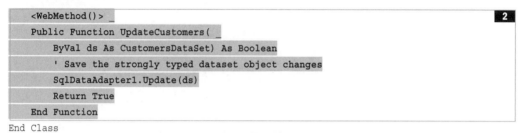
```vb
    <WebMethod()> _
    Public Function UpdateCustomers( _
        ByVal ds As CustomersDataSet) As Boolean
        ' Save the strongly typed dataset object changes
        SqlDataAdapter1.Update(ds)
        Return True
    End Function
```

```vb
End Class
```

FIGURE 32.11 Creating a strongly typed `DataSet` object.

Creating a Web Service That Uses Complex Parameters

The RetrieveCustomers web method **1** returns a strongly typed Customers DataSet object. The UpdateCustomers web method **2** accepts an updated strongly typed Customers DataSet object and saves the DataSet changes to the database.

Build the web service project, and the web service is ready. Now you will build the client Windows application CustomersClient that will invoke web service methods.

Add a web reference to the CustomersService web service (http://localhost/ CustomersService/CustomersService.asmx) in the project by selecting Project, Add Web Reference. Create a Windows Form interface similar to the one shown in Figure 32.12. Add the following event handlers to the Button controls to invoke the web methods shown in Listing 32.4.

LISTING 32.4

Invoking a Web Service That Uses Complex Parameters

```
' Used by both the event handlers
Private dsCustomers As localhost.CustomersDataSet

Private Sub btnRetrieve_Click(ByVal sender As System.Object, _
        ByVal e As System.EventArgs) Handles btnRetrieve.Click

        Dim wsCustomers As localhost.CustomersService
        wsCustomers = New localhost.CustomersService
        dsCustomers = wsCustomers.RetrieveCustomers()
        dgCustomers.DataSource = dsCustomers.Customers.DefaultView
End Sub

Private Sub btnUpdate_Click(ByVal sender As System.Object, _
        ByVal e As System.EventArgs) Handles btnUpdate.Click
        Dim wsCustomers As localhost.CustomersService
        wsCustomers = New localhost.CustomersService
        wsCustomers.UpdateCustomers(dsCustomers)
End Sub
```

Build and run the client application. Click the Retrieve Customers button to invoke the RetrieveCustomers web method and return the strongly typed DataSet object from the web service. The Customers table from the DataSet is then data-bound to the data grid. Make changes to the data in the data grid, and click the Update Customers button to update the changes in the database via the UpdateCustomers web method, as shown in Figure 32.12.

The proxy class makes the complex types available to the client as if they were defined in the client itself.

32

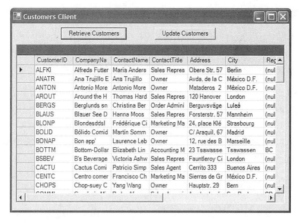

FIGURE 32.12 A web service can accept and
return complex types.

INVOKING A WEB SERVICE ASYNCHRONOUSLY

Depending on how a client application invokes a web service, a web service can be called
either synchronously or asynchronously. Asynchronous calls might make the client
programs more responsive because the client program does not need to wait for the web
service to return results for further processing.

You do not need to modify any server-side code to support asynchronous invocation.
When the proxy class for a web service is created, it generates both the synchronous and
asynchronous versions of the web methods. For each web method, two asynchronous
methods are generated that have the same name as the web method, but they are
prefixed with `Begin` and `End`. The `Begin` method is used to initiate the web service; the
`End` method retrieves the results.

This technique for asynchronous invocation is uniformly followed throughout the .NET
Framework and is explained in Chapter 27, "Multithreading."

Importing a Web Service

The basic idea of the web service is not limited to creating web services for use in
your own applications. Most of the time, you will want to use web services that are
already available. Many well-known companies, including Microsoft, Amazon, and
Google, have provided access to their data through web services.

Using an already available web service is a two-step process:

1. Locate the WSDL information for the web service.

2. Generate a proxy to the web service by using the information in WSDL.

When you have a proxy to the web service, you can invoke methods on the web service.

Discovering a Web Service

As a starting point, you can use the UDDI Registry (http://www.uddi.org) to search the web services of your interest. The catalog-type entry of each web service will provide information such as a link to the WSDL file.

You can also use the .NET Framework Web Service Discovery Tool (`disco.exe`) to find information about web services. The disco.exe tool needs the location of the .disco file. Based on the discovery information in that file, it can generate a set of other files (such as `.wsdl`, `.xsd`, `.disco`, and `.discomap`) that provide complete information about the web service. Note that Disco is a Microsoft standard for discovery, and it might not be used by vendors who provide web services created using non-Microsoft development tools.

Alternatively, if you use a web service from a particular vendor, you might want to ask the vendor to also provide the WSDL and other information for the web service.

Creating a Web Service Proxy

You already know how to generate a web service proxy automatically by using Visual Studio .NET. In this section, you'll learn how to use the .NET Framework SDK Web Service Description tool (`wsdl.exe`) to generate a web service proxy. Table 32.1 shows the various options available with this tool.

TABLE 32.1

Command-Line Options for wsdl.exe

Option	Meaning
`/domain:DomainName` `/d:DomainName`	Specifies the domain name to use when connecting to a server that requires authentication.
`/language:LanguageCode` `/l:LanguageCode`	Specifies the language for the generated class. In the case of Visual Basic .NET, the `LanguageCode` parameter should be `VB`.
`/namespace:Namespace` `/n:Namespace`	Specifies a namespace for the generated class.
`/out:Filename` `/o:FileName`	Specifies the filename for the generated output. If this option is not specified, the filename is derived from the web service name.
`/password:Password` `/p:Password`	Specifies the password to use when connecting to a server that requires authentication.
`/server`	Generates a class to create a server based on the input file. By default, the tool generates a client proxy object.
`/username:Username` `/u:Username`	Specifies the username to use when connecting to a server that requires authentication.
`/?`	Displays full help on the tool.

32

The CapeScience GlobalWeather web page at http://www.capescience.com/webservices/globalweather contains web services that provide weather information around the world. This page also provides the location of the WSDL file for this web service, at http://live.capescience.com/wsdl/GlobalWeather.wsdl.

To generate a web service proxy for this web service, you can use the wsdl.exe tool as follows:

```
wsdl.exe /language:VB /out:GlobalWeatherProxy.vb
➥ http://live.capescience.com/wsdl/GlobalWeather.wsdl
```

When you include the output of this tool, the proxy class, and GlobalWeatherProxy.vb in a Visual Basic project, you can access the remote objects in your programs as if they are locally available in your project.

Customizing Web Services

A web service class definition uses the WebService attributes and WebMethod attributes. The WebService attribute is applied at the class level, and the WebMethod attribute is applied at the method level. As you'll learn in the following sections, these attributes enable you to customize the behavior of a web service as a whole or just its individual methods.

The WebService Attribute

The WebService attribute is applied to the web service class and has a few simple properties to describe the web service class. Table 32.2 shows the properties of the WebService attribute.

32

TABLE 32.2

Properties of the WebService Attribute

Property	Meaning
Description	Specifies the description of the web service.
Name	Specifies the name of the web service.
Namespace	Specifies the default XML namespace for the XML web service. The value is a unique identifier and can be arbitrary; it doesn't need to resolve to an actual web site.

The WebMethod Attribute

The WebMethod attribute is applied to published methods of the web service. You can customize the behavior of web methods by adding properties to this attribute. Table 32.3 shows the properties that you can use to customize the WebMethod attribute.

Customizing Web Services

TABLE 32.3

Properties of the `WebMethod` Attribute

Property	Meaning
BufferResponse	Indicates whether the response should be buffered. If it is set to True (the default), the entire response is buffered by the server and returned to the client as a single message. If it is set to False, the response is sent in chunks of 16KB.
CacheDuration	Specifies the number of seconds that ASP.NET should cache results. The default is 0, which disables caching.
Description	Supplies a description for the web method.
EnableSession	Indicates whether the session state should be enabled. The default is False.
MessageName	Specifies the name by which the method will be called in SOAP messages. The default is the method name.
TransactionOption	If set to TransactionOption.Required or TransactionsOption.RequiredNew, allows the web method to participate as the root object of a transaction.

Caching

The `CacheDuration` property of the `WebMethod` attribute enables caching for the web method output on the web services server. You can improve the performance of a web application that invokes a web service by using output caching. You can read more about output caching in Chapter 19, "Caching."

With output caching, the results of a web page are stored in the output cache for a specified duration. If a similar web request is made, the result can be obtained from the cache instead of actually invoking the web services. In Listing 32.5, the following `CacheDuration` property on the `WebMethod` attribute enables output caching for the web method for a period of 30 seconds.

LISTING 32.5

Enable Output Caching on Web Methods

```
<WebMethod(CacheDuration:=30, _
        Description:="Method that uses caching", _
        MessageName:="CachedTime")> _
Public Function CachedMethod() As String
        Return "The time is " & _
        DateTime.Now.ToLongTimeString()
End Function
```

Note that Listing 32.5 also describes the use of the `Description` and `MessageName` properties of the `WebMethod` attribute.

> **NOTE**
>
> To see the `CacheDuration` property in action, call the web service method from a SOAP client instead of the web browser test page.

State Management

Being part of ASP.NET, web services can make use of the same state-management options as ASP.NET. The web services can access `Application` and `Session` objects through the inherited properties of the base `WebService` class.

Web service methods can make use of Application state just like other ASP.NET applications. Unlike Application state, each web method in a web service must explicitly specify whether it will use the session state. This is done by enabling the `EnableSession` property of the `WebMethod` attribute to `True`. Listing 32.6 shows the usage of session state in web methods in practice.

LISTING 32.6

Enable State Management on Web Methods

```
<WebMethod(EnableSession:=True)> _
Public Function StoreUser(ByVal User As String) As Boolean
    Session("User") = User
    Return True
End Function


<WebMethod(EnableSession:=True)> _
Public Function RetrieveUser() As String
    If Not Session("User") Is Nothing Then
        Return Session("User").ToString()
    Else
        Return ""
    End If
End Function
```

When invoking a web service from a client application, the client needs a way of storing the session cookie. This can be done by the `CookieContainer` property of a web service class:

```
dim ws as new server.webservice()
ws.CookieContainer = new System.Net.CookieContainer()
ws.DoSomething()
```

If you use the same cookie for subsequent calls to a web service, the web service links the request with the same session.

32

Customizing Web Services

Be cautious about using state in a web service because state can tie up server resources for an extended period of time. For more information on state management, refer to Chapter 18, "State Management."

Transactions

XML web service methods can participate in a transaction only as the root of a new transaction. Therefore, if the web methods call other web methods that participate in transactions, the transactions are separate for both the web service methods because the transactions do not flow across XML web service methods.

When the `TransactionOption` property is set to `TransactionOption.Required` or `TransactionsOption.RequiredNew`, the web method can participate as the root object of a transaction. The other options, `TransactionOption.Supported`, `TransactionOption.NotSupported`, and `TransactionOption.Disabled` (the default), do not run the web service methods within the transactions scope.

NOTE

If you're interested in performing transactions within a web service, you should look at the WS-Transaction portion of the Global XML Architecture (GXA) specification, instead of using the `TransactionOption` property. For more information, see www.msdn.com/library/en-us/dnglob-spec/html/ws-transaction.asp.

Creating Custom SOAP Headers

Until now in the chapter, you have learned that when a method call is made on the web service remote object, the call is translated into a SOAP message using the SOAP protocol and is transmitted to the web services server.

A typical SOAP request message sent from the web services client to a web services server appears in Listing 32.7.

LISTING 32.7
A Standard SOAP Message

```xml
<?xml version="1.0" encoding="utf-16"?>
<soap:Envelope
    xmlns:soap="http://schemas.xmlsoap.org/soap/envelope/"
    xmlns:xsi="http://www.w3.org/2001/XMLSchema-instance"
    xmlns:xsd="http://www.w3.org/2001/XMLSchema">
```

LISTING 32.7
Continued

```
<soap:Header>                                              2
  <AuthenticationHeader
    xmlns="http://RectangleService/RectangleService">
    <UserName>user</UserName>
    <Password>password</Password>
  </AuthenticationHeader>
</soap:Header>

<soap:Body>                                                3
  <Area xmlns="http://RectangleService/RectangleService">
    <Length>10</Length>
    <Width>15</Width>
  </Area>
</soap:Body>
```

```
</soap:Envelope>
```

The following points can be derived from this SOAP message format:

▶ The SOAP message consists of an `Envelope` element **1** that encloses the complete message.

▶ The SOAP message consists of a `Body` element **2** that contains the SOAP method request. The method request contains the method name (`Area`) and its parameters (`Length`, `Width`).

▶ The SOAP message consists of a `Header` **3** element that is optional and, therefore, was not created for messages until now. Listing 32.7 points out the location where the `Header`, if provided, would display.

A SOAP `Header` inherits from the `SoapHeader` class of the `System.Web.Services.Protocols` namespace. SOAP `Headers` are applied to web methods using the `SoapHeader` attribute and, therefore, can be applied to multiple web methods easily. SOAP `Headers` are used to provide additional information that is not directly related to the method call.

The best example of SOAP `Headers` is to provide authentication information. This authentication information is vital for the request to execute, but it does not have any role in the underlying business logic and can be separated from the main body of the method.

Begin by creating a SOAP `Header` to the `RectangleService` area web method. Add an `AuthenticationHeader.vb` class to the web service project that contains `UserName` and `Password` properties, as shown in Listing 32.8.

32

Creating Custom SOAP Headers

LISTING 32.8
Creating a SOAP Header

```
Imports System.Web.Services.Protocols

Public Class AuthenticationHeader
    Inherits SoapHeader
    Private _UserName As String
    Private _Password As String

    Public Property UserName() As String
        Get
            Return _UserName
        End Get
        Set(ByVal Value As String)
            _UserName = Value
        End Set
    End Property

    Public Property Password() As String
        Get
            Return _Password
        End Get
        Set(ByVal Value As String)
            _Password = Value
        End Set
    End Property
End Class
```

When you have the SOAP Header defined, you can apply the SOAP Header to the Area web method of RectangleService, as shown in Listing 32.9.

LISTING 32.9
Applying a SOAP Header to a Web Method

```
Imports System.Web.Services.Protocols
    .
    .
    .
```

1 `Public AuthInfo As AuthenticationHeader`

```
<WebMethod(), SoapHeader("AuthInfo", _
    Direction:=SoapHeaderDirection.In)>
```

```
Public Function Area(ByVal Length As Double, _
    ByVal Width As Double) As Double
    ' TODO Verify username and password against database
```

LISTING 32.9
Continued

```
    If AuthInfo.UserName <> "user" Or _                                    2
        AuthInfo.Password <> "password" Then
        Throw New SoapException("Invalid Credentials", SoapException.ClientFaultCode)
    End If
    Return Length * Width
End Function
```

In the web service, you first must define a public member of the SOAP `Header` type and mark the web method with the `SoapHeader` attribute. **1** The attribute is supplied with the name of the public member defined in the class. You can also specify the `Direction` property of the `SoapHeader` attribute. The `SoapHeaderDirection` can be `In` (the default—the web service receives the SOAP header), `Out` (the web service sends the SOAP header), `InOut` (the web service receives and sends the SOAP header), and `Fault` (web service sends the SOAP header when an exception is thrown).

The value of the `UserName` and `Password` properties can then be verified before further execution of the message. **2** If the authentication information is invalid, a `SoapException` can be raised indicating the fault in the client's data.

Now you will see how to send SOAP `Headers` from the `RectangleClient` when calling the `Area` web method in Listing 32.10.

LISTING 32.10
Sending SOAP `Header` from the client

```
Private Sub btnCalculate_Click(ByVal sender As System.Object, _
    ByVal e As System.EventArgs) Handles btnCalculate.Click


    Dim authHeader As localhost.AuthenticationHeader
...
    rectService = New localhost.RectangleService
    If (rbArea.Checked) Then
        authHeader = New localhost.AuthenticationHeader                    1
        authHeader.UserName = "user"
        authHeader.Password = "password"
        rectService.AuthenticationHeaderValue = authHeader
        txtResult.Text = rectService.Area( _
            dblLength, dblWidth).ToString()
...
End Sub
```

32

Creating Custom SOAP Headers

After you update the web reference after the SOAP Header is applied to the web method, the proxy class contains the definition of the newly added SOAP Header. The client needs to create an instance of the SOAP Header object and provide value for its properties: UserName and Password. The instance of the SOAP Header object then needs to be associated with the proxy object using the AuthenticationHeaderValue property. █1 This property is automatically created in the proxy class when the corresponding SOAP Header (AuthenticationHeader, in this case) is applied to a web method.

Of course, in production applications, the authentication details will be validated against some data store, and the data passed will need to be secured; that's the subject of the next chapter, "Security and Web Services Enhancements."

Summary

Web services provide a way to invoke objects over the Internet using standard protocols such as HTTP and XML. A web service can expose one or more web methods, each of which can accept parameters and return objects.

Visual Studio .NET hides the details of the underlying protocol and enables you to work with remote objects as though they are available locally.

The WebMethod attribute provides various ways to customize a web service. SOAP Headers can be used to provide additional information that is not directly related to the method call and that can be applied on multiple web methods.

Further Reading

Scribner, Kenn, and Mark C. Stiver. *Applied SOAP: Implementing .NET XML Web Services*. Pearson Education, 2001.

Eric Newcomer. *Understanding Web Services: XML, WSDL, SOAP, and UDDI*. Addison-Wesley, 2002.

SECURITY AND WEB SERVICES ENHANCEMENTS

IN BRIEF

This chapter discusses techniques for developing secure web service applications. The first part of this chapter discusses platform-level security, which includes the security features offered by IIS and ASP.NET. You'll learn how to authenticate and authorize the web service callers and how to flow security context through a web service.

The second part of this chapter focuses on the message-level security. The chapter discusses how you can use Web Services Enhancements 2.0 for Microsoft .NET to implement the emerging standard of Web Services Security (WS-Security).

WHAT YOU NEED

SOFTWARE REQUIREMENTS	Windows 2000, XP, or 2003 .NET Framework SDK v1.1 Visual Studio .NET 2003 with Visual Basic .NET installed Internet Information Services (IIS) Web Services Enhancements 2.0 for Microsoft .NET
HARDWARE REQUIREMENTS	PC that meets .NET SDK minimum requirements
SKILL REQUIREMENTS	Familiarity with Visual Basic .NET Familiarity with web services Familiarity with ASP.NET security

SECURITY AND WEB SERVICES ENHANCEMENTS AT A GLANCE

Platform-Level Security

A .NET Framework web service runs on a combined platform of Internet Information Services (IIS) and ASP.NET. This means that you can use the full spectrum of authentication and authorization mechanisms provided by ASP.NET and IIS to implement security for web services.

IIS Authentication Strategies

When SOAP messages come in via HTTP on port 80, they are first handled by IIS. This means that you can use IIS to authenticate the caller of the web service by using Anonymous (which means no authentication is performed), Basic, Digest, Integrated (Windows), or Certification authentication.

You can also configure IIS to accept requests from only a specified range of IP addresses. If the incoming SOAP request fails to authenticate (assuming that you have disabled anonymous authentication) or the IP address is not allowed access to the server, that's it; the web service is not called.

ASP.NET Authentication Strategies

After IIS authentication, the SOAP request is passed on to the next level: ASP.NET. Authentication support in ASP.NET can be configured by using the `<authentication>` element in the `web.config` file. This element can have any of the following values: `None`, `Windows (IIS Authentication)`, `Forms`, and `Passport`.

Although Forms authentication and Passport authentication are useful for a web application, they are not easy to support for a web service. Both of these mechanisms are more suitable for end-user interaction because they support things such as logon screen and logon timeout. A web service client, on the other hand, needs programmatic access and, therefore, cannot easily process the logon screen or handle a logon timeout condition.

When the IIS authentication is complete, ASP.NET uses the authenticated identity to authorize access. ASP.NET can propagate the authenticated identity in the application in two different ways:

- Authentication without impersonation
- Authentication with impersonation

Authentication Without Impersonation

Authentication without impersonation is the default ASP.NET setting. In this case, ASP.NET runs the request in the security context of the ASP.NET process identity, regardless of the type of IIS authentication. Authentication without impersonation is useful when all users of your web service should be able to access the same resources after they are authenticated.

33

Platform-Level Security

NOTE

ASP.NET process identity can be configured by using the `<processModel>` element in the `machine.config` file. Note that this is a machine-wide setting instead of an application-level setting.

Authentication with Impersonation

If you need to be able to authorize access to resources based on the caller's identity, you should set up your server to perform Windows authentication with impersonation. Impersonation can be enabled in the `web.config` file for a web service as shown here:

```
<authentication mode="Windows" />
<identity impersonate="true" />
```

When impersonation is enabled as shown here, and if IIS is not configured to allow anonymous access, requests run in the security context of the authenticated Windows user. On the other hand, if impersonation is enabled and you allow anonymous access in IIS, requests run in the security context of the IUSR_*ComputerName* account.

TIP

If you continue to flow a user's authenticated identity to the database, you could end up having different connection strings to the database. This can severely impact SQL Server performance because of the way SQL Server connection pooling works.

It is also possible to configure ASP.NET so that it always impersonates a fixed user identity for all authenticated users. You can do this by modifying the `<identity>` element in the `web.config` file:

```
<identity impersonate="true" userName="Domain\User" password="secret" />
```

This strategy requires storing the password for the fixed identity account in clear text, which is an inherently insecure situation.

DISABLE HTTP-GET AND HTTP-POST ACCESS TO WEB SERVICES

By default, clients can communicate with ASP.NET web services, using three protocols: HTTP-GET, HTTP-POST, and SOAP over HTTP. On production servers, you should disable HTTP-GET and HTTP-POST access to web services, limiting them to SOAP access.

33

This is most important when the web service should be available only to clients on your intranet and those same clients are allowed to browse to the Internet. Under those circumstances, a malicious web page on the Internet could contain a carefully crafted link that would cause the client to invoke the internal-only web service. This is possible only through the HTTP-GET and HTTP-POST protocols because web pages can't create a SOAP message as part of a link. To disable such access, modify the `<webServices>` section of the `machine.config` or `web.config` file as follows:

```
<webServices>
  <protocols>
    <add name="HttpSoap"/>
    <!-- <add name="HttpPost"/> -->
    <!-- <add name="HttpGet"/> -->
    <add name="Documentation"/>
  </protocols>
</webServices>
```

Passing Authentication Credentials to Web Services

When using an ASP.NET web application, a user can be prompted to enter the credentials interactively. Web services, on the other hand, are invoked programmatically, and there should be a way for a web service client to pass the credentials programmatically.

When using Windows authentication, the client program must specify the authentication details in the web service proxy object by using its `Credentials` property. You can do this in two ways.

The first approach is to pass the credentials (username, password, and domain) of the user running the client application. This is done by setting the `Credentials` property of the web service proxy object to `CredentialCache.DefaultCredentials`:

```
Proxy.Credentials = System.Net.CredentialCache.DefaultCredentials
```

The second approach is to pass the credentials of a specific user by using a `NetworkCredential` object:

```
Proxy.Credentials = new NetworkCredential("username", "password", "domainname")
```

This second approach is good for testing, but you should be wary of it in production code because the password is embedded in Microsoft Intermediate Language (MSIL) in plain text.

33

When using either of these approaches to pass the credentials, you can also choose to set the `PreAuthenticate` property:

```
Proxy.PreAuthenticate = True
Proxy.Credentials = System.Net.CredentialCache.DefaultCredentials
```

When this property is set to `True`, the client passes the credentials with the initial SOAP request. If it's set to `False`, the client sends the credentials only if it receives a "401 Access Denied" response from the server, which results in an extra round-trip across the network.

Web Service Authorization

After the user has been authenticated and the identity of ASP.NET requests has been determined, the next line of defense is to restrict the callers to a subset of the functionality that your web service offers based on the caller's identity. You can restrict access at the ASMX file level, at the web method level, or for specific sections of code.

Authorization at the ASMX File Level

One way to restrict access to a web service is to restrict incoming requests to specific URLs. This technique, known as URL authorization, works regardless of the type of authentication that you use.

URL authorization is specified within the `web.config` file as part of the `<authorization>` element. This element enables you to deny access to a resource to unauthenticated users or to grant access to only specified users:

```
<authorization>
    <deny users = "?" />
</authorization>
```

The authorization element is discussed in more detail in Chapter 21, "Security."

If you're using Windows authentication in IIS, you can also protect the file by using file authorization. For file authorization, right-click on the ASMX file in Windows Explorer and select Properties. The Security tab of the Properties dialog box, shown in Figure 33.1, lets you control which Windows users can open the file.

33

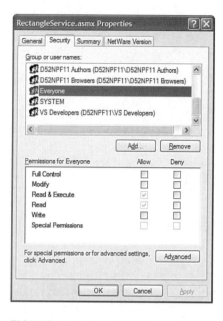

FIGURE 33.1   You can set file authorization properties for a web service via its Properties dialog box.

Authorization at the Code Level

Assuming that the authenticated user can read the ASMX file, the final line of defense is code within the file. You can use imperative or declarative code access security or role-based security within an ASMX file, just as you can inside any other assembly. For example, to demand only that the user is authenticated, you can use this code:

```
<WebMethod(), _
 PrincipalPermission(SecurityAction.Demand, Authenticated:=True)> _
Public Function WebMethod1() As String
    ' Web Method Code
End Function
```

Or, you can use the following code to demand that the authorized user belong to the Manager role:

```
<WebMethod(),   _
 PrincipalPermission(SecurityAction.Demand, Role:="Manager")> _
Public Function WebMethod1() As String
    ' Web Method Code
End Function
```

33

Platform-Level Security

You can also authorize access to specific functionality inside web methods by calling the `IPrincipal.IsInRole()` method:

```
Dim user As GenericPrincipal
' Initialization code goes here
If (user.IsInRole("Manager")) Then
    ' User is authorized to perform this task
End If
```

The `IsInRole()` method returns `True` if the current `GenericPrincipal` is a member of the specified role; otherwise, the method returns `False`.

Message-Level Security

Platform-level security is a workable security solution for tightly coupled intranet scenarios in which you control the configuration of both web service client and server. However, the main goal of web services is to use standards such as HTTP and SOAP to provide interoperability between heterogeneous systems.

An increasing number of companies are exposing their products and services via web services available over the Internet. Web services available in such heterogeneous environments require security to be addressed at the message level instead of the platform level. A number of companies, including IBM and Microsoft, are working together to create a set of standards that addresses these issues. The most recent outcome of this exercise is the Web Services Security (WS-Security) specification.

Microsoft has implemented the WS-Security specification as a part of Web Services Enhancement (WSE) 2.0 for Microsoft .NET, which is a free download available from the Microsoft Web Services Developer Center at www.msdn.com/webservices. The rest of this chapter assumes that you have downloaded and installed WSE 2.0.

Configuring Applications for WSE

To explore the security features that WSE 2.0 offers, you start by creating a simple web service (`MessageService.asmx`) in Visual Studio .NET. The web service contains a single web method, as shown in Listing 33.1.

LISTING 33.1
A Simple Web Method

```
<WebMethod()> _
Public Function DisplayGreetings(ByVal name As String) As String
    Return [String].Format("Hello, {0}!", name)
End Function
```

To test the web service, you can use a console application, as shown in Listing 33.2.

LISTING 33.2
A Web Service Client

```
Module Module1
    Sub Main()
        Dim name As String
        Dim proxy As localhost.MessageService

        Console.WriteLine("Enter Name: ")
        name = Console.ReadLine()
        proxy = New localhost.MessageService
        Console.WriteLine(proxy.DisplayGreetings(name))
        Console.WriteLine("Press any key to continue…")
        Console.ReadLine()
    End Sub
End Module
```

The code creates a new instance of the web service and invokes the
DisplayGreetings web method. **1** Build both the applications and test them.
You should note that currently none of the security features is enabled.

To enable security, start by configuring both the projects to use WSE 2.0. To do this,
right-click the project's name in Solution Explorer and select WSE Settings 2.0, as
shown in Figure 33.2.

FIGURE 33.2   After WSE 2.0 is installed, its
configuration can be accessed through a Visual
Studio .NET project shortcut menu.

33

Message-Level Security

Selecting the WSE Settings 2.0 option brings up a dialog box for WSE settings, as shown in Figure 33.3.

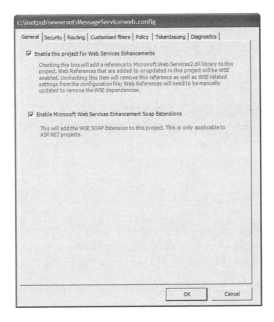

FIGURE 33.3   The dialog box for WSE 2.0 settings.

Two check boxes are available on the General tab. The first check box enables the selected project for WSE. This setting adds a reference to `Microsoft.Web.Services2.dll` in the project and also updates the application configuration file to add support for WSE. The second check box is available only to ASP.NET web applications and web services. When you select the second check box, a WSE SOAP extension is added to the `web.config` file.

After you have configured both the projects for WSE, update the web reference in the web service client. This action re-creates the web service proxy with the WSE configuration.

WSE Authentication

To add WSE authentication to the client application, you need to modify the code of the web service client, as shown in Listing 33.3.

LISTING 33.3
A Web Service Client with WSE Authentication

```
Imports Microsoft.Web.Services2
Imports Microsoft.Web.Services2.Security.Tokens

Module Module1
    Sub Main()
        Dim name, password As String

        Dim proxy As localhost.MessageServiceWse                              1
        Dim token As UsernameToken

        Console.WriteLine("Enter Name: ")
        name = Console.ReadLine()

        Console.WriteLine("Enter Password: ")
        password = Console.ReadLine()

        proxy = New localhost.MessageServiceWse                               2
        token = New UsernameToken(name, password, PasswordOption.SendPlainText)
        proxy.RequestSoapContext.Security.Tokens.Add(token)
        Console.WriteLine(proxy.DisplayGreetings(name))

        Console.WriteLine("Press any key to continue…")
        Console.ReadLine()

    End Sub
End Module
```

The proxy class used in this program is `localhost.MessageServiceWse` instead of `localhost.MessageService`. **1** The WSE automatically adds this new class with the WSE suffix; this is the class that you should use to access the functionality that the WSE offers. To add the credentials to the web service request, the code uses the `UserToken` object and adds it to the `Tokens` collection of the `RequestSoapContext` object. **2**

NOTE

The `UserNameToken` **constructor throws a** `System.ArgumentNullException` **when either the username or password is null or an empty string (" ").**

33

Message-Level Security

When you run this program, the client program asks for a username and password. Enter credentials for a valid Windows account on the web server. The client sends the supplied username and password to the web service. At the web server end, the UsernameToken object tries to validate the username and password against Windows accounts. If the credentials are valid, a greeting is displayed; otherwise, an exception is thrown.

The UsernameToken object here sends passwords in plain text, which is a security risk. However, you can work around this issue by sending the credentials over a secure HTTPS channel:

```
proxy = New localhost.MessageServiceWse
proxy.Url = "https://WebServerName/WebServiceName.asmx"
token = New UsernameToken(name, password, PasswordOption.SendPlainText)
proxy.RequestSoapContext.Security.Tokens.Add(token)
```

WSE Security Tokens

The WSE by itself does not define how authentication will be performed. It just specifies various ways in which the credentials or security tokens can be embedded within a SOAP header. The SecurityToken class is the base class that is used to implement all the security tokens. You can use the SecurityToken class to create a custom security token, but for common applications, the WSE provides implementations of this class in form of the UsernameToken, KerberosToken, and the X509SecurityToken classes. You are already familiar with the UsernameToken class from Listing 33.3.

KerberosToken relies on the Kerberos Network Authentication Service V5, whereas X509SecurityToken relies on an X.509 certificate. Both of these techniques send credentials in an encrypted binary format.

The WSE itself provides a lot of flexibility in how the authentication information is passed. This means that you must make sure that both client and server agree on the same technique for passing tokens. If a client sends a Kerberos token but the server is expecting X.509 token, authentication won't succeed.

WSE Authorization

If the WSE successfully authenticates the credentials of a client request against a Windows account, it creates a Principal object that contains user information and role membership. You can use the IsInRole() method of the Principal object to find out whether the user belongs to a particular rule and then programmatically restrict or allow access to certain resources:

33

```
<WebMethod()> _
Public Function DisplayGreetings (ByVal name As String) As String
    Dim context As SoapContext
    context = RequestSoapContext.Current

    Dim token As SecurityToken
    For Each token In context.Security.Tokens
        Dim user As UsernameToken = token
        If (user.Username = name) Then
            If (user.Principal.IsInRole(System.Net.Dns.GetHostName() _
                    + "\Managers")) Then
                Return [String].Format("Hello, {0}!", name)
            End If
        End If
    Next token
End Function
```

WSE Security Policy

Writing code to authorize access to resources is more work and involves programmers for a job that is best suited for system administrators. WSE Security policy provides a solution for this requirement.

Security policies are defined in an XML document that system administrators easily can edit. General convention is to name the policy file policyCache.xml, but you are free to specify a name that you like. The name and location of the policy file is defined in a configuration file, such as Web.config.

NOTE

The security policy document is stored in plain-text format, so avoid storing any confidential information in this file.

33

A security policy file has two main sections, the <mappings> elements and the <policies> element:

```
<policyDocument xmlns="http://schemas.microsoft.com/wse/2003/06/Policy">
  <mappings xmlns:wse="http://schemas.microsoft.com/wse/2003/06/Policy">
  </mappings>
  <policies xmlns:wsu=
    "http://docs.oasis-open.org/wss/2004/01/oasis-200401-wss-wssecurity-utility-
➥1.0.xsd"
    xmlns:wssp="http://schemas.xmlsoap.org/ws/2002/12/secext"
    xmlns:wsp="http://schemas.xmlsoap.org/ws/2002/12/policy">
  </policies>
</policyDocument>
```

Message-Level Security

The `<policies>` element defines one or more security policies by adding the
`<policy>` element. The `<mappings>` element maps security policies to the web
service endpoints by adding the `<endpoint>` element.

For example, the following XML defines a policy named `Encrypt-Username`:

```
<wsp:Policy wsu:Id="Encrypt-Username">
   <!--The Confidentiality assertion is used to ensure
       that the SOAP Body is encrypted.-->
   <wssp:Confidentiality wsp:Usage="wsp:Required">
     <wssp:KeyInfo>
        <!--The SecurityToken element within the KeyInfo element
            describes which token type must be used for Encryption.-->
        <wssp:SecurityToken>
          <wssp:TokenType>http://schemas.xmlsoap.org/ws/2004/04/security/sc/dk</wssp:
➥TokenType>
          <wssp:Claims>
            <wse:Parent>
              <wssp:SecurityToken wse:IdentityToken="true">
                <wssp:TokenType>
                  http://docs.oasis-open.org/wss/2004/01
➥/oasis-200401-wss-username-token-profile-1.0#UsernameToken
                </wssp:TokenType>
              </wssp:SecurityToken>
            </wse:Parent>
          </wssp:Claims>
        </wssp:SecurityToken>
     </wssp:KeyInfo>
     <wssp:MessageParts
        Dialect="http://schemas.xmlsoap.org/2002/12/wsse#part">
        wsp:Body()
     </wssp:MessageParts>
   </wssp:Confidentiality>
 </wsp:Policy>
```

The following XML maps the `Encrypt-Username` policy to a specific web service:

```
<endpoint uri="http://localhost/MessageService/MessageService.asmx">
   <defaultOperation>
     <request policy="#Sign-Username" />
     <response policy="#Encrypt-Username" />
     <fault policy="" />
   </defaultOperation>
</endpoint>
```

33

The WSE also provides a GUI to create a security policy. After you invoke the WSE Settings dialog box, go to the Policy tab, as shown in Figure 33.4

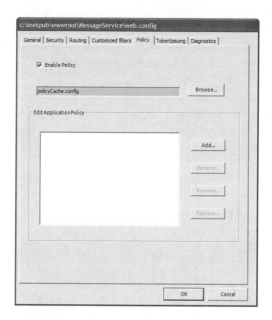

FIGURE 33.4   You can use the WSE 2.0 Settings dialog box to configure security policy.

On the Policy tab, first enable a security policy. Then you can specify the name and location of the policy file, followed by the web services endpoint and policy settings.

Summary

This chapter covered techniques for developing secure web service applications. You first learned about the platform-level web service security features that IIS and ASP.NET provide. These features are useful in an intranet-like scenario in which you have control over the desktops, but they are not suited for heterogeneous scenarios involving interoperability among various operating systems and applications.

The Web Services Enhancement (WSE) 2.0 for Microsoft .NET, on the other hand, implements a message-level security feature that supports the emerging standard for Web Service Security (WS-Security). In this chapter, you also learned how to use WSE 2.0 to create interoperable yet secure web services.

Further Reading

"Improving Web Applications Security: Threats and Countermeasures": www.msdn.com/library/en-us/dnnetsec/html/ThreatCounter.asp.

"WS-Security Drilldown in Web Services Enhancements 2.0": www.msdn.com/library/en-us/dnwse/html/wssecdrill.asp.

Programming with Web Services Enhancements 2.0: www.msdn.com/library/en-us/dnwse/html/programwse2.asp.

Part IX

Enterprise Services

34 INTRODUCTION TO ENTERPRISE SERVICES

IN BRIEF

This chapter explains Enterprise Services, a technology based on COM+. The core building block of Enterprise Services is a `ServicedComponent` that acts as a consumer of services. First, you will learn to build a simple `ServicedComponent`. You also learn how to create a development environment that keeps the builds clean and repeatable. Finally, you will learn about the instrumentation and documentation features of `ServicedComponents`.

WHAT YOU NEED

SOFTWARE REQUIREMENTS	Windows 2000, XP, or 2003
	.NET Framework 1.1 SDK
	Visual Studio .NET 2003 with Visual Basic .NET installed
	Windows Component Services installed
	Local administrator rights on your machine
HARDWARE REQUIREMENTS	PC desktop or laptop
SKILL REQUIREMENTS	Advanced knowledge of Visual Basic .NET
	Advanced knowledge of the .NET Framework

INTRODUCTION TO ENTERPRISE SERVICES AT A GLANCE

Improving Software with *N*-Tier Architectures

In the past, most enterprise software was developed using an architecture with a client and a database back end, which caused many problems. These so-called client/server systems were tightly coupled, making them hard to maintain and making reuse of their parts very difficult.

In these systems, business logic is embedded in either the user interface code, which affects security, or stored procedures in the database, hindering scalability and maintainability.

The solution is to add tiers or layers. The most common practice is to add a business logic layer and a data access layer. However, although this solves the problems inherent in a client/server system, it introduces many new problems. Enterprise Services helps to avoid or mitigate some of these problems. The remaining chapters in this book cover the available services and the issues they solve.

> **TIP**
>
> Multitier systems should use a closed-layer system, meaning that each layer can access only the layer immediately below it. From a "good" practices view, it is acceptable to use a modified closed-layer system that allows calling components in the same layer and in the layer immediately below.

Defining Components with Interfaces

A core principle of modern software engineering is loose coupling between clients and server components. Loosely coupled systems should be built with interfaces, the contracts for your components. Interfaces separate what the consumer (or client) needs to know from the implementation details. .NET encourages building loosely coupled systems with interfaces, but it does not enforce this.

> **TIP**
>
> Interfaces for business logic and data access-layer interfaces contain only methods. A well-factored interface should have between 1 and 10 methods.

34

For correctly built loosely coupled systems, clients should use all objects with interfaces exclusively through their interfaces, not directly through the class, as .NET permits. The server code can enforce this by implementing the interface's methods (and properties) as private methods (and properties). The examples in this chapter illustrate all of this.

INTERFACES PLAY A CENTRAL ROLE IN SERVICE-ORIENTED ARCHITECTURES (SOA)

An SOA-based system defines coarsely grained operations with loose coupling of the components. Service-oriented architectures also acknowledge the inherent chance of failure in distributed components. Web services are the current favorite for SOA (the WSDL defines the actual interface); however, between Windows-based server systems in an intranet scenario, Enterprise Services are a better choice because they have a wider range of composable services and deliver higher performance.

Introduction to the Architecture for Enterprise Services

Components that consume Enterprise Services are called serviced components. They are derived from `ServicedComponent`, which is derived from `ContextBoundObject`. `ServicedComponents` use interception to provide the services, and these services are provided by COM+. In library-activated components, the call to a serviced component itself never leaves managed code; only the interceptors for the COM+ services execute in unmanaged code through .NET interop (see Figure 34.1). Server-activated components execute in another process and incur the marshalling and interop overhead. COM+ provides a rich set of services, as well as an administrative MMC plug-in.

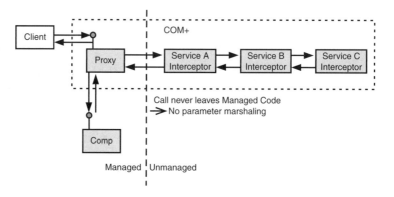

FIGURE 34.1 Enterprise Services interception architecture for a library-activated component.

`ServicedComponents` (just like unmanaged COM+ components) are hosted in a COM+ application. A COM+ application can have any number of components from one or more assemblies. Components must be registered with COM+, which assigns them to an application (see Figure 34.2).

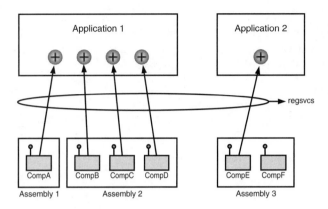

FIGURE 34.2   Components, assemblies, and applications.

COM+ applications are either server-activated or library-activated. Both are created as class libraries (DLLs). Server-activated components are hosted by `dllhost` and may be remote. Library components are loaded into the calling application domain (and, therefore, are always local).

Building a Simple Serviced Component

In this section, you build a simple serviced component with one method: `Method1`. This component uses no services and is library activated.

Start by creating a new solution and one project each for the component and a test application, as follows:

1. Create a new empty solution named `EnterpriseServices`.

2. Add a Windows application named `EsTestApplication`.

3. Add a class library named `BasicServicedComponent`.

4. Rename `Form1` to `MainWindow`, and fix the startup object in Properties.

5. Delete `Class1.vb` from the class library.

6. Add the `System.EnterpriseServices` and `System.Windows.Form` references to `EsTestApplication` and to `BasicServicedComponent` (for trace-information message boxes).

7. Add the `BasicServiceComponent` reference to `EsTestApplication`. Set the `CopyLocal` property for the last reference to `False`. You put this component in the GAC because COM+ requires it.

8. Add a class named `IFirstServicedComponent` to `BasicServicedComponent`. Replace the generated class skeleton code with the interface definition code in Listing 34.1.

34

Introduction to the Architecture for Enterprise Services

9. Add a second class named `FirstServicedComponent`. Replace the generated class skeleton code with the code in Listing 34.2. This prints the process and thread ID as well as the context. **2** Method1 is implemented as private **1**; this enforces its use through the interface.

LISTING 34.1
Interface `IFirstServicedComponent`

```
Imports System.EnterpriseServices

Public Interface IFirstServicedComponent
    Sub Method1()
End Interface
```

LISTING 34.2
Class `FirstServicedComponent`

```
Imports System.EnterpriseServices
Imports System.Text
Imports System.Threading
Imports System.Windows.Forms

Public Class FirstServicedComponent
    Inherits ServicedComponent
    Implements IFirstServicedComponent
```

1
```
    Private Sub Method1() Implements IFirstServicedComponent.Method1
        Dim details As New StringBuilder
```
2
```
        details.Append("Process=")
        details.Append(Process.GetCurrentProcess().Id)
        details.Append(Environment.NewLine)
        details.Append("Thread=")
        details.Append(Thread.CurrentThread.GetHashCode().ToString())
        details.Append(Thread.CurrentThread.GetHashCode().ToString())
        Try
            details.Append(Environment.NewLine)
            details.Append("Context=")
            'Throws COM Exception if zero services requested
            Dim contextID As Guid = ContextUtil.ContextId
            details.Append(ContextUtil.ContextId.ToString())
        Catch ex As Exception
            'Catches exception if no context (zero services requested)
            details.Append("<None>")
        End Try
        MessageBox.Show(details.ToString(), _
            "FirstServicedComponent.Method1 Called")    End Sub
```
```
End Class
```

Next, you need to add the information in `AssemblyInfo.vb` (see Listing 34.3) to enable COM+ to use this component:

1. Add the name of the COM+ application. **1**

2. Add the application activation mode (library activated). **2**

3. Add the signature key. **3** Serviced components must be added to the GAC and, therefore, must be signed with a strong name key.

4. Use `sn -k` to add a strong name file `\KeyFiles\TestServer.snk`.

LISTING 34.3
AssemblyInfo.vb

```
Imports System
Imports System.Reflection
Imports System.Runtime.InteropServices
Imports System.EnterpriseServices

<Assembly: AssemblyCompany("My Company")>
<Assembly: AssemblyProduct("My Product")>
<Assembly: AssemblyCopyright("Copyright 2004, My Company")>
<Assembly: AssemblyTrademark("")>
<Assembly: AssemblyTitle("")>
<Assembly: AssemblyDescription("")>
<Assembly: CLSCompliant(True)>

<Assembly: ApplicationName("FirstServicedApp")>                          1

<Assembly: ApplicationActivation(ActivationOption.Library)>             2
<Assembly: AssemblyVersion("1.0.0.0")>
<Assembly: AssemblyKeyFile("\KeyFiles\TestServer.snk")>                 3
```

You need to add code to your test client testing the serviced component:

1. Add `Imports` statements at the top of the file, as shown in Listing 34.4

2. Change the form's `text` property to Enterprise Service Test Window.

3. Double-click on the form and insert the code in Listing 34.5 (it displays the current process and thread ID).

4. Add a button, and rename it as `m_btnCallBasicServicedComponent`.

5. Change the button text to Call `BasicServicedComponent`.

6. Double-click the button and rename the generated handler as `btnCallBasicServicedComponent_Click`.

7. Insert the code in Listing 34.6. The component is used through its interface. **1**

34

Introduction to the Architecture for Enterprise Services

LISTING 34.4

`Imports` **Statements in** `MainWindow.vb`

```
Imports System.EnterpriseServices
Imports System.Text
Imports System.Threading


Imports BasicServicedComponent
```

LISTING 34.5

MainWindow Load Event Handler

```
Private Sub MainWindow_Load(ByVal sender As System.Object, ByVal e As System.
➥EventArgs) _
    Handles MyBase.Load
    Text += " - Process=" + Process.GetCurrentProcess().Id.ToString()
    Text += " - Thread=" + Thread.CurrentThread.GetHashCode().ToString()
End Sub
```

LISTING 34.6

`Click` **Event Handler**

```
Private Sub btnCallBasicServicedComponent_Click(ByVal sender As System.Object, ByVal
➥e As System.EventArgs) _
    Handles m_btnCallBasicServicedComponent.Click
    Dim component As IFirstServicedComponent
    component = New FirstServicedComponent
    component.Method1()
End Sub
```

You have now created all of the needed code. However, serviced components must be installed in the GAC and registered with COM+. This is contrary to the intent of basic .NET, in which installation in the GAC is a deployment option. Consequently, Visual Studio does not support the necessary steps for this requirement with a simple project property. Additionally, because of the great versioning support in .NET, the COM+ application is quickly polluted with old versions. Use a fully qualified version in `AssemblyInfo.vb` (see Listing 34.3), and increment it manually before each build.

You must adhere to the following process because it is the only way to ensure a repeatable clean build and run:

1. Open the Component Services MMC plug-in and shut down the COM+ application(s) (only for server-activated COM+ applications).

2. Remove all components from the COM+ application (leave the COM+ application).

3. Increment the version number in `AssemblyInfo.cs`.

4. Build the component(s).

5. Uninstall old versions of the assembly from the GAC.

6. Install the assembly in the GAC.

7. Register the component(s) with COM+.

The first two steps must be done manually (later you will learn how to use a tool written by the author to automate all the steps).

Uninstalling or installing an assembly from or into the Global Assembly Cache (GAC) is achieved in one of two ways. You can copy the assembly file from the project's Bin directory to the assembly cache directory, located in `C:\WINDOWS\assembly`. Deleting the assembly in that directory uninstalls it from the GAC. The second choice uses `gacutil`, whose default installation location is `C:\Program Files\Microsoft.NET\SDK\v1.1\Bin`.

Registering the component with COM+ is achieved in one of three ways. You can register the assembly or assemblies programmatically with `RegistrationHelper.InstallAssembly`, or you can have the CLR register the assembly dynamically before the first use. The second choice does not work reliably; specifically, it does not work for server-activated applications that are still running when a client requiring a new version starts. The last choice is to use the utility `regsvcs`. This calls `RegistrationHelper.InstallAssembly` and works. Here you will use `regsvcs`, located in the .NET Framework's directory. On most machines, it is located in `C:\WINDOWS\Microsoft.NET\Framework\v1.1.4322`.

TIP

You should add the two tools' bin directories to your system environment's PATH variable. This avoids typing lengthy absolute filenames for gacutil and regsvcs.

It is vital to automate the GAC and registration steps. Unfortunately, VB .NET projects miss a post-build event to automate this easily. You could write a batch file and run it manually each time the solution is rebuilt, but this is error prone. Instead, here you will use an empty C# project.

If you have not added the paths for `regsvcs` and `gacutil` in your system environment's PATH variable, you should add them now.

First, add the C# project for registration:

1. Add a C# class library project to the solution named `InstallServicedComponents`.

34

2. Delete `Class1.cs`, `AssemblyInfo.cs`, and all references.

3. Right-click on the project and then select Properties.

4. Select Build Events in Common Properties.

5. Click on Post-Build Event Command Line.

6. An ... appears (see Figure 34.3); click on it.

7. Add commands to remove all old versions from the GAC, install the current version to the GAC, and register the components in the assembly with COM+ (see Listing 34.7 and Figure 34.4).

Next, you need to tell the build system to build this project after `BasicServicedComponent` and before `EsTestApplication`:

1. Select Project, Project Dependencies.

2. Select `InstallServicedComponent` in the Projects drop-down box.

3. Check the check box for BasicServicedComponent.

4. Select the project `EsTestApplication`.

5. Check the check box for InstallServicedComponent.

6. Click OK.

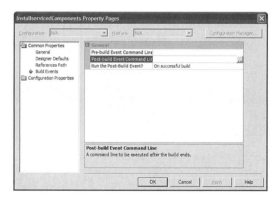

FIGURE 34.3 Property dialog box for the project.

LISTING 34.7

Post-Build Event Command Lines (Add the Necessary Paths to Your Environment First)

```
gacutil -u "BasicServicedComponent"
gacutil -i "$(ProjectDir)\..\BasicServicedComponent\bin\BasicServicedComponent.dll"
regsvcs "$(ProjectDir)\..\BasicServicedComponent\bin\BasicServicedComponent.dll"
```

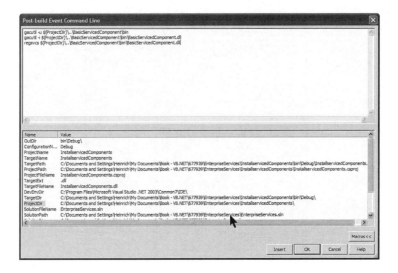

FIGURE 34.4   Command-line dialog box for post-build event.

Run the application and click the button called BasicServicedComponent. Note that the process and thread identifiers are the same in both the client and the serviced component. This is normal for library-activated components. Because no services have been selected and the COM+ application is library activated, no context was created (none was needed).

Next, change the activation mode to server activated and disable access-control security (you will change this later) by adding the code in Listing 34.8 to `AssemblyInfo.vb`.

LISTING 34.8
Changes to `AssemblyInfo.vb`

```
<Assembly: ApplicationActivation(ActivationOption.Server)>
<Assembly: ApplicationAccessControl(False)>
```

Run the application. Note that the process and thread identifiers are different in the client and the serviced component. This is normal for server-activated components because the universal component host, `ddlhost.exe`, hosts them. In the Task Manager under Processes, you can find both the client and the `dllhost` process (see Figure 34.5). Additionally the component is now running in a context. Server-activated components always run in a context. You can think of Remoting as a service.

34

FIGURE 34.5　Test application, component message box, and Task Manager.

Exploring the Component Services MMC Plug-in

You will find the shortcut for this in the Administrative Tools menu as Component Services. Start exploring as follows:

1. Start the MMC plug-in and then double-click on Component Services in tree view (do not click on the + sign because it does not work).

2. Expand My Computer (the + works correctly now).

3. Click on COM+ Applications.

4. You should see FirstServicedApp (this is the name from AssemblyInfo.vb.) Its icon is a ball with a + sign on it in a box. This indicates that it is a server-activated COM+ application; library-activated COM+ applications show the ball outside the box with a red arrow from the ball into the box.

5. Start your test application from earlier and click the button Call BasicServicedComponent. The ball should start spinning, indicating that the process is running. Right-click the icon and select Properties.

6. Check out all the tabs. Most items are best selected with attributes in your code.

34

7. On the `Activation` tab (see Figure 34.6), you can change the activation mode or run a server-activated COM+ application as a Windows service. If you are deploying a distributed system, it is possible to change the server name here.

8. Cancel the dialog box.

9. Expand tree view to show `FirstServicedApp`, `Components` (should have one only), `BasicServicedComponent.FirstServicedComponent`, and `Interfaces`.

10. Right-click on `BasicServicedComponent.FirstServicedComponent` and select Properties (see Figure 34.7). Explore all the tabs.

11. Repeat this for `Interface IFirstServicedComponent`. Interfaces that start with an underscore are auto-generated by .NET for all classes, to allow .NET to call components hosted by COM+ without needing an interface (see Figure 34.8). Note that `FirstServicedComponent` contains no methods because you implemented `Method1` as private and made it accessible through its interface, `IFirstServicedComponent`, only.

12. Collapse COM+ Application in tree view.

13. Open Running Processes. You should see your `FirstServicedApp`. The process ID in parentheses is the same as the process ID displayed by the message box. Obviously, your real components will not display message boxes with that information.

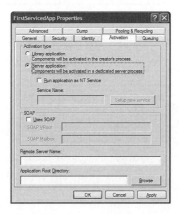

FIGURE 34.6   COM+ application properties—Activation tab.

34

Introduction to the Architecture for Enterprise Services

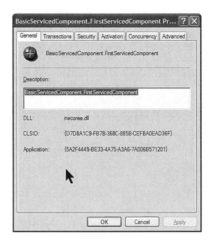

FIGURE 34.7   COM+ component properties.

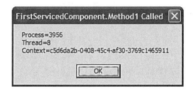

FIGURE 34.8   COM+ running processes.

Debugging Serviced Components

Library-activated COM+ applications can be debugged the same as regular class libraries—just set breakpoints.

Server-activated COM+ applications are best recompiled as library-activated applications. If this is not possible (for example, the problem occurs only when server activation is selected, which is common with security issues), find the process ID for `dllhost` in Running Processes and use it to attach the process in Visual Studio.

Now you will debug the server-activated component you just created:

1. Start the test application in debug mode.

2. Select the Visual Studio menu Debug, Process.

3. Find the `dllhost` with the correct process ID (the process ID can be obtained from `Running Processes`) and select the line (see Figure 34.9). Note that the list of debugged processes already contains your test application.

4. Click Attach.

5. Select Common Language Runtime.

6. Click OK. The list box shows two debugged processes.

7. Click Close and set a breakpoint in `Method1`.

8. Click the test button again. Visual Studio should hit the breakpoint.

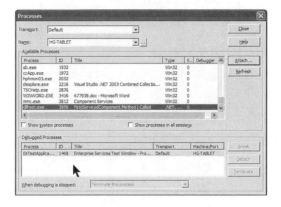

FIGURE 34.9 Visual Studio Attach Process dialog box.

Local versus Remote Deployment

Enterprise Services uses COM+, which has a built-in Remoting infrastructure based on DCOM. It is easily secured through authentication and encryption (the level can be configured). Enterprise Services is completely location transparent for the programmer. Distribution of objects is usually a deployment feature and is handled by qualified systems operations personnel.

In the rare case that you need to test your system in a distributed setting yourself, here are some pointers to get you started. The Component Services MMC plug-in can export a COM+ application as an `.msi` file. You can export a server installation or a client installation. Right-click on the COM+ application and select Export. This leads you to a wizard that guides you through the process (see Figure 34.10).

34

TIP

For compilation, you still need the original serviced component's `DLL`; you cannot use the client proxy. Actually, you need just the metadata; the utility soapsuds can extract the metadata from an assembly. This is a somewhat cumbersome approach; use it only if you have a good reason for not giving the assembly to the client developer.

Client proxies created this way will point back to the computer generating the `.msi`. You can change the server location with the Component Services MMC plug-in on the client machine. Navigate to the installed COM+ application's Property dialog box, select the Activation tab, and change `Remote Server Name` (see Figure 34.11).

Introduction to the Architecture for Enterprise Services

FIGURE 34.10   Exporting a COM+ client proxy.

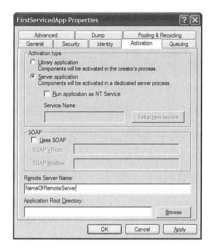

FIGURE 34.11   Changing the Remote Server Name.

Improving Your COM+ Hygiene

As mentioned at the beginning of this chapter, it is hard to build a serviced component correctly and repeatably. This is especially true for server-activated applications because they might still be running, and you cannot replace components in a running COM+ application. Using a repeatable process (as outlined in the section "Building a Simple Serviced Component") is the COM+ equivalent of washing your hands with soap (bar soap, not web services SOAP) before eating. You will improve this process further.

First, add a second serviced component to the solution `EsServices` to implement the improved process:

1. Add a new class library project named `AdvancedServicedComponent` to the solution.

2. Delete `Class1.vb`.

3. Add a reference to `System.EnteriseServices` and `System.Windows.Forms`.

4. Add a new class named `IMyInterface` and replace the code with the code in Listing 34.9.

5. Add a new class named `MyComponent` and replace the code with the code in Listing 34.10.

6. Add a new text file named `SolutionInfo.vb` to the solution. The method `DisplayTraceMessageBox` **1** has been expanded from the one in your `BasicServicedComponent` to display more detail and be more generic.

LISTING 34.9
IMyInterface.vb

```
Imports System.EnterpriseServices

Public Interface IMyInterface
   Sub Method1()
End Interface
```

LISTING 34.10
MyComponent.vb

```
Imports System.EnterpriseServices
Imports System.Text
Imports System.Threading
Imports System.Windows.Forms

Public Class MyComponent
   Inherits ServicedComponent
   Implements IMyInterface

   Private Sub Method1() Implements IMyInterface.Method1
      DisplayTraceMessageBox(Me.GetType().ToString(), "Method1")
   End Sub
```

34

Introduction to the Architecture for Enterprise Services

LISTING 34.10
Continued

```
Private Sub DisplayTraceMessageBox(ByVal className As String, ByVal methodName
  As String)
    Dim details As New StringBuilder
    details.Append("In ")
    details.Append(className)
    details.Append(".")
    details.Append(methodName)
    details.Append(Environment.NewLine)
    details.Append("    Process=")
    details.Append(Process.GetCurrentProcess().Id)
    details.Append(Environment.NewLine)
    details.Append("    Thread=")
    details.Append(Thread.CurrentThread.GetHashCode().ToString())
    Try
        details.Append(Environment.NewLine)
        details.Append("    Context=")
        'Throws COM Exception if zero services requested
        Dim contextID As Guid = ContextUtil.ContextId
        details.Append(ContextUtil.ContextId.ToString())
    Catch ex As Exception
        'Catches exception if no context (zero services requested)
        details.Append("<None>")
    End Try
    MessageBox.Show(details.ToString(), _
        "Show Method Call Detail")
End Sub
```

```
End Class
```

34

Next, you improve the registration process with the utility `RegisterComPlus`. I originally wrote this utility in C# and named it `ComPlusAdmin`. It stops the COM+ application, if running; removes the components in this assembly from the COM+ application; removes all old versions of this assembly from the GAC; installs the current version to the GAC; and registers the serviced components in the assembly with COM+. You will write a clone in VB .NET called `RegisterComPlus` in Chapter 40, "Advanced Enterprise Services Programming."

As before with `BasicServicedComponent`, you need to add a C# project to execute the post-build step. This time, you use the utility `RegisterComPlus`:

1. Copy `RegisterComPlus.exe` to the .NET SDK directory for binaries because you already added this path to your system environment's PATH variable. On my machine, it is C:\Program Files\Microsoft.NET\SDK\v1.1\Bin.

2. Add a C# class library project named `InstallServicedComponentsBetter`.

3. Delete `Class1.cs`, `AssemblyInfo.cs`, and all references.

4. Right-click on the project and select Properties.

5. Select Build Events in Common Properties.

6. Click on `Post-Build Event Command Line`.

7. An … appears. Click on it.

8. Add the `RegisterComPlus` command in Listing 34.11

9. Select Project, Project Dependencies from the menu.

10. Select `InstallServicedComponentBetter` in the Projects drop-down box.

11. Check the check box for `AdvancedServicedComponent`.

12. Select the project `EsTestApplication`.

13. Check the check box for `InstallServicedComponentBetter`.

14. Click OK.

LISTING 34.11
Post-Build Event Command Line

```
RegisterComPlus -r "$(ProjectDir)\..\AdvancedServicedComponent\bin\
➥AdvancedServicedComponent.dll"
```

In addition to the registration issues, most projects have multiple projects with serviced components, each with a different version number. It is advantageous to keep them and other common information the same across all components, to reduce configuration debug issues.

To improve the quality of the solution, factor common items in `AssemblyInfo.vb` into `SolutionInfo.vb`:

1. Add a text file named `SolutionInfo.vb` to the solution (right-click on Solution Enterprise Services [five projects] and select Add New Item).

2. Copy the content of `AssemblyInfo.vb` from `BasicServicedComponent`.

3. Paste it into `AssemblyInfo.vb` in `AdvancedServicedComponent` and into `SolutionInfo.vb` in Solution Items.

4. Change the name of the COM+ application to `AdvancedServicedApp` in `AssemblyInfo.vb`.

5. In `AssemblyInfo.vb`, remove `AssemblyCompany`, `AssemblyProduct`, `AssemblyCopyright`, `AssemblyTrademark`, `CLSCompliant`, `AssemblyVersion`, and `AssemblyKeyFile` (see Listing 34.12). These are shared and are specified in `SolutionInfo.vb`.

34

Introduction to the Architecture for Enterprise Services

6. In `SolutionInfo.vb`, remove `AssemblyTitle`, `AssemblyDescription`, `ApplicationName`, `ApplicationActivation`, and `ApplicationAccessControl`. If you changed the version number previously, set it back to 1.0.0.0 (see Listing 34.13).

7. Add a shared link from the project `AdvancedServicedComponent` to `SolutionInfo.vb`:

   a. Right-click on the project `AdvancedServicedComponent`.

   b. Select Add, Add Existing Item.

   c. Navigate to the parent directory and select `SolutionInfo.vb`.

   d. Click the little down arrow on the Open button and select Link File (see Figure 34.12).

8. A shortcut has been added to the project items. The component is complete!

LISTING 34.12
Project `AdvancedServicedComponent`, File `AssemblyInfo.vb`

```
Imports System
Imports System.Reflection
Imports System.Runtime.InteropServices
Imports System.EnterpriseServices


<Assembly: AssemblyTitle("")>
<Assembly: AssemblyDescription("")>


<Assembly: ApplicationName("AdvancedServicedApp")>
'<Assembly: ApplicationActivation(ActivationOption.Library)>
<Assembly: ApplicationActivation(ActivationOption.Server)>
<Assembly: ApplicationAccessControl(False)>
```

LISTING 34.13
`SolutionInfo.vb`

```
Imports System
Imports System.Reflection
Imports System.Runtime.InteropServices
Imports System.EnterpriseServices


<Assembly: AssemblyCompany("My Company")>
<Assembly: AssemblyProduct("My Product")>
<Assembly: AssemblyCopyright("Copyright 2004, My Company")>
```

LISTING 34.13
Continued

```
<Assembly: AssemblyTrademark("")>
<Assembly: CLSCompliant(True)>

<Assembly: AssemblyVersion("1.0.0.0")>
<Assembly: AssemblyKeyFile("\KeyFiles\TestServer.snk")>
```

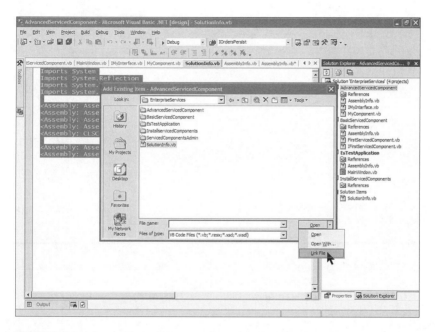

FIGURE 34.12   Adding a shared link to SolutionInfo.vb.

TIP

You can extend the factoring out of additional assembly attributes into other shared `XxxxInfo.vb` files. For example, one file for each COM+ application named `<complusappname>Info.vb` containing the application's activation mode, name, and security attributes.

34

Finally, extend the test client to use the new improved project:

1. Add a reference in the test client to `AdvancedServicedComponent`.

2. Add an `Imports` statement to `AdvancedServicedComponent` at the beginning of `MainWindow.vb`.

Introduction to the Architecture for Enterprise Services

3. Add new buttons to the test client to exercise the new component (see Figure 34.13). Add a group box and four buttons. Rename the buttons m_btnNew, m_btnCall, m_btnDispose, and m_btnAssignNothing.

4. Add a handler for each button (double-click on the button) and change the code as shown in Listing 34.14.

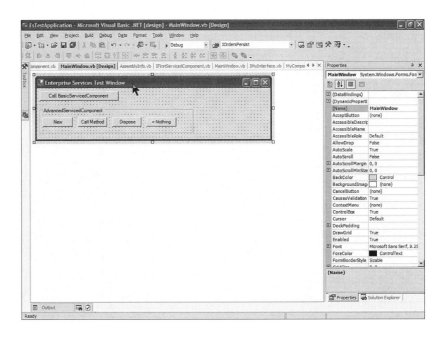

FIGURE 34.13   Test user interface.

LISTING 34.14
Button Handlers for Test UI

```
Private m_AdvancedComponent As IMyInterface

Private Sub btnNew_Click(ByVal sender As System.Object, ByVal e As System.
➡EventArgs) _
     Handles m_btnNew.Click


   m_AdvancedComponent = New MyComponent
End Sub


Private Sub btnCall_Click(ByVal sender As System.Object, ByVal e As System.
➡EventArgs) _
     Handles m_btnCall.Click
```

LISTING 34.14
Continued

```
    m_AdvancedComponent.Method1()
End Sub

Private Sub btnDispose_Click(ByVal sender As System.Object, ByVal e As System.
➥EventArgs) _
     Handles m_btnDispose.Click

   ServicedComponent.DisposeObject(m_AdvancedComponent)
End Sub

Private Sub btnAssignNothing_Click(ByVal sender As System.Object, ByVal e As
➥System.EventArgs) _
     Handles m_btnAssignNothing.Click

   m_AdvancedComponent = Nothing
End Sub
```

Run the application and test it thoroughly.

Adding Instrumentation and Documentation to Serviced Components

COM+ has built-in instrumentation for serviced components. Add an
EventTrackingEnabled attribute **1** before the class MyComponent (see
Listing 34.15).

> **TIP**
>
> You should always use the attribute EventTrackingEnabled because it simplifies debugging for a myriad of problems. Because of this attribute, the Component Services MMC plug-in reflects statistics for component use and transactions.

34

A DescriptionAttribute can be applied to assemblies, serviced components,
interfaces, and methods. It is reflected in the Component Services MMC plug-in. The
code in Listing 34.15 applies the DescriptionAttribute to the serviced component MyComponent.

Adding Instrumentation and Documentation to Serviced Components

TIP
Great naming conventions for your COM+ applications, serviced components, interfaces, and methods are better than using the description attribute. Generally, great naming conventions can eliminate the need for extensive commenting of code.

LISTING 34.15

Changes to `MyComponent`

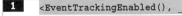

```
<EventTrackingEnabled(), _
 Description("A sample component")> _
Public Class MyComponent
    Inherits ServicedComponent
    Implements IMyInterface

    Private Sub Method1() Implements IMyInterface.Method1
```

Summary

This chapter introduced Enterprise Services, their relationship to *n*-tier systems, and interface-based programming. It also showed how to build a simple serviced component. Finally, it covered how to produce a design pattern that contains serviced components and then how to refine it to avoid common pitfalls in developing serviced components.

Further Reading

Lowy, Juval. *COM and .NET Component Services*. O'Reilly & Associates, 2001.

34

35 ACTIVATION-RELATED SERVICES

IN BRIEF

Clients that hold references to serviced components do not scale because of the amount of system resources consumed. This is exceptionally bad for Internet-scale applications. Just-In-Time activation (JITA) and pooling address (or, at least, mitigate) the scalability problems while maintaining acceptable performance. The service `ConstructionEnabled` mitigates the lack of parameterized constructors in serviced components. Components should also indicate whether they are capable of supporting load balancing. Additional COM+ application-level activation attributes, such as application pooling and recycling, are deployment-oriented services and, therefore, are not covered in this book.

WHAT YOU NEED

SOFTWARE REQUIREMENTS	Windows 2000, XP, or 2003
	.NET Framework 1.1 SDK
	Visual Studio .NET 2003 with Visual Basic .NET installed
	Windows Component Services installed
	Administrative rights on the machine
HARDWARE REQUIREMENTS	PC desktop or laptop
SKILL REQUIREMENTS	Advanced knowledge of Visual Basic .NET
	Advanced knowledge of the .NET Framework
	Basic understanding of COM+ and Enterprise Services

ACTIVATION-RELATED SERVICES AT A GLANCE

Improving Scalability with Just-In-Time Activation (JITA)

Clients that hold references to serviced components do not scale because of the amount of system resources consumed. JITA addresses this by instantiating and destroying the object for each call. Side effects of this architecture are deterministic finalization and automatic concurrency control.

For each call from the client, COM+ creates a new object, calls its constructor, executes the actual call, calls the finalizer, and makes the object eligible for garbage collection. Figure 35.1 shows this behavior as a diagram. This is very similar to remote objects configured as server activated single-call objects.

JITA objects cannot retain any state in memory. If your business logic requires stateful operation, you must store it in a durable store at the end of each method call and retrieve it from the same store at the beginning of each method call. This is very similar to the session-state storage for web pages; however, you have to create the code for persisting and retrieving the state yourself.

The client section of the interception architecture (specifically, the proxy) stays allocated between calls. Creating proxies each time is a significant performance penalty (at least a factor of 2).

This chapter reuses the project from Chapter 34, "Introduction to Enterprise Services," as a starting point.

1. Copy the entire project created in the previous chapter to a new directory, EsActivation.

2. Rename the solution files (.sln and .suo) to EsActivation.

3. Remove the projects BasicServicedComponent and InstallServicedComponents; they are no longer needed.

4. Remove the directories for BasicServicedComponent and InstallServicedComponents.

Listing 35.1 shows how to add JITA to MyComponent:

1. Add the JITA attribute **2**.

2. Add a counter to the class **3**.

3. Add a constructor that initializes the counter to 0 **4**.

4. Add code to Method1 incrementing the counter **5**.

5. Modify the message box to display this counter, and use System.Reflection **1** to retrieve the method name **6**.

35

Improving Scalability with Just-In-Time Activation (JITA)

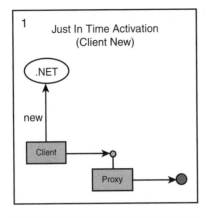
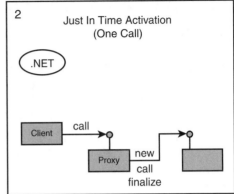
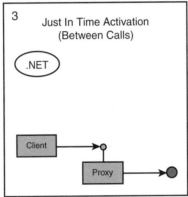
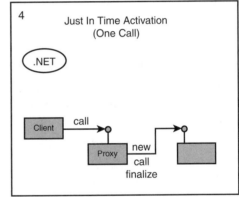
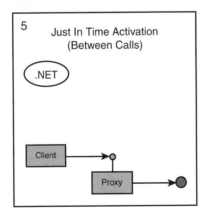
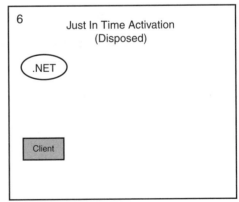

FIGURE 35.1   Just-In-Time activation.

LISTING 35.1
Changes to `MyComponent` for JITA

```
Imports System.EnterpriseServices
Imports System.Text
Imports System.Reflection                                                    1
Imports System.Threading
Imports System.Windows.Forms


<EventTrackingEnabled(), _
 JustInTimeActivation()> _                                                    2
Public Class MyComponent
    Inherits ServicedComponent
    Implements IMyInterface


    Private m_Counter As Integer                                             3


    Public Sub New()
        m_Counter = 0                                                        4
        DisplayTraceMessageBox()
    End Sub


    Protected Overrides Sub Finalize()
        DisplayTraceMessageBox()
    End Sub


    Private Sub Method1() Implements IMyInterface.Method1
        m_Counter += 1                                                       5
        DisplayTraceMessageBox()
    End Sub


    Private Sub DisplayTraceMessageBox()
        Dim className As String                                             6
        Dim methodName As String
        Dim details As New StringBuilder
        Dim sf As New StackFrame(1) ' gets the stack frame calling us
        Dim mi As MethodBase = sf.GetMethod() 'info about the method calling us
        className = mi.DeclaringType.Name 'class declaring the method calling us
        methodName = mi.Name 'the actual name of the method  calling us
        details.Append(className)
        details.Append(".")
        details.Append(methodName)
        details.Append(Environment.NewLine)
        details.Append("   m_Counter=")
        details.Append(m_Counter)
        details.Append(Environment.NewLine)
```

35

Improving Scalability with Just-In-Time Activation (JITA)

LISTING 35.1
Continued

```
    details.Append("   Process=")
    details.Append(Process.GetCurrentProcess().Id)
    details.Append(Environment.NewLine)
    details.Append("   Thread=")
    details.Append(Thread.CurrentThread.GetHashCode().ToString())
    Try
        details.Append(Environment.NewLine)
        details.Append("   Context=")
        'Throws COM Exception if zero services requested
        Dim contextID As Guid = ContextUtil.ContextId
        details.Append(ContextUtil.ContextId.ToString())
    Catch ex As Exception
        'Catches exception if no context (zero services requested)
        details.Append("<None>")
    End Try
    MessageBox.Show(details.ToString(), _
        "Show Method Call Detail")
    End Sub

End Class
```

Next, test this code:

1. Start the test client.

2. Click New. The constructor (.ctor) is invoked.

3. Click Call Method. Method1 with a counter value at 1 is invoked.

4. Click Call Method a second time. Method1 with a counter value at 2 is invoked.

This is not the expected behavior. The JITA attribute only activates the invocation of the IObjectControl interface implemented by ServicedComponent.

For true JITA behavior, all public methods that implement public interfaces must be marked with the attribute AutoComplete **1**. Listing 35.2 shows how to change Method1.

Implementing the COM+ Interface IObjectControl

LISTING 35.2

Changes to MyComponent.Method1 for JITA Autocompletion

```
<AutoComplete()> _
Private Sub Method1() Implements IMyInterface.Method1
    m_Counter += 1
    DisplayTraceMessageBox()
End Sub
```

Next, test this code by following these steps:

1. Start the test client.

2. Click New. The constructor (.ctor) is invoked.

3. Click Call Method. Method1 with a counter value at 1 and Finalize are invoked.

4. Click Call Method a second time. The constructor (.ctor), Method1 with a counter value at 1, and Finalize are invoked.

This is the correct behavior.

TIP

It is possible to use JITA without AutoComplete using ContextUtil.SetComplete. Using AutoComplete is the preferred method, however, because it works better for serviced components with transactions; JITA is frequently used because of transactions. Additionally, every return path from a public method in a JITA serviced component must call this method. This requirement can be satisfied only with a Try-Finally block; this adds unnecessary complexity to your code.

Implementing the COM+ Interface IObjectControl

The framework class ServicedComponent implements IObjectControl (an unmanaged code interface that is not directly visible in managed code). IObjectControl is used only if you specify JITA, object pooling, or transaction support (transaction support implies JITA). Serviced components can override the virtual methods implementing IObjectControl from ServicedComponent.

35

Implementing the COM+ Interface `IObjectControl`

`IObjectControl` contains three methods: `Activate`, `Deactivate`, and `CanBePooled`. For JITA objects, `Activate` is called before any method is called (always after the constructor), and `Deactivate` is called after the call returns (assuming that you specified `AutoComplete`). `CanBePooled` is used for pooled objects only. `Activate` should be used to create or initialize context-specific (or client-specific) objects, such as other serviced components, and to open database connections when using transactions. `Deactivate` should be used to destroy, dispose, or close the context specific objects handled in `Activate`.

Next, add the three `IObjectControl` methods to MyComponent (see Listing 35.3):

1. Open `MyComponent.vb`.

2. Select (Overrides) from the top-left drop-down box, and select Activate from the top-right drop-down box (see Figure 35.2). Visual Studio inserts a skeleton for the overridden method.

3. Repeat for `Deactivate` and `CanBePooled`.

4. Add a call to `DisplayTraceMessageBox()` for each method (see the shaded code in Listing 35.3 **1** **2** **3**).

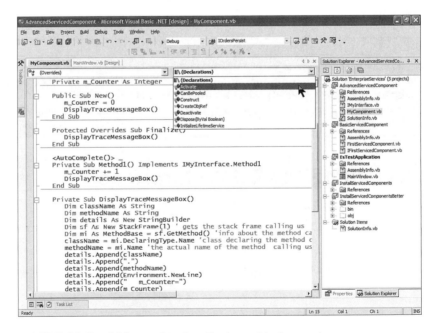

FIGURE 35.2   Adding a virtual method override for `Activate`.

LISTING 35.3

Changes to MyComponent for IObjectControl

```
Protected Overrides Sub Activate()
    DisplayTraceMessageBox()                                              1
End Sub


Protected Overrides Sub Deactivate()
    DisplayTraceMessageBox()                                              2
End Sub


Protected Overrides Function CanBePooled() As Boolean
    DisplayTraceMessageBox()                                              3
    End Function
End Class
```

Next, test this code:

1. Start the test client.

2. Click New. The constructor (.ctor) and Activate are invoked.

3. Click Call Method. Method1 with a counter value at 1, and Deactivate and Finalize are invoked.

4. Click Call Method a second time; the constructor (.ctor), Activate, Method1 with a counter value at 1, Deactivate, and Finalize are invoked.

This is the correct behavior. Figure 35.3 shows a UML activity diagram of the life cycle for a JITA object.

Implementing the COM+ Interface `IObjectControl`

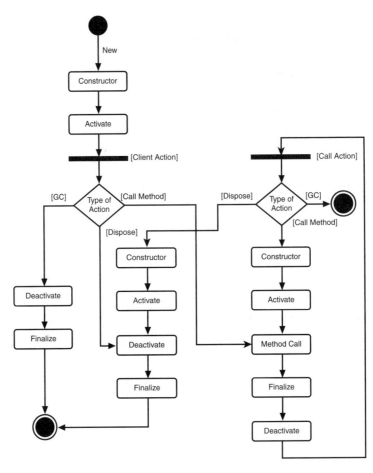

FIGURE 35.3   Activity diagram for JITA.

Improving Performance with Object Pooling

Clients that hold references to serviced components (or remote objects) do not scale due to the amount of system resources consumed. This is exceptionally bad for Internet-scale applications. JITA addresses this by instantiating and destroying the object for each call. However, this is bad if the component is expensive to create. If this creation is common for all clients, you should use object pooling. If the application has few clients with short-duration use cases, object pooling by itself is sufficient. If the application has a large number of clients or a few clients with long-duration use cases, object pooling must be combined with JITA.

For each object creation, COM+ checks whether the pool has an available object and takes it out of the pool. When the client is finished with the object, COM+ returns it to the pool (see Figure 35.4).

Improving Performance with Object Pooling

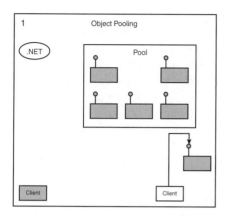

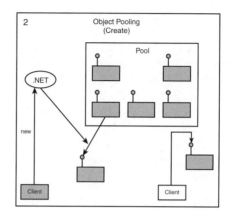

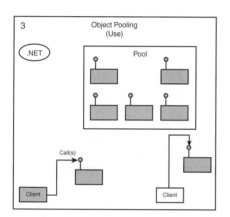

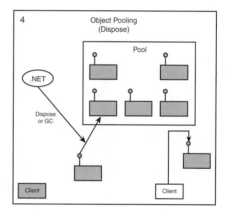

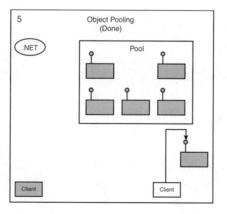

FIGURE 35.4   How pooling works.

35

Improving Performance with Object Pooling

When the first client requests an object (with New), COM+ allocates MinPoolSize objects, activates the first one, and hands it to the client. For later requests, if the pool has an object, COM+ hands it to the client. If the pool has no objects left and the maximum number of pooled objects is not yet reached, COM+ instantiates a new object and hands it to the client. If the pool has no objects left and the pool is full (MaxPoolSize is reached), COM+ blocks the client and waits for an object to be returned to the pool. If the CreationTimeout expires before an object is returned to the pool, an exception is thrown. This is often an indication that you have reached system threshold or need to increase the number of objects pooled—or maybe some other issue, such as a timeout elsewhere, is causing objects not to be released.

Handing an object to the client causes Activate to execute. The client should always call Dispose when it is done with the object. This causes Deactivate to be called. The object is asked if it is okay to be returned to the pool. If CanBePooled returns false, the object is destroyed; otherwise, it is returned to the pool. Figure 35.5 shows a UML activity diagram of the life cycle for a pooled object.

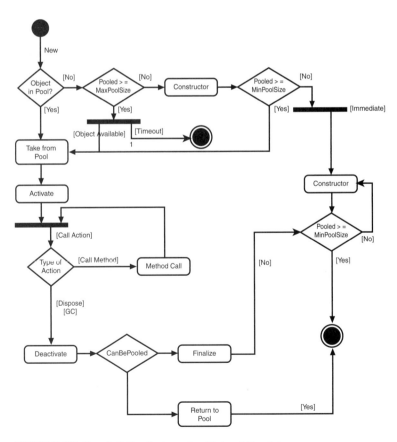

FIGURE 35.5   Activity diagram for ObjectPooling.

The constructor (`Sub New`) does initializations for all clients (for example, ADO.NET objects, such as connections, commands, and adapters), and `Finalize` cleans up those resources shared by all clients. `Activate` and `Deactivate` are called for each client. This allows for client- or context-specific initialization (for example, opening and closing database connections) and cleanup.

Converting the JITA component to `ObjectPooling` is trivial. Listing 35.4 shows how to use a minimum pool size of 2 and a maximum pool size of 4. You also implement `CanBePooled` to ask (with a `MessageBox`) if it should answer `True` or `False`. A real implementation of `CanBePooled` should check the state of "perishable" resources (for example, a database connection object in a bad state):

1. Replace `JustInTimeActivation` with `ObjectPooling(MinPoolSize:=2, MaxPoolSize:=4)` (see Listing 35.4) **1** .

2. Finish the method `CanBePooled` to ask for the behavior to execute (see Listing 35.5 **1**).

LISTING 35.4
Changes to `MyComponent` **for** `ObjectPooling`

```
<EventTrackingEnabled(), _
 ObjectPooling(MinPoolSize:=2, MaxPoolSize:=4)> _        1
Public Class MyComponent
   Inherits ServicedComponent
   Implements IMyInterface


   Private m_Counter As Integer
```

LISTING 35.5
Changes to `MyComponent` **for** `CanBePooled`

```
Protected Overrides Function CanBePooled() As Boolean
   DisplayTraceMessageBox()
      Return DialogResult.Yes = MessageBox.Show( _          1
         "Return the object to the pool?", _
         "CanBePooled", MessageBoxButtons.YesNo)
End Function
```

35

To show the correct behavior of pooled serviced components, add a global counter **1** shared by all clients **2** **3** **4** **7** , and initialize the local `m_Counter` correctly in `Activate` **5** and set it to `-1` in `Deactivate` **6** (see Listing 35.6).

Improving Performance with Object Pooling

LISTING 35.6
MyComponent.vb after the Changes

```vb
Imports System.EnterpriseServices
Imports System.Text
Imports System.Reflection
Imports System.Threading
Imports System.Windows.Forms

<EventTrackingEnabled(), _
 ObjectPooling(MinPoolSize:=2, MaxPoolSize:=4)> _
Public Class MyComponent
    Inherits ServicedComponent
    Implements IMyInterface
```

1
```vb
    Private m_GlobalCounter As Integer
    Private m_Counter As Integer


    Public Sub New()
```
2
```vb
        m_GlobalCounter = 0 'simulate initializing global resources
        m_Counter = -1        'simulate not initializing client specific resources
        DisplayTraceMessageBox()
    End Sub


    Protected Overrides Sub Finalize()
```
3
```vb
        m_GlobalCounter = -1 'simulate releasing global resources
        DisplayTraceMessageBox()
    End Sub


    <AutoComplete()> _
    Private Sub Method1() Implements IMyInterface.Method1
```
4
```vb
        m_GlobalCounter += 1
        m_Counter += 1
        DisplayTraceMessageBox()
    End Sub


    Protected Overrides Sub Activate()
```
5
```vb
        m_Counter = 0        'simulate initializing client specific resources
        DisplayTraceMessageBox()
    End Sub


    Protected Overrides Sub Deactivate()
```
6
```vb
        m_Counter = -1        'simulate not releasing client specific resources
        DisplayTraceMessageBox()
    End Sub
```

35

LISTING 35.6
Continued

```vb
Protected Overrides Function CanBePooled() As Boolean
   DisplayTraceMessageBox()
   Return DialogResult.Yes = MessageBox.Show( _
      "Return the object to the pool?", _
      "CanBePooled", MessageBoxButtons.YesNo)
End Function

Private Sub DisplayTraceMessageBox()
   Dim className As String
   Dim methodName As String
   Dim details As New StringBuilder
   Dim sf As New StackFrame(1) ' gets the stack frame calling us
   Dim mi As MethodBase = sf.GetMethod() 'info about the method calling us
   className = mi.DeclaringType.Name 'class declaring the method calling us
   methodName = mi.Name 'the actual name of the method  calling us
   details.Append(className)
   details.Append(".")
   details.Append(methodName)
   details.Append(Environment.NewLine)
   details.Append("   m_Counter=")
   details.Append(m_Counter)
   details.Append("   m_GlobalCounter=")
   details.Append(m_GlobalCounter)
   details.Append(Environment.NewLine)
   details.Append("   Process=")
   details.Append(Process.GetCurrentProcess().Id)
   details.Append(Environment.NewLine)
   details.Append("   Thread=")
   details.Append(Thread.CurrentThread.GetHashCode().ToString())
   Try
      details.Append(Environment.NewLine)
      details.Append("   Context=")
      'Throws COM Exception if zero services requested
      Dim contextID As Guid = ContextUtil.ContextId
      details.Append(ContextUtil.ContextId.ToString())
   Catch ex As Exception
      'Catches exception if no context (zero services requested)
      details.Append("<None>")
   End Try
   MessageBox.Show(details.ToString(), _
```

7

35

Improving Performance with Object Pooling

LISTING 35.6
Continued

```
        "Show Method Call Detail")
    End Sub

End Class
```

Next, test this code:

1. Start the test client.

2. Click New. the constructor is invoked twice (this is caused by `MinPoolSize:=2`), and `Activate` is invoked once.

3. Click Call Method. `Method1` with an `m_Counter` value at 1 as well as `m_GlobalCounter` at 1 is invoked.

4. Click Call Method a second time; `Activate`, `Method1` with an `m_Counter` value at 2 and `m_GlobalCounter` at 2, `Deactivate`, and `CanBePooled` are invoked.

5. Click Dispose.; `Deactivate` and `CanBePooled` are invoked.

6. Start four more clients, and observe the behavior when clicking New and Call Method. The fifth call to New blocks the client (caused by `MaxPoolSize:=4`). It causes an exception after the default `CreationTimeout`,

7. Select No in `CanBePooled`. The system calls `Finalize`. If you answer three times with No, the number of components in the pool drops below the minimum pool size of 2, and a new object is created to replenish the pool.

Combining JITA with Object Pooling for Improved Scalability and Performance

Unfortunately, object pooling does not scale for a large number of clients or clients with long-duration use cases. Combining JITA and object pooling addresses this problem for most scenarios; therefore, it is arguably the most useful pattern for serviced components. It enables you to create expensive resources once (object pooling), gives you scalability (JITA), and enables you to deal with context-specific initialization (for JITA) in `Activate` and `Deactivate`.

This works similar to object pooling; however, `Activate` and `Deactivate` are called before and after each method call.

Adding JITA to your component with `ObjectPooling` is trivial. Listing 35.7 shows how to add `JustInTimeActivation()` to `ObjectPooling(MinPoolSize:=2, MaxPoolSize:=4)`.

LISTING 35.7

Changes to `MyComponent` **for** `ObjectPooling` **and** `JITA`

```
<EventTrackingEnabled(), _
 JustInTimeActivation(), _
 ObjectPooling(MinPoolSize:=2, MaxPoolSize:=4)> _
Public Class MyComponent
    Inherits ServicedComponent
    Implements IMyInterface


    Private m_GlobalCounter As Integer
```

Retest the modified version. The behavior is very similar to the one for pooled components only, except that the object is retrieved from the pool for each call and returned to it afterward. Repeat the test steps from pooling to observe the correct behavior.

Changing `ObjectPooling` **Parameters During Deployment**

Object pooling has parameters that can and should be adjusted based on the deployment scenario. The parameters for `ObjectPooling` are visible in the `Activation` tab for each component in the COM+ application (see Figure 35.6).

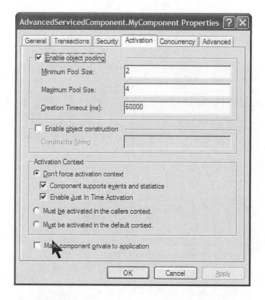

FIGURE 35.6 Activity tab screen shot.

Changing `ObjectPooling` **Parameters During Deployment**

Enabling object pooling is a design decision (as is Just-In-Time activation). Min and max pool sizes should be adjusted based on the application's need and the kind of hardware the application is running on. Creation timeout is 60 seconds, by default; this should not need to be changed. Encountering creation timeouts indicates a flaw in the design or underdimensioned hardware; try throttling back the input. COM+ should select the context needs based on the application activation and services selected.

Passing Run-Time Arguments with a Construction String

Serviced components contain only constructors without parameters because COM+ has no way of passing these parameters. A partial mitigation of this issue uses the constructor string a string configured in the Component Services MMC plug-in. Construction strings are often used for deployment-specific parameters, such as a DB connection string.

Construction strings need to be enabled with the attribute `ConstructionEnabled`, and an override of the virtual method `Construct` needs to be implemented (see Listing 35.8).

1. Comment out the previous object pooling and JITA (to simplify the example) **1**.

2. Add the attribute `ConstructionEnabled` **2**.

3. Add the field `m_ConstructionString` **3**.

4. Add the method `Construct` **4**.

5. Modify `DisplayTraceMessageBox` to display the construction string **5**.

LISTING 35.8
Changes to `MyComponent` **for** `ConstructionEnabled`

```
Imports System.EnterpriseServices
Imports System.Text
Imports System.Reflection
Imports System.Threading
Imports System.Windows.Forms

'<EventTrackingEnabled(), _
'  JustInTimeActivation()> _
'<EventTrackingEnabled(), _
'  ObjectPooling(MinPoolSize:=2, MaxPoolSize:=4)> _
```

35

LISTING 35.8
Continued

```vbnet
'<EventTrackingEnabled(), _                                              1
' JustInTimeActivation(), _
' ObjectPooling(MinPoolSize:=2, MaxPoolSize:=4)> _
<EventTrackingEnabled(), _
ConstructionEnabled(Default:="Our Default String")> _              2
Public Class MyComponent
    Inherits ServicedComponent
    Implements IMyInterface

    Private m_GlobalCounter As Integer
    Private m_Counter As Integer
    Private m_ConstructionString As String                              3

    Public Sub New()
        m_GlobalCounter = 0 'simulate initializing global resources
        m_Counter = -1        'simulate not initializing client specific resources
        DisplayTraceMessageBox()
    End Sub

    Protected Overrides Sub Construct(ByVal s As String)               4
        m_ConstructionString = s
        DisplayTraceMessageBox()
    End Sub

    Protected Overrides Sub Finalize()
        m_GlobalCounter = -1 'simulate releasing global resources
        DisplayTraceMessageBox()
    End Sub

    <AutoComplete()> _
    Private Sub Method1() Implements IMyInterface.Method1
        m_GlobalCounter += 1
        m_Counter += 1
        DisplayTraceMessageBox()
    End Sub

    Protected Overrides Sub Activate()
        m_Counter = 0        'simulate initializing client specific resources
        DisplayTraceMessageBox()
    End Sub

    Protected Overrides Sub Deactivate()
        m_Counter = -1        'simulate not releasing client specific resources
```

35

Passing Run-Time Arguments with a Construction String

LISTING 35.8
Continued

```vb
        DisplayTraceMessageBox()
    End Sub

    Protected Overrides Function CanBePooled() As Boolean
        DisplayTraceMessageBox()
        Return DialogResult.Yes = MessageBox.Show( _
            "Return the object to the pool?", _
            "CanBePooled", MessageBoxButtons.YesNo)
    End Function

    Private Sub DisplayTraceMessageBox()
        Dim className As String
        Dim methodName As String
        Dim details As New StringBuilder
        Dim sf As New StackFrame(1) ' gets the stack frame calling us
        Dim mi As MethodBase = sf.GetMethod() 'info about the method calling us
        className = mi.DeclaringType.Name 'class declaring the method calling us
        methodName = mi.Name 'the actual name of the method  calling us
        details.Append(className)
        details.Append(".")
        details.Append(methodName)
        details.Append(Environment.NewLine)
        details.Append("   Construction string=")
        details.Append(m_ConstructionString)
        details.Append(Environment.NewLine)
        details.Append("   m_Counter=")
        details.Append(m_Counter)
        details.Append(Environment.NewLine)
        details.Append("   m_GlobalCounter=")
        details.Append(m_GlobalCounter)
        details.Append(Environment.NewLine)
        details.Append("   Process=")
        details.Append(Process.GetCurrentProcess().Id)
        details.Append(Environment.NewLine)
        details.Append("   Thread=")
        details.Append(Thread.CurrentThread.GetHashCode().ToString())
        Try
            details.Append(Environment.NewLine)
            details.Append("   Context=")
            'Throws COM Exception if zero services requested
            Dim contextID As Guid = ContextUtil.ContextId
            details.Append(ContextUtil.ContextId.ToString())
        Catch ex As Exception
```

5

35

LISTING 35.8
Continued

```
        'Catches exception if no context (zero services requested)
        details.Append("<None>")
    End Try
    MessageBox.Show(details.ToString(), _
        "Show Method Call Detail")
  End Sub

End Class
```

Enabling Load Balancing

Load balancing is common for web applications. Multiple servers can share the load because the state is stored between HTTP requests. In addition, the session state needs to be stored in a session-state server or a durable store such as a SQL Server.

COM+ supports load balancing in some Windows versions, such as Windows 2000 Advanced Server. Windows XP does not support load balancing. Your components should indicate whether they support load balancing with the class-level attribute `LoadBalancingSupported`. Adding this attribute allows system administrators to install a supported Windows version and enable COM+ load balancing for this component.

> **TIP**
>
> Components with JITA (with or without pooling) or `Transaction` support that are written correctly can and should support load balancing. Components that are "written correctly" retrieve any state information at the beginning of each call and store the changed state information at the end of each call.

Summary

In this chapter, you learned how to use activation-oriented services in COM+ to improve the scalability and deployability of your serviced components. The most useful pattern is a serviced component with pooling and JITA enabled. Planning ahead for realistic deployment scenarios, such as load balancing, improves the robustness of your components.

35

Further Reading

Lowy, Juval. *COM and .NET Component Services*. O'Reilly & Associates, 2001.

36 TRANSACTION SERVICES

IN BRIEF

This chapter explains how transactions simplify transaction handling in simple cases and enable correctness in more complex scenarios that are impossible to handle any other way. You will also learn how to correctly combine transactions with object pooling, Just In Time Activation (JITA) and construction strings, as well as how to integrate transactions with web application and web services.

WHAT YOU NEED

SOFTWARE REQUIREMENTS	Windows 2000, XP, or 2003 .NET Framework 1.1 SDK Visual Studio .NET 2003 Windows Component Services installed Administrative rights on your machine SQL Server 2000 Microsoft Desktop Database Engine or (MSDE) 2000
HARDWARE REQUIREMENTS	PC desktop or laptop
SKILL REQUIREMENTS	Advanced knowledge of Visual Basic .NET Advanced knowledge of the .NET Framework

TRANSACTION SERVICES AT A GLANCE

Simplify Transactional Code with COM+ Transactions

In Chapter 11, "ADO.NET Classes" you learned about transactions for a single database. This works for a simple system (see Figure 36.1). Even in this simple case, however, the handling of transactions requires too much code (creating the transaction, assigning it to all of the command objects, and adding `Try-Catch-Finally` blocks to commit or abort the transaction).

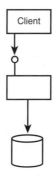

FIGURE 36.1   Simple transaction.

For scenarios that are more complex (see Figure 36.2), it becomes increasingly difficult to determine who opens the database connection and starts the transaction. The resulting sharing of a single connection object can get quite confusing.

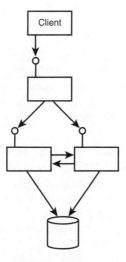

FIGURE 36.2   Simple transaction with multiple components.

36

Simplify Transactional Code with COM+ Transactions

When you use multiple transacted resources (see Figure 36.3), ADO.NET transactions can no longer handle the requirements.

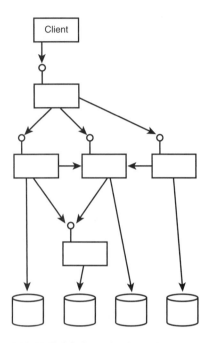

FIGURE 36.3   Distributed transaction.

Transactions that involve multiple resources are called distributed transactions. They were the main reason for the invention of Microsoft Transaction Services (MTS), the predecessor of COM+. Simple ADO.NET transactions can be committed with a single-step process. Distributed transactions require a two-phase commit protocol.

MICROSOFT TRANSACTION CONTROLLER AND COM+ TRANSACTIONS

COM+ transactions are handled by Microsoft's Distributed Transaction Controller (MS DTC). The DTC manages transactions that span multiple resources on one or more machines. Resources that implement a COM+ resource manager can be managed by the DTC (participate in a distributed transaction).

All major database vendors have implemented resource managers. Some vendors require the installation of an option pack to install the resource manager.

Resource managers can be implemented for nondatabase types of resources, as long as they can support database ACID (atomic, consistent, isolated, and durable) properties. Microsoft's Message Queue product implements a resource manager; therefore, it can participate in a distributed transaction to guarantee delivery of the message.

36

Simplify Transactional Code with COM+ Transactions

You will learn how to use the Transaction service for serviced components to simplify your code—and, more important, to make your code work correctly when using multiple components or managed resources, such as databases and message queues.

Transactions and Isolation Levels Explained

Transactions guarantee consistency: All operations within a transaction succeed, or no changes are applied. Most databases and a few other systems provide transactional integrity. The most often used example is money transfer between bank accounts. You and your bank want either all updates to succeed or none to succeed. Database terminology uses the mnemonic ACID for atomic, consistent, isolated, and durable. ACID is a required ingredient for any system that stores state information.

A as in Atomic

Atomic means that all changes to the system are made as one indivisible operation. The changes are applied exactly once or not at all if the system encounters errors. After they are completed, there is no more work to be performed. Failures are handled automatically, and the system is rolled back to the state before the transaction.

C as in Consistent

Transactions must transform the system from one consistent state to a new consistent state (the new state could be the same as the old state). This requirement is the only ACID property that is the application developer's responsibility. The atomic aspect simplifies this requirement by providing automatic error recovery. Additionally, the transaction must release all resources held, such as database locks.

I as in Isolated

Isolated ensures that while the transaction is in progress, no other entity is allowed to see the intermediate (and, therefore, inconsistent) state. If this requirement is violated, an inconsistency occurs. Concurrent transactions must behave the same as transactions executed serially. Most systems enable the developer to relax this requirement through a property called the isolation level. The highest level of isolation is `Serializable`; it is the only one guaranteeing true isolation. `RepeatableRead` locks the data involved in the read and guarantees that rereading the data succeeds; however, it does not prevent phantom data when reading multiple tables. `ReadCommitted` uses shared locks to avoid reading modified data. It results in nonrepeatable reads and phantom data. `ReadUncommitted` does not use locks and does not honor locks issued by other transactions. Data read is often inconsistent.

> **TIP**
>
> You should always use `Serializable` in your system. Lower levels should be used with extreme caution for high-throughput needs. Before lowering the level, use an extensive justification and verification process proving that your data can handle a lower level. Your coding standard should state that you require upper management–level approval to lower isolation levels. Remember that performance is irrelevant if your code produces the wrong results.

36

Simplify Transactional Code with COM+ Transactions

D as in Durable

The consistent states of transactions must persist even if the machines involved in it are turned off or crash. In other words, the results of successful transactions persist even if the machine crashes immediately after deciding to commit the transaction.

Implementing a Transactional Component

Transaction support in COM+ implies JITA. Now you will write a simple system to maintain transfers between bank accounts. You will experience the kind of inconsistency that occurs when not using transactions, and you will see the correct behavior after implementing transactions.

> **NOTE**
>
> The example you are developing is very simple. It is possible to cover the ACID requirements in code without the help of transactions, but all real-life systems deal with much more complicated transactions.

First, you need to create a simple database for the bank accounts as follows:

1. Use Server Explorer in VS .NET to create the database MySimpleBank and the table Accounts with the columns AccountNumber (primary key), Owner, and Balance (see Figure 36.4).

2. Add two accounts: 1, Mary, 10000 and 2, John, 500 (see Figure 36.5).

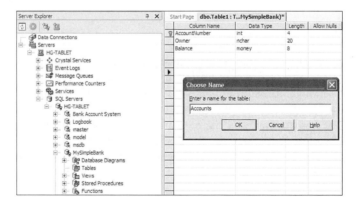

FIGURE 36.4   MySimpleBank database design.

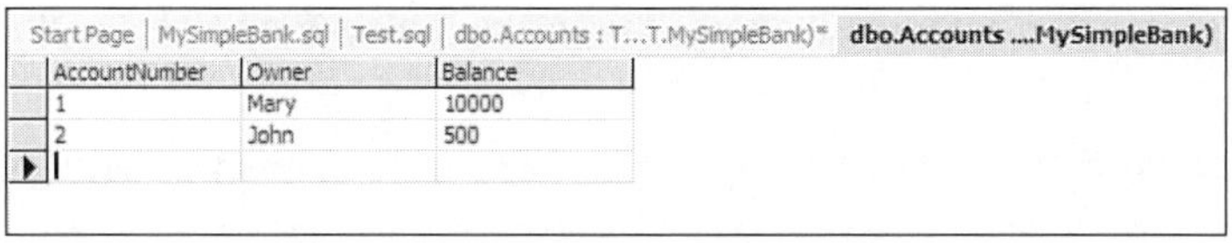

Simplify Transactional Code with COM+ Transactions

FIGURE 36.5   MySimpleBank table Accounts content.

Next, you create a solution with the component `AccountManager` and the test client `WindowsClient`:

 1. Create an empty solution named `Transactions`.

 2. Add a VB class library project named BankServer.

 3. Delete `Class1.vb`.

 4. Add a reference to `Systems.EnterpriseServices`.

 5. Change `AssemblyInfo.vb` and add `SolutionInfo.vb` the same way as in Chapter 34, "Introduction to Enterprise Services," in the section "Improving Your COM+ Hygiene."

 6. Add an interface named `IAccountManager` to the project (see Listing 36.1).

 7. Add a class named `AccountManager` to the project (see Listing 36.2). This class allows for a simple transfer of funds between two accounts. **1** You will add the transaction later. Change `HG-TABLET` to the name of your machine.

 8. Add a VB Windows application project named `WindowsClient` to the solution.

 9. Rename the class `Form1` to `MainWindow`, rename `Form1.vb` to `MainWindow.vb`, and set the project's startup object to `MainWindow`.

10. Change the caption on `MainWindow`.

11. Add all the UI elements in Figure 36.6.

12. Rename the text fields to `m_txtFrom`, `m_txtTo`, and `m_txtAmount`; the button to `m_btnTransfer`; and the grid to `m_AccountsGrid` (see Figure 36.6).

36

Simplify Transactional Code with COM+ Transactions

13. Add the connection and adapter (drag in the table from Server Explorer) and rename them to m_Connection and m_AccountsAdapter (see Figure 36.6).

14. Generate the DataSet AccountsDataset, and rename the resulting instance AccountsDataset1 to m_AccountsDataset.

15. Bind the grid's DataSource to m_AccountsDataset and the DataMember to Accounts.

16. Double-click on the form and on the button to add the handlers.

17. Change the name of the button handler to OnTransfer_Click, **3** and add the code in Listing 36.3 to both handlers. **1** **2** **4**

18. Add a C# project named InstallServicedComponents to execute the post-build step, as shown in Chapter 34, in the section "Improving Your COM+ Hygiene" with the project InstallServicedComponentsBetter. Use the command line RegisterComPlus -r "$(ProjectDir)\..\BankServer\bin\BankServer.dll".

LISTING 36.1
Interface IAccountManager in IAccountmanager.vb

```
Public Interface IAccountManager
    Sub TransferMoney(ByVal fromAccount As Integer, _
        ByVal toAccount As Integer, ByVal amount As Decimal)
End Interface
```

LISTING 36.2
Component AccountManager in Accountmanager.vb

```
Imports System.Data.SqlClient
Imports System.EnterpriseServices

<EventTrackingEnabled()> _
Public Class AccountManager
    Inherits ServicedComponent
    Implements IAccountManager

    Public Sub New()
        InitializeComponent()
    End Sub
```

Simplify Transactional Code with COM+ Transactions

LISTING 36.2
Continued

```vb
<AutoComplete()> _                                                              1
Private Sub TransferMoney(ByVal fromAccount As Integer, _
    ByVal toAccount As Integer, ByVal amount As Decimal) _
    Implements IAccountManager.TransferMoney

    Dim fromBalance As Decimal
    Dim toBalance As Decimal

    toBalance = GetBalance(toAccount)
    toBalance += amount
    StoreBalance(toAccount, toBalance)

    fromBalance = GetBalance(fromAccount)
    fromBalance -= amount
    If fromBalance < 0 Then
        Throw New ArgumentException("Not enough money in account")
    End If
    StoreBalance(fromAccount, fromBalance)

End Sub
```

```vb
Private m_cmdRetrieveBalance As SqlCommand
Private m_cmdStoreBalance As SqlCommand
Private m_MySimpleBankConnection As SqlConnection

Private Sub InitializeComponent()
    ' initialize connection
    m_MySimpleBankConnection = New SqlConnection
    m_MySimpleBankConnection.ConnectionString = "workstation id=""HG-
TABLET"";packet size=4096;integrated security=SSPI;data source=" & _
    """HG-TABLET"";persist security info=True;initial catalog=MySimpleBank"

    'retrieving the balance
    m_cmdRetrieveBalance = New SqlCommand( _
        "SELECT Balance FROM Accounts WHERE AccountNumber = @AccountNumber", _
        m_MySimpleBankConnection)
    m_cmdRetrieveBalance.Parameters.Add( _
        New SqlParameter("@AccountNumber", SqlDbType.Int, 4))
```

36

Simplify Transactional Code with COM+ Transactions

LISTING 36.2
Continued

```vb
        'storing the changed balance back
        m_cmdStoreBalance = New SqlCommand("UPDATE Accounts " & _
            "SET Balance = @Balance WHERE AccountNumber = @AccountNumber", _
            m_MySimpleBankConnection)
        m_cmdStoreBalance.Parameters.Add( _
            New SqlParameter("@AccountNumber", SqlDbType.Int, 4))
        m_cmdStoreBalance.Parameters.Add( _
            New SqlParameter("@Balance", SqlDbType.Money, 8))
    End Sub

    Public Function GetBalance(ByVal account As Integer) As Decimal
        Dim balance As Decimal

        m_MySimpleBankConnection.Open()
        Try
            m_cmdRetrieveBalance.Parameters(0).Value = account
            balance = CType(m_cmdRetrieveBalance.ExecuteScalar(), Decimal)
        Finally
            m_MySimpleBankConnection.Close()
        End Try


        Return balance
    End Function

    Public Function StoreBalance(ByVal account As Integer, _
            ByVal balance As Decimal)

        m_MySimpleBankConnection.Open()
        Try
            m_cmdStoreBalance.Parameters(0).Value = account
            m_cmdStoreBalance.Parameters(1).Value = balance
            m_cmdStoreBalance.ExecuteNonQuery()
        Finally
            m_MySimpleBankConnection.Close()
        End Try
    End Function

End Class
```

36

Simplify Transactional Code with COM+ Transactions

FIGURE 36.6   Test UI.

LISTING 36.3
UI Handlers for Test Client

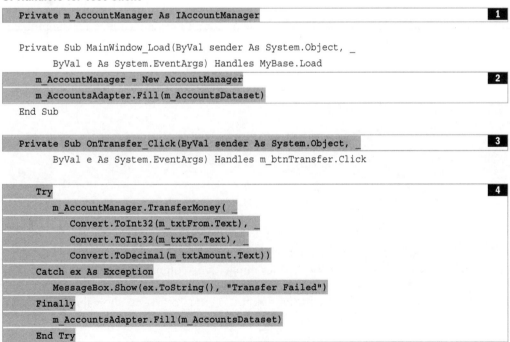

```vb
Private m_AccountManager As IAccountManager                              1

Private Sub MainWindow_Load(ByVal sender As System.Object, _
    ByVal e As System.EventArgs) Handles MyBase.Load
    m_AccountManager = New AccountManager                                2
    m_AccountsAdapter.Fill(m_AccountsDataset)
End Sub

Private Sub OnTransfer_Click(ByVal sender As System.Object, _           3
    ByVal e As System.EventArgs) Handles m_btnTransfer.Click

    Try                                                                 4
        m_AccountManager.TransferMoney( _
            Convert.ToInt32(m_txtFrom.Text), _
            Convert.ToInt32(m_txtTo.Text), _
            Convert.ToDecimal(m_txtAmount.Text))
    Catch ex As Exception
        MessageBox.Show(ex.ToString(), "Transfer Failed")
    Finally
        m_AccountsAdapter.Fill(m_AccountsDataset)
    End Try
End Sub
```

36

Simplify Transactional Code with COM+ Transactions

Test this application by following these steps:

1. Set the startup project to WindowsClient and press F5.

2. Transfer $1,000 from account 1 to account 2, and watch the result in the `DataGrid`. The result is as you expected.

3. Transfer $2,000 from account 2 to account 1. This will fail because of the insufficient balance in account 2. However, account 1 is still credited. This would bankrupt any bank rapidly. This test violates the requirement of being atomic and causes a subsequent inconsistency.

4. Start a second client from a Windows Explorer window.

5. Set a breakpoint in the first client after retrieving the `toBalance` from the database.

6. Transfer $1,000 from account 2 to account 1 in the first client. VS .NET stops at the breakpoint. Do not continue.

7. Transfer $1,000 from account 2 to account 1 in the second client. This works as expected.

8. Continue executing the first client, and observe the wrong behavior. The destination account is not correctly credited. This test violates the requirement of being isolated.

You will now add transactions **1** to the `AccountManager` code to fix the problem (see Listing 36.4).

LISTING 36.4
Adding Transactions to `AccountManager`

```
1    <EventTrackingEnabled(), _
     Transaction()> _

Public Class AccountManager
    Inherits ServicedComponent
    Implements IAccountManager
```

Retest the code according to the previous test plan. Both problems are fixed.

You used `AutoComplete` to control the transaction. Any component that returns normally (without an exception) votes implicitly to commit the transaction. Components that throw an exception veto the transaction (vote to abort it). `ContextUtil.SetAbort` and `ContextUtil.SetComplete` allow for manual control of the transaction.

> **TIP**
>
> Components should stop processing after a transaction is doomed, through a call to `ContextUtil.SetAbort`. Therefore, it is best to use `AutoComplete` and throw an exception to abort both the transaction and all further processing. Obviously, the client should catch the exception and handle the error gracefully.

Controlling Transaction Boundaries and the Isolation Level

The attribute `Transaction` has two properties: `TransactionOption` and `IsolationLevel`. `TransactionOption` controls the participation of a component in a transaction. `IsolationLevel` enables relaxation of the requirement of being isolated in ACID.

Relaxing the Isolation Requirement with `IsolationLevel`

`IsolationLevel` takes one of five enumeration values.
`TransactionIsolationLevel.Serializable` guarantees isolation.
`TransactionIsolationLevel.RepeatableRead`,
`TransactionIsolationLevel.ReadCommitted`, and
`TransactionIsolationLevel.ReadUncommitted` relax the isolation requirement (see the section "Transactions and Isolation Levels Explained," earlier in this chapter). `TransactionIsolationLevel.Any` is the default and runs this component at the same isolation level as its transacted parent component (for transaction roots, `TransactionIsolationLevel.Serializable` is selected). Listing 36.5 shows how to select the isolation level `RepeatableRead`. **1**

LISTING 36.5
Specifying `IsolationLevel` for a Transaction

```
<EventTrackingEnabled(), _
Transaction(Isolation:=TransactionIsolationLevel.RepeatableRead)> _            1


Public Class AccountManager
    Inherits ServicedComponent
    Implements IAccountManager
```

Controlling Transaction Boundaries

`TransactionOption` takes one of five enumeration values that influence the transaction boundaries and the context boundaries (see Figure 36.7). `TransactionOptions` are added as a parameter to the constructor for `TransactionAttribute` (see Listing 36.6). **1**

36

Controlling Transaction Boundaries and the Isolation Level

LISTING 36.6
Specifying `TransactionOption`

```
<EventTrackingEnabled(), _
```
1   `Transaction(TransactionOption.RequiresNew)> _`

```
Public Class AccountManager
    Inherits ServicedComponent
    Implements IAccountManager
```

Components with `TransactionOption.Disabled` never participate in transactions. COM+ does not check the transactional attributes of the client to determine the context. It checks all no-transactional attributes. This setting is the default.

The `TransactionOption.NotSupported` setting is almost the same as `TransactionOption.Disabled`. However, COM+ checks the transactional attributes and all other services attributes of the client to determine the context. This can be useful if the component maintains no persistent state.

The `TransactionOption.Supported` setting indicates that the component should participate in a transaction if the client is in a transaction; otherwise, they run without a transaction. This setting should not be used because the component still incurs the JITA requirement and needs to be written correctly even if it does not need transactions.

If the client is in a transaction, components with `TransactionOption.Required` participate in the client's transaction; otherwise, they start a new transaction. This is the most common option. The default constructor for the attribute `Transaction` sets the option to `Required`.

Components with `TransactionOption.RequiresNew` always start a new transaction.

TIP

It is dangerous to mix transactional and nontransactional components because this impairs consistency. Only when a part of the operation is optional should `Disabled` or `NotSupported` be applied. Even in those cases, it is often best to use `RequiresNew`, which starts a new transaction for the optional processing, keeping the optional part consistent as well.

In other words, you should use `Required` or `RequiresNew`.

36

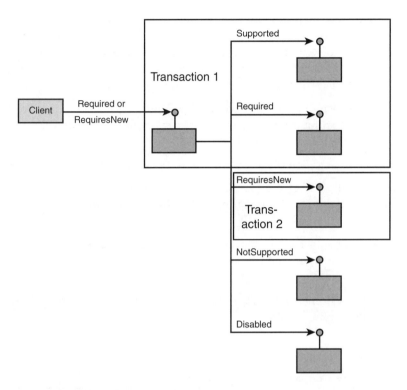

FIGURE 36.7   Transaction boundaries.

Combining Transactions with Pooling and Construction Strings

Transactions imply JITA; therefore, as with JITA, transactions can be combined with pooling. This is especially useful for data access components that require ADO.NET objects. Construction strings are useful in configuring database connection strings.

TIP
Connection strings should be encrypted even when stored in the COM+ Catalog.

36

Combining Transactions with Pooling and Construction Strings

You will now modify `BankServer` to include object pooling and to utilize the construction string to initialize the connection string for the SQL Server connection (see Listing 36.7). You will open the database connection in `Activate` and close it in `Deactivate`. An object is returned to the pool as long as the connection is not damaged. ADO.NET pools connections independently. Change the project as follows:

1. Add attributes for `ConstructionEnabled` and `ObjectPooling`. Copy the construction string from `InitalilizeComponent` to the `Default` for `ConstructionEnabled`. **1**

2. Add overrides for `Construct`, `Activate`, `Deactivate`, and `CanBePooled`.

3. Move the call to `InitializeComponent` from `New` to `Construct`, and add code to store the connection string **2** **3** and consume the string in `InitializeComponent`. **4**

4. Remove the `Try-Finally` blocks from `GetBalance` **5** and `StoreBalance` **6**. Move the `Open` and `Close` calls to the `Activate` **7** and `Deactivate` **8** methods, respectively.

5. Return `True` from `CanBePooled` if the connection is closed correctly (without also being `Broken`). **9**

LISTING 36.7
Adding `ObjectPooling` and `ConstructionEnabled`

```
<EventTrackingEnabled(), _
```
1
```
    ConstructionEnabled(Default:="workstation id=""HG-TABLET"";" & _
        "packet size=4096;integrated security=SSPI;data source=" & _
        """HG-TABLET"";persist security info=True;" & _
        "initial catalog=MySimpleBank"), _
    ObjectPooling(MinPoolSize:=1, MaxPoolSize:=4), _
```
```
    Transaction()> _
Public Class AccountManager
    Inherits ServicedComponent
    Implements IAccountManager
```

2
```
    Public Sub New()
    End Sub
```
```
    Private m_ConnectionString As String
```
```
    Protected Overrides Sub Construct(ByVal s As String)
```
3
```
        m_ConnectionString = s
        InitializeComponent()
```
```
    End Sub
    Private m_cmdRetrieveBalance As SqlCommand
```

LISTING 36.7
Continued

```vb
Private m_cmdStoreBalance As SqlCommand
Private m_MySimpleBankConnection As SqlConnection

Private Sub InitializeComponent()
    ' initialize connection
    m_MySimpleBankConnection = New SqlConnection
    m_MySimpleBankConnection.ConnectionString = m_ConnectionString    4

    'retrieving the balance
    m_cmdRetrieveBalance = New SqlCommand( _
        "SELECT Balance FROM Accounts WHERE AccountNumber = @AccountNumber", _
        m_MySimpleBankConnection)
    m_cmdRetrieveBalance.Parameters.Add( _
        New SqlParameter("@AccountNumber", SqlDbType.Int, 4))

    'storing the changed balance back
    m_cmdStoreBalance = New SqlCommand("UPDATE Accounts " & _
        "SET Balance = @Balance WHERE AccountNumber = @AccountNumber", _
        m_MySimpleBankConnection)
    m_cmdStoreBalance.Parameters.Add( _
        New SqlParameter("@AccountNumber", SqlDbType.Int, 4))
    m_cmdStoreBalance.Parameters.Add( _
        New SqlParameter("@Balance", SqlDbType.Money, 8))
End Sub

Public Function GetBalance(ByVal account As Integer) As Decimal
    Dim balance As Decimal
    m_cmdRetrieveBalance.Parameters(0).Value = account               5
    balance = CType(m_cmdRetrieveBalance.ExecuteScalar(), Decimal)
    Return balance
End Function

Public Function StoreBalance(ByVal account As Integer, _
        ByVal balance As Decimal)
    m_cmdStoreBalance.Parameters(0).Value = account                  6
    m_cmdStoreBalance.Parameters(1).Value = balance
    m_cmdStoreBalance.ExecuteNonQuery()
End Function

Protected Overrides Sub Activate()
    m_MySimpleBankConnection.Open()                                  7
End Sub
```

36

Combining Transactions with Pooling and Construction Strings

LISTING 36.7
Continued

```
Protected Overrides Sub Deactivate()
    m_MySimpleBankConnection.Close()
End Sub


Protected Overrides Function CanBePooled() As Boolean
    return m_MySimpleBankConnection.State = ConnectionState.Closed
End Function


<AutoComplete()> _
Private Sub TransferMoney(ByVal fromAccount As Integer, _
    ByVal toAccount As Integer, ByVal amount As Decimal) _
    Implements IAccountManager.TransferMoney

    Dim fromBalance As Decimal
    Dim toBalance As Decimal

    toBalance = GetBalance(toAccount)
    toBalance += amount
    StoreBalance(toAccount, toBalance)

    fromBalance = GetBalance(fromAccount)
    fromBalance -= amount
    If fromBalance < 0 Then
        Throw New ArgumentException("Not enough money in account")
    End If
    StoreBalance(fromAccount, fromBalance)

End Sub

End Class
```

Using Web Pages and Web Services as Transaction Roots

Web services and web pages have the capability to specify COM+ transaction require-ments. Specifying RequiresNew for a web page or WebMethod makes them the root of a new transaction. They behave like a serviced component.

> **TIP**
>
> Presentation logic code (web pages or web services) should never contain business logic or data access code; therefore, this feature should not be used.

You specify transaction requirements for web pages by adding the `Transaction` attribute **1** to the page directive (see Listing 36.8).

LISTING 36.8
Adding a Transaction to a Web Page

```
<%@ Page Language="vb" AutoEventWireup="false" Codebehind="Transfer.aspx.vb"
Inherits="EsTrWebApplication.Transfer"
Transaction="RequiresNew"%>                                                    1
```

Specify transaction requirements for a web service's `WebMethod` by adding the `TransactionOption` property **1** to the `webMethod` attribute (see Listing 36.9).

LISTING 36.9
Adding Transactions to a `WebMethod`

```
    <WebMethod(TransactionOption:=TransactionOption.RequiresNew)>             1
    Public Function ProcessTransfer(ByVal fromAccount As Integer, _
        ByVal toAccount As Integer, ByVal amount As Decimal) As String
```

Summary

This chapter showed how to use the transaction service in Enterprise Services to simplify transaction handling. Additionally, it provided details on how to influence transaction boundaries.

Further Reading

Lowy, Juval. *COM and .NET Component Services*. O'Reilly & Associates, 2001.

36

37 CONCURRENCY PROTECTION FOR SERVICED COMPONENTS

IN BRIEF

This chapter explains the need for advanced synchronization, details the improvement (from the regular .NET synchronization methods) that the `Synchronization` attribute provides, and also covers interactions with transactions and Just In Time Activation (JITA).

WHAT YOU NEED

SOFTWARE REQUIREMENTS	Windows 2000, XP, or 2003 .NET Framework 1.1 SDK Visual Studio .NET 2003 with Visual Basic .NET installed Windows Component Services installed Local administrator on your machine
HARDWARE REQUIREMENTS	PC desktop or laptop
SKILL REQUIREMENTS	Advanced knowledge of Visual Basic .NET Advanced knowledge of the .NET Framework

CONCURRENCY PROTECTION FOR SERVICED COMPONENTS AT A GLANCE

Multithreading and Resource Protection

Multithreading is useful in several situations. The most common ones are when you want to improve user interface responsiveness, enhance performance on multiple CPU machines, or increase throughput of multiple client requests.

In multithreaded environments, shared resources (memory, files, and so on) must be protected from concurrent access (see Chapter 27, "Multithreading"), to maintain the system's consistency. .NET offers a whole series of methods, from low-level ones such as semaphores to advanced ones such as synchronization domains for context-bound objects.

Traditional locking methods (including all the methods in basic .NET) lock an object based on the physical thread in which the call is executing. Unfortunately, with Enterprise Services as well as Remoting, an object might be called from multiple physical threads that execute the same overall code thread or cause. This is especially true when using callbacks and events. With traditional methods, the callback might cause a deadlock. The synchronization domain for context-bound objects tries to address this with an additional parameter for re-entrancy, but this does not guarantee consistency in all cases.

Improving the Solution with Activity-Based Causality Locks

Enterprise services provide a service called synchronization (the `Synchronization` attribute). This attribute looks very similar to the one for context-bound attributes (see Chapter 27).

Enterprise services use a different kind of lock, based on logical threads instead of physical ones. A logical thread is called a causality (it serves a cause). All objects that participate in a protected causality require a causality lock. If multiple components participate in the same causality, assigning a causality lock per object is inefficient. Through the `Synchronization` attribute, the program controls which components can share a causality lock. COM+ groups all components (which can share a lock) in an activity, to optimize the number of locks needed. Each activity receives one causality lock per process, which is required to avoid expensive cross-process calls to check, lock, or unlock causality locks. Activities are logical items and are independent from processes, application domains, and contexts. COM+ guarantees that each protected component is accessed by only one logical thread at a time. Additional causalities that enter the activity are blocked until the first causality exits the activity.

Adding synchronization to a serviced component is trivial; add the `Synchronization` attribute **1** in front of the class (see Listing 37.1).

Improving the Solution with Activity-Based Causality Locks

LISTING 37.1

Specify Synchronization **Service**

```
<EventTrackingEnabled(), _
    Synchronization()> _
Public Class MyComponent
    Inherits ServicedComponent
    Implements IMyInterface
```

Controlling Activity Boundaries

The Synchronization attribute has one property: SynchronizationOption. This property controls the participation of a component in an activity. The membership in an activity is determined during the instantiation of the serviced component.

SynchronizationOption takes one of five enumeration values that influence the activity boundaries and the context boundaries (see Figure 37.1). SynchronizationOptions are added as a parameter to the constructor **1** for SynchronizationAttribute (see Listing 37.2).

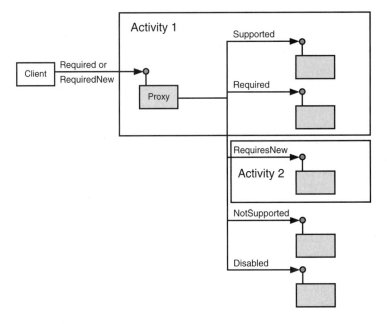

FIGURE 37.1   Synchronization boundaries.

LISTING 37.2

Specifying `SynchronizationOption`

```
<EventTrackingEnabled(), _
Synchronization(SynchronizationOption.RequiresNew)> _                    1
Public Class MyComponent
    Inherits ServicedComponent
    Implements IMyInterface
```

37

Components with `SynchronizationOption.Disabled` never participate in any activity. COM+ does not check the Synchronization attributes of the client to determine the context compatibility; this setting is the default.

The `SynchronizationOption.NotSupported` setting is almost the same as the `SynchronizationOption.Disabled` setting. However, COM+ checks the `Synchronization` attribute of the client to determine context compatibility. This setting can be useful if the component maintains no shared state.

The `SynchronizationOption.Supported` setting indicates that the component should participate in an activity if the client is in an activity; otherwise, it executes without a causality-based lock.

If the client is engaged in an activity, components with `SynchronizationOption.Required` participate in the client's activity; otherwise, they start a new activity. This is the most common option. The default constructor for the `Synchronization` attribute sets the option to `Required`.

Components with `SynchronizationOption.RequiresNew` always start a new activity.

TIP

It is dangerous to mix synchronized and nonsynchronized components because it might lead to deadlocks or inconsistencies. In other words, you should use `Required` or `RequiresNew`.

Combining Activities with JITA, Transactions, and Pooling

Transactions imply JITA, which implies synchronization. Therefore, synchronization is always used with JITA or transactions. JITA allows only `SynchronizationOption.Required` or `SynchronizationOption.RequiredNew`. `TransactionOption.Supported` and `TransactionOption.Required` further restrict the choice to `SynchronizationOption.Required`.

37

> **TIP**
>
> You should not specify `Synchronization` when using the `Transaction` attribute with `TransactionOption.Supported` or `TransactionOption.Required` because the previously mentioned restrictions require synchronization with `SynchronizationOption.Required`. This is enforced by COM+, and it is a bad practice to bloat the code to specify default behavior.

Pooling and synchronization have no dependencies on each other; therefore, they can be mixed without any special consideration.

Summary

This chapter showed how to improve multithreaded resource locking with `System.EnterpriseServices.Synchronization`. This should always be used when building any potentially multithreaded (that is, *every*) serviced component that is neither transactional nor JITA.

Further Reading

Lowy, Juval. *COM and .NET Component Services*. O'Reilly & Associates, 2001.

38 SERVICES FOR LOOSELY COUPLED SYSTEMS

IN BRIEF

This chapter explains the services available to decouple systems. Queued components (QC) are useful in guaranteeing delivery of messages between occasionally connected systems to guarantee. They also smooth loads in systems with high peak loads. Loosely coupled events (LCE) are useful for completely decoupled publish-subscribe scenarios.

WHAT YOU NEED

SOFTWARE REQUIREMENTS	Windows 2000, XP, or 2003 .NET Framework 1.1 SDK Visual Studio .NET 2003 with Visual Basic .NET installed Windows Component Services installed Windows Message Queueing installed Administrative rights on your machine
HARDWARE REQUIREMENTS	PC desktop or laptop
SKILL REQUIREMENTS	Advanced knowledge of Visual Basic .NET Advanced knowledge of the .NET Framework

SERVICES FOR LOOSELY COUPLED SYSTEMS AT A GLANCE

Buffering Requests with Queued Components

Microsoft provides a messaging service (MSMQ) with Windows 2000 or later. This messaging service provides reliable delivery and can participate in COM+ transactions (it implements a Resource Manager interface). The namespace `System.Messaging` contains classes for direct interaction with MSMQ at the message level. COM+ queued components provide asynchronous method call abstractions for easier and more maintainable use of the code.

The component can be written like a normal synchronous component, and the client calls the component in the same way as regular synchronous components. Obviously, any asynchronous component (including QC) must not return any values or return output parameters.

The QC architecture is shown in Figure 38.1. The recorder is a proxy (automatically generated) that implements all queued interfaces implemented by the QC. The proxy serializes every call and the parameters into one message. This message is committed to the recorder queue (for remote components) or directly to the application queue (for local components) after the recorder is released. Releasing the recorder happens when the object created by the client is garbage collected or when `Marshal.ReleaseComObject` (in `System.Runtime.InteropServices`) is called.

> **NOTE**
>
> Despite documentation to the contrary, calling `IDisposable.Dispose` or `ServicedComponent.DisposeObject` does not work; it releases the `IDisposable` interface only. This behavior of `IDisposable.Dispose` and `ServicedComponent.DisposeObject` is unique to queued components.

In remote situations (the client and the queued component reside on different machines), MSMQ transports the message from the recorder queue to the application queue across machine boundaries. This happens immediately or at a future time if the server or the communication channel (DCOM) is unavailable. Transferring the message from the recorder queue to the application queue is always done in a transaction. If the transfer fails, the message stays in the recorder queue for later retries. For queued components that reside on the same machine as the client, only one queue is used and the recorder deposits the message directly into the application queue, eliminating this extra step. The application queue must reside on the machine (local or remote) that contains the QC.

Each COM+ application that receives queued calls has one listener thread, which is started when the COM+ application is started. If the application is not running, no one can know that the application queue has messages. The listener detects new message packets and creates a component-specific player thread.

Buffering Requests with Queued Components

The player retrieves the message from the queue, deserializes each call, and calls the actual method implementation (in the same order as the recording). The message is always removed from the application queue in a transaction. If the processing of any call in the message fails in the component (throws an exception or sets the transaction flag to rollback), the transaction is aborted. This causes the message to be returned to the application queue for later retries.

An application can limit how many concurrent threads are used for players. Additional messages must wait until a thread becomes available. In essence, this creates a thread pool for this component.

> **NOTE**
>
> All threads that COM+ uses are retrieved from the RPC thread pool. If the RPC thread pool runs out of threads before the maximum number of players is reached, no additional players are created.

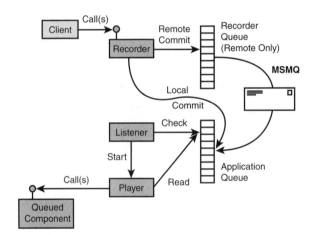

FIGURE 38.1   Queued component architecture.

You have several choices for launching a COM+ application that contains QCs:

- ▶ Use the Component Services MMC plug-in to start the application manually.

- ▶ Provide a simple utility (your system admin can schedule this application to run at startup) that starts the COM+ application with one of two methods:

    1. Program the COM+ catalog (see Chapter 40, "Advanced Enterprise Services Programming").

    2. Instantiate any synchronous component in the COM+ application. You can instantiate the QC itself synchronously (with New).

▸ Use the Component Services MMC plug-in to specify Run as NT Service in the Activation tab. Set the service to start automatically.

NOTE

The utility you are using to register the QC with COM+ (RegisterComPlus) instantiates all components in the COM+ application. This registers the application and components with COM+ and launches the application. This simplifies development because the COM+ application is always started when debugging from Visual Studio. For deployment, it is best to use the third method discussed earlier (Run as NT Service).

Clients that call QC interfaces interact with the recorder; therefore, the method must implement input parameters only and may not return any values.

Parameters have several restrictions. QC cannot handle parameters representing COM, remotable objects (`MarshalByRefObject`), or serviced components. Additionally, only parameters that implement the unmanaged COM interface `IPersistStream` can be used. This limits the parameter types to the primitive types, `String` and arrays of primitive types. To pass other types (user-defined classes), you must manually serialize them into a string. You can use the SOAP formatter or the binary formatter to serialize and deserialize such parameters.

Implementing a Simple Queued Component

The capability to queue a method is related to the interface, not the component. You can tag the interface with the attribute `InterfaceQueuing` or apply the attribute to the call and specify the interface(s) that are queued. Additionally, you need to enable queuing and a listener at the COM+ application level. Listing 38.1 **1** shows how to add `InterfaceQueuing` to an interface definition. This interface defines two methods.

LISTING 38.1
Queued Interface `IQueuedComponent`

```
Imports System.EnterpriseServices
```

```
<InterfaceQueuing()>                                                    1
Public Interface IQueuedComponent
    Sub RegularMethod()
    Sub BadMethod()
End Interface
```

Buffering Requests with Queued Components

You will create a solution with a queued component, a registration project, and a Windows test application. First, you set up the project, create the component, and deal with the registration of the component:

1. Create an empty solution named EsQueuedComponent.

2. Add a VB Windows application project named `TestClient`.

3. Add a VB class project named `MyQueuedComponent`.

4. Delete `Class1.vb`.

5. Complete all design-time configuration settings for a serviced component, such as adding a reference to `System.EnterpriseServices`. For details, see Chapters 34, "Introduction to Enterprise Services," and 35, "Activation-Related Services."

6. Add the interface in Listing 38.1.

7. Add a class named `QueuedComponent` (see Listing 38.2). Note that it does not contain any indication that the component is queued.

8. Modify `AssemblyInfo.vb` (see Listing 38.3) to assign a name to the COM+ application **1**, to enable application queuing and to enable the listener. **2** Optionally, you can specify the number of concurrent players.

LISTING 38.2
Queued Component `QueuedComponent`

```
Imports System.EnterpriseServices
Imports System.Windows.Forms

<EventTrackingEnabled()> _
Public Class QueuedComponent
    Inherits ServicedComponent
    Implements IQueuedComponent

    Public Sub New()
    End Sub

    Public Sub RegularMethod() Implements IQueuedComponent.RegularMethod
        MessageBox.Show("RegularMethod", "QueuedComponent")
    End Sub

    Public Sub BadMethod() Implements IQueuedComponent.BadMethod
        MessageBox.Show("BadMethod", "QueuedComponent")
```

LISTING 38.2
Continued

```
        Throw New ApplicationException("QC processing failure")
    End Sub

End Class
```

38

LISTING 38.3
AssemblyInfo.vb

```
Imports System
Imports System.Reflection
Imports System.Runtime.InteropServices
Imports System.EnterpriseServices


<Assembly: AssemblyTitle("")>
<Assembly: AssemblyDescription("")>

<Assembly: ApplicationName("MyQcServer")>                                      1
<Assembly: ApplicationActivation(ActivationOption.Server)>
<Assembly: ApplicationAccessControl(False)>
<Assembly: ApplicationQueuing(Enabled:=True, QueueListenerEnabled:=True, _    2
                         MaxListenerThreads:=5)>
```

Clients cannot use New to instantiate a queued component; they must call
Marshal.BindToMoniker instead. Monikers are similar to modern URLs and allow
many different types of instantiations in Windows. To create a queued component,
the string passed to BindToMoniker must contain queue:/new: followed by the
fully qualified name of the component. Finally, the returned object must be cast to a
queued interface. BindToMoniker demands unmanaged code permissions.

NOTE

BindToMoniker **has the same functionality as the** GetObject **method on VB6.**

Next, you add a test client named TestClient:

1. In the TestClient project, rename Form1 to MainWindow.

2. Modify the UI as shown in Figure 38.2.

3. Add references to MyQueuedComponent and
   System.EnterpriseServices.

4. Add the button handlers in Listing 38.4.

Buffering Requests with Queued Components

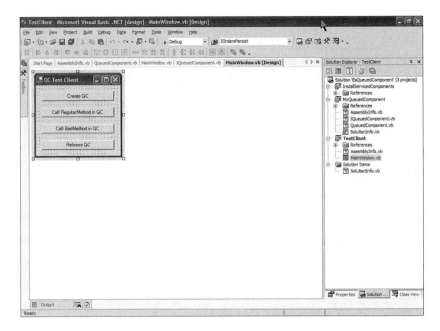

FIGURE 38.2   Test UI.

LISTING 38.4
Button Handlers

```
'Member variable to hold a reference to the QC
Private m_QueuedComponent As IQueuedComponent

Private Sub OnCreate_Click(ByVal sender As Object, ByVal e As EventArgs) _
      Handles m_btnCreate.Click
   'create the recorder object for the queued component with BindToMoniker
   Dim o As Object
   o = Marshal.BindToMoniker("queue:/new:MyQueuedComponent.QueuedComponent")
   m_QueuedComponent = CType(o, IQueuedComponent)
End Sub

Private Sub OnRegular_Click(ByVal sender As Object, ByVal e As EventArgs) _
      Handles m_btnCallRegular.Click
   'call a method on the QC
   m_QueuedComponent.RegularMethod()
End Sub

Private Sub OnBad_Click(ByVal sender As Object, ByVal e As EventArgs) _
      Handles m_btnBadMethod.Click
```

LISTING 38.4
Continued

```
    'Call a queued method that fails (throws an exception
    m_QueuedComponent.BadMethod()
End Sub

Private Sub OnRelease_Click(ByVal sender As Object, ByVal e As EventArgs) _
     Handles m_btnRelease.Click
    'releases the recorder; causes the messages for all called methods
    'to be sent to the actual queued component
    Marshal.ReleaseComObject(m_QueuedComponent)
End Sub
```

Next, test the application for normal operation:

1. Start the test client.

2. Click Create QC.

3. Click Call RegularMethod in QC three times.

4. Click Release QC. The system shows three message boxes. This is the correct behavior.

Handling Errors

The recorder queue and the application queues have retry queues. After each failed attempt, the message is moved to the next retry queue. A progressively larger delay is used before the next retry is attempted. After all attempts have failed, the message is moved to a dead-letter queue.

Specifying a QC exception class enables a last processing step before the message is deposited in the dead-letter queue. A QC exception class can be configured with the attribute ExceptionClass for each component (see Listing 38.5 **1**) or administratively with the Component Services MMC plug-in. Specifying the class administratively allows for deployment-specific implementation of the exception class.

LISTING 38.5
Exception Class Specification

```
<EventTrackingEnabled(), _
ExceptionClass("MyQueuedComponent.QcExceptionHandler")> _                    1
Public Class QueuedComponent
    Inherits ServicedComponent
    Implements IQueuedComponent
```

Buffering Requests with Queued Components

A QC exception class must implement `IPlaybackControl` and all queued interfaces that the QC implements (see Listing 38.6 **1**).

LISTING 38.6
Exception Class `QcExceptionClass` Implementation

```
Imports System.EnterpriseServices
Imports System.Windows.Forms

Public Class QcExceptionHandler
    Inherits ServicedComponent
    Implements IPlaybackControl
    Implements IQueuedComponent

    Public Sub FinalClientRetry() Implements IPlaybackControl.FinalClientRetry
        MessageBox.Show("FinalClientRetry", "QcExceptionHandler")
    End Sub

    Public Sub FinalServerRetry() Implements IPlaybackControl.FinalServerRetry
        MessageBox.Show("FinalServerRetry", "QcExceptionHandler")
    End Sub

    Public Sub BadMethod() Implements IQueuedComponent.BadMethod
        MessageBox.Show("BadMethod", "QcExceptionHandler")
    End Sub

    Public Sub RegularMethod() Implements IQueuedComponent.RegularMethod
        MessageBox.Show("RegularMethod", "QcExceptionHandler")
    End Sub
End Class
```

Client-Side Error Handling for Remote Scenarios

The recorder queue (used only for remote servers) tries to send the message again multiple times. The actual delivery cannot be guaranteed. If all attempts fail, the message is placed in a public and shared (by all clients) dead-letter queue.

If the component has an exception class configured, COM+ calls the local exception class's `IPlaybackControl.FinalClientRetry` and plays the entire message (all the calls) to the local exception class's implementation of the queued interface. If every call returns without an exception, the message is considered handled. If any of the methods throws an exception, the message is put in the dead-letter queue.

The exception handler could attempt alternate delivery mechanisms, just log the failure, or notify the originator (system user) about the failure.

Server-Side Error Handling for Local and Remote Scenarios

The application queue contains five retry queues and one application-specific dead-letter queue. If the original delivery fails (the implementation throws an exception), the message is put in retry queue 0. COM+ retries the processing three times after 1 minute. If all three retries fail, the message is moved to the next retry queue. The retry times are doubled at each retry queue level. If all attempts fail, the message is placed in the application-specific dead-letter queue.

If the component has an exception class configured, COM+ calls the server exception class's `IPlaybackControl.FinalServerRetry` and replays the entire message (all the calls) to the server exception class's implementation of the queued interface. If every call returns without an exception, then the message is considered handled. If any of the methods throws an exception, the message is put in the application-specific dead-letter queue.

You should add the code in Listings 38.5 and 38.6 to the project. Next, test the application for normal operation:

1. Start the test client.

2. Click Create QC.

3. Click Call RegularMethod in QC two times.

4. Click Call BadMethod in QC once.

5. Click Release QC.

The system shows three message boxes. This is the correct behavior. After 1 minute, the three calls are repeated three times. This is repeated for each retry queue. It takes a long time for the exception handler to be called; wait for it. You can view the progress within Administrative Tools by selecting Computer Management. Expand the node Message Queuing and select Private Queues (see Figure 38.3). You need to refresh (from the right-click menu) the display after every retry.

TIP

Exceptions caused by bad data should be caught (and logged) by the QC; otherwise, this poison call is retried repeatedly. This is wasteful because the data will not "magically" repair itself. Only temporary problems should be handled with an exception.

Additionally, you should provide dead-letter queue-management applications for manageability of your product in deployment.

38

Buffering Requests with Queued Components

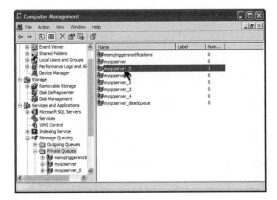

FIGURE 38.3   Viewing queues.

Queued Components, Transactions, and Pooling

You learned in Chapter 36, "Transaction Services," that you should not mix transactional and nontransactional components. The retrieval of a message is always transactional; therefore, queued components and QC exception classes should always be transactional (see Listings 38.7 **1** and 38.8 **1**).

LISTING 38.7
Attribute Transaction for Queued Component

```
<EventTrackingEnabled(), _
    Transaction(), _
ExceptionClass("MyQueuedComponent.QcExceptionHandler")> _
Public Class QueuedComponent
    Inherits ServicedComponent
    Implements IQueuedComponent
```

LISTING 38.8
Attribute Transaction for Exception Class

```
<Transaction()> _
Public Class QcExceptionHandler
    Inherits ServicedComponent
    Implements IPlaybackControl
    Implements IQueuedComponent
```

A queued system does not actually flow the transaction from the client to the server. If the client is in a transaction, the recording of the message in the recorder or application queue is handled in the same transaction. If the transaction is aborted, the message is not committed to the queue. In the remote scenario, the transfer of the message by MSMQ between the two machines is in a new transaction. Finally, the retrieval of the transaction starts a third transaction that should be shared by the queued component.

38

> **TIP**
>
> Avoid configuring the QC to require a new transaction. This causes two additional transactions, one in the client and one in the server.

Building Publish-Subscribe Systems with Loosely Coupled Events (LCE)

.NET provides an event-handling mechanism through delegates. This method still couples the subscriber and publisher and works only if both are running at the same time. This works great for tightly coupled systems, such as a Windows application. The events require explicit setup by both the client and the server.

COM+ provides an event service that decouples this process. A publisher publishes an event to COM+. It does not care whether anyone subscribes to the event. The subscriber (or subscribers) registers its interest with COM+, which calls the event handler when it receives a matching request. This indirection is a very powerful concept to achieve the goal of loosely coupled systems.

Publishers use an event class to publish their event. An event class is a serviced component with the attribute `EventClass` and implements one or more interfaces. The publisher instantiates this class and calls its methods. COM+ does not actually instantiate the event class; it uses the event class as a template for the proxy only.

COM+ provides permanent and transient subscriptions. Permanent subscribers are automatically started when an event of interest fires. Transient subscriptions require a subscriber object to be created first.

Permanent subscriptions are configured in the subscription folder for the component that implements the subscriber. The subscriber must be a serviced component that implements the same interface as the event class.

Transient subscriptions can be created only by programming the COM+ catalog. The subscriber application creates a component and adds the subscription to the Transient Subscriptions collection in the COM+ catalog. Transient subscribers are not required to be serviced components.

Implementing a Simple Loosely Coupled Event

The capability to publish an event requires an event class. **1** Event classes are never called; you should throw an exception of type `NotImplementedException` in each method. Listing 38.9 shows an event class that implements one interface (see Listing 38.10).

LISTING 38.9
Event Class `MyEventClassTemplate`

```
Imports System.EnterpriseServices
```

1 `<EventClass()> _`

```
Public Class MyEventClassTemplate
    Inherits ServicedComponent
    Implements IMyEventSink

    Private Sub SomeEvent() Implements IMyEventSink.SomeEvent
        Throw New NotImplementedException( _
            "Event Classes should not be called directly")
    End Sub
End Class
```

LISTING 38.10
Event Interface `IMyEventSink`

```
Public Interface IMyEventSink
    Sub SomeEvent()
End Interface
```

You will create the solution `EsLooselyCoupledEvent` with the following projects:

1. `InstallServiceComponent`, for COM+ component registration

2. `MyEventClass`, defining the event class and the sink interface

3. `Subscriber`, containing a permanent subscriber

4. `TestPublisher`, to publish events

First, create the solution and all the projects (see Figure 38.4) as follows:

1. Create an empty solution named `EsLooselyCoupledEvent`.

2. Add a VB class project named `MyEventClass`.

3. Delete `Class1.vb`.

Building Publish-Subscribe Systems with Loosely Coupled Events (LCE)

4. Add the setup for a serviced component (reference to `System.EnterpriseServices`, file `AssemblyInfo.cs`, global file `SolutionInfo.cs`). For details, see Chapter 34 or 35.

5. Add a VB class project named Subscriber.

6. Delete `Class1.vb`.

7. Add a reference to the project `MyEventClass`.

8. Add the setup for a serviced component (reference to `System.EnterpriseServices`, file `AssemblyInfo.cs`, global file `SolutionInfo.cs`).

9. Add a VB windows application project `TestPublisher`.

10. Add a reference to the project `MyEventClass`.

11. Add a reference to the project `System.EnterpriseServices`.

12. Add COM+ registration project and project dependencies for `MyEventClass` and `Subscriber`. For details, see Chapter 34 or 35.

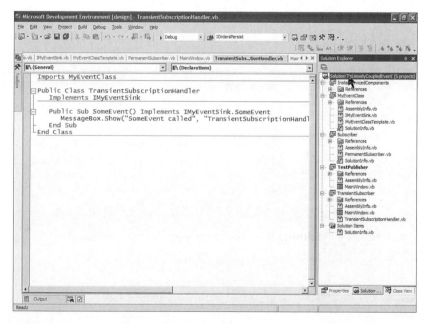

FIGURE 38.4   Creating a loosely couple event.

Next, add the actual event class and the event interface to the project `MyEventClass`. The event interface is also called a sink interface.

Building Publish-Subscribe Systems with Loosely Coupled Events (LCE)

1. Add the interface in Listing 38.10.

2. Add the class `MyEventClass` (see Listing 38.9) and add the attribute `EventClass`.

3. Modify `AssemblyInfo.vb` (see Listing 38.11) to name the COM+ application. You will create a library event class.

LISTING 38.11

AssemblyInfo.vb

```
Imports System
Imports System.Reflection
Imports System.Runtime.InteropServices
Imports System.EnterpriseServices

<Assembly: AssemblyTitle("")>
<Assembly: AssemblyDescription("")>

<Assembly: ApplicationName("MyEventClass")>
<Assembly: ApplicationActivation(ActivationOption.Library)>
<Assembly: ApplicationAccessControl(False)>
```

Next, create a subscriber class named `PermanentSubscriber` (see Listing 38.12). This class is a regular serviced component.

LISTING 38.12

Subscriber Class `PermanentSubscriber`

```
Imports System.EnterpriseServices
Imports System.Windows.Forms
Imports MyEventClass

Public Class PermanentSubscriber
    Inherits ServicedComponent
    Implements IMyEventSink

    Public Sub SomeEvent() Implements IMyEventSink.SomeEvent
        MessageBox.Show("SomeEvent called", "PermanentSubscriber")
    End Sub
End Class
```

Finally, you add a test publisher named `TestPublisher`.

1. In the `TestPublisher` project, rename `Form1` to `MainWindow`.

2. Modify the UI as shown in Figure 38.5.

Building Publish-Subscribe Systems with Loosely Coupled Events (LCE)

3. Add references to `MyEventClass` and `System.EnterpriseServices`.

4. Add the button handler in Listing 38.13.

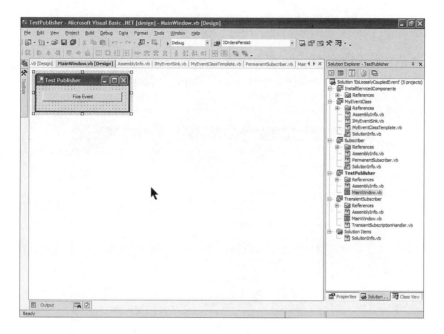

FIGURE 38.5   TestPublisher UI.

LISTING 38.13
Button Handler

```
Private Sub OnFireEvent_Click(ByVal sender As Object, ByVal e As EventArgs) _
    Handles m_btnFireEvent.Click

    Dim sink As IMyEventSink = New MyEventClassTemplate
    sink.SomeEvent()
End Sub
```

Next, test the application for normal operation.

1. Start the test publisher.

2. Click Fire Event.

The event fires correctly; however, no subscribers are configured.

Building Publish-Subscribe Systems with Loosely Coupled Events (LCE)

Adding Persistent Subscriptions to an LCE

Use the Component Services MMC plug-in to add a persistent subscription.

1. Navigate to the application `MyPermanentSubscriber`, component `Subscriber.PermanentSubscriber`, and folder Subscriptions.

2. Right-click and select the menu item New and Subscription (see Figure 38.6).

3. Fill in the wizard pages (see Figures 38.7 through 38.11). The resulting subscription is shown in Figure 38.12.

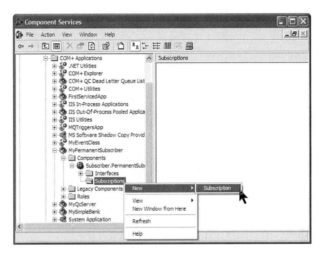

FIGURE 38.6   Component Services MMC plug-in menu to create a subscription.

Test the application for normal operation.

1. Start the test publisher.

2. Click Fire Event.

The event fires correctly, and the subscriber receives the event.

Building Publish-Subscribe Systems with Loosely Coupled Events (LCE)

FIGURE 38.7   COM+ New Subscription Wizard—page 1.

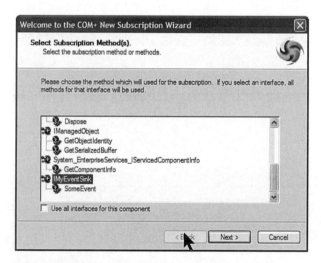

FIGURE 38.8   COM+ New Subscription Wizard: page 2—select the subscription methods.

NOTE

The persistent subscription is lost each time you rebuild our solution. `ComPlusRegister` deletes the component and reregisters the component; this deletes the component and the subscription.

Building Publish-Subscribe Systems with Loosely Coupled Events (LCE)

FIGURE 38.9   COM+ New Subscription Wizard: page 3—select the Event class.

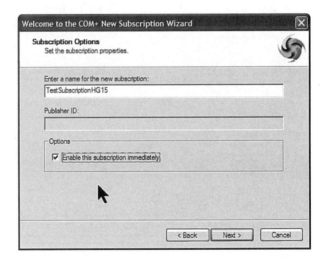

FIGURE 38.10   COM+ New Subscription Wizard: page 4—name and enable the subscription.

Building Publish-Subscribe Systems with Loosely Coupled Events (LCE)

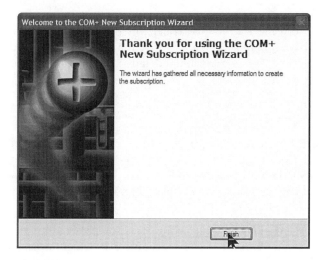

FIGURE 38.11 COM+ New Subscription Wizard: page 5.

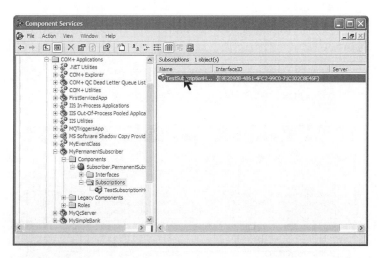

FIGURE 38.12 Result of wizard shown in Component Services MMC plug-in.

Adding Transient Subscriptions to an LCE

Setting up transient subscriptions requires programming the COM+ Catalog with the COM component COM+ 1.0 Admin Type Library. This library's API is not type safe

38

Building Publish-Subscribe Systems with Loosely Coupled Events (LCE)

(it uses strings and generic objects). The general paradigm for programming the COM+ catalog is to retrieve a top-level collection and manipulate it or its members. The following helper library is presented without a detailed explanation. Information on programming the COM+ catalog and a detailed explanation of this class are provided in Chapter 40.

First, add the helper library project LceEx. This library has methods to add and remove transient subscriptions.

The code to add a transient subscription creates a catalog object and retrieves the Transient Subscriptions collection. A subscription object is added to the collection, and the necessary values for the properties are set. The changes are saved. A type-safe version generates the necessary string objects after checking the integrity of the parameters with the reflection API.

The code to remove the subscription creates a catalog object and retrieves the Transient Subscriptions collection. The collection is searched for named subscription. When it is found, the subscription is removed and the changes are saved.

1. Add a VB class project named LceEx.

2. Delete Class1.vb.

3. Add a reference to the project COM component COM+ 1.0 Admin Type Library (see Figure 38.13).

4. Add a reference to System.EnterpriseServices.

5. Add the class TransientSubscriptionManager (see Listing 38.14).

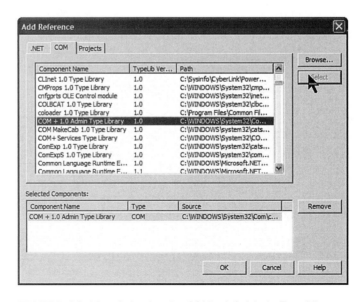

FIGURE 38.13   Selecting the COM+ 1.0 Admin Type Library.

LISTING 38.14
Class TransientSubscriptionManager

```
Imports System.Diagnostics
Imports System.EnterpriseServices
Imports System.Reflection
Imports System.Runtime.InteropServices
Imports COMAdmin


Public Class TransientSubscriptionManager

    Public Shared Function Add( _
            ByVal eventClass As Type, _
            ByVal sinkInterface As Type, _
            ByVal subscriber As Object) As String
        'check parameters -> causes type safety
        Debug.Assert(eventClass.IsClass()) 'eventClass must be a class
        Dim ecaType As Type = GetType(EventClassAttribute)
        Dim eca As Object() = eventClass.GetCustomAttributes(ecaType, True)
        Debug.Assert(eca.Length = 1) 'eventClass must have EventClassAttribute
        Debug.Assert(sinkInterface.IsInterface()) 'interface required
        Debug.Assert(sinkInterface.IsInstanceOfType(subscriber))
        Dim siName As String = sinkInterface.ToString()
        Dim siType As Type = eventClass.GetInterface(siName)
        Debug.Assert(Not siType Is Nothing)
        Debug.Assert(sinkInterface Is siType)
        'add
        Dim eventClassString As String = "{" + eventClass.GUID.ToString() + "}"
        Dim sinkIfString As String = "{" + sinkInterface.GUID.ToString() + "}"
        Return AddNotTypesafe(eventClassString, sinkIfString, "", _
            subscriber, "", "")
    End Function


    Public Shared Function AddNotTypesafe( _
            ByVal eventClassString As String, _
            ByVal sinkInterfaceString As String, _
            ByVal method As String, _
            ByVal subscriber As Object, _
            ByVal filterCriteria As String, _
            ByVal publisherId As String) As String
        'get catalog
        Dim catalog As ICOMAdminCatalog = New COMAdminCatalog
        'get transient collection
        Dim collection As Object
```

38

Building Publish-Subscribe Systems with Loosely Coupled Events (LCE)

LISTING 38.14
Continued

```vb
        Dim transientCollection As ICatalogCollection
        collection = catalog.GetCollection("TransientSubscriptions")
        transientCollection = CType(collection, ICatalogCollection)
        transientCollection.Populate()
        'create subscription name
        Dim subscriptionName As String = Guid.NewGuid().ToString()
        'add subscription
        Dim subscription As ICatalogObject
        subscription = CType(transientCollection.Add(), ICatalogObject)
        subscription.Value("Name") = subscriptionName
        subscription.Value("SubscriberInterface") = subscriber
        subscription.Value("EventCLSID") = eventClassString
        subscription.Value("InterfaceID") = sinkInterfaceString
        subscription.Value("MethodName") = method
        subscription.Value("FilterCriteria") = filterCriteria
        subscription.Value("PublisherID") = publisherId
        transientCollection.SaveChanges()
        'return the name of the newly created subscription
        Return subscriptionName
    End Function

    Public Shared Sub Remove(ByVal subscriptionName As String)
        Debug.Assert(subscriptionName <> "")
        'get catalog
        Dim catalog As ICOMAdminCatalog = New COMAdminCatalog
        'get transient collection
        Dim collection As Object
        Dim transientCollection As ICatalogCollection
        collection = catalog.GetCollection("TransientSubscriptions")
        transientCollection = CType(collection, ICatalogCollection)
        transientCollection.Populate()
        'find subscription to remove
        Dim index As Integer = 0
        For Each item As Object In transientCollection
            Dim subscription As ICatalogObject = CType(item, ICatalogObject)
            If subscription.Name.ToString() = subscriptionName Then
                'found subscription -> remove it
                transientCollection.Remove(index)
                transientCollection.SaveChanges()
                Exit For
            End If
            index += 1
```

Building Publish-Subscribe Systems with Loosely Coupled Events (LCE)

LISTING 38.14
Continued

```
        Next
    End Sub


End Class
```

Next, add a Windows application with a subscriber class; the application uses the previous helper class to subscribe and unsubscribe.

1. Add the project `TransientSubscriber`.

2. In the `TransientSubscriber` project, rename `Form1` to `MainWindow`.

3. Add references to `LceEx`, `MyEventClass`, and `System.EnterpriseServices`.

4. Modify the UI as shown in Figure 38.14.

5. Add the button handler in Listing 38.15. The helper library `LceEx` is used to implement the subscribe and unsubscribe handlers. The generated subscription name (a GUID) is displayed as well.

6. Add the class `TransientSubscriptionHandler` (in Listing 38.16). This class is a regular component; it is possible but not required to make it a serviced component.

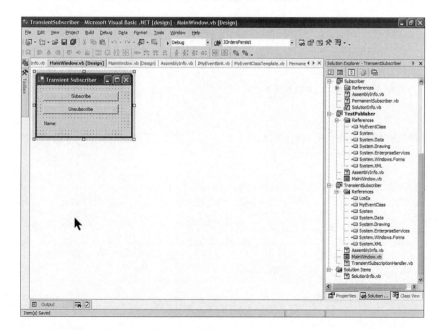

FIGURE 38.14   Transient subscriber UI.

Building Publish-Subscribe Systems with Loosely Coupled Events (LCE)

LISTING 38.15
Button Handlers

```
Private m_MySubscriptionHandler As TransientSubscriptionHandler
Private m_SubscriptionName As String

Private Sub OnSubscribe_Click(ByVal sender As Object, _
      ByVal e As EventArgs) Handles m_btnSubscribe.Click
   m_MySubscriptionHandler = New TransientSubscriptionHandler
   m_SubscriptionName = TransientSubscriptionManager.Add( _
     GetType(MyEventClassTemplate), _
     GetType(IMyEventSink), _
     m_MySubscriptionHandler)
   m_btnSubscribe.Enabled = False
   m_btnUnsubscribe.Enabled = True
   m_lblName.Text = "Name: " + m_SubscriptionName
End Sub

Private Sub OnUnsubscribe_Click(ByVal sender As Object, _
      ByVal e As EventArgs) Handles m_btnUnsubscribe.Click
   TransientSubscriptionManager.Remove(m_SubscriptionName)
   m_MySubscriptionHandler = Nothing
   m_btnSubscribe.Enabled = True
   m_btnUnsubscribe.Enabled = False
   m_lblName.Text = "Name: "
End Sub
```

LISTING 38.16
Class `TransientSubscriptionHandler`

```
Imports MyEventClass

Public Class TransientSubscriptionHandler
   Implements IMyEventSink

   Public Sub SomeEvent() Implements IMyEventSink.SomeEvent
      MessageBox.Show("SomeEvent called", "TransientSubscriptionHandler")
   End Sub
End Class
```

Test the application for normal operation.

1. Start the test publisher.

2. Start the transient subscriber application.

3. Click Fire Event. The event fires correctly; however, no subscribers are configured.

4. Click Subscribe. The text shows the GUID created to name the subscription.

5. Click Fire Event. The event fires correctly. This time the subscriber receives the event.

6. Click Unsubscribe.

7. Click Fire Event. The event fires correctly; however, no subscribers are configured.

38

NOTE

Persistent and transient subscriptions can be used at the same time. This is important for loosely coupled systems because publishers are independent of subscribers, and subscribers are independent of each other.

Advanced LCE Topics

You now learn how to publish events in parallel, publish events asynchronously, design transactions with LCEs, and avoid security pitfalls with inproc-subscribers for LCEs.

Publishing COM+ Events in Parallel

COM+ can publish events in parallel. COM+ uses the RPC thread pool for this; therefore, in systems with large loads or many subscribers, some events are still called serially and control is returned to the client after all subscribers have finished processing the event. You can set a property in the attribute EventClass ▇**1** to specify parallel execution (see Listing 38.17).

LISTING 38.17
Specifying Parallel Processing in Event Class

```
<EventClass(FireInParallel:=True)>                                              1
Public Class MyEventClassTemplate
    Inherits ServicedComponent
    Implements IMyEventSink
```

Publishing COM+ Events Asynchronously

LCE with parallel subscriber processing still exposes the publisher to exceptions thrown by the subscribers and to long processing times. This problem can be solved using queued event classes or queued subscribers. Queued event classes and queued subscribers require the event sink interface(s) to specify the attribute InterfaceQueuing.

Building Publish-Subscribe Systems with Loosely Coupled Events (LCE)

Queued event classes must reside in a COM+ application with queuing and the queue listener enabled.

Queued subscribers must reside in a COM+ application with queuing and the queue listener enabled. Additionally, the subscription must be queued (see Figure 38.15). This instructs the COM+ event mechanism to use `BindToMoniker` instead of `New` for this subscriber.

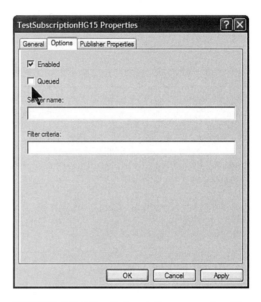

FIGURE 38.15   Subscription property with Queued check box in Component Services MMC plug-in.

LCEs and Transactions

Mixing transactions with LCEs is tricky and contradicts loose coupling.

Transactions cannot be used with transient subscribers because an object participating in the subscriber class transaction is passed to the publishing transaction. This is illegal and leads to serious inconsistencies and system failures.

When using transactions for persistent subscribers, it is best to select `TransactionOption.Required` for the publishing component, the event class, and all the subscribers. This causes all actions in the client and in all subscribers to be committed or aborted. If the client has no transactional needs, each subscriber can require a new transaction, as needed.

> **TIP**
>
> Combining transactions with COM+ events couples the publisher's design to the design of the subscribers. It is better to design a system with queued components.

Security Implications of Inproc-Subscribers

It is a potential security risk to have both the subscriber and the event class library activated. The subscriber component is loaded into the publisher's process space and has the same privileges as the subscriber. This concern is less of an issue for managed code-based subscribers. However, it is possible to run unmanaged subscribers against managed publishers. The event class can specify to disallow inproc-subscribers (see Listing 38.18 **1**).

LISTING 38.18
Specifying to Disallow Inproc-Subscribers in Event Class

```
<EventClass(AllowInprocSubscribers:=False)>                            1
Public Class MyEventClassTemplate
    Inherits ServicedComponent
    Implements IMyEventSink
```

Summary

This chapter showed how to use queued components and loosely coupled events to decouple systems. Queued components are great at flow meters and simplify programming for occasionally connected clients. Loosely coupled events solve the publish-subscribe pattern in a uniform way. Both have issues with transaction boundaries and require extra care in the design.

Further Reading

Lowy, Juval. *COM and .NET Component Services*. O'Reilly & Associates.

39 SECURING SERVICED COMPONENTS

IN BRIEF

This chapter explains the enhanced security features of Enterprise Services for role-based security, communication protection, impersonation control, and identity assignment for trusted subsystems. Additionally, special considerations for queued components and COM+ events are explained.

WHAT YOU NEED

SOFTWARE REQUIREMENTS	Windows 2000, XP, or 2003 .NET Framework 1.1 SDK Visual Studio .NET 2003 with Visual Basic .NET installed Windows Component Services installed Local administrator on your machine
HARDWARE REQUIREMENTS	PC desktop or laptop
SKILL REQUIREMENTS	Advanced knowledge of Visual Basic .NET Advanced knowledge of the .NET Framework Understanding of .NET role-based security

SECURING SERVICED COMPONENTS AT A GLANCE

Controlling Authentication for a COM+ Application

Role-based security (also called authorization) requires authentication of the user or caller. COM+ uses DCOM for authorization. In COM+ (and, therefore, Enterprise Services), authentication, wire-level protection, and authorization are not cleanly separated. To secure a serviced component, a series of decisions must be made.

First, you must decide whether you want the caller of your server-activated serviced component authenticated per session, per method call, or per TCP package. Additionally, you can request the data to be signed or encrypted.

After the caller is authenticated, you must decide whether you want to use this information to only identify the caller for role-based security, impersonate the caller, or allow the caller to be delegated.

You can also specify the granularity of the authorization at the application level or at both the application level and the component level.

Authentication at the application level is controlled with the `ApplicationAccessControl` attribute. The constructor has a Boolean flag to enable COM+ security. This is the security master switch and must be set to `True` to use any security-related features at the application or the component level. `ApplicationAccessControl` has properties that control the access check granularity, the authentication level, data integrity, data privacy, and the impersonation level.

> **TIP**
>
> Library-activated COM+ applications cannot control the authentication and impersonation levels; they receive the settings from the hosting application. A malicious host might pretend to be a user, to circumvent security, so library applications should be used only on the server. They should be hosted only by ASP.NET or a server-activated COM+ application. Never deploy library-activated applications for use in Windows applications or in a regular Remoting host.

The property `AccessChecksLevel` in `ApplicationAccessControl` controls the access control granularity. `AccessChecksLevelOption.Application` enables security checks at the application level only. The caller must be a member of at least one of the roles defined in the application; however, role requirements in the interfaces or components are ignored.

`AccessChecksLevelOption.ApplicationComponent` enables checking at both the application level and the component.

39

Controlling Authentication for a COM+ Application

TIP

All COM+ applications should use `AccessChecksLevelOption.ApplicationCompon` to enable role-based security. `AccessChecksLevelOption.Applicaonti` is useful only for debugging.

The `Authentication` property in `ApplicationAccessControl` controls the authentication level, data integrity, and data privacy for server-activated applications (it has no meaning for library-activated applications). `AuthenticationOption.None` turns off authentication; this turns off security. `AuthenticationOption.Connect` authenticates the client at connection time (usually when the first component in the COM+ application is instantiated). `AuthenticationOption.Call` authenticates the caller for every call. `AuthenticationOption.Packet` authenticates the client for every TCP/IP packet. A single method call can be split into multiple packets for transport. `AuthenticationOption.Integrity` authenticates the client for every TCP/IP packet and signs the data to prevent modification of the data in transit. `AuthenticationOption.Privacy` authenticates the client for every TCP/IP packet, signs the data to prevent modification of the data in transit, and encrypts the data to prevent eavesdropping.

TIP

Server-activated COM+ applications accessed from remote machines should specify `AuthenticationOption.Privacy`. Alternatively, you could specify `AuthenticationOption.Connect` and use a secure transport, such as IPSSEC.

Server-activated COM+ applications accessed locally could specify `AuthenticationOption.Connect` if the server is protected; however, `AuthenticationOption.Privacy` adds extra security.

The `ImpersonationLevel` property in `ApplicationAccessControl` controls the impersonation level for server-activated applications (it has no meaning for library-activated applications). `ImpersonationLevelOption.Anonymous` causes the application to throw away the information about the client; this turns off role-based security. `ImpersonationLevelOption.Identify` causes the application to use the authenticated user's identity for role membership and ACL checks. The application executes under the configured identity (see the later section "Building Trusted Subsystems with Identities"). `ImpersonationLevelOption.Impersonate` causes the application to execute with the same identity as the caller and to access local resources as the caller's identity. `ImpersonationLevelOption.Delegate` causes the application to execute with the same identity as the caller and to access local and remote resources with the caller's identity.

Listing 39.1 illustrates how to specify application security for a server-activated application. **1** Listing 39.2 illustrates how to specify application security for a library-activated application. **1**

LISTING 39.1
`ApplicationAccessControl` **Attribute for Server-Activated Applications**

```
<Assembly: ApplicationName("SecureServicedApp")>
<Assembly: ApplicationActivation(ActivationOption.Server)>
<Assembly: ApplicationAccessControl(True, _                              [1]
        AccessChecksLevel:=AccessChecksLevelOption.ApplicationComponent, _
        Authentication:=AuthenticationOption.Privacy, _
        ImpersonationLevel:=ImpersonationLevelOption.Identify)>
```

39

LISTING 39.2
`ApplicationAccessControl` **Attribute for Library-Activated Applications**

```
<Assembly: ApplicationName("SecureServicedApp")>
<Assembly: ApplicationActivation(ActivationOption.Library)>
<Assembly: ApplicationAccessControl(True, _                              [1]
        AccessChecksLevel:=AccessChecksLevelOption.ApplicationComponent)>
```

Each component can decide whether it needs access control (if the application specified security and `AccessChecksLevel:=AccessChecksLevelOption.ApplicationComponent`). The `ComponentAccessControl` [1] attribute's default constructor enables access control (see Listing 39.3).

LISTING 39.3
`ComponentAccessControl` **Attribute for Library-Activated Applications**

```
<EventTrackingEnabled(), _
ComponentAccessControl(), _                                             [1]
 Description("A secure component")> _
Public Class MyComponent
    Inherits ServicedComponent
    Implements IMyInterface
```

Implementing Role-Based Security in COM+

COM+ role-based security adds an extra level of indirection to the basic .NET role-based security that uses Windows groups as roles. This is extremely useful when deploying software at customer sites. It is unlikely that your customer uses the same role names as your software. COM+ roles are local to a COM+ application and can be defined declaratively in `AssemblyInfo.vb`, programmatically through the COM+ Catalog, or administratively with the Component Services MMC plug-in. Individual Windows users or Windows groups can be assigned programmatically through the COM+ Catalog or administratively with the Component Services MMC plug-in.

Implementing Role-Based Security in COM+

Authorization for a role can be specified for an entire interface, an entire component, or an individual method in a component. The caller must be a member of at least one of the roles authorized to use the method. The roles authorized are the union of roles specified for the interface, the component (class), and the method.

.NET allows components to be used without using the interface either by calling the method in the component directly or by using reflection. This enables a caller to bypass role-based security specified for an interface. The attribute `SecureMethod` prevents this behavior and forces access only through the components' explicitly defined interfaces.

39

Preparing a Test Project

In this section, you create a solution with a serviced component, a registration project, and a Windows test application, as outlined in the following steps:

1. Create an empty solution named EsSecurity.

2. Add a VB windows application project named EsTestApplication.

3. Add a VB class project named MyServicedComponent.

4. Delete `Class1.vb`.

5. Add the setup for a serviced component (reference to `System.`
   `EnterpriseServices`, file `AssemblyInfo.cs`, global file `SolutionInfo.cs`, COM+ registration project, and project dependencies). For details, see Chapters 34, "Introduction to Enterprise Services," or 35, "Activation-Related Services."

6. Add the interface in Listing 39.4.

7. Add the class `MyComponent` in Listing 39.5.

8. In the `EsTestApplication` project, rename `Form1` to `MainWindow`.

9. Modify the UI as shown in Figure 39.1.

10. Add references to `MyServicedComponent` and `System.EnterpriseServices`.

11. Add the button handlers in Listing 39.6.

LISTING 39.4
IMyInterface Interface

```
Imports System.EnterpriseServices

Public Interface IMyInterface
    Sub RegularMethod()
    Sub PrivilegedMethodDeclarative()
    Sub PrivilegedMethodProgrammatic(ByVal value As Integer)
End Interface
```

LISTING 39.5

MyComponent Class

```
Imports System.EnterpriseServices
Imports System.Text
Imports System.Reflection
Imports System.Threading
Imports System.Windows.Forms


<EventTrackingEnabled(), _
Description("A secure component")> _
Public Class MyComponent
    Inherits ServicedComponent
    Implements IMyInterface


    Private Sub PrivilegedMethodDeclarative() _
            Implements IMyInterface.PrivilegedMethodDeclarative
        DisplayTraceMessageBox()
    End Sub


    Private Sub PrivilegedMethodProgrammatic(ByVal value As Integer) _
            Implements IMyInterface.PrivilegedMethodProgrammatic
        DisplayTraceMessageBox()
    End Sub


    Private Sub RegularMethod() Implements IMyInterface.RegularMethod
        DisplayTraceMessageBox()
    End Sub


    Private Sub DisplayTraceMessageBox()
        Dim className As String
        Dim methodName As String
        Dim details As New StringBuilder
        Dim sf As New StackFrame(1) ' gets the stack frame calling us
        Dim mi As MethodBase = sf.GetMethod() 'info about the method calling us
        className = mi.DeclaringType.Name 'class declaring the method calling us
        methodName = mi.Name 'the actual name of the method  calling us
        details.Append(className)
        details.Append(".")
        details.Append(methodName)
        details.Append(Environment.NewLine)
        details.Append("   Process=")
        details.Append(Process.GetCurrentProcess().Id)
        details.Append(Environment.NewLine)
        details.Append("   Thread=")
        details.Append(Thread.CurrentThread.GetHashCode().ToString())
```

39

Implementing Role-Based Security in COM+

LISTING 39.5
Continued

```vb
    Try
        details.Append(Environment.NewLine)
        details.Append("    Context=")
        'Throws COM Exception if zero services requested
        Dim contextID As Guid = ContextUtil.ContextId
        details.Append(contextID.ToString())
        details.Append(Environment.NewLine)
        details.Append("    Security=")
        details.Append(ContextUtil.IsSecurityEnabled().ToString())
        details.Append("; IsInRole(""PrivilegedTestUser"")=")
        details.Append(ContextUtil.IsCallerInRole("PrivilegedTestUser"))
    Catch ex As Exception
        'Catches exception if no context (zero services requested)
        details.Append("<None>")
    End Try
    MessageBox.Show(details.ToString(), _
        "Show Method Call Detail")
    End Sub
End Class
```

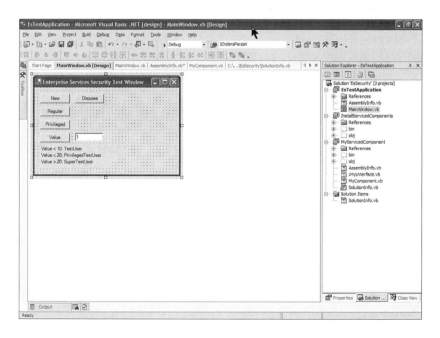

FIGURE 39.1   Test UI.

LISTING 39.6
Security Test Button Handlers

```
Private Sub MainWindow_Load(ByVal sender As System.Object, ByVal e As
➥System.EventArgs) _'
      Handles MyBase.Load
    Text += " - Process=" + Process.GetCurrentProcess().Id.ToString()
    Text += " - Thread=" + Thread.CurrentThread.GetHashCode().ToString()
End Sub


Private m_TestClass As IMyInterface

Private Sub btnNew_Click(ByVal sender As System.Object, ByVal e As
➥System.EventArgs) _
      Handles m_btnNew.Click

    m_TestClass = New MyComponent
End Sub


Private Sub btnDispose_Click(ByVal sender As System.Object, ByVal e As
➥System.EventArgs) _
      Handles m_btnDispose.Click

    ServicedComponent.DisposeObject(m_TestClass)
End Sub


Private Sub OnRegular(ByVal sender As System.Object, _
              ByVal e As System.EventArgs) Handles m_btnRegular.Click
    m_TestClass.RegularMethod()
End Sub


Private Sub OnPrivileged(ByVal sender As System.Object, _
              ByVal e As System.EventArgs) Handles m_btnPrivileged.Click
    m_TestClass.PrivilegedMethodDeclarative()
End Sub


Private Sub OnValue(ByVal sender As System.Object, _
              ByVal e As System.EventArgs) Handles m_btnValue.Click
    Dim value As Integer
    value = Convert.ToInt32(m_txtValue.Text)
    m_TestClass.PrivilegedMethodProgrammatic(value)
End Sub
```

Test the application; all buttons should work normally.

39

Implementing Role-Based Security in COM+

Enabling Role-Based Security

Turn on security at the application and component levels, set authentication to
`AuthenticationOption.Privacy`, and specify `ImpersonationLevel:`
`=ImpersonationLevelOption.Identify`, as follows:

1. Add the modifications in Listing 39.7 **1** to `AssemblyInfo.vb` to enable
   role-based security at the application level.

2. Add the modifications in Listing 39.8 **1** to the `MyComponent` class to enable
   role-based security at the component level and to prevent circumventing security with the attribute `SecureMethod`.

LISTING 39.7

Application Security in `AssemblyInfo.vb`

```
<Assembly: ApplicationName("SecureServicedApp")>
<Assembly: ApplicationActivation(ActivationOption.Server)>
<Assembly: ApplicationAccessControl(True, _
        AccessChecksLevel:=AccessChecksLevelOption.ApplicationComponent, _
        Authentication:=AuthenticationOption.Privacy, _
        ImpersonationLevel:=ImpersonationLevelOption.Identify)>
```

LISTING 39.8

Component-Level Security in `MyComponent.vb`

```
<EventTrackingEnabled(), _
ComponentAccessControl(), _
SecureMethod(), _
Description("A secure component")> _
Public Class MyComponent
    Inherits ServicedComponent
    Implements IMyInterface
```

Test the application; clicking New causes a security exception, which is correct.

You have successfully enabled role-based security without defining roles and granting
access based on roles to the interface, the component, or individual methods.

Defining Roles and Assigning Members

Roles are defined with the assembly-level attribute `SecurityRole` and are applied
to the COM+ application. The attribute `SecurityRole` takes a `String` with the
role name. You can set the optional property `SetEveryoneAccess` to `True` to add
members of the default Windows group Everyone to this role. This enables everyone
to use items protected with an authorization for this role to use it.

COM+ predefines a special role named Marshaler required to instantiate a component. This role is often tagged with `SetEveryoneAccess`. Alternatively, you can add all the users who are allowed to use any functionality in this application to this role.

Add the roles Marshaler, TestUser, PrivilegedTestUser, and SuperTestUser **1** to the COM+ application (see Listing 39.9). The roles Marshaler and TestUser contain everyone.

LISTING 39.9
Define Roles in `AssemblyInfo.vb`

```
<Assembly: ApplicationName("SecureServicedApp")>
<Assembly: ApplicationActivation(ActivationOption.Server)>
<Assembly: ApplicationAccessControl(True, _
        AccessChecksLevel:=AccessChecksLevelOption.ApplicationComponent, _
        Authentication:=AuthenticationOption.Privacy, _
        ImpersonationLevel:=ImpersonationLevelOption.Identify)>
<Assembly: SecurityRole("Marshaler", SetEveryoneAccess:=True)>
<Assembly: SecurityRole("TestUser", SetEveryoneAccess:=True)>
<Assembly: SecurityRole("PrivilegedTestUser")>
<Assembly: SecurityRole("SuperTestUser")>
```

1

Test the application; clicking New and Dispose works because the Marshaler role contains everyone.

Next, you add yourself to the role PrivlegedTestUser. This will not change the behavior of the previous test, as follows:

1. Start the Component Services MMC plug-in.

2. Expand the tree to display My Computer, COM+ Applications, SecureServicedApp, Roles.

3. Expand the tree for every role. The roles Marshaler and TestUser contain the users Everyone. The roles PrivilegedTestUser and SuperTestUser have no users assigned.

4. Right-click on PrivilegedTestUser, Users, and select New, User from the menu (see Figure 39.2).

5. In the Select User or Groups dialog box, click on Advanced.

6. In the advanced Select User or Groups dialog box, click on Find Now.

7. Select your username from the list (see Figure 39.3) and click OK in both dialog boxes. This adds you as a member of the role PrivilegedTestUser.

39

Implementing Role-Based Security in COM+

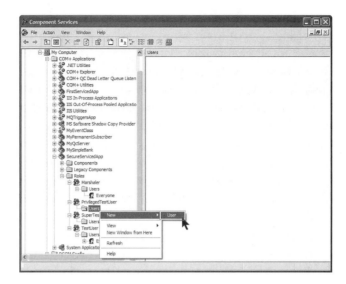

FIGURE 39.2   Adding a new user for a role.

FIGURE 39.3   Selecting the user for a role.

Authorizing Role Members with the `SecurityRole` Attribute

Adding the `SecurityRole` attribute to an interface, a component, **1** or a method **2**, **3** adds the specified role to the roles authorized to execute the method.

Implementing Role-Based Security in COM+

Role membership should be specified where it is most useful. Remember that you can add roles at the component level only to the roles specified at the interface level, and you can add more roles for a method only to the roles specified at the component (class) and interface levels. In other words, you can give permission to execute the method to more roles. Listing 39.10 shows how to apply the attribute SecurityRole to MyComponent.

LISTING 39.10

Declarative Authorization in `MyComponent.vb`

```
<EventTrackingEnabled(), _
 ComponentAccessControl(), _
 SecureMethod(), _
 SecurityRole("SuperTestUser"), _                              1
 SecurityRole("PrivilegedTestUser"), _
 Description("A secure component")> _
Public Class MyComponent
    Inherits ServicedComponent
    Implements IMyInterface

    Private Sub PrivilegedMethodDeclarative() _
            Implements IMyInterface.PrivilegedMethodDeclarative
        DisplayTraceMessageBox()
    End Sub


    <SecurityRole("TestUser")> _                               2
    Private Sub PrivilegedMethodProgrammatic(ByVal value As Integer) _
            Implements IMyInterface.PrivilegedMethodProgrammatic
        DisplayTraceMessageBox()
    End Sub


    <SecurityRole("TestUser")> _                               3
    Private Sub RegularMethod() Implements IMyInterface.RegularMethod
        DisplayTraceMessageBox()
    End Sub
```

TIP

SecurityRole attributes added to a method specification in an interface are ignored.

Test the application; all button clicks succeed. After you remove yourself from the PrivilegedTestUser role and click the New button, clicking the Privileged button fails. Windows roles are cached at login, while COM+ roles are cached at component instantiation.

39

Implementing Role-Based Security in COM+

Authorizing Role Members Programmatically with `ContextUtil` or `SecurityContext`

`ContextUtil` enables simple programmatic role-based security. You can query whether role-based security is enabled and whether the caller is in a specific role.

`SecurityContext` has methods to retrieve information about every aspect of security, including the credentials of every caller in the caller chain.

You will now use `ContextUtil.IsCallerInRole` to decide who will be allowed to use the `PrivilegedMethodProgrammatic` method **1** based on the value parameter passed (see Listing 39.11). You previously specified that every role be allowed to call the method `PrivilegedMethodProgrammatic`.

LISTING 39.11

Programmatic Authorization in `MyComponent.vb`

```vb
<SecurityRole("TestUser")> _
Private Sub PrivilegedMethodProgrammatic(ByVal value As Integer) _
        Implements IMyInterface.PrivilegedMethodProgrammatic
    Dim authorized As Boolean = True
    If value >= 20 Then
        authorized = ContextUtil.IsCallerInRole("SuperTestUser")
        Throw New SecurityException("Not authorized for this operation")
    ElseIf value >= 10 Then
        authorized = ContextUtil.IsCallerInRole("SuperTestUser") Or _
                    ContextUtil.IsCallerInRole("PrivilegedTestUser")
    End If
    If Not authorized Then
        Throw New SecurityException("Not authorized for this operation")
    End If
    DisplayTraceMessageBox()
End Sub
```

TIP

`ContextUtil.IsCallerInRole` always returns `True` if role-based security is disabled. This behavior is correct and allows security to be turned off at deployment time or during debugging without requiring changes to the code.

Alternatively, you can enforce security by testing `ContextUtil.IsSecurityEnabled`, or you can use the `SecurityContext` class to query details about the security of this component. This prevents changes to the security at deployment; however, it might prevent legitimate changes to the security configuration at deployment time.

Building Trusted Subsystems with Identities

In traditional client/server systems, the server executed with the client's security identity. This method can still be applied with the `ImpersonationLevel.Impersonate` or `ImpersonationLevel.Delegate` options. This method is often extended to access to the database. Its advantage is easy auditing. However, it limits the scalability of systems, complicates user management, and gives attackers a straight path to the database if an end-user account is compromised. Therefore, most *n*-tier systems are built with the trusted subsystem model. Additionally, the trusted subsystem model allows each component to execute with the least privilege, another important security principle.

Trusted subsystems authenticate and authorize the actual user at the first server, such as the web server or the business logic layer in COM+. Lower-layer components authenticate and authorize the calling component's identity (not the original caller's identity). The MSDN document referenced in "Further Reading" shows how to implement a trusted subsystem. COM+ supports this for server-activated components with `ImpersonationLevel.Identify` to authenticate and authorize the original caller, and with the capability to set an identity for the COM+ application (see Figure 39.4).

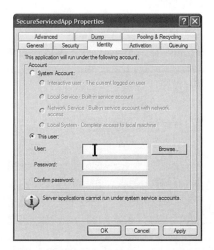

FIGURE 39.4   Setting the identity for a COM+ application.

Securing Queued Components (QCs)

QCs need to capture the client's security credentials when the client uses `BindToMoniker` and send it through MSMQ to the player for later reply. QCs can use the same attributes as regular components to specify their security needs.

Securing Queued Components (QCs)

A QC uses the underlying MSMQ mechanism for authentication. Unfortunately, this is available only for systems with a Message Queuing Primary Enterprise Controller (PEC), which requires a Windows domain controller. In other words, QCs cannot be secured in a Workgroup installation.

QCs do not support client credentials impersonation (or delegation). The designers chose this to prevent impersonation attacks through compromised application queues.

Securing Loosely Coupled Events

LCEs use the same security mechanisms as regular components. The event class is used to enforce security requirements for the publisher; this is the preferred method. However, the subscribers can ask for additional security in the subscriber implementation.

Hiding Components with the Attribute `PrivateComponent`

COM+ applications can contain private components. The class modifier `Friend` is not sufficient protection because it can be circumvented with reflection. COM+ can tag a component as internal to the COM+ application with the attribute `PrivateComponent`.

Summary

This chapter showed how to use COM+ transport and role-based security. COM+ roles add a level of indirection from Windows roles, to simplify deployment. This chapter also covered special issues with security and queued components, as well as the attribute `PrivateComponent`.

Further Reading

Lowy, Juval. *COM and .NET Component Services*. O'Reilly & Associates, 2001.

"Building Secure ASP.NET Applications: Authentication, Authorization, and Secure Communication." MSDN website, http://msdn.microsoft.com/library/default.asp?url=/library/en-us/dnnetsec/html/secnetlpMSDN.asp.

40 ADVANCED ENTERPRISE SERVICES PROGRAMMING

IN BRIEF

This chapter builds on the knowledge gained in the previous chapter by starting with an introduction to programming the COM+ catalog. You will learn this by analyzing the COM+ registration utility used in the previous chapters and the transient subscription helper LceEx used in Chapter 38, "Services for Loosely Coupled Systems."

The chapter then shows you how to use the visual designer for ADO .NET objects with Enterprise Services to enable enterprise-class Rapid Application Development (RAD) for multitier data-driven applications.

WHAT YOU NEED

SOFTWARE REQUIREMENTS	Windows 2000, XP, or 2003 .NET Framework 1.1 SDK Visual Studio .NET 2003 with Visual Basic .NET installed Windows Component Services installed Administrative rights on the machine SQL Server 2000 Microsoft Desktop Database Engine or (MSDE) 2000
HARDWARE REQUIREMENTS	PC desktop or laptop
SKILL REQUIREMENTS	Advanced knowledge of Visual Basic .NET Advanced knowledge of the .NET Framework

ADVANCED ENTERPRISE SERVICES PROGRAMMING AT A GLANCE

Programming the COM+ Catalog

It is sometimes useful to manipulate the COM+ catalog directly. Examples of such uses are registering and unregistering serviced components, writing deployment maintenance utilities, and creating transient subscriptions to loosely coupled events.

The COM+ catalog can be programmed with COM components through the interop library COM+ 1.0 Admin Type Library. The general paradigm for programming the COM+ catalog is to retrieve a top-level collection and manipulate it or its members. The interfaces ICOMAdminCatalog and ICOMAdminCatalog2 (in the component COMAdminCatalog) provide methods for accessing the top-level items in the catalog. The methods execute an action, return a COMAdminCatalogCollection object (accessed through the interface ICatalogCollection), or return a COMAdminCatalogObject (accessed through the interface ICatalogObject).

The catalog is organized into collections (see Figure 40.1). This hierarchy is also used in the Component Services MMC plug-in. The top-level collections (COMAdminCatalogCollection) can be retrieved only through the interface ICOMAdminCatalog. ICatalogCollection can retrieve individual catalog objects (COMAdminCatalogObject) and subordinate as well as related collections (COMAdminCatalogCollection). ICatalogObject can access the properties for the object.

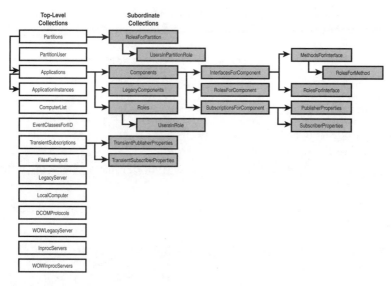

FIGURE 40.1   COM+ catalog structure.

40

TIP
This approach is not type safe and is cumbersome; however, the approach is very extensible. It is best to write a helper library for any work that requires programming of the COM+ catalog.

Now you will learn how to program the catalog through a code walk-through of two samples.

Programming Transient Subscriptions for Loosely Coupled Events

In Chapter 38, "Services for Loosely Coupled Systems," you were instructed to write code to help with adding and removing transient subscription (project LceEx) for loosely coupled events without a detailed explanation. Listing 40.1 is copied from Chapter 38 to help explain the code.

The namespace from the interop library is COMAdmin. **1**

The method Add checks that the parameters passed are the correct type and calls AddNotTypesafe to add the actual subscription. You could have passed a subscription name; instead, the method creates a GUID (subscription names are arbitrary and must be unique).

1. The COMAdminCatalog object is created and the TransientSubscriptions collection is retrieved. **2** You must call the method Populate to retrieve the collection. This is similar to creating the command object in ADO.NET and calling ExecuteReader to retrieve the data.

2. A subscription object is added to the collection. **3**

3. The necessary values for the properties are set. **4**

4. The change to the collection is saved. **5**

The method Remove removes the named subscription. Name is the name returned from the method Add.

1. The COMAdminCatalog object is created and the TransientSubscriptions collection is retrieved. **6**

2. The collection is searched for the named subscription. Once found, the subscription is removed and the changes are saved. **7**

LISTING 40.1

TransientSubscriptionManager Class

```
Imports System.Diagnostics
Imports System.EnterpriseServices
Imports System.Reflection
Imports System.Runtime.InteropServices
Imports COMAdmin                                                        1

Public Class TransientSubscriptionManager

    Public Shared Function Add( _
        ByVal eventClass As Type, _
        ByVal sinkInterface As Type, _
        ByVal subscriber As Object) As String
      'check parameters -> causes type safety
      Debug.Assert(eventClass.IsClass()) 'eventClass must be a class
      Dim ecaType As Type = GetType(EventClassAttribute)
      Dim eca As Object() = eventClass.GetCustomAttributes(ecaType, True)
      Debug.Assert(eca.Length = 1) 'eventClass must have EventClassAttribute
      Debug.Assert(sinkInterface.IsInterface()) 'interface required
      Debug.Assert(sinkInterface.IsInstanceOfType(subscriber))
      Dim siName As String = sinkInterface.ToString()
      Dim siType As Type = eventClass.GetInterface(siName)
      Debug.Assert(Not siType Is Nothing)
      Debug.Assert(sinkInterface Is siType)
      'add
      Dim eventClassString As String = "{" + eventClass.GUID.ToString() + "}"
      Dim sinkIfString As String = "{" + sinkInterface.GUID.ToString() + "}"
      Return AddNotTypesafe(eventClassString, sinkIfString, "", _
        subscriber, "", "")
    End Function

    Public Shared Function AddNotTypesafe( _
        ByVal eventClassString As String, _
        ByVal sinkInterfaceString As String, _
        ByVal method As String, _
        ByVal subscriber As Object, _
        ByVal filterCriteria As String, _
        ByVal publisherId As String) As String
      'get catalog
```

40

Programming the COM+ Catalog

LISTING 40.1
Continued

```
2   Dim catalog As ICOMAdminCatalog = New COMAdminCatalog
    'get transient collection
    Dim collection As Object
    Dim transientCollection As ICatalogCollection
    collection = catalog.GetCollection("TransientSubscriptions")
    transientCollection = CType(collection, ICatalogCollection)
    transientCollection.Populate()
    'create subscription name
    Dim subscriptionName As String = Guid.NewGuid().ToString()
    'add subscription
3   Dim subscription As ICatalogObject
    subscription = CType(transientCollection.Add(), ICatalogObject)

4   subscription.Value("Name") = subscriptionName
    subscription.Value("SubscriberInterface") = subscriber
    subscription.Value("EventCLSID") = eventClassString
    subscription.Value("InterfaceID") = sinkInterfaceString
    subscription.Value("MethodName") = method
    subscription.Value("FilterCriteria") = filterCriteria
    subscription.Value("PublisherID") = publisherId

5   transientCollection.SaveChanges()
    'return the name of the newly created subscription
    Return subscriptionName
End Function

Public Shared Sub Remove(ByVal subscriptionName As String)
    Debug.Assert(subscriptionName <> "")
    'get catalog
6   Dim catalog As ICOMAdminCatalog = New COMAdminCatalog
    'get transient collection
    Dim collection As Object
    Dim transientCollection As ICatalogCollection
    collection = catalog.GetCollection("TransientSubscriptions")
    transientCollection = CType(collection, ICatalogCollection)
    transientCollection.Populate()
```

40

LISTING 40.1
Continued

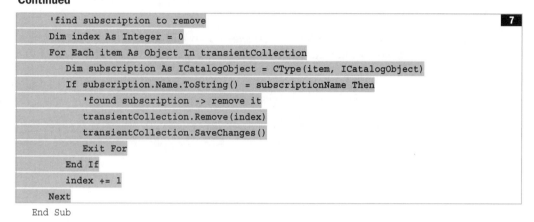

```
        'find subscription to remove                                      7
    Dim index As Integer = 0
    For Each item As Object In transientCollection
        Dim subscription As ICatalogObject = CType(item, ICatalogObject)
        If subscription.Name.ToString() = subscriptionName Then
            'found subscription -> remove it
            transientCollection.Remove(index)
            transientCollection.SaveChanges()
            Exit For
        End If
        index += 1
    Next
End Sub

End Class
```

40

Shutting Down a COM+ Application and Removing Components

You used the provided utility RegisterComPlus in Chapters 34, "Introduction to Enterprise Services," through 39, "Securing Serviced Components." This utility shows command-line parsing, reflection programming, and the execution of external processes. Finally, it shows how to use the COM+ catalog to find and shut down the application instances for the components in the assembly, and how to remove the actual component without removing the COM+ application.

Listing 40.2 shows the uninstall code, including the GAC uninstall in the class ComPlusRegistrar.

First, it searches for the application using m_Catalog, a private instance of ICOMAdminCtalog created in the class's constructor.

1. The collection Applications is retrieved. **1** You must call the method Populate to retrieve the collection. This is similar to creating the command object in ADO.NET and calling ExecuteReader to retrieve the data.

2. The collection's objects are searched until a match of the application object's property Name with the application name from the assembly to be uninstalled is found. **2**

3. The subordinate collection Components is retrieved. **3** You must call the method Populate to retrieve the collection. This is similar to creating the command object in ADO.NET and calling ExecuteReader to retrieve the data.

Programming the COM+ Catalog

Next, the uninstall code checks for running instances of the application and initiates a shutdown. This code checks whether the shutdown was successful. It attempts 200 tries at 100-millisecond intervals before failing. **4**

1. The private method `IsRunning` retrieves the top-level collection `ApplicationInstances` from the collection `Applications`. **10** You must call the method `Populate` to retrieve the collection. This is similar to creating the command object in ADO.NET and calling `ExecuteReader` to retrieve the data. The application is running if one or more instances are running.

2. The private method `InitiateShutdown` uses a global method in `ICOMAdminCatalog` and handles errors. **11** The application is running if one or more instances are running.

Finally, the uninstall code finds all the components in the COM+ application, which are defined in the assembly to be unregistered, and removes them from the application.

1. The method `GetComPlusComponents` in class `AssemblyHelper` uses reflection to collect an array of strings containing the fully qualified names of all the serviced components in the assembly. **5**

2. The code loops through all the components in the `Components` collection retrieved when we found the application and extracts the `Name` property. **6**

3. The code checks the component name in the catalog against the name of each component in the assembly. **7**

4. If it matches, the component is removed from the collection Components. **8** The index variable `j` is decremented to adjust for the removed object in the list.

5. The changes to the collection `Components` are saved. **9**

LISTING 40.2
Uninstalling COM+ Components

```
Public Sub Uninstall(ByVal theAssembly As AssemblyHelper)
    Dim application As String = theAssembly.ComPlusApplicationName

    'find the COM+ application, if it exists
    Dim appCollection As ICatalogCollection = _
        CType(m_Catalog.GetCollection("Applications"), ICatalogCollection)
    appCollection.Populate()
    Dim appCount As Integer = appCollection.Count
    Dim i As Integer
    Dim currentName As String = ""
    Dim appKey As Object = New Object
    Dim app As ICatalogObject = Nothing
```

LISTING 40.2
Continued

```vb
Dim compCollection As ICatalogCollection = Nothing
Dim found As Boolean = False
i = 0
While i < appCount AndAlso Not found
    app = CType(appCollection.Item(i), ICatalogObject)          2
    currentName = CType(app.Value("Name"), String)
    If currentName = application Then
        'we found the COM+ application
        appKey = app.Key                                        3
        compCollection = _
            CType(appCollection.GetCollection("Components", appKey), _
            ICatalogCollection)
        compCollection.Populate()
        found = True
    End If
    i += 1
End While
If found Then
    'is application running?                                     4
    Dim tries As Integer = 0
    While IsRunning(appCollection, appKey)
        'COM+ application is (still) running -> stop it
        InitiateShutdown(application)
        If IsRunning(appCollection, appKey) Then
            'COM+ application is still running
            If tries > 200 Then
                'fail
                WriteLine( _
                    "Failed to shutdown COM+ application {0} in 20 seconds", _
                    application)
                Throw New ApplicationException( _
                    "Could not shutdown COM+ application " + application)
            Else
                'wait for 100 ms and try to stop it again
                Thread.Sleep(TimeSpan.FromMilliseconds(100))
                tries += 1
            End If
        End If
    End While
```

40

Programming the COM+ Catalog

LISTING 40.2
Continued

```
5   'remove component(s) from COM+ application
    Dim servicedComp As String() = theAssembly.GetComPlusComponents
    Dim j As Integer = 0
6   While j < compCollection.Count
        Dim compObj As ICatalogObject = CType(compCollection.Item(j), _
            ICatalogObject)
        Dim compName As String = CType(compObj.Name, String)
        Dim k As Integer = 0
7       While k < servicedComp.Length
            If servicedComp(k) = compName Then
8               compCollection.Remove(j)
                j -= 1
                WriteLine( _
                    "Removed component {0} from COM+ application {1}", _
                    compName, application)
                Exit While
            End If
            k += 1
        End While
        j += 1
    End While
9   compCollection.SaveChanges()
    End If

    'uninstall from GAC
    Dim name As String = theAssembly.AssemblyName
    WriteLine("Removing {0} from the GAC", name)
    Dim args As String = "-silent -u """ + name + """"
    Dim info As ProcessStartInfo = New ProcessStartInfo("gacutil.exe ", args)
    info.CreateNoWindow = True
    info.WindowStyle = ProcessWindowStyle.Hidden
    Dim process As Process = process.Start(info)
    process.WaitForExit()

End Sub

Private Function IsRunning(ByVal appCollection As ICatalogCollection, _
        ByVal appKey As Object) As Boolean
    'check catalog
```

LISTING 40.2
Continued

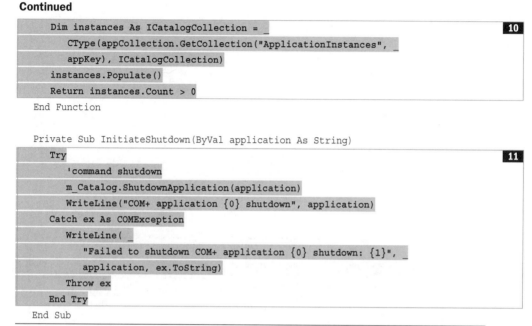

```
    Dim instances As ICatalogCollection = _                              10
        CType(appCollection.GetCollection("ApplicationInstances", _
        appKey), ICatalogCollection)
    instances.Populate()
    Return instances.Count > 0
End Function


Private Sub InitiateShutdown(ByVal application As String)
    Try                                                                  11
        'command shutdown
        m_Catalog.ShutdownApplication(application)
        WriteLine("COM+ application {0} shutdown", application)
    Catch ex As COMException
        WriteLine( _
            "Failed to shutdown COM+ application {0} shutdown: {1}", _
            application, ex.ToString)
        Throw ex
    End Try
End Sub
```

40

Combining Rapid Application Development and Enterprise Services

Rapid Application Development (RAD) uses the visual designer to design the data access components and to design the user interface.

The visual designer in VS .NET 2003 works only for classes derived from `System.ComponentModel.Component`, while components using Enterprise Services must derive from `System.EnterpriseServices.ServicedComponent`. This prevents the use of the visual designer.

One solution uses a compile-time switch for the class definition in the data access component. When the compile-time switch is set to `RAD_MODE`, the code derives the class from `Component`; otherwise, it is derived from `ServicedComponent`.

You will develop a simple multitier system, shown in Figure 40.2. Each tier has a single component. All middle-tier components are transacted. The data-access tier component can be switched between RAD mode and deployment mode with the conditional compile symbol `RAD_MODE`. The project `Utils` contains the shared elements, such as the middle-tier interface `ICustomerAccess` and `CustomerDataSet`.

Combining Rapid Application Development and Enterprise Services

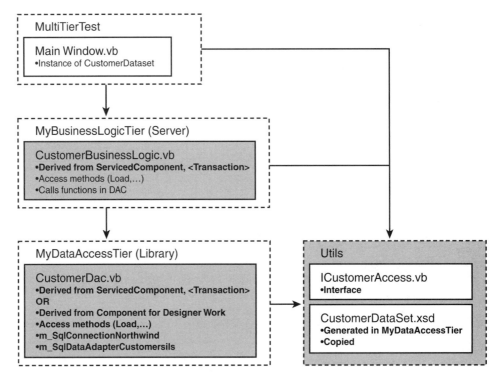

FIGURE 40.2   Three-tier architecture.

Multitier systems are built from the bottom up. A solution with all the projects, the setup for Enterprise Services, and the installation project dependencies have been created for you (see Figure 40.3).

First, you add the data access component, prepare it for switching between design and deployment modes, design the data access, and generate the DataSet. Here you will use the Customers table in the Northwind database. Add the data access component named CustomerDac as follows:

1. Add a component named CustomerDac to the project MyDataAccessTier.

2. Switch from design view to code view.

3. Add a custom constant named RAD_MODE=True in MyDataAccessTier Property Pages for All Configurations (see Figure 40.4).

4. Change the definition of the class CustomerDac to derive the component differently based on the definition of RAD_MODE (see Listing 40.3 **1**). Specify the services required.

5. Rebuild the solution.

Combining Rapid Application Development and Enterprise Services

6. You might need to exit and re-enter Visual Studio. Visual Studio does not always parse the switch between RAD_MODE=False and RAD_MODE=True correctly.

7. Drag the table Customers from the Northwind database in Server Explorer.

8. Rename the connection to m_SqlConnectionNorthwind and the adapter to m_SqlDataAdapterCustomers.

9. Generate the DataSet CustomerDataSet (see Figure 40.5).

FIGURE 40.3   Three-tier solution structure.

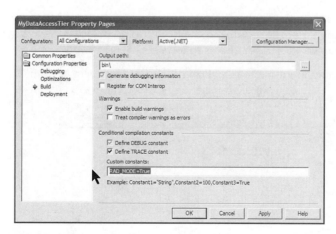

FIGURE 40.4   Adding the constant RAD_MODE.

Combining Rapid Application Development and Enterprise Services

LISTING 40.3
Modified Component `CustomerDac`

```vb
Imports System.ComponentModel
Imports System.EnterpriseServices

Imports Utils

<EventTrackingEnabled(), _
 Transaction(), _
 ObjectPooling(MinPoolSize:=1, MaxPoolSize:=1), _
 ComponentAccessControl(), _
 SecureMethod(), _
 SecurityRole("TestUser")> _
Public Class CustomerDac
#If RAD_MODE Then
    Inherits Component
#Else
    Inherits ServicedComponent
#End If
    Implements ICustomerAccess
```

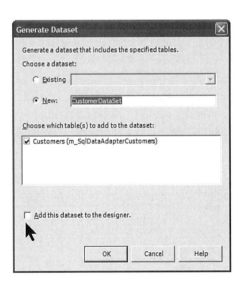

FIGURE 40.5 Generate `CustomerDataSet`.

Combining Rapid Application Development and Enterprise Services

Next, you move the generated `DataSet` to the project Utils, switch to deployment mode, and build the rest of the data access and business logic tier.

1. In Solution Explorer, drag the file `CustomerDataSet.xsd` from project MyDataAccessTier to the project Utils.

2. Right-click `CustomerDataSet.xsd` and select Run Custom Tool to regenerate the strongly typed `DataSet` in file `CustomerDataSet.vb`.

3. Change the custom constant RAD_MODE=True in MyDataAccessTier Property Pages for All Configurations (see Figure 40.4) to RAD_MODE=False.

4. Rebuild the solution.

5. Add a method to retrieve the data in the table Customers to the interface `ICustomerAccess` (see Listing 40.4 **1**).

6. Implement the interface `ICustomerAccess` in the class `CustomerDac` (see Listing 40.5).

7. Add the class `CustomerBusinessLogic` to the project MyBusinessLogicTier.

8. Change the class `CustomerBusinessLogic` into a serviced component, and implement the interface `ICustomerAccess` in the class `MyBusinessLogicTier` (see Listing 40.6).

9. Rebuild the solution.

LISTING 40.4
Interface `ICustomerAccess`

```
Public Interface ICustomerAccess
    Function GetData() As CustomerDataSet                                    1
End Interface
```

LISTING 40.5
Implementation of Interface `ICustomerAccess` in the Class `CustomerDac`

```
<AutoComplete()> _
Private Function GetData() As CustomerDataSet _
     Implements ICustomerAccess.GetData
   Dim ds As New CustomerDataSet
   m_SqlDataAdapterCustomers.Fill(ds)
   Return ds
End Function
```

Combining Rapid Application Development and Enterprise Services

LISTING 40.6
Implementation of the Interface `ICustomerAccess` in the Class `CustomerBusinessLogic`

```
Imports System.EnterpriseServices
Imports MyDataAccessTier
Imports Utils

<EventTrackingEnabled(), _
 Transaction(), _
 ComponentAccessControl(), _
 SecureMethod(), _
 SecurityRole("TestUser")> _
Public Class CustomerBusinessLogic
    Inherits ServicedComponent
    Implements ICustomerAccess

    <AutoComplete()> _
    Private Function GetData() As CustomerDataSet _
         Implements ICustomerAccess.GetData
       Dim dac As CustomerDac = New CustomerDac
       Dim dacInterface As ICustomerAccess = dac
       Dim ds As CustomerDataSet = dacInterface.GetData()
       ServicedComponent.DisposeObject(dac)
       Return ds
    End Function
End Class
```

Next, you add the UI to display the customer data in a `DataGrid`:

1. Add a `DataGrid` to the window; use the entire space. Rename it to `m_CustomerDataGrid`.

2. Add a `DataSet` to the window. Select `ReferencedDataSet` from the drop-down list (see Figure 40.6). Select `Utils.CustomerDataSet`.

3. Rename the `DataSet` to `m_CustomerDataSet`.

4. Set the DataGrid property set `DataSource` to `m_CustomerDataSet` and the property `DataMember` to `Customers`.

5. Add a load event handler, as in Listing 40.7, to the form `MainWindow`.

6. Run the application.

Combining Rapid Application Development and Enterprise Services

LISTING 40.7
Implementation of Load Event Handler in Class `MainWindow`

```
Private m_BusinessLogic As Utils.ICustomerAccess
Private Sub MainWindow_Load(ByVal sender As System.Object, _
     ByVal e As System.EventArgs) Handles MyBase.Load
  m_BusinessLogic = New MyBusinessLogicTier.CustomerBusinessLogic
  m_CustomerDataSet.Clear()
  m_CustomerDataSet.Merge(m_BusinessLogic.GetData())
End Sub
```

Finally, here you will modify the data design to learn how to modify an n-tier system developed with RAD methodology with the same RAD tools. You will remove the column Fax from the query and the DataSet, and reflect the change in the UI. Follow these steps to change the system:

1. Change the custom constant RAD_MODE=False in MyDataAccessTier Property Pages for All Configurations (see Figure 40.4) to RAD_MODE=True.

2. Rebuild the solution. An error is reported in the class CustomerBusinessLogic; ignore it.

3. You might need to exit and re-enter Visual Studio. Visual Studio does not always parse the switch between RAD_MODE=False and RAD_MODE=True correctly.

4. Open CustomerDac.vb in designer mode.

5. Right-click on the adapter m_SqlAdapterCustomers and select the menu item Configure Data Adapter.

6. Use the wizard's default choices (you might need to re-enter the database connection) until you reach Generate the SQL statements.

7. Click on the button Query Builder.

8. Deselect the check box for Fax in the list of table columns (see Figure 40.6).

9. Use the wizard's default choices for the remaining screens.

10. Generate the DataSet CustomerDataSet (see Figure 40.5).

11. In Solution Explorer, drag the file CustomerDataSet.xsd from the project MyDataAccessTier to the project Utils.

12. Right-click CustomerDataSet.xsd and select Run Custom Tool to regenerate the strongly typed DataSet in the file CustomerDataSet.vb.

13. Change the custom constant RAD_MODE=True in MyDataAccessTier Property Pages for All Configurations (see Figure 40.4) to RAD_MODE=False.

40

Combining Rapid Application Development and Enterprise Services

14. Rebuild the solution.

15. Run the application; the column Fax is not present.

TIP

Close all open UI design windows before you change the DataSet. If the DataSet is temporarily unavailable while a UI design window with this DataSet is open, the designer will remove the DataSet and all data bindings for the DataSet. You will need to re-create them.

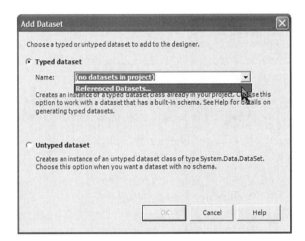

FIGURE 40.6 Change query for m_SqlDataAdapterCustomers.

Summary

This chapter showed you how to program the COM+ catalog for maintenance and execution time utilities. The knowledge you gained should enable you to write enterprise-class solutions with great deployment and maintenance support.

The second part of the chapter introduced you to the process of enabling visual database design tools and Enterprise Services to coexist.

Further Reading

Lowy, Juval. *COM and .NET Component Services.* O'Reilly & Associates, 2001.

Visual Studio Help. "COM+ Administration Collections" in "Platform SDK: COM+ (Component Services)."

Index

ExecutablePath property (Application object), 126

ExecuteNonQuery( ) method (Command object), 312

ExecuteReader( ) method, 306

Command object, 311

ExecuteScalar( ) method, 306

Command object, 311-312

ExecuteXmlReader( ) method, 306

Command object, 313

execution

ASP.NET files, order of, 530-531

ASP.NET web pages, 541

global.asax file methods, order of, 625

Exists() method (File class), 693

Exit method (Application object), 127

Exit statement, 50-51

ExitThread method (Application object), 127

expiration date, cookies, 608

expiration parameter (CacheDependency object), 613

explicit Remoting, 822

activation call types, 822-823

expressions, conditional, 55

F

File class, 693-694

file format compatibility, images, 206

File menu (menu controls, 171

File System Editor (deployment projects), 221

configuring, 221-222

special folders, adding items to, 223-224

File Types Editor (deployment projects), 221

configuring, 225-226

FileInfo class, 693

files

ASP.NET types, handlers for, 660

DPAPI and, 654

FileStream class, 694-695

performance improvement, 696

Fill( ) method (Data Form Wizard), 424

FillDataSet( ) method (Data Form Wizard), 424

fills, shapes, 199

filters, accessing class members, 763

Finalize method, dereferencing objects, 79

Find method (IBindingList interface), 476

FindString method (ComboBox control), 168

FindString property (ListBox control), 160

FindStringExact property (ListBox control), 160

FlatStyle property (Button control), 153

Flatten method (GraphicsPath class), 203

floating-point numbers, data types and, 97

Flush() method (FileStream class), 695

folders

IIS root, path and contents, 523

projects, 115

Font class, 207-208

Drawing namespace, 186

Font object (Graphics class), 191

Font property, 127

Button control, 153

Label control, 156

FontDialog control, 277

FontFamily class (Drawing namespace), 186

fonts, storing in databases, 460

FontStyle enumeration (Font class), 208

For/Next structure, 48-49

ForEach/Next structure, 49-50

ForeColor property, 127

foreign key tables, 366

Form class, 117

controls, adding, 119

Forms Designer, 117-118

I

IAsyncResult interface, 752

IBindingList interface, 474

ICOMAdminCatalog interface, 1021

ICOMAdminCatalog2 interface, 1021

Icon property, 123

IConfigurationSectionHandler interface (ASP.NET), custom configuration files, 630

icons, forms, displaying, 123-124

identities (ASP.NET security), 638

identity (web.config configuration section), 626

IDL (Interface Definition Language), metadata and, 27-28

IEnumerable interface, ForEach/Next structure, 50

If/Then structure, 44

If/Then/Else structure, 44

IHttpHandler interface, required members, 665

IHttpModule interface, 662

IIdentity interface, authorization, 799

IIS (Internet Information Server)

   ASP.NET applications and, 523

   authentication strategies, 891

   console, 523

   default website address, 523

   request processing (ASP.NET), 659

   root folder, path and contents, 523

   version 6.0 performance, request processing and, 659

   Windows authentication (ASP.NET), 639

     enabling, 639

IIS Manager (ISM), 639

ildasm.exe (MSIL Disassembler tool), 757

IList interface

   classes, 449

   data binding, 446-448

Image class, 206

   Drawing namespace, 186

Image control (ASP.NET), 543

Image property (RadioButton control), 157

ImageButton control (ASP.NET), 543

ImageIndex property (TreeView control), 282

ImageList property (RadioButton control), 157

ImageList property (TreeView control), 282

images

   button backgrounds, 153

   file type compatibility, 206

   forms background, changing, 122-123

immediate signing (assemblies), 792-793

ImpersonationLevel attribute, trusted subsystems, 1017

ImpersonationLevel property (ApplicationAccessControl attribute), 1006

implementation, defined, 74-75

implementing (IObjectControl interface), 937-939

importing web services, 879

   discovery, 880

Imports keyword, namespaces, 39-40

in-process Remoting, 818-821

Indent property (TreeView control), 282

Indeterminate (CheckBox control), 158

Index constant (HelpNavigator enumeration), 271

IndexOf method (IList interface), 447

IndexOf method (String class), 104

inheritance, 85-87

   implementing, 266-267

   object-oriented programming, 67

   overriding methods, 87-88

   web services classes, 869

IsValid property

ASP.NET Page object, 548

ASP.NET validation controls, 548

IsValid property (PrinterSettings class), 256

Item property (IList interface), 448

Items property (ComboBox control), 166

J

JIT compiler, 16

JITA (Just-In-Time Activation)

combining with object pooling, 946-947

scalability, 933-937

synchronization and, 973-974

testing functionality, 936

Join method (String class), 104

Just-In-Time Activation. See JITA

K

keyboard, event handling, 141-143

KeyCode property (keyboard events), 143

KeyData property (keyboard events), 143

KeyEventArgs object, properties, 142

KeyPressed event, 142

KeyValue property (keyboard events), 143

KeywordIndex constant (HelpNavigator enumeration), 271

keywords

Class, 68-69

ConnectionString property, 297

spaces and, 297

variable declarations, 34

Keywords property (deployment projects), 219

L

Label control, 156-157

Label control (ASP.NET), 543

labels (Data Form Wizard), 409

Landscape property (PageSettings class), 257

languages, third-party, compatible languages, 29

LastIndexOf method (String class), 104

late binding, 763-765

.NET components, invoking from COM applications, 723

Launch Conditions Editor (deployment projects), 221

configuring, 226-227

Launch Conditions section (Launch Conditions Editor), 227

launching COM+ applications with QCs, 978

LCase string function, 59

LCE (loosely coupled events), publish-subscribe systems, 987

COM+ event asynchronously, 1001

COM+ event in parallel, 1001

implementing, 988-991

persistent subscriptions, 992

securing, 1018

security, 1003

transactions and, 1002

transient subscriptions, 995-1001

lease managers (remote objects), 849

lease managers (Remoting), sponsors, 852-859

Leave event (TextBox control), 152

Left string function, 59

legacy code. See compatibility

Len string function, 59

Length property (FileStream class), 695

How can we make this index more useful? Email us at indexes@samspublishing.com